Plazas

For Pima Community College

Robert Hershberger | Susan Navey-Davis
Guiomar Borrás Álvarez

Australia • Brazil • Japan • Korea • Mexico • Singapore • Spain • United Kingdom • United States

Plazas: For Pima Community College

Executive Editors:
Maureen Staudt
Michael Stranz

Senior Project Development Manager:
Linda deStefano

Marketing Specialist:
Courtney Sheldon

Senior Production/Manufacturing Manager:
Donna M. Brown

PreMedia Manager:
Joel Brennecke

Sr. Rights Acquisition Account Manager:
Todd Osborne

Cover Image:
Getty Images*

*Unless otherwise noted, all cover images used by Custom Solutions, a part of Cengage Learning, have been supplied courtesy of Getty Images with the exception of the Earthview cover image, which has been supplied by the National Aeronautics and Space Administration (NASA).

Printed in the United States of America

PLAZAS, LUGAR DE ENCUENTROS, FOURTH EDITION
Hershberger | Navey-Davis | Álvarez

ISBN-13: 978-1-133-35524-3

ISBN-10: 1-133-35524-2

Cengage Learning
5191 Natorp Boulevard
Mason, Ohio 45040
USA

Cengage Learning is a leading provider of customized learning solutions with office locations around the globe, including Singapore, the United Kingdom, Australia, Mexico, Brazil, and Japan. Locate your local office at: **international.cengage.com/region.**

Cengage Learning products are represented in Canada by Nelson Education, Ltd.
For your lifelong learning solutions, visit **www.cengage.com/custom.**
Visit our corporate website at **www.cengage.com.**

Custom Contents

Scope and Sequence

Scope and Sequence

Scope and Sequence

	CAPÍTULO 10	CAPÍTULO 11
CHAPTER	**CAPÍTULO 10** **Las relaciones sentimentales: Honduras y Nicaragua** ... 319	**CAPÍTULO 11** **El mundo del trabajo: Panamá** ... 353
COMMUNICATIVE GOALS	• Communicate about personal relationships and marriage • Indicate things that people do for one another • Share information about events that have taken place • Express frequency of actions and state how they are done • **¡A comunicarnos!**	• Communicate about occupations and professions, job responsibilities, and the search for employment • Share information about personal finances • Make recommendations and attempt to exert influence on others • **¡A comunicarnos!**
VOCABULARY	• Personal relationships ... 320 • Receptions and banquets ... 334	• Professions and trades ... 354 • The office, work, and the job hunt ... 366 • Personal finances ... 372
STRUCTURES	• The present perfect tense ... 326 • Reciprocal constructions with **se, nos,** and **os** ... 330 • Adverbs and adverbial expressions of time and sequencing of events ... 338 • Relative pronouns ... 342 • **¡A repasar!** ... 350	• **Por** vs. **para** ... 360 • The subjunctive mood ... 370 • The present subjunctive with statements of volition ... 374 • **¡A repasar!** ... 386
CULTURAL INFORMATION	• Rubén Darío ... 332 • Benigno Gómez López ... 333 • Copán, Honduras ... 333 • Nicaragua Libre, "La danza del cielo" ... 333 • **¡A leer!** "Epigrama V" by Ernesto Cardenal ... 346	• Archipiélago de Bocas del Toro ... 364 • Canal de Panamá ... 364 • Olga Sinclair, *Inocencia* ... 365 • Rubén Blades, "País portátil" ... 365 • **¡A leer!** Los negocios y la etiqueta ... 382

Acknowledgments

A very special thanks goes to Heather Bradley Cole, Acquisitions Editor, who has helped us enormously through her encouragement, flexibility, and dedication to the excellence of this edition. We are also indebted to Marissa Vargas-Tokuda, whose careful eye and ear have made this edition a work we are all immensely proud of. Our gratitude and special thanks for her hard work, reflected throughout the book, go to Aileen Mason, Senior Content Project Manager. We would like to recognize Ben Rivera, Senior Marketing Manager, and express our appreciation for his hard work on campus nationwide and, in particular, for his outstanding contributions to the marketing and promotional materials. We appreciate the creative thinking and welcome improvements that Morgen Murphy, Media Editor, has brought to the ***Plazas,*** Fourth Edition, media package. Our thanks also go to Bill Smith Group, the compositor, and in particular to Carol Thompson, the Project Manager, for her dedication and hard work. And, finally, we would also like to thank Sara Dyer, Editorial Assistant, for her masterful coordination of the ***Plazas,*** Fourth Edition, Advisory Board as well as numerous other reviewing activities, and Jennifer Carlson for her focused work with the authors of the ***Plazas,*** Fourth Edition, components.

Student Activities Manual

Jill Pellettieri, *Santa Clara University*
Silvia Rolle-Risetto, *California State-San Marcos*
Verónica Añover, *California State-San Marcos*
We would like to acknowledge the helpful suggestions and useful ideas of our Advisory Board, whose input was invaluable to the fourth edition.

iLrn: Heinle Learning Center Diagnostics

Daniela Schuvaks Katz, *Indiana University-Purdue University Indianapolis*

PowerLecture Instructor's Resource CD-ROM

Florencia Henshaw, *University of Illinois at Urbana-Champaign* (Instructor's Resource Manual)
Rachel López, *Kutztown University* (Activity File)
Karen Rauch, *Kutztown University* (Activity File)
Alberto Ribas-Casasayas, *California State University San Marcos* (PowerPoint Presentations)
Carmen Scales, *Arizona State University* (Testing Program)

Premium Website

Margaret Eomurian, *Houston Community College* (Web quizzes)
Ed Stering, *City College of San Francisco* (Web search activities)

We would like to acknowledge the helpful suggestions and useful ideas of our Advisory Board, whose input was invaluable to the fourth edition.

Fourth Edition Advisory Board

Amy Adrian, *Ivy Tech Community College–Central Indiana*
Frances Alpren, *Vanderbilt University*
Carlota Babilon, *City College of San Francisco–Ocean*
Valeria Barragán, *Saddleback College*
Anne Becher, *University of Colorado*
Andrzej Dabrowski, *University of Hawaii–Leeward Community College*
Michelle Faust, *Arizona Western College*
Rodolfo García, *Metropolitan State College of Denver*
Valerie Job, *South Plains College–Reese Center*
Nuria Ibañez, *University of North Florida*
Rachel López, *Kutztown University*
Regina Roebuck, *University of Louisville*
Christine Sabin, *Sierra College*
Daniela Schuvaks Katz, *Indiana University-Purdue University Indianapolis*
Virginia Shen, *Chicago State University*
Carolyn Wright, *North Carolina State University*
Francisco Zermeño, *Chabot College*

Acknowledgments

We would also like to thank the many instructors at colleges and universities across the country who contributed comments and suggestions on how to improve the fourth edition.

Fourth Edition Reviewers

Pilar Alcalde, *The University of Memphis*
Gunnar Anderson, *State University of New York–Potsdam*
Ann Baker, *University of Evansville*
Lisa Barboun, *Coastal Carolina University*
Marie Blair, *The University of Nebraska*
Kristy Britt, *University of South Alabama*
Donna M. Brown, *Longwood University*
Julia Bussade, *The University of Mississippi*
Mónica Cantero, *Drew University*
Eduardo Castilla Ortiz, *Missouri Western State University*
Cal Chandler, *St. Charles Community College*
Silvia Choi, *Huntington University*
Robert Colvin, *Brigham Young University–Idaho*
Raquel Cortés, *Elon University*
Linda Crawford, *Salve Regina University*
Karen Díaz Reátegui, *Washburn University*
María DiFrancesco, *Ithaca College*
Patrick Duffey, *Austin College*
María Forcadell, *DePauw University*
Leslie Frates, *California State University–East Bay/ Hayward*
Elliot H. Gaffer, *North Carolina State University*
Carmen García, *Texas Southern University*
Scott Gibby, *Austin Community College*
Curtis Goss, *Southwest Baptist University*
Luis F. Guzmán, *Longwood University*
Hsing Ho, *Rio Hondo College*
Laurie Huffman, *Los Medanos College*
Todd Hughes, *Vanderbilt University*
Carolina Ibañez-Murphy, *Pima Community College*
Scott Infanger, *University of North Alabama*
William Jensen, *Snow College*
Michael A. Kistner, *The University of Toledo*
Julie Kleinhans-Urrutia, *Austin Community College*
Tim Lee Catawba, *Valley Community College*
Pamela H. Long, *Auburn University–Montgomery*
Guadalupe López-Cox, *Austin Community College*
Paula Luteran, *Hutchinson Community College*
Lunden MacDonald, *Metropolitan State College of Denver*
Maríadelaluz Matus-Mendoza, *Drexel University*
Karin Meyer, *Canisius College*
David Migaj, *Wilbur Wright College*
Deanna Mihaly, *Eastern Michigan University*
Elaine Miller, *Christopher Newport University*
Matthew O'Neill, *Oklahoma State University*
Danae Orlins, *Transylvania University*
Roberto Pérez Galluccio, *Rochester Institute of Technology*
Pablo Pintado-Casas, *Kean University*
Silvia T. Pulido, *Brevard Community College*
Graziella Rondon-Pari, *State University of New York–Brockport*
Angela Shaheen, *Antelope Valley College*
Roger Simpson, *Clemson University*
Jon Sirko, *Longwood University*
Karen Tharrington, *North Carolina State University*
Jonnie Wilhite, *Kalamazoo Valley Community College*
Bel Winemiller, *Glendale Community College*
Jason Youngkeit, *Missouri Western State University*

Finally, we would like to express our appreciation to Sara Dyer, Editorial Assistant, for her tireless coordination of the Fourth Edition review boards, in particular the Advisory Board.

To my two lovely daughters, Kate and Annie. To my family and to my colleagues and students at DePauw University.

Robert Hershberger

To my husband, Mike. To my parents, Bob and Sally. To my colleagues and students at NC State University.

Susan Navey-Davis

To my wonderful family. To my mother, Gisela, to my son, Santiago, to my brother Tommy and his family, Gloria and María Rebeca. To my extraordinary colleagues at the Communication and World Languages Department, Bel, JT, and Joyce and to my remarkable students at Glendale Community College in Arizona and around the world.

Guiomar Borrás Álvarez

To the Student

Dear Student,

Spanish has become a major second language of the United States. Although southern and costal states have seen dramatic increases in Spanish-speaking populations for years, the presence of Latino communities in every large city throughout the nation is now a reality. Spanish radio and television stations are multiplying and playing to huge audiences, and Latino entertainers are soaring to the top of U.S. charts with smash hits. Spanish can be seen on road signs, menus, and product literature. Even in your local supermarket, chances are that some of the products you buy are marketed to Spanish-speaking customers. In the entertainment, leisure, and travel industries, Spanish is more prevalent than ever before. Business people, teachers, civil servants, store clerks, and especially emergency and hospital personnel are scrambling to keep up with an increasingly Spanish-speaking client base. Questions about our national immigration policy and our country's relationship to our neighbors to the south are in the headlines.

Just recently, peoples of Hispanic descent have become the largest minority group in the United States and are shaping social and political agendas in a profound way. By 2042, according to the U.S Census Bureau, current minority groups in the United States will constitute a majority, and the fastest growing minority group will be of Hispanic background. Real-world incentives to learn Spanish are all around you. ***Plazas*** welcomes you to join a community of Spanish speakers not only in your class, but also in your neighborhood, work environment, or travel destination. ***Plazas*** is based on the Five Cs of Communication, Communities, Connections, Comparisons, and Culture to ensure that your interaction with the Spanish-speaking world is dynamic and profound. In ***Plazas***, we not only introduce you to a language, but also to the people—through their history, traditions, and culture—who speak the language.

Learning Spanish successfully requires determination, good study habits, and patience. You must commit yourself to learning the language every day. Mastery is the result of daily study and practice. Everything you learn relies, to a certain extent, on previous material. If you invest time from the beginning, what you learn over time will build naturally upon a solid foundation of understanding and competence.

We wish you the very best in your introduction to Spanish and welcome you to the communities of ***Plazas***.

Bob Hershberger
Susan Navey-Davis
Guiomar Borrás Álvarez

MAR CARIBE
Barranquilla
Cartagena
Maracaibo
Caracas
Puerto España
TRINIDAD Y TOBAGO
R. Orinoco
Georgetown
Paramaribo
Cayenne
OCÉANO ATLÁNTICO
Medellín
VENEZUELA
GUYANA
SURINAM
GUAYANA FRANCESA
Manizales
Bogotá
Cali
COLOMBIA
ECUADOR
Quito
Guayaquil
ECUADOR
R. Amazonas
Belem
Manaus
Iquitos
PERÚ
R. Madeira
Cajamarca
Recife
BRASIL
Machu Picchu
Lima
Ayacucho
Cusco
Salvador
BOLIVIA
L. Titicaca
Arequipa
La Paz
Brasilia
Arica
Sucre
Iquique
Potosí
Belo Horizonte
São Paulo
Río de Janeiro
Santos
OCÉANO PACÍFICO
Antofagasta
PARAGUAY
Asunción
Salta
CHILE
Tucumán
R. Paraná
R. Uruguay
Porto Alegre
Córdoba
Mendoza
Valparaíso
Rosario
URUGUAY
Santiago
Buenos Aires
Montevideo
La Plata
Concepción
ARGENTINA
Río de la Plata
Bahía Blanca
TRÓPICO DE CAPRICORNIO
Puerto Montt
CORDILLERA DE LOS ANDES
0 200 400 600 800 millas
0 200 400 600 800 kilómetros
ISLAS MALVINAS
Punta Arenas
TIERRA DEL FUEGO
Cabo de Hornos
Estrecho de Magallanes

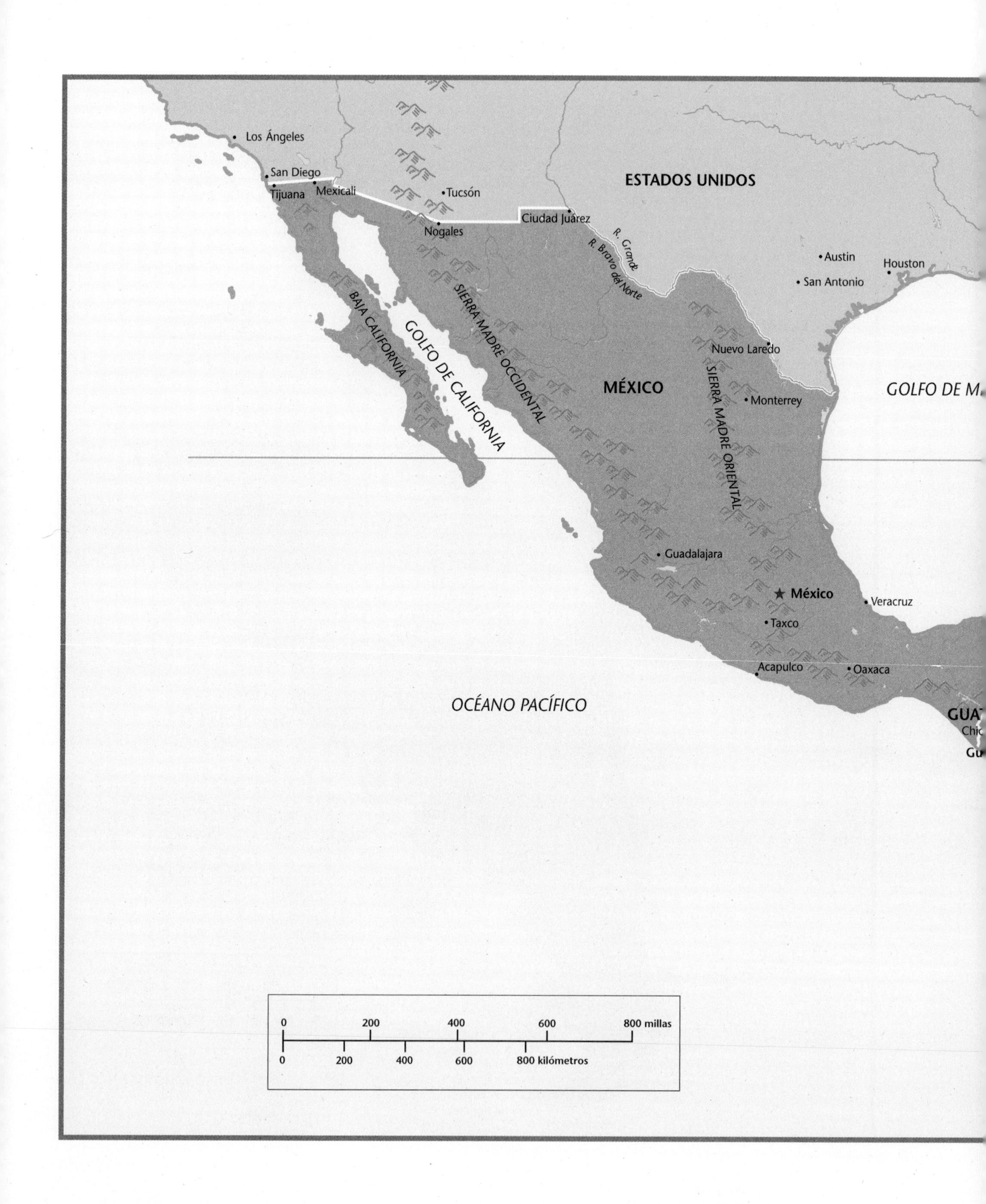
Los Ángeles
San Diego
Tijuana
Mexicali
Tucsón
Nogales
Ciudad Juárez
ESTADOS UNIDOS
R. Grande
R. Bravo del Norte
Austin
Houston
San Antonio
BAJA CALIFORNIA
GOLFO DE CALIFORNIA
SIERRA MADRE OCCIDENTAL
Nuevo Laredo
MÉXICO
SIERRA MADRE ORIENTAL
Monterrey
Guadalajara
México
Veracruz
Taxco
Acapulco
Oaxaca
OCÉANO PACÍFICO
0
200
400
600
800 millas
0
200
400
600
800 kilómetros

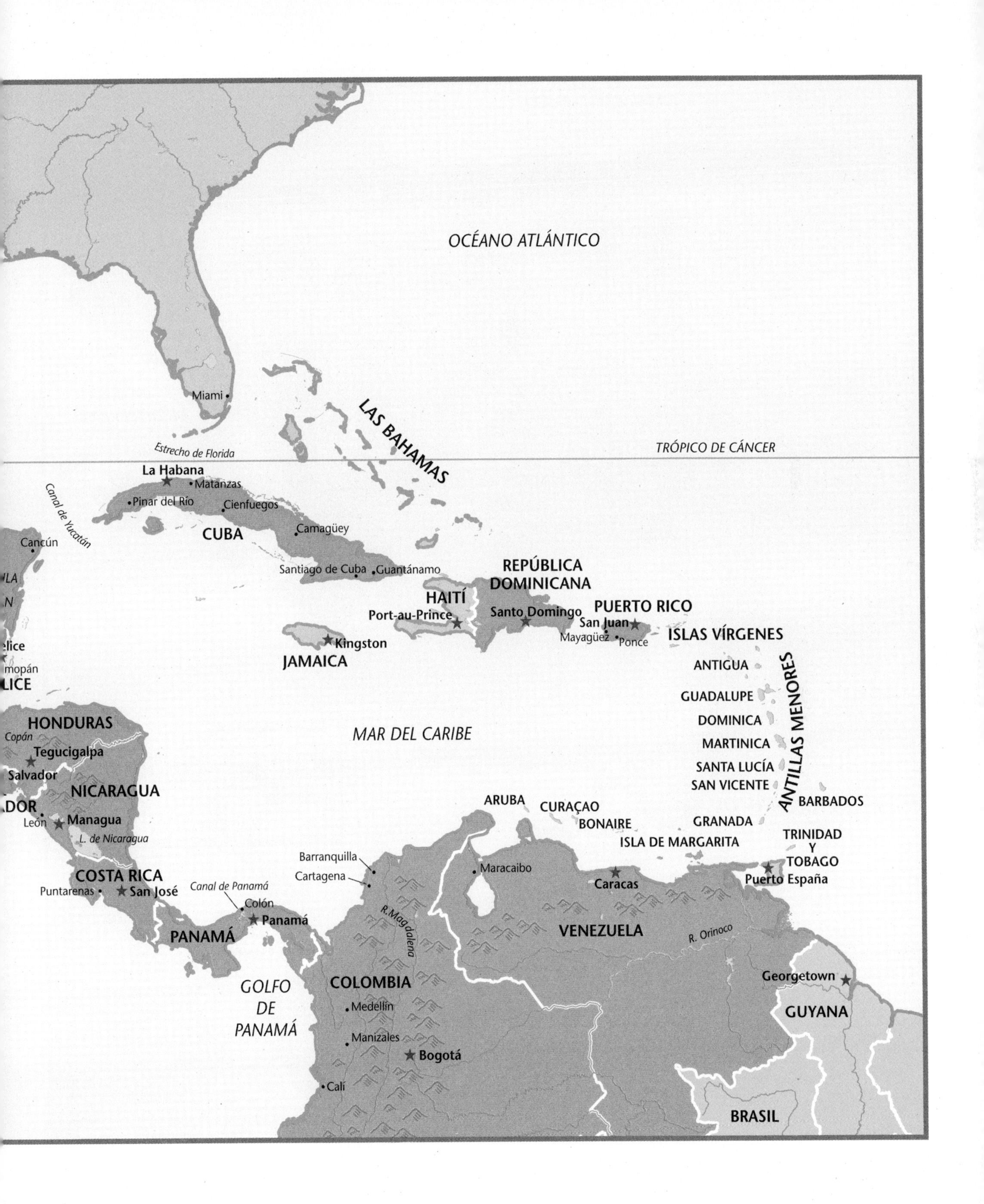
OCÉANO ATLÁNTICO
Miami
LAS BAHAMAS
Estrecho de Florida
TRÓPICO DE CÁNCER
La Habana
Matanzas
Pinar del Río
Cienfuegos
Canal de Yucatán
Cancún
Camagüey
CUBA
Santiago de Cuba
Guantánamo
REPÚBLICA DOMINICANA
HAITÍ
Port-au-Prince
Santo Domingo
PUERTO RICO
San Juan
Mayagüez
Ponce
ISLAS VÍRGENES
Kingston
JAMAICA
ANTIGUA
ANTILLAS MENORES
GUADALUPE
DOMINICA
MARTINICA
SANTA LUCÍA
SAN VICENTE
BARBADOS
MAR DEL CARIBE
HONDURAS
Copán
Tegucigalpa
Salvador
NICARAGUA
DOR
León
Managua
L. de Nicaragua
ARUBA
CURAÇAO
BONAIRE
GRANADA
ISLA DE MARGARITA
TRINIDAD Y TOBAGO
Barranquilla
Cartagena
Maracaibo
Caracas
Puerto España
COSTA RICA
Puntarenas
San José
Canal de Panamá
Colón
Panamá
PANAMÁ
R. Magdalena
VENEZUELA
R. Orinoco
GOLFO DE PANAMÁ
COLOMBIA
Medellín
Manizales
Bogotá
Calí
Georgetown
GUYANA
BRASIL

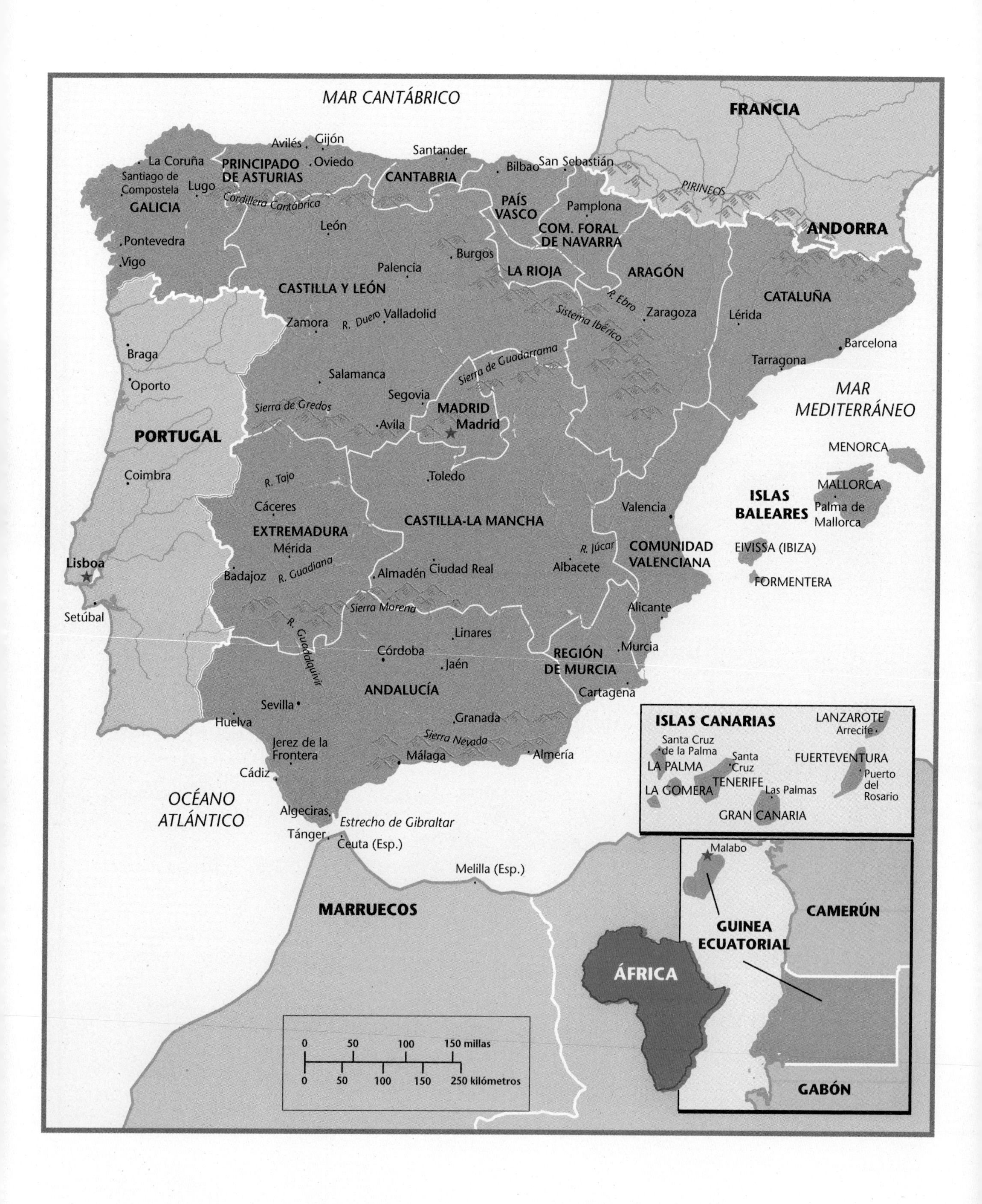

MAR CANTÁBRICO
FRANCIA
Avilés
Gijón
La Coruña
PRINCIPADO DE ASTURIAS
Oviedo
Santander
Bilbao
San Sebastián
Santiago de Compostela
Lugo
CANTABRIA
PIRINEOS
GALICIA
Cordillera Cantábrica
PAÍS VASCO
Pamplona
León
COM. FORAL DE NAVARRA
ANDORRA
Pontevedra
Burgos
Vigo
Palencia
LA RIOJA
ARAGÓN
CASTILLA Y LEÓN
R. Ebro
CATALUÑA
Zamora
R. Duero
Valladolid
Zaragoza
Lérida
Sistema Ibérico
Braga
Barcelona
Sierra de Guadarrama
Tarragona
Salamanca
Oporto
MAR MEDITERRÁNEO
Segovia
Sierra de Gredos
MADRID
Madrid
Avila
PORTUGAL
MENORCA
Coimbra
R. Tajo
Toledo
MALLORCA
ISLAS BALEARES
Palma de Mallorca
Cáceres
Valencia
CASTILLA-LA MANCHA
EXTREMADURA
Mérida
R. Júcar
COMUNIDAD VALENCIANA
EIVISSA (IBIZA)
Lisboa
R. Guadiana
Almadén
Ciudad Real
Albacete
Badajoz
FORMENTERA
Setúbal
Sierra Morena
Alicante
R. Guadalquivir
Linares
Córdoba
REGIÓN DE MURCIA
Murcia
Jaén
ANDALUCÍA
Cartagena
Sevilla
Huelva
Granada
Sierra Nevada
Jerez de la Frontera
Málaga
Almería
Cádiz
ISLAS CANARIAS
LANZAROTE
Arrecife
Santa Cruz de la Palma
LA PALMA
Santa Cruz
FUERTEVENTURA
LA GOMERA
TENERIFE
Las Palmas
Puerto del Rosario
GRAN CANARIA
OCÉANO ATLÁNTICO
Algeciras
Estrecho de Gibraltar
Tánger
Ceuta (Esp.)
Malabo
Melilla (Esp.)
MARRUECOS
CAMERÚN
GUINEA ECUATORIAL
ÁFRICA
0
50
100
150 millas
0
50
100
150
250 kilómetros
GABÓN

CAPÍTULO

¡Mucho gusto!

El mundo hispano

Plaza de Armas, Cusco, Perú

Chapter Objectives

Communicative Goals

In this chapter, you will learn how to . . .

- Greet others, introduce yourself, and say good-bye
- Exchange personal information such as name, origin, and address
- Identify quantities of objects

Structures

- Subject pronouns and the present tense of the verb **ser**
- The verb form **hay**
- Question words

▲ Have you visited any Spanish-speaking countries? If so, which one(s)?

▲ For your next visit to a Spanish-speaking area, would you like to visit a big city or a small town?

▲ Which Spanish-speaking country or city would you visit?

Visit it live on **Google Earth!**

A saludar y a conocer a la gente *(Greeting and meeting people)*

In this section, you will learn how to greet and say good-bye to people in Spanish in both formal and informal situations. How do you greet your professor? How do you greet your friends?

Saludos *Greetings*

Buenos días. *Good morning.*

Buenas tardes. *Good afternoon.*

Buenas noches. *Good evening/night.*

¡Hola! *Hi! (informal)*

Presentaciones *Introductions*

Me llamo... *My name is . . .*

(Yo) Soy... *I am . . .*

Encantada. *Nice to meet you. (women say this)*

Encantado. *Nice to meet you. (men say this)*

Mucho gusto. *Nice to meet you. (men and women say this)*

El gusto es mío. *The pleasure is mine. (men and women say this)*

Despedidas *Farewells*

Adiós. *Good-bye.*

Buenas noches. *Good night.*

Chao. *Bye.*

Hasta luego. *See you later.*

Hasta mañana. *See you tomorrow.*

Hasta pronto. *See you soon.*

Nos vemos. *See you later.*

Títulos *Titles*

señor (Sr.) *Mr.*

señora (Sra.) *Mrs., Ms.*

señorita (Srta.) *Miss*

Una situación formal *(A formal situation)*

Una situación informal *(An informal situation)*

Cultura

The form **usted** is abbreviated as **Ud.** and is used in formal situations with people whom you would address on a last-name basis. The abbreviation **Ud.** is pronounced just like **usted.**

Nota lingüística

When you ask questions in Spanish the voice rises on the last syllable of the last word in the question. It falls on the last syllable of the last word in a statement. For example:

¿Cómo está usted? **Soy de California.**

Preguntas formales

Formal questions

¿Cómo está usted? *How are you?*

¿Cómo se llama usted? *What is your name?*

¿De dónde es usted? *Where are you from?*

¿Y usted? *And you?*

Preguntas informales

Informal questions

¿Cómo estás? *How are you?*

¿Cómo te llamas? *What is your name?*

¿De dónde eres? *Where are you from?*

¿Qué hay? *What's new?*

¿Qué tal? *What's up?*

¿Cómo te va? *How's it going?*

¿Y tú? *And you?*

Respuestas *Replies*

Bastante bien. *Pretty well.*

Bien, gracias. *Fine, thanks.*

Más o menos. *So-so.*

(Muy) Bien. *(Very) Well.*

Me llamo... *My name is...*

(Yo) Soy de... *I'm from...*

Palabras útiles

con permiso *pardon me, excuse me (to ask permission to pass through)*

disculpe *pardon me (to formally ask for someone's forgiveness or to get someone's attention)*

perdón *pardon me, excuse me (to ask for someone's forgiveness)*

por favor *please*

Palabras útiles are presented to help you enrich your personal vocabulary. The words here will help you interact in Spanish.

¡A practicar! *(Let's practice!)*

Nota lingüística

In some countries, such as Chile, Colombia, and Venezuela people say **chao** (**chau** in Argentina, Bolivia, Peru, and Uruguay) to express *good-bye*, due to the influence of Italian immigrants.

Nota lingüística

The expressions **nos vemos** and **chao** are used in informal situations with the expectation that you will see the other person(s) in the near future or the following day. On the other hand, **adiós** is used when you do not expect to see the person again right away.

P-1 **¿Qué dices?** ***(What do you say?)*** Match the situations on the left with an appropriate expression from the list on the right. Remember to distinguish between formal and informal situations.

1. You're introduced to Sra. Fuertes. ______
2. You're asking a child where he/she is from. ______
3. You're greeting a stranger on the way to class at 8:00 a.m. ______
4. You're saying good-bye to a friend going on vacation. ______
5. You're asking your mother's friend how she's doing. ______
6. You're saying hello to a friend. ______
7. You're leaving a party at a friend's house at 2:00 a.m. ______
8. You're asking an an old man in the park what his name is. ______
9. You're walking to an afternoon class and you see your TA. ______

a. ¡Hola!
b. ¿De dónde eres?
c. Mucho gusto, señora.
d. ¿Cómo está usted?
e. ¡Buenos días!
f. ¡Adiós!
g. ¡Chao!
h. ¿Cómo se llama usted?
i. ¡Buenas tardes!
j. ¡Buenas noches!

P-2 **¡Mucho gusto!** Complete the following brief dialogues with the appropriate expressions.

1. —¿______________ eres?
   —Soy de Orlando.
2. —¿______________ estás?
   —Bastante bien.
3. —¿______________ usted?
   —______________ Rosario Vargas. ¿Y ______________?
   —Me llamo Manuel Ramos.

P-3 **Los estudiantes internacionales** Listen to the short messages from three new students who were asked to call to confirm that they will be moving into the international dormitory where you work. For each student, you must write the first name of the student and his or her home country and, when possible, indicate when the call was made. Circle **a.m.** to indicate morning, **p.m.** to indicate afternoon, or **¿?** to indicate that the time cannot be determined.

AUDIO CD
CD 1, TRACK 2

Nombre de pila *(First name)*	País *(Country)*	Hora de la llamada *(Time of the call)*
		a.m. p.m. ¿?
		a.m. p.m. ¿?
		a.m. p.m. ¿?

Workbook *P-1 – P-3*
Lab Manual *P-1 – P-3*

¡A conversar! *(Let's talk!)*

P-4 **Al revés *(The other way around)*** Working with a partner, change each informal dialogue in activity P-2 to a formal interaction and change the formal dialogue to an informal interaction. Role-play each new dialogue with a partner.

P-5 **Una fiesta** Pretend that you are attending a party given at the beginning of the semester for all students in your Spanish class. You want to speak to as many students in the class as possible.

Part I:
Work with one or two other students to practice the questions and answers that you will use to introduce yourself to all students and find out who they are. Practice asking students their names, how they are doing, and where they are from, and practice answering these questions. Also practice expressing pleasure in meeting each new student.

Part II:
All students move around the classroom, greeting classmates, and asking and answering questions about their names and other information. Speak to as many people as possible and ask as many different questions as you can. Your goal is to speak to each student. Speak only Spanish!

P-6 **Conversaciones** Work with a partner to act out the three conversations depicted in the drawings. Use the information below to help you decide if each interaction is formal or informal. Then include appropriate greetings, ask appropriate questions, and give appropriate answers. After practicing with your partner, be prepared to present at least one conversation to the class.

1. José Ramón and Ricardo, two old friends, happen to see one another on the street at 8 p.m. one evening.

2. Professor Sánchez greets a new colleague in the university medical center where they work, at 9 a.m. The new colleague is Dra. (**doctora**) Matos, but Professor Sánchez does not know her name.

3. At 2 p.m. Mrs. Calderón sees a young neighbor whose family has just moved to the area. She does not know his name, but wants to get to know him. Jaime, the young man, politely responds to Mrs. Calderón's questions.

Heinle/Cengage Learning

EN CONTEXTO

In this section you are presented with a dialogue that models (in bold) many of the grammatical structures you will learn later in the chapter. Listen for as many cognates as possible to help you establish meaning.

AUDIO CD
CD 1, TRACK 3

The dialogue describes the Ortega family's first meeting with Raquel, the new babysitter, at their home in Miami. Read the statements below before you listen to the dialogue. As you listen to the conversation, establish whether these statements are **cierto** *(true)* or **falso** *(false).*

1. El señor Ortega es cubano. ________
2. Raquel es de Nueva York. ________
3. Raquel habla español muy bien. ________
4. El padre de Raquel es de Cuba. ________
5. Hay muchas personas hispanas en Florida. ________
6. María José tiene siete años. ________

Raquel: ¡Buenas noches, señor!

Sr. Ortega: ¡Buenas noches! **¿Es usted** la señorita Gandía?

Comentario cultural In Florida, it is common to see Spanish colonial-style houses. These houses feature low roofs with red roof tiles, stucco siding, and numerous arches above doors and main windows. Thick walls provide relief from the hot summer temperatures.

Raquel: Sí, **soy yo.** Me llamo Raquel.

Sr. Ortega: Mucho gusto, Raquel. **Yo soy** Ricardo Ortega.

Raquel: Encantada, señor Ortega.

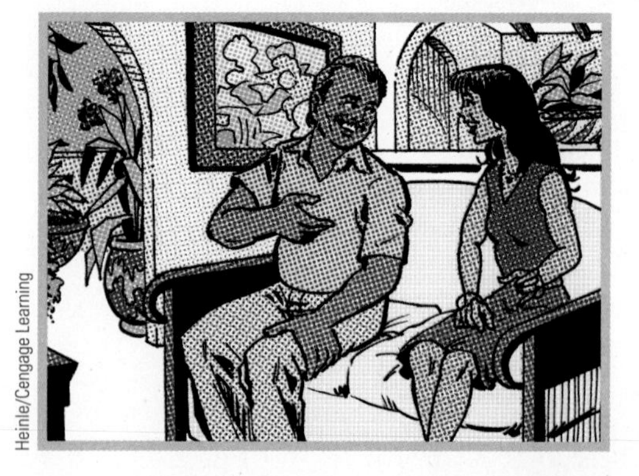

Sr. Ortega: **¿De dónde es usted**?

Raquel: **Yo soy** de aquí… de Miami. ¿Y ustedes?

Comentario cultural According to the 2008 Census, Miami Dade County, Florida, is 62.4 percent (1,496,505 individuals) Hispanic or Latino, a result of large-scale immigration, especially from Cuba, Puerto Rico, and the Dominican Republic.

Expresiones en contexto

aquí *here*
barrio *neighborhood*
de allí *from there*
mucha gente *a lot of people*
nena/nene *boy/girl, used when an adult wants to get a young person's attention (Puerto Rico)*
nuestro(a) *our*
¿Cuántos años tienes tú? *How old are you?*
¡Dios mío! *My God! My goodness!*
habla tan bien *speak so well*
Llevamos un año aquí. *We have been here for a year.*
Pareces mayor. *You look older.*
¿Sólo nueve años? *Only nine years old?*
¿Y cómo es que... ? *And how is it that . . . ?*
Yo tengo nueve años. *I am nine years old.*

Sr. Ortega: **Nosotros somos** de La Habana, Cuba. Llevamos un año aquí. ¿Y **cómo es** que usted habla tan bien el español?

Raquel: Mi padre **es** de Puerto Rico y en mi barrio **hay** mucha gente de allí, de Cuba y de la República Dominicana.

Comentario cultural Cuba is truly a melting pot of several different African and European cultures. This original Creole culture has been further diversified by more recent migrations of French, Chinese, Jamaicans, Haitians, and Mexicans.

Sr. Ortega: Raquel, quiero presentarle a mi hija, María José.

María José: ¡Hola!

Raquel: ¡Hola, María José! **¿Cómo** estás**?**

María José: Bien, gracias, ¿y usted?

Comentario cultural Notice how Mr. Ortega and Raquel use the formal form of **usted** to address each other. However, when Raquel meets Mr. Ortega's daughter, María José, she talks to the child using the informal **tú** form, appropriate when addressing someone younger than the speaker.

Raquel: Muy bien, gracias. ¿Y **cuántos** años tienes tú, nena?

María José: Yo tengo nueve años.

Raquel: ¡Dios mío! ¿Sólo nueve años? Pareces mayor.

Comentario cultural Certain exclamations carry less of a stigma in the Spanish language than they do in the English language. ¡Dios mío!, for example, literally translates to *My God!*, yet the strength of its meaning is closer to a phrase like *My goodness!*

Una experiencia como niñera *(babysitter)* You will be meeting the parents of a child, for whom you will babysit, for the first time. With a partner, take turns role-playing the situation. The babysitter should greet the parents, greet the child, and introduce himself or herself. Each person may invent a background of Hispanic origin. Use the expressions from **En contexto** as a model for your dialogue.

El mundo hispano

En los Estados Unidos

• Do you have friends who speak Spanish? Where do they live? Where do they come from?

According to the U.S. Census Bureau, there are more than 46.9 million Hispanics in the United States (2009). Hispanics are now the largest minority group in the nation, making up around 15.1 percent of the total population of the United States. The projected Hispanic population of the United States for July 1, 2050 is 132.8 million people. According to this projection, Hispanics will then constitute 30 percent of the nation's population.

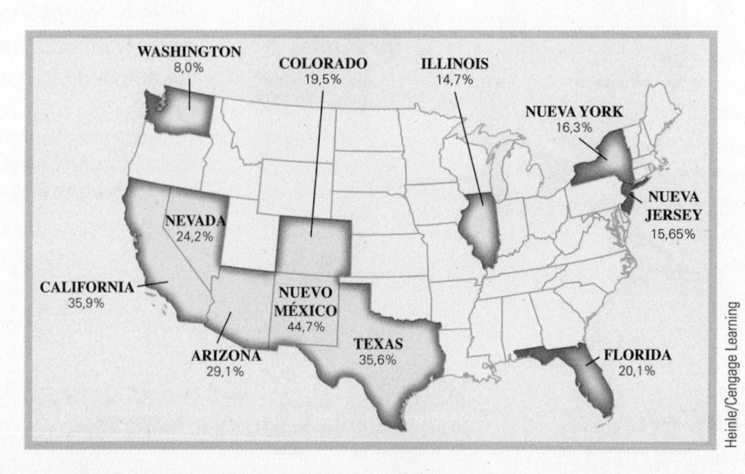

Heinle/Cengage Learning

1. **In which states do you find the largest concentrations of Hispanics? Why do you think this is?**
2. **After studying this map, discuss the importance of learning Spanish.**

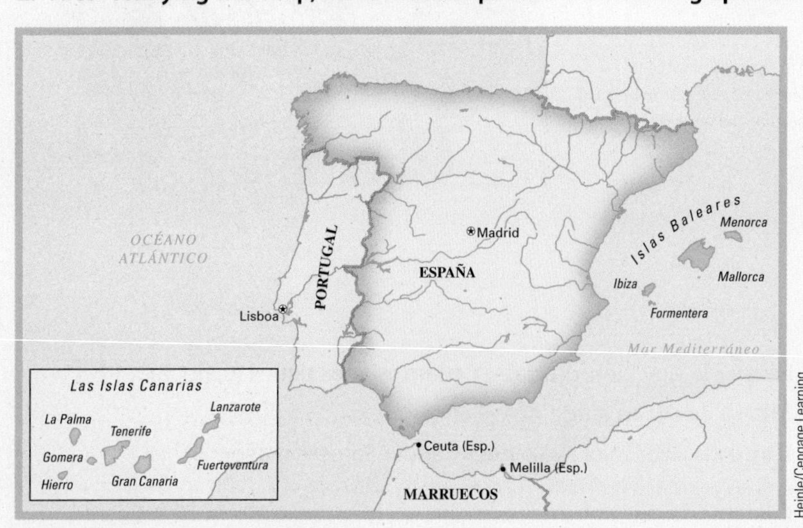

Heinle/Cengage Learning

España

• What facts do you know about Spain?

Spain and Portugal make up the Iberian Peninsula. Spain shares a border with Portugal to the west, France and Andorra to the north, and Gibraltar (a British Colony) to the south, and through its cities in North Africa (Ceuta and Melilla), Morocco. Its population includes speakers of Castilian Spanish, as well as speakers of regional languages in certain autonomous communities, such as Catalan in Cataluña and the Baleares Islands, Euskera or the Basque language in the Basque country, and Navarra and Galician in Galicia.

1. **What do you think about the fact that different languages are spoken in Spain?**
2. **Would you like to visit Spain? If so, which city or region would you be interested in visiting?**

México

• What do you know about Mexico?

The population of Mexico is ethnically diverse: 60 percent of the population is mestizo (indigenous-Spanish), 30 percent is indigenous, 9 percent is white, and 1 percent is classified as "other." The capital, Mexico City, has more than eight million inhabitants, which makes it one of the most populated cities in the world. The Yucatan Peninsula in Mexico is popular for its warm beaches and amazing Mayan ruins. Outside of the Yucatán, one can find famous beaches in Acapulco, Puerto Vallarta, Mazatlan, and the trendy Los Cabos in Baja California.

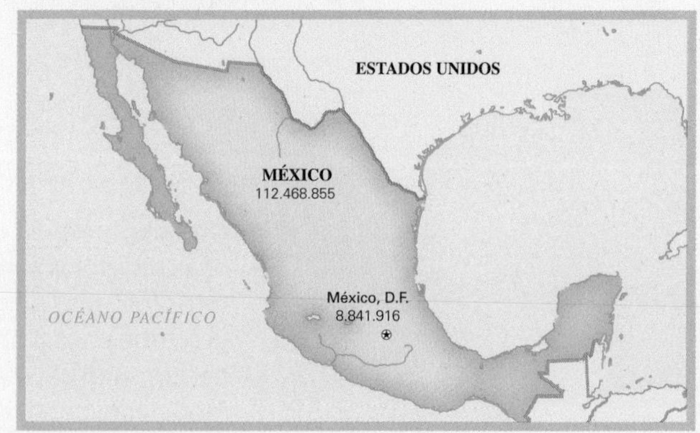

Heinle/Cengage Learning

1. **Would you like to live in a big city like Mexico City? Explain why or why not.**
2. **Which part of Mexico would you prefer to visit, the sandy beaches or the Mayan ruins?**

En América Central y el Caribe

- What facts do you know about Central America and the Caribbean islands?

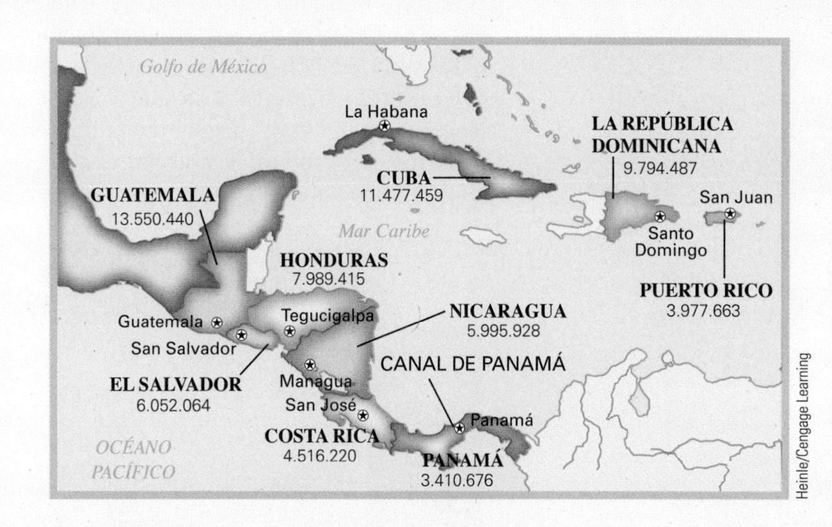

With the exception of El Salvador and Belize, the countries of Central America have two coasts: one on the Pacific Ocean and one on the Caribbean Sea. This distinguishing characteristic makes beach tourism very popular in these countries. Additionally, Panama's control of the Panama Canal—a 77-kilometer (48-mile) shipping canal that connects the Caribbean Sea (Atlantic Ocean) to the Pacific Ocean—is of international importance. Of the over 7,000 islands in the Caribbean Sea, the three largest islands are Spanish-speaking. The Caribbean nations of Cuba, the Dominican Republic, and Puerto Rico use Spanish as their official language. Puerto Rico, a United States territory with Commonwealth status, has a second official language: English.

1. **Why do you think the Panama Canal is important to the world?**
2. **Puerto Rico has two official languages: Spanish and English. Do you think this is a good idea? Explain why or why not.**

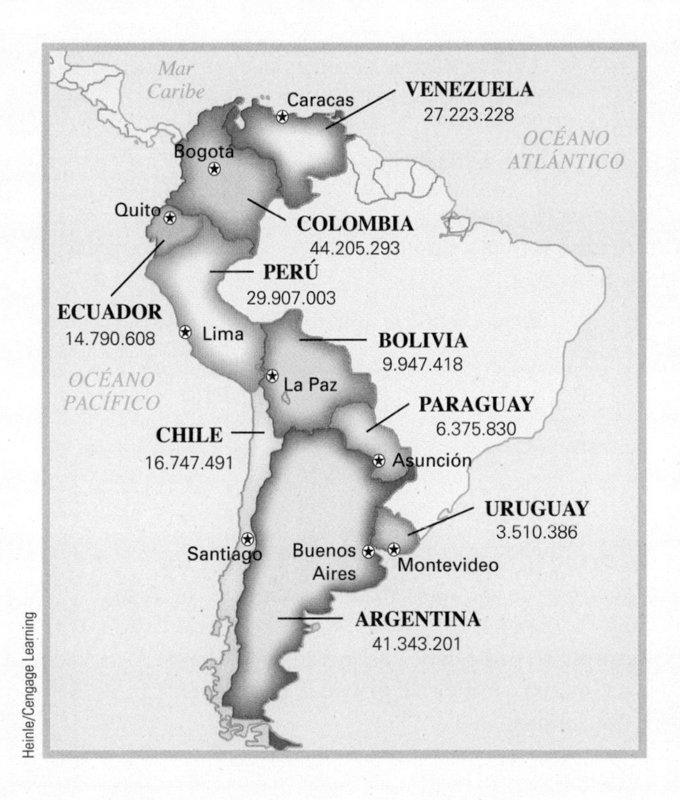

En América del Sur

- Can you name any natural wonders in South America?

Similar to North and Central America, South America is named for Amerigo Vespucci, the first European to suggest that the Americas were not in fact the Indies—as Christopher Columbus had thought—but rather a new continent, unknown to the Europeans. Despite their similar names, their geographic situations make North America and South America opposites of sorts.

Since South America is situated in the southern hemisphere, its seasons are opposite to those of North America. For instance, in South America, in countries such as Argentina and Chile, people ski in June, July, and August, and are at the beaches in December, January, and February.

1. **Are you aware of other differences between the southern and northern hemispheres in terms of climate, weather, and geography?**
2. **Which South American country would you most like to visit? When would you travel there, and what type of trip would you take?**

**In most of the Spanish-speaking world, periods and commas in numbers are reversed from the way they are used in English.*

Subject pronouns and the present tense of the verb *ser*

A *verb* is a word that expresses action (*run, jump,* etc.) or indicates a state of being (*is, seems,* etc.). The *subject* of the verb is either a *noun* or *pronoun* that identifies who does the action of the verb. Subjects that are nouns include names, such as *Mary, Fred, Jerome,* and so forth. Subjects that are pronouns include words, such as *you, we, they,* etc. Spanish, as a Romance language, exhibits both gender (masculine and feminine) and number. The subject pronouns **nosotros(as) vosotros(as)** and **ellos(as)** are plural forms and are shown with both masculine **-os** and feminine **-as** endings.

	Subject pronoun	*ser* (to be)	
Singular	yo	soy	*I am*
	tú	eres	*you* (informal) *are*
	él/ella, usted	es	*he/she is, you* (formal) *are*
Plural	nosotros(as)	somos	*we are*
	vosotros(as)	sois	*you* (informal: Spain) *are*
	ellos(as) , ustedes	son	*they are, you are*

Note that in most of Spain, the plural form of **tú** is **vosotros** (referring to males only or to a mixed group of males and females) and **vosotras** (referring to females only).

vosotros *you* } **sois** *are*
vosotras *you* }

David y María, **vosotros sois** mis amigos.
David and María, you are my friends.

Alicia y Regina, **vosotras sois** muy sinceras.
Alicia and Regina, you are very sincere.

In Latin America, **ustedes** is the plural form for both **tú** and **usted.**

The easiest way to negate a sentence in Spanish is to place **no** in front of the verb. If the sentence is already negated, remove the **no** before the verb.

Raquel es la madre de María José. — *Raquel is María José's mother.*
Raquel **no** es la madre de María José. — *Raquel is not María José's mother.*

¿Recuerdas?

Heinle/Cengage Learning

Sr. Ortega: **Nosotros somos** de La Habana, Cuba. Llevamos un año aquí. ¿Y cómo es que usted habla tan bien el español?
Raquel: Mi padre **es** de Puerto Rico y en mi barrio hay mucha gente de allí, de Cuba y de la República Dominicana.

¡A practicar!

P-7 **¿Sí o no?** Say whether you agree (**sí**) or disagree (**no**) with the following statements and repeat the sentence. To make a sentence negative, place **no** before the verb.

Modelos Penélope Cruz es actriz.
Sí. Penélope Cruz es actriz.

Penélope Cruz es profesora.
No. Penélope Cruz no es profesora.

1. Salma Hayek es elegante.
2. Alex Rodríguez no es atlético.
3. Mis profesores son cómicos.
4. Mis amigas son independientes.
5. Mi papá es profesor.
6. Mi mamá es bailarina.
7. Yo soy sentimental.

P-8 **¿Quiénes somos? ¿Quiénes son? *(Who are we? Who are they?)*** Complete the sentences below with the correct form of the verb **ser.**

Modelo George López *es* un cómico famoso.

1. Nosotros ______ estudiantes de español.
2. Tú ______ mi compañero(a) de clase.
3. América Ferrera y Cristián de la Fuente ______ dos actores famosos.
4. Carlos Santana ______ un músico famoso.
5. Ustedes ______ de Costa Rica.
6. Yo ______ estudiante de español.

P-9 **¿Ser o no ser?** Use the elements in each group to form a complete sentence. You must conjugate the verb **ser** to agree with the subject pronouns.

Modelo yo / ser / responsable
Yo soy responsable.

1. Buenos Aires / ser / la capital de Argentina
2. Javier Bardem y David Bisbal / ser / de España
3. mis amigos y yo / no / ser / profesores
4. el señor Ortega / ser / de Cuba y el padre de Raquel / ser / de Puerto Rico
5. Uds. / ser / generosos
6. tú / no / ser / introvertido

Workbook *P-4 – P-5*
Lab Manual *P-4 – P-6*

¡A conversar!

P-10 **¿Quién entre nosotros? *(Who among us?)*** Working with a partner, form questions using the adjectives listed below to ask your classmate. To ask a question in Spanish, place the verb before the adjective.

Modelo cómica *(a woman)*
E1: *¿Es cómica Katie?*
E2: *Sí, Katie es cómica.*
o *No, Katie no es cómica.*

1. responsable *(your professor)*
2. admirable *(you)*
3. extrovertidos *(two men)*
4. serios *(we)*
5. inteligentes *(a man and a woman)*
6. generosas *(two women)*
7. honesto *(a man)*
8. introvertida *(a woman)*

P-11 **¿Quién soy yo? ¿Quiénes son Uds.?** In groups of four or five students, make a list of ten well-known people who fit at least one of the criteria listed below. One group member introduces himself/herself as the first person on the list and gives one additional piece of information. The second person introduces himself/herself as the second person on the list and gives additional information, then repeats who the first person is and the information about him/her. Continue with the remaining names on the list. If time allows, create a new list of people and start again.

Modelo **E1:** *Soy Jeff García. Soy atleta.*
E2: *Soy Salma Hayek. Soy de México. Él es Jeff García. Es atleta.*

Características	**Profesiones**	**Nacionalidades**
arrogante	actor	de España
responsable	atleta	de Cuba
inteligente	músico(a)	de México
extrovertido(a)	político(a)	de Venezuela
elegante	artista	de los Estados Unidos

Hay and numbers 0–30

A useful Spanish verb form is **hay,** which means *there is* and *there are* (or *Is there... ?* and *Are there... ?* in questions). Use **hay** to indicate the existence of people, places, and things; **hay** may be followed by a singular or plural noun. Be careful not to confuse this verb form with the verb **ser**, which also means *to be* but does not express the idea of *there is/there are.*

¿Cuántas personas **hay** en tu clase de español?
*How many people **are there** in your Spanish class?*

Hay una profesora y veintisiete estudiantes.
***There is** one teacher and twenty-seven students.*

Numbers 0–30			
0 cero	8 ocho	16 dieciséis	24 veinticuatro
1 uno	9 nueve	17 diecisiete	25 veinticinco
2 dos	10 diez	18 dieciocho	26 veintiséis
3 tres	11 once	19 diecinueve	27 veintisiete
4 cuatro	12 doce	20 veinte	28 veintiocho
5 cinco	13 trece	21 veintiuno	29 veintinueve
6 seis	14 catorce	22 veintidós	30 treinta
7 siete	15 quince	23 veintitrés	

- Note that **uno** has three different forms.

  1. When counting, the form **uno** is used.

     Uno, dos, tres... *One, two, three . . .*

  2. When preceding a singular masculine noun, the **-o** is dropped to form **un (un señor, un profesor...).**

     Hay **un** profesor en la clase.
     *There is **one** professor in the class.*

  3. Before a singular feminine noun, **una** is used **(una señora, una profesora...).**

     Hay **una** cafetería buena en esta universidad.
     *There is **one** good cafeteria in this university.*

- The number **veintiuno** changes to **veintiún** before a plural masculine.

  Hay **veintiún** estudiantes.
  *There are **twenty-one** students.*

- The numbers 16 to 19 and 21 to 29 can be written either as one word (e.g., **dieciséis**) or as three words (e.g., **diez y seis**). In most Spanish-speaking countries, people prefer to use the single word.

- Note that some numbers when written as one word, will need a written accent to maintain stress on the proper syllable: **dieciséis, veintiún, veintiséis.**

¡A practicar!

P-12 **¿Cuántos hay?** ***(How many are there?)*** State how many units there are of the following items.

Modelo 18 computadoras
Hay dieciocho computadoras.

1. 1 auto
2. 5 libros *(books)*
3. 12 estudiantes
4. 6 profesores
5. 27 bicicletas
6. 30 clases
7. 15 personas

P-13 **Problemas de matemáticas** Do the following math problems with another student.

Modelo 2 + 2 = ¿? **[+ más]**
E1: *¿Cuántos son dos más dos?*
E2: *Dos más dos son cuatro.*

3 – 1 = ¿? **[– menos]**
E1: *¿Cuántos son tres menos uno?*
E2: *Tres menos uno son dos.*

1. 11 + 4 = ¿?
2. 16 + 10 = ¿?
3. 7 + 3 = ¿?
4. 25 – 11 = ¿?
5. 7 – 4 = ¿?
6. 30 – 9 = ¿?
7. 18 – 1 = ¿?
8. 22 + 7 = ¿?

P-14 **La lotería** Your friend purchased lottery tickets and found some of the results on the Internet. He was not able to find all of them so he asked you to listen to the radio announcement and complete the information that he was unable to find. Write the numbers in the appropriate spaces to complete the information that he needs.

AUDIO CD
CD 1, TRACK 4

Argentina: 2 3 1 7
Colombia: ______ ______ ______ ______
Chile: 7 9 12 14
Ecuador: ______ ______ ______ ______ ______
Uruguay: ______ ______ ______

Workbook *P-6 – P-8*
Lab Manual *P-7 – P-9*

¡A conversar!

P-15 **¿Hay o no hay?** In pairs, answer these questions about your class. Follow the model, then switch roles.

Modelo hombres *(men)*
—¿Hay hombres en la clase?
—Sí. Hay doce hombres.

1. mujeres *(women)*
2. hombres y mujeres
3. profesores
4. sillas *(chairs)*
5. calendarios
6. . . .

¿Cuántos estudiantes hay en la foto?

P-16 **¡BINGO!** Work in groups of four to six students. One student writes a list of numbers between 0 and 30 in random order. Every other student draws a grid of 16 squares, 4 across and 4 down, and puts a different number between 0 and 30 in each square. The student who made the list of numbers calls out a number (in Spanish, of course!), and students who have the number in their grid cross it out. The caller continues until one student crosses out four numbers in a row—vertical, horizontal, or diagonal—and says ¡Bingo! Continue the game so several students can achieve Bingo.

ESTRUCTURA 2

Question words

As an English speaker, there are a few basic linguistic points to keep in mind when using Spanish question words.

¿Cuál? ***(Which?)*** is used far more frequently in Spanish than in English. It has the same meaning as *What?* when someone's name, address, or telephone number is being asked. When it refers to a plural noun, it becomes **¿Cuáles?**

> **¿Cuál** es tu nombre?
> ***What*** *is your name?*
>
> **¿Cuál** es tu número de teléfono?
> ***What*** *is your telephone number?*
>
> **¿Cuál** es tu dirección?
> ***What*** *is your address?*
>
> **¿Cuáles** son tus amigos?
> ***Which ones*** *are your friends?*

¿Quién?, like **¿Cuál?,** must be made plural when referring to two or more people.

> **¿Quiénes** son tus padres?
> ***Who*** *are your parents?*

¿Cuánto(a)? and **¿Cuántos(as)?** must agree in number (singular or plural) and gender (masculine or feminine) with the nouns they describe.

> **¿Cuántos** hombres hay en la clase?
> ***How many*** *men are in the class?*
>
> **¿Cuántas** personas hay en tu familia?
> ***How many*** *people are in your family?*

Notice that all question words carry accents. The accent indicates that the word is being used as an interrogative. For example, **que** without an accent means *that* (e.g., *The one that got away.*) The word means *What?* only when it appears as **¿Qué?**

Commonly used question words	
¿Cómo? How?	**¿De dónde?** From where?
¿Cuál(es)? Which?	**¿Dónde?** Where?
¿Cuándo? When?	**¿Por qué?** Why?
¿Cuánto(a)? How much?	**¿Qué?** What?
¿Cuántos(as)? How many?	**¿Quién(es)?** Who?

¿Recuerdas?

Heinle/Cengage Learning

Sr. Ortega: ¿**De dónde** es usted?
Raquel: Yo soy de aquí… de Miami. ¿Y ustedes?

¡A practicar!

P-17 ¿Cuál es? Choose the correct interrogative word to complete each question.

1. ¿(Cómo / Quién) es la clase de literatura?
2. ¿(Dónde / De dónde) eres?
3. Marisela, ¿(cuánto / cuál) es tu clase favorita?
4. ¿(Quién / Dónde) es la profesora? ¿Es la doctora Martín?
5. ¿(Cuándo / Cuántos) estudiantes hay en la clase?
6. ¿(Por qué / Cuáles) hay computadoras en la clase?

P-18 Preguntas A friend of yours is doing a survey in a Spanish-speaking neighborhood. Help him fill in the missing question words. Are the survey questions addressed formally or informally?

Modelo ¿Cómo se llama usted?

1. ¿De ______ es usted?
2. ¿______ es su *(your)* dirección *(address)*?
3. ¿______ personas hay en su familia?
4. ¿______ son sus padres?
5. ¿______ es su número de teléfono?
6. ¿De ______ es su familia?
7. ¿______ es su cumpleaños *(birthday)*?
8. ¿______ le gusta este barrio *(do you like this neighborhood)*?

P-19 Información personal Read the answers that a student gave to the questions posed by classmates. Write the question that was used to elicit each answer.

Modelo —Soy de España.
—*¿De dónde eres?*

1. Me llamo Carolina.
2. Estoy bien.
3. Los profesores de español son el doctor Garza y la doctora Valenzuela.
4. Hay veinte estudiantes en la clase.
5. El número de teléfono de la profesora Valenzuela es el 725-2519.

Workbook *P-9 – P-11*
Lab Manual *P-10 – P-12*

¡A conversar!

P-20 Información personal Circulate around your classroom to obtain the phone numbers and addresses of at least three different classmates. Be sure to use the appropriate mode of address (informal or formal).

Modelo —*¿Cuál es tu número de teléfono?*
—*Es el dos, veintinueve, quince, once (229-1511). ¿Y el tuyo?* (And yours?)
—*Es el cuatro, veinticinco, diez, trece (425-1013). ¿Cuál es tu dirección?*
—*Camino Linda Vista, número tres, cinco, cuatro, siete (3547); apartamento número once (11).*

Cultura

In most Spanish-speaking countries, telephone numbers have 7 digits, but they have only 5 or 6 in some areas. When expressing a telephone number with an uneven number of digits, it is common to begin with a single digit but express the remaining numbers in groups of two. If your telephone number contains numbers that you are not yet able to express in pairs, you may present each number individually, such as dos, cuatro, uno, ocho, nueve, seis, cero for 241-8960.

P-21 ¿Qué? ¿Cuántos? ¿Cómo? Create questions in Spanish in order to find out personal information about two classmates. You want to get the following information:

- their names
- where they come from
- who their best friend *(mejor amigo[a])* is
- how many people there are in their family *(familia)*
- how they are feeling

Take turns asking each other the questions you come up with.

ENCUENTRO CULTURAL

Let's continue to get acquainted with the Spanish-speaking world. Below you will find the information you need to answer the following questions:

1. Do you know how many people speak Spanish as a first language?
2. Do you know how many countries use Spanish as an official language? Can you name some of these countries?
3. Do you know what other languages have influenced the Spanish language?

Heinle/Cengage Learning

Native speakers of Spanish
There are 329 million native speakers of Spanish. Spanish ranks second as the language most widely spoken by native speakers. It is slightly ahead of English (328 million) but far behind Chinese (1.2 billion).

Spanish as an official language
There are 21 countries where Spanish is used as an official language: 1 country in Europe, 1 country in Africa, 1 country in North America, 9 countries in Central America and the Caribbean, and 9 countries in South America.

Languages that have influenced the Spanish language
Spanish developed from Latin with influences from Greek, Basque, Arabic, and German, in addition to elements from Nahuatl in Mexico and Quechua in Bolivia, Ecuador, and Peru.

© Andre Jenny/Alamy

Personas notables Simon Bolivar, one of South America's greatest generals, was born in Caracas, Venezuela, in 1783 and died in Santa Marta, Colombia, in 1830. His victories over the Spaniards during the War of Independence won independence for Bolivia, Colombia, Ecuador, Peru, and Venezuela. He is known as **El Libertador** *(The Liberator)* throughout Latin America. In Venezuela, on the anniversaries of both his birth and his death, people come together in the Plaza Bolívar to honor his memory.

Who are the defenders of freedom in your community? Is there an important plaza, park, or street in your town or city dedicated to these individuals?

Historia Teotihuacan (300 B.C. – 450 A.C.) is the largest-known pre-Columbian city in the Americas. The city is located approximately 40 km (approx. 25 miles) northeast of present-day Mexico City. Archaeological evidence indicates that Teotihuacan was a multiethnic site. The presence of several different pre-Columbian communities, such as the Zapotecs, the Mixtecs, the Maya, the Nahua, the Totonacs, and finally the Aztecs, has been detected. The name Teotihuacan was coined by the Aztecs centuries after the fall of the city; it translates roughly to "the place where men became gods."

Are there historical monuments in your community that date back to ancient times? Can you describe them?

© Fotos and Photos/Photolibrary

© Color Point Photo/Photolibrary

Lugares mágicos When traveling to Spain, one of the most famous Moorish palaces to visit there is **La Alhambra**, which is situated on the southeastern border of the city of Granada. This ancient palace, mosque, and fortress complex was the residence of the Muslim kings and their courts. The majority of the structures that visitors appreciate today were constructed between 1333 and 1391. When touring the complex, one can delight in the royal quarters and the salons. One can also visit numerous fountains, interior and exterior patios, and extensive gardens. La Alhambra is an amazing architectural representation of the Arab presence and influence in Spain.

Do you have a building or structure in your town, city, or state that exhibits the presence or influence of other cultures? Can you describe it?

Visit it live on **Google Earth!**

Ritmos y música In Cuba, many former slaves were forced to join the Catholic Church, which led to the development of a new religion called **santería.** In **santería,** each deity is associated with colors, emotions, and a saint from the Catholic Church, plus specific drum patterns called **toques.** By the twentieth century, elements of Santería music—particularly the percussion patterns—began appearing in popular and folk music. Some of the resulting popular Cuban rhythms are **conga, son montuno,** and **rumba.**

Listen to the classic Cuban song "Son de la loma", performed by The Cuban All Star Band. *Access the iTunes playlist on the **Plazas** website.*

Do you like this type of Cuban music? What do you like about this rhythm?

© Lou Jones/Photolibrary

¡Busquen en Internet!

1. Personas notables: Simón Bolívar
2. Historia: Teotihuacán, México
3. Lugares mágicos: La Alhambra, Granada, España
4. Ritmos y música: el son cubano, The Cuban All Star Band

VOCABULARIO ESENCIAL

 AUDIO CD
CD 1, TRACK 5

 PERSONAL TUTOR

Cómo saludar	How to greet
Buenos días.	Good morning.
Buenas tardes.	Good afternoon.
Buenas noches.	Good evening/night.
¿Cómo estás?	How are you? (informal)
¿Cómo está usted?	How are you? (formal)
¡Hola!	Hi! (informal)
¿Qué tal?	What's up? (informal)
¿Qué hay?	What's new? (informal)

Cómo contestar	How to answer
Bastante bien.	Pretty well.
Bien, gracias. ¿Y usted?	Fine thanks. And you?
Más o menos.	So-so.
(Muy) Bien.	(Very) Well.

Cómo despedirse	How to say good-bye
Adiós.	Good-bye.
Buenas noches.	Good night.
Chao.	Bye. (informal)
Hasta luego.	See you later.
Hasta mañana.	See you tomorrow.
Hasta pronto.	See you soon.
Nos vemos.	See you later.

Cómo pedir información	How to ask for information
¿Cómo se llama usted?	What's your name? (formal)
¿Cómo te llamas?	What's your name? (informal)
¿Cómo te va?	How's it going?
¿Cuál es tu nombre?	What's your name? (informal)
¿Cuál es tu número de teléfono?	What's your telephone number? (informal)
¿Cuál es tu dirección?	What's your address? (informal)
¿De dónde es usted?	Where are you from? (formal)
¿De dónde eres tú?	Where are you from? (informal)

Presentaciones	Introductions
Encantado(a).	Nice to meet you.
El gusto es mío.	The pleasure is mine.
Me llamo...	My name is . . .
Mucho gusto.	Nice to meet you.
(Yo) Soy...	I am . . .
(Yo) Soy de...	I'm from . . .

Títulos	Titles
señor (Sr.)	Mr.
señora (Sra.)	Mrs., Ms.
señorita (Srta.)	Miss

Los números del 0 al 30	Numbers from 0 to 30
cero	0
uno	1
dos	2
tres	3
cuatro	4
cinco	5
seis	6
siete	7
ocho	8
nueve	9
diez	10
once	11
doce	12
trece	13
catorce	14
quince	15
dieciséis	16
diecisiete	17
dieciocho	18
diecinueve	19
veinte	20
veintiuno	21
veintidós	22
veintitrés	23
veinticuatro	24
veinticinco	25
veintiséis	26
veintisiete	27
veintiocho	28
veintinueve	29
treinta	30

Pronombres personales	
yo	I
tú	you (informal)
usted (Ud.)	you (formal)
él	he
ella	she
nosotros(as)	we
vosotros(as)	you (informal: Spain)
ustedes (Uds.)	you
ellos(as)	they

Palabras interrogativas	
¿Cómo?	How?
¿Cuál(es)?	Which?
¿Cuándo?	When?
¿Cuánto(a)?	How much?
¿Cuántos(as)?	How many?
¿De dónde?	From where?
¿Dónde?	Where?
¿Por qué?	Why?
¿Qué?	What?
¿Quién(es)?	Who?

Verbos	
hay	there is, there are
ser	to be

CAPÍTULO 1

En una clase de español

Los Estados Unidos

©Gunnar Kullenberg/Photolibrary

Plaza México, Lynwood, California, EE. UU.

Chapter Objectives

Communicative Goals

In this chapter, you will learn how to . . .

- Identify people, places and things in an educational setting
- Specify colors
- Communicate about everyday activities
- Tell time and indicate days of the week

Structures

- Definite and indefinite articles, the gender of nouns, and how to make nouns plural
- Present tense of regular **-ar** verbs

▲ Do you remember which states have the largest concentration of Hispanics?

▲ Have you visited any of these states? If so, did you notice any influence of Hispanic culture in those places?

▲ Do you think it is important to know how to speak Spanish in the U.S.? Why or why not?

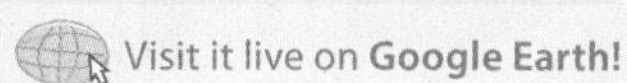

En la clase de la profesora Muñoz *(In Professor Muñoz's class)*

In this section, you will learn how to identify people and things in the classroom. How does Professor Muñoz's class compare to your own?

Heinle/Cengage Learning

Otras cosas *Other things*

el dinero *money*
el examen *exam*
la lección *lesson*
la palabra *word*
la tarea *homework*

Otras personas *Other people*

el (la) amigo(a) *friend*
el (la) compañero(a) de clase *classmate*
el (la) compañero(a) de cuarto *roommate*
el hombre *man*
la mujer *woman*
el (la) novio(a) *boyfriend/girlfriend*

Palabras útiles

el (la) consejero(a) *adviser*
el (la) decano(a) *dean*
el (la) maestro(a) *teacher*
el (la) presidente/rector(a) de la universidad *president of the university*
la sala de clase *classroom*

Palabras útiles are presented to help you enrich your personal vocabulary. The terms provided here will help you talk about your classes and the people you interact with on campus.

Nota lingüística

In Spain, the most common word for *computer* is **el ordenador** and for *marker* is **el rotulador**.

¡A practicar!

Nota lingüística

The color brown has more than one name in Spanish. It translates to **marrón,** but it can also be **color café, castaño,** or **pardo. Color café** tends to refer to the color of eyes, while **castaño** refers to hair color, and **pardo** refers to a darker brown.

1-1 ¿De qué color es? Match each of the following foods with the color or colors most often associated with it. **¡Ojo!** The foods are cognates so you should be able to identify them.

1. ______ la banana — a. rojo o verde
2. ______ el café — b. amarillo
3. ______ el tomate — c. marrón
4. ______ el chocolate — d. amarillo o verde
5. ______ el limón — e. negro

1-2 ¿Cierto o falso? Study the drawing of Professor Muñoz's classroom and decide whether each of the following statements is true (**cierto**) or false (**falso**). If a statement is false, correct it.

Modelo Hay tres mapas en la pared.
Falso. Hay un mapa en la pared.

1. La tiza es azul.
2. La señorita Muñoz es profesora de biología.
3. Hay tres luces.
4. La silla de la profesora es marrón.
5. Hay una calculadora en una silla.
6. Es una clase de matemáticas.
7. Hay una pluma en un pupitre.
8. Hay cinco chicos y cinco chicas en la clase de la profesora Muñoz.

1-3 ¿Cuántos hay en la clase? Say how many of each of the following items appear in Professor Muñoz's classroom. Remember that **uno** changes to **una** before a singular feminine noun and changes to **un** before a singular masculine noun.

Modelo Hay ___*quince*___ estudiante(s) en la clase.

1. Hay ______________ tiza(s) en la clase.
2. Hay ______________ calculadora(s) en la clase.
3. Hay ______________ computadora(s) en la clase.
4. Hay ______________ luz (luces) en la clase.
5. Hay ______________ mapa(s) en la clase.
6. Hay ______________ cosas (*things*) en la pared (*wall*): un reloj, ______________, ______________, ______________ y ______________.

Workbook *1-1 – 1-4*
Lab Manual *1-1 – 1-3*

¡A conversar!

1-4 **Cosas y colores** Ask a partner if the following items are in his/her backpack. If they are, he/she should state the color of the object. Your partner may also choose to identify another object.

Modelo un bolígrafo
E1: *¿Hay un bolígrafo?*
E2: *Sí, hay un bolígrafo y es azul.*
o **E2:** *No, no hay un bolígrafo. Hay un lápiz y es rojo.*

1. un libro
2. un diccionario
3. un lápiz
4. un cuaderno
5. un marcador
6. un mapa

1-5 **La clase ideal** Working with a partner, design the ideal classroom. One person describes the room to the other person who draws it. The one who draws the classroom should explain the design to the class.

Modelo *En la clase ideal hay muchos* (a lot of) *amigos, pero no hay profesor…*

1-6 **Una clase** With a partner, look at the photo of an English class at a Latin American university and identify as many items as possible. Note colors and numbers whenever possible. Compare the class to a typical classroom in your institution. Follow the model.

Modelo *En la clase hay tres mapas, un profesor y once estudiantes. En la clase de español hay una profesora y veinte estudiantes.*

© Davis Barber/PhotoEdit

1-7 **Una encuesta *(A survey)*** Form groups of four or five students. As a group, make a list of ten things a student might have in his/her dorm room or apartment. One person in the group asks every other group member if that item is in his/her room and records the number of yes and no responses.

Modelo **E1:** *¿Hay un mapa?*
E2: *Sí, hay un mapa.*
E3: *No, no hay mapa.*

Continue until all group members have answered and all questions have been asked. Conclude with a summary: *Hay cinco sillas y cinco relojes. Hay dos mapas.*

Nota lingüística

The indefinite article (**un/una**) is often omitted after **no hay. No hay mapa en la clase** means *There is no map in the class* or *There isn't a map in the class.*

EN CONTEXTO

Ana Guadalupe Camacho Ortega, a prospective student at the University of Chicago whose family plans to move to Illinois from Puerto Rico next year, is talking to Claudio Fuentes, a teaching assistant for Professor Muñoz. Ana is telling Claudio about her studies at the **Universidad de Puerto Rico.**

AUDIO CD
CD 1, TRACK 6

Listen to the conversation and establish whether the following statements are true (**cierto**) or false (**falso**). If a statement is false, correct it.

1. Ana es estudiante en la Universidad de Chicago.
2. Ana es de Yucatán.
3. Claudio estudia historia española.
4. Ana estudia ciencias.
5. Hay pocos (*few*) hispanohablantes en las clases de español.
6. Muchos estudiantes usan el español cuando (*when*) trabajan en otros países.

Claudio: ¡Hola! Soy Claudio Fuentes. ¿Cómo te llamas?

Ana: Ana Camacho. Mucho gusto.

Claudio: El gusto es mío. ¿De dónde eres, Ana?

Ana: Soy de Puerto Rico. Ahora **estudio** en **la** Universidad de Puerto Rico en Río Piedras. ¿Y tú?

Comentario cultural The University of Puerto Rico was established in 1903 and today has 11 campuses. Approximately 70,000 students attend the university under the instruction of over 5,000 professors.

Claudio: Este… Originalmente mi familia es de Mérida, Yucatán, pero yo soy de **los** Estados Unidos. **Estudio** en esta universidad hace dos años. ¿Qué **estudias** allí en Puerto Rico, Ana?

Comentario cultural The pyramid of Kukulkan is the most popular attraction of the Mayan ruins in Chichén Itzá, located near the city of Mérida.

Heinle/Cengage Learning

Ana: **Estudio** sicología, geografía, francés, alemán e inglés.

Claudio: Ah, eres estudiante de lenguas, ¿verdad?

Ana: Sí. **Deseo** ser intérprete. Y tú, ¿qué **estudias** aquí en Chicago?

Comentario cultural El Morro is a fortress located in Old San Juan, Puerto Rico. The fort has a labyrinth of tunnels, and features dungeons, ramps, barracks, and sentry boxes.

Expresiones en contexto

a ellos les gusta estudiar *they like to study / lit. studying is pleasing to them*
ahora *right now*
allí *there*
hace dos años *for two years*
muchos hispanohablantes *many Spanish-speakers*
intérprete *interpreter*
varios *several*
cuando trabajan *when they work*
deseo ser *I want to be*
la verdad es que *the truth is that*
lo usan después *they use it later*
parece que *it appears that*
por eso *for this reason*
que hablan *that speak*
que toman *that take*
tienen *they have*

Claudio: Yo **estudio** literatura y cultura latinoamericana.

Ana: ¡Genial! ¿Hay muchos hispanohablantes en tus clases?

Comentario cultural The U.S. Census Bureau indicates that approximately 44.3 million Hispanics reside in the United States; this number equates to 15.1 percent of the U.S. population. 64 percent of Hispanics in the United States are of Mexican descent. 9 percent are of Puerto Rican background, 3.4 percent Cuban, 3.1 percent Salvadoran, and 2.8 percent Dominican.

Claudio: Sí, hay varios. Algunos de ellos tienen dos especialidades. Ahora hay estudiantes que combinan **el** español con **el** inglés, con **la** computación, con **la** administración de empresas o con **las** ciencias...

Ana: ¡Parece que **el** español es muy popular!

Comentario cultural Most academic institutions in the United States offer a broad liberal arts education as part of their undergraduate degrees, which allows students to take several elective courses outside of their majors. Conversely, many universities in Spanish-speaking countries offer a curriculum in which students focus on a single subject.

Claudio: ¡Sí! Pues, **la** verdad es que ahora hay muchas personas en **los** Estados Unidos que **hablan** español. **Los** estudiantes que **toman** clases de español aquí frecuentemente lo **usan** después cuando **trabajan** en ciudades como aquí en Chicago, Miami, Nueva York, Phoenix o Los Ángeles. Por eso, a ellos les gusta estudiar español en **la** universidad.

Comentario cultural California had the largest Hispanic population (13.2 million) of any state as of July 1, 2007, followed by Texas (8.6 million) and Florida (3.8 million). In New Mexico, Hispanics comprised the highest proportion of the total population (44 percent), with California and Texas (36 percent each) next in line.

Nota lingüística

The word **y** (*and*) becomes **e** before a word beginning with **i** or **hi.** The conjunction **o** (*or*) becomes **u** before a word beginning with **o** or **ho.** Both of these changes occur for pronunciation reasons. Note examples: **Hablo español e inglés. Padre e hijo son amables. ¿Te llamas Omar u Óscar? ¿Estudiamos mañana u hoy?**

 **¡Buenos días, compañero(a)!** Working with a partner, take turns role-playing the situation of a student from a Spanish-speaking country talking to a classmate that he/she is meeting for the first time. Be sure to vary the nationalities and interests of the two speakers. Use the expressions from **En contexto** as a model for your dialogue.

ESTRUCTURA 1

Definite and indefinite articles, gender, and how to make nouns plural

A noun names a person (**Ana, estudiante**), a place (**Mérida, ciudad**), a thing (**libro, computadora**), or a concept (**clase, español**). In Spanish, all nouns are classified as having a gender—either masculine or feminine. This gender is indicated by an article that precedes the noun. There are definite articles, **el, la, los, las** (*the*), and indefinite articles, **un, una** (*a, an*), **unos, unas** (*some*). The words **un** and **una** can also mean *one*, depending on the context. Both definite and indefinite articles agree in gender and number with the nouns they modify.

el libro *the book*	las mochilas *the backpacks*
un libro *a book*	unas mochilas *some backpacks*

How to determine gender of nouns

1. In Spanish, nouns referring to males and most nouns ending in **-o** are masculine. Nouns referring to females and most nouns ending in **-a** are feminine. Definite and indefinite articles must match the gender (masculine or feminine) of the nouns they refer to.

   el/un amigo — **la/una** amiga
   el/un escritorio — **la/una** biblioteca

2. Most nouns ending in **-l** or **-r** are masculine, and most nouns ending in **-d** or **-ión** are feminine

   el/un papel — **la/una** universidad
   el/un borrador — **la/una** lección

3. Many words that end in **-ma** and **-ta** are masculine:

   el problema — *problem*
   el tema — *theme*
   el cometa — *comet*
   el planeta — *planet*

4. Some nouns do not conform to the rules stated above. One way to remember the gender of these nouns is to learn the definite articles and the nouns together, for example: **la clase, el día** (*day*), **el mapa,** and **la mano** (*hand*).

How to make nouns plural

Like in English, all nouns in Spanish are either singular or plural. Definite and indefinite articles (**el, la, los, las; un, una, unos, unas**) must match the number (singular or plural) of the nouns they refer to. To make Spanish nouns plural, add **-s** to nouns ending in a vowel, and **-es** to nouns ending in a consonant.

Definite articles

Singular	Plural
el amigo	los amigos
la amiga	las amigas

Indefinite articles

Singular	Plural
una clase	unas clases
un profesor	unos profesores
una universidad	unas universidades

Here are two additional rules for making nouns plural:

1. For nouns ending in **-án, -és,** or **-ión,** drop the accent mark before adding **-es.**

   el/un alemán — **los/unos** alemanes
   el/un japonés — **los/unos** japoneses
   la/una lección — **las/unas** lecciones

2. For nouns ending in **-z,** drop the **-z,** then add **-ces.**

   el/un lápiz — **los/unos** lápices

Spanish speakers do not consider nouns as being male or female (except when referring to people or animals). Therefore, the terms "masculine" and "feminine" are simply labels for classifying nouns.

¿Recuerdas?

Heinle/Cengage Learning

Ana: ¡Parece que **el** español es muy popular!

¡A practicar!

1-8 **¿El, la, los o las?** Supply the definite article for each noun below.

Modelo __*las*__ mochilas

1. ______ mapa
2. ______ universidad
3. ______ exámenes
4. ______ tarea
5. ______ bolígrafo
6. ______ lecciones

1-9 **¿Qué es? ¿Qué son?** Identify the following objects using the indefinite articles **un, una, unos,** or **unas.**

Modelo calendario
Es un calendario.

1. 

2. 

3.

4. 

Heinle/Cengage Learning

1-10 **¿Qué hay en la clase?** You are one of several teaching assistants assigned to a new classroom. Another assistant visits the room and leaves you a voice mail about what he finds. Listen to the voice mail and write down the items he says are in the classroom and the number of each one so you are prepared for your class. Write only the items that are present, not those that are not.

AUDIO CD
CD 1, TRACK 7

1. ____________________
2. ____________________
3. ____________________
4. ____________________
5. ____________________
6. ____________________

Workbook *1-5 – 1-7*
Lab Manual *1-4 – 1-6*

¡A conversar!

1-11 **Cuestionario: ¿Cuántos hay?** Form the plural of each of the nouns below and then ask two of your classmates how many of each there are.

Modelo libro
E1: *¿Cuántos libros hay?*
E2: *Hay dos libros de texto en la mochila.*

CUESTIONARIO

En esta clase
1. pizarra ____________________
2. luz ____________________
3. mapa ____________________

En la mochila
4. libro ____________________
5. bolígrafo ____________________
6. calculadora ____________________

En el cuarto
7. computadora ____________________
8. silla ____________________
9. televisor ____________________

1-12 **¿Qué necesitas?** ***(What do you need?)*** Working with a partner, indicate at least one item that you need in each of the following situations. Include more than one when possible.

Modelo en la clase de español
E1: *Necesito* (I need) *un lápiz y papel.*
E2: *Necesito un libro de texto, un cuaderno y un bolígrafo.*

1. en la clase de matemáticas
2. en la clase de geografía
3. en la clase de computación
4. en la oficina del profesor
5. en el centro estudiantil
6. en la residencia

Los Estados Unidos

Watch the video about the United States and discuss the following questions:

1. Do you know why San Antonio, Texas, is such an interesting and cheerful city?
2. Mention some facts that you already know about Miami, Florida.
3. What Hispanic city would you like to visit in the United States? Why?

See the *Workbook,* **Capítulo 1, 1-15–1-17** for additional activities.

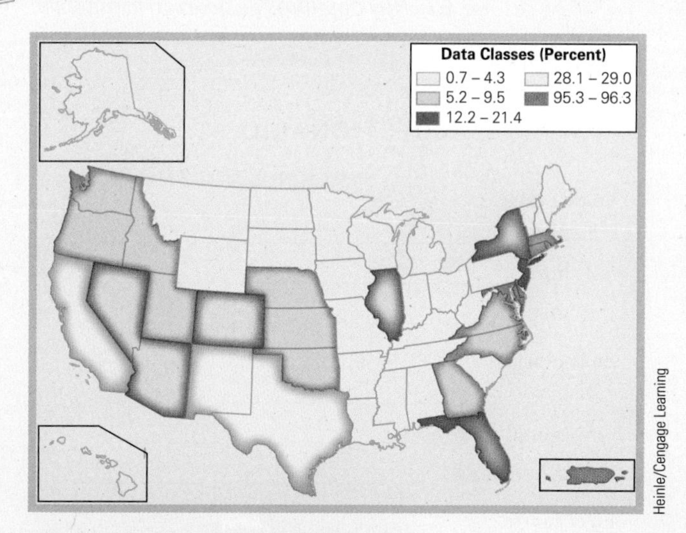

The estimated Hispanic population of the United States as of July 2008 constituted 15% of the nation's total population. This percentage makes people of Hispanic origin the nation's largest ethnic minority.

The size of the U.S. Hispanic population is the second largest worldwide, as of 2008. Only Mexico (111 million) had a larger Hispanic population than the United States (46.9 million).

There were 34 million of U.S. residents five years and older who spoke Spanish at home in 2006.

Sonia Sotomayor

Personas notables Sonia María Sotomayor (1954) es la primera jueza *(first judge)* de origen hispano y la tercera *(third)* mujer en la Corte Suprema de Justicia de los Estados Unidos. Ella se gradúa con honores de la secundaria en el Bronx, recibe una beca *(scholarship)* para la Universidad de Princeton donde también *(also)* se gradúa con honores, y finalmente estudia Derecho *(Law)* en la Universidad de Yale. Antes de *(Prior to)* ser jueza de la Corte Suprema, ella trabaja exitosamente *(successfully works)* como abogada *(lawyer)* y fiscal *(district attorney)*.

¿Hay personas de origen hispano en la administración de tu ciudad *(your city)* o estado? ¿Y en tu universidad?

Lugares mágicos La ciudad de San Agustín en Florida es la ciudad más antigua *(oldest)* de origen hispano en los Estados Unidos. La ciudad abre *(opens)* sus puertas en 1565, gracias al trabajo del español Pedro Menéndez de Avilés. La escuela más antigua de madera *(wood)* está en San Agustín también. Es la primera escuela en los Estados Unidos que recibe a chicos y chicas en una sala de clase.

¿Cómo es tu escuela secundaria? ¿Cómo es tu universidad o colegio universitario? ¿Es histórico(a)?

La escuela más antigua en los Estados Unidos, San Agustín, Florida

Visit it live on **Google Earth!**

North wall of a mural depicting Detroit Industry, 1932-33 (fresco) (see also 139315-7 & 112945 & 47) by Diego Rivera (1886-1957) Detroit Institute of Arts, USA/ Gift of Edsel B. Ford/ The Bridgeman Art Library

***Industria de Detroit o Hombre y Máquina* de Diego Rivera (Instituto de Artes de Detroit, Detroit, Michigan)**

Artes plásticas La pintura mural es una de las formas más antiguas de expresión artística. El notable muralista mexicano Diego Rivera es famoso por sus murales realistas de contenido social. Un ejemplo de su arte se observa en el Instituto de Arte de Detroit. En este mural, Rivera representa la gloria de la industria mecánica de los Estados Unidos.

¿Qué colores hay en este mural? ¿Hay murales en tu ciudad?

Ritmos y música En la actualidad (*Nowadays*) es muy común la colaboración musical entre artistas. En algunos casos, esta colaboración supera (*surpasses*) fronteras y estilos musicales. Por ejemplo, el cantante de pop español Alejandro Sanz combina su talento con el de la cantante de R&B Alicia Keys para producir su éxito "Buscando el paraíso" (*Looking for paradise*).

Access the iTunes playlist on the ***Plazas*** *website.*

¿Cuál es tu tipo de música preferido?

Alejandro Sanz y Alicia Keys en los Grammy Latinos

¡Busquen en Internet!

1. Personas notables: Sonia Sotomayor
2. Lugares mágicos: San Agustín, Florida *(Oldest Wooden School)*
3. Artes plásticas: Diego Rivera
4. Ritmos y música: Alejandro Sanz y Alicia Keys

VOCABULARIO 2

El campus y los cursos universitarios *(Campus and university classes)*

In this section, you will learn how to talk about university buildings and academic courses in Spanish. What classes are you taking this semester?

Cursos, lenguas extranjeras y lugares en la universidad

Nota lingüística

The word **facultad** is a false cognate. It refers to school or department rather than faculty.

Más cursos y especializaciones

More courses and majors

el arte *art*
la computación *computer science*
la economía *economics*
la geografía *geography*
la historia *history*
la literatura *literature*
las matemáticas *mathematics*
la música *music*
la sicología *psychology*
la sociología *sociology*
el teatro *theater*

Las lenguas extranjeras

Foreign languages

el alemán *German*
el chino *Chinese*
el español *Spanish*
el francés *French*
el inglés *English*
el italiano *Italian*
el japonés *Japanese*
el portugués *Portuguese*
el ruso *Russian*

Palabras útiles

la arquitectura *architecture*
la biología *biology*
el colegio universitario *community college or two-year college*
la contabilidad *accounting*
la filosofía *philosophy*
la física *physics*
las humanidades *humanities*
las materias *subjects, courses*
la química *chemistry*

Palabras útiles are presented to help you enrich your personal vocabulary. The terms provided here will help you talk about your courses.

¡A practicar!

1-13 ¿Dónde...? During a typical day, Pilar visits many parts of the campus. Identify the places where she does the following activities.

Modelo Aquí tomo *(I have)* un café después de clases.
En el centro estudiantil.

1. Aquí compro *(I buy)* mis libros de texto.
2. Aquí estudio *(I study)* para los exámenes.
3. Aquí hablo *(I speak)* con mis compañeros de clase y compro comida.
4. Aquí toco *(I play)* la trompeta para los partidos de baloncesto *(basketball games).*

1-14 Profesiones What subjects did the people in the following professions study in school? More than one answer may be possible for a profession.

1. economista ____________________
2. actor ____________________
3. sicólogo(a) ____________________
4. médico(a)/doctor(a) ____________________
5. artista ____________________
6. periodista ____________________
7. educador(a) ____________________
8. sociólogo(a) ____________________

Nota lingüística

In many Spanish-speaking countries, the name for the language **el español** alternates with **el castellano,** or "Castillian Spanish." It is one of the four main languages that are spoken in Spain. The other languages are Basque, Catalan, and Galician.

1-15 ¿Qué lengua habla? ***(What language does he/she speak?)*** Note where each of the following people is from and identify the native language he/she speaks (**él habla, ella habla**). Do you speak any other languages besides English and Spanish?

1. El emperador Akihito es de Japón. Habla ______________.
2. Nicolas Sarkozy es de Francia. Habla ______________.
3. Yao Ming es de China. Habla ______________.
4. Fernanda Montenegro es de Costa Rica. Habla ______________.
5. Vladimir Vladimirovich Putin es de Rusia. Habla ______________.
6. Yo soy de ______________ y yo hablo ______________, ______________, ...

1-16 Instituto de verano Listen to the podcast about a summer institute in international studies. Write down information to share with students you know who may be interested.

AUDIO CD
CD 1, TRACK 8

1. Clases de lenguas: ________, ________, ________, ________, ________, ________ y ________.
2. Otras clases: ________________, ________, ________, ________, ________ y ________.
3. Número de teléfono para más información: ______ - ______ - ______

Workbook *1-8 – 1-10*
Lab Manual *1-7 – 1-9*

¡A conversar!

1-17 **¿Cierto o falso?** Alternating with a classmate, make each of the following statements. If the statement your classmate makes is false, correct it.

Modelo **E1:** Normalmente hay muchos libros en el gimnasio.
E2: *No, es falso. Normalmente hay muchos libros en la biblioteca.*

1. Hay libros de español en la sala de clase de ciencias.
2. Hay muchas copias de ***Plazas*** en la librería.
3. Hay comida japonesa en el centro estudiantil.
4. En nuestra (*our*) universidad hay clases de ruso.
5. Por la noche (*At night*), hay muchos estudiantes en la biblioteca.
6. En mi residencia, hay estudiantes de Francia.

1-18 **En la librería** You work in the campus bookstore and are helping Pilar and Felipe, two international students, find the textbooks they need for the courses they have jotted down. Of course, they've written their lists in Spanish! With a classmate in the role of either Pilar or Felipe, ask what general subject area each course is in just to make sure you read their lists correctly. Then, describe the book(s) they need including the title (in English), the color(s) of the book cover, and any other details you may wish to add.

Modelo Cálculo 3
E1: *La clase se llama Cálculo 3.*
E2: *Es una clase de matemáticas/computación, ¿verdad?*
E1: *Sí. / No, es una clase de matemáticas.*
E2: *El libro de texto se llama* Five Easy Steps to Calculus. *Es verde y azul.*

Felipe: Escritores británicos; Interacción social; Fonética francesa; Sicología anormal; Revolución mexicana

Pilar: Finanzas; Diez dramas; Guitarra clásica; Televisión ; Estadística

1-19 **Mis clases** Prepare a list of your classes, in Spanish. Include classes from the current semester as well as others you will take this academic year. Share your list with a partner saying **Este año estudio...** *(This year I'm studying . . .)* and have your partner tell you what he/she is studying. Use the following expressions to comment on your classes and those of your partner. Choose the plural form when appropriate. Follow the model.

Modelo *Este año estudio biología. Es interesante.*
Estudio matemáticas...

Es interesante / Son interesantes
Es fascinante / Son fascinantes
Es importante / Son importantes
Es necesario(a) / Son necesarios(as)
Es fácil *(It's easy)* / Son fáciles
Es difícil *(It's hard)* / Son difíciles

1-20 **Lenguas extranjeras** Think of all the people you know who speak languages other than English. Tell a classmate who the people are and what languages they speak.

Modelo *La profesora Li es profesora de sicología. Habla* (She speaks) *chino.*
Karl y Greta son estudiantes. Hablan (They speak) *alemán.*

Present tense of regular *-ar* verbs

How to form the present tense

An infinitive is an unconjugated verb form, such as **hablar** (to speak; to talk). In Spanish, infinitives end in **-ar, -er,** or **-ir.** All Spanish infinitives have two parts: a stem (**habl-**) and an ending (**-ar**).

To form the present tense of Spanish verbs ending in **-ar,** drop the infinitive ending and add a personal ending to the stem.

hablar		
yo	habl**o**	*I speak*
tú	habl**as**	*you* (informal) *speak*
usted, él/ella	habl**a**	*you* (formal) *speak, he/she speaks*
nosotros(as)	habl**amos**	*we speak*
vosotros(as)	habl**áis**	*you* (informal: Spain) *speak*
ustedes, ellos/ellas	habl**an**	*you speak, they speak*

How to use the present tense

Use the present tense to express

(1) what people do in a general sense: Anita studies languages.

(2) what they're doing in a particular instance: Anita is studying languages this semester.

(3) what they do habitually: She studies a lot in the evening.

(4) what they intend to do at a later time: Tomorrow she's studying with Laura.

In this sense the present tense in Spanish is more flexible than in English.

(1) Anita estudia lenguas.
Anita studies languages.

(2) Anita estudia lenguas este semestre.
Anita is studying languages this semester.

(3) Ella estudia mucho por la noche.
She studies a lot in the evening.

(4) Mañana estudia con Laura.
Tomorrow she's studying with Laura.

In this chapter, you have already seen some **-ar** verbs in the **En contexto** section on pages 24–25. Now study the following verbs with useful example phrases:

descansar por una hora	*to rest for an hour*	Yo descanso por una hora.
escuchar música	*to listen to music*	Tú escuchas música en tu cuarto *(room).*
estudiar en la biblioteca	*to study in the library*	Él estudia español en la biblioteca.
llegar a la clase	*to arrive at class*	Ella llega a la clase de historia.
mandar cartas/mensajes	*to send letters/messages*	Usted manda cartas a su mamá.
regresar a casa	*to return home*	Vosotros regresáis a casa.
tomar clases/exámenes	*to take classes/tests*	Nosotros tomamos un examen mañana.
trabajar por la noche	*to work at night*	Ellos trabajan por la noche.

Here are some more common **-ar** verbs:

ayudar	*to help*	**llamar**	*to call; to phone*
bailar	*to dance*	**mirar**	*to watch*
buscar	*to look for*	**necesitar**	*to need*
caminar	*to walk*	**pagar**	*to pay*
cantar	*to sing*	**pasar tiempo**	*to spend (time); to pass*
comprar	*to buy*	**practicar**	*to practice*
contestar	*to answer*	**preguntar**	*to ask (a question)*
desear	*to want; to wish*	**terminar**	*to finish*
dibujar	*to draw*	**tocar**	*to touch; to play an instrument*
enseñar	*to teach*	**usar**	*to use*
entrar	*to enter*	**viajar**	*to travel*
esperar	*to hope; to expect; to wait*	**visitar**	*to visit*

Much like the phrases in English *to want, to hope,* and *to need,* the Spanish verbs **desear, esperar,** and **necesitar** are often followed by the infinitive of another verb. **Deseo/Espero/Necesito estudiar** means *I want/hope/need to study.*

The following words and phrases are used in Spanish to express how well, how often, or how much you do something: **(muy) bien** *(very) well,* **(muy) mal** *(very) poorly,* **todos los días** *everyday,* **siempre** *always,* **a veces** *sometimes,* **nunca** *never,* **mucho** *a lot,* **(muy) poco** *(very) little.*

¿Recuerdas?

Heinle/Cengage Learning

Ana: **Estudio** sicología, geografía, francés, alemán e inglés.
Claudio: Ah, eres estudiante de lenguas, ¿verdad?
Ana: Sí. **Deseo** ser intérprete. Y tú, ¿qué **estudias** aquí en Chicago?

¡A practicar!

1-21 **¡Juan tiene una vida loca! *(Juan has a crazy life!)*** Juan's busy student life is described in the following paragraph. Conjugate the verbs in parentheses to agree with the subjects.

Yo soy Juan y tengo una vida loca. Mi compañero de cuarto, Miguel, y yo ______________ *(1. tomar) seis clases este semestre. Miguel también* ______________ *(2. trabajar) quince horas a la semana* (a week) *en la biblioteca. Yo* ______________ *(3. necesitar) más* (more) *dinero pero no* ______________ *(4. trabajar) porque* (because) *yo* ______________ *(5. tocar) el saxofón en una banda de jazz. Dos días a la semana yo* ______________ *(6. enseñar) español a unos chicos* (kids) *de la escuela primaria* (elementary school). *¡Ellos* ______________ *(7. practicar) mucho! Por la noche, Miguel y yo* ______________ *(8. estudiar),* ______________ *(9. hablar) por teléfono con las novias o* ______________ *(10. descansar). Yo* ______________ *(11. bailar) en las fiestas* (parties) *con mi novia, Carmen. Mis padres y yo* ______________ *(12. visitar) a la abuela* (grandmother) *y* ______________ *(13. pasar) tiempo con la familia.*

1-22 **La vida en la universidad** Describe what the following people do, using appropriate phrases from the right column and conjugating the verbs correctly.

Modelo María y yo — bailar muy bien
María y yo bailamos muy bien.

1. yo	desear tocar la guitarra
2. mi amiga	mirar la televisión
3. mis compañeros de clase	descansar por la noche
4. nosotros	pagar los libros de texto
5. el (la) profesor(a)	cantar con la música del radio
6. mi compañero de cuarto	escuchar música en español
7. ¿...?	estudiar español

1-23 **El primer *(first)* día de clases** Complete the paragraph by selecting the correct verb for each blank and conjugating it in the proper form. Each verb will be used only one time.

ayudar	comprar	mandar
buscar	contestar	necesitar
caminar	llegar	regresar

El primer día en la universidad, Liliana 1. ______________ *rápidamente a la clase de español y 2.* ______________ *a clase temprano* (early). *Los estudiantes 3.* ______________ *las preguntas de la profesora. Un estudiante 4.* ______________ *ayuda, y Liliana 5.* ______________ *al estudiante. Después* (After) *de clase, Liliana y otros estudiantes 6.* ______________ *la librería en el mapa. En la librería ellos 7.* ______________ *los libros. Más tarde, Liliana 8.* ______________ *a la residencia y 9.* ______________ *correos electrónicos* (e-mails) *a muchos amigos.*

Workbook *1-11 – 1-12*
Lab Manual *1-10– 1-12*

¡A conversar!

1-24 Mi rutina diaria *(My daily routine)* In pairs, read each of the following statements and decide whether it is **cierto** *(true)* or **falso** *(false)* for you. Correct false statements to make them true for you.

Modelo Yo hablo mucho español en la clase.
E1 *Sí, yo hablo mucho español en la clase.*
E2 *Sí, yo también* (also) *hablo mucho español en la clase.*
o No, no hablo mucho español en la clase.

1. Yo descanso después de la clase.
2. Mis compañeros y yo hablamos español en la residencia.
3. El (La) profesor(a) llega tarde a la clase.
4. Después de la clase mis compañeros regresan a casa.
5. Yo trabajo por la noche.
6. Nosotros practicamos el vocabulario en la clase.
7. Yo tomo cinco clases este semestre.
8. Nosotros necesitamos estudiar mucho.

1-25 Nuevos amigos *(New friends)* The people in the photo have just arrived at the home they will be sharing in Puerto Rico. They are getting to know one another and sharing information about their favorite activities. Form sentences to learn something about each one and then tell your partner if you and your friends enjoy the same activities.

Modelo Alejandra: bailar
Alejandra baila. Yo bailo mucho. Mi amiga Sally baila, pero mis amigos Tom y Linda no bailan.

1. Sofía: estudiar mucho; viajar a Italia frecuentemente; buscar un apartamento en Puerto Rico
2. Antonio: escuchar música; pasar tiempo con amigos; estudiar administración de empresas
3. Javier: mirar fútbol en la tele *(TV)*; practicar fútbol con amigos; no desear ser médico
4. Alejandra: tomar clases de fotografía; desear tomar más clases; bailar mucho
5. Valeria: viajar mucho; comprar mucho; hablar con amigos por teléfono

1-26 Entrevista *(Interview)* Ask a classmate what he/she does around campus. Why is the **tú** form used in this activity?

1. ¿Estudias mucho en la biblioteca? ¿Qué estudias?
2. ¿Hablas por teléfono con estudiantes de otras residencias? ¿Con quién hablas?
3. ¿Qué compras en la librería?
4. ¿Llegas a la universidad en auto, en autobús, en bicicleta o a pie *(on foot)*?
5. Cuando regresas a casa, ¿estudias, trabajas o descansas?
6. ¿Tocas un instrumento?
7. ¿Qué programas de televisión miras?
8. ¿Caminas mucho en el campus?

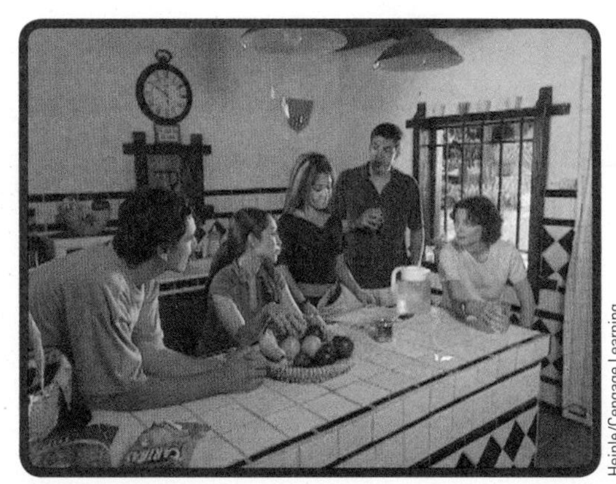
Heinle/Cengage Learning

La hora y los días de la semana

¿Qué hora es? ***(What time is it?)*** can be answered in different ways, depending on the time and whether you are using the 12-hour or the 24-hour system.

- The 12-hour system is used in informal situations such as when you are speaking with friends and family.
- The 24-hour system is used for class schedules, airline and train schedules, medical and business appointments, and formal and official gatherings. In this system 1 a.m. is the first hour of the day and hours are numbered consecutively to 24.

1. On the hour

Informal: **Es la una de la tarde.**

Formal: **Son las trece (horas).**
It's one o'clock p.m.

Informal: **Son las siete de la mañana.**

Formal: **Son las siete (horas).**
It's seven o'clock a.m.

2. On the quarter or the half hour

Son las siete y cuarto de la mañana. Son las siete y quince.

It's a quarter past seven a.m.
It's seven fifteen.

Son las siete y media de la mañana. Son las siete y treinta.

It's seven thirty a.m.

Son las ocho menos cuarto de la mañana.
Son las siete y cuarenta y cinco.

It's a quarter to eight a.m.
It's seven forty-five.

3. Minutes before and after the hour

Es la una y diez de la mañana.
Es la una y diez.

It's ten after one a.m.
It's one ten.

Son las ocho menos diez de la noche.
Son las diecinueve y cincuenta.

It's ten till eight p.m.
It's seven fifty.

Use **es** to tell time between 12:35 (**Es la una menos veinticinco**) and 1:30 (**Es la una y media**). Otherwise, use **son** because it refers to more than one hour (it is plural).

To ask or tell what time an event occurs, use the word **a: ¿A qué hora es la clase de matemáticas? A las once de la mañana.**

Other time expressions include **a tiempo** *on time,* **en punto** *on the dot,* **ahora** *now,* **tarde** *late, tardy,* **temprano** *early,* **la medianoche** *midnight,* and **el mediodía** *noon.*

¿Qué día es hoy? *(What day is today?)*

Hoy es...

lunes *Monday*
martes *Tuesday*
miércoles *Wednesday*
jueves *Thursday*
viernes *Friday*
sábado *Saturday*
domingo *Sunday*

Notice that the days of the week are not capitalized in Spanish as they are in English.

Other important words and expressions when talking about the days of the week are:

el día *day*
la semana *week*
el fin de semana *weekend*
todos los días *every day*
hoy *today*
mañana *tomorrow*

¡A practicar!

1-27 ¿Qué hora es? Indicate the time shown on each of the clocks below. Use the 12-hour system.

1. ____________________

2.  ____________________

3. 

____

4.  ____________________

5.  ____________________

1-28 ¿Qué día es mañana? Complete the following sentences.

1. Hoy es domingo. Mañana es ________________.
2. Hoy es viernes. Mañana es ________________.
3. Hoy es jueves. Mañana es ________________.
4. Hoy es sábado. Mañana es ________________.
5. Hoy es lunes. Mañana es ________________.
6. Hoy es martes. Mañana es ________________.

Workbook *1-13 – 1-14*
Lab Manual *1-13 – 1-14*

¡A conversar!

1-29 Mi horario *(My schedule)* You and a friend have just received your schedules for a study-abroad experience in Venezuela. Share information about the classes you will take as well as the days and times of the classes in order to determine if you have classes and free time in common. Note that the schedules use the 24-hour-clock system, but when you speak to your friend you will use the 12-hour-clock system.

Modelo **E1:** *Mi clase de sociología es a las nueve de la mañana los lunes y miércoles.*
E2: *Mi clase de sociología es a la una y media de la tarde los martes y jueves. Mi clase de historia es a las once y quince los miércoles y viernes.*

HORARIO DE CLASES Universidad Central de Venezuela Facultad de Ciencias Sociales		
LUNES/MIÉRCOLES	9.00	Sociología
MIÉRCOLES/VIERNES	11.15	Historia
LUNES/MIÉRCOLES	13.30	Economía aplicada
MARTES/JUEVES	15.45	Sicología
LUNES/MIÉRCOLES	18.45	Economía internacional

HORARIO DE CLASES Universidad Central de Venezuela Facultad de Ciencias Sociales		
LUNES/MIÉRCOLES	9.00	Derecho civil
MIÉRCOLES/VIERNES	11.15	Historia
MARTES/JUEVES	13.30	Sociología
MARTES/JUEVES	16.30	Antropología
LUNES/MIÉRCOLES	18.45	Economía internacional

1-30 Los días Ask your partner when he or she is doing the following things.

Modelo estudiar en la casa
—*¿Cuándo estudias en la casa?*
—*Estudio en la casa el lunes.*

1. mirar televisión
2. bailar en el cuarto
3. comprar libros
4. trabajar en el campus
5. mirar una película *(movie)* con amigos
6. comprar comida en la cafetería de la universidad

Heinle/Cengage Learning

Los nuevos compañeros de casa
You are about to meet five young people who will be sharing a house in Puerto Rico. Throughout the ***Plazas*** video episodes, you will observe the roommates interact, get to know each other, form friendships, and make plans for the future.

In this segment, the new roommates meet each other for the first time and explore their new home, **Hacienda Vista Alegre.** You will learn where they are from, what they are studying, and a little bit about their personalities.

Javier

Alejandra

Antonio

Sofía

Valeria

Heinle/Cengage Learning

Antes de ver

Expresiones útiles The following are some new expressions you will hear in the video.

¡Bienvenida!	*Welcome!*
¿Cómo te va?	*How's it going?*
Qué aburrido, ¿no?	*How boring!*
¡Ay... es una broma!	*Oh, it's just a joke!*

Enfoque estructural The following are expressions in the video with regular –**ar** verbs:

*Javier:	Me **llamo** Javier, mucho gusto.
Javier	¿Te **llevo** las maletas?
Antonio:	Yo te **ayudo**.
Antonio:	¿Por qué **preguntas**?
*Sofía:	**Estudio** filología española en la universidad.
*Alejandra:	Además, **trabajo** como asistente de un fotógrafo.
*Valeria:	**Cantas** música norteña.

1. **Recordemos** *(Let's remember)* What expressions have you learned to use to introduce yourself and greet others? What are the typical responses when you meet someone?
2. **Practiquemos** *(Let's practice)* For each of the statements in **Enfoque estructural** marked by an asterisk, supply a question in Spanish that would produce the statement.
3. **Charlemos** *(Let's chat)* Generate a list of possible fields of study that these five students might pursue. Of these, which are the five most popular among your classmates?

Después de ver

1. Así soy yo Now that you have seen the video, can you write statements below that each person might make about himself or herself? Use the word bank to help you.

Argentina	Colombia	cómico	España	Italia
inteligente	medicina	Texas	tomar fotos	Venezuela

- Alejandra: *Me llamo Alejandra. Soy de Colombia y tomo fotos.*
- Valeria: ____________________
- Sofía: ____________________
- Antonio: ____________________
- Javier: ____________________

2. ¿Qué estudias? After you have watched the video a few times, see if you can match each roommate with his/her specialization.

Javier estudia	filología española.
Antonio estudia	medicina.
Sofía estudia	danza moderna.
Valeria estudia	administración de empresas.
Alejandra estudia	diseño.

Filología, or philology in English, is the study of language use in literature.

3. Entre nosotros Now that you have identified what each roommate of **Hacienda Vista Alegre** studies, do a similar inventory of your classmates. Talk to at least five different students and record the information on the chart below. Be sure to ask the appropriate question for each category of information.

Nombre	Lugar de origen	Especialización académica

4. Presentaciones Choose one of your classmates that you interviewed for **Entre nosotros** and present this individual to the class. Have students guess what he or she studies.

See the *Lab Manual,* **Capítulo 1, 1-17 – 1-19** for additional activities.

Antes de leer

Strategy: Recognizing cognates

Cognates (**cognados**) are words from different languages that are identical or very similar in spelling and meaning. There are many cognates in Spanish and English; your ability to recognize them and guess their meaning will help you to read Spanish more efficiently. However, you should also be aware of "false cognates" in Spanish and English, such as **éxito,** which means *success,* **dirección,** which means *address,* **lectura,** which means *reading,* and **librería,** which means *bookstore.*

While reading the following advertisement, identify five cognates.

¡ESPAÑOL PARA TU FUTURO!

—Cursos intensivos, lecciones individuales para estudiantes de universidades o de colegios universitarios desde Santa Fe, Nuevo México
—Actividades diarias: vocabulario, estructuras gramaticales y práctica auditiva y oral
—La práctica oral es en Skype®: los instructores y los estudiantes hablan y practican español cara a cara en línea
—Horario: todos los días, dos horas diarias en persona en línea y cuatro horas de práctica con tarea en la computadora

Now, can you deduce the meaning of these cognates? List each of the cognates and its meaning.

____________	____________
____________	____________
____________	____________
____________	____________
____________	____________

Español en línea

Skim the following advertisement about Spanish language learning **(Español en línea con Skype®)** and identify as many cognates as you can. Then, indicate what you think each cognate means in English. Feel free to guess if you need to. Based on the cognates you have identified, what do you think is the purpose of the ad? Compare your answers with those of a classmate.

© Andresr/Shutterstock

Heinle/Cengage Learning

Después de leer

A escoger. Read the advertisement once more and answer the following questions.

1. What is this advertisement about?
   a. getting a new computer
   b. getting a new program to study languages
   c. learning a new language, Spanish, through a computer course
2. This advertisement is directed toward…
   a. children
   b. professionals
   c. college students
3. According to the advertisement, your plan of study should be:
   a. 4 hours online with Skype® and 1 hour of online homework
   b. 2 hours online with Skype® and 4 hours of online homework
   c. 2 hours online with Skype®and 2 hours of online homework
4. According to the advertisement, the students will meet with their instructors:
   a. face to face online
   b. face to face in the classroom at the university
   c. face to face at the library

¿Cierto o falso? Indicate whether each statement is **cierto** *(true)* or **falso** *(false)*. Then correct the false statements.

1. ______ To take this Spanish course, you will have to have access to a computer.
2. ______ To take this class, you have to register with other students.
3. ______ The conversation classes are available every day, 24 hours a day.
4. ______ Students have to pay 53 dollars per credit.

¡A conversar! With two or three of your classmates, write and design an advertisement for your ideal Spanish course, using as many cognates as you can. Be sure to include the following details.

- Method of delivery (online, classroom, hybrid, video conference)
- Types of exercises (oral, written)
- Class size
- Cost of the course

When you have finished, present your ad to the class.

Strategy: Organizing your ideas

A good way to improve your writing is to organize the ideas you want to express before you actually begin composing your document.

Task: Writing a short personal profile

Short personal profiles occur in many contexts, such as newspapers, newsletters, and websites of companies, campus groups, and civic organizations. They are often used to introduce a new member of a group or to highlight a recent accomplishment of an individual. In this activity you will write a profile of a student at your university for the International Club newsletter.

Paso 1 Look at the chart below and familiarize yourself with the information about María Sánchez Pérez.

Nombre	María Sánchez Pérez	**Escuela**	Universidad de Miami
Nación	Estados Unidos	**Cursos**	francés, contabilidad, periodismo, economía
Lenguas	español e inglés	**Intereses**	tocar el piano, escuchar música clásica, cantar

Paso 2 Now read the following description of María Sánchez Pérez. Note how the information in the chart is used in this paragraph.

> María Sánchez Pérez es de los Estados Unidos. Ella habla español e inglés. María es estudiante de la Universidad de Miami, en Florida. Estudia francés, contabilidad, periodismo y economía. Toca el piano, escucha música clásica y canta muy bien.

Paso 3 Now interview a classmate to fill out the third column on the chart with information about him/her. Then write a similar descriptive paragraph about him/her.

Nombre	María Sánchez Pérez	Tu compañero(a) de clase:
Nación	Estados Unidos	
Lenguas	español e inglés	
Escuela	Universidad de Miami	
Cursos	francés, contabilidad, periodismo, economía	
Intereses	tocar el piano, escuchar música clásica, cantar	

Paso 4 Exchange your paragraph with a classmate. Check over each other's work for mistakes and correct any mistakes that you find. Discuss the corrections and comments you made, and then return his/her paragraph. You may wish to share your paragraphs with other classmates, either by distributing them in class or by posting them on a class website.

Communicative Goals:

- Identify people, places and things in an educational setting
- Specify colors
- Communicate about common activities
- Tell time and indicate days of the week

Paso 1

Review the Communicative Goals for **Capítulo 1** and determine if you are able to accomplish the goals. If you are not certain that you have achieved all of the goals, review the pertinent portions of the chapter.

Paso 2

Look at the components of a conversation, which address the communicative goals for this chapter. The percentages will help you evaluate your ability to successfully participate in the conversation featured below. Your instructor may use the same rubric to assess your oral performance.

Components of the conversation	%
☐ Appropriate greeting	10
☐ Suitable introduction	10
☐ Information about city or country of origin	10
☐ Questions and answers about at least two pieces of information regarding academic life	20
☐ Indication of having a job or not having one	10
☐ Information about at least three activities that you do regularly	30
☐ Information about at least one activity that you do not do or do not do very much	10

En acción Work with a partner to carry out the conversation outlined below. You meet one another on campus at 2:00 in the afternoon. Be sure to address each specified item. Look at the following list of steps that you and another person might use in an informal conversation and consider how information will be exchanged. Note how questions should be asked and how answers will be given.

1. Greet one another appropriately according to the formality or informality of the situation and the time of day or night.
2. Introduce yourselves and shake hands.
3. Ask and tell each other where you are from.
4. Exchange information about:
   a. your academic life (classes, instructors, activities, important places on campus)
   b. your work or job, if you have one (where you work, your work schedule)
   c. several thing you do regularly and at least one you do not do (school, work and leisure activities)

¡A REPASAR!

Definite and indefinite articles

A noun is often preceded by a definite article: **el, la, los, las** *(the)*, or by an indefinite article: **un, una** *(a, an)*, **unos, unas** *(some)*. Both definite and indefinite articles agree in number and gender with the nouns they modify.

el libro, un libro	las mochilas, unas mochilas

¡A recordar! 1 In Spanish, what endings typically denote masculine nouns? What about feminine nouns?

How to make nouns plural

To make Spanish nouns plural, add **-s** to nouns ending in a vowel, and **-es** to nouns ending in a consonant.

Singular	Plural	Singular	Plural
el amigo	los amigos	un profesor	unos profesores
la amiga	las amigas	una universidad	unas universidades

¡A recordar! 2 How is the plural formed for nouns ending in **-án, -és,** or **-ión**? What about for nouns ending in **-z**?

Present tense of regular *-ar* verbs

To form the present tense of Spanish verbs ending in **-ar,** drop the infinitive ending and add a personal ending to the stem.

hablar	
(yo)	hablo
(tú)	hablas
(usted, él/ella)	habla
(nosotros/nosotras)	hablamos
(vosotros/vosotras)	habláis
(ustedes, ellos/ellas)	hablan

¡A recordar! 3 In what four instances might someone use the present tense?

Common *-ar* verbs

ayudar, bailar, cantar, comprar, dibujar, enseñar, entrar, mirar, necesitar, practicar, preguntar, usar, viajar, visitar

¡A recordar! 4 What other common **-ar** verbs can you remember from Chapter 1?

Telling time

The 12-hour system is used in informal situations such as when you are speaking with friends and family: Son las tres de la tarde.
The 24-hour system is used for class schedules, airline and train schedules, medical and business appointments, and formal and official gatherings. In this system 1 a.m. is the first hour of the day and hours are numbered consecutively to 24: **Son las quince horas.**

¡A recordar! 5 How do you say *It is one o'clock in the afternoon?*

Actividad 1 Los artículos For each item, write the appropriate definite article **(el, la, los, las)** in the first blank and the appropriate indefinite article **(un, una, unos, unas)** in the second blank.

1. ________ domingo es ________ día.
2. ________ medianoche es ________ hora.
3. ________ educación es ________ curso.
4. ________ ingeniería es ________ profesión.
5. ________ lápices son ________ objetos útiles.
6. ________ mapa es ________ representación del mundo *(world)*.
7. ________ profesores son ________ personas importantes de la universidad.
8. ________ Golfo de México es parte de ________ océano.
9. ________ gimnasio es ________ edificio.
10. ________ ciencias son ________ clases interesantes.

Actividad 2 ¿Qué hay en la clase? Write the appropriate plural form of the words in parentheses to tell what is in the classroom.

En la clase hay...

1. 20 ________________ (libro de texto)
2. 15 ________________ (borrador)
3. 18 ________________ (mochila)
4. 28 ________________ (pupitre)
5. 2 ________________ (borrador)
6. 12 ________________ (lápiz)
7. 15 ________________ (bolígrafo)
8. 2 ________________ (reloj)
9. 20 ________________ (papel)
10. 4 ________________ (luz)

Actividad 3 Una noche en la residencia estudiantil Complete the paragraph with the correct form of each verb in parentheses.

Yo ______________ (llegar) a la residencia y ______________ (visitar) a mis amigos. Mario ______________ (estudiar) y ______________ (tomar) café. Él y yo ______________ (hablar) un poco. Luisa ______________ (escuchar) música y ______________ (preparar) una presentación para una clase. Diana ______________ (ayudar) con la presentación. Ramón y Tonia ______________ (practicar) español. Catalina y Javier ______________ (usar) la computadora. Paco ______________ (necesitar) estudiar, pero ______________ (desear) dormir una siesta. Él ______________ (descansar) por quince minutos. Pilar ______________ (tocar) la guitarra y ______________ (cantar). Los amigos ______________ (bailar). Jorge y Carlos ______________ (mirar) la televisión. Federico ______________ (trabajar) en la cafetería y yo ______________ (llamar) a la cafetería porque yo ______________ (desear) hablar con él.

Actividad 4 Las actividades de los estudiantes Choose the correct verb from the list to complete each sentence and write the appropriate form in the blank.

caminar	hablar	practicar
comprar	mandar	regresar
descansar	pagar	tomar
enseñar	pasar	usar

1. Los amigos de Marta ______________ español porque son de España.
2. Mi madre ______________ los libros de texto que ______________ en mis clases.
3. Yo ______________ mucho tiempo en la biblioteca.
4. Los estudiantes ______________ libros en la librería.
5. Mi amigo y yo ______________ café en la cafetería estudiantil.
6. Tú ______________ mucho correo electrónico, ¿no?
7. Mis compañeros ______________ a clase.
8. Muchos estudiantes ______________ a la residencia tarde los sábados y ______________ los domingos.
9. Mis amigos y yo ______________ fútbol y tenis.
10. La profesora ______________ clases en dos universidades.

Actividad 5 ¿Qué hora es? Tell the time shown by the clocks.

Modelo *Son las cinco* de la tarde.

1. ______________ de la mañana.

2. ______________ de la noche.

3. ______________ de la tarde.

4. ______________ de la tarde.

5. ______________ de la mañana.

Heinle/Cengage Learning

Refrán

Heinle/Cengage Learning

El propósito de ________ *(to work)* es llegar a ________ *(to rest).*

VOCABULARIO ESENCIAL

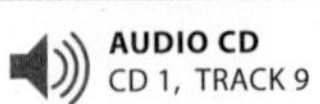
AUDIO CD
CD 1, TRACK 9

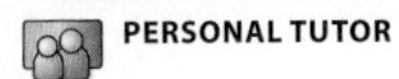
PERSONAL TUTOR

Objetos en la clase	Objects in the classroom
el bolígrafo	ballpoint pen
el borrador	eraser
la calculadora	calculator
el calendario	calendar
la computadora	computer
el cuaderno	notebook
el diccionario	dictionary
el dinero	money
el escritorio	desk
el examen	test
el lápiz (los lápices)	pencil(s)
la lección	lesson
el libro (de texto)	(text)book
la luz (las luces)	light(s)
el mapa	map
el marcador	marker
la mochila	backpack
la palabra	word
la pantalla	screen
el papel	paper
la pizarra	chalkboard
la pluma	fountain pen
el pupitre	student desk
el reloj	watch
la silla	chair
la tarea	homework
la tiza	chalk

Personas en la clase	People in the classroom
el (la) amigo(a)	friend
el (la) chico(a)	boy/girl
el (la) compañero(a) de clase	classmate
el (la) compañero(a) de cuarto	roommate
el (la) estudiante	student
el hombre	man
el (la) muchacho(a)	boy/girl
la mujer	woman
el (la) novio(a)	boyfriend/girlfriend
el (la) profesor(a)	professor

Colores	Colors
amarillo	yellow
anaranjado	orange
azul	blue
blanco	white
marrón	brown
morado	purple
negro	black
rojo	red
verde	green

El campus	Campus
el apartamento	apartment
la biblioteca	library
la cafetería	cafeteria
el centro estudiantil	student center
la facultad	school, department
el gimnasio	gymnasium
la librería	bookstore
la oficina	office
la residencia	dormitory

Cursos y especializaciones	Courses and majors
la administración de empresas	business administration
el arte	art
las ciencias	science
las ciencias sociales	social science
la computación	computer science
el derecho	law
la economía	economics
la educación	education
la geografía	geography
la historia	history
la ingeniería	engineering
las lenguas extranjeras	foreign languages
la literatura	literature
las matemáticas	math
la medicina	medicine
la música	music
el periodismo	journalism
la sicología	psychology
la sociología	sociology
el teatro	theater

Las lenguas extranjeras	Foreign languages
el alemán	German
el chino	Chinese
el español	Spanish
el francés	French
el inglés	English
el italiano	Italian
el japonés	Japanese
el portugués	Portuguese
el ruso	Russian

Los días de la semana	Days of the week
el lunes	Monday
el martes	Tuesday
el miércoles	Wednesday
el jueves	Thursday
el viernes	Friday
el sábado	Saturday
el domingo	Sunday

La hora	Time
ahora	now
a tiempo	on time
de (por) la mañana (tarde/noche)	in the morning (afternoon/evening)
en punto	on time
el fin de semana	weekend
hoy	today
mañana	tomorrow
la medianoche	midnight
el mediodía	noon
el reloj	clock
tarde	late
temprano	early
todos los días	every day
¿A qué hora...?	At what time...?
¿Qué hora es?	What time is it?

Artículos	
el	the (masc.)
la	the (fem.)
los	the (masc. pl.)
las	the (fem. pl.)
un	a (masc.)
unos	some (masc.)
una	a (fem.)
unas	some (fem.)

Verbos	
ayudar	to help
bailar	to dance
buscar	to look for
caminar	to walk
cantar	to sing
comprar	to buy
contestar	to answer
descansar	to rest
desear	to want; to wish
dibujar	to draw
enseñar	to teach
entrar	to enter
escuchar	to listen
esperar	to hope; to expect
estudiar	to study
llamar	to call; to phone
llegar	to arrive
mandar	to send
mirar	to watch
necesitar	to need
pagar	to pay
pasar tiempo	to spend (time); to pass
practicar	to practice
preguntar	to ask (a question)
regresar	to return
terminar	to finish
tocar	to touch; to play an instrument
tomar	to take
trabajar	to work
usar	to use
viajar	to travel
visitar	to visit

CAPÍTULO

En una reunión familiar

2

México

Plaza de los Laureles, Guadalajara, México

Chapter Objectives

Communicative Goals

In this chapter, you will learn how to . . .

- Identify and discuss family relationships
- Indicate ownership and possession
- Describe people and things and indicate nationality
- Communicate about daily activities at home or at school
- Express obligation or desire to do something

Structures

- Possession with **de(l)** and possessive adjectives
- Common uses of the verb **ser**
- Agreement with descriptive adjectives
- Present tense of -**er** and -**ir** verbs
- Common uses of the verb **tener**

▲ Do you go to the park with your family and friends?

▲ When do you get together with your family?

▲ Whom do you include when you mention family?

▲ Do you have family reunions? How often? Where? What do you do at family gatherings?

 Visit it live on **Google Earth!**

La familia de Juan Carlos García Martínez

In this section, you will practice talking about family relationships by learning about the family of Juan Carlos. Do you know of any families like Juan Carlos's that have relatives living in two or more countries?

Cultura

D.F. stands for *Distrito Federal* and is commonly used to refer to Mexico City.

¡Hola! Me llamo Juan Carlos. Mi **padre** se llama Jorge y mi **madre** se llama Ana María. **Papá** es del D.F. y **mamá**, de Los Ángeles. Mi **hermana** se llama Juana y mi **hermano** se llama Rafael. Nuestro **perro** se llama Hércules. Mis **abuelos**, Pedro y Elena, son de Guadalajara. Papá tiene dos hermanos: mi **tío** Tomás y mi **tía** Esperanza. Mi tía Esperanza y su **esposo** Paco tienen dos **hijos**: mis **primos** Gabriela y Felipe. Ellos tienen un **gato** que se llama Tigre.

Jorge: el padre (papá)
Ana María: la madre (mamá)
Rafael: el hermano
Juana: la hermana
Juan Carlos
Hércules: el perro

Más parientes *More relatives*

el (la) cuñado(a) *brother-in-law/sister-in-law*
el (la) esposo(a) *husband/wife*
el (la) hijo(a) *son/daughter*
el (la) nieto(a) *grandson/granddaughter*
la nuera *daughter-in-law*
los padres *parents*
el (la) sobrino(a) *nephew/niece*
el (la) suegro(a) *father-in-law/mother-in-law*
el yerno *son-in-law*

Más mascotas *More pets*

el pájaro *bird*
el pez *fish*

Nombres *Names*

el apellido *last name*
el nombre *first name*

Palabras útiles

el (la) hermanastro(a) *stepbrother / stepsister*
la madrastra *stepmother*
el (la) medio(a) hermano(a) *half brother (sister)*
el (la) niño(a) *child*
el padrastro *stepfather*
casado(a) *married*
divorciado(a) *divorced*
separado(a) *separated*
soltero(a) *single*

Palabras útiles are presented to help you enrich your personal vocabulary. The words here will help you talk about family relationships.

¡A practicar!

2-1 **¿Cierto o falso?** Indicate if each of the statements about Juan Carlos' family is **cierto** or **falso**.

_______ 1. Juan Carlos tiene *(has)* dos primas.
_______ 2. Pedro y Elena tienen tres nietos en total.
_______ 3. Tomás tiene dos hijas.
_______ 4. Ana María y Tomás son cuñados.
_______ 5. Hay dos mascotas en la familia.
_______ 6. Pedro es el suegro de Jorge.
_______ 7. Ana María es la nuera de Elena.
_______ 8. Hay un pez en la familia.
_______ 9. Gabriela es la sobrina de Tomás.
_______ 10. El yerno de Pedro es Jorge.

2-2 **La familia de Juan Carlos** Complete the following sentences with the correct relationship based on the drawing.

Modelo Ana María es *la esposa* de Jorge.

1. Juan Carlos es _______________ de Juana.
2. Felipe es _______________ de Esperanza.
3. Gabriela y Felipe son _______________.
4. El esposo de Esperanza es _______________ de Tomás.
5. Elena es _______________ de la hija de Jorge y Ana María.
6. La hija de Jorge y Ana María es _______________ de Esperanza.
7. Tomás es _______________ de los hijos de Jorge y Ana María.
8. Pedro es _______________ de Elena.

2-3 **En otras palabras** Indicate the relationships between the family members listed below.

Modelo yo / mi tía
Yo soy el (la) sobrino(a) de mi tía.
mi abuelo / mi padre
Mi abuelo es el padre de mi padre.

1. mi hermano(a) / mi abuelo
2. mi hijo(a) / mi hermano(a)
3. mi madre / mi hijo(a)
4. mi primo / mi mamá
5. mi padre / mi abuela
6. mi tío / mi primo(a)
7. mi padre / mi madre
8. mi abuela / mi padre

Workbook *2-1 – 2-4*
Lab Manual *2-1 – 2-3*

¡A conversar!

2-4 **Adivinanzas *(Riddles)*** Ask a classmate the following questions, keeping in mind that some of them may be purely hypothetical. Then, add three questions of your own.

Modelo **E1**: *¿Quién es el padre de tu madre?*
E2: *Mi abuelo.*

¿Quién es... ?

1. la madre de tu padre
2. el (la) hermano(a) de tu madre
3. la hija de tu tío
4. el (la) hijo(a) de tu padre
5. el hijo de tu hija

2-5 **Un árbol genealógico *(A family tree)***

Primera parte Create your own family tree, real or imagined, based on the categories below. Be artistic if you'd like!

Mis abuelos

______ ______ ______ ______

Mis padres

Mis tíos	**(papá)**	**(mamá)**	**Mis tíos**
______	______	______	______
______			______

Mis primos	**Mis hermanos**	**Yo**	**Mis primos**
______	______	______	______
______	______		______

Segunda parte Now describe your family relationships in Spanish to a partner. You should also mention your family pet(s). Your partner will then review your family tree with you before presenting it to the class.

2-6 **¿Quién en tu familia... ?** Identify people in your family who fit the characteristics listed below. Tell your partner the name of the person and his/her relationship to you. Continue by identifying people who do not fit the characteristics.

Modelo *Mi primo Jamal es cómico. Mi tía Elizabeth no es...*

artístico(a)	extrovertido(a)	paciente
atlético(a)	generoso(a)	responsable
dramático(a)	inteligente	sincero(a)

EN CONTEXTO

Juan Carlos and his sister, Juana, live in Los Angeles and are always eager to share their experiences in the United States with their grandparents, who continue to live in Mexico.

AUDIO CD
CD 1, TRACK 10

Listen to the conversation and establish whether the following statements are true (**cierto**) or false (**falso**). If a statement is false, correct it.

1. Los abuelos no tienen información sobre la vida de Juan Carlos en los Estados Unidos.
2. Juan Carlos no tiene muchos amigos en el nuevo barrio.
3. Todos los amigos de Juan Carlos hablan español.
4. Juana tiene una amiga que habla español y es de México.

Juana: ¡Hola, abuelos! ¿Cómo están? ¡Qué lindo el departamento! ¡Qué chido!

Juan Carlos: ¡Hola, abuelito! ¡Hola, abuelita! ¿Cómo están? ¡**Tengo** muchas noticias sobre **mi vida** en los Estados Unidos!

Comentario cultural Spanish-speakers use the diminutive forms of certain nouns to express affection. Juan Carlos addresses his grandparents as **abuelito** and **abuelita** (literally "*little grandfather*" and "*little grandmother*"). Another term of affection commonly used in Mexico is the contraction **m'hijo** or **m'hija** (from **mi hijo, mi hija**) to mean *my son, my daughter*.

Elena: ¡Ay, qué bueno, Juan Carlos! **Tenemos tus cartas y tus postales**, pero deseamos tener más información. Y Juana, las fotos que **tenemos** de **tu escuela** son **preciosas**.

Comentario cultural The Aztec calendar you see on the wall, also known as the Sun Stone, has two distinct functions. As a religious calendar, called the **tonalpohualli**, the sun stone marks a 260-day ritual cycle. As a day calendar, called the **xiuhpohualli**, it marks 365 days. These two cycles together form a 52-year-long "century."

Pedro: Y ahora **viven** en un **barrio nuevo. Debe ser** muy **diferente**. **¿Tienen** muchos amigos allí?

Comentario cultural According to legend, in 1531, Juan Diego, an Aztec descendant, had a vision of the Virgin Mary, who instructed him to build a church on the site of his vision. After the visit, Mary left her impression on Juan's tilma, a cloak made of cactus cloth. The cloth is displayed in a basilica in Mexico City where it is visited by over 10 million people a year.

Expresiones en contexto

el barrio *neighborhood*
las cartas *letters*
en la próxima manzana *on the next block*
entonces *so*
mis cuates *my friends (Mexico)*
la misma edad *the same age*
las noticias *news*
¡Qué lindo...! *How cute . . . !*
nunca crecen *never grow up*
por supuesto *of course*
las postales *postcards*
¡Qué chido! *Cool! (Mexico)*

Juan Carlos: Sí, abuelito. **Tengo** muchos compañeros, ¡y dos de **mis cuates** hablan español! Los padres de **mis amigos son mexicanos,** del D.F., y sus abuelos viven aquí. Los abuelos de mi amigo Enrique, don Ramón y doña Lucía, son muy simpáticos.

Comentario cultural The forms **don** and **doña** may be used before first names to show respect or affection (while maintaining formality); they are generally used for addressing one's elders or superiors. Juan Carlos's grandparents, for example, might be addressed as **don Pedro** and **doña Elena**. At one time, **don** stood for **de origen noble**.

Elena: ¡Entonces, muchas personas **tienen** nietos en los Estados Unidos!

Juan Carlos: Sí, por supuesto. Hay una **familia cubana** que **vive** en la calle Cuarenta y Dos, en la próxima manzana, y ellos **tienen** una hija de catorce años, de la misma edad que Juana.

Juana: Sí, ella se llama Lupe, y es **mi mejor amiga**. También **tengo** algunos amigos.

Comentario cultural Another indication of the importance of religion in Mexico is the Tree of Life, **Árbol de la vida**, a ceramic product of Metepec, Mexico. These creations consist of clay pieces in the shape of a tree, featuring biblical figures, flowers and leaves. The design is a blend of Aztec influences and the teachings of Franciscan monks.

Pedro: **¿Mi Juanita tiene catorce años y tiene amigos?** ¡Imposible!

Elena: ¿Ves cómo **tu abuelo vive** en el pasado, m'hija? Él **cree** que los niños nunca crecen.

 **Diálogo entre abuelo(a) y nieto(a)** Working with a partner, take turns role playing the situation of grandparents being reunited with their grandchildren. The grandchildren should indicate where they live and who they like to play with, etc.

Possession with *de(l)* and possessive adjectives

Possession with *de(l)*

One way English speakers express possession is to attach an apostrophe and an "s" to a noun. Spanish speakers show the same relationship by using **de** before the noun. Note that when using **de** + **el**, Spanish speakers form the contraction **del.**

Ariana es la hermana **de** Juan.
Ariana is Juan's sister.

El libro es **de la** tía Julia.
The book is Aunt Julia's.

Aquí está el perro **del** señor Roque.
Here is Mr. Roque's dog.

Possessive adjectives

Another way to indicate relationships or ownership is to use possessive adjectives. In Spanish, possessive adjectives must match the number (singular or plural) and, in the cases of **nosotros(as)** and **vosotros(as)**, the gender (masculine or feminine) of the nouns they describe.

	Singular	Plural
my	mi abuelo	mis abuelos
your (informal, singular)	tu gato	tus gatos
his, her, its, your (formal, singular)	su familia	sus familias
our	nuestro hijo	nuestros hijos
	nuestra hija	nuestras hijas
your (informal, plural: Spain)	vuestro primo	vuestros primos
	vuestra prima	vuestras primas
their, your (plural)	su madre	sus madres

Heinle/Cengage Learning

Juan Carlos: ¡Hola, abuelito! ¡Hola, abuelita! ¿Cómo están? ¡Tengo muchas noticias sobre **mi vida** en los Estados Unidos!

¡A practicar!

2-7 Cada uno con lo suyo *(To each his own)* Members of Juan Carlos's family have strong preferences for certain colors. Use **del, de la, de las**, or **de los** to indicate to whom the following objects belong.

Modelo La pluma _____ es _____ esposo de Ana María.
La pluma azul es del esposo de Ana María.

1.

2. 

3. 

4. 

Heinle/Cengage Learning

1. La bicicleta _______ es _______ abuela.
2. Las mochilas _______ son _______ nieta.
3. El coche _______ es _______ tíos de Juan Carlos.
4. Las computadoras _______ son _______ esposo de Ana María.

2-8 Las memorias de Maximiliano Imagine you are listening to Maximiliano, emperor of Mexico, describe his family and residence in Mexico. Complete the following paragraph with the indicated possessive adjective.

1. _______ *(My)* padres y abuelos viven en Austria, pero 2. _______ *(our)* familia vive en México. 3. _______ *(My)* hermano Francisco José es emperador de Austria. 4. _______ *(His)* palacio es enorme. 5. _______ *(My)* palacio, en el parque de Chapultepec, también es grande y majestuoso. Es aquí donde mi esposa y yo pasamos la mayoría de 6. _______ *(our)* tiempo. El nombre de mi esposa es Marie-Charlotte-Amélie-Augustine-Victoire-Clémentine-Léopoldine, pero para 7. _______ *(her)* amigas es Carlota.

Cultura

Maximilian was born in Austria in 1832. He was a member of the Hapsburg dynasty. He went to Mexico in 1864 with his wife Carlota to rule over a new empire in Mexico, after the current President Benito Juárez decided not to pay interest on foreign loans.

Workbook *2-5 – 2-6*
Lab Manual *2-4 – 2-6*

¡A conversar!

2-9 ¿Es tu libro o mi libro? Working in groups of three or four, take turns role-playing a forgetful student. When the student asks the others to whom an item in the classroom belongs, they respond in either the affirmative or negative. Use as many items as you can.

Modelo libro
E1 *¿Es mi libro?*
E2 *No, no es tu libro. Es el libro de David.*

tizas
E1 *¿Son mis tizas?*
E2 *Sí, son tus tizas.*

1. la mochila
2. el reloj
3. los lápices
4. el escritorio
5. el cuaderno
6. las calculadoras
7. el libro de español
8. los diccionarios
9. los papeles
10. la silla

2-10 Entrevista Ask a classmate the following questions to learn more about his/her family and friends.

1. ¿Es grande tu familia? ¿Cuántas personas hay en tu familia? ¿Hay una mascota? ¿De dónde son tus padres? ¿Trabajan mucho tus padres? ¿Mira la tele mucho tu hermano(a)? ¿Cómo se llaman tus tíos y tías? ¿Cómo se llaman sus esposos y sus hijos? ¿Estudian o trabajan tus primos?
2. ¿Son tus mejores *(best)* amigos(as) de aquí? ¿Qué estudian tus amigos? ¿Cuáles son sus clases favoritas? ¿Caminan Uds. mucho en la universidad? ¿Bailan Uds. mucho? ¿Baila bien tu mejor amigo(a)?

Common uses of the verb *ser*

As you learned in **Capítulo preliminar**, the present tense of **ser** is formed as follows:

	subject pronoun	*ser* (to be)	
singular	yo	soy	*I am*
	tú	eres	*you (informal) are*
	él/ella, usted	es	*he/she is, you (formal) are*
plural	nosotros(as)	somos	*we are*
	vosotros(as)	sois	*you (informal: Spain) are*
	ellos(as), ustedes	son	*they are, you are*

The verb **ser** *(to be)* is used:

1. to identify essential characteristics of people and things.

   Carlos Fuentes **es** inteligente y creativo.
   Carlos Fuentes is intelligent and creative.

   Sus libros **son** interesantes.
   His books are interesting.

2. to indicate profession or vocation.

   Carlos Fuentes **es** escritor. *Carlos Fuentes is a writer.*
   Yo **soy** músico. *I am a musician.*
   Tú **eres** doctora. *You are a doctor.*

3. to express nationality . . .

   Carlos Fuentes **es** mexicano. *Carlos Fuentes is Mexican.*

   . . . and origin with the preposition **de.**

   El Sr. Fuentes **es de** México. *Mr. Fuentes is from Mexico.*

4. to talk about time.

   Son las cinco. *It's five o'clock.*
   Es la una. *It's one o'clock.*

5. to talk about days of the week, months, and dates.

   Hoy **es** lunes. *Today is Monday.*
   Mañana **es** el 4 de mayo. *Tomorrow is May 4.*

Nota lingüística

In Spanish, adjectives of nationality are not capitalized. Example: Hans es alemán. *Hans is German.*

¿Recuerdas?

Heinle/Cengage Learning

Juana: Sí, ella se llama Lupe, y **es** mi mejor amiga. También tengo algunos amigos.

¡A practicar!

2-11 ¡A emparejar! Choose the item(s) on the right that best complete(s) each statement on the left.

1. Yo soy ______.	a. difíciles.
2. Son las ______.	b. el cuatro de octubre.
3. Susana es ______.	c. estudiante.
4. Carlos es ______.	d. maestro de español.
5. Hoy es ______.	e. dos de la tarde.
6. Los problemas son ______.	f. simpática y sincera.

2-12 Imágenes de una civilización Fill in the blanks with the appropriate form of **ser** to learn some interesting facts about Mexico.

Modelo *Juan es de Aguascalientes, México.*

1. El Popocatépetl ______ un volcán activo cerca de la ciudad de México.
2. El emperador Maximiliano y su esposa ______ de Austria.
3. El Día de los Muertos ______ un día festivo muy importante para los mexicanos.
4. Felipe Calderón ______ el presidente de México.
5. Vosotros ______ españoles, pero en México, en vez de usar *vosotros*, la forma correcta ______ *ustedes*.
6. Rocío y Memo ______ estudiantes en la Universidad Nacional Autónoma de México.
7. El Zócalo ______ la plaza más grande y más conocida de México.
8. Las playas de México ______ muy hermosas.

2-13 Diego Diego Mejía writes an email to his host sister in Spain to introduce himself. Complete the email with the appropriate forms of **ser**.

¡Hola, María! Yo ______ Diego Mejía. ______ estudiante de ingeniería en la Universidad de las Américas, en Puebla, México. ¡Puebla ______ un lugar precioso! ¿Cómo ______ Madrid?
Yo ______ muy estudioso y tranquilo. Mis padres y yo ______ muy unidos (*close*). ¿Y cómo ______ tú? ¿Cómo ______ tus padres y tus hermanos?

¡Hasta pronto!

Diego

Workbook *2-7 – 2-8*
Lab Manual *2-7 – 2-9*

¡A conversar!

2-14 ¿Es cierto o no es cierto? Working with a partner, form sentences from the elements below, using the verb **ser** as needed and conjugating it correctly. Then read each sentence aloud and indicate if it is true (**Es cierto**) or not (**No es cierto**). Change elements in statements that are not true so that they are true.

1. Hoy / sábado y mañana / domingo.
2. Hoy / el dos de enero.
3. Yo / estudiante y estudio mucho.
4. Mis amigos / creativos.
5. Mis amigos y yo / inteligentes.
6. Mi madre / de Guadalajara, México.

2-15 Una presentación Prepare a short presentation for a partner or small group based on answers to the questions below. After each student has presented, combine information from the different presentations to create a new presentation.

1. ¿Qué día es hoy?
2. ¿Cuál es la fecha?
3. ¿Quién eres tú?
4. ¿De dónde eres?
5. ¿Cómo eres?
6. ¿Quién es una persona de tu familia?
7. ¿Cómo es él (ella)?

2-16 ¿Quiénes son las personas de la clase?

Paso 1:
Work in groups of three or four to identify all the students in your class by name. Speaking first with your group, use the verb **ser** to identify as many students as possible. **(Él es Bill. Ella es Ramona...)**. If you do not know the names of some students, get out of your seats and ask your classmates their names—in Spanish, of course!

Paso 2:
Your instructor will call up to ten students at a time to the front of the class and will ask one of them to identify himself or herself and as many others as possible. If the student cannot identify someone, he or she can ask the student. After everyone in one group has been identified, another group is called forward.

Modelo *Soy Anna. Ella es Kari, él es Dre y ellos son Marcus y Zhou. Y tú, ¿eres Samuel? Sí, eres Samuel.*

Agreement with descriptive adjectives

Heinle/Cengage Learning

Nota lingüística

It is common for Mexicans to use the word **güero(a)** to describe someone who is blond. **Pelirrojo** means red-haired.

The words modeled in the drawings are *adjectives* and are used to describe *nouns* or *pronouns*. In Spanish, descriptive adjectives must match the *gender* (masculine or feminine) and the *number* (singular or plural) of the noun or pronoun they describe.

How to match adjectives with their nouns

1. Spanish adjectives agree in number and gender with the nouns they modify. Adjectives ending in **-o** change to **-a** to indicate feminine gender and add an **-s** to indicate plural.

	Singular	Plural
Masculine	abuelo generos**o**	abuelos generos**os**
Feminine	abuela generos**a**	abuelas generos**as**

2. Adjectives ending in **-e** or in most consonants are invariable for gender. That is, they use the same form for the masculine and the feminine. For the plural of adjectives ending in **-e**, add **-s**. For the plural of adjectives ending in a consonant, add **-es**.

	Singular	Plural
Masculine	tío interesante hermano intelectual	tíos interesant**es** hermanos intelectual**es**
Feminine	tía interesante hermana intelectual	tías interesant**es** hermanas intelectual**es**

3. Most adjectives of nationality ending in a consonant add **-a** for the feminine form. To form the plural, add **-es** to masculine adjectives and **-s** to feminine adjectives. Most adjectives that end in **-dor, -án, -ón**, and **-ín** also follow this pattern.

	Singular	Plural
Masculine	primo español primo trabaja**dor** tío alem**án**	primos españo**les** primos trabajado**res** tíos alema**nes**
Feminine	prima españo**la** prima trabajador**a** tía aleman**a**	primas españo**las** primas trabajador**as** tías aleman**as**

Where to place adjectives

1. Most Spanish adjectives follow the nouns they describe.

   un escritorio viejo

   las estudiantes altas

2. Spanish adjectives of quantity precede the nouns they describe, as in English. Remember that in Spanish, when the number one is used to quantify a singular masculine noun, speakers drop the **-o: un libro, un papel.**

   Necesito cuatro plumas y un lápiz.

3. The adjectives **bueno** *(good)* and **malo** *(bad)* can be placed before or after the noun they describe. When they come before a singular masculine noun, the **-o** is dropped: **buen** and **mal**.

   Nuestro primo es un **buen** actor. Nuestro primo es un actor **bueno**.

   Su abuelo no es un **mal** hombre. Su abuelo no es un hombre **malo**.

The adjective **grande** can also be used before or after the noun it describes. When it precedes a singular noun (either masculine or feminine), it drops the **-de** to become **gran**. When **gran** precedes a noun, it takes on the figurative meaning of *great* or *impressive*. When **grande** follows a noun, it assumes its more literal meaning of *large* or *big*. For example,

Es una gran familia. *It's a great family.*

Es una familia grande. *It's a big family.*

Commonly used adjectives

aburrido(a) boring	**perezoso(a)** lazy
antipático(a) unpleasant	**pobre** poor
buen(o)(a) good	**rico(a)** rich
divertido(a) fun	**simpático(a)** nice, pleasant
listo(a) smart, ready	**tacaño(a)** stingy
mal(o)(a) bad	**tonto(a)** silly, foolish
nuevo(a) new	**trabajador(a)** hardworking

Cognates

Cognates are words of similar or identical spelling that share the same meaning between two languages. Many adjectives are cognates in Spanish and English.

arrogante arrogant	**generoso(a)** generous	**moderno(a)** modern
artístico(a) artistic	**honesto(a)** honest	**paciente** patient
atlético(a) athletic	**indeciso(a)** indecisive	**reservado(a)** reserved
bilingüe bilingual	**intelectual** intellectual	**responsable** responsible
cómico(a) humorous, comical	**inteligente** intelligent	**sincero(a)** sincere
dramático(a) dramatic	**introvertido(a)** introverted	**tímido(a)** timid
extrovertido(a) outgoing, extroverted	**irresponsable** irresponsible	**tolerante** tolerant

¡A practicar!

2-17 Descripciones de familiares y amigos Choose from the adjectives you've learned in this section to describe what the following people are and are not like. Be sure the adjectives agree in gender and number with the nouns they describe. Compare your answers with those of a classmate.

Modelo *Mi madre es trabajadora pero no es atlética.*

1. Mi mejor amigo(a) es... pero no es...
2. Mis abuelos son... pero no son...
3. Mis compañeros de clase son... pero no son...
4. Mi padre es... pero no es...
5. Los estudiantes de esta universidad son... pero no son...
6. El (La) profesor(a) es... pero no es...
7. Mi perro/gato es... pero no es...

2-18 ¿Cómo es/son? Describe the following people, using descriptive adjectives and the appropriate form of the verb **ser**. Use adjectives that precede a noun in at least three of your sentences.

Modelo Gael García Bernal
Gael García Bernal es delgado, moreno y reservado.

1. Salma Hayek
2. Carlos Santana
3. mi compañero de cuarto
4. mi mejor amigo(a)
5. mi familia y yo
6. mis hermanos(as)
7. mis primos(as)
8. yo

Cultura

Gael García Bernal is a Mexican actor who has appeared in several Oscar-nominated films: **De tripas, corazón; Amores perros; El crimen del padre Amaro; Y tú mamá también; Diarios de motocicleta,** and **Babel.** He also starred in *Letters to Juliet* (2010) with Amanda Seyfried.

2-19 Mi familia In groups of four or five, prepare two lists, one list consisting of ten family members and another consisting of ten personal characteristics. One person in the group presents a family member and a characteristic and the others form sentences about that member of their families with the characteristic, saying if it is accurate or not. Take turns presenting the words from the lists. Follow the model and pay attention to agreement of nouns and adjectives.

Modelo padre, perezoso — *Mi padre no es perezoso.*
abuela, simpático — *Mi abuela es muy simpática.*

2-20 Entrevista (*Interview*) en la radio *Radio Guadalajara* is speaking with students around the city and airing the short interviews. You and your friends very much want to be interviewed. Listen to the first installment of the series and note the topics of information included in the interview, so you and your friends will be prepared to meet the roving interviewer. Check each topic that is discussed. If a topic is not included, leave it blank.

AUDIO CD
CD 1, TRACK 11

_______ los estudios
_______ otras actividades
_______ la fecha, el día y la hora
_______ la familia
_______ las características de unas personas
_______ las mascotas
_______ las lenguas extranjeras
_______ los lugares de la universidad

Workbook *2-9 – 2-10*
Lab Manual *2-10 – 2-12*

¡A conversar!

2-21 **¿Quién puede ser? *(Who could it be?)*** Describe someone in the class for your classmates to identify.

Modelo **E1**: *Es alta, delgada y atlética. Es morena.*
E2: *¿Es Michelle?*
E1: *¡Sí!*

2-22 **Personas ideales** Working with a partner, develop an ideal profile for the following people.

Modelo el profesor
E1: *Para mí (For me), el profesor ideal es inteligente, tolerante y paciente.*
E2: *Para mí, el profesor ideal es liberal, intelectual y un poco rebelde.*

1. el (la) compañero(a) de cuarto
2. los amigos
3. la abuela
4. los padres
5. el presidente
6. el (la) hermano(a)

2-23 **Nuestras familias** Working with a partner, assume the roles of two students who have lived with host families in Mexico during a study abroad experience. Below are photos of the two families that have hosted you and your partner. Each of you will identify and describe at least five members of your host family. Identify each person by his (her) relationship to others in the family and describe each member, including at least two physical and/or personality characteristics.

Los Ramírez

Los Trelles

México

Watch the video about Mexico and discuss the following questions.

1. Where was Mexico City built?
2. What is the *Zócalo?* Why is this place so important in the city?
3. Why is the Anthropology Museum so relevant to Mexican culture?
4. Have you ever visited Mexico? Where did you go and why? If you've never been, what part of Mexico would you choose to visit and why?

See the *Workbook*, **Capítulo 2, 2-25–2-27** for additional activities.

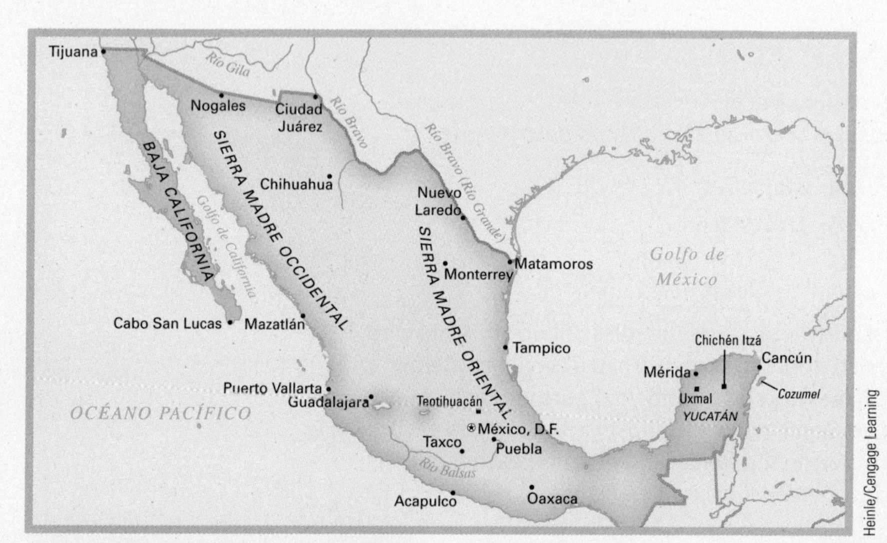

Población: 112.468.855 habs.

Área: 1.952.201 km^2, representa un quinto del territorio de los Estados Unidos. México es casi tres veces el tamaño *(size)* de Texas.

Capital: Distrito Federal (8.841.916 habs.)

Ciudades principales: Guadalajara (1.500.000 habs.); Monterrey (1.100.000 habs.); Puebla (1.100.000 habs.); Tijuana (1.500.000 habs.)

Moneda: el peso

Lenguas: el español, lenguas indígenas (el maya, el náhuatl y otras)

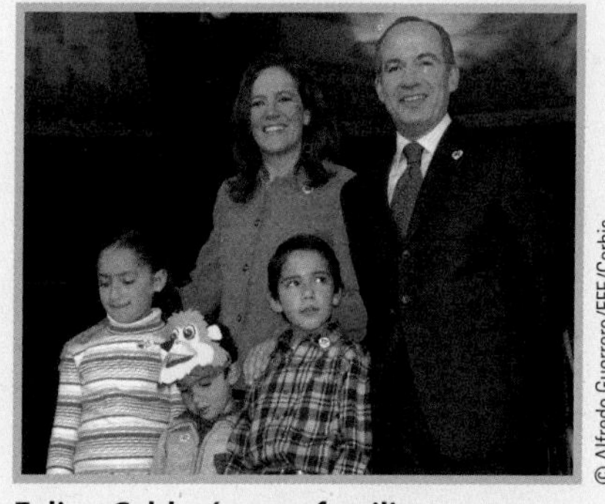

Felipe Calderón y su familia

Personas notables El Sr. Felipe Calderón es el presidente de México hasta el año 2012. El presidente y su familia viven en la ciudad de México o Distrito Federal (D.F.). Su esposa se llama Margarita Zavala y sus hijos se llaman María, Luis Felipe y Juan Pablo. Hasta las elecciones del año 2000, en México dominó un partido político, el Partido Revolucionario Institucional (PRI). Ahora en México hay tres partidos importantes: el Partido Acción Nacional (PAN) (Vicente Fox y Felipe Calderón son de este partido), el Partido de la Revolución Democrática (PRD) y el Partido Revolucionario Institucional (PRI).

Describe a la familia presidencial de México. Describe a la familia presidencial de los Estados Unidos. ¿Son similares?

Historia Algunos de los grupos indígenas que viven en la región de México y Centroamérica, desde hace más de 4.000 años, son los olmecas, toltecas, zapotecas, aztecas y mayas. En la cultura maya, las mujeres son muy importantes para la economía familiar porque preparan la comida para la familia y para las celebraciones religiosas, trabajan en la elaboración de cerámica y cuidan a *(take care of)* los animales. En la cultura maya, los padres deciden el matrimonio de los hijos para tener más poder económico y político dentro de la sociedad. El esposo vive bajo *(under)* las órdenes del suegro por un período de hasta cinco años.

¿Hay responsabilidades específicas para los hombres y las mujeres de tu comunidad?

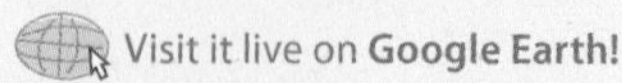

Visit it live on **Google Earth!**

Ruinas mayas en Uxmal

Frieda y Diego Rivera **de Frida (Frieda) Kahlo**

Artes plásticas Frida Kahlo (1907-1954) y Diego Rivera (1886-1957) son artistas importantes y esposos famosos dentro del arte mexicano. El tema de la obra *(work)* de Kahlo es personal y autobiográfico con elementos de fantasía, mientras *(while)* que el tema de Rivera es político y presenta la lucha (*struggle*) de los trabajadores (*workers*). Hoy en día la casa de Frida y Diego en la ciudad de México es un museo que se llama "La Casa Azul". Es importante visitar también el Museo Mural Diego Rivera y el Museo de Bellas Artes.

¿Visitas museos? ¿Cuál es tu museo favorito y por qué?

Ritmos y música El «son» mexicano es un tipo de música con influencias indígenas, españolas y africanas. Los instrumentos varían de región a región. Un grupo de «sones» se conoce como *(is known as)* el «jarabe». Existen jarabes como el Tapatío, el Mixteco, el del Valle, etcétera. La música mexicana moderna incluye, entre otros tipos de música, el rock en español. Como el son, el rock es también una mezcla de estilos musicales.

Desde 2002 uno de los grupos musicales más importantes dentro de la música pop en español es el grupo mexicano Reik. De su último álbum, que se llama *Un día más*, la canción «Inolvidable» es una de las más populares. *Access the iTunes playlist on the* ***Plazas*** *website.*

¿Qué tipo de música escuchas? ¿Cuál es tu grupo de música favorito?

Grupo Reik

¡Busquen en Internet!

1. Personas notables: El presidente de México, Felipe Calderón y su familia
2. Historia: La cultura maya
3. Artes plásticas: Frida Kahlo y Diego Rivera
4. Ritmos y música: El son mexicano, el pop en español, Reik

¿De dónde eres?

In this section, you will learn to talk about nationalities of individuals who live in many different parts of the world. Do you know someone who is from another country?

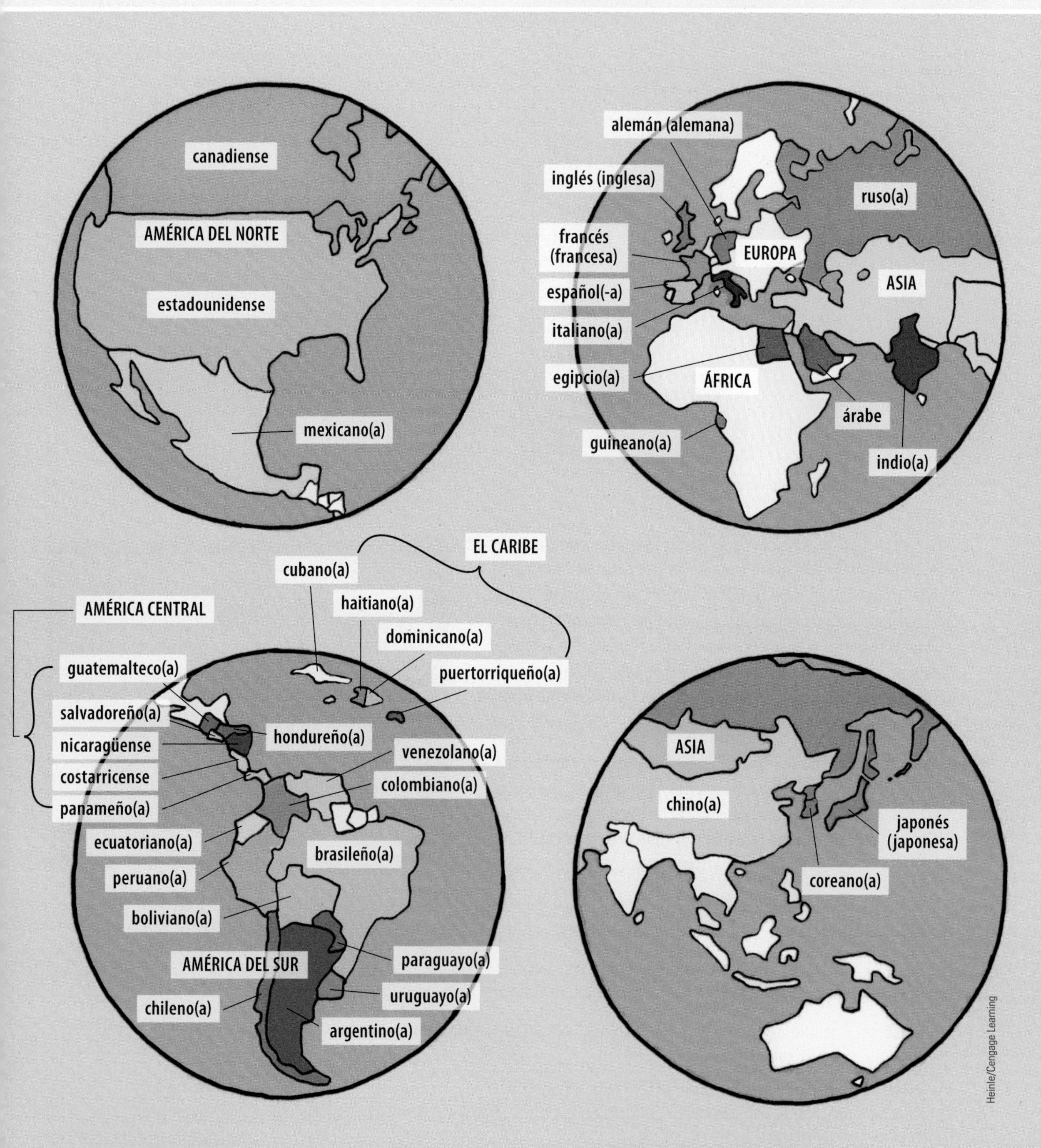

¡A practicar!

2-24 Lenguas y nacionalidades Identify the nationalities of the following people. In some cases there may be various possibilities.

1. Jorge es de América del Sur y habla portugués. Él es ________.
2. Masako es de Asia y habla japonés. Ella es ________.
3. Paquita y Mar son de Europa y hablan español. Ellas son ________.
4. Teresita es de San Juan y habla español. Ella es ________.
5. Tito y Florentina viven en Roma. Ellos son ________.
6. Hans es de Bonn y habla alemán. Él es ________.
7. Pierre es de América del Norte y habla francés e inglés. Él es ________.
8. María es de América del Sur y habla español. Ella es ________ ________.
9. Yo soy ________.
10. Mi profesor(a) es ________.

2-25 Orígenes Use adjectives of nationality to indicate the origins of the following items.

1. El sushi es una comida ________.
2. El BMW es un automóvil ________.
3. El tango es un baile ________.
4. Las enchiladas son ________.
5. Los espaguetis son ________.
6. El mejor *(The best)* café del mundo es ________.
7. Las pirámides de Giza son ________.

Nota lingüística

Another way to say **costarricense** is **tico(a)**. **Puertorriqueños** are also known as **boricuas**.

Workbook *2-11 – 2-12*
Lab Manual *2-13 – 2-15*

¡A conversar!

2-26 ¿De dónde son? Take turns naming as many people as possible of a given nationality and have your partner state the nationality. Start with the examples below and continue with lists that you create.

Modelo **E1**: Gloria Estefan, Andy García y Fidel Castro
E2: *Ellos son cubanos.*

1. Shakira, Juanes y Sofía Vergara (de la serie *Modern Family*)
2. Hugo Chávez, Andrés Galarraga y Carolina Herrera
3. Gael García Bernal, Salma Hayek y Carlos Santana
4. Penélope Cruz, Sergio García y Plácido Domingo
5. Yao Ming, Jackie Chan y Ang Lee
6. Los príncipes William y Harry, David Beckham y su esposa Victoria Beckham

2-27 Categorías Working in groups of four, begin by dividing into pairs and setting a timer for five minutes. Each pair makes a list of well-known people from many different countries in the professions listed below and writes the nationality of each person (in Spanish!).

músico(a) *musician* | **escritor(a)** *writer*
político(a) *politician* | **artista** *artist*
atleta *athlete* | **actor/actriz** *actor/actress*

One pair then presents a profession to the group, and other members identify a person in the profession and state his/her nationality. If the presenters of the list have someone of that nationality (the same person or a different one), they score a point. If the other group members identify a nationality not represented on the original list, they score a point.

After one pair presents a list and others identify individuals of as many nationalities as possible, the other pair presents its list to the group, and the competition continues.

ESTRUCTURA 4

Present tense of *-er* and *-ir* verbs

In Spanish, in order to form the present tense of infinitives ending in **-er** and **-ir**, you need to add the appropriate personal ending to the stem.

com**er** *(to eat)*			viv**ir** *(to live)*	
yo	com**o**	*I eat*	viv**o**	*I live*
tú	com**es**	*you* (informal) *eat*	viv**es**	*you* (informal) *live*
Ud., él/ella	com**e**	*you* (formal) *eat, he/she eats*	viv**e**	*you* (formal) *live, he/she lives*
nosotros(as)	com**emos**	*we eat*	viv**imos**	*we live*
vosotros(as)	com**éis**	*you* (informal: Spain) *eat*	viv**ís**	*you* (informal: Spain) *live*
Uds., ellos(as)	com**en**	*you eat, they eat*	viv**en**	*you live, they live*

The following are several useful **-er** and **-ir** verbs presented in sentences.

abrir	*to open*	Abr**o** la puerta cuando entro a la sala de clase. *I open the door when I enter the classroom.*
aprender	*to learn*	Tú aprend**es** español. *You learn (are learning) Spanish.*
asistir a	*to attend*	Ella asist**e** a clase. *She attends class.*
beber	*to drink*	Ud. beb**e** mucho café. *You drink a lot of coffee.*
comprender	*to understand*	Él comprend**e** la tarea. *He understands the homework.*
creer	*to believe*	Nosotros cre**emos** en la importancia de nuestra familia. *We believe in our family's importance.*
deber	*ought to, must*	Vosotros deb**éis** hablar con mi primo. *You must talk to my cousin.*
escribir	*to write*	Ustedes escrib**en** cartas. *You write (are writing) letters.*
leer	*to read*	Ellos le**en** un libro. *They read (are reading) a book.*
recibir	*to receive*	Yo recib**o** una tarjeta de mi sobrino. *I receive a card from my nephew.*
vender	*to sell*	¿Vend**es** tú mis libros? *Are you selling my books?*
vivir	*to live*	Viv**imos** con nuestros amigos. *We live with our friends.*

Nota lingüística

Deber is used before other verbs to communicate the idea of obligation. In Spanish, as in English, when two verbs are used together the first is conjugated and the second appears in the infinitive form: **Yo debo ir a la fiesta.** / ***should (must, ought to)* go** *to the party.*

¿Recuerdas?

Heinle/Cengage Learning

Elena: ¿Ves cómo tu abuelo **vive** en el pasado, m'hija? Él **cree** que los niños nunca crecen.

¡A practicar!

2-28 Mi compañero y yo Complete the following sentences with the appropriate form of the **-er** and **-ir** verbs in parentheses to learn about Tomás's roommate at UNAM.

1. José, mi compañero de cuarto, y yo __________ (vivir) en un apartamento.
2. Nosotros __________ (asistir a) la UNAM.
3. Todos los días él __________ (recibir) noticias *(news)* de su familia.
4. Su hermana __________ (escribir) mucho por correo electrónico *(e-mail).*
5. A veces yo __________ (leer) los mensajes *(messages)* de ella.
6. Mis abuelos __________ (creer) que las computadoras son importantes, pero todavía no tienen computadora en casa.

© csp/shutterstock

Biblioteca Central de la Universidad Nacional Autónoma de México (UNAM)

2-29 Dos compañeros Complete the following paragraph with the correct form of the most appropriate verb from the previous page.

¡Hola! Soy estudiante de la UNAM, donde estudio para ser intérprete. 1. ______ mucho de la cultura y la lengua de los estadounidenses en mis clases. Yo 2. ______ clases con mi amigo Juan. Él es mi compañero en la clase de inglés. Juan y yo estudiamos en la cafetería donde también 3. ______ café y 4. ______ sándwiches.

Workbook *2-13 – 2-16*
Lab Manual *2-16 – 2-17*

¡A conversar!

2-30 Actividades diarias Working with a partner, take turns sharing information, selecting items from each of the three columns to form logical sentences.

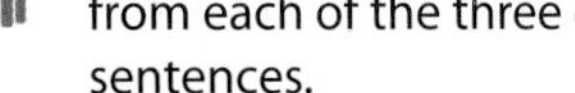

Modelo **E1**: *¿Beben café tus padres en casa?*
E2: *No, mis padres no beben café en casa. Beben café en la cafetería.*

¿Quién?	¿Qué?	¿Dónde?
tú y tus amigos	leer el periódico	en la residencia
tu compañero(a)	comer	en casa
tú	beber café	en la cafetería
el (la) profesor(a)	vivir	en clase
tus padres	aprender el vocabulario	en la biblioteca

2-31 Entrevista Find out more about your classmate by asking him/her the following questions. Then report your findings to the rest of the class.

1. ¿Dónde vives ahora? ¿Con quién vives? ¿Cuál es tu dirección *(address)*?
2. ¿Aprendes mucho en tus clases? ¿Debes estudiar mucho?
3. En general, ¿eres un(a) estudiante bueno(a) o malo(a)?
4. ¿Lees mucho o poco? ¿Lees novelas, el periódico o páginas de Internet?
5. ¿Dónde comes? ¿Qué tipo de comida comes? ¿Bebes mucho café?

2-32 Mi compañero(a) Using the information gathered in your interview, write a short composition about your classmate. Write 5 to 7 sentences and include at least 5 of the verbs listed below.

aprender	escribir
beber	estudiar
comer	leer
comprender	ser
deber	vivir

Common uses of the verb *tener*

The verb **tener** is irregular and conjugated as follows:

yo	**tengo**	*I have*
tú	**tienes**	*you* (informal) *have*
usted, él/ella	**tiene**	*you* (formal) *have, he/she has*
nosotros(as)	**tenemos**	*we have*
vosotros(as)	**tenéis**	*you* (informal: Spain) *have*
ustedes, ellos(as)	**tienen**	*you have, they have*

To indicate possession

—¿Cuántas hermanas **tienes**? *How many sisters do you have?*
—Yo **tengo** dos hermanas. *I have two sisters.*

—¿**Tienen** hijos tus hermanas? *Do your sisters have any children?*
—No, no **tienen** hijos. *No, they don't have any children.*

To express age

Mirta **tiene** solamente **dieciocho** años y Margarita **tiene veinte** años. *Mirta is only eighteen years old and Margarita is twenty years old.*

To express certain states or conditions

tener calor *to be hot*	**tener paciencia** *to be patient*
tener celos *to be jealous*	**tener prisa** *to be in a hurry*
tener éxito *to be successful*	**tener razón** *to be right*
tener frío *to be cold*	**tener sed** *to be thirsty*
tener hambre *to be hungry*	**tener sueño** *to be tired/sleepy*
tener miedo (de) *to be afraid (of)*	

Note that although Spanish speakers use **hacer** to say it *is cold* or *it is hot* (**hace frío, hace calor**), the verb **tener** is used with these two nouns when a person says *I am cold* (**Yo tengo frío**) or *She is hot* (**Ella tiene calor**).

To indicate desire to do something

When you want to say that you feel like doing something, use the expression **tener ganas de** + *infinitive*. Simply conjugate *tener* and use the infinitive form of the verb that expresses what you feel like doing.

¿**Tienes ganas de pintar** la casa? *Do you feel like painting the house?*
Tenemos ganas de ver una película. *We feel like watching a movie.*

To indicate obligation to do something

The verb **tener** is also used in the construction **tener que** + *infinitive*, which means *to have to do something.* It is used in the same way as the verb **deber**, but it carries a stronger sense of obligation. **Deber** normally carries the meaning of *should*, whereas **tener que** often means *must.* Note that both of these verb forms must be followed by an infinitive.

Deseo mirar la televisión, pero **tengo que estudiar.** *I want to watch TV, but I have to (must) study.*
Tenemos que regresar a casa. ¡Es tarde! *We have to (must) return home. It's late!*

¡A practicar!

2-33 ¿Qué tienen? Provide the correct form of **tener** to complete each sentence.

Modelo Yo tengo una mochila nueva.

1. Nosotros ______ calor en julio *(July)*.
2. Ellos ______ el nuevo CD de Reik.
3. Roberto estudia mucho y ______ éxito en su clase de español.
4. Después de hacer ejercicio yo ______ sed.
5. Mi hermanita, Paqui, ______ nueve años.
6. ¡Tú siempre ______ sueño! Debes descansar más.
7. Mi compañero de cuarto y yo ______ un perro.
8. ¿Por qué ustedes no ______ paciencia con José?

2-34 ¿Qué tienen que hacer? Complete the following sentences with **tener que** + *infinitive* in order to tell what some students have to do.

Modelo mis amigos / estudiar la lección
Mis amigos tienen que estudiar la lección.

1. nosotros / tomar cuatro clases este semestre
2. Juan y Antonio / trabajar por la noche
3. Marta / regresar a la biblioteca
4. Guadalupe / visitar a su familia este fin de semana
5. tú / asistir a una conferencia
6. ¿yo?

2-35 Una reunión familiar Marcos is planning a family reunion. Listen to descriptions of family members from an audio file that he has prepared. Write each person's first name, his or her relationship to Marcos, and at least two pieces of additional information. Follow the model.

AUDIO CD
CD 1, TRACK 12

Modelo Nombre: Catalina
Relación con Marcos: madre
Otra información: bonita, inteligente, generosa, su esposo es Mario Luis, tiene cuatro hijos

Workbook *2-17 – 2-21*
Lab Manual *2-18 – 2-19*

¡A conversar!

2-36 Conversemos Ask the following questions of a partner and compare answers.

1. ¿Cuándo tienes sueño? ¿En clase o por la noche?
2. ¿Cuándo tienes prisa? ¿Siempre llegas a tiempo a la clase?
3. ¿Tienes mucho éxito en la vida? ¿De qué tienes miedo?
4. ¿Tenemos mucha tarea en esta clase? ¿De qué tienes miedo?
5. ¿Tienes celos de un(a) amigo(a)? ¿Por qué?
6. ¿Siempre tiene razón el (la) profesor(a)?
7. ¿Tienes mucha paciencia cuando estudias español? ¿Tienes que estudiar mucho?
8. ¿Tienes hambre ahora? ¿Tienes sed?
9. ¿Tienes ganas de estudiar después *(after)* de clase?
10. ¿Cuándo tienes miedo?

2-37 ¿Cuántos primos tienes? Working with a partner, find out more about each other's family by asking questions with **tener**.

Modelo **E1:** *¿Cuántos primos: tienes?*
E2: *Yo tengo tres primos: una prima y dos primos. Y tú, ¿tienes primos?*
E1: *Sí, yo tengo una prima. Mi prima se llama Carolina.*
E2: *¿Y cuántos años tiene Carolina?*
E1: *Ella tiene dieciocho años...*

2-38 Preferencias y obligaciones Working with a partner, form five sentences that express something that you feel like doing in combination with something that you have to do.

Modelo esta noche:
Yo tengo ganas de descansar, pero tengo que estudiar.

1. hoy por la tarde:
2. esta noche:
3. mañana por la mañana:
4. este fin de semana:
5. en el verano (*summer*):

Numbers 30 to 100

30 treinta	35 treinta y cinco
31 treinta y uno	36 treinta y seis
32 treinta y dos	37 treinta y siete
33 treinta y tres	38 treinta y ocho
34 treinta y cuatro	39 treinta y nueve

40 cuarenta
50 cincuenta
60 sesenta
70 setenta
80 ochenta
90 noventa
100 cien/ciento

The numbers **treinta y uno, cuarenta y uno, cincuenta y uno**, etc. are used in counting. When followed by a noun, they change to agree with the noun in gender. When preceding a masculine noun, the **–o** is dropped to form **un**.

treinta y un libros
cincuenta y una sillas

Note that the short form of **cien** is used before nouns and in counting. You will practice **ciento** later when you learn to count above one hundred.

cien libros
... noventa y ocho, noventa y nueve, **cien**...

Numbers 30–90 always end in **-a**, such as **setenta** and **noventa.** Numbers 31–99 must be written as three words. Remember, however, that the numbers 16–29 are often written as one word: **dieciocho, veintitrés.**

Heinle/Cengage Learning

Juan Carlos: Sí, por supuesto. Hay una familia cubana que vive en la calle **Cuarenta y Dos**, en la próxima manzana, y ellos tienen una hija de catorce años, de la misma edad que Juana.

¡A practicar!

2-39 Problemas de matemáticas Working with a partner, quiz each other using the following equations. Take turns reading the questions to one another.

+ y/más **– menos** **= son**

Modelos 30 + 41=

E1: *¿Cuántos son treinta* ***y (más)*** *cuarenta y uno?*

E2: *Treinta* ***y (más)*** *cuarenta y uno* ***son*** *setenta y uno.*

50 – 25 =

E1: *¿Cuántos* ***son*** *cincuenta* ***menos*** *veinticinco?*

E2: *Cincuenta* ***menos*** *veinticinco* ***son*** *veinticinco.*

1. 15 + 15 = ______
2. 80 + 17 = ______
3. 77 – 22 = ______
4. 60 – 19 = ______
5. 59 + 7 = ______
6. 100 – 25 = ______
7. 22 + 24 = ______
8. 16 + 36 = ______
9. 99 – 10 = ______
10. 73 + 27 = ______

2-40 ¿Cuántos...? Answer each question with the correct number between 0 and 100. Spell out each number. Use your knowledge of cognates to help you understand any unfamiliar words. Use the Internet to find any information you do not know.

1. ¿Cuántas horas hay en dos días? ¿en tres días? ¿en cuatro días?
2. ¿Cuántos estados hay en los Estados Unidos? ¿en México?
3. ¿Cuántos puntos son necesarios para aprobar *(pass)* un examen de cien puntos en tu universidad? ¿para sacar *(get)* una "A"?, ¿una "B"?, ¿una "C"?
4. ¿Cuántas semanas hay en un año?
5. ¿Cuántos años debe tener una persona para votar en las elecciones en los Estados Unidos?, ¿para ser presidente de los Estados Unidos?, ¿para ser presidente de México?

Workbook *2-22 – 2-24*
Lab Manual *2-20 – 2-22*

¡A conversar!

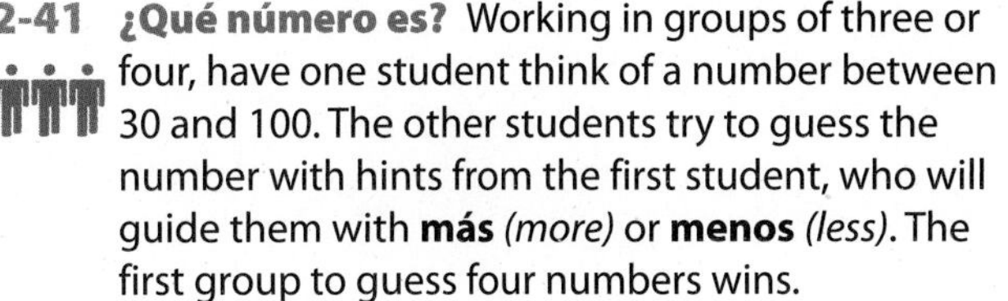

2-41 ¿Qué número es? Working in groups of three or four, have one student think of a number between 30 and 100. The other students try to guess the number with hints from the first student, who will guide them with **más** *(more)* or **menos** *(less)*. The first group to guess four numbers wins.

Modelo **E1:** *¿Es cincuenta?*

E2: *No, no es cincuenta. Es menos.*

E3: *¿Es cuarenta?*

E2: *No, no es cuarenta. Es más.*

E1: *¿Es cuarenta y nueve?*

E2: *¡Sí! Tienes razón.*

2-42 Más números Work in groups of four to five students. Each student should make ten flashcards and write one number on each card, beginning with 0 and ending with 9. The group leader will designate two people to each hold up one card. The leader calls on another group member to state the two-digit number that those two people are holding up. For example, one student holds up a 3 and the other holds up a 6. The number to be stated is 36, **treinta y seis**. After completing several numbers, designate a new group leader. Be sure that everyone participates!

2-43 ¿Qué hacen Uds? Work with a partner to form sentences about what you and other people do in a week, a month, a semester, and so on.

Modelo *En una semana yo asisto a catorce clases.*

Período	Personas	Actividades	Cosas
En un día	yo	asistir a	clases
En una semana	mi amigo(a)	aprender	palabras en español
En un mes	mis amigos	comprar	composiciones
En un semestre	mis amigos y yo	escribir	libros
En un año	mis padres	leer	mensajes de correo electrónico
	¿...?	recibir	exámenes
		leer	
		recibir	
		tener	
		vender	

¡A VER!

Heinle/Cengage Learning

¿Cómo es tu familia? In this segment, the five housemates begin to settle in and get to know each other. After they share a little information about their families, they begin to reveal opinions they are forming about their new housemates. You will also begin to form your own opinions about each character as you watch them interact on a typical morning.

Antes de ver

Expresiones útiles The following are some new expressions you will hear in the video.

hace un rato	*a little while ago*
se trae un rollo	*has a big problem*

Enfoque estructural The following are expressions in the video with the verb **tener** and common uses of the verb **ser**:

*Javier:	Yo **tengo** un hermano mayor. **Tiene** 29 años y es médico.
*Valeria:	¡Por supuesto que **tengo** familia! Mi papá **es** un famoso arquitecto en Venezuela y mi mamá **es** una modelo jubilada.
Sofía:	Tu padre **es** moreno y tu madre **es** blanca de pelo negro, y bajita como tú.
Alejandra:	¡**Somos** una familia de contrastes!
Alejandra:	Y éstos **son** mis perros, Gitano y Lady.

1. **Recordemos** What expressions have you learned to ask about someone's family? How would you describe your own family?
2. **Practiquemos** For each of the statements above marked by an asterisk, supply a question in Spanish that would produce the statement. You might have to ask several different questions using **tener** and **ser**.
3.  **Charlemos** Interview one of your classmates about his/her family. Be sure to ask about how many family members he or she has, their ages, their physical features, and their professions.

Después de ver

¿Cierto o falso? Now that you have watched the video segment, recall what each housemate said about his/her family, then decide if each of the following statements is **cierto** or **falso**, and correct those that are false.

1. Alejandra tiene dos gatos, Gitano y Lady. ____________________.
2. Javier solamente (*only*) tiene una hermana. ____________________.
   ____________________.
3. La madre de Valeria es arquitecta. ____________________.
   ____________________.
4. Valeria tiene dos hermanas que practican el modelaje. ____________________.
5. La madre de Alejandra es alta y rubia. ____________________.

Resumen de la acción Use the correct form of the verbs below to complete the paragraph summarizing the events of the video.

abrir	entrar	contestar	tener éxito
tener prisa	necesitar	ser	llamar

1. __________ las ocho y treinta y cinco de la mañana. Sofía 2. __________ porque ya es muy tarde, pero Valeria está en el baño. Todos 3. __________ usar el baño y se ponen muy impacientes con Valeria. Por fin, Antonio 4. __________ a Valeria. Ella no 5. __________, entonces Antonio 6. __________ la puerta, 7. __________ al baño y sorprende a Valeria. Su plan 8. __________ porque Valeria grita y sale del baño muy rápidamente.

Heinle/Cengage Learning

Entre nosotros Write a detailed description of either Alejandra, Javier or Valeria. Be sure to include physical characteristics, nationality, personality and details about family members. Share your descriptions with a classmate and see if he/she can guess who you are describing.

Nombre	Características físicas	Personalidad	Familia

Presentaciones With a partner, choose one of the characters you described in **Entre nosotros** and present this individual to the class. Who is the character that was described the most?

See the *Lab Manual,* **Capítulo 2, 2-25– 2-26** for additional activities.

Antes de leer

Strategy: Recognizing cognates

As we have seen on page 61, cognates (**cognados**) are words of similar or identical spelling that share the same meaning between two languages, in this case, Spanish and English. Your ability to recognize them and guess their meaning will help you to read Spanish more efficiently. However, you should also be aware of "false cognates" such as **éxito**, which means *success*, **dirección**, which means *address*, **lectura**, which means *reading*, and **librería**, which means *bookstore*.

Strategy: Skimming and scanning

In addition to using cognates to make reading material more comprehensible, you will find the following strategies useful: skimming and scanning.

- Skimming is useful for quickly getting the gist or the general idea.
- Scanning allows you to find specific information.

Scan the document and write down any cognates and their meanings.

GLORIA & TOMÁS
Desean invitar a su querida
familia a su boda
el sábado 18 de febrero a
las 8 de la noche
en el Hotel Presidente Monterrey
José Vasconcelos 300,
San Pedro Garza García
Nuevo León, México

After identifying the cognates, skim the document to gain a general understanding of what it is about. Use this information to answer the following questions.

1. What type of document is this?
2. What is its purpose?

La fiesta de quince años

Underline the cognates and then skim the following document to get the gist of it, and answer the following questions.

1. What type of document is this?
2. What is its purpose?
3. Where would you get this document? In what country or from what country?

¡Es una celebración de quince años para María Rebeca!

Los padres de María Rebeca,
los señores Alejandro Martínez Escribano y
Rebeca Hernández de Martínez,
desean invitar a Ud. y a su distinguida familia
a la fiesta de cumpleaños
de su hija María Rebeca
con motivo de sus Quince Años
el sábado 7 de agosto a las nueve de la noche.

Hotel Fiesta Americana
Aurelio Aceves 225,
Guadalajara, Jalisco 44110 • México

Después de leer

Detalles Scan the document in order to answer the following questions.

1. What occasion is being celebrated?
2. Who are the hosts? What are their names?
3. When and where is the celebration taking place?
4. What type of gifts do you think Alexandra would like to receive?

¿Cierto o falso? Indicate whether each statement is **cierto** or **falso**. Then correct the false statements.

1. ______ María Rebeca is celebrating her sweet sixteen birthday.
2. ______ María Rebeca's whole family is hosting the party.
3. ______ The party will be in a hotel.
4. ______ In the invitation, the guests are asked to reply if they are coming to the party.
5. ______ The party will be in April.

¡A conversar! With two or three of your classmates, discuss the differences and similarities between the celebrations in Spanish-speaking countries and those in the United States, in particular the celebration of the **quince años** and sweet sixteen.

- who hosts the party
- replies to the invitations (RSVP vs. no RSVP)
- time to arrive at the party
- time to leave the party
- appropriate gifts

¡A escribir! With a classmate write an invitation:

- Decide what type of invitation you will write (**fiesta de cumpleaños, graduación, boda** [wedding]...)
- Who the hosts are
- Time and place of the invitation
- Accepting or not accepting gifts
- Decide if you need to know the number of people attending this event.

After you write the invitation, share it with the rest of the class and explain why or why not you need to know the number of guests for the event.

Strategy: Learning Spanish word order

Word order refers to the meaningful sequence of words in a sentence. The order of words in Spanish sentences differs somewhat from English word order. Some common rules of Spanish word order are:

- Definite and indefinite articles precede nouns.
  Los gatos y los perros son animales.
  Tengo **un gato** y **un perro**.
- Subjects usually precede their verbs in statements.
  Mi gato es negro.
- Subjects usually follow their verbs in questions.
  ¿**Tiene usted** animales en casa?
- Adjectives of quantity usually precede nouns.
  Tengo **dos animales** en casa.
- Adjectives of description usually follow nouns.
  El **perro pardo** *(brown)* se llama Bandido.
- Possession is often expressed by using **de** with a noun.
  Tigre es **el gato de Sara**.

Task: Writing a family profile

Family profiles may occur in many contexts. Some common contexts are informal letters of introduction such as ones written to a key pal or a host family for a study-abroad student; newsletters of organizations, civic groups, or religious groups; and websites of such organizations and groups or individuals. In this activity you will write a short family profile to include in a letter to a key pal.

Paso 1 Unscramble the words in the following sentences. Then rewrite them in their correct sequence. Be sure to capitalize the first word of every sentence and to end each one with a period. Begin and end questions with appropriate question marks.

Modelo *es Anita Camacho de México*
Anita Camacho es de México.

1. es Anita una universitaria estudiante
2. Carlos Suárez su clase compañero se llama de
3. años tienen cuántos ellos ¿?
4. tiene Anita hermanos cuántos ¿?
5. gato tiene un Anita
6. Pecas llama Anita se gato de el

Paso 2 Now work with a classmate. Compare your sentences and check for errors in word order, spelling, capitalization, and punctuation.

Paso 3 Imagine that you are Anita's new key pal and that you are writing her a letter introducing yourself and your family. Describe your family as accurately as possible, including information such as names, ages, physical descriptions, personality traits, and favorite activities.

Paso 4 Share your letter with one or more classmates. Encourage your partner(s) to respond to what you have written and to ask questions about any information that is not clear.

Communicative Goals:

- Identify and discuss family relationships
- Describe people and things and indicate nationality
- Indicate ownership and possession
- Communicate about daily activities
- Express obligation or desire to do something

Paso 1

Review the Communicative Goals for **Capítulo 2** and determine if you are able to accomplish the goals. If you are not certain that you have achieved all of the goals, review the pertinent portions of the chapter.

Paso 2

Look at the components of a conversation which addresses the communicative goals for this chapter. The percentages will help you evaluate your ability to successfully participate in the conversation that is featured below. Your instructor may use the same rubric to assess your oral performance.

Components of the conversation	%
☐ Greeting, presentation of names, where each person is from and where each one lives	20
☐ Identification of at least three people or pets by name and by relationship to the speaker	20
☐ Information about at least one characteristic of each family member, friend or pet	10
☐ Questions and answers about at least two pieces of information regarding academic life	20
☐ Information about at least two other common activities and about one activity that the speaker must do or desires to do	20
☐ Appropriate closure of the conversation	10

En acción Think about a conversation that might take place between two students who are getting to know one another. Consider the sort of information that might be exchanged and how the speakers will communicate it. Make sure you and your partner include the following steps in the development of the conversation.

1. The individuals greet one another and then ask and answer questions about names, home town or city and current residence.
2. They exchange information about family members, good friends, and pets, identifying at least three people or pets by name and relationship to the speaker and providing at least one description of a physical characteristic or personality trait about each one.
3. The speakers ask and answer questions about activities and items related to academic life.
4. They converse about other activities, each speaker naming at least two activities that he or she does or does not do and at least one he or she wants to do or has to do.
5. The speakers conclude the conversation and say goodbye to one another.

¡A REPASAR!

Possession with *de(l)* and possessive adjectives

Spanish speakers show possession in one of two ways: using **de** before the noun, and using a possessive adjective.

Singular	Plural	Singular	Plural
mi	mis	nuestro(a)	nuestros(as)
tu	tus	vuestro(a)	vuestros(as)
su	sus		

¡A recordar! 1 In Spanish, how is the combination **de + el** simplified? Which possessive adjectives must agree in gender and number with the object?

Present tense of the verb *ser*

yo	soy	nosotros(as)	somos
tú	eres	vosotros(as)	sois
él, ella, Ud.	es	ellos, ellas, Uds.	son

¡A recordar! 2 For what purposes is the verb **ser** used?

Agreement with descriptive adjectives

In Spanish, descriptive adjectives must agree in *gender* and *number* with the noun or pronoun they modify.

una mujer **alta** dos hombres **tímidos**

¡A recordar! 3 Do adjectives ending in **-e** or in a consonant change to match gender? How are plural forms generated for adjectives ending in a consonant or in **-e?** How is the feminine form for adjectives of nationalities formed? What about plural forms of these same adjectives? What are the agreement rules for adjectives that end in **-dor, -án, -ón,** and **-ín?**

Present tense of *-er* and *-ir* verbs

To form the present tense of Spanish infinitives ending in **-er** and **-ir**, add the appropriate personal ending to the stem of each.

	comer	vivir
yo	com**o**	viv**o**
tú	com**es**	viv**es**
él, ella, Ud.	com**e**	viv**e**
nosotros(as)	com**emos**	viv**imos**
vosotros(as)	com**éis**	viv**ís**
ellos, ellas, Uds.	com**en**	viv**en**

¡A recordar! 4 How many **-er** or **-ir** verbs can you recall from the chapter?

Common uses of the verb *tener*

The verb **tener** (*to have*) can be used to indicate possession or to express age. **Tener** is also part of a number of idiomatic expressions and special constructions.

¡A recordar! 5 How many **tener** idioms can you remember from the chapter?

Actividad 1 Un correo electrónico *(An e-mail)*

Complete the following e-mail with the correct possessive adjectives.

Enviar Guardar Archivos

Querida Verónica:

¿Cómo es ________ (*your*) familia? ________ (*My*) padres se llaman Alfredo y Pilar y ________ (*my*) hermano mayor es Pepe. ________ (*His*) esposa se llama Miranda. ________ (*Their*) hijo se llama Juan Carlos y ________ (*their*) perros son Paco y Fifi. Visitamos mucho a ________ (*our*) abuelos y ________ (*our*) familia tiene una reunión todos los años en julio.

Actividad 2 Personas y lugares *(People and places)*

Choose the correct form of the verb **ser** to complete each sentence.

1. Yo ________ alto.
   a. soy b. eres c. es
2. Carolina y yo ________ estudiantes.
   a. somos b. sois c. son
3. El D. F. ________ la capital de México.
   a. soy b. son c. es
4. Tú ________ inteligente.
   a. eres b. es c. sois
5. Perú y Bolivia ________ países de Sudamérica.
   a. soy b. eres c. son
6. Mis amigos y yo ________ jóvenes.
   a. soy b. somos c. son
7. Mis primos ________ simpáticos.
   a. es b. son c. somos
8. El abuelo ________ de Guadalajara, México.
   a. es b. eres c. sois
9. Ud. y su esposa ________ muy generosos.
   a. son b. sois c. soy
10. Nosotras ________ inteligentes y extrovertidas.
    a. eres b. son c. somos

Actividad 3 ¿De dónde son? *(Where are they from?)* Complete each sentence with the correct adjective of nationality in the correct form.

1. Los tacos son ______________.
2. El tango es un baile ______________.
3. Rafael Nadal y Penélope Cruz son ______________.
4. Hugo Chávez, el presidente de Venezuela, es ______________.
5. Nicolas Sarkozy es de París. Es ______________.
6. El mejor café del mundo es ______________.
7. Sammy Sosa y Manny Ramírez son ______________.
8. El Toyota y el Honda son automóviles ______________.
9. LeBron James y Kobe Bryant son ______________.
10. El Hyundai es un automóvil ______________.

Actividad 4 Los estudiantes Complete the following paragraphs about the activities of some university students. Choose the correct verb from the list to complete each sentence in a logical manner and write the correct form of each verb.

abrir	aprender	asistir
beber	comer	comprender
creer	deber	escribir
leer	recibir	tener que
vender	vivir	

Yo ________ a mi clase de español los martes y jueves. Yo ________ mucho y generalmente ________ las lecciones. Mis compañeros y yo ________ el libro y ________ con lápiz o bolígrafo en la clase. Mi amigo José ________ buenas notas en la clase. Todos nosotros ________ estudiar mucho todo el semestre.

Después de (*After*) clase unos estudiantes ________ café y ________ sándwiches en la cafetería de la residencia. Yo ________ en un apartamento y yo voy allí (*go there*) después de clase. Yo ________ mis libros inmediatamente porque yo ________ estudiar. Al fin del semestre tú ________ tu libro, ¿no? ¡Yo no! ¡Yo ________ que el libro es muy importante!

Actividad 5 ¡A emparejar! Match the elements below with the logical **tener** expression.

______ 1. Preparo tacos y burritos.
______ 2. Mi nota en la clase de español es A⁺.
______ 3. Necesito agua.
______ 4. Estoy (*I am*) en el sur de Chile en agosto.
______ 5. Estoy en Cancún.
______ 6. Deseo descansar.
______ 7. Escribo en mi cuaderno «El D.F. es la capital de México».
______ 8. Son las dos menos uno y mi clase es a las dos.
______ 9. ¡Veo un perro muy grande!
______ 10. Mi amiga va a México y yo deseo ir.

a. Tengo prisa.
b. Tengo sueño.
c. Tengo éxito.
d. Tengo hambre.
e. Tengo miedo.
f. Tengo frío.
g. Tengo calor.
h. Tengo razón.
i. Tengo sed.
j. Tengo celos.

Refrán

Heinle/Cengage Learning

A casa de _____ *(your)* ________ *(sister)*, una vez a la semana.
A casa de ________ *(your brother)*, una vez al año.
A casa de _____ *(your aunt)*, más pero no cada día.

VOCABULARIO ESENCIAL

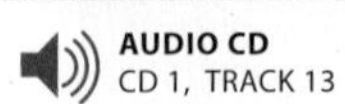 AUDIO CD
CD 1, TRACK 13

 PERSONAL TUTOR

Miembros de la familia y otros parientes	Members of the family and other relatives
el (la) abuelo(a)	grandfather/grandmother
el (la) cuñado(a)	brother-in-law/ sister-in-law
el (la) esposo(a)	husband/wife
el (la) hermano(a)	brother/sister
el (la) hijo(a)	son/daughter
la madre (mamá)	mother
el (la) nieto(a)	grandson/ granddaughter
la nuera	daughter-in-law
el padre (papá)	father
los padres	parents
el (la) primo(a)	cousin
el (la) sobrino(a)	nephew/niece
el (la) suegro(a)	father-in-law/ mother-in-law
el (la) tío(a)	uncle/aunt
el yerno	son-in-law

Los nombres	Names
el apellido	last name
el nombre	first name

Verbos	Verbs
abrir	to open
aprender	to learn
asistir a	to attend
beber	to drink
comer	to eat
comprender	to understand
creer	to believe
deber	ought to, must
escribir	to write
leer	to read
recibir	to receive
vender	to sell
vivir	to live

Expresiones con tener	
tener... años	to be . . . years old
tener calor	to be hot
tener celos	to be jealous
tener éxito	to be successful
tener frío	to be cold
tener ganas de...	to feel like . . . (*doing something*)
tener hambre	to be hungry
tener miedo (de)	to be afraid (de)
tener paciencia	to be patient
tener prisa	to be in a hurry
tener razón	to be right
tener sed	to be thirsty
tener sueño	to be tired/sleepy

Las mascotas	House pets
el (la) gato(a)	cat
el pájaro	bird
el (la) perro(a)	dog
el pez	fish

Los números	Numbers
treinta	30
treinta y uno	31
treinta y dos	32
treinta y tres	33
treinta y cuatro	34
treinta y cinco	35
treinta y seis	36
treinta y siete	37
treinta y ocho	38
treinta y nueve	39
cuarenta	40
cincuenta	50
sesenta	60
setenta	70
ochenta	80
noventa	90
cien/ciento	100

Las nacionalidades	Nationalities
alemán(-ana)	German
árabe	Arab
argentino(a)	Argentinian
boliviano(a)	Bolivian
brasileño(a)	Brazilian
canadiense	Canadian
chileno(a)	Chilean
chino(a)	Chinese
colombiano(a)	Colombian
coreano(a)	Korean
costarricense	Costa Rican
cubano(a)	Cuban
dominicano(a)	Dominican
ecuatoriano(a)	Ecuadorian
egipcio(a)	Egyptian
español(-a)	Spanish
estadounidense	from the United States
francés (-esa)	French
guatemalteco(a)	Guatemalan
guineano(a)	Guinean
haitiano(a)	Haitian
hondureño(a)	Honduran
indio(a)	Indian
inglés (-esa)	English
italiano(a)	Italian
japonés (-esa)	Japanese
mexicano(a)	Mexican
nicaragüense	Nicaraguan
panameño(a)	Panamanian
paraguayo(a)	Paraguayan
peruano(a)	Peruvian
puertorriqueño(a)	Puerto Rican
ruso(a)	Russian
salvadoreño(a)	Salvadorean
uruguayo(a)	Uruguayan
venezolano(a)	Venezuelan

Adjetivos	Adjectives
aburrido(a)	boring
alto(a)	tall
antipático(a)	unpleasant
arrogante	arrogant
artístico(a)	artistic
atlético(a)	athletic
bajo(a)	short
bilingüe	bilingual
bonito(a)	pretty
buen(o)(a)	good
cómico(a)	humorous
corto(a)	short
delgado(a)	thin
divertido(a)	fun
dramático(a)	dramatic
extrovertido(a)	outgoing
feo(a)	ugly
generoso(a)	generous
gordo(a)	fat
grande	big
guapo(a)	handsome
honesto(a)	honest
indeciso(a)	indecisive
intelectual	intellectual
inteligente	intelligent
interesante	interesting
introvertido(a)	introverted
irresponsable	irresponsible
joven	young
largo(a)	long
listo(a)	smart, ready
mal(o)(a)	bad
moderno(a)	modern
moreno(a)	brunette
nuevo(a)	new
paciente	patient
pequeño(a)	small
perezoso(a)	lazy
pobre	poor
reservado(a)	reserved
responsable	responsible
rico(a)	rich
rubio(a)	blonde
simpático(a)	nice, pleasant
sincero(a)	sincere
tacaño(a)	stingy
tímido(a)	timid
tolerante	tolerant
tonto(a)	silly, foolish
trabajador(a)	hardworking
viejo(a)	old

CAPÍTULO 3

El tiempo libre

Colombia

Plaza de Santo Domingo, Cartagena de Indias, Colombia

Chapter Objectives

Communicative Goals

In this chapter, you will learn how to . . .

- Communicate about leisure activities
- Express likes and dislikes
- Indicate plans and intentions
- Share information about when and where common activities are done

Structures

- **Gustar** + *infinitive* and **gustar** + *nouns*
- **Ir** and **Ir a**
- Verbs with irregular **yo** forms
- **Saber, conocer,** and the personal **a**
- Expressing weather with **hacer** and **estar**

▲ What do you like to do during your free time? What are your pastimes?

▲ What sports do you like to play?

▲ What place would you like to visit in Colombia and what activity would you like to do there?

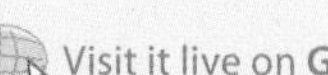 Visit it live on **Google Earth!**

El tiempo libre *(Spare time/Free time)*

In this section, you will learn how to talk about leisure-time activities and sports. What do you like to do in your spare time?

Más pasatiempos y deportes *More pastimes and sports*

bailar *to dance*
dar un paseo / pasear *to go for a walk*
jugar... *to play . . .*
- **al béisbol** *baseball*
- **al fútbol** *soccer*
- **al fútbol americano** *football*
- **al golf** *golf*
- **al tenis** *tennis*

ir... *to go . . .*
- **a tomar un café** *to drink coffee*
- **a un bar** *to a bar*
- **a un club** *to a club*
- **a un concierto** *to a concert*
- **a una discoteca** *to a dance club*
- **a una fiesta** *to a party*
- **al cine** *to the movies*
- **de compras** *shopping*

mirar la tele *to watch TV*
practicar deportes *to play sports*
tocar la guitarra *to play the guitar*
ver una película *to watch a movie*
visitar un museo *to visit a museum*

Otros sustantivos *Other nouns*

el campo de... *. . . field/course*
la cancha de... *. . . court*
el partido *game*

Otros verbos *Other verbs*

ganar *to win*
hacer planes *to make plans*

Palabras útiles

la bicicleta *bicycle* **el juego** *game*
el estadio *stadium* **la pelota** *ball*

Palabras útiles are presented to help you enrich your personal vocabulary. The terms provided here will help you talk about leisure-time activities.

¡A practicar!

Cultura

Alberto Contador is a professional road bicycle racer from Spain and winner of the 2007, 2009, and 2010 Tour de France. Manny Ramírez, from the Dominican Republic, is a baseball player who plays left field. Manú Ginóbili is a basketball player from Argentina who plays for the San Antonio Spurs. Paco de Lucía is a Spanish composer and famous flamenco guitarist. Lorena Ochoa is a Mexican golfer who retired in 2010. Rafael Nadal, a Spanish tennis player, ranked number 1 in 2010.

3-1 **Asociaciones** What activities do you associate with the following people?

Modelo Shakira, Juanes, Beyoncé
cantar

1. Roberto Alomar, Manny Ramírez, Alex Rodríguez
2. Manu Ginóbili, Pau Gasol, LeBron James
3. Mia Hamm, Diego Maradona, David Beckham
4. Carlos Santana, Eric Clapton, Paco de Lucía
5. Ángel Cabrera, Lorena Ochoa, Tiger Woods
6. Miguel Indurain, Lance Armstrong, Alberto Contador
7. Pancho González, Rafael Nadal, Mary Joe Fernández
8. John Leguizamo, Penélope Cruz, Gael García Bernal

3-2 **¿Qué podemos hacer?** ***(What can we do?)*** List as many activities as possible that you and your friends can do in the following places.

Modelo en las montañas
esquiar y caminar

1. en la casa
2. en el parque
3. en el centro comercial *(shopping mall)*
4. en el gimnasio
5. en la playa *(beach)*
6. en el campo *(country)*

3-3 **El Centro Deportivo Atlas** You hear a radio advertisement for a new sports complex that is offering a discount when five or more people join together. Listen carefully to the advertisement and write down information that you can share with your friends to convince them to join with you.

AUDIO CD
CD 1, TRACK 14

Write five sports activities that can be enjoyed in Centro Deportivo Atlas.

1. ____________________
2. ____________________
3. ____________________
4. ____________________
5. ____________________

Write two other activities that are mentioned in the advertisement.

1. ____________________
2. ____________________

Nota lingüística

El baloncesto is also called **el básquetbol** and **la pelota** is also called **el balón** or **la bola.**

Workbook *3-1 – 3-3*
Lab Manual *3-1 – 3-3*

¡A conversar!

3-4 **Un fin de semana típico** Incorporate the items below in questions to ask a classmate about his/her weekend activities. Upon answering the questions, change the information in the questions so that it is true for you.

Modelo tú / pasear en el parque / los sábados
E1: *¿Paseas en el parque los sábados?*
E2: *Sí, paseo en el parque con mi amiga Jill.*
o **E2:** *No, mis amigas y yo nadamos los sábados.*

1. tú / bailar en las fiestas / los viernes por la noche
2. tú y tu compañero(a) de cuarto / mirar la tele / los sábados por la tarde
3. tú y tu(s) amigo(a)(s) / tomar café / los sábados por la noche
4. tú / visitar un museo / los domingos por la mañana
5. tú / andar en bicicleta / los domingos por la tarde
6. tú y tus padres / tocar el piano y cantar / los domingos por la noche
7. tú / montar a caballo / los sábados por la mañana
8. tus amigos / sacar fotos / los sábados por la noche

Nota lingüística

To form **sí/no** questions, make your voice rise at the end of the questions. Another way is to invert the order of the subject and verb, in addition to making your voice rise at the end of the question:

¿Miguel regresa a las seis?

¿Regresa Miguel a las seis?

3-5 **Actividades en el parque** Work with a partner to ask and answer questions about what the people in the picture do in the park. Also indicate if you do those activities or not. If you do, tell on which day or days you most often do them.

Modelo El señor Martínez camina.
Yo camino a clase los lunes, miércoles y viernes.

Heinle/Cengage Learning

3-6 **¿Cuándo y con quién?** Discuss with your partner when you do the activities on the list and with whom.

Modelo bailar en una discoteca: *Bailo en una discoteca los sábados por la noche. Bailo con mis amigos Paul, Gabe y Caroline.*

1. tomar un café
2. mirar una película
3. practicar deportes
4. tocar la guitarra
5. correr
6. visitar un museo
7. mirar la tele
8. pescar
9. nadar
10. sacar fotos

EN CONTEXTO

Three Colombian students, Catalina, Isabel, and Gerardo, are discussing plans for an upcoming party at Catalina's apartment in Bogotá, Colombia. As you listen to their conversation, pay attention to the form of address used among the three friends.

AUDIO CD
CD 1, TRACK 15

Listen to the conversation and establish whether the following statements are true (**cierto**) or false (**falso**). If a statement is false, correct it.

1. Isabel va a hacer una fiesta.
2. Gerardo practica la guitarra todos los días.
3. La fiesta es el sábado por la noche en la casa de Catalina.
4. La amiga de Gerardo es muy tímida.
5. Gerardo no va a ir a la fiesta.

Gerardo: ¡Hola, Catalina! Isabel dice que usted **va a hacer** una fiesta este fin de semana.

Catalina: ¡Sí! Los invito a usted y a su hermano Pepe. Ustedes tienen que venir.

Comentario cultural It is common for Colombians to use the **usted** form even when addressing friends.

Gerardo: Mmm... ¿Cuándo es?

Catalina: El sábado a las nueve en mi casa. Cuento con usted para la música y con su hermano para sacar fotos.

Comentario cultural Young people in Colombia can often be seen wearing indigenous products, such as backpacks, handbags, and hats. These products are typically made from **cabuya,** a locally harvested plant. Yellow, blue, and red—often the colors of choice—are the colors of the Colombian flag.

Gerardo: Bueno, **no sé.** No toco la guitarra mucho en estos días y...

Isabel: ¡Venga, Gerardo! **Va a ser** una fiesta chévere y usted nunca practica. ¡Es un maestro de la guitarra!

Comentario cultural Colombian-born Juanes (Juan Esteban Aristizábal Vásquez) is a very popular artist in the Latin music scene. Juanes won five Latin Grammys in 2008 and one in 2009.

Expresiones en contexto

chévere *fantastic, cool (Colombia, Venezuela, and the Caribbean)*
Cuento con usted *I'm counting on you*
en estos días *these days*
puede venir *can come*
sensible *sensitive*
un buen rato *a good time*
un poquitico *a little bit (Colombia)*
¡Venga! *Come on!*

Gerardo: Es un poquitico complicado. Tengo planes con una amiga para **ir a un club** el sábado. No sé si...

Catalina: ¡Pues! ¡Ella también puede venir a pasar un buen rato con nosotros!

Comentario cultural Colombia is renowned in the world marketplace for its exquisite coffee, beautiful orchids and other flowers, as well as for its emeralds.

Isabel: **Vamos a bailar** mucho y **yo sé** cómo **le gusta bailar a su hermano.**

Gerardo: Bueno, acepto, pero mi compañera es muy sensible y...

Comentario cultural Cumbia is the national music of Colombia and is derived from Spanish and African influences. Salsa, of Cuban origin and then popularized by Puerto Ricans in New York City, is also highly popular in Colombia. Both types of music are associated with dances of the same names.

Catalina: ¡Ay! La mujer misteriosa de Gerardo debe ser muy especial.

Isabel: ¡Claro que sí! **Tú sabes,** Catalina, que todas las amigas de Gerardo son especiales.

Comentario cultural Fernando Botero is Colombia's most famous painter. Botero, influenced by the works of Spanish painters Velázquez and Goya, is known for his corpulent subjects and playful themes.

Diálogo entre compañeros Working with a partner, take turns role-playing the situation you have just studied in **En contexto,** using only two speakers. Be sure to vary the interests of the speakers. Use the expressions from **En contexto** as a model for your dialogue.

Gustar + infinitive and *gustar* + nouns

To express likes and dislikes, Spanish speakers often use the verb **gustar** *(to be pleasing [to someone])*. The verb **gustar** can be used in two constructions: **gustar** + *infinitive* and **gustar** + *nouns.*

— ¿Qué **te gusta hacer?**
What do you like to do?

— **Me gusta correr.**
I like to run (go running).

— A mi papá **le gusta correr** también.
My dad likes to run (go running), too.

— Pero a mi madre y a mí **nos gusta el ciclismo.**
But my mom and I like cycling.

— Y a mi hermano **le gusta el baloncesto.**
And my brother likes basketball.

Gustar + infinitive

The verb **gustar** can be used with infinitives to express that an activity or action is pleasing to someone. To express to whom an action or activity—talking, running, shopping—is pleasing, use one of the following pronouns with the verb form **gusta** plus an infinitive. Note that these indirect object pronouns below indicate *to whom* or *for whom* an action is pleasing.

me	*to me*	+ **gusta** + infinitive
te	*to you* (informal)	
le	*to you* (formal), *to him/her*	
nos	*to us*	
os	*to you* (informal, plural: Spain)	
les	*to you* (plural), *to them*	

Gustar + nouns

When you use **gustar** with nouns, its form changes depending on whether you are talking about one thing or more than one thing.

— A Carlos le **gusta** el tenis.
Carlos likes tennis.

— A Carlos le **gustan** los deportes.
Carlos likes sports.

El tenis, in the first example, is singular, so you use the singular form of **gustar: gusta. Los deportes,** in the second example, is plural, so you use the plural form of the verb **gustar: gustan.** Note that with the **gustar** + *noun* construction, the noun is usually preceded by the definite article (**el** tenis, **los** deportes).

In order to clarify or emphasize to whom something is pleasing, you can use the preposition **a** plus the person(s)'s name(s) or a pronoun. For instance, **a Catalina** and **a tus amigos** in the examples below are used to clarify to whom something is pleasing. However, **a mí, a ti,** and **a nosotros** are used for emphasis.

— ¿A **Catalina le** gusta tomar el sol?
Does Catalina like to sunbathe?

— Sí. También **le** gusta nadar.
Yes. She also likes to swim.

— ¿A **ti te** gusta nadar?
Do you like to swim?

— Sí, a **mí me** gusta nadar mucho.
I very much like to swim.

— ¿A **tus amigos les** gusta tomar café?
Do your friends like to drink coffee?

— Sí, **les** gusta tomar café colombiano.
Yes, they like to drink Colombian coffee.

— ¿A **ustedes les** gusta esquiar en el agua?
Do you like to water ski?

— Sí, **a nosotros nos** gusta.
Yes, we do.

¿Recuerdas?

Heinle/Cengage Learning

Isabel: Vamos a bailar mucho y yo sé cómo **le gusta bailar a su hermano.**

¡A practicar!

3-7 Los fines de semana Use **me, te, le, nos,** or **les** to complete the following statements describing what Gerardo, Pepe, and their friends like.

1. A ti ______ gusta sacar fotos.
2. A mí ______ gusta tocar la guitarra.
3. A Catalina y a Isabel ______ gusta escuchar música.
4. A la familia de Isabel ______ gustan los partidos de fútbol.
5. A un compañero de Pepe ______ gusta sacar fotos.
6. A nosotros ______ gusta hacer fiestas los fines de semana.

3-8 Un niño difícil Use the correct form of the verb **gustar** and the appropriate indirect object pronoun to complete the following dialogue between a babysitter and a difficult child.

Niñera: Pepito, ¿te gusta mirar la tele?

Pepito: No. A mí no 1. ____________ los programas de esta noche.

Niñera: Pues, yo creo que a tu hermana 2. ____________ los dibujos animados *(cartoons).*

Pepito: No es cierto. A mi hermana y a mí solamente 3. ____________ mirar las películas de horror.

Niñera: ¿A ustedes 4. ____________ las canciones de Shakira? Yo tengo el nuevo CD de ella.

Pepito: No. No 5. ____________ escuchar música porque a mí no 6. ____________ cantar y a mi hermana no 7. ____________ bailar. Por eso no 8. ____________ la música.

Cultura

Shakira Isabel Mebarak Ripoll is a Colombian singer of Latin alternative folk-rock. In 2010, Shakira was honored by the United Nations for her humanitarian efforts in helping needy children around the world.

Workbook *3-4 – 3-6*
Lab Manual *3-4 – 3-6*

¡A conversar!

3-9 Preferencias personales Ask a classmate about his/her family members' preferences regarding the following objects and activities. When necessary, use **a** + the family member to specify the person.

Modelo el fútbol
E1: *¿A tu papá le gusta el fútbol?*
E2: *Sí, le gusta el fútbol.*
o **E2:** *No, no le gusta el fútbol. A mi papá le gusta el tenis.*

1. la música de Shakira
2. caminar por las montañas
3. las películas románticas
4. el café colombiano
5. el fútbol americano
6. bailar

3-10 ¿Qué te gusta hacer? Write at least five leisure activities that you like to do. Working in pairs, tell your partner about one of the activities you like to do and then ask if he or she likes to do the activity. Continue the conversation with information about when and where you do it and ask your partner questions about that activity or others. Discuss all of the activities on the lists and provide as much information as possible.

Modelo **E1:** *Me gusta levantar pesas en el gimnasio. ¿Te gusta levantar pesas?*
E2: *No, no me gusta levantar pesas. Me gusta correr.*
E1: *¿Dónde corres?*
E2: *En el parque. Corro todos los días.*

3-11 Más gustos Compose sentences using items from the three columns in order to discuss with a partner what you and other people like to do, where, and with whom.

Modelo **E1:** *Me gusta nadar en la piscina con mis amigos. ¿Te gusta nadar?*
E2: *Sí, me gusta nadar.*
E1: *¿Dónde y con quién?*
E2: *Me gusta nadar en la piscina con mi familia.*

¿Qué?	¿Dónde?	¿Con quién?
sacar fotos	el parque	mis amigos(as)
mirar la tele	la residencia	mi amigo(a)
bailar	el gimnasio	mi familia
escuchar música	las fiestas	mis padres
hacer ejercicio	el centro estudiantil	mi hermano(a)

Colombia

Watch the video about Colombia and discuss the following questions.

1. Describe the historic places you will be able to visit when in Bogotá, Colombia's capital.
2. What products does Colombia export?
3. What places would you like to visit and what activities would you like to do when visiting Colombia?

See the *Workbook*, **Capítulo 3, 3-20–3-22** for additional activities.

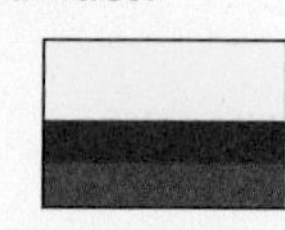

Población: 44.205.293 de habitantes

Área: 1.138.910 km^2, casi dos veces el tamaño de Texas

Capital: Santa Fe de Bogotá (7.259.597 habs.)

Ciudades principales: Medellín (5.988.984 habs.); Cali (4.337.909 habs.); Barranquilla (2.284.840 habs.); Cartagena (1.959.597 habs.)

Moneda: el peso colombiano

Lenguas: el español

Lugares mágicos El Parque Nacional Natural Tayrona es uno de los parques más importantes del país. Situado al norte de Colombia, en Santa Marta, este parque fascinante tiene bahías, playas, manglares *(mangroves)*, bosques, más de 100 especies de mamíferos, 200 especies de aves *(birds)*, 50 especies de reptiles y algunas ruinas arqueológicas de los indígenas tayronas, uno de los pueblos prehispánicos más interesantes de Colombia. La gente puede visitar el parque y hacer muchos deportes, como caminar por las montañas, nadar, esquiar en el agua, pescar, bucear *(scuba dive)* y caretear (hacer esnórquel), además de jugar al fútbol, al voleibol y al baloncesto.

Visit it live on **Google Earth!**

¿Te gusta visitar los parques nacionales en los Estados Unidos? ¿Te gusta caminar por las montañas o los bosques?

Carlos Vives, Miguel Bosé, Ricardo Montaner, Juan Luis Guerra, Juanes y J. Fernando Velasco en el concierto *Paz sin fronteras*

Oficios y ocupaciones Los cantantes y músicos colombianos tienen mucho éxito en los Estados Unidos. En el mundo de los cantantes están: Carlos Vives, famoso por su música de vallenatos (una música popular con influencia de la cumbia), y Juanes, con diecisiete premios Grammy desde el año 2002. Juanes canta canciones políticas y trabaja para la organización colombiana que tiene como misión eliminar las minas terrestres *(land mines)*. En marzo de 2008, Juanes organiza un concierto por la paz *(peace)* de Colombia, Ecuador y Venezuela en la frontera *(border)* entre Colombia y Venezuela. Al concierto asisten más de 50.000 personas. Shakira es conocida internacionalmente por sus canciones y sus bailes "Whenever, Wherever", "La Tortura", "Hips Don't Lie" y "She Wolf". Ella también trabaja por la paz en Colombia con su Fundación Pies Descalzos para ayudar a los niños afectados por la guerra en Colombia, el terremoto *(earthquake)* en Haití (2010) y los niños de Sudáfrica.

¿Te gustan las canciones de Carlos Vives, de Juanes o de Shakira? ¿Tus cantantes favoritos participan en organizaciones humanitarias? ¿Cuáles?

La calle de Fernando Botero

The Street, 1987 (oil on canvas) by Fernando Botero (b. 1932) Private Collection/James Goodman Gallery, New York, USA/ The Bridgeman Art Library © Fernando Botero, courtesy Marlborough Gallery, New York

Artes plásticas
Fernando Botero es el artista colombiano más reconocido del mundo por sus figuras grandes y redondas. Botero es de Medellín y su familia es muy pobre porque su papá muere *(dies)* joven. Botero expresa: "La vida es una gran aventura cuando la persona es pobre". Muchas de sus obras representan los pasatiempos colombianos como la música, el baile, las corridas de toros *(bullfights)*, pasear por las calles (*streets*) y plazas, hacer un picnic, tomar el sol y montar a caballo.

Describe a las personas de la calle de Botero. ¿Qué pasatiempos identificas?

¿Qué significa: "La vida es una gran aventura cuando la persona es pobre"?

Ritmos y música En Colombia, el ritmo nacional es la cumbia. La cumbia es una mezcla de música española y africana. En el siglo XIX, aparece la influencia de la música indígena, con el vallenato y el porro. Ahora, la música colombiana moderna tiene influencias de la música electrónica, del rock, del punk, del mariachi, del son cubano, del bolero y del flamenco.

La música de Juanes es un ejemplo perfecto de la música moderna colombiana. Su música es una fusión de rock con ritmos colombianos como el vallenato y la cumbia. Los temas de sus canciones son políticos, sociales y románticos. La canción "Me enamora" es de su álbum *La vida es un ratico* que vende más de 6 millones de canciones electrónicas. *Access the iTunes playlist on the* ***Plazas*** *website.*

¿Te gusta ir a conciertos? ¿Qué tipo de música te gusta escuchar: música clásica, rock, hip-hop, reggae, ska?

© Juergen Schwarz/AFP/Getty Images

Juanes

¡Busquen en Internet!
1. Lugares mágicos: Parque Nacional Natural Tayrona
2. Oficios y ocupaciones: Músicos en Colombia
3. Artes plásticas: Fernando Botero
4. Ritmos y música: Cumbia, Juanes

Siempre Verde, un pueblo colombiano

In this section, you will learn the names of places in a town. How does the imaginary town of **Siempre Verde** compare with your own?

El centro *Downtown*

Palabras útiles

la carnicería *butcher shop*
la ferretería *hardware store*
la frutería *fruit store*
la gasolinera *gas station*
la joyería *jewelry store*
la papelería *stationery store*
la peluquería *hair salon*
la tienda de antigüedades (de música/de discos, de ropa) *antiques (music, clothing) store*

Palabras útiles are presented to help you enrich your personal vocabulary. The terms provided here will help you talk about the places in your city/town.

Nota lingüística

El almacén is another word for **la tienda;** it can sometimes mean *department store, warehouse,* or even *grocery store*, depending on the region

¡A practicar!

3-12 Lugares y actividades Match each place with the activity or activities most commonly done in that location.

_______ 1. El museo
_______ 2. La iglesia
_______ 3. El parque
_______ 4. El supermercado
_______ 5. La calle

a. Compramos vegetales, frutas y otras cosas que comemos.
b. Miramos obras *(works)* de arte.
c. Paseamos en auto o motocicleta.
d. Participamos en una misa *(mass)* u otro servicio religioso.
e. Caminamos, practicamos deportes y hablamos con amigos.

3-13 Asociaciones What places do you associate with the following activities?

Modelo caminar
el parque

1. ir de compras
2. ir a tomar un café
3. comer
4. mandar cartas
5. ver una película
6. nadar
7. depositar dinero
8. jugar deportes

3-14 En mi pueblo hay... / no hay... Form sentences to describe the town where you live or study.

Modelo *En mi pueblo hay seis restaurante(s). Mi restaurante favorito se llama Marvin's.*

1. En mi pueblo hay _______ parques. Mi parque favorito es _______.
2. En mi pueblo hay _______ supermercados. Generalmente compro cosas en _______.
3. En mi pueblo hay _______ cafés. El café más popular es _______.
4. En mi pueblo hay _______ cine(s). Generalmente voy al cine _______.
5. Vivo en la calle _______.
6. En mi pueblo hay _______ piscina(s) pública(s).

Workbook *3-7 – 3-8*
Lab Manual *3-7 – 3-8*

¡A conversar!

3-15 ¿Te gusta el cine? Ask a classmate whether he/she likes the following places in your town or city. If your classmate does like a particular place, ask what he/she does there.

Modelo **E1:** *¿Te gusta el café Maggie's?*
E2: *Sí, me gusta el café Maggie's.*
E1: *¿Estudias mucho allí?*
E2: *No, hablo y tomo café con mis amigos.*

1. la plaza
2. el mercado
3. la tienda
4. el centro comercial
5. el parque
6. la oficina de correos
7. el restaurante
8. el banco
9. la discoteca
10. el museo

3-16 Un estudio de mi pueblo Ask a partner to identify the number of places in his/her town and then to indicate what places or buildings he/she feels are needed. Your partner should also express what kinds of buildings or places are not needed.

Modelo *En mi pueblo hay seis bancos, tres cines, ocho restaurantes, dos parques y tres tiendas de video. Nosotros necesitamos un museo y una discoteca. No necesitamos más restaurantes de comida china.*

3-17 Un turista en Siempre Verde Work with a partner. One person plays the role of a resident of Siempre Verde, Colombia, the town shown on page 94; the other plays the role of a visitor to the town. Ask and answer at least five original questions about places in the town, things to do, and likes and dislikes. Follow the model.

Modelo **E1:** ¿Hay un cine en el pueblo?
E2: Sí, hay un cine. ¿A Ud. le gusta mirar películas?
E1: Sí, me gusta mucho.

Ir and *ir a*

In this section, you will learn how to talk about future plans with the verb **ir** *(to go)*. First you will learn how to conjugate the verb **ir** and then you will learn about two structures that you can use with this verb, **ir a** + *destination,* and **ir a** + *infinitive,* in order to express plans.

Present tense of the verb *ir (to go)*

The verb **ir** has the following irregular conjugation in the present tense:

yo	**voy**	*I go*
tú	**vas**	*you* (informal) *go*
Ud., él, ella	**va**	*you* (formal) *go, he/she goes*
nosotros(as)	**vamos**	*we go*
vosotros(as)	**vais**	*you* (informal: Spain) *go*
Uds., ellos(as)	**van**	*you go, they go*

Ir a + destination

To tell where people are going, use a form of the verb **ir** plus the preposition **a,** followed by a destination.

—¿Adónde van Uds.?	*Where are you going?*
—Yo voy a la piscina.	*I'm going to the pool.*
—Y yo voy al parque.	*And I'm going to the park.*
—Nosotros vamos a la plaza.	*We're going to the plaza.*
—José va al museo.	*José is going to the museum.*

In Capítulo 2, you learned how to form the contraction **del** in talking about possessive constructions. Another common contraction in Spanish is **a + el = al,** as shown in the example **Yo voy al parque.** The preposition **a** *(to)* combines with the definite article **el** *(the)* to form the word **al** *(to the).*

Ir a + infinitive

To express future plans, use a form of the verb **ir** plus the preposition **a,** followed by an infinitive.

—¿Qué vas a hacer ahora?	*What are you going to do now?*
—Voy a jugar al tenis.	*I'm going to play tennis.*
—Ellos van a ir de compras al centro comercial.	*They're going shopping at the mall.*
—Tú vas a comer al restaurante italiano.	*You're going to eat at the Italian restaurant.*

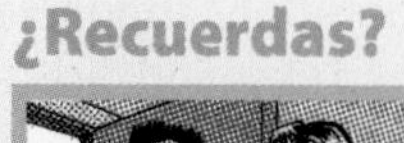

Heinle/Cengage Learning

Gerardo: ¡Hola, Catalina! Isabel dice que usted **va a hacer** una fiesta este fin de semana.

¡A practicar!

3-18 Una invitación Complete this conversation between two friends who are planning to go to a party. Use **ir, voy, vas, va, vamos,** and **van.** After completing the dialogue, practice the conversation with a classmate.

Ana: ¡Hola, Paco! ¿Adónde 1. ______ ahora?

Paco: (Yo) 2. ______ al cine. 3. ¿______ conmigo?

Ana: No, tengo que estudiar y después mi hermana y yo 4. ______ al parque.

Paco: ¿Qué 5. ______ a hacer el fin de semana?

Ana: ¡(Yo) 6. ______ a la fiesta! Y tú, 7. ¿______ a la fiesta también?

Paco: No, no 8. ______ a la fiesta. Tengo que 9. ______ a la casa de mis abuelos. Mis padres 10. ______ también. Es el aniversario de mis abuelos y nosotros 11. ______ a comer en un restaurante muy bueno.

Ana: ¡Qué chévere!

3-19 ¡Vamos a conocer Bogotá! Imagine that you are with a group of students who are visiting Bogotá and are explaining to one student what the other students are going to do. Use the contraction **al** as necessary.

Modelo Megan / el Banco Nacional
Megan va al Banco Nacional.

1. Roger y Erika / el parque Simón Bolívar ______
2. tú y Claire / el estadio El Campín ______
3. Mark / la plaza de toros Santamaría ______
4. Amber y Darius / el Museo del Oro ______
5. nosotros / el Centro Histórico ______
6. yo / la Zona Rosa ______

3-20 Los favores Listen to the voicemail that your host mother for your study abroad experience has left for you in response to your request to borrow her car to go to the shopping center. After listening, write down the 4 things that you must do for her in exchange for using the car.

AUDIO CD
CD 1, TRACK 16

1. ______
2. ______
3. ______
4. ______

Workbook *3-9 – 3-10*
Lab Manual *3-9 – 3-11*

¡A conversar!

3-21 Planes para un fin de semana Using the subjects listed below, ask a classmate questions about his/her activities for the next weekend. Choose a day for each subject listed.

Modelo tú / el viernes por la noche
E1: *¿Qué vas a hacer* (to do) *el viernes por la noche?*
E2: *Yo voy a ir al cine y luego mis amigas y yo vamos a una fiesta.*

1. tú	el viernes por la noche
2. tu compañero(a) de cuarto	el sábado por la mañana
3. tus padres	el sábado por la tarde
4. tú y tus amigos(as)	el sábado por la noche
5. tus abuelos	el domingo por la tarde
6. tu hermano(a)	el domingo por la noche

3-22 ¡Vamos al festival de música! Look at the schedule for the **Festival de Música Vivelatino** and decide what performances you wish to attend. Working with a partner, discuss where you are going and try to figure out if you can go to some of the performances together.

Modelo **E1:** *Voy al escenario verde a las cinco y cuarto para escuchar a Ritmo caribeño.*
E2: *¡Yo también! Y después voy al escenario rojo a las seis y media para ver a Decadencia. ¡Tengo prisa!*

Heinle/Cengage Learning

Verbs with irregular *yo* forms

The verb **hacer** *(to do; to make)* is a regular **-er** verb except for the **yo** form **(yo hago)**. You have already seen the verb **hacer** used in this chapter to pose questions.

¿Qué **haces** en tu tiempo libre? — *What do you do in your free time?*

¿Qué **hacen** tus amigos los domingos? — *What do your friends do on Friday?*

Hacer is conjugated as follows:

yo	**hago**	*I do*
tú	**haces**	*you* (informal) *do*
Ud., él, ella	**hace**	*you* (formal) *do, he/she does*
nosotros(as)	**hacemos**	*we do*
vosotros(as)	**hacéis**	*you* (informal: Spain) *do*
Uds., ellos(as)	**hacen**	*you do, they do*

There are other Spanish verbs that, like **hacer,** have irregular **yo** forms in the present tense.

conocer *to know; to meet*
Conozco a Carlos Suárez.

dar *to give*
Doy una fiesta el viernes.

estar *to be (location and health)*
Estoy en el cine. **Estoy** bien, gracias.

poner *to put (on)*
Pongo música rock en casa.

saber *to know (how)*
Sé jugar bien al béisbol.

salir *to leave; to go out*
Salgo todos los sábados.

traer *to bring*
Traigo la tarea mañana.

ver *to see*
Veo a mi profesora en la tienda.

The other present-tense forms of these verbs are regular with the small exception of **dar** and **ver,** which do not carry an accent on the **a** or **e** of the **vosotros(as)** form as other **-ar** and **-er** verbs do.

	conocer	dar	estar	poner	saber	salir	traer	ver
yo	conozco	doy	estoy	pongo	sé	salgo	traigo	veo
tú	conoces	das	estás	pones	sabes	sales	traes	ves
Ud., él/ella	conoce	da	está	pone	sabe	sale	trae	ve
nosotros(as)	conocemos	damos	estamos	ponemos	sabemos	salimos	traemos	vemos
vosotros(as)	conocéis	dais	estáis	ponéis	sabéis	salís	traéis	veis
Uds., ellos(as)	conocen	dan	están	ponen	saben	salen	traen	ven

¿Recuerdas?

Heinle/Cengage Learning

Gerardo: Bueno, **no sé.** No toco la guitarra mucho en estos días y...

¡A practicar!

3-23 Un mensaje electrónico de Bogotá Claire is writing an e-mail in Spanish to her friend Ramón in the United States. Help her conjugate the verbs in parentheses.

Enviar Guardar Archivos

¡Hola, Ramón!

¿Cómo estás? ¡Bogotá es increíble! 1. Yo ______ *(salir)* mucho con mis compañeros de clase por la ciudad, especialmente durante los fines de semana. Normalmente los sábados nosotros 2. ______ *(hacer)* muchas actividades juntos. A veces *(Sometimes)* 3. ______ *(ver)* películas en el cine o en casa. Anne, mi compañera de casa, casi nunca *(almost never)* 4. ______ *(estar)* en casa los sábados por la tarde porque 5. ______ *(salir)* con su novio, Juanjo. Pero por la noche todos 6. ______ *(estar)* juntos para ir a fiestas. Por ejemplo, una amiga colombiana, Luisa Gómez, 7. ______ *(dar)* una fiesta en su casa mañana. Yo 8. ______ *(saber)* que tú no 9. ______ *(conocer)* a Luisa, pero es una chica muy simpática. Nosotros 10. ______ *(salir)* con frecuencia, pero generalmente 11. ______ *(estar)* en la casa de un amigo o una amiga y 12. ______ *(poner)* música en la radio. Anne siempre 13. ______ *(poner)* música rock y yo siempre cambio de música y 14. ______ *(poner)* jazz. Durante la semana, en casa yo 15. ______ *(hacer)* mucho ejercicio. Ahora yo 16. ______ *(estar)* en casa y voy a descansar un poco.

Un abrazo muy fuerte,
Claire

3-24 Diferencias Complete the sentences with the correct forms of the verbs in parentheses to see how these friends and family members are different from one another.

1. *(hacer)* Yo ______ la tarea por la tarde pero mi amiga Sarita ______ la tarea por la noche.
2. *(estar)* Yo ______ bien pero mi hermano ______ enfermo hoy.
3. *(ver)* Mis amigos y yo ______ muchas películas pero yo no ______ películas de horror.
4. *(conocer)* Yo ______ Bogotá pero mi amigo Luis no ______ la ciudad.
5. *(traer)* Nosotros ______ los libros a clase. Yo ______ mi libro todos los días.

Workbook *3-11 – 3-13*
Lab Manual *3-12 – 3-14*

¡A conversar!

3-25 Correspondencia Using the e-mail from Julieta as a guide, tell your partner about your life at the university. Include information about going to class, doing homework, playing sports, listening to or playing music, going out with friends, and weekend activities. Listen as your partner tells you about his/her activities. Ask questions and share as much information as possible.

Enviar Guardar Archivos

Queridos papis:

Pues, estoy aquí en Cartagena, ¡qué increíble! Ya *(Already)* conozco a mucha gente de todas partes del mundo. Todos los días voy a clase por cuatro horas y hago la tarea después. Generalmente pongo música cuando estudio y a veces toco mi guitarra cuando no deseo estudiar más. Mis amigos Sofía y Jesús tocan un poco, pero no muy bien. A veces les doy lecciones a ellos y a otras personas. También tengo tiempo para jugar un poco. ☺ Practico deportes con mis amigos por la tarde y por la noche salgo con ellos a las discotecas. Sí, sí, sé que necesito tener cuidado. No salgo sola de noche. En la residencia veo la tele o escucho música antes de dormirme *(go to sleep)*. Este fin de semana voy a la playa con mi amigo Jorge Luis y sus primos. Bueno, debo ir a estudiar.
¡Escríbanme pronto!

Besitos, Julieta

3-26 Entrevista In order to know what your classmate does during the weekend and to compare that with your activities, ask a classmate the following questions with the verbs **hacer, estar, saber, conocer, dar, traer, salir, poner,** and **ver.**

1. ¿Cuándo haces planes para el fin de semana? ¿Qué vas a hacer este fin de semana? ¿Vas a estar en casa o vas a salir? ¿Sales mucho durante la semana?
2. Cuando tienes una fiesta, ¿qué tipo de música pones? ¿Llevan tus amigos comida *(food)* a la fiesta? ¿Saben tus padres que vas a tener una fiesta? ¿Sabe tu compañero(a) de cuarto? ¿Siempre conoces a todas las personas de la fiesta?
3. Cuando haces ejercicio, ¿sales de tu cuarto? ¿Ves videos cuando haces ejercicio? ¿Pones la tele o el estéreo cuando haces ejercicio?

Saber, conocer, and the personal *a*

As you have seen earlier, the verbs **saber** and **conocer** both mean *to know,* and they have irregular **yo** forms (**sé/conozco**). These verbs represent two different kinds of knowledge, however.

Saber

Use the verb **saber** to express knowing something (information) or knowing how to do something.

—¿**Saben ustedes que** Juanes es de Medellín, Colombia?	*Do you know that Juanes is from Medellín, Colombia?*
—¿**Sabes que** Carlos Vives canta vallenatos?	*Do you know that Carlos Vives sings vallenatos?*
—¿**Sabes jugar** al tenis?	*Do you know how to play tennis?*
—No, pero **sé jugar** al golf.	*No, but I know how to play golf.*
—**¿Sabes qué?** ¡Me gusta el golf!	*Do you know what? I like golf!*

Conocer and the personal *a*

Use the verb **conocer** to express being acquainted with a person, place, or thing. Note that Spanish speakers use the preposition **a** immediately before a direct object that refers to a specific person or persons.

Cultura

Vallenato is a type of Colombian folk music—usually played on the accordion—that celebrates everyday events, passions, and village folklore.

—¿Quieres **conocer a** mi amiga?	*Do you want to meet my friend?*
—Ya **conozco a** tu amiga, Luisa.	*I already know your friend, Luisa.*
—¿**Conoces** Bogotá?	*Do you know Bogota?*
—No, pero **conozco** Cali.	*No, but I know Cali.*
—**¿Conocen** la música de vallenato?	*Do you know vallenato music?*
—**¿Conoces** la música de Juanes?	*Do you know Juanes's music?*

Note in the first example the use of the personal **a** with a direct object that is a person. The direct object of a verb is the person or thing that receives the action of the verb. For example, in the sentence *I know Carlos,* the direct object is **Carlos.** The personal **a,** which has no English equivalent, is usually used before each noun or pronoun; however, it is usually not used with the verb **tener** even when the direct object is a person.

Conozco **a** Carlos.	*I know Carlos.*
Conozco **a** Carlos y **a** Juan.	*I know Carlos and Juan.*
Carlos y Juan tienen muchos amigos.	*Carlos and Juan have many friends.*

¿Recuerdas?

Heinle/Cengage Learning

Isabel: ¡Claro que sí! **Tú sabes,** Catalina, que todas las amigas de Gerardo son especiales.

¡A practicar!

3-27 ¿Saber o conocer? Decide whether to use **saber** or **conocer** to talk about the following people, places, and activities.

1. jugar al tenis ______
2. mi amigo José Alfredo ______
3. el arte de Botero ______
4. Barranquilla, Colombia ______
5. Cartagena, Colombia ______
6. bailar vallenato ______
7. hablar español ______
8. Gabriel García Márquez ______

Cultura

Gabriel García Márquez is the most famous Colombian writer. He received the Nobel Prize for literature in 1982.

3-28 La *a* personal When should you use the personal ***a***? Decide whether or not you need to use the construction in the following sentences. Don't forget that **a + el = al**!

1. Yo no conozco ______ Bogotá.
2. Mis amigos conocen ______ mi hermano Pablo.
3. Joaquín conoce ______ (el) novio de Anne.
4. Julieta y Penélope conocen bien ______ la música de Carlos Vives.
5. ¿Conoces tú ______ (el) profesor de francés?
6. ¿Tienes ______ amigos en tu clase de español?
7. Conocemos ______ varias ciudades de Colombia.
8. Tengo ______ tres amigos en Cali.
9. ¿Conocen Uds ______ mi amiga Luisa?
10. Muchas personas conocen ______ el arte de Botero.

Workbook *3-14 – 3-16*
Lab Manual *3-15 – 3-17*

¡A conversar!

3-29 ¡Yo sé... ! ¡Yo conozco... ! Now, with a classmate, talk about your familiarity with the items of activity **3-27**.

Modelo jugar al tenis
E1: *Yo no sé jugar al tenis. ¿Sabes tú jugar al tenis?*
E2: *Sí, sé jugar al tenis.*
E2: *No, no sé jugar al tenis.*

3-30 Entrevista You are going to interview a classmate. You need to know who he/she knows, the places he/she is familiar with, and what things he/she knows how to do. Write four questions; then take turns answering.

Modelo *¿Conoces Bogotá?*
¿Sabes esquiar?
¿Conoces el arte de Fernando Botero?
¿Conoces al (a la) presidente de la universidad?

3-31 ¿Quién soy yo? Form groups of 3–4 students. Each person will choose a well-known person but not reveal the name to the other members of the group. Group members will try to identify the well-known person chosen by each member by asking questions about what and whom his or her secret person knows and is familiar with. When one person identifies the secret person of another group member, the activity continues with the other group members asking him or her questions to identify his or her secret person. Consider the following categories for forming questions.

- Personas (actores/actrices, políticos/as, etc.)
- Ciudades (en los Estados Unidos o en otros países)
- Lugares (un restaurante, un campo de golf, etc.)
- Deportes (el tenis, el fútbol, etc.)
- Habilidades especiales (cantar, cocinar, etc.)

Expressing time and weather with *hacer* and *estar*

In this section, you will learn how to talk about the months, seasons, and weather conditions.

Los meses

ENERO

L	M	M	J	V	S	D
1	2	3	4	5	6	7
8	9	10	11	12	13	14
15	16	17	18	19	20	21
22	23	24	25	26	27	28
29	30	31				

FEBRERO

L	M	M	J	V	S	D
			1	2	3	4
5	6	7	8	9	10	11
12	13	14	15	16	17	18
19	20	21	22	23	24	25
26	27	28				

MARZO

L	M	M	J	V	S	D
			1	2	3	4
5	6	7	8	9	10	11
12	13	14	15	16	17	18
19	20	21	22	23	24	25
26	27	28	29	30	31	

ABRIL

L	M	M	J	V	S	D
						1
2	3	4	5	6	7	8
9	10	11	12	13	14	15
16	17	18	19	20	21	22
23/30	24	25	26	27	28	29

MAYO

L	M	M	J	V	S	D
	1	2	3	4	5	6
7	8	9	10	11	12	13
14	15	16	17	18	19	20
21	22	23	24	25	26	27
28	29	30	31			

JUNIO

L	M	M	J	V	S	D
				1	2	3
4	5	6	7	8	9	10
11	12	13	14	15	16	17
18	19	20	21	22	23	24
25	26	27	28	29	30	

JULIO

L	M	M	J	V	S	D
						1
2	3	4	5	6	7	8
9	10	11	12	13	14	15
16	17	18	19	20	21	22
23/30	24/31	25	26	27	28	29

AGOSTO

L	M	M	J	V	S	D
		1	2	3	4	5
6	7	8	9	10	11	12
13	14	15	16	17	18	19
20	21	22	23	24	25	26
27	28	29	30	31		

SEPTIEMBRE

L	M	M	J	V	S	D
					1	2
3	4	5	6	7	8	9
10	11	12	13	14	15	16
17	18	19	20	21	22	23
24	25	26	27	28	29	30

OCTUBRE

L	M	M	J	V	S	D
1	2	3	4	5	6	7
8	9	10	11	12	13	14
15	16	17	18	19	20	21
22	23	24	25	26	27	28
29	30	31				

NOVIEMBRE

L	M	M	J	V	S	D
			1	2	3	4
5	6	7	8	9	10	11
12	13	14	15	16	17	18
19	20	21	22	23	24	25
26	27	28	29	30		

DICIEMBRE

L	M	M	J	V	S	D
					1	2
3	4	5	6	7	8	9
10	11	12	13	14	15	16
17	18	19	20	21	22	23
24/31	25	26	27	28	29	30

In Spanish, the names of the months do not begin with a capital letter as in English, although calendars may print the months in all uppercase letters.

Hoy es martes, 20 de **julio.**
Today is Tuesday, July 20th.

Mi cumpleaños es el 19 de **diciembre.**
My birthday is December 19.

Nota lingüística

In Latin America and Spain, the date is typically written differently than in the United States. The day is presented first and the month is presented second. Thus, when written in Spanish, December 19 is written as 19/12.

Las estaciones

el invierno

la primavera

el verano

el otoño

El tiempo

The verb **hacer** is used to talk about the weather in the following phrases.

hace buen tiempo *the weather is nice*
hace fresco *it's chilly*
hace calor *it's hot*
hace sol *it's sunny*
hace frío *it's cold*
hace viento *it's windy*

The verbs **llover** *(to rain)* and **nevar** *(to snow)* are used in the third person singular.

llueve *it's raining*
nieva *it's snowing*

The nouns derived from these verbs are:

la lluvia *rain*
la nieve *snow*

The verb **estar** is used to indicate whether the sky is overcast or clear.

está despejado *it's clear*
está nublado *it's cloudy*

¡A practicar!

3-32 Los días festivos *(Holidays)* Complete the following sentences with the appropriate months.

Los días festivos de Colombia	
20/7	Día de la Independencia
1/11	Día de Todos los Santos
12/10	Día de la Raza
8/12	Fiesta de la Inmaculada Concepción

1. El Día de la Raza es el 12 de ________.
2. El primer *(first)* día del año es el primero de ________.
3. La Navidad *(Christmas)* es el 25 de ________.
4. El Día de la Independencia de Colombia es el 20 de ________.
5. La fiesta de la Inmaculada Concepción es el 8 de ________.
6. Mi cumpleaños *(birthday)* es el ________ de ________.

3-33 ¿Qué tiempo hace? Look at the drawings and complete the statements.

En el ________ hace mucho ________ y a veces ________. El cielo *(sky)* está ________.

En la ________ hace ________ y a veces ________.

En el ________ hace ________ y ________. El cielo está ________.

En el ________ hace ________.

Workbook *3-17 – 3-19*
Lab Manual *3-18 – 3-19*

¡A conversar!

3-34 Un día típico Working with a partner, state each of the following dates in Spanish, identify the season and describe typical weather conditions. Continue the conversation by sharing information about what you typically do on each date or what you like to do on the date.

Modelo 13/5
E1: Es el trece de mayo. Es la primavera y aquí hace buen tiempo en mayo. Voy al parque y camino o corro. Si *(If)* es el fin de semana, voy a la playa.
E2: Me gusta ir al café y tomar té con mis amigos pero estudio mucho en mayo porque tengo exámenes.

1. 22/12
2. 25/7
3. 3/9
4. 1/4
5. 29/8
6. 7/10
7. 27/4
8. hoy

3-35 La realidad y la fantasía Working with a partner, discuss what you generally like to do during the following periods and then tell what you have to do.

Modelo los sábados *(Saturdays in general)*
Me gusta descansar los sábados pero tengo que estudiar.

1. los veranos
2. los fines de semana
3. por la tarde
4. los días festivos
5. por la mañana
6. los inviernos
7. los domingos
8. por la noche
9. los viernes
10. los lunes

Heinle/Cengage Learning

¿Qué haces en tu tiempo libre? In this segment, the housemates are about to go on an excursion to Old San Juan. As they get ready, they talk about some of the things they like to do in their free time. When they arrive in the heart of Old San Juan, each person shares his or her plan for the day. Watch and see if the day turns out the way they expect it to!

Antes de ver

Expresiones útiles The following are some new expressions you will hear in the video.

Pensándolo bien...	*Now that I think about it . . .*
Estoy de acuerdo...	*I agree . . .*
No vale la pena...	*It's not worth the trouble . . .*
Es hora de vernos con los demás...	*It's time to meet up with the others . . .*

Enfoque estructural The following are expressions in the video with the verb **gustar** and uses of **ir a** + infinitive.

Sofía: Así que **a ti** Javier **te gusta** jugar al fútbol... Y a ti Antonio, al fútbol americano. ¿Qué otros deportes **les gustan**?

Antonio: Y **a mí me gusta** el baloncesto, el... ¡ah! y mucho, el hockey sobre hielo.

Alejandra: Yo **voy a tomar** muchas fotos.

Antonio: Tú ten cuidado. Si te pierdes, yo no quiero **ir a buscarte.**

1. **Recordemos** What pastimes/hobbies have you learned in this chapter? How would you express likes and dislikes? How would you communicate three things that you are going to do this weekend?
2. **Practiquemos** Using the statements above as a model, develop a short survey that 1. asks people what they like to do in their free time and 2. asks people about their plans/intentions for the weekend.

3. **Charlemos** Conduct the survey you developed above in order to determine who is unique in the classroom in terms of his/her pastimes and/or his/her plans for the weekend.

Después de ver

1. ¿A quién le gusta? Based on the activities listed, decide which of the five housemates is being described.

1. ¿A quién le gusta el alpinismo, el buceo, el esnórkel y todas las actividades al aire libre?
2. ¿A quién le gusta ver el ver el hockey sobre hielo por televisión y le gusta también el fútbol americano y el baloncesto?
3. ¿Quién practica el piano?
4. ¿A quién no le gustan los deportes?
5. ¿A quién le gusta ir de compras?
6. ¿Quién practica el yoga y el tenis?

2. ¿Qué quieren hacer y qué hacen al final? What did the housemates originally plan to do and what did they actually end up doing?

1. Alejandra quiere ______________.
2. Sofía quiere ______________. Al final Javier y Sofia ______________, pero ______________.
3. Valeria quiere ______________.
4. Antonio quiere ______________. Al final Antonio y Alejandra ______________ y Alejandra ______________ pero ______________.

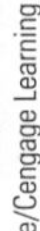

Heinle/Cengage Learning

Entre nosotros Write a detailed description of your ideal itinerary for the day based on activities mentioned in the video. Choose at least two things to do and explain why. Share your plans with a classmate and see if your ideas are compatible.

Presentaciones With a partner, develop a new character for the story. Present this individual to the class. Be sure to include details about where this person is from and what he/she likes to do in his/her free time. Decide with whom the character would most likely have gone during the day in Old San Juan.

See the *Lab Manual*, **Capítulo 3, 3-22– 3-23** for additional activities.

Antes de leer

Strategy: Using context to predict content

In addition to the reading strategies previously presented—identifying cognates and skimming and scanning—efficient readers like you may use other strategies to determine the meaning of unfamiliar words and phrases in a reading selection. One of these strategies is the use of context to predict content. You may identify the context of a reading selection in the following ways:

- by looking at the photos or images that accompany the reading
- by reading the title and subtitles of the selection

Use this chapter's reading strategy to answer the following questions with a classmate.

Context

1. What types of photos do you see in the selection?
2. What do the titles and subtitles say? What are the titles of the various sections?

Predictions

1. What type of reading selection is this? What is the subject?
2. Who wrote this selection?
3. Who are its probable readers?

¡Vamos a Colombia!

1. Scan the reading selection and write down any cognates you encounter and their meanings.
2. Now, skim the selection, trying to understand the gist of the content. Then, scan the selection to find the following information. Discuss this information with a partner.
   a. What can tourists do in the Caribbean Region in Colombia?
   b. What can tourists do in the Andean Region in Colombia?
   c. What is the weather like in the Caribbean Region?
   d. What is the best region to scuba dive, to snorkel or to sail?
   e. What is the best region to bike or to glide?
3. Read the article again and try to guess the meaning of some words. Discuss your predictions with a partner.
   a. ¡Si desean tomar el sol, nadar, navegar y esquiar en **el mar,** las **Islas** del Rosario en Cartagena, **las playas** del Parque Tayrona y las playas de Rodadero en Santa Marta son maravillosas!
   b. En la región andina de Colombia, existen muchas montañas con nieve, bosques, **lagos y valles.**
   c. Hay muchas **riquezas** naturales y por eso existen muchos parques nacionales **para proteger** la naturaleza y donde hacer paseos ecológicos.

Después de leer

¿Cierto o falso? Indicate whether each statement is **cierto** *(true)* or **falso** *(false)*. Then correct the false statements.

1. ______ The people in the Caribbean Region are open and happy. They like **cumbia** which is influenced by African rhythms.
2. ______ The National Park of Tayrona cannot be visited by tourists.
3. ______ The people from the Andean Region do not want to show off the beauty of their region.
4. ______ The Andean mountains are exciting for mountain biking.

¿Qué saben ustedes de los pasatiempos de los colombianos?

¿Qué saben ustedes de los deportes de aventuras?

Región Caribe

- **Bailar**
- **Bucear** *(to scuba dive)*
- **Navegar**
- **Nadar**
- **Caretear** *(to snorkel)*
- **Esquiar**

En la región caribe de Colombia hace mucho calor y mucho sol.

Las personas de la región son alegres, espontáneas y muy simpáticas. A ellos les gusta el mar y también les gusta la música y el baile. La música tiene influencia africana y los ritmos son la cumbia, el vallenato y el porro.

¡Si desean tomar el sol, nadar, navegar y esquiar en el **mar**, las **Islas** del Rosario en Cartagena, **las playas** del Parque Tayrona y las playas de Rodadero en Santa Marta son maravillosas!

¡Si desean aprender a bucear, a caretear o a esquiar, las playas son el paraíso!

¡Si desean caminar por las montañas y hacer paseos ecológicos, el Parque Nacional Tayrona es el parque perfecto!

¡Si desean aprender a bailar cumbia o vallenato, los carnavales de Barranquilla, de Cartagena o de Santa Marta son ideales!

Región Andina

- **Parapente** *(paragliding)*
- **Canotaje** *(canoeing/kayaking)*
- **Ciclomontañismo** *(mountain biking)*

© Joel Carillet/istockphoto.com

En la región andina de Colombia, existen muchas montañas con nieve, bosques, **lagos y valles.** En la región hace fresco y a veces hace mucho frío también.

Las personas son muy amables y desean mostrar la belleza de su país.

Hay muchas **riquezas** naturales y por eso existen muchos parques nacionales **para proteger** la naturaleza y donde hacer caminatas ecológicas.

¡Si practican el parapente o el ciclomontañismo, las montañas de la región andina son fabulosas!

¡Si practican el canotaje, los ríos y lagos son ideales para este deporte!

¡A conversar! With three or four of your classmates, discuss the following topics.

1. After reading this brochure about sports and adventures in Colombia, discuss your impressions of Colombia and its people before reading this guide and your ideas of Colombia after reading it. Mention at least four of each. Have your ideas changed about Colombia? How?
2. Did you find this short brochure to be useful? Mention three other topics that you would like to read about.
   a. ____________________
   b. ____________________
   c. ____________________
3. Would you like to do Xtreme sports in Colombia or any other country? Explain which country and what sports.

Strategy: Combining sentences

Learning to combine simple sentences into more complex ones can help you improve your writing style immensely. In Spanish, there are several words you can use as connectors to combine sentences and phrases:

y	*and* (**y** becomes **e** before **i**, or **hi**)
o	*or* (**o** becomes **u** before **o** or **ho**)
que	*that; which; who*
pero	*but*
porque	*because*

Paso 1 Read the following blog posting that Kelly wrote about what she is doing during her summer vacation. Circle all of the connectors used in the following sentences.

> *¡Saludos a todos!*
> *Estoy de vacaciones en Santa Marta, Colombia. Ustedes saben que me gusta practicar muchos deportes, como el tenis, la natación, el ciclismo y el baloncesto. Hago todas las actividades aquí en Santa Marta. Me gusta nadar todos los días, pero cuando llueve, voy de compras o miro la tele en casa. También paso mucho tiempo con mi amigo Carlos. Carlos tiene veintitrés años y es un chico muy simpático. Nos gusta salir por la noche los fines de semana e ir a las discotecas que están en el centro. Carlos conoce Santa Marta muy bien y, gracias a él, ahora conozco la ciudad también. Bueno, en pocos minutos vamos al cine porque deseamos ver una película.*
> *¡Hasta pronto!*

Paso 2 Now that you have seen how connectors were used in the blog posting, combine the following sets of sentences, using **y, pero, que,** and **porque** appropriately.

Modelo Estudio en la Universidad de Bogotá. Me gustan mis clases.
Estudio en la Universidad de Bogotá y me gustan mis clases.

Tengo muchos amigos. Son muy simpáticos.
Tengo muchos amigos que son muy simpáticos.

1. Me gusta practicar deportes. No tengo mucho tiempo libre.
2. Mi amiga corre todos los días. Le gusta correr.
3. Deseo mirar un partido de fútbol en la tele. Necesito estudiar.
4. Tengo muchos amigos. Esquían en el invierno.

Task: Writing an informal blog posting

Paso 1 Using Kelly's blog posting as a model, write a similar one telling friends what you do in your free time. Be sure to include a description of several activities, and mention who (if anyone) you like to do these activities with as well as when and where you do them. Use connectors appropriately.

Paso 2 Work with one or more classmates, exchanging and reading one another's postings. Ask questions about the activities, the people who do them, and the places where they are done.

Communicative Goals:

- Communicate about leisure activities
- Express likes and dislikes
- Indicate plans and intentions
- Share information about when and where common activities are done

Paso 1

Review the Communicative Goals for **Capítulo 3** and determine if you are able to accomplish the goals. If you are not certain that you have achieved all of the goals, review the pertinent portions of the chapter.

Paso 2

Look at the components of a conversation which addresses the communicative goals for this chapter. The percentages will help you evaluate your ability to successfully participate in the conversation that is featured below. Your instructor may use the same rubric to assess your oral performance.

Components of the conversation	%
☐ Asking a general question about leisure activities	10
☐ Communicating about at least two activities and when, where and/or with whom they are done.	30
☐ Communicating about at least two additional activities and when, where and/or with whom they are done.	30
☐ Stating something that must be done or has to be done, including information about when or where.	20
☐ Concluding the conversation and saying good-bye.	10

En acción Think about how a conversation between two friends who are discussing leisure activities might develop. Determine the sort of information that could be shared and how the friends would exchange the information. You may find it helpful to write down some ideas about what might be included. Consider the following steps:

1. One friend asks the other what he or she likes to do during free time.
2. The second person responds, mentioning at least two activities and providing details about when, where, and/or with whom they are done.
3. That person asks the first person what activities he or she likes.
4. The first person responds with appropriate information.
5. The conversation continues with each person mentioning a total of at least four activities and, for each one, additional information about when, where, and with whom they are done.
6. One person states that he or she must or has to do something, including when and/or where, and the other person replies with similar information.
7. The conversation concludes as the friends say good-bye to one another.

Gustar + infinitive

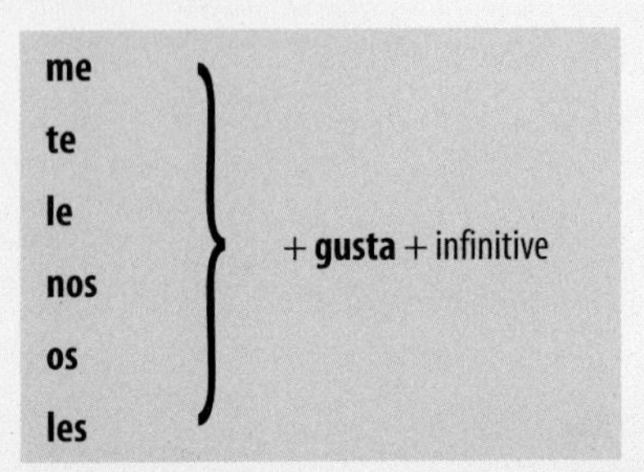

Spanish-speakers use indirect object pronouns to indicate *to whom* or *for whom* an action is pleasing.

¡A recordar! 1 In Spanish, how does one clarify to whom something is pleasing?

Gustar + nouns

When you use gustar with nouns, its form changes to reflect whether you are talking about one thing or more than one thing.

—A Carlos le **gusta** la piscina. —A Carlos le **gustan** los deportes.

¡A recordar! 2 Which type of article (definite or indefinite) usually precedes the noun in the **gustar** + *noun* construction?

Verbs with irregular *yo* forms

conocer	**Conozco** a Carlos Suárez.
dar	**Doy** una fiesta el viernes.
estar	**Estoy** en la discoteca.
hacer	**Hago** mucho ejercicio.
poner	**Pongo** música rock en casa.
saber	**Sé** jugar bien al béisbol.
salir	**Salgo** todos los sábados.
traer	**Traigo** mis discos compactos a la fiesta.
ver	**Veo** a mi profesora en la tienda.

¡A recordar! 3 How are the conjugations of **dar** and **ver** different from the conjugations of the other verbs listed above?

Ir and *ir a...*

To tell where people are going, use a form of the verb **ir** plus the preposition **a,** followed by a destination. To express future plans, use a form of the verb **ir** plus the preposition **a,** followed by an infinitive.

¡A recordar! 4 What does the combination **a** + **el** yield in Spanish?

Saber, conocer, and the personal *a*

Use the verb **saber** to express knowledge of something (information) or of how to do something.
—¿**Sabes jugar** al tenis?

Use the verb **conocer** to express an acquaintance with a person, place, or thing.
—¿**Conoces** Bogotá?
—¿Quieres **conocer a** mi amiga?

¡A recordar! 5 In what instances do you use the personal **a?**

Expressing time and weather with *hacer* and *estar*

The verb **hacer** is used to talk about the weather. The verb **estar** is used to indicate whether the sky is overcast or clear.

hace sol *it's sunny* **hace frío** *it's cold*
está despejado *it's clear* **está nublado** *it's cloudy*

¡A recordar! 6 What's the weather like in July in the Southern hemisphere?

Actividad 1 Los gustos Complete each sentence to express what various people like. Write the correct indirect object pronoun in the first blank and the correct form of **gustar** in the second blank.

1. A mis hermanos ______ ______ practicar el tenis.
2. A mí ______ ______ el baloncesto. También ______ ______ los deportes acuáticos.
3. A nuestro padre ______ ______ los conciertos.
4. A mi primo ______ ______ montar a caballo.
5. A todos nosotros ______ ______ la natación.
6. A ti ______ ______ el béisbol y el fútbol, ¿no?

Actividad 2 ¿Qué hacen estas personas? Complete each sentence with the appropriate verb forms to express things these people do. Use the verb that is in the first sentence and write the correct forms according to the new subjects.

1. Luisa hace la tarea por la mañana. Yo ______ la tarea por la noche. ¿Cuándo ______ la tarea tú?
2. Muchas personas ponen la tele cuando estudian. Mi hermano ______ la tele frecuentemente. Tú ______ la tele cuando descansas, ¿no?
3. Jorge y yo damos una fiesta el sábado. Jorge ______ muchas fiestas pero yo no ______ muchas fiestas.
4. Todos los estudiantes traen sus libros a clase. Yo ______ mi libro y la profesora ______ su libro todos los días.
5. Mis amigos y yo salimos los viernes y los sábados. Unos amigos ______ los jueves también pero yo ______ solamente el fin de semana.
6. Yo no veo mucha tele, pero mis amigos ______ mucho fútbol en la tele. Y tú, ¿______ mucha tele?
7. Estoy en la residencia. Gerardo y David ______ en la residencia también. ¿Dónde ______ Mariana?
8. Alejandra sabe montar a caballo. Yo no ______ montar a caballo, pero mis primos tienen muchos caballos y ______ montar.

Actividad 3 El fin de semana Form sentences with the given elements and the correct form of the verb **ir** to express where people are going and what they are going to do.

1. Sofía / el parque
2. Mis amigos y yo / mirar un partido de fútbol.
3. Tú / el concierto
4. Celia / la piscina
5. Celia y sus amigos / nadar
6. Antonio / las montañas
7. Tú / el café después del concierto
8. Yo / la discoteca

Actividad 4 Cosas familiares Choose the correct verb to complete each sentence in order to tell what various people know. Pay careful attention to context and to form.

1. ¿ Uds. ______ a mi hermano?

   a. saben c. conoces
   b. sabe d. conocen

2. Yo ______ Bogotá, la capital de Colombia.

   a. sé c. sabe
   b. conozco d. conocen

3. Manolo y yo ______ esquiar en el agua.

   a. sabes c. sabemos
   b. conocemos d. conocen

4. Mi amiga ______ muchos verbos en español.

   a. sabe c. conoces
   b. conoce d. sabes

5. Los jóvenes ______ jugar al fútbol.

   a. sabes c. conocen
   b. saben d. conocemos

6. ¿Tú ______ a Fernando Botero? ¡Imposible!

   a. conoces c. sabes
   b. conozco d. saben

7. Mi profesor ______ cuántas personas viven en Cartagena, Colombia.

   a. sabes c. conoces
   b. sabe d. conoce

Actividad 5 ¿Qué tiempo hace? Match each phrase in the first column with the most closely associated weather expression in the second column.

______ 1. en julio en Tampa, Florida	a. Hace viento.
______ 2. en Chile en los Andes en agosto	b. Hace calor.
______ 3. en Puerto Rico durante un huracán (*hurricane*)	c. Llueve.
______ 4. en Nueva York en octubre	d. Hace fresco.
______ 5. en Seattle muchos días del año	e. Hace frío.
______ 6. en el desierto del Sahara	f. Casi (*almost*) no llueve.

Refrán

Treinta días ______ (*bring*) ______ (?), con ______ (?), ______ (?) y ______ (?). Veintiocho sólo ______ (*bring*) uno y los demás treinta y uno.

VOCABULARIO ESENCIAL

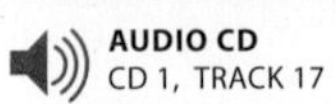
AUDIO CD
CD 1, TRACK 17

PERSONAL TUTOR

Los pasatiempos y deportes	Pastimes and Sports
andar en bicicleta	to ride a bike
bailar	to dance
caminar por las montañas	to hike/walk in the mountains
correr	to run
dar un paseo	to go for a walk
esquiar	to ski
esquiar en el agua	to water-ski
hacer ejercicio	to exercise
hacer un picnic	to go on a picnic
jugar...	to play...
al baloncesto	basketball
al béisbol	baseball
al fútbol	soccer
al fútbol americano	football
al golf	golf
al tenis	tennis
al voleibol	volleyball
ir...	to go ...
a tomar un café	to drink coffee
a un bar	to a bar
a un club	to a club
a un concierto	to a concert
a una discoteca	to a dance club
a una fiesta	to a party
al cine	to the movies
de compras	shopping
levantar pesas	to lift weights
mirar la tele	to watch TV
montar a caballo	to go horseback riding
nadar	to swim
pasear	to go for a walk
patinar en línea	to in-line skate
practicar deportes	to play sports
pescar	to fish
sacar fotos	to take pictures
tocar la guitarra	to play the guitar
tomar el sol	to sunbathe
ver una película	to watch a movie
visitar un museo	to visit a museum

Otras palabras relacionadas con el tiempo libre	Other words related to spare time
Sustantivos	
el campo de...	... field/course
la cancha de...	... court
el ciclismo	cycling
la natación	swimming
el partido	game
la pesca	fishing
Verbos	
ganar	to win
hacer planes	to make plans

Los lugares en el pueblo	Places in town
el banco	bank
el café	café
la calle	street
el centro	downtown
el centro comercial	mall
el cine	movie theater
la iglesia	church
el mercado (al aire libre)	(outdoor) market
el museo	museum
la oficina de correos	post office
el parque	park
la piscina	pool
la plaza	plaza
el restaurante	restaurant
el supermercado	supermarket
la tienda	store

Los meses del año	Months of the year
enero	January
febrero	February
marzo	March
abril	April
mayo	May
junio	June
julio	July
agosto	August
septiembre	September
octubre	October
noviembre	November
diciembre	December

Las estaciones	Seasons
el invierno	winter
la primavera	spring
el verano	summer
el otoño	fall

El tiempo	Weather
está despejado	it's clear
está nublado	it's cloudy
hace buen tiempo	the weather is nice
hace calor	it's hot
hace fresco	it's chilly
hace frío	it's cold
hace sol	it's sunny
hace viento	it's windy
llueve	it's raining
la lluvia	rain
nieva	it's snowing
la nieve	snow

Otros verbos	Other Verbs
conocer	to know; to meet
dar	to give
estar	to be (location and health)
hacer	to do; to make
poner	to put (on)
saber	to know (how)
salir	to leave; to go out
traer	to bring
ver	to see

CAPÍTULO 4

En la casa

España

© Carlos Nieto/Photolibrary

Plaza de España, Vejer de la Frontera, España

Chapter Objectives

Communicative Goals

In this chapter, you will learn how to . . .

- Describe features and contents of homes and other residences
- Give instructions to friends and family members
- State locations
- Indicate feelings
- Communicate about actions in progress

Structures

- Present tense of stem-changing verbs **(e → ie, o → ue, u → ue, e → i)**
- Affirmative **tú** commands
- The verb **estar** and the present progressive

- ¿Deseas visitar España con tu familia o con tus amigos? Explica con quién y por qué.
- ¿En qué estación del año deseas visitar España?
- ¿Qué actividades te gusta hacer en tu casa? ¿Es similar tu casa a las casas de la foto?

 Visit it live on **Google Earth!**

En la Casa de la Troya de doña Rosa

In this section, you will practice talking about household rooms and furniture. Are there any student houses on your campus? How do they compare with doña Rosa's?

Nota lingüística

In Spain, **el piso** refers to the apartment as a whole. **El suelo** is the term used for *floor.*

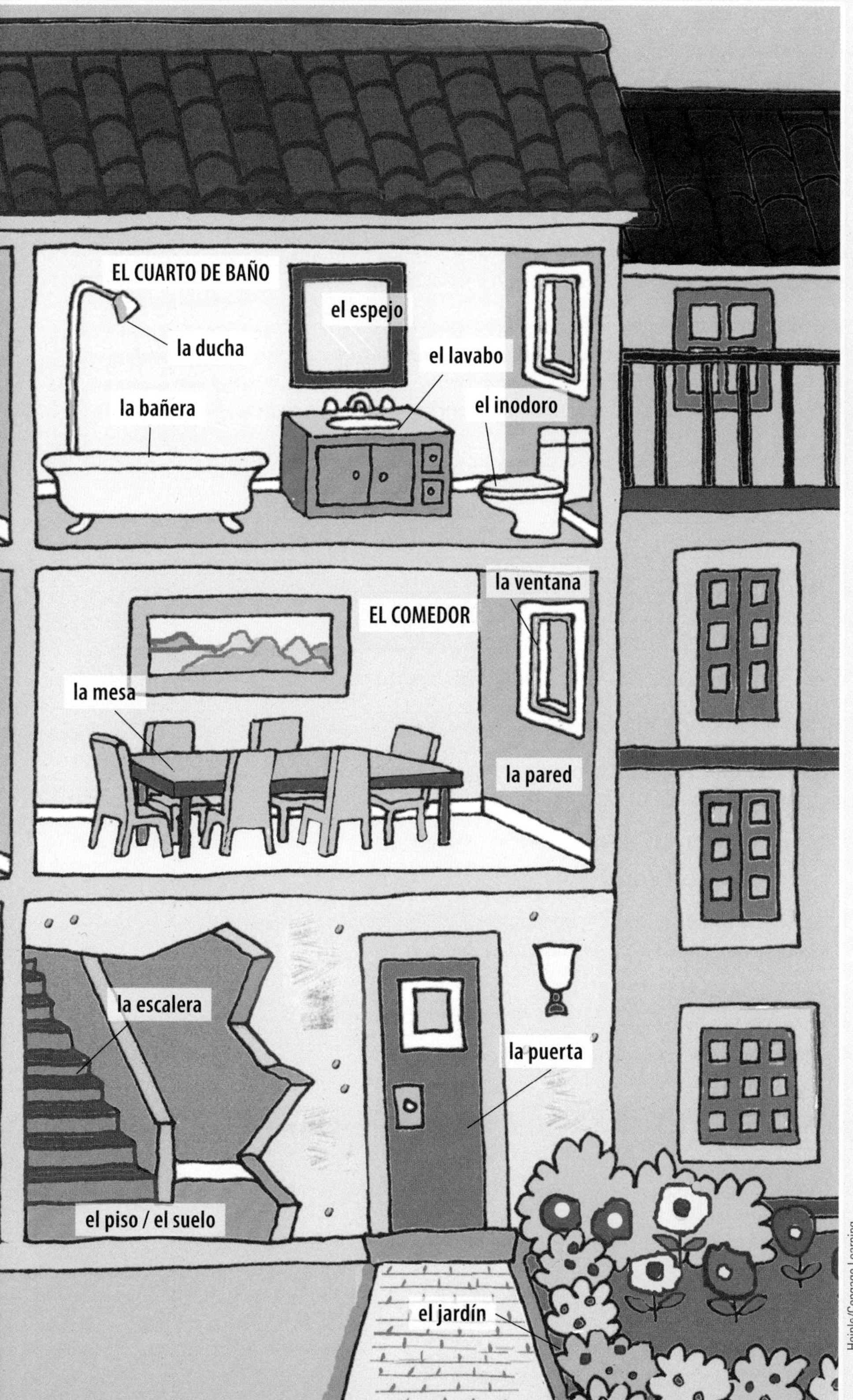

Heinle/Cengage Learning

Más palabras relacionadas con la casa

el cuarto *room*

la decoración *decoration*

el (aparato) electrodoméstico *electrical appliance*

el mueble *piece of furniture*

Palabras útiles

el aire acondicionado *air conditioning*

el balcón *balcony*

la calefacción *heat*

la chimenea *fireplace, chimney*

el condominio *condominium*

el garaje *garage*

el hogar *home*

el techo *roof*

la terraza *terrace/patio*

el tocador *dresser*

la vivienda *housing*

Palabras útiles are presented to help you enrich your personal vocabulary. The terms provided here will help you talk about housing and household areas.

Cultura

Santiago de Compostela, in northwest Spain, is home to one of the major universities in Spain. **La Casa de la Troya** is Santiago de Compostela's most famous student residence. This building is typical of the architecture from the XVII century in this part of Spain. It served as a student hostel during the end of the XIX century.

¡A practicar!

4-1 **¿Dónde pongo los muebles nuevos?** Doña Rosa necesita poner los muebles nuevos en la Casa de la Troya. Indica el cuarto apropiado para cada *(each)* mueble.

Modelo Usted debe poner el estante _en el dormitorio_.

1. Es lógico poner el lavaplatos en ______________.
2. Usted debe poner la cama y la cómoda en ______________, ¿no?
3. El sofá debe estar en ______________.
4. La nevera debe estar en ______________.
5. ¿La ducha, la bañera, el inodoro y el lavabo? En ______________, ¡por supuesto!
6. Es necesario poner la mesa y las sillas en _______.

Nota lingüística

La habitación, el cuarto, la alcoba, la recámara, and **la pieza** are all synonyms for **el dormitorio** (which does not mean *dormitory*). **La habitación** is more commonly used in Spain.

4-2 **¿Qué hay en la casa de doña Rosa?** Describe los muebles y las otras cosas de cada cuarto de la casa con la expresión verbal **hay...**

Modelo el dormitorio / la habitación
En el dormitorio / la habitación hay un estante, un armario, una cómoda, una cama, un despertador, una tabla de planchar y una plancha.

1. la sala: ______________________________
____
____
2. el comedor: ______________________________
3. la cocina: ______________________________
____
____
4. el cuarto de baño: ______________________________
____

4-3 **¿Y qué hay en tu casa?** Completa las siguientes oraciones con los muebles y electrodomésticos de tu casa o residencia.

Modelo En el cuarto de baño hay _un lavabo, un inodoro y una bañera._

1. En mi casa hay _______ (#) dormitorio(s)/habitación (habitaciones) y _______ (#) cuarto(s) de baño.
2. Hay _______ (#) puerta(s) y _______ (#) ventana(s).
3. En la cocina hay _______.
4. En el dormitorio / la habitación hay _______.
5. En la sala hay _______.
6. En el comedor hay _______.
7. En el garaje hay _______.
8. ¿Tienes un jardín o un sótano?

Workbook *4-1 – 4-5*
Lab Manual *4-1 – 4-4*

¡A conversar!

4-4 **Lugares preferidos** Habla con un(a) compañero(a) sobre las siguientes actividades. Dile en qué parte de la casa te gusta hacer estas actividades.

Modelo leer libros
Me gusta leer libros en el dormitorio.

1. estudiar
2. comer con la familia
3. mirar la tele
4. comer solo(a)
5. hablar por teléfono
6. escuchar música
7. descansar
8. hacer la tarea

4-5 **Se alquila piso *(Apartment for rent)*** Tú y un(a) amigo(a) van a pasar dos semanas de vacaciones en España y desean alquilar un piso o una casa pequeña. Uds. leen en Internet información sobre una casa y un apartamento. Tienen que decidir cuál de los dos prefieren y explicar por qué.

Modelo Me gusta la casa porque tiene Internet.

Estudiante A: Encuentras un anuncio para un apartamento en Costa del Sol.

- 2 habitaciones: 1 habitación con una cama matrimonial y armario; 1 habitación con 2 camas sencillas y 1 escritorio
- salón con sofá cama, mesa y televisor
- cocina con horno de microondas, mesa de comedor y tostadora
- baño moderno con ducha, lavabo e inodoro
- electricidad incluida en el precio
- 5 minutos del centro de la ciudad, donde hay muchos bares de tapas, tiendas, iglesias y plazas; en una zona muy segura
- Precio: 60 euros/noche; 360 euros/semana; 1.200 euros/mes

Estudiante B: Encuentras un anuncio para una casa pequeña en Costa del Sol.

- 2 habitaciones: 1 habitación con cama matrimonial y un armario; 1 habitación con 2 camas sencillas y 1 escritorio
- cocina: nevera, microondas, plancha y mesa de planchar; comestibles básicos (aceite, vinagre, sal, azúcar, café, té)
- comedor: mesa de centro, mesa de comedor extensible con 4 sillas, TV a color por cable, ordenador con conexión permanente de Internet
- baño: lavabo, WC, ducha, espejo
- con terraza para sentarse al aire libre, comer, hacer barbacoas, etc.
- ubicación: está a sólo 1 minuto de la parada de autobuses más cercana y a 15 minutos del centro de la ciudad
- cerca: tiendas, bares, restaurantes, bancos, farmacias y supermercado
- Precio: 150 euros/día; 856 euros/semana; 3.424 euros/mes

EN CONTEXTO

Alberto, un estudiante de medicina de la Universidad de Santiago de Compostela, expresa sus opiniones sobre un apartamento desastroso que él visita con su amigo Francisco.

AUDIO CD
CD 2, TRACK 2

Escucha la conversación entre Alberto y Francisco e indica cuatro cosas que no le gustan a Alberto del apartamento.

Modelo *Todo está sucio y desordenado.*

En la calle...

Alberto: Vaya... las plantas en el balcón **están muertas.** ¡No puedo entrar!

Francisco: ¿Tienes miedo? ¡Hombre! **Espera** un momento para ver el interior. Seguro que **está mejor.**

Comentario cultural Large lawn areas are uncommon in Spain; however, apartment-dwellers often take great pride in their flowerboxes and it is not uncommon to hear caged songbirds singing from balconies.

En el salón...

Alberto: ¡Dios mío! ¡Qué desastre de apartamento! Hay ropa por todas partes y en el sillón hay un montón de libros.

Francisco: Seguro que las personas que viven aquí son estudiantes. **¿Quieres** ver la cocina?

Comentario cultural In Spain, it is more common for students to have cell phones in lieu of a traditional land line due to the expense of having a permanent phone installed.

En la cocina...

Alberto: ¡Qué barbaridad! Todos los platos **están sucios.** Y todavía no han quitado la mesa. Parece que nadie limpia aquí. Y para colmo, ¡una bolsa de basura en la terraza!... No **puedo** imaginar cómo viven aquí.

Comentario cultural In Spain, washing machines are typically located in the kitchen. Dryers are rarely used; instead, clothes are hung on clothes lines or on indoor drying racks. To fuel hot water heaters and gas stoves or ovens, Spaniards often use orange, refillable propane containers.

Expresiones en contexto

el alquiler *rent*
antes de *before*
apenas puedo verla *I can barely see it*
qué mal huele *it smells awful*
inquilinos *tenants*
un montón *a lot (informal, Spain)*
ni siquiera *not even*
...no han quitado la mesa *... haven't cleared the table*
¡No puedo más! *I can't take anymore!*
para colmo *and on top of that*
vivir al aire libre *to live outdoors*
¡Qué barbaridad! *How atrocious!*
¡Qué desastre de apartamento! *What a disastrous apartment!*
salón *living room (Spain)*
seguro *surely*
súper *really (adverb, Spain)*

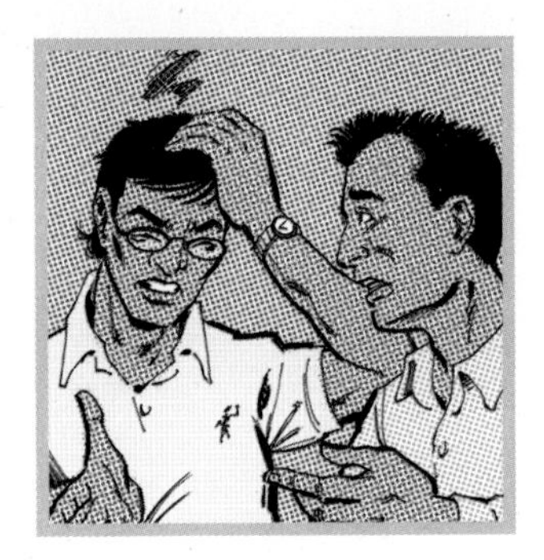

Francisco: **Ten** paciencia, Alberto. ¿Vamos a ver la habitación?

En la habitación...

Alberto: No veo la cama... Ah, allí está. Apenas **puedo** verla debajo de la ropa. Y ni siquiera hay un libro en el estante.

Francisco: Creo que todos **están en el sillón** del salón. Bueno, Alberto,... tienes razón. El piso **está un poco desordenado.** Pero **ven** conmigo para ver el cuarto de baño antes de decidir.

Comentario cultural Fernando Alonso, the world-champion formula 1 race-car driver, and Raúl, the team captain who plays for Real Madrid, are popular figures among Spanish youth.

En el cuarto de baño...

Alberto: Mira cómo está la bañera... y qué mal huele aquí. No **puedo** vivir con esta gente... Los inquilinos de este piso son un desastre. Y el alquiler es súper alto. **Prefiero** vivir al aire libre. En fin, ya me voy... ¡No puedo más!

Comentario cultural In Spain, not all apartments have a bathtub because of space. It is also common in parts of Europe for bathrooms to have a **bidet**, which is used for personal hygiene.

Donde yo vivo Haz un dibujo *(drawing)* de tu casa, piso o cuarto en la residencia, e incluye por lo menos 3 detalles *(details)* desagradables *(unpleasant/disagreeable)*. Luego, explica tu dibujo a un(a) compañero(a) de clase y comenta el dibujo de él/ella.

ESTRUCTURA 1

Present tense of stem-changing verbs *(e → ie; o → ue; u → ue; e → i)*

In this section, you will learn how to conjugate verbs that change—either **e** to **ie**, **o** to **ue**, **u** to **ue**, or **e** to **i**—in the stem of the verb. The stem is the part of an infinitive to which one adds personal endings. For example, the stem of **hablar** is **habl-**. The above-mentioned types of vowel changes occur in all stressed syllables. Since the stress does not fall on the stem in the **nosotros(as)** and **vosotros(as)** forms, there is no stem change.

The present tense of *e → ie* stem-changing verbs

Infinitive	comenzar (ie)	pensar (ie)	preferir (ie)	querer (ie)	venir (ie)
	(to begin)	*(to think)*	*(to prefer)*	*(to want; to love)*	*(to come)*
Stem	**comienz-**	**piens-**	**prefier-**	**quier-**	**vien-**
	com**ie**nzo	p**ie**nso	pref**ie**ro	qu**ie**ro	vengo
	com**ie**nzas	p**ie**nsas	pref**ie**res	qu**ie**res	v**ie**nes
	com**ie**nza	p**ie**nsa	pref**ie**re	qu**ie**re	v**ie**ne
	comenzamos	pensamos	preferimos	queremos	venimos
	comenzáis	pensáis	preferís	queréis	venís
	com**ie**nzan	p**ie**nsan	pref**ie**ren	qu**ie**ren	v**ie**nen

Other frequently used *e* to *ie* stem-changing verbs are:

cerrar (ie) *to close*
empezar (ie) *to begin*
entender (ie) *to understand*
perder (ie) *to lose; to miss (an event)*
regar (ie) *to water*

The present tense of *o → ue/u → ue* stem-changing verbs

Infinitive	almorzar (ue)	dormir (ue)	jugar (ue)	volver (ue)	poder (ue)
	(to have lunch)	*(to sleep)*	*(to play)*	*(to return)*	*(to be able)*
Stem	**almuerz-**	**duerm-**	**jueg-**	**vuelv-**	**pued-**
	alm**ue**rzo	d**ue**rmo	j**ue**go	v**ue**lvo	p**ue**do
	alm**ue**rzas	d**ue**rmes	j**ue**gas	v**ue**lves	p**ue**des
	alm**ue**rza	d**ue**rme	j**ue**ga	v**ue**lve	p**ue**de
	almorzamos	dormimos	jugamos	volvemos	podemos
	almorzáis	dormís	jugáis	volvéis	podéis
	alm**ue**rzan	d**ue**rmen	j**ue**gan	v**ue**lven	p**ue**den

The present tense of *e → i* stem-changing verbs

Infinitive	decir (i)	pedir (i)	servir (i)
	(to say; to tell)	*(to ask for)*	*(to serve)*
Stem	**dic-**	**pid-**	**sirv-**
	digo (irregular **yo** form)	p**i**do	s**i**rvo
	d**i**ces	p**i**des	s**i**rves
	d**i**ce	p**i**de	s**i**rve
	decimos	pedimos	servimos
	decís	pedís	servís
	d**i**cen	p**i**den	s**i**rven

¡A practicar!

4-6 Entrevista a doña Rosa Raquel Navarro es reportera. Ella quiere escribir un artículo sobre la gente de edad *(the elderly)*. En este momento ella habla con doña Rosa. Completa su conversación con la forma correcta de los siguientes verbos:

comenzar pensar preferir querer tener venir

Raquel: Yo 1. ______________ hablar con usted, doña Rosa. ¿Está bien?
Doña Rosa: Sí. 2. ¿ ______________ (nosotras) con mi vida *(life)* personal?
Raquel: Muy bien. 3. ¿ ______________ usted hijos?
Doña Rosa: Sí, 4. ______________ cuatro. Dos de ellos viven aquí.
Raquel: Y los demás... 5. ¿ ______________ mucho por aquí?
Doña Rosa: Bueno, no 6. ______________ mucho porque viven en Madrid.
Raquel: Sé que Ud. tiene que trabajar mucho pero, ¿qué hace cuando no trabaja?
Doña Rosa: Me gusta mirar la tele. (Yo) 7. ______________ ver telenovelas. Mi telenovela favorita se llama «El amor en tiempos inciertos». El programa 8. ______________ en una hora. 9. ¿ ______________ Ud. verlo conmigo esta tarde?
Raquel: Sí, gracias. Me gusta mucho el programa. ¡Qué guay! *(Cool!)*

4-7 Planes para el sábado Beti y su compañero Tomás, dos estudiantes de medicina en Santiago de Compostela, hablan de sus planes. Completa su conversación con la forma correcta de los siguientes verbos:

almorzar dormir jugar poder volver

Beti: ¿Por qué no 1. ______________ (nosotros) al tenis esta tarde?
Tomás: Yo no 2. ______________ bien al tenis, Beti. Y después de *(after)* mi accidente, no 3. ______________ hacer mucho ejercicio por una semana.
Beti: Pues, vamos al cine. ¿Quieres? (Nosotros) 4. ______________ ver la nueva película de Amenábar.
Tomás: Bien. Antes *(before)* del cine, 5. ¿ ______________ (nosotros) en la calle Franco?
Beti: ¡Perfecto! Y después de almorzar, (nosotros) 6. ______________ a casa. Yo siempre 7. ______________ la siesta.
Tomás: ¿Cómo? Tú 8. ______________ dormir la siesta, si quieres, pero yo no.

Cultura

La calle Franco is one of the more popular streets for dining in Santiago de Compostela. The street is in the old part of the city where car traffic is prohibited and features numerous street musicians and other attractions.

4-8 Un anuncio Tú y dos amigos van a vivir en un apartamento nuevo y tienen una lista de cosas que necesitan comprar. Escucha el anuncio de la tienda *Muebles Jiménez* y marca las cosas que venden.

AUDIO CD
CD 2, TRACK 3

______ Un sofá
______ Dos sillones
______ Dos mesitas
______ Una alfombra
______ Una mesa de comedor y sillas
______ Tres camas
______ Tres armarios
______ Un espejo
______ Tres escritorios
______ Cuatro lámparas
______ Una aspiradora
______ Un horno de microondas

Workbook *4-6 – 4-8*
Lab Manual *4-5 – 4-7*

¡A conversar!

Cultura

Las tapas are a Spanish tradition that started in the 12th century when King Alfonso X outlawed drinking in bars without eating food. The word **tapa** *(lid)* was used to describe what was placed above the wine glass to cover it, such as a piece of bread. Nowadays in Spain, people go to tapas bars before lunch from 11:00 to 2:00 and before dinner from 7:00 to 11:00.

4-9 ¿Es verdad? Con un(a) compañero(a) de clase, respondan a las siguientes observaciones. En este ejercicio los verbos **pedir, servir** y **decir** son importantes.

Modelos Tú pides mucha comida en la cafetería.
No es verdad. Yo no pido mucha comida en la cafetería.

Tú y tus amigos siempre *(always)* dicen la verdad.
Sí, es verdad. Nosotros siempre decimos la verdad.

1. Tú y tus amigos(as) siempre dicen cosas buenas sobre los profesores.
2. Tus amigos sirven tapas en las fiestas.
3. Tú siempre dices cosas interesantes de tus compañeros de clase.
4. Tú siempre pides ayuda cuando no entiendes una cosa.
5. Vosotros pedís tarea adicional a los profesores.
6. Los restaurantes de la universidad sirven buena comida.

4-10 ¿Quién...? ¿Quién en tu clase hace las siguientes cosas *(following things)*? Con las siguientes frases, formula preguntas para tus compañeros(as) para saber si *(if)* ellos(as) hacen o no hacen esas cosas.

Modelo querer una casa con sótano
E1: *¿Quieres una casa con sótano?*
E2: *Sí, yo quiero una casa con sótano.*

1. almorzar en la sala
2. preferir una casa a un apartamento
3. pensar tener una fiesta en la casa de tus padres
4. poder ir a tomar un café después *(after)* de la clase
5. jugar al fútbol americano
6. pedir postres *(desserts)* en los restaurantes
7. decir cosas atrevidas *(bold)*
8. servir comida deliciosa en las fiestas

4-11 Entrevista Trabaja con un compañero de clase y hazle preguntas sobre cómo vive.

1. ¿Prefieres vivir en un apartamento, una casa o una residencia? ¿Almuerzas en casa o en una cafetería? ¿Van de visita mucho tus padres a tu casa o apartamento?
2. ¿Cierras las ventanas de tu dormitorio por la noche? ¿Duermes bien cuando estás solo(a) *(alone)* en casa?
3. ¿Haces muchas fiestas en tu casa? ¿En qué lugar de la casa prefieres recibir a tus amigos? ¿A qué hora vuelves de una fiesta, generalmente?
4. ¿Pierdes muchas cosas en tu dormitorio? ¿Puedes estudiar bien en tu dormitorio? ¿Duermes bien en tu dormitorio? ¿Qué muebles y decoraciones tienes en tu dormitorio?

4-12 Acorazado *(Battleship)* Clasifica las palabras de la siguiente lista de verbos en categorías según el tipo de cambio: **e → i, e → ie, o → ue, u → ue,** y escríbelas en los lugares apropiados de la cuadrícula *(grid).*

almorzar
cerrar
comenzar
decir
dormir
empezar
entender
jugar
pedir
pensar
perder
poder
preferir
querer
regar
servir
tener
venir
volver

e → i	e → ie	o → ue / u → ue

Ahora vas a jugar el juego **Acorazado.** Usa la cuadrícula que aparece a continuación *(below).* Dibuja cinco submarinos en diferentes partes de la cuadrícula, pero, ¡nadie debe verlos! Quieres destruir los submarinos de tu compañero(a) y vas a hacer preguntas con los verbos de la cuadrícula.

Modelo la profesora / preferir
¿La profesora prefiere café?

Si tu compañero(a) tiene un submarino en ese lugar, él/ella contesta: *Sí, prefiere café,* y ¡tú ganas el punto!

Si tu compañero no tiene un submarino en ese lugar, él/ella contesta: *No, no prefiere café.*

Túrnense *(Take turns)* para hacerse preguntas hasta que una persona destruya *(destroys)* todos los submarinos de la otra persona.

	poder hablar francés	jugar al tenis	dormir ocho horas	preferir café
tú				
la profesora				
Rosa y Luis				
nosotros				

España

Veamos *(Let's see)* el video de España para luego comentarlo.

1. ¿Qué lugares pueden visitar en Madrid, la capital de España?
2. ¿Qué es y qué hay en la Gran Vía?
3. ¿Qué actividades pueden hacer en el Parque del Retiro?

See the *Workbook*, **Capítulo 4, 4-22 – 4-25** for additional activities.

Heinle/Cengage Learning

Población: 40.548.753 habs.

Área: 504.782 km^2, más o menos dos veces el tamaño de Oregón

Capital: Madrid (3.213.271 habs.)

Ciudades principales: Barcelona (1.605.602 habs.); Bilbao (354.860 habs.); Málaga (568.305 habs.); Sevilla (703.206 habs.); Valencia (814.208 habs.); Santiago de Compostela (95.092 habs.)

Moneda: el euro

Lenguas: el español, el catalán, el euskera (vasco), el gallego

Personas notables Antonio Gaudí y Cornet (1852–1926) es uno de los arquitectos más creativos y prestigiosos de España. Su estilo personal, inspirado en la naturaleza, combina perfectamente la tradición e innovación. Originario de Barcelona, muchas de sus obras más importantes están en esa ciudad: Templo de la Sagrada Familia *(Church of the Holy Family)*, Parque Güell, Casa Batlló y Casa Milà. La Casa Milà, también llamada La Pedrera, es un edificio *(building)* de apartamentos con dos escaleras, siete chimeneas, dos patios y acceso al techo *(flat roof)*, donde la gente va a ver la magnífica vista de la ciudad de Barcelona, a tomar una soda y a escuchar música por la noche.

¿Cuál es la casa más fascinante o innovadora que conoces? ¿Dónde está? Describe sus habitaciones, decoración y muebles.

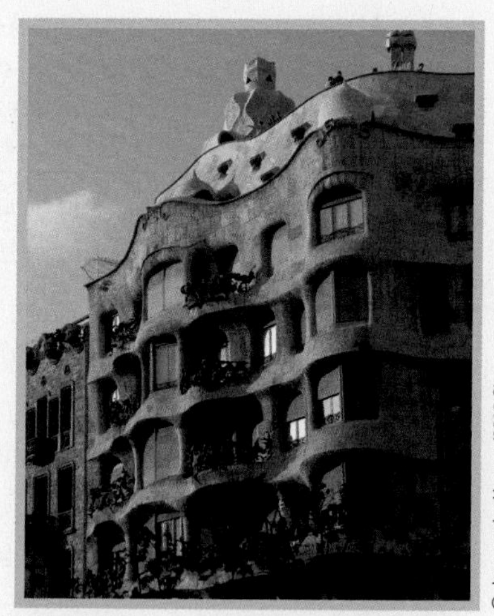

Casa Milà o La Pedrera en Barcelona

La Familia Real Española

Lugares mágicos El Palacio de la Zarzuela es la residencia del Rey de España, don Juan Carlos I, y su esposa, la Reina doña Sofía. El palacio está cerca de Madrid y tiene una colección muy interesante de porcelanas, muebles y relojes. El hijo de los Reyes de España, el Príncipe Felipe de Asturias, su esposa, la Princesa Letizia, y sus hijas, la Infanta Leonor y la Infanta Sofía, viven en un nuevo palacio dentro del área del Palacio de la Zarzuela.

¿Deseas vivir en un palacio? ¿Por qué? ¿Te gusta vivir en la residencia estudiantil, en un apartamento, en una casa? ¿Por qué?

Museo Guggenheim Bilbao

Artes plásticas El Museo Guggenheim Bilbao (1997) está en el País Vasco y es una obra del arquitecto estadounidense Frank O. Gehry. Es un magnífico edificio y un gran ejemplo de la arquitectura vanguardista del siglo XX. El objetivo del museo es investigar y exponer el arte moderno y el arte contemporáneo dentro de la historia del arte. El museo tiene exposiciones permanentes de la segunda mitad del siglo XX, con obras de Willem de Kooning, Robert Motherwell, Clyfford Still, Louise Bourgeois y Andy Warhol. También tiene una extensa colección de obras de artistas españoles como Abigail Lazkoz, Maider López, Manu Arregui, Sergio Prego y Cristina Iglesias.

¿Te gusta visitar museos? ¿Qué piensas de la arquitectura del Museo Guggenheim Bilbao? ¿Prefieres la arquitectura moderna o la clásica? ¿Qué otros museos conoces?

Ritmos y música En España, cada *(each)* región tiene su música y sus bailes. Por ejemplo, en el siglo XVIII, en Andalucía, al sur *(south)* de España, se origina el flamenco. Las personas que cantan, tocan la guitarra y bailan flamenco expresan sentimientos muy profundos y con mucha emoción. El flamenco es una manera de vivir.

Uno de los cantantes españoles más importantes hoy en día es David Bisbal. Originario de Almería, en Andalucía, Bisbal comienza a cantar en el 2002 y en el 2009 aparece el CD *Sin mirar atrás,* con su canción más famosa «Esclavo de sus besos», que es un éxito. *Access the iTunes playlist on the **Plazas** website.*

David Bisbal

¿Te gusta bailar o escuchar música? ¿Qué tipo de música te gusta?

¡Busquen en Internet!

1. Personas notables: Antonio Gaudí y Cornet (1852–1926)
2. Lugares mágicos: Palacio de la Zarzuela
3. Artes plásticas: Museo Guggenheim Bilbao
4. Ritmos y música: el flamenco, David Bisbal

Los quehaceres domésticos en la Casa de la Troya

In this section, you will talk about the chores that are done in and outside the house. What household chores do you do?

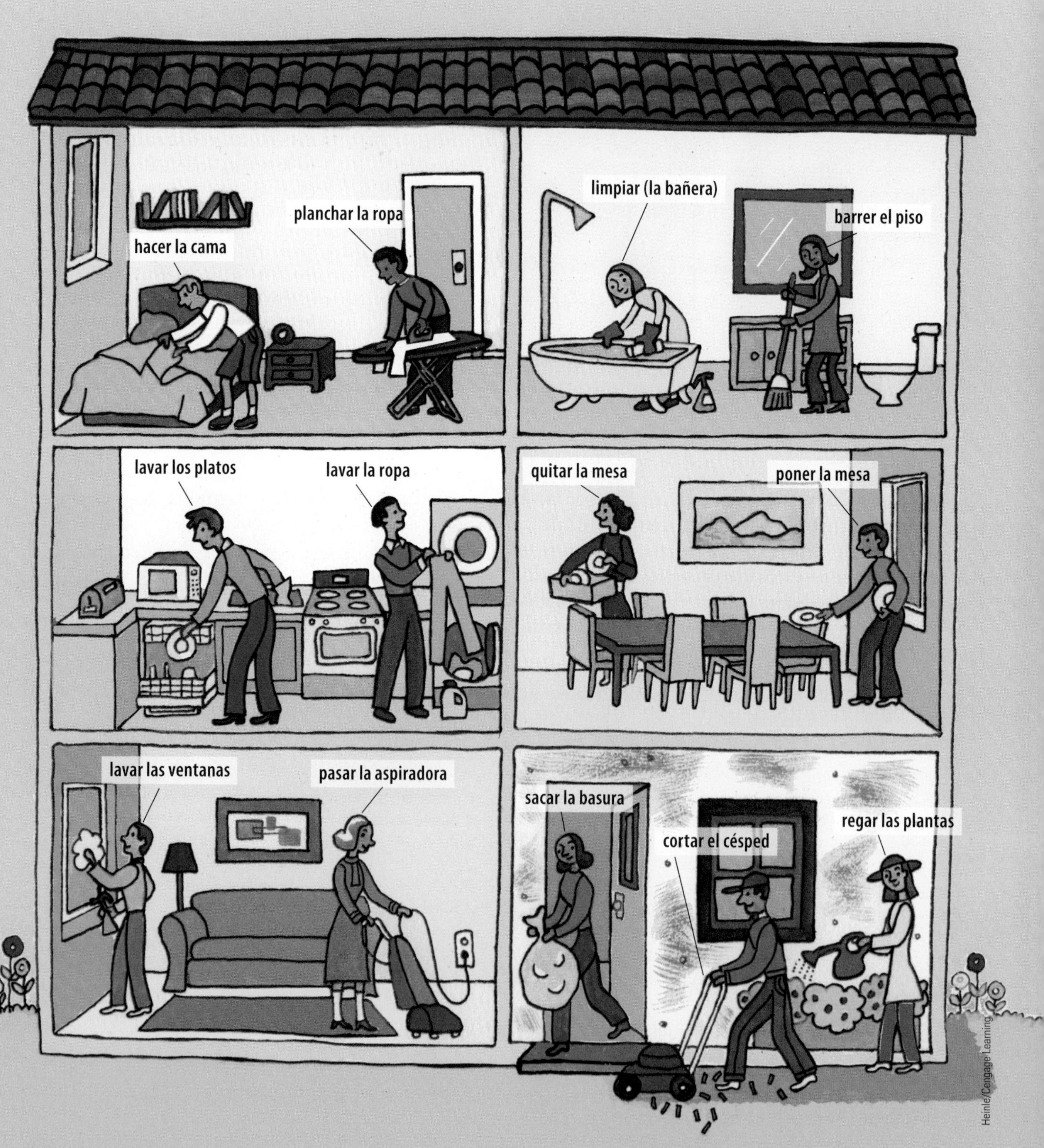

¡A practicar!

4-13 ¿Quién hace qué? *(Who is doing what?)* Doña Rosa siempre ayuda a los estudiantes con los quehaceres domésticos. Completa las siguientes oraciones para identificar lo que cada uno hace en la casa.

1. Manuel y David: Nosotros _______ la mesa antes de comer.
2. Carlos _______ la mesa después de comer.
3. Doña Rosa y Marcos _______ los platos en la cocina.
4. Doña Rosa: Pepe, tú _______ la basura.
5. Manuel y David _______ la casa los fines de semana.
6. Ramón: Yo _______ el césped y _______ las plantas en junio, julio y agosto.
7. Los estudiantes _______ la cama todas las mañanas.
8. La hija de doña Rosa _______ la ropa y _______ el piso.

Cultura

Unlike in the U.S., in Spanish homes it is rare to find carpeted floors. Most floors are either hardwood or tiled.

4-14 ¿Te ayudo? Manuel siempre ayuda a su madre con los quehaceres en la casa, especialmente cuando hay mucho que hacer. ¿Qué tiene que hacer Manuel?

Modelo La cama está sin hacer *(unmade)*.
Manuel tiene que hacer la cama.

1. Los platos están sucios *(dirty)*.
2. Hay mucha basura en la casa.
3. La ropa está arrugada *(wrinkled)*.
4. La casa está sucia.
5. El piso está sucio.
6. Las plantas necesitan agua.

Workbook *4-9 – 4-11*
Lab Manual *4-8 – 4-10*

¡A conversar!

4-15 ¿Qué haces para limpiar la casa? Pregúntale a un(a) compañero(a) de clase si hace los siguientes quehaceres. Si tu compañero(a) no hace el quehacer, debe indicar quién lo hace.

Modelo sacar la basura
E1: *¿Sacas la basura?*
E2: *No, no saco la basura. Mi padre saca la basura.*

1. poner la mesa
2. lavar los platos
3. planchar la ropa
4. lavar la ropa
5. pasar la aspiradora
6. hacer la cama
7. cortar el césped
8. barrer el piso
9. regar las plantas

4-16 Entrevista Trabaja con un(a) compañero(a) de clase y pregúntale sobre los quehaceres domésticos que él/ella hace en casa.

1. ¿Qué quehaceres domésticos haces todos los días?
2. ¿Te gusta cocinar? ¿Poner la mesa? ¿Quitar la mesa? ¿Lavar los platos?
3. ¿Qué hace(n) tu(s) hermano(a)(s) o tu(s) compañero(s) de cuarto?
4. ¿Quién plancha la ropa en la familia? ¿Usas la lavadora y la secadora?
5. ¿Cuántas veces *(times)* al mes limpias la casa? ¿Y la nevera?
6. ¿Tienes que cortar el césped?
7. ¿Quién riega las plantas en tu casa?
8. ¿Quién saca la basura en tu casa o apartamento?
9. ¿Prefieres pasar la aspiradora o barrer el piso?
10. De todos los quehaceres domésticos, ¿cuál es el que prefieres no hacer?

Affirmative *tú* commands

Spanish speakers use affirmative informal commands mainly to tell children, close friends, relatives, and pets to do something. You have already seen these commands in the direction lines of each exercise telling you (**tú**) what to do.

For most Spanish verbs, use the third-person singular (the **él/ella** verb forms) of the present indicative for the **tú** command form.

Espera un momento.
Wait a minute.

Pide un postre, si quieres.
Order dessert, if you want to.

In Spain, to form the informal vosotros command, replace the final **-r** in the infinitive with **-d: hablar → hablad, comer → comed, escribir → escribid.**

Infinitive	3rd person present indicative	*tú* command
hablar	habla	**habla (tú)**
comer	come	**come (tú)**
escribir	escribe	**escribe (tú)**
cerrar	cierra	**cierra (tú)**
dormir	duerme	**duerme (tú)**

Eight verbs have irregular affirmative **tú** commands.

decir	**di**	salir	**sal**
hacer	**haz**	ser	**sé**
ir	**ve**	tener	**ten**
poner	**pon**	venir	**ven**

—**Ven** conmigo para ver el piso.
***Come** with me to see the apartment.*

—Sí, pero **ten** paciencia, Alberto.
*Yes, but **be** patient, Alberto.*

—**Pon** la dirección en el bolsillo, Francisco.
***Put** the address in your pocket, Francisco.*

—**Dime** tu opinión del piso.
***Tell me** your opinion of the apartment.*

¿Recuerdas?

Heinle/Cengage Learning

Francisco: ¿Tienes miedo? ¡Hombre! **Espera** un momento para ver el interior. Seguro que está mejor.

¡A practicar!

4-17 A sus órdenes, doña Rosa Completa la siguiente conversación entre doña Rosa y los chicos de la casa, usando los mandatos informales *(informal commands)* de la lista. Puedes usar los verbos más de una vez *(more than once)*.

espera	llama	quita	ten
haz	pon	riega	ven

Doña Rosa: ¡Chicos! Ya es tarde. Ayudadme con los quehaceres. Hay mucho por hacer.

Manuel: Ahora mismo *(Right now)*, señora. Alberto, 1. ______ conmigo para lavar los platos.

Alberto: 2. ______ un minuto. Tengo que terminar la tarea.

Manuel: Alberto, 3. ______ la tarea después. La señora necesita nuestra ayuda ahora.

Alberto: ¿No me oyes, Manuel? 4. ______ paciencia. ¿No puedes esperar dos minutos?

Manuel: En dos minutos entonces. Te espero en el comedor.

Alberto: Muy bien. 5. ______ la mesa y te ayudo en la cocina con los platos.

Francisco: Manuel, ¿necesitas ayuda?

Manuel: ¡Sí! Gracias. 6. ______ los platos en el lavaplatos y luego 7. ______ las plantas del patio. Antes de empezar, 8. ______ a Alberto. Él no tiene ganas de ayudar hoy.

4-18 Nuevo apartamento Te mudas *(You are moving)* a un nuevo piso en Madrid. ¿Qué le dices a tu compañero(a) de casa? Sigue el modelo y usa los siguientes verbos para dar seis mandatos.

Modelo ir a la cocina
¡Ve a la cocina!

1. poner la mesa
2. hacer la cama
3. limpiar el baño
4. barrer el piso
5. lavar los platos
6. quitar la mesa

Workbook *4-12 – 4-14*
Lab Manual *4-11 – 4-13*

¡A conversar!

4-19 Consejos *(Advice)* para un nuevo estudiante

La supervisora hace recomendaciones a un nuevo estudiante de la casa. ¿Qué le dice? Trabaja con un(a) compañero(a) para dar consejos. Usa mandatos informales afirmativos.

Modelo ayudar / con los quehaceres domésticos
Ayuda con los quehaceres domésticos.

1. barrer / el piso de tu habitación todas las semanas
2. lavar / tu ropa los fines de semana
3. comer / a las horas establecidas
4. hacer / la cama todos los días
5. salir / para hacer ejercicio con los otros chicos
6. ir / al mercado los domingos por la mañana
7. llamar / a tus padres todas las semanas
8. dormir / la siesta

Nota lingüística

Many Spaniards will say **echar una siesta** instead of **dormir la siesta**. It is still common for Spaniards to return home for lunch and then take a short nap, before returning to work or school.

4-20 ¿Qué recomiendas?

Ahora un estudiante universitario de España te escribe una carta. Dale consejos para tener éxito en tu universidad. Trabaja con un(a) compañero(a) de clase para hacer una lista de mandatos afirmativos. Luego practica con el (la) otro(a) estudiante.

Modelo *Come en la cafetería grande. ¡La comida en la otra es horrible!*

4-21 Para conocer la ciudad

Ahora el estudiante español está en tu ciudad. Con un(a) compañero(a), túrnense para decirle al nuevo estudiante qué hacer y adónde ir. Utilicen mandatos informales.

Modelo *¿Quieres pasear? Camina por el parque. Luego visita el museo.*

ESTRUCTURA 3

The verb *estar*

The verb *to be* in English is translated in Spanish by either the verb **ser** or **estar**. As you learned in **Capítulo 2**, **ser** is used to identify essential or inherent characteristics, profession, nationality or origin, time, and dates. You learned the conjugation of **estar** in **Capítulo 3.** In this section, you will learn three functions of the verb **estar**.

Location

To state the location of people and things, use **estar** + preposition of location + location.

Papá **está en** el comedor. — *Dad is in the dining room.*

La aspiradora **está detrás del** sofá, **en** la sala. — *The vacuum cleaner is behind the sofa in the living room.*

La tarea **está encima de** la mesa, **debajo del** libro de texto. — *The homework is on top of the table, under the textbook.*

Prepositions of location often used with the verb **estar**:

al lado de	*next to, beside*	**detrás de**	*behind*
cerca de	*near*	**en**	*in; on*
con	*with*	**encima de**	*on top of*
debajo de	*under, below*	**entre**	*between, among*
delante de	*in front of*	**lejos de**	*far from*
dentro de	*inside of*	**sobre**	*on; over*

Emotional and physical states

To describe how people are feeling or the physical state of something, use **estar** + *adjective*.

¿Cómo **estás**, Elena? — *How are you, Elena?*

Estoy muy cansada, pero contenta. — *I'm very tired, but happy.*

Here are some adjectives commonly used with **estar** to describe emotional and physical states:

aburrido(a)	*bored*	**furioso(a)**	*furious*
cansado(a)	*tired*	**limpio(a)**	*clean*
contento(a)	*happy*	**ocupado(a)**	*busy*
desordenado(a)	*messy*	**ordenado(a)**	*neat*
emocionado(a)	*excited*	**preocupado(a)**	*worried*
enfermo(a)	*sick*	**sucio(a)**	*dirty*
enojado(a)	*angry*	**triste**	*sad*

Note that **estar** can also be used with the adverbs **bien** and **mal**.

¿Cómo **estás**? — *How are you?*

Yo **estoy bien (mal).** — *I'm well (sick).*

Actions in progress

The **present progressive** tense is used to describe actions in progress. To form the present progressive, use a present tense form of **estar** plus a present participle, which is formed by adding **-ando** to the stem of **-ar** verbs, and **-iendo** to the stem of **-er** and **-ir** verbs.

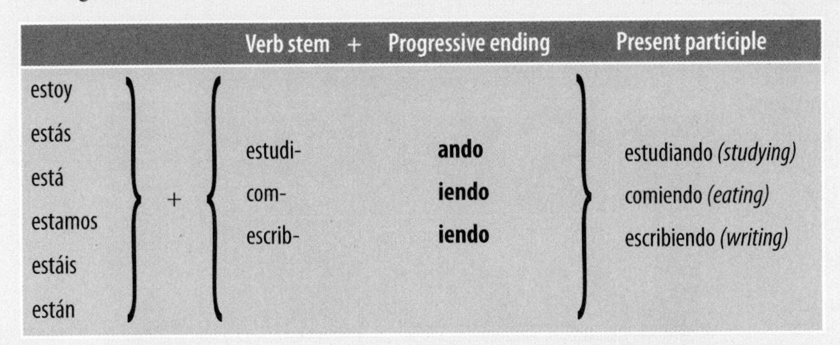

		Verb stem +	Progressive ending	Present participle
estoy estás está estamos estáis están	+	estudi- com- escrib-	**ando** **iendo** **iendo**	estudiando *(studying)* comiendo *(eating)* escribiendo *(writing)*

Two irregular present participles are **leyendo** *(reading)* and **trayendo** *(bringing)*. Verbs that end in **-ir** and have a stem change, such as the verbs **dormir, pedir,** and **servir,** change in the stem from **o** to **u** or **e** to **i** (forming **durmiendo, pidiendo,** and **sirviendo,** respectively).

While Spanish speakers often use the simple present tense to describe routine or habitual actions, they use the present progressive tense to describe what is happening right now—at this very moment. Compare the two examples.

Happens habitually

Generalmente, Lorena **come** con su familia en casa. — *Usually, Lorena eats with her family at home.*

Happening right now

Pero en este momento Lorena **está comiendo** en una cafetería. — *But right now Lorena is eating in a cafeteria.*

¿Recuerdas?

Heinle/Cengage Learning

Francisco: Creo que **todos están en el sillón** del salón. Bueno, Alberto,... tienes razón. El piso **está un poco desordenado**. Pero ven conmigo para ver el cuarto de baño antes de decidir.

¡A practicar!

4-22 **¿Dónde está...?** Ayuda a doña Rosa a encontrar las siguientes cosas en la casa. Usa **estar** + *preposition* para indicarle dónde están.

Modelo la lámpara *La lámpara está cerca de la ventana.*

1. la aspiradora
2. los libros
3. el espejo
4. la ropa
5. el sofá
6. el gato

Heinle/Cengage Learning

4-23 **¿Cómo está(n)?** Mira los siguientes dibujos y decide cómo están las personas. Usa la forma apropiada de los adjetivos de la lista de la página 130 y el verbo **estar.**

1. ______________ 2. ______________ 3. ______________ 4. ______________

5. ______________ 6. ______________ 7. ______________ 8. ______________

4-24 **La casa nueva** Tus padres, tus abuelos y dos de tus hermanos están en su casa nueva. Tú y tu hermano viven en la universidad, así que tu madre te llama para darte información sobre cada miembro de la familia. Escucha el mensaje telefónico y escribe la información necesaria para dársela *(give it)* a tu hermano.

AUDIO CD
CD 2, TRACK 4

Persona	Dónde está	Otra información (cómo está, qué está haciendo, etc.)
1. ________	________	______________________________
2. ________	________	______________________________
3. ________	________	______________________________
4. ________	________	______________________________
5. ________	________	______________________________
6. ________	________	______________________________

Workbook *4-15 – 4-18*
Lab Manual *4-14 – 4-16*

¡A conversar!

4-25 ¿Dónde está Joaquín? En parejas, usando la siguiente información, indiquen dónde están Joaquín y su esposa Silvia. Varias respuestas son posibles.

Modelo Silvia y Joaquín almuerzan juntos.
Están en el comedor.

1. Joaquín duerme profundamente *(deeply)*.
2. Silvia comienza a leer una novela.
3. Joaquín piensa sacar la basura.
4. Joaquín empieza a cantar una canción.
5. Silvia y Joaquín vuelven de su trabajo y cierran la puerta.
6. Joaquín piensa en los ingredientes de la tortilla española.
7. Joaquín corre y juega con su perro.

Cultura

Tortilla española is a popular dish that is served either hot or cold. It is made with eggs, potatoes, and onions.

4-26 Situaciones y emociones Trabajando con un(a) compañero(a) de clase, túrnense *(take turns)* para identificar sus emociones en las siguientes situaciones, y expliquen por qué.

Modelo Cuando hace sol, estoy...
Cuando hace sol, estoy muy contento(a); me gusta mucho el sol.

1. Cuando saco una mala nota *(bad grade)*, estoy...
2. Cuando tengo que hablar en español, estoy...
3. Cuando mi hermano tiene que limpiar el cuarto de baño, está...
4. Cuando estoy con mis amigos, nosotros estamos...
5. Cuando mi compañero(a) pierde un documento en la computadora, está...
6. Cuando los estudiantes no tienen clase, están...

4-27 ¿Qué están haciendo? Con un(a) compañero(a), túrnense para saber qué están haciendo otras personas de la clase o alguien que ustedes conocen. Un compañero elige a la persona y hace la pregunta. El otro responde usando el presente progresivo.

Modelo **E1:** *¿Qué está haciendo el profesor/tu hermano ahora?*
E2: *Está escribiendo en la pizarra./Está trabajando.*

4-28 ¡Actuemos! En grupos de tres personas, túrnense para actuar (*act out*) y adivinar *(guess)* varios quehaceres domésticos. Una persona hace la pantomima y el resto del grupo hace preguntas sobre lo que está haciendo, usando el presente progresivo.

Modelo **E1:** *¿Estás lavando la ropa?*
E2: *No, estoy en la cocina.*
E3: *¿Estás lavando los platos?*
E2: *¡Sí! Estoy lavando los platos porque están muy sucios.*

Numbers 100 to 1,000,000

100 cien (ciento + *número*)
200 doscientos(as)
300 trescientos(as)
400 cuatrocientos(as)
500 quinientos(as)
600 seiscientos(as)
700 setecientos(as)
800 ochocientos(as)
900 novecientos(as)
1.000 mil
1.000.000 un millón

1. The **y** never occurs directly after the number **ciento: ciento uno(a).**
2. Numbers ending in **un**- and **cien**- agree in gender with the nouns they modify: **doscientos libros,** but **doscientas sillas.**
3. The word **mil,** which can mean *a thousand* or *one thousand,* is not usually used in the plural form when counting but can be in other contexts. **Un millón** *(a million or one million),* however, has the plural form **millones,** in which the accent is dropped.
4. When expressing numbers greater than 1,000, use **mil.** For expressing hundreds of thousands, numbers ending in **un**- and **cien**- must agree in gender with the nouns they modify.

   2.000 — dos mil
   300.055 — trescient**os** mil cincuenta y cinco **estudiantes**
   200.000 — doscient**as** mil **personas**

5. For expressing dates, the numbers 200–900 will be plural masculine to agree with the implied or stated masculine plural noun **años.**

   1835 — mil ochocientos treinta y cinco
   1998 — mil novecientos noventa y ocho
   2012 — dos mil doce

   Use the preposition **de** to connect the day, month, and year.

   Nací *(I was born)* el 24 **de** junio **de** 1986.

6. Note that when writing numbers, Spanish uses a period where English uses a comma, and vice versa.

   English: $1,500.75
   Spanish: $1.500,75

   As in English, years are never written with a period nor a comma.

   1999 1969 1492

   Unlike in English, years must be spelled out (**mil, novecientos, noventa y nueve**) rather than broken into two-digit groupings (*nineteen, ninety-nine*).

¡A practicar!

4-29 Eventos históricos de España Para cada fecha histórica, escribe la fecha y luego dile la frase completa a un compañero(a) de clase.

Modelo Barcelona celebra los Juegos Olímpicos en 1992.
Barcelona celebra los Juegos Olímpicos en mil novecientos noventa y dos.

1. Los romanos llegan a España en el año 218 a.C. (antes de Cristo).
2. Los árabes invaden desde África en el año 711 d.C. (después de Cristo).
3. Los Reyes Católicos, Fernando e Isabel, conquistan Granada en 1492.
4. El príncipe Juan Carlos de Borbón es nombrado sucesor al trono de España en 1969.

4-30 ¿Cuánto cuesta? *(How much does it cost?)* Escribe los precios en español.

1. un pequeño condominio en Madrid, España: 227.834,00 euros
2. un año de estudios en una universidad privada en los Estados Unidos: 42.000,00 dólares
3. una lavadora: 515,00 euros
4. un televisor de plasma: 1.300,00 dólares
5. un sofá: 2.199,00 euros
6. una casa con 2 habitaciones y un baño en Bilbao, España: 379.500,00 euros

4-31 ¿Cuántos hay? Utilizando números mayores de 100, completa las siguientes oraciones. Debajo de la oración escribe ese número en español.

1. En mi ciudad hay ______ casas. [Usa un número aproximado.]
____
2. En la universidad hay ______ estudiantes. [Usa un número aproximado.]
____
3. El libro de español tiene ______ páginas.
____
4. Sevilla tiene ______ habitantes *(inhabitants)* y Valencia tiene ______. [La respuesta está en la página 124.]
____

Workbook *4-19 – 4-21*
Lab Manual *4-17*

¡A conversar!

4-32 ¿Cómo se dice... en español? Escribe los siguientes números y luego exprésalos a un(a) compañero(a) de clase. Indica si el número es o no es importante para ti.

Modelo la fundación de esta universidad
1825: mil ochocientos veinticinco
Para mí no es muy importante.

1. el año de tu nacimiento *(birth)*
2. el año de tu graduación de la escuela secundaria
3. la cantidad de dinero que esperas tener en el banco en el año 2020
4. el número de días en el año
5. el número de horas que duermes en un mes
6. el número de personas en tu ciudad o pueblo

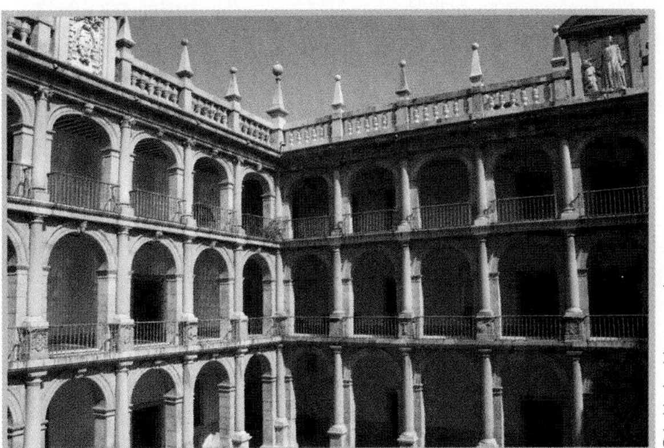

La Universidad de Alcalá de Henares es uno de los 890 lugares declarados por la UNESCO como Patrimonios de la Humanidad. ¿Conoces otros?

4-33 ¿Cuántos de cada? Haz preguntas a tu compañero sobre cantidades de cosas, personas o lugares, basándote en los números dados *(given)*. Tu compañero responde eligiendo un número de la lista. Luego, tu compañero pregunta y tú respondes.

Modelo **E1:** *¿Cuántos salones de clase hay en la universidad?*
E2: *Hay mil quinientos sesenta y dos.*

1. 768
2. 12.889
3. 55.015
4. 1.000.000
5. 1.562
6. 203.245

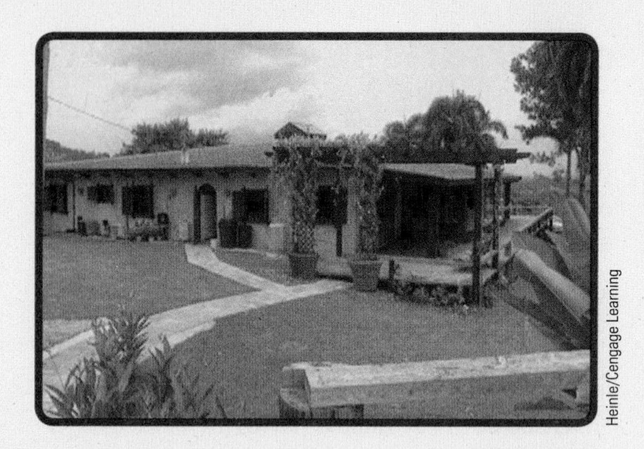
Heinle/Cengage Learning

En la Hacienda Vista Alegre En este segmento del video, los cinco compañeros de casa ya se conocen bien y están muy contentos en su nueva casa, la Hacienda Vista Alegre. Vas a ver varias escenas en la casa, incluso escenas del primer día en la Hacienda. Los jóvenes recuerdan *(remember)* las diferentes partes de la casa y cómo dividieron *(how they divided)* las habitaciones.

Antes de ver

Expresiones útiles The following are some new expressions you will hear in the video.

si no les molesta	*if it doesn't bother you all*
vale	*okay*
¿No te da miedo?	*Doesn't it frighten you?*

Enfoque estructural The following are expressions in the video with present tense stem-changing verbs and the verb **estar**.

Javier: Hay tres habitaciones. **Antonio y yo podemos** ocupar la doble.

Valeria: Si no les molesta, yo **prefiero** dormir sola. Porque... es que me encanta la privacidad. Y además tengo muchas cosas.

Antonio: Entonces Valeria, **tu cuarto está al lado** del mío. Oye ¿tú sabes que yo camino cuando **estoy dormido**? ¿No te da miedo?

1. **Recordemos** ¿Cómo describes tu propio cuarto, incluyendo los muebles y electrodomésticos que tienes? Imagina que necesitas la ayuda de tu compañero(a) de cuarto para hacer 3 quehaceres domésticos, ¿qué le dices a él o ella?
2. **Practiquemos** Con un compañero, imagina que llegan a un hotel y que uno de ustedes prefiere dormir solo. La persona que prefiere dormir sola tiene que convencer al otro de su preferencia. (Pueden usar las oraciones de **Enfoque estructural** como modelo).
3. **Charlemos** Ahora comparte tus argumentos de **Practiquemos** con otros miembros de la clase. ¿Quién de la clase tiene las mejores razones para querer dormir solo?

Después de ver

1. Inventario de la Hacienda Vista Alegre Ahora completa el siguiente inventario de la casa.

Número total de:

A. Habitaciones

____

B. Baños

____

C. Muebles en el cuarto de Alejandra

____

Ocupantes de las habitaciones:

1. ________ y ________
2. ________ y ________
3. ________ y ________

2. Reacciones emocionales ¿Cómo se sienten los compañeros de la Hacienda Vista Alegre? Completa las siguientes oraciones con la emoción apropiada y la forma correcta del verbo **estar.**

contento emocionado enojado triste

Sofía ____________ porque la habitación no tiene escritorio.

Antonio ____________ porque le gusta molestar *(to bother)* a Valeria.

Valeria ____________ con Antonio porque él siempre hace bromas *(jokes around).*

Alejandra ____________ porque va a compartir el cuarto con Sofía.

Entre nosotros Imagina que eres uno de los personajes *(characters)* de Vista Alegre. Escoge tres estados emocionales y explícalos a otro miembro de la casa.

Presentaciones Con un compañero(a) de clase, escribe una escena corta en la que los dos expresan mucha emoción sobre una situación en la casa. ¡Utiliza tu imaginación y tu sensibilidad melodramática! Luego, presenta la escena a la clase.

See the *Lab Manual,* **Capítulo 4, 4-19– 4-20** for additional activities.

Antes de leer

Strategy: Clustering words

Reading one word at a time slows down your reading speed and is inefficient. Reading one word at a time may also lead to a great deal of frustration, as in many instances you will not know the meaning of every word in a given passage. It is more efficient to read meaningful groups or clusters of words. For instance, when reading the following biographical information for a twentieth century Spanish writer, it will be easier if you process groups of two, three or four words in order to get the gist of the content. You'll notice that these clusters are already identified for you. Use the clustering strategy to determine the main ideas of this biographical information. What are the main points?

> Alejandro Rodríguez Álvarez (1903-1965), conocido con el nombre de Alejandro Casona, es un escritor español muy importante dentro de la literatura española y latinoamericana del siglo XX. Cuando comienza la Guerra Civil Española (1936–1939), viaja a Francia y luego visita Puerto Rico, Cuba, Venezuela y México como director de sus obras de teatro *(plays)*. Decide vivir en Buenos Aires, Argentina, hasta 1962, donde escribe y dirige más obras de teatro. Casona es famoso por combinar temas diarios y ordinarios con elementos mágicos que crean ilusiones en sus personajes *(characters)*. En su obra, *Los árboles mueren de pie*, Casona usa la ilusión y la fantasía para remediar lo negativo de la vida.

If you and your classmates determined that this is a short biography of a Spanish playwright, Alejandro Casona, whose play deals with the difficulties of life and the role of fantasy in overcoming them, you used the clustering strategy correctly.

Los árboles mueren de pie

Estrategia: Con un(a) compañero(a) de clase, dividan las descripciones de los actos del drama en grupos de palabras *(clusters of words)* para hacer más fácil la lectura.

Lectura activa: Después de identificar los grupos de palabras, lean las tres descripciones. Con un(a) compañero(a) de clase, discutan los siguientes temas.

1. Acto Primero: ¿Qué hay en esta oficina moderna? ¿Qué objetos hay que representan la imaginación y la fantasía? ¿Qué representan los objetos? ¿Cómo son las oficinas modernas hoy?
2. Acto Segundo: Describan la casa de la Abuela. ¿Quién es la "Abuela"? ¿Qué representa la "amplia escalera con barandal"? ¿Por qué la casa es cómoda?
3. Acto Tercero: ¿Quién llama por teléfono? ¿Para qué llama?
4. ¿Cuál o cuáles creen ustedes que son las estaciones del año en los actos? ¿Qué hora del día es en los actos?

Acto primero

A primera vista *(at first sight)* estamos en una gran oficina moderna, del más aséptico (limpio) capitalismo funcional. Archivos metálicos… teléfonos, audífono y toda la comodidad mecánica… La mitad derecha del foro *(backstage)* está ocupada por una librería *(bookshelves)*…

En contraste con el aspecto burocrático hay acá y allá un rastro sospechoso *(a suspicious trail)* de fantasía: redes de pescadores *(fisherman's nets)*,… un globo terráqueo *(a globe)*, armas inútiles, mapas de países que no han existido nunca *(have never existed)*…

Acto segundo

En casa de la Abuela. Salón con terraza al foro sobre el jardín. Primera derecha *(Front right)*, puerta a la cocina. Primera izquierda, a las habitaciones. A la izquierda, segundo término, una amplia escalera con barandal *(banister)*. Todo aquí tiene el encanto esfumado *(hazy charm)* de los viejos álbumes y la cómoda cordialidad de las casas largamente vividas *(long lived in)*.

Acto tercero

En el mismo lugar unos días después. Tarde. La escena sola. Llama el teléfono….

Después de leer

A escoger Después de leer las descripciones para los tres actos, contesta las siguientes preguntas:

1. En el acto primero, la oficina es moderna porque tiene:
   a. Un teléfono y una librería
   b. Un teléfono y un audífono
   c. Un teléfono y unos archivos metálicos
   d. Todas las opciones
2. ¿Cómo es la decoración en el acto primero?
   a. Es una decoración simple.
   b. Es una decoración moderna.
   c. Es una decoración moderna y fantástica.
   d. Es una decoración simple y moderna.
3. En el acto segundo, la casa de la Abuela es muy cómoda porque:
   a. Tiene jardín y habitaciones.
   b. Tiene habitaciones y cocina.
   c. Tiene cocina, jardín y habitaciones.
   d. Tiene habitaciones, cocina, jardín y un ambiente cordial.
4. En el acto tercero, ¿qué interrumpe la escena sola?
   a. Alguien llama a la puerta.
   b. Alguien llama por teléfono.
   c. Alguien visita a la Abuela.
   d. La Abuela entra en escena.

¿Cierto o falso? Indica si las siguientes oraciones son **ciertas** o **falsas**. Corrige las oraciones falsas.

1. ______ En el acto primero hay un contraste entre los muebles y la decoración fantástica.
2. ______ En el acto primero hay un globo terráqueo y mapas de países reales.
3. ______ En el acto segundo, la casa de la Abuela tiene un ambiente antiguo pero muy cómodo.
4. ______ En el acto segundo, la escalera no tiene barandal.
5. ______ En el acto tercero, en la escena es muy temprano por la mañana.

¡A conversar! Con tres de sus compañeros de clase comenten los siguientes temas:

1. **La casa de sus sueños** *(dreams)*. Describan la casa en la que ustedes quieren vivir, considerando lo siguiente *(considering the following)*:
   - el tamaño de la casa y el número de habitaciones
   - el tamaño de la cocina
   - los electrodomésticos
2. **En venta.** Después de describir la casa o el apartamento de sus sueños, diseñen *(design)* un anuncio para alquilar o vender un piso o una casa en Internet. ¿Qué tipo de información van a incluir? Para ver ejemplos, pueden buscar "Anuncios de casas" en Internet. Presenten su anuncio a la clase.

Strategy: Writing topic sentences

The first step in writing a well-structured paragraph is to formulate a clear, concise topic sentence. A good topic sentence has the following characteristics:

- It comes at the beginning of a paragraph.
- It states the main idea of the paragraph.
- It focuses on only one topic of interest.
- It makes a factual or personal statement.
- It is neither too general nor too specific.
- It attracts the attention of the reader.

Paso 1 Below you will find four possible topic sentences for a paragraph a student has written about the house in which he lives in the north of Spain. Discuss the sentences with a classmate, focusing on the characteristics listed above.

1. Hay cuatro habitaciones y dos baños en la casa.
2. La cocina no es muy grande, pero tiene los electrodomésticos más importantes.
3. La casa, situada en una parte histórica de la ciudad, es el lugar ideal para un estudiante universitario.
4. El jardín es muy bonito porque los residentes de la casa riegan las plantas frecuentemente.

Paso 2 In your opinion, which is the best sentence to begin the paragraph? Why?

Task: Writing a property description

Property descriptions often appear in several different contexts. For example, individuals who wish to sell or rent property provide them for prospective tenants and buyers. In this activity, you will prepare a property description. You may choose a real property or an imaginary one to describe.

Paso 1 Choose a property to describe. It may be your current house or apartment, one you know from the past, or one you hope to live in one day. Write a topic sentence for a paragraph describing the property, keeping in mind the characteristics listed above.

Paso 2 Write five or six sentences about the property, developing the idea stated in your topic sentence. If you have a photograph of the property or wish to prepare a sketch of it, you may want to submit it with your written description.

Paso 3 Share your paragraph with a classmate and discuss how you might improve the topic sentence, focusing on the characteristics of a good topic sentence and its relationship to the rest of the paragraph. You may use the following checklist questions as a guide: Does the topic sentence . . .

1. come at the beginning of the paragraph? ______ yes ______ no
2. state the main idea of the paragraph? ______ yes ______ no
3. focus on only one topic of interest? ______ yes ______ no
4. make a factual or personal statement? ______ yes ______ no
5. seem neither too general nor too specific? ______ yes ______ no
6. attract the attention of the reader? ______ yes ______ no

Paso 4 Share your paragraph with several other class members. After you have read several descriptions, identify one or two properties that you find particularly interesting.

Communicative Goals:

- Describe features and contents of homes and other residences
- Give instructions to friends and family members
- State locations
- Indicate feelings
- Communicate about actions in progress

Paso 1

Review the Communicative Goals for **Capítulo 4** and determine if you are able to accomplish the goals. If you are not certain that you have achieved all of the goals, review the pertinent portions of the chapter.

Paso 2

Look at the components of a conversation which addresses the communicative goals for this chapter. The percentages will help you evaluate your ability to successfully participate in the conversation that is featured below. Your instructor may use the same rubric to assess your oral performance.

Components of the conversation	%
☐ Greetings, each person asks how the other person is feeling, each responds and explains why he (she) is feeling a particular way	20
☐ Response, followed by indication that apartment is messy, must be cleaned and why	20
☐ Agreement, statement that another roommate cannot help and explanation	20
☐ Statement by each person of at least two household chores that the person is going to do	15
☐ Commanding that roommate do at least two household chores	15
☐ Polite conclusion of conversation	10

En acción Think about a conversation that might take place between apartment mates on a Saturday morning. Their apartment needs to be cleaned because visitors are expected. Three apartment mates share the apartment but only two are available and those two participate in the conversation. Consider the sort of information that might be exchanged and how the speakers will communicate the information. You and your partner must include the following steps in the development of the conversation.

1. The individuals greet one another, ask how they are feeling, provide information about their current conditions and explain why they are feeling as they are.
2. One person indicates that the apartment is messy and says that they need to clean it because friends are coming to visit soon.
3. The second person says that their other apartment mate should also help but says that he (she) cannot and explains where that person is and what he (she) is doing at that moment.
4. One person states at least two chores that he (she) is going to do and then tells (commands) the other person to do two chores.
5. The other person responds, stating at least two chores that he (she) will do and then tells (commands) the other person to do two other chores.
6. The individuals politely end the conversation so they can begin their work.

¡A REPASAR!

Present tense of *e > ie* verbs

Infinitive	pensar (ie)	querer (ie)	preferir (ie)
Stem	piens-	quier-	prefier-
	p**ie**nso	qu**ie**ro	pref**ie**ro
	p**ie**nsas	qu**ie**res	pref**ie**res
	p**ie**nsa	qu**ie**re	pref**ie**re
	pensamos	queremos	preferimos
	pensáis	queréis	preferís
	p**ie**nsan	qu**ie**ren	pref**ie**ren

¡A recordar! 1 What other common **e** > **ie** verbs did you learn in this chapter? Which common **e** > **ie** verbs have irregular **yo** forms?

Present tense of *o > ue, u > ue* verbs

Infinitive	jugar (ue)	poder (ue)	dormir (ue)
Stem	jueg-	pued-	duerm-
	juego	**pue**do	**due**rmo
	juegas	**pue**des	**due**rmes
	juega	**pue**de	**due**rme
	jugamos	podemos	dormimos
	jugáis	podéis	dormís
	juegan	**pue**den	**due**rmen

¡A recordar! 2 What other common **o** > **ue** verbs did you learn in this chapter?

Present tense of *e > i* verbs

Infinitive	pedir (i)	decir (i)
Stem	pid-	dic-
	pido	**di**go
	pides	**di**ces
	pide	**di**ce
	pedimos	decimos
	pedís	decís
	piden	**di**cen

¡A recordar! 3 What other common **e** > **i** verbs did you learn in this chapter? Why is **digo** the **yo** form of **decir**?

Affirmative *tú* commands for regular verbs

Infinitive	3rd person present indicative	*tú* command
hablar	habla	**habla (tú)**
comer	come	**come (tú)**
escribir	escribe	**escribe (tú)**

¡A recordar! 4 What are the **tú** commands for the verbs **dormir** and **cerrar**? What are the eight verbs that have irregular affirmative **tú** commands?

Estar and the present progressive

Infinitive		Present participle
estar	+	estud**iando** com**iendo** escrib**iendo**

¡A recordar! 5 What are the present participle endings for **leer** and **traer**? What are the participles for stem-changing verbs such as **dormir, pedir,** and **servir**? What other uses of **estar** do you remember from the chapter?

Actividad 1 Los planes de esta noche Completa el diálogo entre unos amigos sobre los planes de esta noche, usando la forma apropiada de los verbos que están entre paréntesis.

— ¿Uds. 1. ______ (poder) salir a las nueve esta noche? Nosotros 2. ______ (pensar) ver una película.

— Mi hermano tiene que limpiar su dormitorio y se 3. ______ (dormir) temprano, pero yo 4. ______ (poder) salir a las nueve. Yo 5. ______ (preferir) ir a un restaurante a cenar, porque no 6. ______ (querer) ver una película.

— Sí, yo 7. ______ (entender). Entonces, nosotros 8. ______ (querer) pasar por tu casa a las ocho. Hay un restaurante muy bueno en la calle Segovia. Ellos 9. ______ (servir) una paella muy rica.

— Sí. Mi madre también 10. ______ (decir) que es excelente. Ella 11. ______ (almorzar) allí con mi tía y ellas siempre 12. ______ (pedir) paella.

Actividad 2 La rutina de dos chicos Usa los verbos de la lista para completar el párrafo sobre los hijos de los señores Saavedra.

almorzar	jugar	preferir	venir
dormir	pensar	tener	volver

Los señores Saavedra 1. ______ dos hijos. Jorge, el mayor, 2. ______ al tenis pero Ramón, el menor, 3. ______ jugar al fútbol. Él 4. ______ que el tenis es aburrido. Los sábados los niños practican deportes por la mañana. Ellos 5. ______ a casa y 6. ______ a las dos de la tarde. A veces ellos 7. ______ la siesta después de comer, pero generalmente unos amigos 8. ______ a su casa y no hay tiempo para la siesta.

Actividad 3 ¿Qué dice? Forma el mandato afirmativo de los verbos que están entre paréntesis para saber qué tienes que hacer.

1. ¡_______ (Venir) aquí!
2. ¡_______ (Limpiar) la cocina!
3. ¡_______ (Poner) la mesa!
4. ¡_______ (Hacer) la cama!
5. ¡_______ (Regar) las plantas!
6. ¡_______ (Barrer) el piso!
7. ¡_______ (Ir) a la tienda con tu madre!
8. ¡_______ (Escribir) un correo electrónico a tu tía!
9. ¡_______ (Tener) paciencia con tu hermana!
10. ¡_______ (Ser) simpático!

Actividad 4 ¿Dónde está? Completa los espacios en blanco con la(s) palabra(s) que completa(n) las oraciones lógicamente.

1. El banco está _______ (encima / al lado) de la iglesia.
2. Boston está _______ (cerca / lejos) de Atlanta; a 935 millas.
3. Los libros están _______ (encima / entre) de la cama.
4. Las camisas están _______ (con / en) la secadora.
5. Voy a cortar el césped que está _______ (cerca del / sobre el) condominio.
6. El número 526 está _______ (entre / sobre) el 525 y el 527.
7. En el mapa, México está _______ (debajo / detrás) de los Estados Unidos.
8. Yo estoy viviendo _______ (en / con) un amigo.
9. Los lápices están _______ (dentro / lejos) de la mochila. Abre la mochila y toma un lápiz.
10. No puedo ver el despertador. Está _______ (delante / detrás) de la lámpara.

Actividad 5 ¿Cómo están? Escribe oraciones con las palabras dadas, usando el verbo **estar** y el adjetivo. Presta atención a la concordancia del verbo y el adjetivo.

cansado contento furioso sucio desordenado

1. Mi hermano _______________. ¡No tiene dinero!
2. Amalia y Sandra _______________ porque estudian y trabajan.
3. La profesora _______________ porque sacamos una "A".
4. Luisito, _______________. ¡Ve a la ducha!
5. ¡Enrique! Tu dormitorio _______________. Tienes que hacer tu cama.

Actividad 6 ¿Qué están haciendo? Completa cada frase con la forma apropiada del verbo en el presente progresivo para saber qué están haciendo los residentes de la Casa de la Troya según doña Rosa.

1. Nosotros _______________ (preparar) la cena.
2. Yo _______________ (poner) la mesa.
3. Dos estudiantes _______________ (trabajar) en la cocina.
4. Una estudiante _______________ (abrir) el refrigerador.
5. Tú _______________ (hacer) la tortilla, ¿no?

Refrán

_______ (Hacer) bien; pero _______ (mirar) cómo y a quién.

VOCABULARIO ESENCIAL

AUDIO CD
CD 2, TRACK 5

PERSONAL TUTOR

En la casa	In the house
la bañera	bathtub
la cocina	kitchen
el comedor	dining room
el cuarto	(bed)room
el cuarto de baño	bathroom
el dormitorio	bedroom
la ducha	shower
la escalera	stairs
la habitación	(bed)room
el inodoro	toilet
el jardín	garden
el lavabo	bathroom sink
la pared	wall
el piso	floor; apartment (Spain)
la puerta	door
la sala	living room
el salón	living room
el sótano	basement
el suelo	floor
la ventana	window

Los muebles y las decoraciones	Furniture and decorations
la alfombra	carpet
el armario	wardrobe, armoire, closet
la cama	bed
la cómoda	dresser
el cuadro	painting
el espejo	mirror
el estante	bookshelf
la lámpara	lamp
la mesa	table
la mesita	coffee (side) table
el sillón	easy chair, armchair
el sofá	sofa, couch

Los electrodo-mésticos y otros artículos del hogar	Appliances and other household goods
la aspiradora	vacuum cleaner
el despertador	alarm clock
la estufa	stove
el horno (de microondas)	(microwave) oven
la lavadora	washing machine
el lavaplatos	dishwasher
la nevera	refrigerator
la plancha	iron
el refrigerador	refrigerator
la secadora	clothes dryer
la tabla de planchar	ironing board
la tostadora	toaster

Los quehaceres domésticos	Household chores
barrer el piso	to sweep the floor
cortar el césped	to mow the lawn
hacer la cama	to make one's bed
lavar (los platos, la ropa, las ventanas)	to wash (dishes, clothes, windows)
limpiar (la casa)	to clean (the house)
pasar la aspiradora	to vacuum
planchar (la ropa)	to iron (clothes)
poner la mesa	to set the table
quitar la mesa	to clear the table
regar (ie) las plantas	to water the plants
sacar la basura	to take out the garbage

Estados emocionales y físicos	Emotional and physical states
aburrido(a)	bored
cansado(a)	tired
contento(a)	happy
desordenado(a)	messy
emocionado(a)	excited
enfermo(a)	sick
enojado(a)	angry
furioso(a)	furious
limpio(a)	clean
ocupado(a)	busy
ordenado(a)	neat, orderly
preocupado(a)	worried
sucio(a)	dirty
triste	sad
bien	good
mal	bad

Expresiones de lugar	
al lado de	next to, beside
cerca de	near
con	with
debajo de	under, below
delante de	in front of
dentro de	inside of
detrás de	behind
en	in; on
encima de	on top of
entre	between; among
lejos de	far from
sobre	on; over

Otros verbos	
almorzar (ue)	to have lunch
cerrar (ie)	to close
comenzar (ie)	to begin
decir (i)	to say, to tell
dormir (ue)	to sleep
empezar (ie)	to begin
entender (ie)	to understand
jugar (ue)	to play
pedir (i)	to ask for
pensar (ie)	to think
perder (ie)	to lose; to miss (an event)
poder (ue)	to be able to
preferir (ie)	to prefer
querer (ie)	to want; to love
servir (i)	to serve
venir (ie)	to come
volver (ue)	to return

Los números de 100 a 1.000.000	
100	cien
200	doscientos(as)
300	trescientos(as)
400	cuatrocientos(as)
500	quinientos(as)
600	seiscientos(as)
700	setecientos(as)
800	ochocientos(as)
900	novecientos(as)
1.000	mil
1.000.000	un millón

CAPÍTULO 5

La salud

Bolivia y Paraguay

Plaza Murillo, La Paz, Bolivia

Chapter Objectives

Communicative Goals

In this chapter, you will learn how to . . .

- Identify parts of the body and communicate about health conditions
- Describe daily activities
- Express what you and others have just finished doing
- Communicate about characteristics and conditions of people and things

Structures

- Reflexive pronouns and present tense of reflexive verbs
- **Acabar de** + *infinitive*
- **Ser** vs. **estar**
- Demonstrative adjectives and pronouns

▲ ¿Cómo estás? ¿Estás enfermo(a) o estás preocupado(a) o estás triste?

▲ ¿Cuándo visitas al (a la) doctor(a) o al (a la) dentista?

▲ ¿Qué tomas cuando estás enfermo(a)?

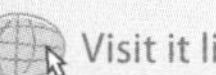 Visit it live on **Google Earth!**

En el consultorio de la doctora Aguilar

In this section, you will learn how to talk about parts of the body by viewing a scene in the office of Dr. Aguilar, a medical doctor in Bolivia who is examining a patient. Does this office resemble medical offices that you have visited?

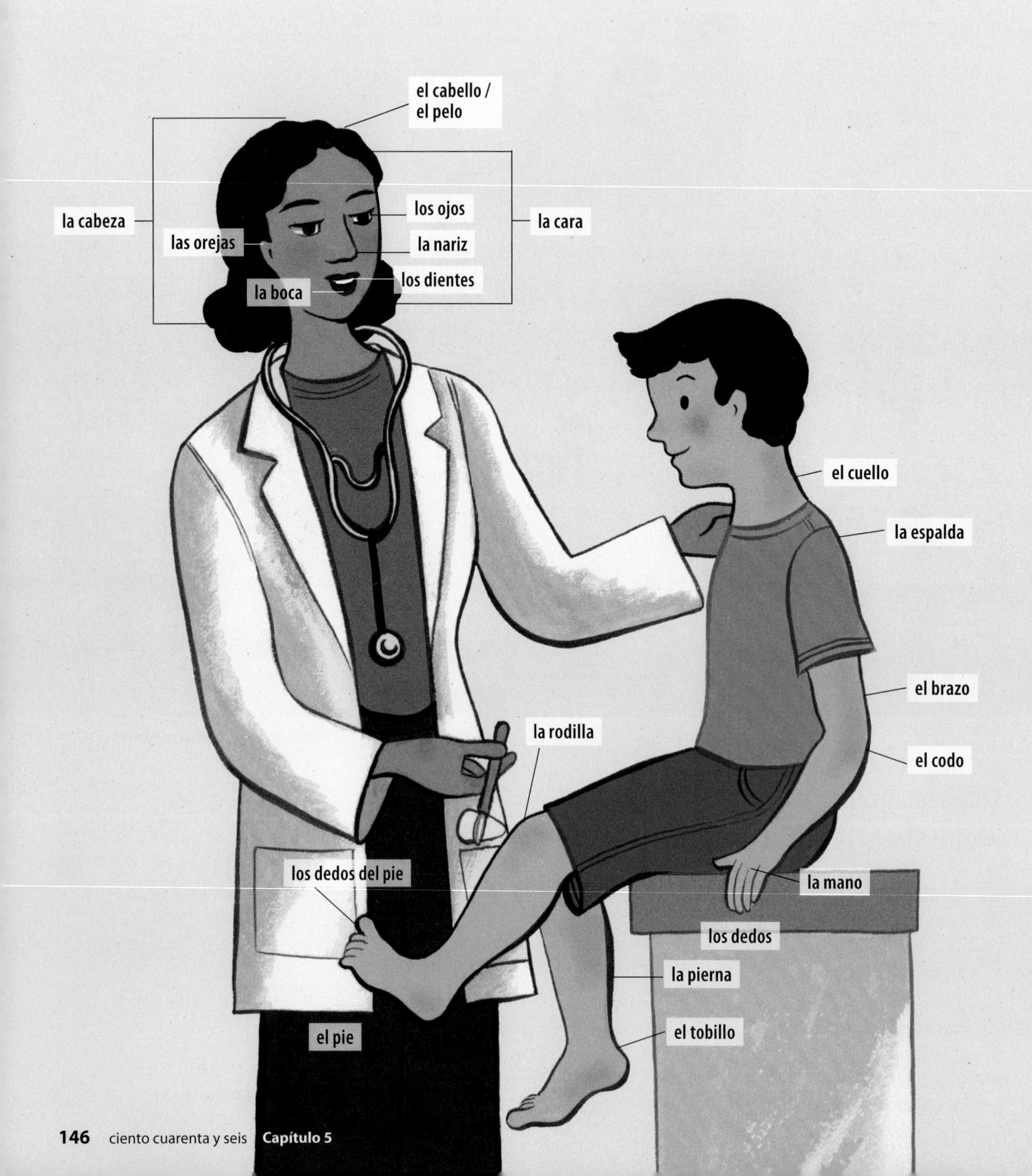

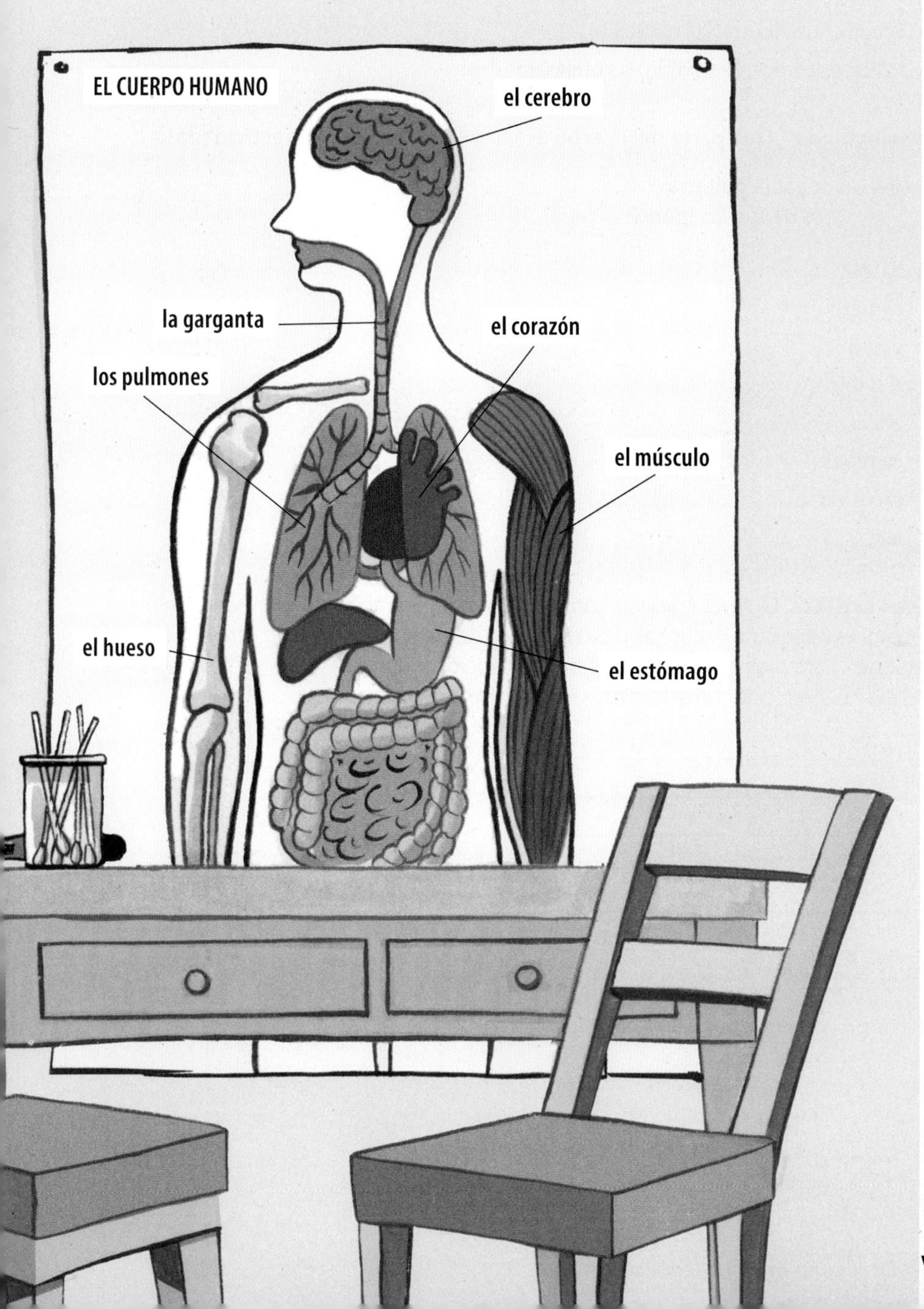

Palabras útiles

la cadera *hip*
las cejas *eyebrows*
los labios *lips*
la lengua *tongue*
el oído *(inner) ear*
el pecho *chest*
las pestañas *eyelashes*
la piel *skin*
las uñas *fingernails*

Palabras útiles are presented to help you enrich your personal vocabulary. The terms provided here will help you talk about parts of the body.

Nota lingüística

El cabello and **el pelo** are words that refer to hair. It is usually more polite to refer to **el cabello** when describing a person's hair.

¡A practicar!

5-1 **¡No es lógico!** Identifica la palabra que no va con el grupo y explica por qué.

Modelo los dedos, las manos, los dientes
Los dientes son partes de la cabeza;
los dedos y las manos son partes del brazo.

1. la boca, la cara, el brazo
2. el corazón, el pelo, el estómago
3. los pulmones, la nariz, el músculo
4. los dedos, las rodillas, los tobillos
5. la garganta, las orejas, el estómago
6. los pies, los codos, los dedos de los pies
7. el codo, los dientes, las manos
8. los ojos, la boca, la espalda, las orejas, los dientes

5-2 **Asociaciones** ¿Qué parte del cuerpo asocias con las siguientes actividades?

Modelo tocar la guitarra
los dedos, las manos

1. hablar
2. comer
3. pensar
4. escribir
5. beber
6. caminar
7. escuchar
8. leer

5-3 **¿Eres artista?** Quieres trabajar como artista para la policía de tu ciudad. En el trabajo, es necesario escuchar descripciones de personas y dibujar *(draw)* a las personas. Para practicar, escucha esta descripción y dibuja a la persona. Luego, escribe las siete características más importantes de la persona.

AUDIO CD
CD 2, TRACK 6

1. ______________________________
2. ______________________________
3. ______________________________
4. ______________________________
5. ______________________________
6. ______________________________
7. ______________________________

Workbook *5-1 – 5-3*
Lab Manual *5-1 – 5-3*

¡A conversar!

5-4 **Entrevista** Hazle a tu compañero(a) las siguientes preguntas.

Modelo **E1**: *¿Tienes la nariz grande o pequeña?*
E2: *Tengo la nariz grande.*

1. ¿De qué color tienes el pelo?
2. ¿De qué color tienes los ojos?
3. ¿Tienes las orejas grandes o pequeñas?
4. ¿Tienes los pies grandes o pequeños?
5. ¿Usas las manos para hablar?
6. De tus amigos o tu familia, ¿quién usa las manos para hablar?
7. Cuando haces ejercicio, ¿qué parte del cuerpo usas más?
8. ¿Por qué es malo el tabaco?

5-5 **Retratos *(Portraits)* de un extraterrestre** Descríbele a un(a) compañero(a) las características físicas de un extraterrestre *(alien)* mientras *(while)* tu compañero(a) lo dibuja. Después de dibujar, tu compañero(a) tiene que explicarte los atributos.

Modelo *El extraterrestre tiene piernas cortas, pero dos brazos muy largos. Tiene pelo azul y largo. Tiene ojos anaranjados. La cara es pequeña pero la boca es grande. Tiene dos orejas enormes.*

5-6 **¡Manos a la obra!** Muchas partes del cuerpo son importantes para varios trabajos académicos, trabajos profesionales y quehaceres domésticos. Trabajando en grupos de dos o tres personas, miren la lista de actividades asociadas con varios tipos de trabajo y digan las partes del cuerpo necesarias para hacer los trabajos. Identifiquen más actividades en cada categoría y continúen la discusión identificando las partes del cuerpo necesarias para hacer esas actividades también. Sigan el modelo.

Modelo *Para escribir la tarea, necesito los brazos, las manos y los dedos para escribir con bolígrafo o lápiz, o para usar la computadora. Necesito los ojos para ver el papel o la computadora.*

Los trabajos académicos	Los trabajos profesionales	Los quehaceres domésticos
escribir la tarea	trabajar en un banco	cortar el césped
leer un libro	vender ropa en una tienda	hacer la cama
escuchar el disco compacto *(CD)* de español	ayudar a los clientes en la oficina de correos	poner la mesa
dibujar algo para la clase de arte	trabajar en una piscina	limpiar el baño
cantar una canción y tocar el piano para la clase de música	recibir dinero de los clientes en un restaurante	sacar la basura
tomar un examen de matemáticas	dar información a los visitantes en el museo	cocinar la cena

EN CONTEXTO

La señora Mendoza y su hija Carolina están en una clínica médica. Acaban de llenar su historial clínico y ahora están hablando con el doctor Chávez. Carolina piensa que está muy enferma.

AUDIO CD
CD 2, TRACK 7

Escucha el diálogo y contesta las siguientes preguntas basándote en el diálogo.

1. ¿Está realmente enferma Carolina?
2. ¿Qué síntomas tiene?
3. ¿Por qué recomienda una operación el doctor Chávez? ¿Quiere asustarla *(to scare her)*?
4. ¿Por qué se siente mejor Carolina al final?

Dr. Chávez: ¿Cómo **se siente** su hija hoy, señora Mendoza?

Sra. Mendoza: Dice que **está muy mal** y que no puede asistir a la escuela. Hoy por la mañana empiezan las clases y es la primera vez que Carolina va solita a la escuela. Lleva tres días en cama mirando la tele. Generalmente **es** una niña muy **sana**.

Comentario cultural Two highland Indian groups, the Quechua and Aymara, account for roughly 55 percent of the population in Bolivia. **Mestizos** or **cholos** (those of mixed ancestry) constitute about 30 percent. European descendants of Spaniards constitute less than 15 percent of the population.

Dr. Chávez: Mmm... Carolina, ¿te duele el estómago?

Carolina: ¡Ayyy! Sí, me duele mucho el estómago.

Comentario cultural Numerous diseases, including hepatitis A and typhoid fever, are transmitted in Bolivia by contaminated water. Rural wastewater treatment rates are at approximately 60 percent in Bolivia. With more and more people migrating to the large cities of La Paz and Santa Cruz from the countryside, supplying safe drinking water is becoming increasingly challenging. Rural populations are most at risk for becoming ill from untreated water.

Heinle/Cengage Learning

Dr. Chávez: ¿Tienes fiebre?

Sra. Mendoza: Dice que sí, pero **acabo de tomarle la temperatura** y tiene 37 grados, o sea, normal.

Comentario cultural Bolivia, similar to most other countries worldwide, uses the metric system. To convert Celsius temperatures into Fahrenheit, begin by multiplying the Celsius number by 9. Next, divide the answer by 5 and then add 32. To convert Fahrenheit temperatures into Celsius, begin by subtracting 32 from the Fahrenheit number. Next, divide the answer by 9 and then multiply that answer by 5.

Expresiones en contexto

historial clínico *medical history*
hoy por la mañana *this morning*
la primera vez *the first time*
llenar *to fill out*
llevar + *time* + *present participle* *to have been experiencing a condition for a period of time*
me encuentro *I'm feeling*
o sea *I mean, in other words*
solito(a) *all by him/herself*

Dr. Chávez: Vamos a ver... ¿Tienes dolor de cabeza?

Carolina: ¡Sí! Y tengo tos y estoy mareada y... y **este** lado del cuerpo me duele mucho.

Comentario cultural Often known as the "Tibet" of South America, Bolivia is traversed by three very high and long Andean ranges. For those unaccustomed to the altitude of the **Altiplano** (roughly 3,658 meters or 12,000 feet high) headaches, dizziness, and difficulty sleeping are common. High-altitude sickness in Bolivia is called **el soroche** and is often treated with **mate de coca**, a local herbal tea derived from the coca plant.

Dr. Chávez: Parece que estás muy grave, Carolina. **Tenemos que operarte** inmediatamente. Creo que tienes la «escuelacitis». Es una condición del cerebro.

Comentario cultural Bolivia has a population of 9 million people with an under-five mortality rate of 65 per 1,000 births, down from a previous estimate of 125 per 1,000 births. As vaccinations for measles, mumps, rubella, diphtheria, and tuberculosis are sometimes financially unavailable to Bolivia's poor, world health organizations, such as UNICEF, support free vaccination programs that target children.

Heinle/Cengage Learning

Carolina: ¿Una operación? ¿El cerebro? Pues... la verdad es que ahora **me encuentro** un poco mejor.

Comentario cultural Bolivia often hosts brigades of international medical volunteers, including plastic surgeons, anesthesiologists, nurses, pediatricians, dentists, and speech pathologists, who provide free medical evaluations and reconstructive surgery to children suffering with facial deformities, such as cleft lip and cleft palate.

 **Diálogo entre doctor y paciente** Trabajando con un(a) compañero(a) de clase, túrnense *(take turns)* para practicar el diálogo que acaban de estudiar en **En contexto**. Deben cambiar *(change)* las nacionalidades y condiciones de los hablantes. Usen expresiones de **En contexto** como modelo para su diálogo.

Reflexive pronouns and present tense of reflexive verbs

A reflexive construction consists of a **reflexive pronoun** and a verb. In English, reflexive pronouns end in *-self* or *-selves;* for example: *myself, yourself, ourselves.* In Spanish, reflexive pronouns are used with some verbs (called **reflexive verbs**) that reflect the action back to the subject of a sentence, meaning that the subject of the verb also receives the action of the verb. In the following example, notice how Juan Carlos is both the subject and recipient of the action of getting himself up.

Subject	Reflexive Pronoun	Verb	
↓ Juan Carlos	↓ **se**	↓ levanta	a las ocho.
Juan Carlos	*gets (himself) up*		*at eight.*

Conjugating reflexive constructions

Reflexive verbs are identified by the pronoun **-se** attached to the end of the infinitive form of the verb. To conjugate these verbs, use a reflexive pronoun (e.g., **me**) with its corresponding verb form (e.g., **levanto**), according to the subject of the sentence (e.g., **yo**).

Reflexive infinitive: levantarse *(to get up)*

Subject	Reflexive Pronoun + Verb Form	
yo	**me** levant**o**	*I get up*
tú	**te** levant**as**	*you* (informal) *get up*
Ud., él/ella	**se** levanta	*you* (formal) *get up, he / she gets up*
nosotros(as)	**nos** levant**amos**	*we get up*
vosotros(as)	**os** levant**áis**	*you* (informal: Spain) *get up*
Uds., ellos(as)	**se** levant**an**	*you get up, they get up*

Note that when reflexive verbs are used with parts of the body or with clothing items, the definite article (**el, la, los, las**) precedes the noun.

Juan Carlos se cepilla **los** dientes.
Juan Carlos brushes his teeth.

Tomás va a lavarse **el** cabello.
Tomás is going to wash his hair.

Placing reflexive pronouns

- Place the pronoun in front of the conjugated verb.

  Juan Carlos **se levanta** a las ocho.
  Juan Carlos gets up at eight.

- When a reflexive verb is used as an infinitive or as a present participle, place the pronoun either before the conjugated verb (if there are two or more verbs used together) or attach it to the infinitive or to the present participle.

  Sara **se va a levantar** pronto.

  or

  Sara **va a levantarse** pronto.
  Sara is going to get up soon.

  Sara **se está levantando** ahora.

  or

  Sara **está levantándose** ahora.
  Sara is getting up now.

- When a reflexive pronoun is attached to a present participle (e.g., **levantándose**), an accent mark is added to maintain the correct stress.

Reflexive vs. nonreflexive verbs

When the action is performed on another person (as indicated by the addition of the personal **a** before **mi mamá**) a reflexive pronoun is not used. Compare these two examples:

Me despierto a las ocho.
I wake up at eight o'clock.

Despierto a mi mamá a las ocho.
I wake up my mom at eight.

Verbos reflexivos de la rutina diaria y personal

acostarse (ue) to go to bed	**levantarse** to get up
afeitarse to shave	**maquillarse** to put on makeup
bañarse to take a bath	**peinarse** to comb one's hair
cepillarse los dientes to brush one's teeth	**pintarse** to put on makeup
cuidarse to take care (of oneself)	**ponerse (la ropa)** to put on (one's clothes)
despertarse (ie) to wake up	**quitarse (la ropa)** to take off (one's clothes)
dormirse (ue) to fall asleep	**secarse (el cuerpo)** to dry off (one's body)
ducharse to take a shower	**vestirse (i)** to get dressed
lavarse to wash up	

¡A practicar!

5-7 Los domingos por la mañana Completa las siguientes oraciones, usando las formas correctas de los verbos entre paréntesis y tu información personal.

Modelo (afeitarse) *Todos los días Juan Carlos se afeita, pero yo nunca me afeito.*

1. (levantarse)
   Los domingos Juan Carlos y Sara ________ a las ocho, y Tomás, su hijo, ________ a las nueve. Yo ________ a las diez.
2. (cepillarse)
   Después, el esposo y la esposa siempre ________ los dientes.
3. (ducharse)
   Juan Carlos y Tomás se bañan en la bañera, pero Sara prefiere ________ .
   Yo también prefiero ________ .
4. (vestirse)
   Juan Carlos y Sara ________ con ropa elegante y Tomás ________ de jeans.
   Yo ________ de jeans también.

5-8 ¡Qué mujer más ocupada! Para comprender la vida diaria que tiene Sara durante la semana, completa las siguientes descripciones conjugando los verbos entre paréntesis.

Sara:
Los días de trabajo yo ________ (1. despertarse) a las siete. Primero, voy al baño, donde ________ (2. ducharse) por diez minutos. Después, ________ (3. secarse) bien todo el cuerpo y ________ (4. peinarse).

Juan:
Entonces Sara ________ (5. vestirse) con ropa elegante, ________ (6. maquillarse) la cara y ________ (7. ponerse) un poco de perfume. Luego ella ________ (8. cepillarse) los dientes y sale de la casa. Sara trabaja por cinco horas hasta *(until)* la una de la tarde. Luego vuelve a casa. Ella ________ (9. lavarse) las manos y almuerza con nosotros.

5-9 Las actividades diarias de Tomás Basándote en los dibujos, escribe lo que hace Tomás en cada dibujo.

Modelo *Tomás se despierta a las seis. Me despierto a las ocho.*

1. Primero
2. Luego
3. Después
4. Más tarde
5. Finalmente

Workbook *5-4 – 5-6*
Lab Manual *5-4 – 5-6*

¡A conversar!

5-10 Preferencias personales Con un(a) compañero(a), compara lo que hacen las siguientes personas durante la semana con lo que hacen durante los fines de semana. Túrnense para escoger *(choose)* el sujeto que va con los verbos. Usen el pronombre reflexivo correcto. Sigan el modelo.

Modelo levantarse: *yo*
Entre semana me levanto a las seis, pero los fines de semana, me levanto a las nueve.

yo
tú
mi mejor amigo(a) y yo
nuestro(a) profesor(a)
nuestros(as) compañeros(as) de clase

1. peinarse
2. vestirse
3. ducharse
4. acostarse
5. dormirse

5-11 Tus actividades diarias Con un(a) compañero(a) de clase, contesten las siguientes preguntas.

1. ¿A qué hora te levantas normalmente? ¿Te levantas inmediatamente después de despertarte?
2. ¿Te bañas en la bañera o te duchas? ¿Prefieres bañarte por la mañana o por la noche?
3. ¿Desayunas *(do you have breakfast)* con tu compañero(a) de cuarto/casa? O, si vives con tu familia, ¿desayunas con tu familia? ¿Siempre te cepillas los dientes después del desayuno?
4. Si eres mujer, ¿te maquillas todos los días? Si eres hombre, ¿te afeitas los fines de semana?
5. ¿Te peinas durante el día o solamente antes de salir?
6. ¿A qué hora almuerzas normalmente? ¿Duermes la siesta a veces después del almuerzo?
7. De noche, ¿comes algo para la cena? ¿Ayudas a lavar los platos después?
8. ¿A qué hora te gusta acostarte? Normalmente, ¿te duermes fácilmente? En general, ¿miras la tele o lees algún libro antes de dormir?

5-12 Mi rutina Explica tu rutina diaria a un(a) compañero(a) de clase. Tu compañero(a) debe dibujar tus actividades y usar el dibujo para explicarle las actividades a la clase.

Acabar de + infinitive

Acabar de + *infinitive* is a way speakers of Spanish talk about things that have just taken place without using the past tense. Literally, **acabar de** + *infinitive* means *to have just finished doing something.* The verb **acabar** is regular and is used in all forms of the present tense to communicate what has just been done.

yo	**acabo**
tú	**acabas**
Ud., él/ella	**acaba**
nosotros(as)	**acabamos**
vosotros(as)	**acabáis**
Uds., ellos(as)	**acaban**

Acabamos de abrir una clínica en Bolivia.
We have just opened a clinic in Bolivia.

El doctor Chávez **acaba de ver** a tres pacientes.
Dr. Chávez has just seen three patients.

Cuatro pacientes **acaban de llegar** a la clínica.
Four patients have just arrived at the clinic.

Acabo de hablar con dos pacientes.
I have just spoken to two patients.

Remember that when the infinitive is a reflexive verb, the reflexive pronoun may be placed either before the conjugated verb, in this case **acabar,** or attached to the infinitive verb.

Son las siete. **Me acabo de levantar.**

Son las siete. **Acabo de levantarme.**

It´s seven o´clock. I have just woken up.

¿Recuerdas?

Heinle/Cengage Learning

Dr. Chávez: ¿Tienes fiebre?

Sra. Mendoza: Dice que sí, pero **acabo de tomarle la temperatura** y tiene 37 grados, o sea, normal.

¡A practicar!

5-13 Mamá, ¡acabo de hacerlo! Tu mamá sugiere varias actividades para algunas personas de la familia. Dile que ya están hechas *(are done)*, usando **acabar de**.

Modelo ¿Por qué no te bañas?
(Yo) me acabo de bañar.
o *(Yo) acabo de bañarme.*

1. ¿Por qué no se cepillan los dientes tú y tu hermana después del almuerzo?
2. ¿Por qué no se visten ellos para la fiesta de sus amigos?
3. ¿Por qué no se afeita tu padre?
4. ¿Por qué no tomas una siesta?
5. ¿Por qué no se peina tu mejor amiga?

5-14 ¡Adivina lo que acaba de hacer esa gente! Las siguientes personas acaban de hacer algo. Tú y un(a) compañero(a) de clase tienen que adivinar *(guess)* lo que acaban de hacer, basándose en la información que tienen.

Modelo Sara sale del baño. Tiene el cabello mojado *(wet)*.
Sara acaba de bañarse.

1. Tomás se levanta de la cama.
2. Sarita y Tomás se levantan de la mesa. Son las ocho de la mañana.
3. Juan Carlos sale de su cuarto. Tiene puesta *(He's wearing)* ropa elegante para una fiesta.
4. El doctor Chávez entra por la puerta de la clínica. Son las nueve de la mañana.
5. La señora Martínez sale del consultorio *(doctor's office)* del doctor Chávez.
6. Juan Carlos está en la cama y apaga *(turn off)* la luz.
7. Sara va a una fiesta en 15 minutos. Su pelo está diferente.

Workbook *5-7 – 5-9*
Lab Manual *5-7 – 5-8*

¡A conversar!

5-15 Antes y después Mira los dibujos y di qué acaban de hacer estas *(these)* personas y qué van a hacer. Luego, indica si tú acabas de hacer la actividad o no, y/o cuándo vas a hacerla. Después pregúntale a tu compañero(a) de clase si él/ella acaba de hacer la actividad o no, y/o cuándo va a hacerla.

Modelo E1: *Acaba de ducharse y va a vestirse. Acabo de ducharme y vestirme. ¿Y tú?*

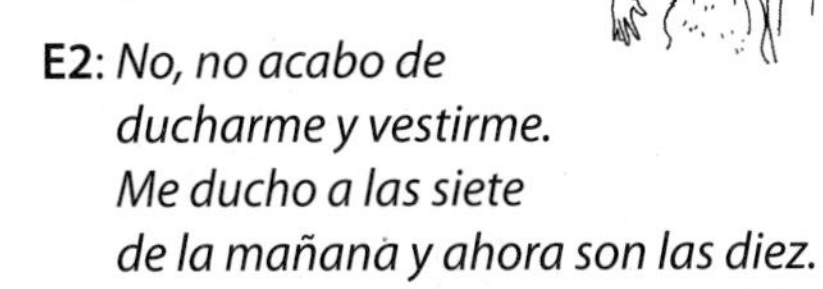

E2: *No, no acabo de ducharme y vestirme. Me ducho a las siete de la mañana y ahora son las diez.*

1.

2.

3.

Bolivia y Paraguay

Veamos los videos de Bolivia y Paraguay para comentarlos.

1. Describan la población boliviana.
2. ¿Qué ciudades o lugares interesantes pueden visitar en Bolivia?
3. ¿Qué significa la palabra "Paraguay" en guaraní, la lengua indígena oficial?

See also the *Workbook*, **Capítulo 5, 5-20 – 5-23** for additional activities.

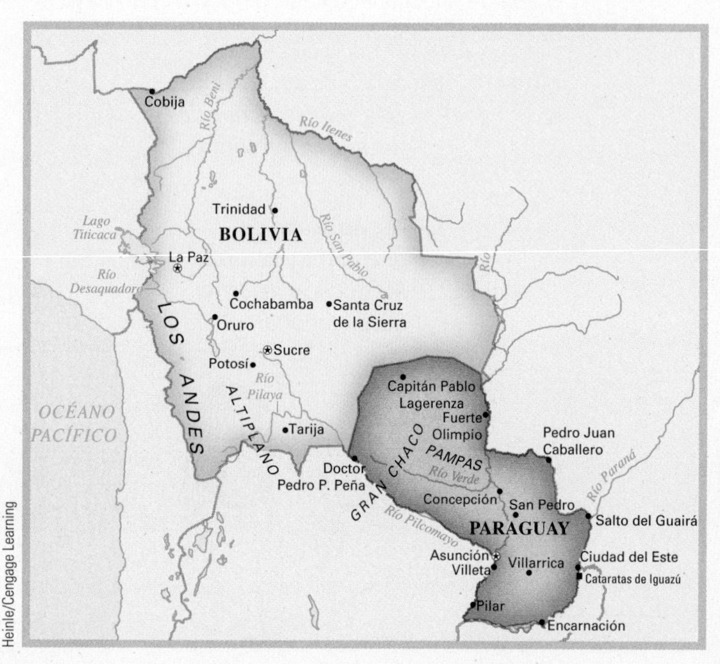

Heinle/Cengage Learning

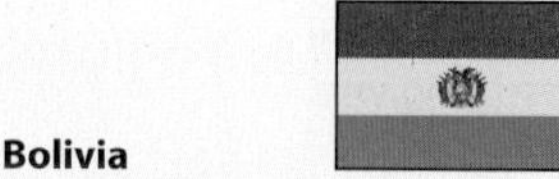

Bolivia

Población: 9.947.418 habs.

Área: 1.098.580 km², aproximadamente tres veces el tamaño de Montana

Capital: La Paz (sede de gobierno [2.757.000 habs.]); Sucre (sede jurídica [631.100 habs.])

Ciudades principales: Santa Cruz (2.626.700 habs.); Cochabamba (1.786.000 habs.); Potosí (780.400 habs.)

Moneda: el peso boliviano

Lenguas: el español y 36 lenguas indígenas, incluyendo el quechua y el aimara (lenguas oficiales)

Paraguay

Población: 6.375.830 habs.

Área: 406.752 km², el tamaño de California.

Capital: Asunción (2.870.000 habs.)

Ciudades principales: Ciudad del Este (558.672 habs.); Encarnación (70.000 habs.); Villarrica (83.000 habs.)

Moneda: el guaraní

Lenguas: el español y el guaraní (lenguas oficiales), el fronterizo (lengua no oficial)

Lugares mágicos La Eco-reserva Mbatoví es el parque de eco-aventura más popular de Paraguay y está situado en la Cordillera de los Altos a 72 km (*44 miles*) de Asunción, la capital. El parque ofrece distintas actividades y algunas de ellas requieren tener una buena condición física. Por ejemplo, es posible caminar sobre puentes colgantes *(suspended bridges)* instalados en el bosque *(forest)* y terminar la excursión en un tramo de tirolesa *(canopy)* de 105 metros (*344 feet*) de largo y 40 metros (*141 feet*) de alto. Los visitantes también pueden caminar por el parque para ver cataratas *(waterfalls)*, arroyos (*creeks*), flores como las orquídeas y una gran variedad de animales.

¿Conoces parques como este en los Estados Unidos? Si *(If)* es así, ¿qué actividades puedes hacer en esos lugares?

Courtesy Reserva Mbatov=ED, Paraguay www.mbatovi.com.py

Un tramo de tirolesa en la eco-reserva Mbatoví

Visit it live on **Google Earth!**

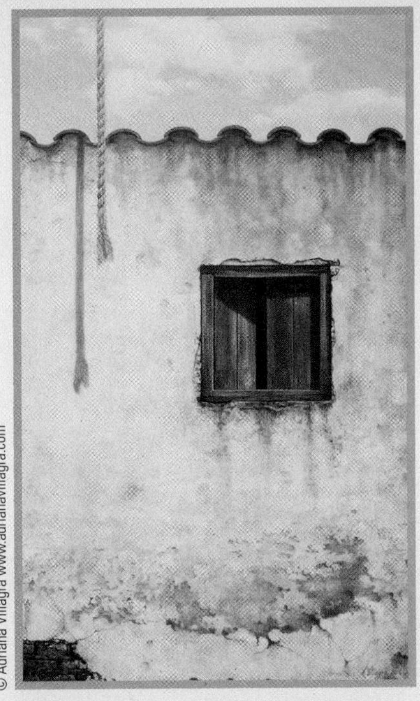
© Adriana Villagra www.adrianavillagra.com

Pintura realista de Adriana Villagra

Artes plásticas Adriana Villagra (1978) es una pintora de Ciudad del Este, en Paraguay. Es una artista autodidacta *(self-taught)*, aprende a dibujar y a pintar por su propia cuenta y con la ayuda de su madre, que también es autodidacta. Estudia la carrera de Diseño Gráfico en la Universidad Católica de Asunción y se gradúa con honores. Tiene exposiciones en Argentina, México, Paraguay y los Estados Unidos y obtiene premios *(awards)* importantes como el 1er. Premio en el V Concurso Juvenil de Pintura organizado por el Centro Cultural Paraguayo Americano en 2006.

¿Conoces a artistas autodidactas? ¿Crees que es necesario estudiar arte para ser un buen pintor? ¿Qué título puedes darle a la pintura de Villagra?

Oficios y ocupaciones El pueblo aimara de la civilización Tiwanaku existe desde hace 2000 años en la región del lago Titicaca, entre Bolivia y Perú. Desde entonces, sus médicos, llamados «kallawayas», caminan por las montañas y los valles para curar a las personas, física y espiritualmente. Los kallawayas curan usando hierbas como las hojas de coca, el clavel *(carnation)*, el romero *(rosemary)*, la manzanilla *(chamomile)* y el algodón *(cotton)*; además conocen los beneficios de más de 300 plantas medicinales.

¿Crees en la medicina natural? ¿Qué piensas de los médicos como los kallawayas? ¿Tomas té de plantas medicinales?

© Mel Longhurst / Impact / HIP / The Image Works South

Kallawaya da una ofrenda a la Madre Tierra (*Pachamama*) en la Isla del Sol, Bolivia

© Melvyn Longhurst/Alamy

Instrumentos musicales de los Andes

Ritmos y música En relación a la música, Bolivia es el país de los Andes que está más unido a la música indígena. La zampoña y la quena son dos tipos de flautas tradicionales de los Andes y están hechas de bambú. A diferencia de la música boliviana, la música paraguaya es totalmente europea, aunque en la letra *(lyrics)* de las canciones se usa la lengua indígena, el guaraní. En Paraguay, el 90% de la población habla español y guaraní. El guaraní se usa para la comunicación diaria y el español se usa solamente en situaciones formales. El instrumento musical más importante en Paraguay es el arpa *(harp)*.

Escucha lo mejor del arpa paraguaya interpretada por Oscar Benito (*Best of the Paraguayan Harp*, 2004) y la canción «Mombyryete Che Retägui» donde podemos escuchar el arpa paraguaya y el idioma guaraní.

¿Conoces a cantantes o grupos de música folclórica en inglés? ¿Existen instrumentos musicales asociados con ese tipo de música?

¡Busquen en Internet!

1. Lugares mágicos: Eco-reserva Mbatoví
2. Artes plásticas: Adriana Villagra
3. Oficios y profesiones: los kallawayas
4. Ritmos y música: los instrumentos andinos y el arpa paraguaya

En una clínica de Potosí

In this section, you will learn how to talk about common illnesses and discuss treatments and remedies. In the drawing below, Dr. Carlos Chávez is busy treating patients. How often do you go to the doctor?

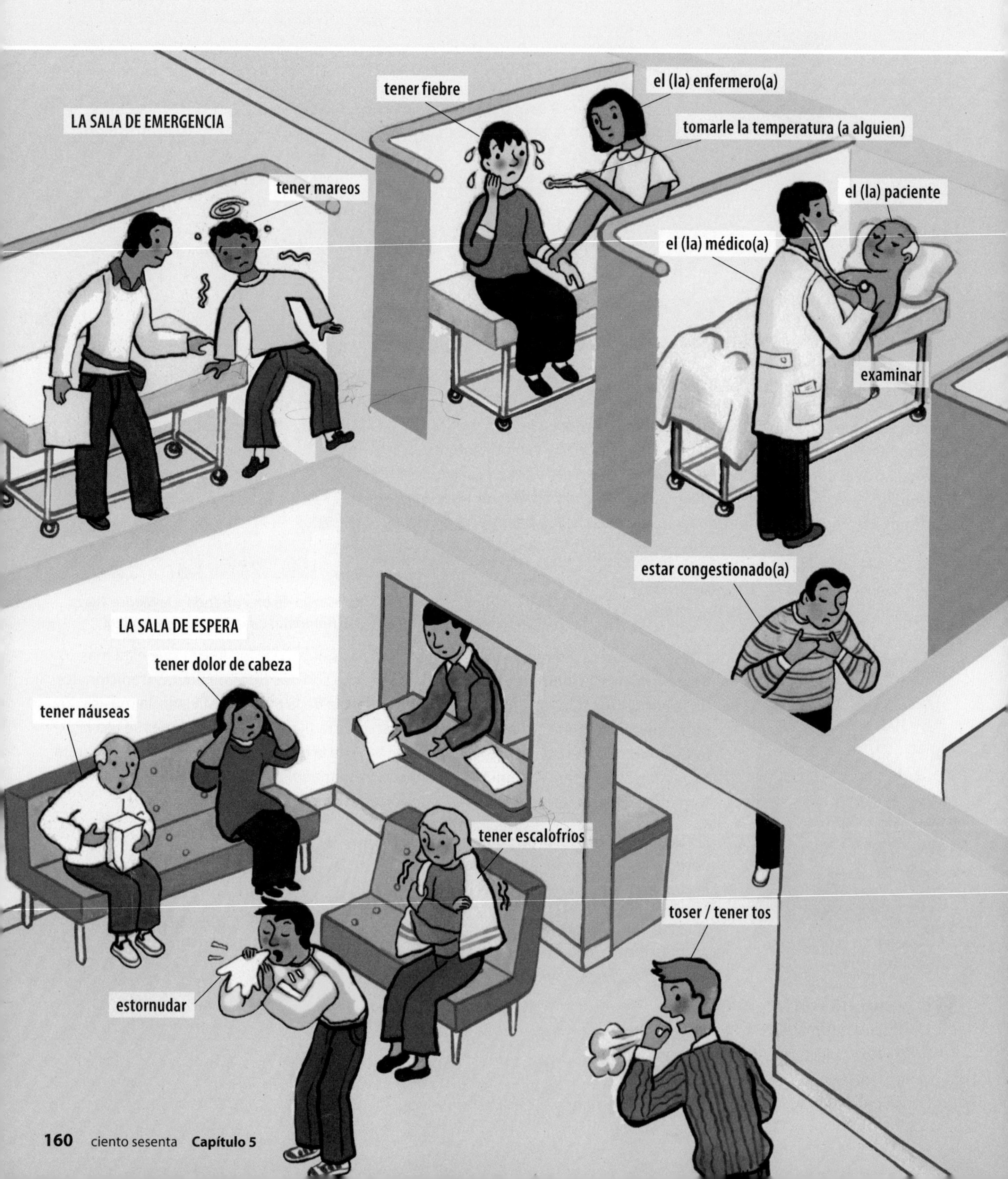

Cultura

The city of Potosí is one of the highest cities in the world (13,420 feet). During the period of Spanish rule, the city contained the richest silver mine in the world.

Heinle/Cengage Learning

Más problemas médicos *More medical problems*

la alergia *allergy*
el catarro *cold*
la enfermedad *illness*
el resfrío *cold*

Más expresiones y verbos

doler (ue) (a alguien) *to be painful (to someone); to hurt*
enfermarse *to get sick*
estar enfermo(a) *to be sick*
estar resfriado(a) *to have a cold*
guardar cama *to stay in bed*
resfriarse *to catch a cold*
sentirse (bien/mal) *to feel (good/ill)*
tener gripe *to have a cold or flu*

Palabras útiles

la ambulancia *ambulance*
el antiácido *antacid*
el diagnóstico *diagnosis*
la inyección *shot*
la radiografía *X-ray*
el tratamiento *treatment*

Palabras útiles are presented to help you enrich your personal vocabulary. The terms provided here will help you talk about health and health care.

Nota lingüística

The verb **doler** *(to hurt, to be painful)* is used like the verb **gustar: Me duele la cabeza. / Le duelen los pies.**

¡A practicar!

5-16 Asociaciones ¿Qué partes del cuerpo afecta cada enfermedad?

Modelo estar resfriado(a)
la nariz y los pulmones

1. el catarro
2. las alergias
3. el mareo
4. la tos
5. estar congestionado
6. tener náuseas

5-17 ¿Qué recomiendas? Empareja cada enfermedad con el tratamiento *(treatment)* apropiado.

Modelo Una persona que tiene *catarro* debe *tomar jarabe.*

Una persona que tiene...	debe...
1. fiebre	tomar jarabe
2. gripe	descansar un poco
3. dolor de cabeza	tomar Pepto-Bismol
4. tos	tomar antibióticos
5. un problema grave	tomar aspirina
6. dolor de estómago	hablar con un(a) médico(a)
7. náuseas	ir a una clínica
8. escalofríos	guardar cama

5-18 Recomendaciones para la salud Escucha el podcast del sitio Internet *Para tu salud.* Tu amigo quiere entender el podcast, pero no comprende el español muy bien y necesita tu ayuda. Completa la información.

AUDIO CD
CD 2, TRACK 8

Nota lingüística

As with reflexive verbs, when one is using **doler** to talk about a body part, the definite articles **(el, la, los, las)** are used.

Si te duele(n)...	debes...
la cabeza	____________________
	____________________
las piernas y los pies	____________________
	____________________
la espalda	____________________
	____________________
el estómago	____________________
	____________________

Workbook *5-10 – 5-13*
Lab Manual *5-9 – 5-10*

¡A conversar!

5-19 Los dolores En parejas, miren los dibujos y para cada uno completen la oración *(sentence)* para indicar qué le(s) duele y expliquen por qué.

Modelo A Esteban... *le duele la mano porque tuvo un accidente.*

1. A mí...

2. A ellos...

3. A ti...

4. A nosotros...

5-20 Conversación sobre la salud Con un(a) compañero(a) de clase, contesta las siguientes preguntas sobre la salud.

1. ¿Qué haces cuando tienes catarro? ¿Tomas alguna medicina? ¿Tienes escalofríos cuando tienes catarro?
2. ¿Tienes dolor de cabeza mucho o poco? ¿Qué haces cuando tienes dolor de cabeza? ¿Tomas aspirina?
3. ¿Qué haces cuando tienes náuseas? ¿Tomas Pepto-Bismol? ¿Te sientes mareado(a) frecuentemente *(frequently)*? Si tienes náuseas, ¿guardas cama?
4. ¿Estás resfriado(a) más frecuentemente en el verano o en el invierno? ¿Tienes fiebre? ¿Qué otros síntomas tienes cuando estás resfriado(a)? ¿Estornudas a veces? ¿Tienes tos?

¿Tienes alergias en la primavera?

Ser vs. estar

As you have learned, the verbs **ser** and **estar** both mean *to be*, but they are used to express different kinds of information. In this section you will review the uses of **ser** and **estar** and learn to better distinguish between the contexts for both verbs.

The verb **ser** often implies a fundamental quality or characteristic that describes or defines the essence of a person, thing, place, or idea. Use **ser** to express the following information:

ser	
Identity	—**Soy** el doctor Carlos Dardo Chávez. —¡Mucho gusto!
Origin and nationality	**Soy** de Bolivia. **Soy** boliviano.
Profession	El Dr. Chávez **es** médico.
Characteristics of people and places	El doctor **es** alto e inteligente. La Paz **es** una ciudad muy bonita.
Possession	La clínica **es** de la comunidad.
Time of day and dates	**Son** las dos de la tarde. **Es** sábado. **Es** el 22 de julio.
Intentions	**Es** para ti, Sara. **Es** para tu cumpleaños.
Impersonal statements	**Es** importante comer frutas y vegetales.
Mathematical equations	Cinco más treinta **son** treinta y cinco.
Location of events	La fiesta **es** en mi casa.

The verb **estar** often indicates a state or condition of a person, place, thing, or action at a given moment, which may be the result of a change or a deviation from the norm. Use **estar** to express the following information:

estar	
Location of people	**Estoy** en casa.
Location of things	La clínica **está** en Asunción.
Location of places	Asunción **está** en Paraguay.
Physical condition	**Estoy** cansado.
Emotional condition	**Estoy** preocupada.
Action in progress	**Estoy** trabajando.
Weather expressions	**Está** despejado. **Está** lloviendo.

Ser and **estar** can be used with the same adjectives to communicate different ideas. In some cases, the choice of **ser** or **estar** can radically change the meaning of the sentence. Consider the following examples:

ser	estar
Carlos **es guapo**. *Carlos is handsome.*	Carlos **está** muy **guapo** hoy. *Carlos looks very handsome today.*
Los voluntarios **son listos**. *The volunteers are smart.*	Los voluntarios **están listos**. *The volunteers are ready.*
Sara **es aburrida**. *Sara is boring.*	Sara **está aburrida**. *Sara is bored.*
La fruta **es verde**. *The fruit is green (color).*	La fruta **está verde**. *The fruit is unripe.*

¡A practicar!

5-21 Una visita a Bolivia: ¿Ser o estar? Las personas que visitan Bolivia deben aprender un poco sobre el país antes de viajar allí. Indica si debes usar **ser** o **estar** para completar las siguientes oraciones de una guía turística sobre este país.

Modelo Bolivia es / está un país de América del Sur.
Bolivia es un país de América del Sur.

1. La Paz es / está la capital de Bolivia.
2. La ciudad de La Paz es / está en la cordillera de los Andes.
3. La Paz es / está la ciudad más alta de América del Sur.
4. La ciudad de Cochabamba es / está al sureste *(southeast)* de La Paz.
5. El presidente de Bolivia es / está presidente durante cinco años.
6. El lago Titicaca, un lago muy importante entre Bolivia y Perú, es / está el lago navegable más alto del mundo.
7. Los turistas dicen que los bolivianos son / están muy simpáticos.
8. Hay muchos conciertos de música andina, la música típica de la región. Esta noche el concierto es / está en la ciudad de Santa Cruz.
9. Muchas personas no saben dónde son / están las ruinas de Tihuanaco, un sitio arqueológico cerca del lago Titicaca.
10. Esta guía turística es / está para las personas que van a visitar el país.

5-22 La fiesta de los voluntarios Completa la siguiente descripción y conversación con las formas correctas de los verbos **ser** y **estar**.

Hoy 1. ______ sábado, 22 de julio. 2. ______ las dos de la tarde. Hace calor y 3. ______ lloviendo un poco. La temperatura 4. ______ a 26 grados centígrados. Juan Carlos, su familia y unos amigos de la clínica 5. ______ comiendo un pastel con Roberto, un voluntario de los Estados Unidos. La fiesta 6. ______ en su apartamento. Roberto 7. ______ hablando con su amiga Rachel.

Roberto: Mmm. ¡Qué pastel más rico, Rachel!
Rachel: ¿Te gusta? 8. ______ mi pastel favorito.
Roberto: Pero 9. ______ muy grande, Rachel.
Rachel: Sí, claro. El pastel 10. ______ para todas las personas que 11. ______ aquí hoy.
Roberto: Perdón, ¿dónde 12. ______ el Dr. Chávez?
Rachel: Él 13. ______ durmiendo ahora, Roberto.
Roberto: ¿14. ______ enfermo?
Rachel: No, 15. ______ un poco cansado.
Roberto: Él 16. ______ trabajando mucho estos días.
Rachel: Sí. Él 17. ______ muy dedicado.

Workbook *5-14 – 5-16*
Lab Manual *5-11 – 5-12*

¡A conversar!

5-23 Datos personales Con un(a) compañero(a) de clase, haz y contesta preguntas con los verbos **ser** y **estar** sobre los siguientes temas.

1. **La personalidad**: Ask about his/her personality in general.
2. **La salud:** Ask about his/her emotional and physical state today.
3. **El pueblo:** Ask about his/her hometown, where it is, what it looks like, and whether it's big or small.
4. **La familia:** Ask about his/her family (size, ages, physical features, personalities).

5-24 Busca a alguien que... Tienes dos minutos para buscar a una persona de tu clase para cada una de las siguientes categorías. Después de identificar a una persona para una categoría, la persona debe escribir su nombre en tu papel. Al final del juego, habla con tus compañeros(as) sobre lo que acabas de averiguar *(find out)*. Ten cuidado con el uso de **ser** y **estar** en esta actividad.

Modelo ser de Indiana
Tú: *Brian, ¿eres de Indiana?*
Brian: *Sí, soy de Indianápolis.* (Brian firma tu lista.)
o **Brian:** *No, no soy de Indiana. Yo soy de Colorado.*
Al final: *Brian (no) es de Indiana... Cecilia está contenta... Bob es estudiante de medicina...*

1. estar enfermo(a)____________________
2. ser una persona muy sana____________________
3. estar contento(a)____________________
4. ser estudiante de ciencias____________________
5. estar congestionado(a)____________________
6. ser trabajador(a)____________________

5-25 ¿Quién soy yo? Juega con un(a) compañero(a) este juego. Sigue los siguientes pasos:

1. Completa estas preguntas con la forma correcta de **ser** o **estar**:
   ¿De dónde ______ tú?
   ¿Dónde ______ (tú) ahora?
   ¿Cómo ______ (tú) físicamente *(physically)*? ¿y tu personalidad?
   ¿Cuál ______ tu profesión?
   ¿Qué ______ (tú) haciendo ahora?
   ¿Cómo ______ (tú) ahora? ¿Por qué?
2. Cada estudiante tiene una nueva identidad. Puede ser una persona famosa o una persona de la clase.
3. Un(a) estudiante hace las preguntas para determinar la nueva identidad de su compañero(a). (Si no sabes la respuesta, debes responder de una manera lógica.)
4. Después de determinar la identidad de la primera persona, cambien de papeles para identificar a la otra persona.

5-26 Un cuento *(A story)* Trabaja con un(a) compañero(a) para escribir un cuento original. Sigue estos pasos *(steps)*:

A. Cada persona escribe en su papel la siguiente información:

1. El nombre de una persona (persona famosa, estudiante de la clase, etcétera)
2. Una profesión
3. Una característica física
4. Una característica de personalidad
5. Una ciudad, un país
6. Un número entre 1 y 28
7. Un mes
8. Un número entre 1 y 12
9. Un número entre 1 y 29
10. Una característica del tiempo
11. Una ciudad, un país
12. Una emoción
13. Un verbo de acción en la forma progresiva (**-ando, -iendo**)

B. Intercambien los papeles. Cada persona escribe los elementos de su lista en los blancos con los números correspondientes. Luego, debe escribir las formas de **ser** y **estar** apropiadamente según *(according to)* el contexto. Es importante prestar *(pay)* mucha atención al contexto para escoger el verbo apropiado en cada caso.

_____ (1) _____ (ser o estar) _____ (2).

_____ (ser o estar) _____ (3) y _____ (4).

_____ (ser o estar) de _____ (5), _____ (5).

Hoy _____ (ser o estar) el _____ (6) de _____ (7)

y ahora _____ (ser o estar) las _____ (8) y

_____ (9), según el reloj. El cielo _____ (ser o estar)

_____ (10). Ahora _____ (ser o estar) en _____ (11),

_____ (11). _____ (ser o estar) _____ (12)

porque _____ (ser o estar) _____ (13).

C. Después de terminar los cuentos, intercambien los papeles otra vez. Cada persona le lee su cuento a su compañero(a). Algunas personas pueden leerle su cuento a la clase.

Demonstrative adjectives and pronouns

In this section, you will learn how to specify people, places, things, and ideas.

Demonstrative adjectives

You can use demonstrative adjectives to point out a specific noun. Note that these adjectives must agree in gender (masculine or feminine) and number (singular or plural) with the noun to which they refer.

Singular	Plural
este(a) *this*	**estos(as)** *these*
ese(a) *that*	**esos(as)** *those*
aquel (aquella) *that (over there)*	**aquellos(as)** *those (over there)*

Note that in order to point out people, things, and places that are far from the speaker and from the person addressed, and to indicate something from a long time ago, Spanish speakers use forms of the demonstrative adjective **aquel**. For example:

Este paciente tiene dolor de estómago, **ese paciente** en la otra cama tiene fiebre y **aquel paciente** en la otra sala tiene náusea. **Estos pacientes** que tenemos hoy no están tan enfermos como *(as sick as)* **aquellos pacientes** del mes pasado.

Demonstrative pronouns

Demonstrative pronouns are used in place of nouns and must agree with them in gender (masculine or feminine) and number (singular or plural). The forms below once carried accents to distinguish them from the demonstrative adjectives, but in 2005, the Real Academia ruled that accents are not necessary unless there is room for confusion.

The Real Academia Española was founded as an institution in 1713. Its purpose was to study and maintain beauty, elegance, and purity in the Spanish language. Today, its purpose is to explain and keep track of the changes in the language.

Singular	Plural
este(a)	**estos(as)**
ese(a)	**esos(as)**
aquel (aquella)	**aquellos(as)**

—¿Quieres ir a esa farmacia? *Do you want to go to that pharmacy?*
—Sí, a **esa**. *Yes, to **that one**.*
—¿Son tuyos aquellos libros? *Are those books (over there) yours?*
—Sí, **aquellos** son míos. *Yes, **those** are mine.*

Neuter demonstrative pronouns

The words **esto** *(this)*, **eso** *(that)*, and **aquello** *(that over there)* can refer either to nonspecific things that are not yet identified or to ideas that were already mentioned. Note that neuter demonstrative pronouns never carry accents.

—¿Qué es **esto**, mamá? *What's **this**, Mom?*
—Es un termómetro. *It's a thermometer.*
La clínica no tiene muchas ambulancias, y **eso** es grave. *The clinic doesn't have many ambulances, and **that** is serious.*

¡A practicar!

5-27 La nueva clínica de la Cruz Roja Al doctor Chávez le gusta mucho la nueva clínica de la Cruz Roja. Habla con unos visitantes en la clínica, Roberto y Rachel. Completa sus comentarios usando **este, esta, estos** o **estas**.

Dr. Chávez: Amigos, entramos aquí, por esta puerta.

Roberto: ¡Qué bonita! 1. ______ clínica tiene de todo.

Dr. Chávez: Sí, por fin la gente de 2. ______ barrio tiene un buen lugar para recibir tratamiento médico.

Rachel: ¿Y 3. ______ personas? ¿Todas vienen para consultas *(consultations)* hoy?

Dr. Chávez: Sí, en 4. ______ días tenemos muchos pacientes.

Roberto: ¿Cuánto tienen que pagar 5. ______ personas por las consultas?

Dr. Chávez: 6. ______ consultas no son totalmente gratis *(free)*, pero solamente cobramos *(we charge)* según la capacidad *(according to the means)* de cada persona.

5-28 Para aclarar Imagínate que estás en la librería de tu universidad comprando cosas para tus clases. Responde a las preguntas de modo positivo o negativo usando los adjetivos demostrativos **ese, esa, esos** o **esas**. Luego repite tus respuestas a las preguntas usando los pronombres demostrativos.

Modelo ¿Quieres este libro?
Sí, quiero ese libro. o *No, no quiero ese libro.*
Quiero este / ese / aquel.

1. ¿Quieres estos bolígrafos?
2. ¿Necesitas estas mochilas?
3. ¿Quieres ver este cuaderno?
4. ¿Compras este libro de texto?
5. ¿Buscas esta alfombra para tu cuarto?
6. ¿Estás aquí con estas personas?

Workbook *5-17 – 5-19*
Lab Manual *5-13*

¡A conversar!

5-29 Una venta *(sale)* en la clase Con tres o cuatro compañeros(as) de clase, arregla *(arrange)* las siguientes cosas en una mesa: dos libros, dos mochilas y dos bolígrafos. Una persona es el (la) vendedor(a) *(the seller)* y los otros son los clientes *(customers)*. El (La) vendedor(a) y los clientes deben usar las formas correctas de los adjetivos o pronombres demostrativos en la conversación.

Modelo **E1:** *¿Quieres comprar este libro?*
E2: *No, no quiero ese libro. Prefiero aquel libro.*
E1: *¿Ese?*
E2: *No, aquel.*

Me gusta este bolígrafo blanco. ¿Cuál te gusta a ti?

5-30 ¿Conoces a aquel chico? Trabajando con un(a) compañero(a) de clase, haz preguntas sobre los miembros de tu clase, usando adjetivos o pronombres demostrativos. Cada persona debe hacer cinco preguntas y dos de ellas deben ser en la forma plural.

Modelo **E1:** *¿Conoces a aquellos chicos?*
E2: *¿Los chicos altos y morenos?*
E1: *Sí, aquellos.*
E2: *Sí, son Darius y Renault.*

La clase de baile En este segmento del video, los compañeros de casa van a aprender un baile folclórico llamado bomba puertorriqueña. Desafortunadamente, uno de ellos también sufre de un problema de salud.

Antes de ver

Expresiones útiles The following are some new expressions you will hear in the video.

¿Qué les parece? — *How does that sound to you?*
Me lastimé el tobillo. — *I hurt my ankle.*
De acuerdo. — *Okay.*
No me quedó otra opción. — *I didn't have any other choice.*

Enfoque estructural The following are expressions in the video with reflexive verbs and their corresponding reflexive pronouns.

Valeria: No **se preocupen,** que yo no voy a bailar.

Instructor: Bueno, si no vas a bailar, **siéntate** por allá.

Alejandra: Sí. Es que me lastimé el tobillo y no puedo apoyar la pierna al suelo. Es que yo **me rompí** la pierna hace un año.

1. **Recordemos** ¿Cómo describes tu rutina diaria? Describe a un(a) compañero(a) de clase 3 cosas que haces antes de comer el desayuno.

2. **Practiquemos** Con dos compañeros de clase, comparen cuándo y con qué frecuencia hacen las siguientes actividades.

ACTIVIDAD	ESTUDIANTE A	ESTUDIANTE B	ESTUDIANTE C
ducharse			
cepillarse los dientes			
lavarse las manos			
peinarse			

3. **Charlemos** Ahora comparen los resultados de la actividad anterior. ¿Quién es la persona más higiénica? ¿Quién debe prestar más atención a la higiene personal?

Después de ver

1. El accidente de Alejandra Piensa en el accidente de Alejandra. Lee las siguientes oraciones y ponlas *(put them)* en orden cronológico según el video.

______ Alejandra se lastima el tobillo y no puede bailar.

______ Alejandra decide descansar, ¡pero solamente si puede salir con el instructor esa noche!

______ Los jóvenes llegan al salón de baile.

______ Valeria no quiere bailar y se sienta.

______ El instructor dice que Alejandra no puede bailar más y que necesita descansar.

______ Alejandra dice que es la mejor *(best)* bailarina de todo el grupo.

______ Valeria tiene que bailar con Antonio.

______ Alejandra se sienta y habla con el instructor sobre el dolor.

______ El instructor explica los pasos del baile y los cuatro empiezan a bailar un poco.

______ Alejandra dice que no le duele la rodilla, pero que el pie le duele mucho. También dice que se rompió *(she broke)* la pierna hace un año *(a year ago)*.

Heinle/Cengage Learning

2. ¿Que acaban de hacer? Indica lo que acaba de hacer cada persona, escogiendo de la siguiente lista de acciones.

aprender a bailar	bailar con Antonio
invitar a Alejandra a salir	lastimarse

Alejandra: ______________________________

Valeria: ______________________________

Javier: ______________________________

Sofía: ______________________________

Víctor: ______________________________

Entre nosotros En este segmento, Alejandra no se siente bien porque le duele el pie. Ahora imagina que tú estas enfermo(a), y tu compañero(a) es el (la) médico(a). Describe tus síntomas a él/ella. ¿Tienes tos? ¿Estás mareado? ¿Te duele algo? Luego cambien de papel. ¡Sean creativos! *(Be creative!)*

Presentaciones Con un compañero(a) de clase, escoge *(choose)* uno de los personajes de Vista Alegre y escribe una lista de actividades que normalmente él o ella hace durante el día. Por ejemplo, ¿se levanta tarde o temprano? ¿Se ducha o se baña? Comparte tus ideas con la clase para ver si ellos están de acuerdo.

See the *Lab Manual,* **Capítulo 5, 5-15 – 5-16** for additional activities.

Antes de leer

Strategy: Recognizing Spanish affixes

An affix is added to the beginning (prefix), or to the end (suffix) of a word stem to create a new word. Knowing the meaning of Spanish affixes can significantly increase your ability to read Spanish effectively.

Study the list of affixes (**afijos**) to learn the basic meaning of each prefix (**prefijo**) or suffix (**sufijo**) in English and in Spanish.

Español	Inglés	Ejemplos
Prefijos		
auto-	*self-*	**auto**estima
des-	*negation*	**des**afortunado
mono-	*mono-* (one)	**mono**lingüe
mal-	*bad, ill*	**mal**estar
bi-	*bi-* (two)	**bi**lingüe
tri-	*tri-* (three)	**tri**lingüe
im-	*negation*	**im**posible
in-	*negation*	**in**creíble
infra-	*inferior*	**infra**humano
Sufijos		
-mente	*-ly*	rápida**mente**
-ado,	*-ed*	ocup**ado**
-ada	*-ed*	present**ada**
-oso,	*-ous*	maravill**oso**
-osa	*-ous*	fabul**osa**
-dad,	*-ty*	oportuni**dad**
-tad	*-ty*	liber**tad**
-ción,	*-sion,-tion*	ac**ción**
-sión	*-sion,-tion*	televi**sión**

Curaméricas Global

Now you can apply the strategies that you have learned thus far—recognizing cognates and affixes, reading titles and subtitles, and looking at photos and maps to predict the topic of an article and thereby make the reading easier.

1. Escriban cinco cognados y sus significados.
2. **Afijos.** Escriban seis palabras con prefijos o con sufijos y sus significados.
3. ¿Qué significa el título de la lectura?
4. ¿Qué subtítulos tiene el artículo? ¿Qué pueden predecir con estos subtítulos?
5. ¿De qué país son la foto y el mapa?

Heinle/Cengage Learning

Después de leer

A escoger Después de leer el artículo, contesten las siguientes preguntas.

1. ¿Qué tipo de artículo es?
   a. un anuncio para mejorar la salud de comunidades
   b. un anuncio para educar a la comunidad con respecto a la salud
   c. un anuncio para ayudar a los gobiernos a mejorar la salud
2. ¿A quién está dirigido este anuncio?
   a. a la comunidad en general
   b. a los gobiernos
   c. a los estudiantes de medicina
3. ¿Cuáles son los problemas que Curaméricas Global, Inc. ayuda a combatir en las comunidades?
   a. los problemas respiratorios y digestivos
   b. los problemas emocionales y físicos
   c. los problemas educativos y económicos

Curando comunidades

una persona a la vez

Matthew Totten/Alamy

HISTORIA DE CURAMÉRICAS GLOBAL, INC.

Henry Perry III y Alice Weldon, dos médicos de Carolina del Norte, fundan Curaméricas Global, Inc. en 1983. El objetivo principal de esta organización es prevenir *(prevent)* enfermedades y muertes *(deaths)* innecesarias en poblaciones pobres, con pocos recursos económicos, en países como Bolivia, Guatemala, Haití y Liberia. Los médicos, enfermeros, enfermeras y voluntarios visitan las casas en una comunidad específica y estudian la manera de ayudar a las familias que tienen más riesgos *(risks)* de contraer enfermedades.

CURAMÉRICAS GLOBAL, INC. EN BOLIVIA

En Bolivia, esta organización ayuda a muchas familias en el Altiplano y en la región de Montero en los últimos años. Estas familias reciben ayuda y educación médica porque la combinación de la poca infraestructura y las condiciones infrahumanas de la población hacen de Bolivia uno de los países más pobres *(one of the poorest countries)* de América del Sur. Muchas comunidades no tienen agua potable y si la gente se enferma tiene que caminar más de un día para llegar a una clínica. Debido a la altitud y a una dieta desequilibrada, las mujeres y los niños mueren de pulmonía, diarrea y problemas del estómago. El programa de Curaméricas Global, Inc. trabaja en más de 200 comunidades para enseñar a estas personas a cuidarse de estas enfermedades.

RESULTADOS

Gracias a los servicios de Curaméricas Global, Inc. en las comunidades bolivianas, la tasa de mortalidad *(death rate)* de los niños bolivianos se reduce un 62% en comparación con otras comunidades donde Curaméricas Global, Inc. no trabaja todavía.

¿Cómo pueden ustedes ayudar a Curaméricas Global, Inc.?

- Pueden donar dinero a la organización Curaméricas Global, Inc. y su donativo es deducible de impuestos *(taxes)*.
- Pueden ser voluntarios en la oficina de la organización o pueden mandar medicinas a los proyectos en los diferentes países.
- Pueden trabajar como voluntarios o pueden hacer sus prácticas *(internships)* de medicina, enfermería, mercadeo y publicidad *(marketing)* y recursos humanos *(human resources)* en uno de estos países: Bolivia, Guatemala, Haití y Liberia.

4. Curaméricas Global, Inc. necesita ayudar a las familias en Bolivia porque...
   a el país no tiene agua potable.
   b. el país es uno de los más pobres de Sudamérica.
   c. el país no tiene muchos doctores en lugares remotos.

¿Cierto o falso? Indica si las oraciones son **ciertas** o **falsas**. Luego, corrige las falsas.

1. _____ Dos médicos de Carolina del Norte, Henry Perry III y Alice Weldon fundan Curaméricas Global, Inc. en 1983 para prevenir enfermedades y muertes *(deaths)* innecesarias en poblaciones pobres.
2. _____ Los voluntarios visitan todas las casas de un país y estudian la manera de ayudar a las familias que tienen más riesgos *(risks)* de contraer enfermedades.
3. _____ La combinación de la poca infraestructura y las condiciones infrahumanas de la población hacen de Bolivia uno de los países más pobres de Sudamérica.
4. _____ Debido al frío, las mujeres y los niños mueren de pulmonía, diarrea y problemas del estómago.
5. _____ La gente puede ayudar a Curaméricas Global, Inc. donando dinero, mandando medicinas o trabajando como voluntaria.

¡A conversar! Con sus compañeros de clase comenten:

- El trabajo que hace Curaméricas Global, Inc. en Latinoamérica.
- La manera en que ustedes pueden ayudar a estas comunidades necesitadas.
- Si ustedes conocen otras organizaciones como Curaméricas Global, Inc., expliquen lo que hacen estas organizaciones y los lugares donde trabajan.
- Si ustedes hacen trabajo comunitario en sus comunidades, expliquen lo que ustedes hacen, para quién y con quién.

Strategy: Using a bilingual dictionary

A bilingual dictionary is a useful tool that, when used properly, can enhance the quality, complexity, and accuracy of your writing in Spanish. It is very important, however, that you learn to use it correctly. Here are some suggestions to help you use your bilingual dictionary properly.

1. When you look up the Spanish equivalent of an English word, you will often find several meanings for the same word, often appearing like this:

   cold: *n.* **frío, catarro, resfriado**
   adj. **frío**

2. In larger dictionaries, additional information may be given that will clarify meanings and uses.

   cold: *n.* **frío** *(low temperature)*; **catarro** *(illness)*; **resfriado** *(illness)*
   adj. **frío**

3. Pay attention to certain abbreviations in your dictionary that will tell you what type of word you have found. Notice the abbreviations *n.* and *adj.* in the examples above, indicating that the word is a noun or an adjective. Some of the more common abbreviations you will find are listed below. Their Spanish equivalents are in parentheses.

n.	noun	(**sustantivo**)	*conj.*	conjunction	(**conjunción**)
adj.	adjective	(**adjetivo**)	*prep.*	preposition	(**preposición**)
adv.	adverb	(**adverbio**)	*v.*	verb	(**verbo**)

4. Looking up a lot of different words in a bilingual dictionary when you are writing is inefficient. It is wiser and faster to use the phrases you already know in Spanish as much as possible, rather than trying to translate too many new words you don't know from English to Spanish.

Task: Writing a health report

Health reports may be written in a variety of situations and they may be official or unofficial, formal or quite informal. Individuals may prepare health reports before they undertake new or strenuous activity, such as participation in a sport. You will now write a report of your own health that might be given to a health care provider, coach, or other person who needs information about your current condition.

Paso 1 Prepara una lista de seis aspectos importantes de tu condición física actual *(current)*. Puedes incluir aspectos positivos como: **Tengo mucha energía porque hago ejercicio regularmente,** y problemas como: **Me duele la cabeza cuando estudio mucho.**

Paso 2 Decide si tu estado físico es, en general, bueno o malo basándote en el **Paso 1.**

Paso 3 Escribe un informe de diez oraciones, explicando tu condición física e incluyendo la siguiente información.

- cuántos años tienes
- si tu condición es, en general, buena o mala
- un mínimo de cinco aspectos

Paso 4 Intercambia tu informe con un(a) compañero(a) de clase y lee el suyo *(his/hers)*. Después, comenta con él/ella los aspectos positivos y negativos presentados en los informes y decide si uno(a) o los (las) dos necesita(n) hacer una cita con el (la) médico(a).

Communicative Goals:

- Identify parts of the body and communicate about health conditions
- Describe daily activities
- Express what you and others have just finished doing
- Communicate about characteristics and conditions of people and things

Paso 1

Review the Communicative Goals for **Capítulo 5** and determine if you are able to accomplish the goals. If you are not certain that you have achieved all of the goals, review the pertinent portions of the chapter.

Paso 2

Look at the components of a conversation which addresses the communicative goals for this chapter. The percentages will help you evaluate your ability to successfully participate in the conversation that is featured below. Your instructor may use the same rubric to assess your oral performance.

Components of the conversation	%
☐ Greetings, questions and answers about how the patient is feeling, information about what the patient has just done	10
☐ Questions and answers about at least two body parts that may hurt or cause pain	20
☐ Questions and answers about medications	20
☐ Information about at least four daily activities and when they take place	20
☐ Information regarding physical characteristics and/or personality traits and health conditions of two family members	20
☐ Polite conclusion of conversation	10

En acción Role-play a conversation between a doctor and patient, following the steps given. Then switch roles and repeat.

1. The individuals greet one another in a professional manner, the doctor asks the patient how he (she) is feeling; the patient responds and indicates what he (she) has just done.
2. The doctor asks if two specific parts of the body ache or cause pain, the patient responds and explains why or why not.
3. The doctor asks if the patient takes any medications, the patient responds and explains why or why not.
4. The doctor inquires about typical daily activities and the patient replies with information about at least four activities and when they are done.
5. The doctor asks about two family members, requesting information about their physical characteristics and/or personality traits (what they are like) and their health conditions.
6. The patient provides information about two family members, specifying at least two physical or personality traits for each and giving information about health conditions.
7. The patient and the doctor conclude the conversation in a professional manner.

¡A REPASAR!

Reflexive pronouns and the present tense of reflexive verbs

Reflexive verbs are identified by the pronoun **-se** attached to the end of the infinitive form of the verb. To conjugate these verbs, use a reflexive pronoun (e.g., **me**) with its corresponding verb form (e.g., **levanto**), according to the subject of the sentence (e.g., **yo**).

Subject	Reflexive pronoun + Verb form
yo	me levanto
tú	te levantas
Ud., él/ella	se levanta
nosotros(as)	nos levantamos
vosotros(as)	os levantáis
Uds., ellos(as)	se levantan

¡A recordar! 1 When are definite articles used with reflexive verbs? Where are reflexive pronouns placed in relation to the verb?

Acabar de + infinitive

Acabar de + infinitive means *to have just finished doing something*.

¡A recordar! 2 How is **acabar** conjugated in the present tense?

Ser versus *estar*

Ser implies a fundamental quality or characteristic that describes or defines the essence of a person, thing, place, or idea. **Estar** indicates the location or the state or condition of a person, thing, place, or action at a given moment, which may be the result of a change or a deviation from the norm.

¡A recordar! 3 Which qualities or conditions require the use of the verb **ser**? Which states or conditions are expressed by the verb **estar**? Which adjectives can change meaning depending on their use with either **ser** or **estar**?

Demonstrative adjectives and pronouns

Demonstrative adjectives must agree in gender (masculine or feminine) and number (singular or plural) with the noun to which they refer. Demonstrative pronouns must agree in gender and number with the nouns they replace. Both adjectives and pronouns have the same form.

Singular	Plural
este(a)	estos(as)
ese(a)	esos(as)
aquel (aquella)	aquellos(as)

¡A recordar! 4 When are the neuter demonstrative pronouns used?

Actividad 1 Las actividades de un día típico

Completa cada frase con las formas correctas del verbo indicado. Escoge las formas reflexivas y no reflexivas apropiadamente según el contexto.

1. **levantar(se):** Sara y su esposo Mario ______________ a las seis. A las seis y media Sara ______________ a sus hijos.
2. **bañar(se):** Sara ______________ por la mañana, pero ella ______________ a su hijo menor *(youngest)* por la noche.
3. **afeitar(se):** ¡Sara y Mario no ______________ a los niños! Mario ______________ por la mañana.
4. **peinar(se):** Generalmente, los niños ______________ solos, pero si es un día especial, como el día de fotografías en la escuela, Sara ______________ a su hijo menor.
5. **poner(se):** Yo ______________ mis libros en la mochila y después ______________ la chaqueta *(jacket)* y salgo para la escuela.
6. **dormir(se):** Yo ______________ siete u ocho horas cada noche. ¡Yo no ______________ en la clase!
7. **maquillar(se), pintar(se):** ¿ ______________ tú todos los días? ¡Yo no! Yo ______________ a veces *(at times)* cuando tengo tiempo.
8. **lavar(se):** Nosotros ______________ las manos antes de comer y ______________ los platos después.
9. **cuidar(se):** Estás resfriado otra vez. Tú no ____________ . Yo nunca me enfermo. ____________ muy bien.
10. **vestir(se):** Lola tiene cuatro años. No puede ____________ sola *(by herself)*, pero sí puede ____________ a su muñeca *(doll)* Dora.

Actividad 2 ¿Qué acaban de hacer? Forma oraciones con la expresión **acabar de** para expresar las actividades que las personas acaban de hacer.

1. Mis amigos / jugar al tenis
____
2. Nuestro tío / levantar pesas
____
3. Yo / correr en el parque
____
4. Tú / bailar con amigos
____
5. Mi amigo y yo / hablar por teléfono
____
6. El enfermero / despertarse
____

Actividad 3 Preguntas Escoge el verbo correcto para completar cada pregunta.

1. ¿Dónde es / está la sala de emergencia?
2. ¿Quién es / está la médica?
3. ¿Es / Está necesario completar un historial clínico?
4. ¿Están / Son Uds. enfermos?
5. ¿Son / Están simpáticos los enfermeros?
6. ¿Qué está / es leyendo Ud.?

Actividad 4 Un día en la vida de Cristina
Completa cada oración con la forma correcta de **ser** o **estar**, según el contexto.

Cristina Vargas Ramos 1. ________ médica en un hospital de La Paz. El hospital 2. ________ cerca de su casa y ella camina al trabajo. Ahora ella 3. ________ caminando al hospital y 4. ________ un poco preocupada porque hay muchos pacientes que 5. ________ muy enfermos esta semana. Todos los médicos 6. ________ inteligentes y dedicados, pero hay mucho trabajo y 7. ________ difícil ayudar a todos. Hace buen tiempo y el cielo 8. ________ despejado. Por eso las personas en la calle 9. ________ contentas. Cristina sabe que su trabajo 10. ________ importante y que ella ayuda a muchas personas.

Actividad 5 Unas cosas importantes Identifica la palabra apropiada para completar cada oración.

1. ______ libro de anatomía que está aquí es interesante.
2. ______ papeles que están allí son de David.
3. El médico escribe ______ recetas que están aquí para Felipe.
4. Los enfermeros recomiendan ______ medicina que está aquí.
5. —Debes tomar las pastillas que están allí, para la infección.
   —¿Cuáles? ¿ ______ ?
6. Necesito hablar con ______ medica que está allí.
7. Necesito ______ documentos que están aquí.
8. —¿Trabaja tu amiga en el hospital que está allí, cerca de la plaza?
   —Sí, trabaja en ______ .

a. este
b. esta
c. estos
d. estas
e. ese
f. esa
g. esos
h. esas

Refrán

Heinle/Cengage Learning

________ (*Eyes*) que no ________ (*see*),
________ (*heart*) que no ________ (*feel*).

VOCABULARIO ESENCIAL

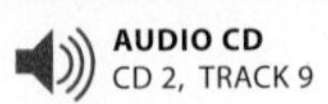
AUDIO CD
CD 2, TRACK 9

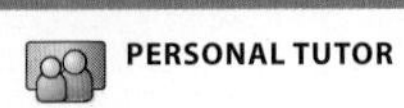
PERSONAL TUTOR

Las partes del cuerpo	*Body parts*
la boca	mouth
el brazo	arm
el cabello	hair
la cabeza	head
la cara	face
el cerebro	brain
el codo	elbow
el corazón	heart
el cuello	neck
los dedos	fingers
los dedos del pie/de los pies	toes
los dientes	teeth
la espalda	back
el estómago	stomach
la garganta	throat
el hueso	bone
la mano	hand
el músculo	muscle
la nariz	nose
los ojos	eyes
las orejas	(outer) ears
el pelo	hair
el pie	foot
la pierna	leg
los pulmones	lungs
la rodilla	knee
el tobillo	ankle

La salud	*Health*
Sustantivos	
la alergia	allergy
el antibiótico	antibiotic
la aspirina	aspirin
el catarro	cold
el consultorio	doctor's office
el dolor de cabeza	headache
la enfermedad	illness
el (la) enfermero(a)	nurse
la farmacia	pharmacy
la fiebre	fever
el jarabe	cough syrup
el mareo	dizziness
la medicina	medicine
el (la) médico(a)	physician, doctor
el (la) paciente	patient
la pastilla	pill
la receta	prescription
el resfrío	cold
la sala de emergencia	emergency room
la sala de espera	waiting room
Verbos y expresiones	
dolerle (ue) (a alguien)	to be painful (to someone); to hurt
enfermarse	to get sick
estar congestionado(a)	to be congested
estar enfermo(a)	to be sick
estar resfriado(a)	to have a cold
estornudar	to sneeze
examinar	to examine
guardar cama	to stay in bed
resfriarse	to catch a cold
sentirse (ie) (bien/mal)	to feel (good/bad)
tener dolor de cabeza	to have a headache
tener escalofríos	to have chills
tener fiebre	to have a fever
tener gripe	to have a cold/the flu
tener náuseas	to be nauseous
tener tos	to have a cough
tomarle la temperatura (a alguien)	to take (someone's) temperature
toser	to cough

Verbos de la rutina diaria y personal	*Daily and personal routine verbs*
acostarse (ue)	to go to bed
afeitarse	to shave
bañarse	to take a bath
cepillarse los dientes	to brush one's teeth
cuidarse	to take care (of oneself)
despertarse (ie)	to wake up
dormirse (ue)	to fall asleep
ducharse	to take a shower
lavarse	to wash up
levantarse	to get up
maquillarse	to put on makeup
peinarse	to comb one's hair
pintarse	to put on makeup
ponerse (la ropa)	to put on (one's clothes)
quitarse (la ropa)	to take off (one's clothes)
secarse (el cuerpo)	to dry off (one's body)
vestirse (i)	to get dressed

Adjetivos y pronombres demostrativos	
este(a)	this
estos(as)	these
ese(a)	that
esos(as)	those
aquel (aquella)	that (over there)
aquellos(as)	those (over there)

CAPÍTULO

¿Quieres comer conmigo esta noche?

Venezuela

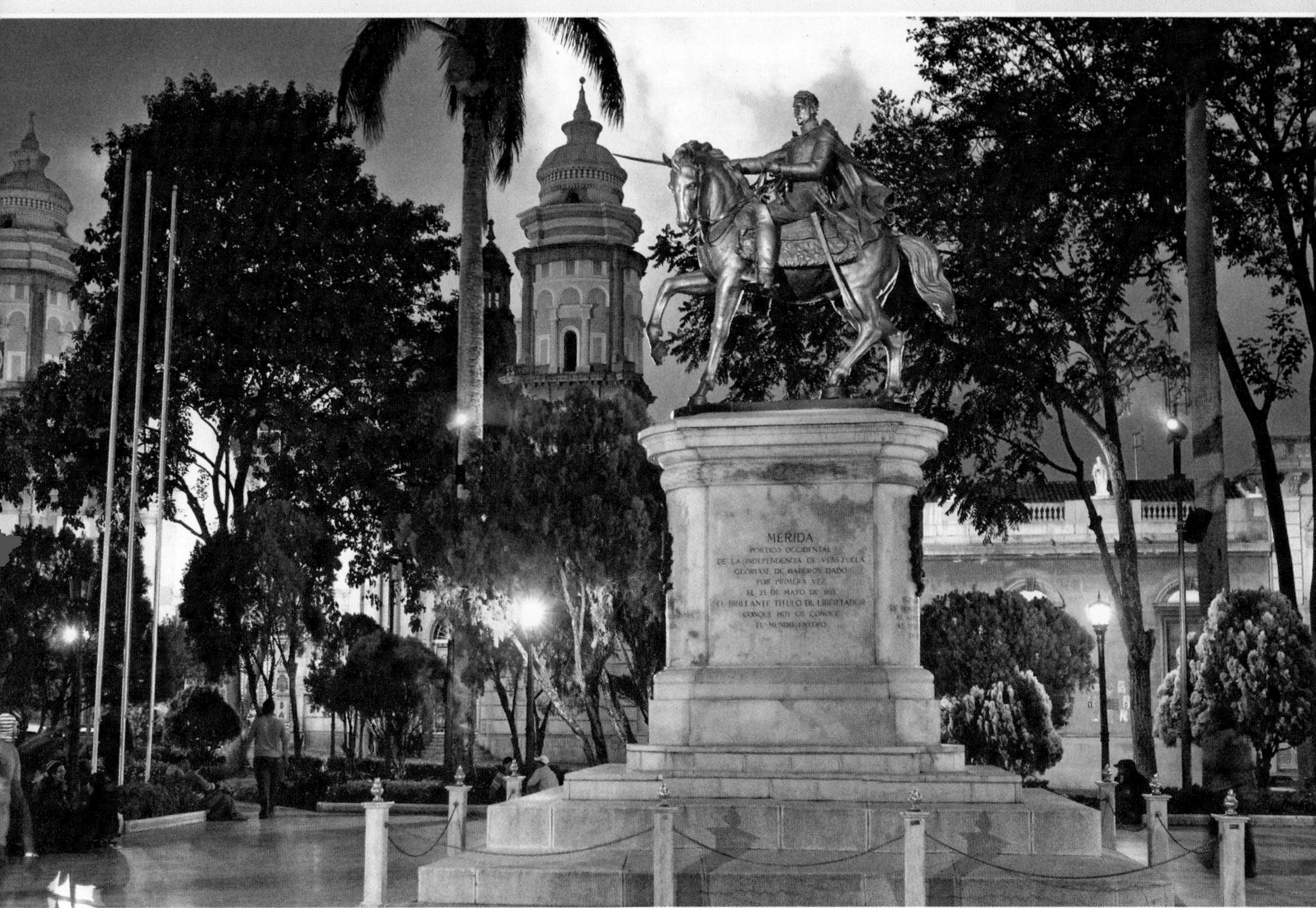

Plaza Bolívar, Mérida, Venezuela

Chapter Objectives

Communicative Goals

In this chapter, you will learn how to . . .

- Communicate about foods, beverages, and dining
- Make comparisons and express superlatives
- Order food and beverages in a restaurant
- Communicate about past events and actions

Structures

- Comparatives and superlatives
- Regular verbs and verbs with spelling changes in the preterite
- Verbs with stem changes in the preterite

▲ ¿Tienes hambre ahora? ¿Tienes sed?

▲ ¿Dónde tienes ganas de comer?

▲ ¿Qué tipo de comida te gusta?

 Visit it live on **Google Earth!**

En el restaurante de doña Margarita

In this section, you will practice talking about foods and table utensils by learning about doña Margarita's restaurant, **El Criollito,** on the east side of Caracas. What do you like to order when you go to a restaurant?

Otras bebidas *Other beverages*

el agua mineral sin gas *noncarbonated mineral water*

el café *coffee*

el jugo de fruta *fruit juice*

el té (helado) *(iced) tea*

Otros condimentos *Other condiments*

el aceite *oil*

el azúcar *sugar*

el vinagre *vinegar*

Modos de preparación *Cooking methods*

asado(a) *roasted*

frito(a) *fried*

tostado(a) *toasted*

Las comidas *Meals*

el almuerzo *lunch*

la cena *dinner, supper*

el desayuno *breakfast*

Verbos

almorzar (ue) *to have (eat) lunch*

cenar *to have (eat) dinner (supper)*

desayunar *to have (eat) breakfast*

Cultura

Arepas, fried or baked corn pancakes, either plain or with a filling, such as shredded meat, beans, cheese or avocado, are a staple for most Venezuelans and can be found in restaurants and in small food stands called **areperas.**

¡A practicar!

Nota lingüística

In Spain, **las papas** are referred to as **las patatas** and **el jugo de naranja** is referred to as **el zumo de naranja.** In Puerto Rico, however, **el jugo de naranja** is referred to as **el jugo de china.**

6-1 Combinaciones Combina cada elemento de la primera columna con el elemento apropiado de la segunda columna.

1. ______ Las carnes — a. el café y el jugo
2. ______ Las verduras — b. el jamón y el pollo
3. ______ Los mariscos — c. la sal y la pimienta
4. ______ Los condimentos — d. el flan y el helado
5. ______ Las bebidas — e. la langosta y los camarones
6. ______ Los postres — f. la lechuga y la papa

6-2 Un menú desorganizado Doña Margarita está organizando el menú para su restaurante. Ayúdala a encontrar la comida que no forma parte del grupo. En cada grupo, también indica lo que tienen en común los otros tres artículos *(items)*.

Nota lingüística

There are several ways to say "banana" in Spanish. **La banana** and **el plátano** are often used. **El banano** is common in Central America, **el guineo** is used in the Caribbean, and **el cambur** is preferred in Venezuela.

1. las chuletas, los camarones, el helado, el pescado
2. el café, el té, el huevo, el agua mineral
3. el bistec, los calamares, la langosta, el pescado
4. los postres, los tenedores, los entremeses, los platos principales
5. los champiñones, las papas, las manzanas, la lechuga
6. la leche, la manzana, la naranja, la banana
7. la sal, el azúcar, el aceite, el sándwich

6-3 ¿Qué bebidas te gustan? Escogiendo de la lista de bebidas de la derecha, completa las siguientes oraciones para expresar tus preferencias.

1. Para el desayuno, prefiero tomar...
2. Cuando estudio en casa, tomo...
3. Cuando tengo mucha sed, bebo...
4. Para el almuerzo, me gusta beber...
5. En las fiestas siempre tomo...
6. Los fines de semana me gusta tomar...
7. Para la cena prefiero beber...
8. Cuando estoy en el cine, tomo...

leche
café
té
vino tinto/blanco
agua mineral
jugo de naranja
un refresco
una cerveza

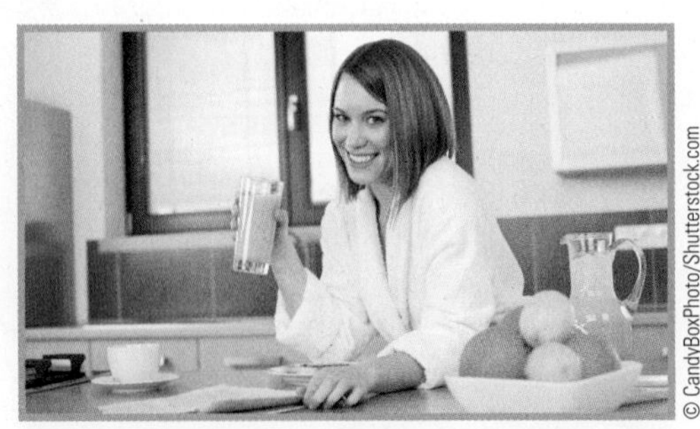

Alicia toma jugo de naranja todas las mañanas. Y tú, ¿qué tomas normalmente?

Workbook *6-1 – 6-3*
Lab Manual *6-1 – 6-3*

¡A conversar!

6-4 **Una invitación** Conversa con un(a) compañero(a) de clase para hacer planes para una comida para el fin de semana. ¡Sé creativo(a)!

Estudiante A	**Estudiante B**
1. Saluda a tu amigo(a).	2. Contéstale a tu amigo(a) y pregúntale cómo está él/ella. Después invita a tu amigo(a) a un almuerzo en casa el sábado.
3. Dile que no puedes aceptar su invitación. Habla de los planes que ya tienes.	4. Reacciona a lo que dice tu amigo(a). Invítalo(la) a almorzar otro día.
5. Acepta la invitación. Dale las gracias a tu amigo(a). Pregúntale sobre la invitación (día, hora, etc.).	6. Respóndele sus preguntas.
7. Pregúntale si su familia va a estar en el almuerzo o no.	8. Contesta si tu familia va a estar en el el almuerzo o no.
9. Dile adiós a tu amigo(a).	10. Responde.

6-5 **Entrevista** Pregúntale a otro(a) compañero(a) de clase sobre su rutina a la hora de comer. Después comparte esta información con la clase. ¿Tienen mucho en común tus compañeros de clase?

1. **el desayuno:** ¿A qué hora desayunas? ¿Desayunas solo(a) o con otras personas? ¿Qué prefieres tomar por la mañana, café, té, leche o jugo? ¿Qué te gusta comer para el desayuno?
2. **el almuerzo:** Normalmente, ¿dónde almuerzas? ¿Con quién te gusta almorzar? ¿A qué hora almuerzas? ¿Qué comes para el almuerzo?
3. **la cena:** Normalmente, ¿a qué hora cenas? ¿Cenas con tu familia, con otras personas o solo(a)? ¿Comes mucho o poco en la cena? Por ejemplo, ¿qué comes?

6-6  **Dietas especiales** Uds. trabajan en un restaurante y tienen clientes con necesidades especiales. Planeen un menú para cada cliente de la lista, considerando sus preferencias y necesidades. Para cada persona, escriban un mínimo de tres platos y una bebida. Después de planear los menús deben presentarlos y explicar sus decisiones a la clase.

1. Gustavo es un hombre de 45 años, bastante gordo. Trabaja en una oficina y no hace mucho ejercicio. Siempre tiene mucha hambre pero quiere adelgazar *(lose weight).*
2. Amalia es una estudiante universitaria de 21 años. Come poca carne, pero come pescado y mariscos. Le gustan mucho las frutas y las verduras.
3. Felipe es un hombre muy deportista de 25 años. Consume muchas proteínas y mucho calcio en su dieta.
4. Marisol tiene 12 años. Le gustan mucho los postres, pero su madre le recomienda carne y verduras.
5. Doña Soledad es una mujer de 70 años. No es muy activa y tiene algunos problemas de salud. Necesita comida saludable para cuidar su corazón y su salud en general.

EN CONTEXTO

El siguiente diálogo tiene lugar en el nuevo restaurante **El Criollito** de doña Margarita. Doña Margarita está hablando con sus primeros clientes, Rosa y Simón, y quiere servirles una cena perfecta.

AUDIO CD
CD 2, TRACK 10

Escucha el diálogo e identifica la oración del diálogo que explica las siguientes decisiones.

Modelo A Rosa le gusta sentarse en la terraza.
Rosa dice: «En la terraza. ¡Las flores que tienen allí son muy bonitas!».

1. Simón va a tomar una cerveza.
2. Rosa y Simón van a comer arepas.
3. Rosa va a pedir los calamares fritos.
4. Simón pide un plato del menú.
5. Rosa quiere comer postre.

Doña Margarita: ¡Bienvenidos al Criollito! ¿Quieren sentarse adentro o en la terraza?

Rosa: En la terraza. ¡Las flores que tienen allí son muy bonitas!

Doña Margarita: Gracias. Pasen por aquí, entonces.

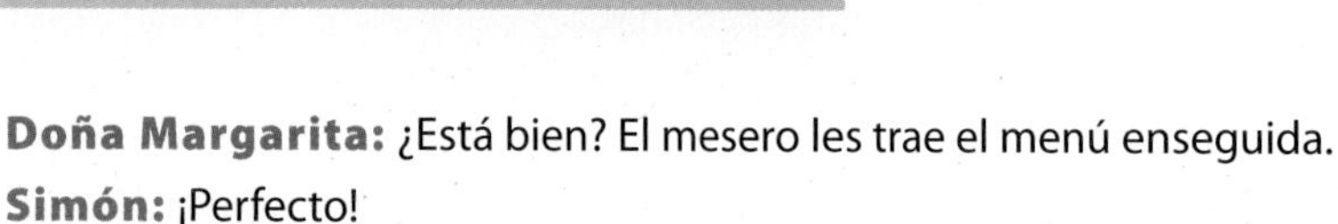

Doña Margarita: ¿Está bien? El mesero les trae el menú enseguida.

Simón: ¡Perfecto!

Comentario cultural Mercal, Venezuela's leading food distributor, is dedicated to giving foods produced in the country priority over imported foods. It is estimated that Venezuela still imports nearly 75 percent of its food. The three major imports are rice, chicken, and beans.

El mesero: ¡Buenas noches! Aquí tienen el menú. ¿Desean tomar algo?

Rosa: Para mí, un jugo de naranja con hielo.

Simón: Y para mí, una cerveza. Me gusta **más** la cerveza **que** el jugo cuando hace un poquito de calor.

El mesero: Muy bien. Seguro que quieren unas arepas para empezar, ¿no? ¡Son **las mejores de toda la ciudad!** Es la especialidad de la casa.

Simón: ¡Cómo no!

Expresiones en contexto

bien cocido *well done*
¡Cómo no! *Of course!*
de vez en cuando *occasionally*
enseguida *right way*
¿Desean tomar algo? *Would you like something to drink?*
¡Están para chuparse los dedos! *They're finger-licking good!*
¡Están riquísimas! *They're delicious!*
mesero(a) *waiter or waitress*
no nos mataría *it wouldn't kill us*
tiene lugar *takes place*
vamos a ver *let's see*
Yo quisiera... *I would like*

El mesero: Aquí están las arepas que **pidieron.**

Simón: ¡Están riquísimas!

Rosa: ¡Están para chuparse los dedos!

El mesero: Están muy frescas. La cocinera **preparó** muchas esta mañana. ¿Quieren pedir algo del menú? Les recomiendo el pabellón criollo.

Comentario cultural Venezuela has a long Caribbean coastline and, therefore, has been strongly influenced in its history, culture, and gastronomy by the Caribbean islands. Some culinary favorites include **arepas** *(meat or cheese-filled cornmeal pockets)*, **caraotas negras** *(black beans)*, **guasacaca** *(avocado salsa)*, **pabellón criollo** *(shredded beef with beans, rice, and plantains)*, and **tajadas de plátano maduro** *(fried ripe plantains)*.

Rosa: Sí. Vamos a ver. Yo quisiera los calamares fritos. ¿Están frescos?

El mesero: Sí, señora. **Recibimos** los mariscos esta mañana. Y los calamares son **los mejores del día.** Seguro que le van a gustar. ¿Y para el señor? ¿El pabellón criollo?

Simón: No, gracias. Hoy quisiera el bistec bien cocido con champiñones.

El mesero: ¿Algo más? ¿Postre? ¿Café?

Simón: Un cafecito y la cuenta, por favor.

Rosa: ¿Por qué **pediste** la cuenta, mi amor? No nos mataría un postre de vez en cuando.

Nota lingüística

In several Latin American countries it is quite common to use the diminutive form when requesting common beverages such as **un cafecito** *(little coffee)* or **una cervecita** *(little beer)*. Also note that in Latin America, it is more appropriate to use **(yo) quisiera...** *(I would like)* when ordering food. In Spain, it is more common to use the more direct present tense form **(yo) quiero...**

Diálogo entre mesero(a) y cliente Trabaja con un(a) compañero(a) de clase. Túrnense para practicar el diálogo que acaban de estudiar en **En contexto.** Deben cambiar las selecciones del menú. Pueden consultar Internet para obtener más ideas. Usen expresiones de **En contexto** como modelo para su diálogo.

Comparatives and superlatives

In this section, you will learn how to make comparative and superlative statements.

I. Comparative statements

English speakers make comparisons by adding the ending *-er* to an adjective (e.g., *warmer*) or by using the words *more* or *less* with an adjective (e.g., *more interesting, less expensive*). Spanish speakers make comparisons in the following manner.

Comparisons of inequality

- Use **más** *(more)* or **menos** *(less)* before an adjective, an adverb, or a noun, and use **que** *(than)* after it.

Making comparisons

más		adjective **(tímido)**		
	+	adverb **(pronto)**	+	que
menos		noun **(hambre)**		

Ana quiere comer **más pronto que** Elena. — *Ana wants to eat **sooner than** Elena.*

Elena tiene **menos hambre que** Matilde. — *Elena is **less hungry than** Matilde.*

- Use **más que** or **menos que** after a verb form.

Lorena come **más que** Roberto. — *Lorena eats **more than** Roberto.*

- Use the preposition **de** to express *than* before a number.

Elena tiene **más de** diez amigos. — *Elena has **more than** ten friends.*

Irregular comparatives

mejor(es)	*better*	**peor(es)**	*worse*
menor(es)	*younger*	**mayor(es)**	*older*

—El tiempo en Caracas es **mejor que** en Maracaibo. — *The weather in Caracas is **better than** in Maracaibo.*

—Sí, y la humedad en Maracaibo es **peor que** en Caracas. — *Yes, and the humidity in Maracaibo is **worse than** in Caracas.*

Elena es **menor que** Roberto, y Lorena es **mayor que** su hermana Matilde. — *Elena is **younger than** Roberto, and Lorena is **older than** her sister Matilde.*

Comparisons of equality

- Use **tan** *(as)* before an adjective or an adverb and **como** *(as)* after it.

		adjective **(nublado)**		
tan	+		+	**como**
		adverb **(frecuentemente)**		

A veces está **tan** nublado en Caracas **como** en Maracaibo. — *Sometimes it is **as** cloudy in Caracas **as** in Maracaibo.*

Además no llueve **tan** frecuentemente en Maracaibo **como** en Mérida. — *Also, it doesn't rain **as** frequently in Maracaibo **as** in Merida.*

Note that **tan** can also be used by itself to show a great degree of a given quality; for example, ¡Qué día **tan** perfecto! *What a perfect day!*

- Use **tanto(a)** *(as much)* or **tantos(as)** *(as many)* before a noun, and **como** *(as)* after it.

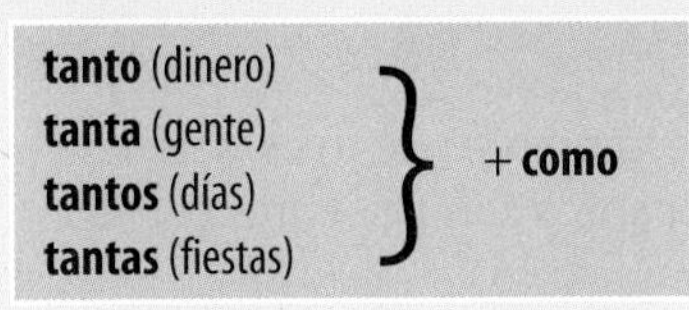

tanto (dinero)
tanta (gente)
tantos (días)
tantas (fiestas)
} + **como**

—¿Hace **tanto** calor en Puerto Ayacucho **como** en Ciudad Guayana? — *Is it **as** hot in Puerto Ayacucho **as** in Ciudad Guayana?*

—Sí, y hay **tantas** tormentas en Puerto Ayacucho **como** en Ciudad Guayana. — *Yes, and there are **as many** storms in Puerto Ayacucho **as** in Ciudad Guayana.*

Tanto(s)/Tanta(s) can also be used without **como** to show a great amount of something; for example, ¡Hace **tanto** calor! *It's so hot!*

- To make comparisons of equality with verbs, use **tanto como** after the verb, followed by the person (or pronoun) that is being compared to the subject.

Tú estudias **tanto como** yo. — *You study **as much as** I.*

II. Superlative statements

English speakers single out someone or something from a group by adding the ending *-est* to an adjective (e.g., *warmest*) or by using the phrases *the most* or *the least* with an adjective (e.g., *the most elegant, the least expensive*).

Spanish speakers form superlatives by using a definite article before the person or thing being compared + **más** *(most)* or **menos** *(least)* + adjective. To introduce the group to which the person or thing is being compared (*the most/least . . . in the class/world/city*, etc.), the preposition **de** + noun is used.

el (sobrino)			
la (familia)		**más**	
	+		+ *adjective* (+ **de** + *noun*)
los (amigos)		**menos**	
las (compañeras)			

Tengo...
la familia más inteligente...
el esposo más guapo...
los amigos más generosos...
de Caracas.

I have . . .
the most intelligent family . . .
the most handsome husband . . .
the most generous friends . . .
in Caracas.

Irregular superlatives

el (la, los, las)	**mejor(es)**	*best*
el (la, los, las)	**mayor(es)**	*oldest*
el (la, los, las)	**peor(es)**	*worst*
el (la, los, las)	**menor(es)**	*youngest*

—¡El Criollito es **el mejor** restaurante **de** Caracas! — *El Criollito is the best restaurant in Caracas!*

—Sí. Y El Mesón es **el peor** restaurante. — *Yes. And El Mesón is the worst restaurant.*

Elena es **la menor de** las niñas. — *Elena is the youngest of the girls.*

Matilde es **la mayor.** — *Matilde is the oldest.*

¡A practicar!

6-7 **¡La mejor comida de la ciudad!** Pensando en los restaurantes de tu ciudad, forma expresiones superlativas para describir los siguientes componentes con los adjetivos dados.

Modelo comida / sana *(healthy)*
El restaurante con la comida más sana es El Gourmet Vegetariano.

1. los meseros / simpático
2. los precios / bajo
3. el ambiente / popular
4. el menú / variado
5. los platos / delicioso
6. En tu opinión, ¿cuál es el mejor restaurante de tu ciudad? ¿Cuál es el peor restaurante?

6-8 **Los intereses de Matilde y Elena** Matilde y Elena tienen muchos intereses en común. Completa las siguientes oraciones apropiadamente, usando **tan, tanto, tanta, tantos** o **tantas.**

Modelo Matilde es *tan* inteligente como Elena.

1. Matilde tiene ______ energía como Elena.
2. Matilde juega ______ como su hermana.
3. Y a Elena le gusta hacer ______ ejercicio como a Matilde.
4. Matilde juega al tenis ______ bien como Elena.
5. También Matilde es ______ activa como Elena.
6. Elena tiene ______ amigos como Matilde.
7. A Elena le gusta ir al cine ______ como a Matilde.

6-9 **El restaurante Las Palmas** Escuchas un anuncio en la radio para el restaurante Las Palmas y decides que es el lugar perfecto para celebrar tu cumpleaños *(birthday)* con tu familia. Escribe cinco cosas que oyes en el anuncio para decirles a tus padres y convencerlos *(convince them)* de que deben hacer la celebración en Las Palmas.

AUDIO CD
CD 2, TRACK 11

1. ______________________
2. ______________________
3. ______________________
4. ______________________
5. ______________________

Workbook *6-4 – 6-8*
Lab Manual *6-4 – 6-6*

¡A conversar!

6-10 Dos cocineros *(cooks)* y tú Imagínate que quieres trabajar en el restaurante de doña Margarita. ¿Cómo te comparas con dos cocineros que ya trabajan allí? Vas a compararte con los dos cocineros, Pablo y Memo, para averiguar *(find out)* qué tienen Uds. en común. Vas a usar construcciones comparativas y construcciones superlativas.

Completa el siguiente cuadro *(table)* y después usa la información para comparar a Pablo con su amigo Memo. Luego compárate con los dos. Hazle las preguntas a un(a) compañero(a) de clase.

Modelo —¿Quién es más joven?
—Pablo es más joven que Memo.
—¿Eres tú menor o mayor que Memo?
—Soy menor que Memo; tengo veinte años.

Persona	Edad	Horas	Experiencia	Intereses
Pablo	23	8 al día	5 años	libros, arte, conciertos
Memo	26	9 al día	5 años	fútbol, tenis, rap, fiestas
Tú	¿?	¿?	¿?	¿?

1. ¿Quién es mayor? ¿Eres tú menor o mayor que Pablo? ¿Cuántos años tienes?
2. ¿Quién tiene más años de experiencia? ¿Tienes tú más o menos años de experiencia que Memo?
3. ¿Quién es más trabajador(a)? ¿Eres tú más o menos trabajador(a) que Memo?
4. ¿A quién le gusta más practicar deportes? ¿Qué deportes practicas tú? ¿Qué otros intereses tienes?

6-11 Lo que me gusta hacer... Usa las siguientes frases para describirle tus gustos y situaciones personales a un(a) compañero(a) de clase. Usa **más... que** o **menos... que** en cada oración. Después, dile a la clase si tú y tu compañero(a) tienen mucho en común.

Modelo Me gusta nadar más (en el invierno/en el verano)

Me gusta nadar más en el invierno que en el verano. ¿Y a ti?
o *Me gusta nadar menos en el invierno que en el verano. ¿Y a ti?*
o *Me gusta nadar más en el verano que en el invierno. ¿Y a ti?*

1. Me gusta caminar más (en el invierno/en el verano)
2. Me gusta dormir más (cuando hace frío/cuando hace calor)
3. Me gusta ducharme más (por las mañanas/por las noches)
4. Me enfermo más (en la primavera/en el otoño)
5. Tengo más dolores de cabeza (durante el semestre/durante las vacaciones)
6. Tomo menos bebidas (cuando hace calor/cuando hace fresco)

6-12 ¿Cuál es el mejor/peor? Trabaja con dos o tres compañeros(as) de clase para elegir tres figuras públicas: un(a) deportista, un(a) actor/actriz, un(a) criminal. Describan a la persona usando el superlativo de tres adjectivos diferentes. Luego, presenten sus figuras a la clase y voten sobre cuál es la mejor o peor persona en cada categoría.

Venezuela

Veamos el video de Venezuela para luego comentarlo.

1. ¿Cómo es la ciudad de Caracas, la capital de Venezuela?
2. Describan la zona colonial.
3. ¿Qué edificios quieres visitar en Caracas: el Nuevo Circo, el Observatorio Cagigal o la Plaza Bolívar?

See the *Workbook,* **Capítulo 6, 6-21 – 6-24** for additional activities.

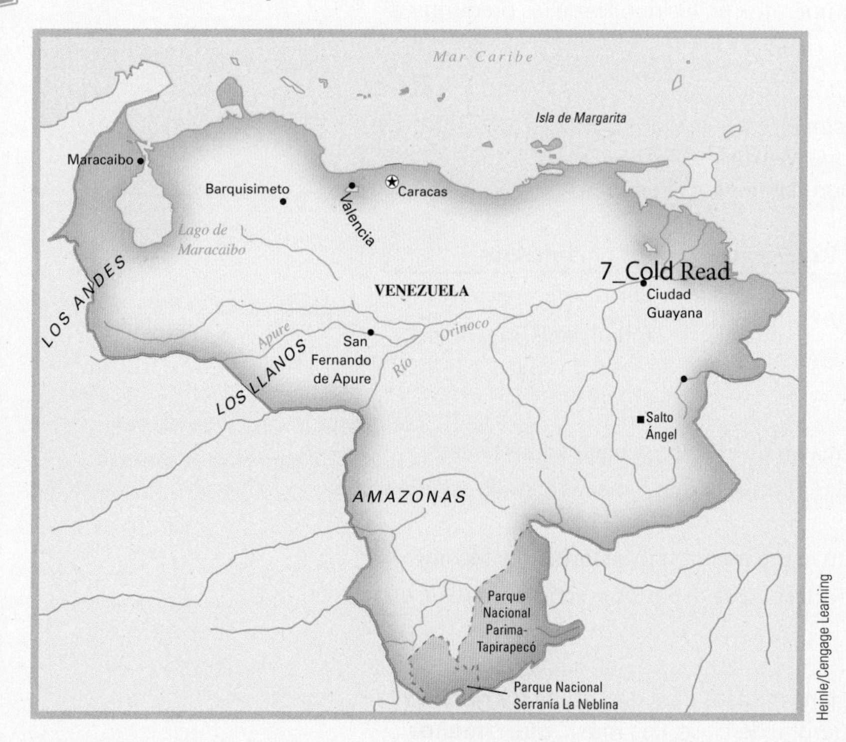

Población: 27.223.228 de habitantes

Área: 912.051 km^2, más de dos veces el tamaño de California

Capital: Caracas (5.254.700 habs.)

Ciudades principales: Maracaibo (2.200.000 habs.); Valencia (1.700.000 habs.); Barquisimeto (1.200.000 habs.)

Moneda: el bolívar

Lenguas: el español y 35 lenguas indígenas

Lugares mágicos En el parque Nacional Canaima está el salto de agua *(waterfall)* más alto del mundo, el Salto Ángel, con 979 metros (3.212 pies) de altura. Los turistas pueden ver el salto desde una avioneta (*small plane*) o pueden hacer una excursión de tres horas por los ríos Carrao y Churún. El Salto Ángel tiene ese nombre en honor al aviador aventurero norteamericano Jimmy Angel, quien reporta ver el salto a las autoridades en 1937. Los indígenas de la zona, los pemones, lo llaman **Churún Merú,** que significa «Salto del lugar más profundo». Para visitar el Parque Nacional Canaima hay que quedarse *(to stay)* en cabañas *(cabins)* rústicas, donde se puede comer pescado originario de la zona, pollo asado y fruta fresca del lugar, así como mangos, bananas, piñas (*pineapples*) y papayas.

¿Conoces otros saltos de agua? ¿Crees que es más interesante ver los saltos de agua desde una avioneta o en una canoa?

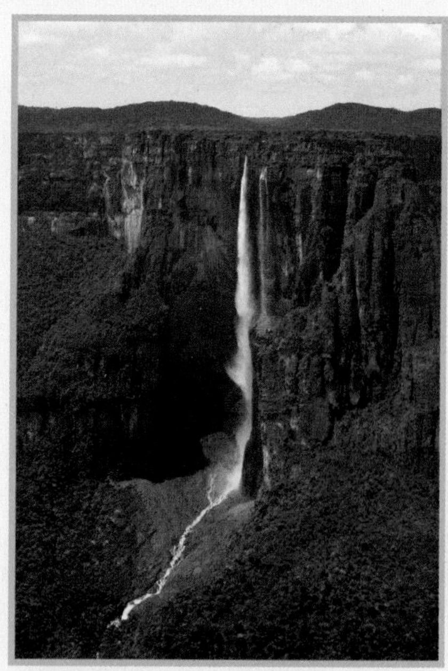

El Salto Ángel (Churún Merú)

 Visit it live on **Google Earth!**

© Marcos Delgado/EFE/Corbis

Penetrable de Jesús Rafael Soto

Artes plásticas Jesús Rafael Soto (1923–2005), artista venezolano, es el creador del arte cinético en 1950. En el arte cinético, las partes de la obra *(work)* tienen movimiento o dan una impresión de movimiento. Soto estudia en la Escuela de Artes en Caracas y sus obras se encuentran en el Museo de Arte Moderno y el Museo Guggenheim en Nueva York y el Centro Georges Pompidou en París, Francia. Soto es famoso por sus esculturas «penetrables» donde las personas pueden caminar y experimentar el movimiento dentro de las esculturas.

¿Te gusta la idea de caminar dentro de una escultura? ¿Qué tipo de arte te gusta más: el cinético o el tradicional?

© Gastromedia / Alamy

La hallaca

Creencias y costumbres La hallaca es un plato típico venezolano en el que se puede notar las presencia de las tres culturas que forman las tradiciones y la historia de Venezuela: la española, la indígena y la africana. La hallaca es una mezcla de carnes de res, de cerdo y de pollo, aceitunas *(olives)* y pasas *(raisins)*, que son los ingredientes que traen los españoles a América. Estas carnes se ponen dentro de una masa de maíz, que es el principal ingrediente indígena. Todo esto va envuelto *(wrapped)* en hojas de plátano *(plantain leaves)*, que es uno de los ingredientes que usan los africanos y los indígenas para envolver sus comidas. La tradición es que todos los miembros de la familia ayudan a hacer las hallacas en diciembre. Las hallacas se comen durante el mes de diciembre hasta el 6 de enero, el Día de los Reyes Magos *(Three Kings Day)*.

¿Existe alguna tradición en tu familia de preparar una comida particular durante una fecha especial? ¿Qué platos preparan?

Ritmos y música La música venezolana tiene una variedad de ritmos, dependiendo de las regiones geográficas. En el oeste del país, en la ciudad de Maracaibo, la gaita es la música tradicional navideña *(Christmas)*. Los instrumentos principales son los tambores *(drums)*, la flauta *(flute)*, el cuatro —una guitarra pequeña con cuatro cuerdas *(strings)*— y las maracas, de influencia africana.

Uno de los mejores grupos de gaitas es Betulio y Maracaibo 15. Vas a escuchar su canción «Aguinaldos venezolanos» del CD *De vuelta a casa* (2005). *Access the iTunes playlist on the **Plazas** website.*

¿Conoces el instrumento venezolano llamado el cuatro? ¿Tocas algún instrumento?

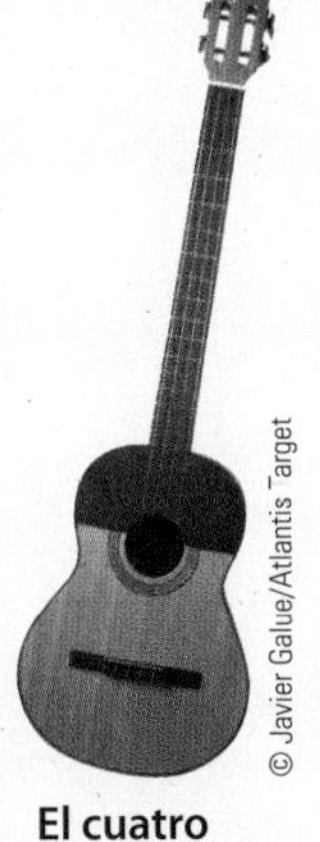
© Javier Galue/Atlantis Target

El cuatro

¡Busquen en Internet

1. Lugares mágicos: el Salto Ángel
2. Artes plásticas: Jesús Rafael Soto
3. Creencias y costumbres: las hallacas
4. Ritmos y música: la gaita venezolana, Betulio y Maracaibo 15

VOCABULARIO 2

El Sr. y la Sra. Tovar cenan en El Mesón de Caracas

In this section, you will learn vocabulary and expressions associated with eating in a restaurant. When you eat in a restaurant, what questions do you ask your server?

Nota lingüística

It is customary in Spanish-speaking countries to say **¡Buen provecho!** when others begin to eat. Another word for **el (la) mesero(a)** es **el (la) camarero(a).**

Las personas

el (la) cliente(a) *client*
el (la) mesero(a) *waiter (waitress)*

Características de la comida

caliente *hot (temperature)*
fresco(a) *fresh*
ligero(a) *light (meal, food)*
pesado(a) *heavy (meal, food)*
rico(a) *delicious*

Verbos

cocinar *to cook*
dejar una (buena) propina *to leave a (good) tip*
pedir (i) *to order (food)*
picar *to eat appetizers; to nibble*
preparar *to prepare*
recomendar (ie) *to recommend*

Expresiones idiomáticas

¡Buen provecho! *Enjoy your meal!*
¡Cómo no! *Of course*
Estoy a dieta. *I'm on a diet.*
Estoy satisfecho(a). *I'm satisfied.*
La cuenta, por favor. *The check, please.*
No puedo más. *I can't (eat) any more.*
¿Qué desean/quieren comer (beber)? *What would you like to eat (to drink)?*
¡Salud! *Cheers!*
Te invito. *It's on me (my treat).*
Yo quisiera... *I would like . . .*

Nota lingüística

Estoy lleno(a) is a less formal way to say **Estoy satisfecho(a).**

¡A practicar!

6-13 ¿Lógico o no? Lee las conversaciones breves entre los meseros y los clientes y decide si cada una es lógica o no. Si no es lógica, cambia la respuesta para completar la conversación de una manera lógica.

Modelo: **Cliente:** *¿Está fresca la langosta?*
Mesero: *Te invito.*
No es lógico. El mesero debe decir *«¡Cómo no! Está muy fresca.»*

1. **Cliente:** ¿Podemos ver el menú?
   Mesero: ¡Salud!
2. **Mesero:** ¿Y para beber?
   Cliente: Las arepas, por favor.
3. **Mesero:** ¿Algo para picar?
   Cliente: Quisiera agua mineral sin gas.
4. **Mesero:** ¿Desean ver la lista de postres?
   Cliente: Ay, no puedo. Estoy a dieta.
5. **Mesero:** ¿Desean algo más?
   Cliente: No, gracias. La cuenta, por favor.

6-14 Un mesero algo *(a bit)* confundido Pepe, el mesero, está un poco confundido. Ayúdalo a poner en orden lógico las frases que les dice a los clientes.

_____ Traigo la cuenta ahora mismo.
_____ ¿Qué quieren comer?
_____ De postre hay helado.
_____ ¿Y para beber?
_____ ¿Dos para cenar?
_____ Les recomiendo los mariscos.
_____ ¡Buenas noches!
_____ ¡Buen provecho!
_____ ¿Desean algo más?
_____ Gracias, señores, y buenas noches.
_____ Aquí tienen el menú.

6-15 Impresiones de Pepe Pepe, el mesero, siempre les sirve a don Fernando y a doña Olga cuando ellos vienen a comer al restaurante El Mesón. Completa el párrafo siguiente sobre sus impresiones de la pareja. Usa las siguientes frases, palabras y expresiones.

yo te invito	ensalada	agua mineral	¿qué desean?	propina
algo ligero	picar	menú	piden	está a dieta

Hola. Yo llevo muchos años trabajando (I have been working many years) *aquí en El Mesón. Conozco bien a don Fernando y a doña Olga: son clientes muy buenos. Siempre les pregunto a ellos: 1. «__________». Don Fernando siempre pide ver el 2. __________. Él siempre pide una cerveza Polar muy fría y 3. __________ para 4. __________. Les gustan mucho los mariscos: casi siempre 5. __________ langosta o pescado. Claro, ¡nuestro restaurante tiene el mejor pescado de Caracas! Como doña Olga es un poco gorda, siempre 6. __________. Por eso, normalmente ella pide 7. __________ para beber y una 8. __________ para comer con su plato principal. Realmente son unas personas especiales y muy románticas. Después de comer, don Fernando siempre le dice de broma* (jokingly) *a su esposa: 9. «__________, cariño». Ellos siempre dejan una buena 10. __________.*

Workbook *6-9 – 6-11*
Lab Manual *6-7 – 6-9*

¡A conversar!

6-16 Una noche en el restaurante Esmeralda Trabajen en grupos para presentar las siguientes escenas en el restaurante:

1. Unos amigos van al restaurante Esmeralda para celebrar el fin del semestre. Quieren empezar con algo para picar y después quieren varios platos, postres y bebidas. Una mujer es un poco quisquillosa *(finicky)*, pero en general les gusta mucho la comida y se divierten en el restaurante.
2. *Los señores Villafranca cenan en el restaurante Esmeralda todos los viernes. Conocen al mesero Luis muy bien y casi siempre (almost always)* piden la especialidad de la casa. Esta noche el señor Villafranca quiere pedir algo diferente, pero no puede decidir qué quiere. Por fin él toma una decisión y le gusta mucho el nuevo plato.
3. *La familia Martín va a cenar en el restaurante Esmeralda. La señora y sus hijos esperan al señor Martín, que no llega a tiempo. Los niños se ponen impacientes pero cuando comen algo, están más contentos y la familia lo pasa bien (has a good time).*

Nota lingüística

Here are some other expressions to talk about food: **¡Qué delicioso!** *(How delicious!)* and **¡Qué sabroso!** *(How tasty!)* While **caliente** means *hot*, it refers to the temperature of something. **Picante** means *hot*, as in *spicy*: **¡Qué picante!** *(How spicy!)*

6-17 Entrevista Trabaja con un(a) compañero(a). Háganse *(Ask one another)* las siguientes preguntas. Después, compartan la información con la clase.

1. Si vas a celebrar un día especial, ¿a qué restaurante prefieres ir? ¿Por qué?
2. Si sales a comer con un grupo de amigos y no tienes mucho dinero, ¿adónde vas? ¿Por qué?
3. ¿Cuál es el restaurante más elegante que conoces? Describe el restaurante, la comida y el servicio.
4. ¿Qué restaurante recomiendas para el desayuno? ¿el almuerzo? ¿la cena? ¿Cuáles son los mejores platos que sirve cada restaurante?
5. ¿Qué restaurante sirve comida muy fresca? ¿comida rica? ¿comida ligera? ¿comida pesada?
6. ¿Trabajas en un restaurante? ¿Tus amigos trabajan en restaurantes? ¿Te gusta el trabajo en un restaurante? ¿Por qué?

Making statements about quantity

In this section, you will learn how to express quantities of foods that you would ask for when shopping or cooking.

I. En el supermercado

Dependiente:	¿En qué puedo servirle?	*How may I help you?*
Cliente:	Quiero 5 **rodajas** de queso blanco.	*I want 5 slices of white cheese*
Dependiente:	¿Le corto el queso en **rodajas finas o gruesas**?	*Shall I cut the cheese for you in thin or thick slices?*
Cliente:	En **rodajas finas,** por favor.	*In thin slices, please.*
Dependiente:	¿Quiere algo más?	*Would you like anything else?*
Cliente:	Sí, necesito medio **kilo** de jamón, también en **rodajas finas.**	*Yes, I also need a half a kilo of ham, also in thin slices.*
Dependiente:	Por supuesto, aquí tiene el queso y el jamón.	*Of course, here is the cheese and the ham.*
Cliente:	Gracias.	*Thanks.*
Dependiente:	A sus órdenes.	*At your service.*

II. En la cocina

Para la receta de flan casero necesitamos los siguientes ingredientes:

1 **lata** de leche condensada	*1 can of condensed milk*
1 **lata** de leche	*1 can of milk*
6 huevos	*6 eggs*
1 **cucharadita** de vainilla	*1 teaspoon of vanilla*
1 **taza** de azúcar hecha caramelo	*1 cup of sugar made into caramel*

Flan casero

III. Más cantidades

una botella *bottle*
una caja *box*
una cucharada *tablespoon*
un galón *one gallon*
un gramo *gram*
una libra *pound*
un litro *liter*
una onza *ounce*
un frasco *jar, pot, jug*
un vaso *glass*

¡A practicar!

6-18 ¿Cuánto compro? Estás en el supermercado y tienes una lista de compras. Usa palabras del vocabulario relacionadas con cantidades lógicas para saber qué cantidad vas a comprar de cada cosa. No repitas información.

1. Una ________ de cereal
2. Dos ________ de refresco (aproximadamente medio *(half a)* galón)
3. Un ________ de azúcar
4. Una ________ de queso
5. Un ________ de comida para bebé *(baby)*
6. Una ________ de sopa
7. Una ________ de vinagre
8. Tres ________ de agua

6-19 Una cena especial Vas a preparar una cena especial para tres amigos. Piensas preparar un entremés, un plato principal y un postre. Decide qué platos vas a hacer y luego haz una lista de los ingredientes que necesitas para preparar cada uno de estos platos. ¡No te olvides *(Don't forget)* de incluir las cantidades de los ingredientes!

Entremés: ________________
1. ________________
2. ________________
3. ________________
4. ________________

Plato principal: ________________
1. ________________
2. ________________
3. ________________
4. ________________

Postre: ________________
1. ________________
2. ________________
3. ________________
4. ________________

Workbook *6-12*
Lab Manual *6-10*

¡A conversar!

6-20 Lista de compras Con un(a) compañero(a), preparen una lista con cosas que compran cada semana en el supermercado para el desayuno, el almuerzo y la cena. Incluyan al menos cuatro artículos para cada comida y las cantidades que compran.

Modelo *Para el desayuno compramos dos litros de leche, un kilo de azúcar, seis huevos y 500 gramos de queso.*
Para el almuerzo...

6-21 Recetas y cantidades Con un(a) compañero(a), inventen dos recetas: una para un plato principal y una para un postre. Digan qué ingredientes necesitan y qué cantidades.

Modelo *Mi comida se llama "pollo con mantequilla". Necesitamos dos kilos de pollo, cien gramos de mantequilla, una cucharada de aceite...*
Mi postre se llama...

6-22 Platos del día Con un(a) compañero(a), hablen sobre lo que comen en su casa todos los días.

Modelo *Generalmente en el desayuno tomo café con leche y como cereal.*

- ¿Qué desayunan?
- ¿Qué almuerzan?
- ¿Qué comen?
- ¿Comen o beben algo entre comidas?

Javier bebe 6 vasos de agua al día. ¿Cuántos bebes tú?

ESTRUCTURA 2

Regular verbs and verbs with spelling changes in the preterite

Spanish speakers use the preterite tense to describe what occurred in the past.

Regular verbs in the preterite

- To form the preterite for most Spanish verbs, add the following endings to the verb stem.

	hablar	comer	vivir
yo	habl**é**	com**í**	viv**í**
tú	habl**aste**	com**iste**	viv**iste**
Ud., él/ella	habl**ó**	com**ió**	viv**ió**
nosotros(as)	habl**amos**	com**imos**	viv**imos**
vosotros(as)	habl**asteis**	com**isteis**	viv**isteis**
Uds., ellos(as)	habl**aron**	com**ieron**	viv**ieron**

Note the identical endings for **-er** and **-ir** verbs.

Mis padres **hablaron** en español con el mesero.
*My parents **spoke** in Spanish with the waiter.*

Ella **comió** mucho ayer.
*She **ate** a lot yesterday.*

- **-ar** and **-er** stem-changing verbs in the present tense have no stem change in the preterite; use the same verb stem as you would for the **nosotros(as)** form.

	pensar	volver
yo	pens**é**	volv**í**
tú	pens**aste**	volv**iste**
Ud., él/ella	pens**ó**	volv**ió**
nosotros(as)	pens**amos**	volv**imos**
vosotros(as)	pens**asteis**	volv**isteis**
Uds., ellos(as)	pens**aron**	volv**ieron**

Yo **pensé** mucho en doña Margarita.
*I **thought** a lot about doña Margarita.*

Volvió a casa a la 1:00.
*She **returned** home at 1:00.*

Verbs with spelling changes in the preterite

- Verbs ending in **-car, -gar,** and **-zar** have a spelling change in the **yo** form of the preterite tense. This change is necessary to maintain the sound of the original consonant.

c changes to **qu**	**g** changes to **gu**	**z** changes to **c**
tocar > to**qué**	llegar > lle**gué**	comenzar > comen**cé**

Yo **llegué** a las 2:00 y **almorcé** con su familia.
*I **arrived** at 2:00 and **had lunch** with his family.*

Toqué la guitarra y **saqué** unas fotos.
*I **played** the guitar and **took** some photos.*

Jugué a las cartas con toda la familia.
*I **played** cards with the whole family.*

- Verbs ending in **-er** and **-ir** that have a vowel before the infinitive ending require the following change in the **Ud./él/ella** and **Uds./ellos/ellas** forms of the preterite tense: the **e** or **i** between the two vowels changes to **y**.

	creer	leer	oír
Ud., él/ella	cre**y**ó	le**y**ó	o**y**ó
Uds., ellos(as)	cre**y**eron	le**y**eron	o**y**eron

Margarita y su esposo Jorge **leyeron** un poco.
*Margarita and her husband Jorge **read** a bit.*

Jorge **oyó** algo raro en la calle.
*Jorge **heard** something strange in the street.*

Nadie le **creyó** el cuento.
*Nobody **believed** his story.*

Uses of the preterite

Spanish speakers use the preterite tense to express the beginning and completion of past actions, conditions, and events. Basically, the preterite is used to tell what did or did not happen or to tell what someone did or did not do. Observe the use of the preterite in the following examples.

Ayer Jorge **se despertó** un poco tarde porque no **oyó** el despertador.
*Yesterday, Jorge **woke up** a little late because he **didn't hear** the alarm clock.*

Margarita **llamó** a su esposo dos veces y finalmente él se levantó.
*Margarita **called** her husband two times and finally he **got up.***

Luego Jorge **se duchó** y **desayunó** con sus tres hijos.
*Then, Jorge **showered** and **ate breakfast** with his three children.*

Here are some common expressions used to refer to the past:

anoche	*last night*
anteayer	*the day before yesterday*
ayer	*yesterday*
la semana pasada	*last week*
el mes pasado	*last month*
el año pasado	*last year*

¿Recuerdas?

Heinle/Cengage Learning

El mesero: Aquí están las arepas que **pidieron.**
Simón: ¡Están riquísimas!
Rosa: ¡Están para chuparse los dedos!
El mesero: Están muy frescas. La cocinera **preparó** muchas esta mañana.

¡A practicar!

6-23 Cómo preparamos las arepas Doña Olga explica cómo ella, su esposo Fernando y sus tres hijos, Alberto, Pedro y Óscar, prepararon las arepas ayer. Escribe su historia con la siguiente información.

Modelo nosotros / entrar / a la cocina / para preparar arepas
Nosotros entramos a la cocina para preparar arepas.

1. mi esposo Fernando / leer / la receta
2. yo / comenzar / a buscar los ingredientes
3. mis hijos Pedro y Alberto / formar / las arepas
4. nosotros / cocinar / las arepas / en el horno
5. mi hijo Óscar / beber / un refresco y no / ayudar
6. yo / sacar / todas las arepas / del horno
7. Óscar, Pedro y Alberto / comer / las arepas / en seguida
8. Óscar / limpiar / la cocina

6-24 Preparaciones para una fiesta Escucha el mensaje telefónico de tu mejor amigo. Acaba de volver del supermercado, donde compró parte de la comida que Uds. necesitan para una fiesta que van a dar el sábado. Mira la lista de comida que Uds. escribieron ayer y marca con X las cosas que tu amigo compró.

AUDIO CD
CD 2, TRACK 12

_______ la carne de res
_______ las papas
_______ el queso
_______ la lechuga
_______ el pan
_______ los champiñones
_______ el tomate
_______ los refrescos
_______ el helado
_______ los camarones

6-25 Un secreto Alberto, el hijo mayor de doña Olga y don Fernando, está secretamente enamorado *(in love)* de Matilde, la hija de doña Margarita. Una noche, él va con sus hermanos a la casa de Matilde y le dan una serenata. Usando los verbos de la lista, completa el siguiente párrafo en el que Matilde describe lo que pasó.

acostarse	descubrir	invitar	llegar
cantar	despertarse	leer	recibir
cerrar	escuchar	llamar	volver

Anoche, yo 1. _______ un poco antes de dormir. A las 11:00, yo 2. _______. ¡Siempre estoy cansada después de trabajar en el restaurante con mamá! Una hora después, a las 12:00, 3. _______. Mi hermana Elena y yo 4. _______ algo fuera de la casa. Cuando yo 5. _______ a la ventana, 6. _______ a Óscar, Alberto y Pedro. ¡Qué sorpresa! Bueno. La semana pasada, yo 7. _______ un mensaje electrónico de Alberto en que él me hablaba de su amor por mí. Y ayer, él me 8. _______ por teléfono y me 9. _______ a cenar con él. ¡Ay, ay, ay! ¡Yo no quiero ser la novia de Alberto! Pero anoche, él y sus dos hermanos me 10. _______ una canción de amor. Elena y yo 11. _______ la ventana y 12. _______ a acostarnos. ¡Esos muchachos!

Workbook *6-13 – 6-16*
Lab Manual *6-11 – 6-13*

¡A conversar!

6-26 Lo que yo hice Dile a otro(a) compañero(a) de clase lo que tú hiciste *(you did)* la semana pasada. A continuación hay varias posibilidades que puedes usar si las necesitas. Luego comparte con la clase la información que tienes de tu compañero(a).

Modelo levantarse tarde
Yo me levanté tarde.

1. **En el trabajo...**
   a. no trabajar mucho
   b. recibir un cheque
   c. hablar con mi jefe(a)
   d. conocer a otro(a) empleado(a)
   e. ¿?
2. **En la universidad...**
   a. jugar a un deporte
   b. comer en la cafetería
   c. aprender mucho español
   d. tomar un examen difícil
   e. ¿?
3. **En el restaurante...**
   a. pedir algo para picar
   b. beber agua mineral
   c. comer pescado frito
   d. pagar la cuenta
   e. ¿?

6-27 Ayer yo... ¿Qué comió tu compañero(a) ayer? Pregúntale qué comió y después cuéntale *(tell him/her)* lo que tú comiste. Pide muchos detalles sobre lo que comió, con quién, cuánto, a qué hora, dónde, si lo preparó él/ella, etcétera.

Modelo el desayuno
—¿Qué comiste para el desayuno?
—Comí cereal con leche.

1. el desayuno
2. el almuerzo
3. la cena

6-28 ¿Quién...? Tienes dos minutos para buscar a alguien de tu clase que haya hecho *(has done)* las siguientes cosas. Después de encontrar a alguien para una categoría, pídele que firme *(sign)* la actividad en tu papel. Al final, cuéntales a tus compañeros(as) de clase lo que acabas de descubrir.

Modelo comer camarones ayer
Tú: *Bonnie, ¿comiste camarones ayer?*
Bonnie: *Sí, comí camarones ayer.* (Bonnie signs next to the activity.)
o *No, no comí camarones ayer.* (Bonnie doesn't sign and you look for someone else.)
Al final: *Bonnie (no) comió camarones ayer...*

1. comer una hamburguesa anteayer: ________________
2. oír música venezolana alguna vez: ________________
3. leer una receta en Internet la semana pasada: ________________
4. tocar la guitarra anoche: ________________
5. llegar tarde a clase el mes pasado: ________________
6. pagar la cuenta en un restaurante ayer: ________________

Verbs with stem changes in the preterite

Spanish -**ir** verbs that have a stem change in the present tense also have a stem change in the third-person singular and plural forms (**Ud./él/ella** and **Uds./ellos/ellas**) of the preterite. In these cases, **e** becomes **i**, and **o** becomes **u**. Remember, stem-changing -**ar** and -**er** verbs do not show stem changes in the preterite.

servir *(to serve)*

Present (i)		Preterite (i)	
sirvo	servimos	serví	servimos
sirves	servís	serviste	servisteis
sirve	sirven	sirvió	sirvieron

divertirse *(to have fun)*

Present (ie)		Preterite (i)	
me divierto	nos divertimos	me divertí	nos divertimos
te diviertes	os divertís	te divertiste	os divertisteis
se divierte	se divierten	se divirtió	se divirtieron

dormir *(to sleep)*

Present (ue)		Preterite (u)	
duermo	dormimos	dormí	dormimos
duermes	dormís	dormiste	dormisteis
duerme	duermen	durmió	durmieron

Here are other -**ir** stem-changing verbs that exhibit the same changes as the three verbs shown above. Many of these you have already learned. Note below that the first vowel(s) in the parentheses indicate(s) the stem change in the present tense, and the second vowel indicates the stem change in the preterite.

conseguir (i, i) to get, obtain
despedir(se) (i, i) (de) to say good-bye (to)
dormirse (ue, u) to fall asleep
morir(se) (ue, u) to die
pedir (i, i) to request, order; to ask for
preferir (ie, i) to prefer
reírse (i, i) to laugh
sentirse (ie, i) to feel
sonreír (i, i) to smile
sugerir (ie, i) to suggest
vestirse (i, i) to get dressed

To form the third-person forms of **sonreír**, drop the **i** in the stem before adding the ending (**sonrió, sonrieron**). Similarly, the third-person forms of **reírse** are **se rio** and **se rieron**. Note, however, that **se rio** does not carry a written accent on the **o**. (In 1999, the **Real Academia Española** introduced a spelling convention in which one-syllable words should not carry written accents.)

¡A practicar!

6-29 Unas vacaciones para Julio Julio es el gerente *(manager)* del Restaurante del Lago, en Maracaibo, y normalmente va de vacaciones a Caracas, la capital. Él nos cuenta qué pasa en su viaje. Cambia las oraciones del presente al pasado para indicar lo que pasó en su último viaje

Modelo Consigo un boleto *(ticket)* de avión para Caracas.
Conseguí un boleto de avión para Caracas.

1. Cuando llego al aeropuerto, los agentes me piden el boleto.
2. Al llegar a Caracas, prefiero ir a la Casa de Bolívar y al Capitolio Nacional primero.
3. Varias personas me sugieren unas discotecas en el distrito Las Mercedes.
4. Me visto con chaqueta, pero sin corbata para ir a las discotecas.
5. Me siento cansado cuando vuelvo a mi hotel y me duermo muy rápido.

6-30 Una pequeña fiesta de doña Margarita y don Jorge El sábado pasado doña Margarita y don Jorge hicieron una fiesta en su apartamento de Altamira, en Caracas, para celebrar su aniversario con unos amigos. Doña Margarita describe los preparativos y lo que pasó en la fiesta.

El sábado durante el día, nosotros ______________ *(1. empezar) a prepararnos para la fiesta. Yo fui* (I went) *a hacer las compras para la comida.*

A las 7:00, Jorge y yo nos duchamos y luego ______________ *(2. vestirse). Yo* ______________ *(3. vestirse) con un vestido largo y Jorge también* ______________ *(4. vestirse) elegantemente. A las 9:30 de la noche llegaron los primeros invitados. Yo* ______________ *(5. servir) unas empanadas de carne y unas arepas de queso. Todos* ______________ *(6. divertirse) mucho en la fiesta.*

Cultura

Apartments in Altamira are very nice because of their proximity to El Ávila. This hill protects the city of Caracas from the winds.

Workbook *6-17 – 6-20*
Lab Manual *6-14 – 6-16*

¡A conversar!

6-31 Una cena memorable en un restaurante inolvidable Pregúntale a un(a) compañero(a) de clase sobre una cena especial. Luego descríbele a la clase las experiencias de tu compañero(a).

1. ¿Dónde comiste? ¿Quiénes comieron contigo? ¿Por qué decidieron ir a ese restaurante? ¿Qué platos recomendó el mesero? ¿Comieron entremeses? ¿Qué plato principal pediste tú y qué platos principales pidieron las otras personas? ¿Qué bebieron?
2. ¿Comiste en un restaurante grande o en un restaurante pequeño? ¿A qué hora llegaste (llegaron Uds.) al restaurante? ¿Se divirtieron tú y tus amigos? ¿Se rieron mucho durante la comida? ¿Pediste algo especial de postre?
3. ¿Después de cuánto tiempo volviste a casa? ¿A qué hora te acostaste cuando llegaste a casa? ¿Te sentiste contento(a) después de la cena? ¿Por qué? ¿Te dormiste inmediatamente o no?

6-32 Un restaurante nuevo Trabajen en grupos de tres o cuatro estudiantes para crear y presentar una escena sobre la primera noche con clientes en un restaurante nuevo. Escojan a diferentes personas del grupo para hacer las siguientes actividades. Dramaticen *(Act out)* la escena mientras varias personas del grupo se turnan para describir lo que pasó. ¡Claro que la narración tiene que ser en el pretérito!

Los clientes: llegar, sentarse, pedir el menú

El mesero: sonreír, sugerir bebidas

Los clientes: pedir bebidas y comidas

Un(a) cliente: sentirse mal, salir

El mesero: servir bebidas y comidas

Los clientes: comer, divertirse

Un(a) cliente: pedir la cuenta

Los clientes: despedirse, volver a casa

Heinle/Cengage Learning

¿Qué vas a cocinar? En este segmento del video, Valeria decide sorprender a los muchachos con una cena especial. Desafortunadamente, no obtiene los resultados deseados.

Antes de ver

Expresiones útiles The following are some new expressions you will hear in the video.

A ver	*Let's see*
¿Yo qué sé?	*What do I know?*
Se hace lo que se puede	*One does what one can*
quemarse	*to burn*
encontrar	*to find*

Enfoque estructural The following is Valeria's testimonial at the end of the video segment, featuring several preterite-tense verbs.

La cena **resultó** todo un desastre. Los chiles **se** me **quemaron** y el queso que **usé** estaba muy salado. Le **eché** mucho picante a la salsa. Estaba todo horrible. Pero a pesar de todo, Antonio **fue** *(was)* muy cortés y **se comió** todo un chile relleno...

1. **Recordemos** ¿Cómo describes algo que pasó en el pasado? Imagina que quieres contar un incidente cómico/desastroso *(disastrous)* que te pasó en un restaurante elegante. Describe por lo menos tres cosas que ocurrieron durante la comida. ¿Dejaste una buena propina? ¿Saliste del restaurante sin pagar la cuenta?
2. **Practiquemos** Trabaja con un(a) compañero(a) de clase e identifica el sujeto *(the subject)* para cada verbo **en letra negrita** en la anécdota de Valeria. Luego, identifica tres errores que cometió Valeria en la cocina y explícaselos a tu compañero(a).
3. **Charlemos** ¿Recuerdas la última vez *(last time)* que cocinaste algo y no salió bien? Explica ese incidente a un(a) compañero(a) de clase, indicando los errores que cometiste. Luego, eschucha lo que dice tu compañero y explícaselo a otros compañeros de la clase. ¿Quién es el(la) peor cocinero(a) de la clase?

Después de ver

1. Una cena típica mexicana Completa el siguiente párrafo con el pretérito de los verbos apropiados de la lista para describir lo que pasó cuando Valeria intentó *(tried)* preparar algo típico mexicano para sorprender *(to surprise)* a Antonio.

comer	comprar	decidir	empezar	encontrar
leer	volver	quemarse	salir	

Un día, Valeria 1. ________ sorprender a los chicos con una cena típica mexicana. Alejandra y Valeria 2. ________ libros de recetas y Alejandra 3. ________ una receta de chiles rellenos al horno. Las chicas 4. ________ los ingredientes en el mercado, 5. ________ a la Hacienda Vista Alegre y Valeria 6. ________ a cocinar. Desafortunadamente, ¡Valeria no es muy buena cocinera! Los chiles 7. ________ y la cena fue *(was)* un desastre. Antonio 8. ________ un poco, pero al final todos 9. ________ a un restaurante.

2. La lista de ingredientes ¿Cuáles son los ingredientes que usó Valeria? Mira la siguiente lista y pon una «X» para indicar los ingredientes que mencionó. Compara tus respuestas con las de un(a) compañero(a). ¿Se acordaron de todo?

Ingredientes para los chiles rellenos al horno

________ chiles poblanos

________ camarones

________ aceite

________ arroz blanco guisado

________ crema

________ vinagre

________ cebollitas de cambray

________ champiñones

________ sal

________ jamón

________ caldillo de jitomate

________ queso añejo

Heinle/Cengage Learning

Entre nosotros ¿Cuál es tu cena ideal? Imagina que puedes pedir cualquier cosa *(anything)* sin preocuparte por el precio o la preparación. ¿Tienes un restaurante favorito adonde quieres ir, o prefieres que alguien cocine algo en casa? ¿Pides algo para empezar? ¿Tienes un postre favorito? ¿Qué quieres beber? Comparte tu menú ideal con un(a) compañero(a) de clase.

Presentaciones Con dos compañero(a)s de clase, escribe una escena corta en la que una pareja va a cenar a un restaurante elegante. Si eres el/la mesero/a, usa los menus de Entre nosotros. ¿Qué vas a pedir? ¿Vas a pedir algo para picar? ¿Vas a probar la especialidad de la casa? ¿Quieres ver la lista de postres? Luego, presenta la escena a la clase.

See the *Lab Manual,* **Capítulo 6, 6-18– 6-19** for additional activities.

Antes de leer

Strategy: Improving your reading efficiency: Organizational features of a passage, cognates, background knowledge and skimming

Reading efficiently involves a bit of guessing. By considering the organizational features of a passage, you can often make intelligent guesses as to the content of a passage before reading it. You should use all of the information available to you—cognates, titles, subtitles (if present), pictures, photos, and personal knowledge. You should also skim through the passage before closely reading it in order to ascertain the gist of the reading.

Identify the organizational features of the reading selection to answer the following questions.

1. What is the title of this selection?
2. What do you see in the photo? Describe the person.
3. What would you guess this selection to be about?
4. What do you know about food from Venezuela?

Now, skim the passage to answer these questions.

5. Can you find four cognates and their meanings?
6. Who is the selection about?
7. What is the purpose of the selection?

Doña Bárbara en el cine

Doña Bárbara

Primera parte: Capítulo VI: El recuerdo de Asdrúbal

... doña Bárbara acaba de sentarse a la mesa...

... Doña Bárbara come acompañada de Balbino Paiba, persona con quien [Melquíades] no simpatiza. Trata [Melquíades] de revolverse *(tries to turn around)*, a tiempo que ella le dice:

—Entra, Melquíades.

—Yo vuelvo más tarde. Siga comiendo tranquila.

Y Balbino, con sorna *(irony, sarcasm)* y a la vez que se enjuaga *(wipes away)* a manotadas los gruesos bigotes *(mustache)* impregnados del caldo grasiento *(greasy broth)* de las sopas, dice:

—Entre, Melquíades. No tenga miedo, que aquí no hay perros. [...]

[Melquíades] saca varias monedas de oro *(gold coins)*, que luego pone apiladas en la mesa diciendo:

—Cuente a ver si está completo.

Balbino las mira de soslayo *(sideways)*, y aludiendo a la costumbre de doña Bárbara de enterrar *(to bury)* todo el oro que le caía *(would fall into)* en las manos, exclama:

—¿Morocotas? *(gold coins)* ¡Ojos que te vieron!

Y sigue masticando *(chewing)* el trozo de carne que le llena la boca pero sin apartar de las monedas la codiciosa *(greedy)* mirada.

Después de leer

A escoger Lee el fragmento de la novela nuevamente para responder las siguientes preguntas.

1. Doña Bárbara acaba de...
   a. pensar en Melquíades
   b. conversar con Balbino
   c. sentarse a la mesa
2. La comida principal en este fragmento está compuesta de...
   a. sopa y pollo
   b. sopa y carne
   c. sopa y pescado
3. Melquíades tiene...
   a. tanto miedo como Balbino de doña Bárbara
   b. más miedo que Balbino de doña Bárbara
   c. menos miedo que Balbino de doña Bárbara
4. Doña Bárbara esconde *(hides)* sus morocotas o monedas de oro en...
   a. la tierra
   b. el banco
   c. la cama

¿Cierto o falso? Indica si las siguientes oraciones son **ciertas** *(true)* o **falsas** *(false)*. Corrige las oraciones falsas.

1. ______ Melquíades respeta y no quiere molestar a doña Bárbara en el momento de la comida.
2. ______ Balbino se limpió la grasa de la sopa de los bigotes.
3. ______ Melquíades saca varias monedas de oro y luego cuenta las monedas enfrente de doña Bárbara.
4. ______ Balbino no ve las morocotas y sigue comiendo la carne tranquilamente.

Análisis Con un compañero(a) de clase responde las siguientes preguntas.

1. ¿Cuándo se usa el título **doña**? Si no lo recuerdan, miren el **Comentario cultural** de la página 55.
2. ¿Por qué Melquíades no quiere molestar a doña Bárbara?
3. ¿Por qué Melquíades quiere que doña Bárbara cuente *(counts)* las morocotas de oro?
4. ¿Qué actitud muestra doña Bárbara al enterrar sus morocotas de oro?
5. Después de leer este fragmento, ¿qué idea tienen de doña Bárbara?

¡A escribir! Con dos compañeros de clase, imaginen que tienen que escribir una reseña *(review)* corta de 4 ó 5 líneas para el periódico de la universidad y describir la película Doña Bárbara basándose en la foto y en la descripción de la comida. ¿Cómo es doña Bárbara? ¿Por qué la llaman "doña" si no es muy mayor? ¿Es rica o pobre?

Strategy: Adding details to a paragraph

In **Capítulo 4,** you learned how to write a topic sentence for a paragraph. The other sentences in the paragraph should contain details that develop the main idea stated in the topic sentence. The following procedure will help you develop a well-written paragraph in Spanish.

1. Write a topic sentence about a specific subject.
2. List some details that develop your topic sentence.
3. Cross out any details that are unrelated to the topic.
4. Number the remaining details in a clear, logical order.
5. Write the first draft of a paragraph based on your work.
6. Cross out any ideas that do not contribute to the topic.
7. Write the second draft of your paragraph as clearly as possible.

Read the topic sentence below and then read the sentences that follow it. Indicate if each sentence on the list adds appropriate details based on the topic sentence or not.

Oración principal: Mi restaurante favorito es Chez Claude.

Detalles:	**¿Oración relacionada?**	
El restaurante Chez Claude sirve comida francesa.	Sí	No
Mis amigos y yo comemos en casa a veces.	Sí	No
Chez Claude tiene muchos tipos de refrescos.	Sí	No
Los precios son altos, pero la comida es deliciosa.	Sí	No

Task: Writing a restaurant review

You will now write a brief review of your favorite restaurant, being careful to include only pertinent details. Use the strategies you have practiced and follow the directions below.

Paso 1 ¿Cuál es tu restaurante favorito? Escribe un párrafo sobre tu restaurante favorito siguiendo el procedimiento descrito anteriormente.

Paso 2 Ahora trabaja con un(a) compañero(a) de clase. Uds. deben...

- eliminar los detalles que no estén relacionados con la oración principal.
- añadir *(add)* unos detalles, si es necesario.
- corregir los errores de vocabulario, de gramática o de ortografía *(spelling)*.

Paso 3 Intercambia tu reseña con otros compañeros de clase. Lee los párrafos de varios estudiantes e identifica algunos restaurantes que quieras visitar.

Communicative Goals:

- Communicate about foods, beverages and dining
- Make comparisons and express superlatives
- Order food and beverages in a restaurant
- Communicate about past events and actions

Paso 1

Review the Communicative Goals for **Capítulo 6** and determine if you are able to accomplish the goals. If you are not certain that you have achieved all of the goals, review the pertinent portions of the chapter.

Paso 2

Look at the components of a conversation which addresses the communicative goals for this chapter. The percentages will help you evaluate your ability to successfully participate in the conversation that is featured below. Your instructor may use the same rubric to assess your oral performance.

Components of the conversation	%
☐ Greetings, questions and answers about a beverage order	10
☐ Information about a daily special and question about ordering a meal	10
☐ Statement of food and/or beverages consumed yesterday and desire to order something different today	20
☐ Comparison of two items on the menu	20
☐ Placing of order and proper response	10
☐ Question about desire to order additional items and proper response	10
☐ Request of check and positive comment	10
☐ Appropriate conclusion of the conversation	10

En acción Role-play a conversation that might take place between a diner and a server in a restaurant. Follow the steps below to carry out the conversation with a partner. After you have executed the conversation, switch roles and change as many details as possible.

1. The server greets the diner and asks what he (she) would like to drink; the diner responds.
2. The server describes a daily special and asks what the diner would like to order.
3. The diner states what he (she) ate or drank yesterday and indicates that he (she) prefers something different today.
4. The server suggests two items on the menu, the diner asks a question about how the two items compare to one another, and the server responds.
5. The diner orders at least three items, the server responds and departs to place the order.
6. Later the server returns to ask if the diner would like to order more food or drink.
7. The diner declines to order more but makes a positive comment about the food or the dining experience and then requests the check.
8. The server presents the check, thanks the diner and ends the conversation appropriately.

¡A REPASAR!

Comparisons of inequality

- Use **más** or **menos** before an adjective, an adverb, or a noun, and **que** after it.
- Use **más que** or **menos que** after a verb form.
- Irregular comparatives
  mejor(es) **peor(es)**
  mayor(es) **menor(es)**

¡A recordar! 1 What preposition is used before a number in a comparison of inequality?

Comparisons of equality

- Use **tan** before an adjective or an adverb and **como** after it.
- Use **tanto(o)** or **tantos(as)** before a noun, and **como** after it.

¡A recordar! 2 How can one change a comparison of equality to one of inequality? When would one use **tanto(s)/tanta(s)** without **como?**

Superlative statements

Superlatives are formed by using a definite article before the person or thing being compared + **más** or **menos** + an adjective. To introduce the group to which the person or thing is being compared, the preposition **de** + noun is used.

¡A recordar! 3 What are the four irregular superlative forms?

Verbs regular in the preterite

To form the preterite for most Spanish verbs, add the following endings to the verb stem.

	hablar	comer	vivir
yo	habl**é**	com**í**	viv**í**
tú	habl**aste**	com**iste**	viv**iste**
Ud., él, ella	habl**ó**	com**ió**	viv**ió**
nosotros(as)	habl**amos**	com**imos**	viv**imos**
vosotros(as)	habl**asteis**	com**isteis**	viv**isteis**
Uds., ellos(as)	habl**aron**	com**ieron**	viv**ieron**

¡A recordar! 4 Do **-ar** and **-er** stem-changing verbs in the present tense have stem changes in the preterite? What spelling change in the **yo** form do preterite tense verbs ending in **-car, -gar,** and **-zar** have? For verbs ending in **-ir** and **-er** that have a vowel before the infinitive ending, what changes are required in the **usted/él/ella** and **ustedes/ellos/ellas** forms of the preterite tense?

Verbs with stem changes in the preterite

Spanish **-ir** verbs that have a stem change in the present tense also have a stem change in the third-person singular and plural forms **usted/él/ella** and **ustedes/ellos/ellas** of the preterite. In these cases **e** becomes **i**, and **o** becomes **u**.

¡A recordar! 5 How many Spanish **-ir** verbs can you think of that have stem changes in the third-person singular and plural forms of the preterite?

Actividad 1 ¡A emparejar! Escoge la frase más apropiada de la segunda columna para cada comparación de la primera columna.

1. El mesero Raúl tiene 23 años y el mesero Gabriel tiene 21 años. Raúl es ________.
2. Este restaurante es malo pero el otro es terrible. El otro es ________.
3. El Criollito tiene 5 estrellas, Tarzilandia tiene 4 y Las palmas tiene 3. El Criollito es ________.
4. Gabriel tiene 21 años y su hermano tiene 25. Gabriel es ________.
5. Las arepas de El Criollito son riquísimas. Son ________.

a. el mejor
b. mayor
c. menor
d. las mejores de la ciudad
e. peor que este

Actividad 2 Comparaciones Completa las frases para comparar las siguientes comidas y bebidas.

1. las bananas + las manzanas: Matilde cree que las bananas son ________ deliciosas ________ las manzanas.
2. el jugo = la leche: Pablo dice que el jugo es ________ importante ________ la leche.
3. las papas fritas – la lechuga: El médico insiste en que las papas fritas son ________ nutritivas ________ la lechuga.
4. el bistec = la langosta: En este restaurante, el bistec es ________ caro ________ la langosta.
5. ensaladas = postres: En el menú, hay ________ ensaladas ________ postres.

Actividad 3 Más comparaciones Ahora compara a las siguientes personas.

1. María trabaja mucho. Pablo trabaja mucho.
   ____
2. Tú cocinas mal. Alicia cocina bien. ________________
   ____
3. Felipe bebe 3 litros de agua al día. Sandra bebe 1 litro de agua al día. ________________________
   ____
4. Mi hermano estudia todos los días. Yo estudio todos los días. ________________________________
5. Los niños duermen 8 horas. Sus padres duermen 6 horas. ________________________________
   ____

Actividad 4 ¿Qué pasó? Escoge la respuesta correcta para cada oración para saber qué pasó en la fiesta. Presta atención al contexto para escoger el verbo lógico y la forma apropiada.

1. Yo ______ unas decoraciones muy bonitas para la fiesta.

   a. conseguí c. sonreí
   b. consiguió d. sonreíste

2. Mi amiga Verónica preparó y ______ comida muy rica.

   a. serví c. se sintió
   b. sirvió d. se sintieron

3. Pablo contó chistes *(jokes)* pero tú no ______. ¿Por qué?

   a. sugerí c. se rio
   b. sugirió d. te reíste

4. Muchas personas comieron su plato de comida y ______ más.

   a. pidieron c. se despidieron
   b. pedí d. se despidió

5. Una persona ______ en el sofá, pero se despertó un poco después.

   a. se vistió c. se durmió
   b. me vestí d. te dormiste

Actividad 5 Una noche en el restaurante Cambia cada verbo al pretérito para narrar la historia de una cena memorable.

Mi familia (1. come) ______ en Tarzilandia. Mi madre (2. empieza) ______ con unas arepas y vino tinto, mi padre (3. bebe) ______ una cerveza y mis hermanos menores (4. toman) ______ jugo. (5. Decido) ______ probar un mojito. El cocinero (6. prepara) ______ un plato especial para nuestra familia y a todos nos (7. gusta) ______ mucho. (8. Hablamos) ______ mucho y (9. comemos) ______ toda la comida. Sólo mi padre (10. come) ______ un postre. (11. Camino) ______ al apartamento de mi amigo después, pero los otros (12. vuelven) ______ a casa en coche. Mi amigo y yo (13. bailamos) ______ en la discoteca por varias horas.(14. Llego) ______ a casa muy tarde y (15. entro) ______ sin hacer ruido *(without making noise)* para no despertar a mis padres y mis hermanos.

Actividad 6 Un día en Caracas Completa el siguiente párrafo con la forma correcta del pretérito de cada verbo.

Enviar | Guardar | Archivos

Mis amigos y yo ______ (1. pasar) un día estupendo ayer. Yo ______ (2. despertar) a mi compañera de cuarto a las ocho y ella ______ (3. vestirse) rápidamente. Ella ______ (4. pasar) la aspiradora y nosotras ______ (5. limpiar) toda la casa. A las diez mi primo Arturo ______ (6. llegar) de Valencia. Él ______ (7. conocer) a los otros residentes de la casa y todos nosotros ______ (8. hablar) de muchas cosas diferentes. Más tarde nosotros ______ (9. salir) para el centro de Caracas. En un café, algunas personas ______ (10. pedir) arepas. Varias personas ______ (11. beber) café, pero yo ______ (12. pedir) un refresco. Arturo ______ (13. divertirse) mucho hasta que él ______ (14. despedirse) de nosotros a la medianoche. ¿ ______ (15. divertirse) tú ayer? Espero que sí. Hasta pronto.

Refrán

Heinle/Cengage Learning

______ (*Stomach*) lleno, ______ (*heart*) contento.

VOCABULARIO ESENCIAL

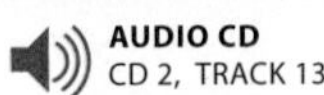
AUDIO CD
CD 2, TRACK 13

PERSONAL TUTOR

Las comidas	*Meals*
el almuerzo	lunch
la cena	dinner
el desayuno	breakfast

Los entremeses y otras comidas	*Appetizers and other foods*
las arepas	cornmeal pockets
el arroz	rice
la ensalada	salad
el huevo duro	hard-boiled egg
el jamón	ham
el pan (tostado)	(toasted) bread
el queso	cheese
la sopa	soup

Los platos principales	*Main dishes*
el bistec	steak
los calamares (fritos)	(fried) calamari
los camarones	shrimp
la carne (de res)	meat (beef)
la chuleta (de cerdo)	(pork) chop
la hamburguesa	hamburger
la langosta	lobster
los mariscos	shellfish, seafood
el pavo	turkey
el pescado	fish
el pollo (asado)	(roasted) chicken
el sándwich	sandwich

Los postres	*Desserts*
el flan (casero)	(homemade) caramel custard
el helado	ice cream

Las bebidas	*Beverages*
el agua (f.) mineral sin/ con gas	(non)carbonated mineral water
el café	coffee
la cerveza	beer
el jugo de fruta	fruit juice
la leche	milk
el refresco	soft drink
el té (helado)	(iced) tea
el vino (blanco, tinto)	(white, red) wine

Las frutas y verduras	*Fruits and vegetables*
la banana	banana
los champiñones	mushrooms
la lechuga	lettuce
la manzana	apple
la naranja	orange
las papas (fritas)	(French fried) potatoes
el tomate	tomato

Los condimentos	*Condiments*
el aceite	oil
el azúcar	sugar
la mantequilla	butter
la pimienta	pepper
la sal	salt
la salsa	sauce
el vinagre	vinegar

El restaurante	*The restaurant*
Sustantivos	
el (la) cliente(a)	client
la cuenta	check, bill
la especialidad de la casa	house specialty
el menú	menu
el (la) mesero(a)	waiter (waitress)
Adjetivos	
caliente	hot (temperature)
fresco(a)	fresh
ligero(a)	light (meal, food)
pesado(a)	heavy (meal, food)
rico(a)	delicious
Verbos	
almorzar (ue)	to have (eat) lunch
cenar	to have (eat) dinner
cocinar	to cook
dejar (una) propina	to leave a tip
desayunar	to have (eat) breakfast
pedir (i, i)	to order (food)
picar	to eat appetizers; to nibble
preparar	to prepare
recomendar (ie)	to recommend
Expresiones idiomáticas	
¡Buen provecho!	Enjoy your meal!
¡Cómo no!	Of course!
Estoy a dieta.	I'm on a diet.
Estoy satisfecho(a).	I'm satisfied. I'm full.
La cuenta, por favor.	The check, please.
No puedo (comer) más.	I can't (eat) any more.
¿Qué desean/quieren comer(beber)?	What would you like to eat (to drink)?
¡Salud!	Cheers!
Te invito.	It's on me (my treat).
Yo quisiera...	I would like . . .

La mesa	*The table*
la copa	goblet, wine glass
la cuchara	spoon
el cuchillo	knife
el plato	plate
la servilleta	napkin
la taza	cup
el tenedor	fork
el vaso	glass

Las medidas	*Measurements*
una botella	bottle
una caja	box
una cucharada	tablespoon
una cucharadita	teaspoon
un frasco	jar, pot, jug
un galón	gallon
un gramo	gram
un kilogramo (kilo)	kilogram
una lata	can, tin
una libra	pound
un litro	liter
una onza	ounce
una rodaja	slice

Otros verbos	
conseguir (i, i)	to get, obtain
despedir(se) (i, i) (de)	to say good-bye (to)
divertirse (ie, i)	to have fun
dormirse (ue, u)	to fall asleep
morir(se) (ue, u)	to die
pedir (i, i)	to order; to ask for
preferir (ie, i)	to prefer
reírse (i, i)	to laugh
sentirse (ie, i)	to feel
servir (i, i)	to serve
sonreír (i, i)	to smile
sugerir (ie, i)	to suggest
vestirse (i, i)	to get dressed

Expresiones de tiempo	
anoche	last night
anteayer	the day before yesterday
el año pasado	last year
ayer	yesterday
el mes pasado	last month
la semana pasada	last week

Comparativos y superlativos	
más/menos *[noun, adj., adv.]* que	more/less *[noun, adj., adv.]* than
***[verb]* más/menos que**	*[verb]* more/less than
tan *[adj., adv.]* como	as *[adj., adv.]* as
***[verb]* tan como**	*[verb]* as much as
tanto(a) *[noun]* como	as much *[noun]* as
tantos(as) *[noun]* como	as many *[noun]* as
mayor(es)	older
mejor(es)	better
menor(es)	younger
peor(es)	worse
el (la, los, las) mayor(es)	oldest
el (la, los, las) mejor(es)	best
el (la, los, las) menor(es)	youngest
el (la, los, las) peor(es)	worst

CAPÍTULO

De compras

Argentina y Uruguay

Plaza de Mayo, Buenos Aires, Argentina

Chapter Objectives

Communicative Goals

In this chapter, you will learn how to . . .

- Identify articles of clothing and accessories
- Communicate about shopping experiences
- Describe ongoing and habitual actions and feelings in the past

Structures

- Stressed possessive adjectives and pronouns
- Irregular verbs in the preterite
- Direct object pronouns
- The imperfect tense

▲ ¿Cuándo y con quién vas de compras?

▲ ¿Qué te gusta comprar?

▲ ¿Conoces un mercado al aire libre? ¿Qué venden?

 Visit it live on **Google Earth!**

VOCABULARIO 1

La ropa de última moda en Buenos Aires

In this section, you will learn how to talk about clothing and related accessories. What kinds of clothing are fashionable for people today? Do you think fashions in Spanish-speaking countries are ahead of or behind styles currently popular in the United States?

Estilos y telas *Styles and fabrics*

a/de cuadros *plaid*
a/de lunares *polka-dotted*
a/de rayas *stripped*
el algodón *cotton*
el cuero *leather*
la lana *wool*
la seda *silk*

Verbos

llevar *to wear; to take, to carry*
usar *to wear; to use*
ponerse *to put on*

Palabras útiles

el bolsillo *pocket*
el botón *button*
el cierre / la cremallera *zipper*
los gemelos *cufflinks*
la prenda *article of clothing*
el smoking *tuxedo*

Palabras útiles are presented to help you enrich your personal vocabulary. The words here will help you talk about clothing and accessories.

Nota lingüística

In Argentina and Uruguay, a skirt is called **la pollera** instead of **la falda;** a jacket is called **la campera** instead of **la chaqueta;** and in Argentina **las camisetas** are called **las remeras.**

¡A practicar!

Nota lingüística

In Argentina, **la cartera** refers to a woman's purse, while **la billetera** is a wallet.

7-1 Asociaciones La dependienta de La última moda necesita organizar la ropa de la tienda. Encuentra la palabra que no forma parte de cada grupo y explica por qué.

1. la cartera, la bolsa, el abrigo, el anillo
2. la chaqueta, los pantalones cortos, la camiseta, el suéter
3. el sombrero, las medias, los zapatos, las sandalias
4. el traje, el vestido, el cinturón, la corbata
5. los guantes, el traje de baño, el impermeable, el abrigo

7-2 Definiciones Escoge la definición apropiada para cada elemento.

______ 1. Es la ropa que llevamos para nadar.	a. el traje
______ 2. Son zapatos informales que muchas personas llevan en el verano.	b. los vaqueros
______ 3. Son pantalones informales.	c. la cartera
______ 4. Incluye una chaqueta y unos pantalones o una falda.	d. el traje de baño
______ 5. Es una camisa informal.	e. el impermeable
______ 6. Son para las manos, especialmente cuando hace frío.	f. la camiseta
______ 7. Es un abrigo que ofrece protección de la lluvia.	g. las sandalias
______ 8. Es donde ponemos el dinero.	h. los guantes

Nota lingüística

The verb **llevar** means to take or carry, such as **Llevo mi libro a clase,** but it also means to wear clothes. Some Spanish speakers use the phrase **llevar puesto(a)** when talking about wearing clothing. You may hear, for example, either **Llevo vaqueros** or **Llevo puestos vaqueros. Usar** is a cognate which means to use, but it can also mean to wear clothing.

7-3 ¿Para hombres o mujeres? Decide si los siguientes artículos se asocian más con los hombres, las mujeres o con ambos *(both)*. Luego, trata de encontrar a una persona en la clase que lleve los mismos artículos de ropa.

Modelo la bufanda
Es para hombres y mujeres. Soledad lleva una bufanda.

1. la blusa
2. la camisa
3. las botas
4. los pantalones de lana
5. la minifalda
6. los guantes
7. los calcetines
8. las medias
9. los aretes
10. la corbata

Marcelo lleva una camisa de cuadros, una camiseta blanca y unos vaqueros. ¿Qué llevas tú hoy?

Workbook *7-1 – 7-3*
Lab Manual *7-1 – 7-3*

¡A conversar!

7-4 **Tus preferencias** Habla con un(a) compañero(a) acerca de *(with regard to)* sus preferencias. Después de contestar tus preguntas, él/ella va a preguntarte sobre tus preferencias.

Modelo botas negras de cuero / zapatos de tenis
E1: *¿Qué prefieres tú, unas botas negras de cuero o unos zapatos de tenis?*
E2: *Mmm, yo prefiero unas botas negras. No me gustan mucho los zapatos de tenis. ¿Y tú?...*

1. bufanda de cuadros / bufanda de lana
2. sombrero de vaquero *(cowboy)* / gorra de béisbol
3. minifalda / falda larga
4. guantes de seda / guantes de algodón
5. abrigo de lana / chaqueta de esquiar
6. pantalones de cuero / los vaqueros
7. traje o vestido formal / ropa cómoda *(comfortable)*
8. pantalones cortos / pantalones largos

Nota lingüística

Las zapatillas and **los tenis** are other common ways to say tennis shoes in many Spanish-speaking countries.

7-5 **La ropa y el clima** Pregúntale a otro(a) compañero(a) qué ropa se necesita para las siguientes situaciones. ¿Están de acuerdo?

1. Es octubre, hace sol y no hace viento. Tú y dos amigos quieren caminar por la ciudad de Buenos Aires. ¿Qué ropa van a ponerse?
2. Tú y tu mejor amigo(a) piensan ir de vacaciones a Punta del Este en Uruguay por dos semanas en enero, cuando hace buen tiempo allí. ¿Qué ropa van a llevar?
3. Una amiga te invita a visitar San Carlos de Bariloche, por cinco días en agosto, durante el invierno. Tú aceptas la invitación y ahora tienes que decidir qué ropa vas a llevar.

Cultura

Punta del Este, Uruguay, is one of South America's most glamorous beach resorts. It has beautiful beaches, elegant seaside homes, yacht clubs, and expensive hotels and restaurants.

7-6 **¿Qué llevan?** Trabaja con un(a) compañero(a) para hablar de la ropa, el tiempo y las situaciones en las ilustraciones. Para cada ilustración, conversen sobre lo siguiente:

1. Describe la ropa que lleva(n) la(s) persona(s).
2. Describe el tiempo o la situación.

Modelo *El hombre lleva un traje, una camisa, una corbata y zapatos. Está nublado y posiblemente va a llover* (rain). *Por eso tiene el paraguas y el impermeable.*

1. 

2. 

3. 

4. 

EN CONTEXTO

Hoy es sábado 18 de diciembre. Julio y Silvia Sepúlveda y su hijo están en una tienda de la calle Florida, en Buenos Aires. Silvia está probándose *(is trying on)* un vestido que quiere llevar para una fiesta que ella y su esposo van a dar la semana que viene. Julio está esperándola con su hijo Juan Carlos.

Escucha el diálogo y contesta las siguientes preguntas basándote en el diálogo.

1. ¿Qué están haciendo los Sepúlveda en este momento?
2. ¿Qué van a hacer después?
3. ¿Dónde va a ser la fiesta?
4. ¿Los zapatos de Juan Carlos son viejos o nuevos?

Silvia: ¿Qué te parece este vestido, Julio? ¿Cómo me queda?

Julio: ¡Me gusta mucho! Te queda muy bien. Vos estás muy elegante.

Comentario cultural **La calle Florida** is a pedestrian-only street that features many boutiques and shops. It is the most frequented shopping zone in the city of Buenos Aires, and features high-end boutiques.

Silvia: Gracias. Me gusta este color porque va bien con las joyas.

Julio: Pero, ¿qué joyas?

Silvia: **Las mías.** Las que me **diste** para mi cumpleaños. Creo que el vestido va a ser perfecto para nuestra fiesta, ¿verdad?

Comentario cultural Unlike other countries that are known for jewels or precious metals, Argentina does not enjoy international recognition in this area. Nevertheless, silver is mined in Argentina, as are most kinds of gemstones.

Heinle/Cengage Learning

Julio: ¡Claro que sí! ¿Te acordás de la fiesta tan estupenda que **dieron** Jorge y Hortensia el año pasado cuando **hacía** tanto frío y **llovía?**

Silvia: Nunca **voy a olvidarla.** ¡Cómo nos divertimos! ¿No? Comimos tantas cosas ricas y conocimos a tanta gente, y vos bailando con todo el mundo.

Comentario cultural In Argentina, Paraguay, and Uruguay and on a limited basis in southern Mexico, Central America, and northwestern South America, **vos** is used in lieu of **tú.**

Expresiones en contexto

aguantar *to put up with*
cambiar *to exchange*
cariño *my dear*
ir bien con *to go well with*
las joyas *jewelry/jewels*
las que *the ones that*
olvidar *to forget*
quedar *to fit*

Julio: Sí, sí. La fiesta **fue** fabulosa. Bueno, ahora voy a pagar el vestido con mi tarjeta de crédito. ¿Cuánto cuesta, Silvia?

Silvia: Menos de 100 pesos. Es un buen precio, ¿no te parece, Julio?

Comentario cultural In June 2010, the Argentine peso was worth 25 U.S. cents. Argentina's economy is still recovering from a crisis in 2002, caused by a national debt default. The situation was made worse when panicked citizens rushed to the banks to withdraw their money. The acclaimed film *Nueve reinas* derives its context from this crisis. Today, Argentina appears to be stabilizing economically.

Julio: Creo que sí... Che, Silvia, tenemos que volver a la zapatería para cambiar estos zapatos que le compramos a Juan Carlos la semana pasada. Le quedan un poco grandes.

Juan Carlos: ¡No quiero ir a otra tienda! ¡Tengo hambre!

Comentario cultural Although Argentina is world-renowned for its beef, its high-quality leather goods are still undervalued. Especially attractive to foreign shoppers are articles made of soft, spotted, velvety suede. This leather comes from **carpincho** *(capibarra)*, which is the largest rodent in the world.

Silvia: Bueno. Y después vamos a casa porque Juan Carlos tiene hambre y estoy cansada de tanta actividad.

Julio: Cómo no, cariño. Juan Carlos, tenés que aguantar un poco más.

Comentario cultural In Argentina, the siesta is observed typically between 1:00 p.m. and 4:00 p.m. In some regions of Argentina, the siesta affects business hours; stores and businesses are usually open from 8:00 to 12:00 and from 4:00 to 8:00. In bigger cities, such as Buenos Aires, businesses have adopted the standard schedule of 9:00 to 5:00.

Diálogo entre dos clientes

Trabaja con un(a) compañero(a) de clase y practica el diálogo que acabas de escuchar y leer. Cambien el lugar de las compras y la ropa que quieren comprar. Usen expresiones de **En contexto** como modelo para el diálogo.

Stressed possessive adjectives and pronouns

Possessives are used to express ownership. In **Capítulo 2,** you learned how to indicate possession by using **de (El vestido es *de* Silvia)** and by using unstressed possessive adjectives: **mi(s), tu(s), su(s), nuestro(a)(s), vuestro(a)(s), su(s).** In English, we place emphasis on the possessive by using intonation *(This is **my** dress),* or by using the forms *of mine, of his, of hers,* etc. In Spanish, emphasis is placed on the possessive by using the stressed forms identified below:

- **mío(a)(s)** *my, (of) mine*
- **tuyo(a)(s)** *your* (informal), *(of) yours*
- **suyo(a)(s)** *your* (sing. formal), *(of) yours; his, (of) his; her, (of) hers; its, (of) its*
- **nuestro(a)(s)** *our, (of) ours*
- **vuestro(a)(s)** *your* (plural informal: Spain), *(of) yours*
- **suyo(a)(s)** *your* (plural), *(of) yours; their, (of) theirs*

Stressed possessive adjectives

The stressed possessive adjective must come after the noun and, like most other adjectives, agree in number and gender.

Unstressed: Estos son mis guantes. — *These are my gloves.*
Stressed: Estos guantes son **míos.** / Son **míos.** — *These gloves are mine. / They are mine.*

Unstressed: Es su blusa. — *It's her blouse.*
Stressed: Es una blusa **suya.** / Es **suya.** — *It's a blouse of hers. / It's hers.*

Stressed possessive pronouns

Stressed possessives often function as pronouns, substituting the omitted noun. When used as a pronoun, stressed possessives are preceded by a definite or indefinite article.

Silvia no tiene chaqueta. — *Silvia doesn't have a jacket.*
Le doy **la mía.** — *I'll give her mine.*

Mi camiseta está sucia. — *My shirt is dirty.*
Préstame **una tuya.** — *Lend me one of yours.*

Note that with **ser** the article is omitted unless there is a choice between items.

Este sombrero **es mío.**
but
Este sombrero **es el mío** y ese **es el tuyo.**

¿Recuerdas?

Heinle/Cengage Learning

Julio: Pero, ¿qué joyas?
Silvia: **Las mías.** Las que me diste para mi cumpleaños.

¡A practicar!

7-7 ¿A quién le pertenece *(belong)*? Llena los espacios con la forma correcta del pronombre posesivo enfático.

Modelo Es mi falda. *Es mía.*

1. Son los zapatos de Tamara. Son ______
2. Es la corbata de Sebastián. Es ______
3. Son tus pantalones. Son ______
4. Es mi chaqueta. Es ______
5. Son las sandalias de Mauricio. Son ______
6. Estos trajes son de Marcos y míos. Son ______
7. Las camisetas son de vosotros. Son ______
8. Estos son mis zapatos de tenis. Son ______
9. Es tu gorra de béisbol. Es ______
10. Estos aretes, collares y pulseras son de mi mamá y mi abuela. Son ______

7-8 Confusión en la lavandería Dos chicos acaban de lavar la ropa y tienen que separar las prendas *(articles)*. Utiliza la forma correcta del adjetivo o del pronombre posesivo entre paréntesis.

Daniel: Esos pantalones no son ______ *(mine)*; son ______ *(yours)*.

Tomás: ¡Imposible! Son muy grandes. Son de Óscar. Son ______ *(his)*.

Daniel: Y esa camiseta, ¿también es ______ *(his)*?

Tomás: No, esa camiseta es ______ *(mine)*.

Daniel: ¡Ay! Me olvidé de separar estos vaqueros de la blusa blanca de mi hermana. ¡Mira la blusa ______ *(hers)*!

Tomás: No importa. Mi hermana le puede prestar ______ *(hers)* para la fiesta esta noche.

Daniel: Perfecto. Mi hermana tiene la misma talla que ______ *(yours)*.

Tomás: Y tú, ¿a quién vas a ver esta noche, a los amigos de tu hermana o a ______ *(ours)*?

Daniel: ¡Qué pregunta! Ya sabes que mi hermana y yo somos independientes. Ella con sus cosas y yo con ______ *(mine)*.

Workbook *7-4 – 7-5*
Lab Manual *7-4 – 7-6*

¡A conversar!

7-9 ¿De quién son... ?  Con un(a) compañero(a) de clase, contesten las siguientes preguntas sobre de quién son estas cosas que encontramos en nuestro salón de clase en un día de invierno. En sus respuestas, usen el pronombre posesivo correcto.

Modelo **E1:** *¿Son estos mis guantes?*
E2: *Sí, son los tuyos.*
o **E2:** *No, no son los tuyos. Son los míos.*

1. ¿Es este mi libro?
2. ¿Son estos nuestros lápices?
3. ¿Son estos nuestros cuadernos?
4. ¿Son estos sus abrigos (de ellos)?
5. ¿Son estas sus gafas de sol (de Uds.)?
6. ¿Es esta mi bufanda?
7. ¿Es este tu impermeable?
8. ¿Es este su sombrero (de él)?

7-10 ¿Es tuya? Basándote en el vocabulario que ya sabes de este capítulo, hazles ocho preguntas a dos compañeros(as) de clase sobre las prendas de ropa que encuentres *(you may find)* en la clase.

Modelo **E1:** *Jason, ese abrigo, ¿es tuyo?*
E2: *No, no es mío. Es de mi compañero de cuarto. Es un abrigo suyo.*

7-11 Lotería de posesivos Con un(a) compañero(a), preparen seis trozos *(pieces)* de papel y en cada uno escriban lo siguiente:

Papel 1: tu nombre y el de tu compañero(a)
Papel 2: tu nombre
Papel 3: el nombre de tu compañero(a)
Papel 4: el nombre de otro(a) compañero(a)
Papel 5: los nombres de dos compañeros(as)
Papel 6: la palabra <<vosotros>>

Tú escoges una prenda de vestir y preguntas de quién es. Tu compañero saca un papel y contesta con el pronombre posesivo apropiado.

Modelo **E1:** *¿De quiénes son los calcetines?*
E2: (saca el papel con el nombre de una compañera) *Son suyos.*

Irregular verbs in the preterite

As you know, Spanish speakers use the preterite tense to express the beginning and ending/completion of past actions, conditions, and events. Some Spanish verbs have irregular verb stems in the preterite and their endings have no accent marks.

dar	di, diste, dio, dimos, disteis, dieron
hacer	hice, hiciste, hizo, hicimos, hicisteis, hicieron
ir	fui, fuiste, fue, fuimos, fuisteis, fueron
poder	pude, pudiste, pudo, pudimos, pudisteis, pudieron
poner	puse, pusiste, puso, pusimos, pusisteis, pusieron
saber	supe, supiste, supo, supimos, supisteis, supieron
querer	quise, quisiste, quiso, quisimos, quisisteis, quisieron
venir	vine, viniste, vino, vinimos, vinisteis, vinieron
estar	estuve, estuviste, estuvo, estuvimos, estuvisteis, estuvieron
tener	tuve, tuviste, tuvo, tuvimos, tuvisteis, tuvieron
decir	dije, dijiste, dijo, dijimos, dijisteis, dijeron
traer	traje, trajiste, trajo, trajimos, trajisteis, trajeron
ser	fui, fuiste, fue, fuimos, fuisteis, fueron
ver	vi, viste, vio, vimos, visteis, vieron

Note the spelling change from **c** to **z** in the **Ud./él/ella** form of the verb **hacer.**

Note that the preterite stems of **decir** and **traer** end in **-j.** With these two verbs, the **-i** is dropped in the **Uds./ellos/ellas** form to become **dijeron** and **trajeron,** respectively.

- Note that the preterite forms for **ir** and **ser** are identical; context clarifies their meaning in a sentence.

Fui dependiente por un día.	*I was a salesclerk for a day.*
Fui a la tienda de ropa ayer.	*I went to the clothing store yesterday.*

- Also note that **poder, poner, saber, querer, venir, estar,** and **tener** share the same endings:

poder	pud-	
poner	pus-	-e
saber	sup-	-iste
querer	quis-	-o -imos
venir	vin-	-isteis
estar	estuv-	-ieron
tener	tuv-	

Andar also follows this pattern: **anduve, anduviste, anduvo, anduvimos, anduvisteis, anduvieron.**

- The preterite of **hay** is **hubo.**

Ayer **hubo** una gran oferta en la calle Florida pero no **hubo** muchos clientes.	*Yesterday, there was a big sale on Florida street but there weren't many customers.*

Heinle/Cengage Learning

Julio: Sí, sí. La fiesta **fue** fabulosa.

¡A practicar!

7-12 Un mensaje telefónico Recibes un mensaje de tu hermana que está de vacaciones en Montevideo. Como tu madre no pudo hablar con ella ayer, tienes que llamarla para contarle sobre las actividades que hizo ayer tu hermana. Escribe cinco actividades que tu hermana menciona en el mensaje.

AUDIO CD
CD 2, TRACK 15

Modelo *Fue a la tienda de ropa.*

1. ______________________________
2. ______________________________
3. ______________________________
4. ______________________________
5. ______________________________

7-13 De compras Silvia fue de compras un sábado con su amiga Andrea. Conjuga los verbos entre paréntesis para saber adónde fue de compras Silvia.

Silvia se levantó temprano...

1. Ella ______ (tener) que ir de compras para buscar ropa para su esposo y su hijo.
2. Ella le ______ (decir) «adiós» a su esposo a las 9 de la mañana.
3. Silvia y su amiga Andrea ______ (ir) a la calle Florida.
4. Cuando llegaron a la calle Florida, Andrea preguntó: <<¿Silvia, ______ (traer) tu paraguas? Hoy va a llover?>>
5. Las dos amigas ______ (ir) a la tienda más grande de Buenos Aires.
6. Ellas ______ (poder) comprar muchas cosas.
7. Las dependientas ______ (ser) muy simpáticas con ellas.
8. Silvia ______ (querer) pagar con su tarjeta de crédito.
9. Silvia ______ (tener) que mostrar un documento para confirmar su identidad.
10. Silvia y Andrea ______ sus compras en el auto y regresaron a sus casas.

Cultura

Argentina is especially famous for its leather goods: jackets, handbags, gloves, wallets, and shoes. Stores specializing in leather can be found in all of Argentina's major cities.

7-14 ¡Qué generoso es Julio! Julio, el esposo de Silvia, se enteró de *(found out about)* que su esposa fue de compras esa misma noche. Él nos cuenta cómo lo supo y qué le regaló Silvia a él. Completa el siguiente párrafo con la forma correcta del pretérito de los infinitivos entre paréntesis.

Ayer por la noche yo ______ (1. saber) que mi esposa Silvia fue de compras con su amiga Andrea. Por la mañana, ella no me ______ (2. decir) lo de las compras. Ella salió a las 9:00 de la mañana. Primero, ella y Andrea ______ (3. ir) a la calle Florida, donde las dos compraron zapatos. Después, tomaron un café en la Recoleta. En la Recoleta, ellas entraron a una tienda muy grande y compraron muchas cosas. ¡Menos mal que Silvia usó su tarjeta de crédito! Cuando ella ______ (4. venir) a casa anoche, me habló de su día: «Lo siento, Julio, pero ¡______ (5. haber) unas rebajas (sales) *fantásticas en la Recoleta, y Andrea y yo no ______ (6. poder) resistir la tentación de comprar!» Ella me ______ (7. hacer) un regalo* (gift) *muy bonito: ¡una billetera de cuero! Yo le ______ (8. dar) un beso* (kiss) *a mi esposa. Nosotros ______ (9. tener) una cena deliciosa con nuestro hijo Juan Carlos. La noche ______ (10. ser) muy buena. Todos nos acostamos contentos.*

Cultura

La Recoleta is an upscale section of Buenos Aires, known for elegant shops, galleries, parks, and cafés in a pedestrian-friendly setting. French style architecture is seen in many fine homes and other buildings in the area.

Workbook *7-6 – 7-9*
Lab Manual *7-7 – 7-9*

¡A conversar!

7-15 Entrevista: Una cena en un restaurante Quieres saber más sobre tu compañero(a) de clase. Forma preguntas con los elementos indicados y hazle las preguntas a tu compañero(a) para hablar de una cena que él (ella) tuvo en un restaurante. Después, tu compañero(a) debe hacerte las preguntas a ti.

Modelo cuándo / ir / tú / a cenar en un restaurante
E1: *¿Cuándo fuiste a cenar en un restaurante?*
E2: Fui a cenar en un restaurante el fin de semana pasado.

1. otras personas / ir / también
2. poder comer / tú / tu comida favorita
3. querer tomar / tú / café
4. qué / beber y comer / otras personas
5. cuánto tiempo / estar / tú / en el restaurante
6. qué / decir / tú / al final de la cena
7. tener que pagar la cuenta / tú
8. ser / una buena experiencia
9. que / hacer / tú / después

7-16 De compras... Descríbele a un(a) compañero(a) de clase una experiencia que ocurrió cuando fuiste al centro comercial Alto Palermo, en la avenida Santa Fe de Buenos Aires. Considera las siguientes preguntas en tu descripción. ¡Sé creativo(a)!

- ¿Adónde y con quién fuiste?
- ¿Llevaste las tarjetas de crédito?
- ¿Qué compraste? ¿Por qué compraste eso?
- ¿Cuánto costó (costaron)?
- ¿Tuviste que pedirle ayuda a un(a) dependiente(a)?
- ¿Pudiste encontrar alguna oferta o ganga *(bargain)*?
- ¿Compraste ropa para otras personas?
- ¿Qué más hiciste?
- ¿Estuviste contento(a) con tus compras?
- ¿Hablaste de tus compras con tus padres / tu novio(a) / tu esposo(a)?

Centro comercial Alto Palermo

7-17 El primer día de clases Piensa en el primer día de clases en la universidad. Usando las categorías y algunos *(some)* de los verbos a continuación, forma diez frases sobre lo que tú y tus compañeros hicieron ese día. Comparte *(Share)* las frases con un(a) compañero(a) para comparar y contrastar sus experiencias.

La rutina diaria:	despertarse, levantarse, bañarse, vestirse, peinarse, acostarse
La comida:	comer, beber, cocinar, preparar, comprar, pedir
Las clases:	ir, sentarse, poner, escribir, contestar, aprender
Los profesores:	llegar, empezar, dar, decir, traer, terminar
Los amigos:	ver, hablar, preguntar, caminar, llamar, conocer
Las actividades:	jugar, tocar, mirar, escuchar, visitar, leer

7-18 Una gran fiesta En una gran fiesta, cada persona de la clase hizo algo diferente. Lo que hicieron todos está en la lista y el (la) profesor(a) va a determinar quién hizo cada actividad, ¡pero sólo él (ella) sabe la información! Tú y tus compañeros tienen que hacerles preguntas a todas las personas de la clase para determinar quién hizo cada actividad. Al determinar quién hizo una actividad, escribe su nombre al lado de la actividad y sigue haciendo preguntas hasta completar la lista con todos los nombres.

Modelo **E1:** Nick, ¿limpiaste la casa?
E2: No, *no limpié la casa.*
E1: ¿Invitaste *a la profesora?*
E2: *Sí, invité a la profesora.* (E1 writes the name of E2 next to the activity.)

1. escribir las invitaciones ____________
2. hacer las decoraciones ____________
3. limpiar la casa ____________
4. poner la mesa ____________
5. comprar las bebidas ____________
6. invitar al (a la) profesor(a) ____________
7. llegar (muy) temprano ____________
8. sacar muchas fotos ____________
9. traer muchos discos compactos ____________
10. tocar la guitarra ____________
11. no querer bailar ____________
12. comer mucha pizza ____________
13. llevar zapatos rojos ____________
14. servir la comida ____________
15. dormirse en el sofá ____________
16. perder las llaves del coche ____________
17. dar lecciones de tango y salsa ____________
18. lavar los platos ____________
19. tener que salir de la fiesta temprano ____________
20. no poder participar ____________

Argentina y Uruguay

Veamos los videos de Argentina y Uruguay para luego comentarlos.

1. ¿Por qué se conoce Buenos Aires, Argentina?
2. ¿Cuál es la plaza más importante en Buenos Aires? ¿Qué representa esta plaza?
3. ¿Qué pueden ver en la Ciudad Vieja en Montevideo, Uruguay?

See the *Workbook*, **Capítulo 7, 7-21–7-24** for additional activities.

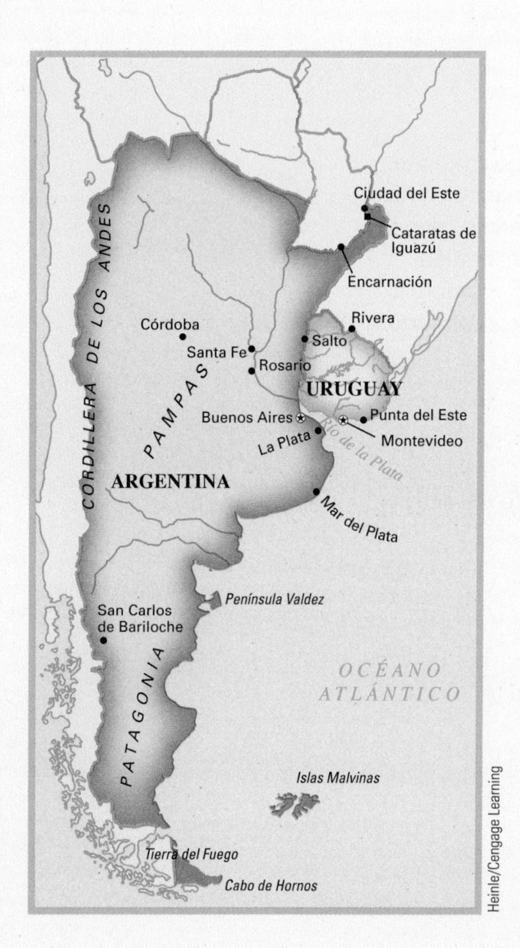

Argentina

Población: 41.343.201 de habitantes

Área: 2.779.221 km^2, cuatro veces el tamaño de Texas

Capital: La Ciudad de Buenos Aires, (3.050.728 habs.); Gran Buenos Aires (12.925.000 habs.)

Ciudades principales: Córdoba (1.400.000 habs.); Rosario (1.200.000 habs.); Mendoza (110.993 habs.); Mar del Plata (683.700 habs.)

Moneda: el peso

Lenguas: el español

Uruguay

Población: 3.510.386 de habitantes

Área: 176.220 km^2, un poco más pequeño que el estado de Washington

Capital: Montevideo, (1.300.000 habs.)

Ciudades principales: Salto (123.120 habs.); Rivera (104.921 habs.); Punta del Este (8.252 habs.); Minas (37.925 habs.)

Moneda: el peso

Lenguas: el español

Historia Visitar el centro histórico de Colonia del Sacramento en Uruguay es como volver al pasado, cuando el portugués Manuel de Lobo fundó la ciudad en 1680. Esta ciudad se conoce por sus calles de piedras y sus casas pintadas de diferentes colores, que recuerdan el centro histórico de Lisboa, capital de Portugal. Colonia fue el centro de luchas *(fights)* entre los portugueses y los españoles por más de un siglo *(century)* y por esto el gobierno de la ciudad cambió trece veces *(times)* de manos, de portuguesas a españolas y viceversa. Hoy en día sigue siendo un puerto para una región rica en agricultura y ganadería *(livestock)*, además de ser una ciudad turística para divertirse y descansar. La ciudad mantiene su sabor colonial y en 1995, la ciudad fue declarada "Patrimonio de la Humanidad" por la UNESCO (Organización de las Naciones Unidas para la Educación, la Ciencia y la Cultura).

¿Conoces ciudades históricas en los Estados Unidos? Descríbelas. ¿Crees que las ciudades coloniales deben mantener sus tradiciones?

Colonia del Sacramento, Uruguay

***Pareja* de Alejandro Xul Solar**

Artes plásticas El MALBA (Museo de Arte Latinoamericano de Buenos Aires) es un museo dedicado al arte latinoamericano del siglo XX. Expone pinturas, esculturas, dibujos, *collages* y fotografías de artistas de países latinoamericanos, desde México y el Caribe hasta Argentina. Uno de los artistas presentes en la colección permanente del museo es Alejandro Xul Solar (Argentina, 1887–1963). Xul Solar usó su conocimiento sobre religiones, mitologías e idiomas para realizar sus pinturas y buscar conexiones entre las personas, los pueblos y sus pensamientos *(thoughts)*.

Describe los colores, las formas y el significado de la obra *Pareja* de Xul Solar. ¿Cuál es tu estilo de pintura favorito: el contemporáneo, el vanguardista o el clásico?

Oficios y ocupaciones Uno de los oficios más difíciles, pero uno de los más nobles, es el trabajo de los gauchos. El gaucho, que tiene su equivalente en los Estados Unidos en el *cowboy*, es un símbolo importante en Argentina y en Uruguay; es la persona honesta, fuerte, valiente y defensora de su tierra *(piece of land)* y de sus animales. La ropa del gaucho es muy característica y consiste en un **poncho** y unos pantalones muy anchos *(wide)* llamados **bombachas.** El estilo de estas prendas de vestir influye en la moda en los Estados Unidos. Por ejemplo, los pantalones Capri o gauchos de pierna ancha, que son similares a las bombachas del gaucho, así como *(as well as)* los ponchos y las botas que se usan en el invierno y en la primavera.

Gauchos argentinos

¿Hay una relación entre el gaucho argentino o el gaucho uruguayo y el vaquero norteamericano? ¿Te gusta la moda al estilo gaucho? ¿Por qué?

Bailarines *(Dancers)* de tango

Ritmos y música Es difícil hablar de Argentina y de Uruguay sin mencionar el tango. Al comienzo, el tango se cantó en los bares de los barrios *(neighborhoods)* bajos del puerto de Buenos Aires, Argentina, y de Montevideo, Uruguay, pero desde 1924 todos los círculos sociales cantan y bailan al ritmo del tango.

Uno de los grupos famosos de música electrónica, Gotan Project, reinventa la música del tango para los jóvenes, y por eso combina los elementos tradicionales de este ritmo con los elementos electrónicos. El nombre del grupo es Gotan, que significa *Tango,* pero usando las dos sílabas invertidas *(backwards)*. La canción «Santa María (del buen ayre)» del CD *La Revancha del Tango* aparece en la película *Shall We Dance?* (2004) con Jennifer López y Richard Gere y es un buen ejemplo del tango electrónico. *Access the iTunes playlist on the* ***Plazas*** *website.*

¿Qué piensas del tango electrónico? ¿Te gusta el sonido y el ritmo? ¿Qué piensas de la modernización de la música tradicional?

¡Busquen en Internet!

1. Historia: Colonia del Sacramento
2. Artes plásticas: MALBA, Alejandro Xul Solar
3. Oficios y ocupaciones: los gauchos
4. Ritmos y música: el tango, Gotan Project

VOCABULARIO 2

En las tiendas de la Recoleta

In this section, you will practice vocabulary and expressions for shopping by learning more about one of the most famous shopping areas in Buenos Aires. Where do you like to shop?

Cultura

In Buenos Aires, the most luxurious boutiques can be found in the Recoleta neighborhood. Other popular shopping areas in Buenos Aires are the calle Florida, Alto Palermo, and Galerías Pacífico.

Sustantivos

el cheque *check*
el descuento *discount*
el efectivo *cash*
la liquidación *sale (Lat. Am.), reduction (in price)*
el número *shoe size*
la oferta *sale (Lat. Am.)*
el... por ciento *...percent*
el precio *price*
la rebaja *sale (Spain), reduction (in price)*
la talla *size (clothing)*
la tarjeta de crédito *credit card*

Adjetivos

barato(a) *inexpensive, cheap*
caro(a) *expensive*

Verbos

cambiar *to change, exchange*
costar (ue) *to cost*
gastar *to spend (money)*
hacer juego con *to match*
ir (bien) con *to go (well) with*
mostrar (ue) *to show*
probarse (ue) *to try on*
quedarle (a uno) *to fit (someone)*
rebajar *to reduce (in price)*

Expresiones idiomáticas

¿Cómo me queda? *How does it look/fit me?*
¿Cuánto le debo? *How much do I owe you?*
¿En qué puedo servirle? *How can I help you?*
¡Es una ganga! *It's a bargain!*
¡Está de (última) moda! *It's the (latest) style!*
¡Me quedan muy pequeños! *They're too small!*

¡A practicar!

Nota lingüística

Spanish sometimes "borrows" words from English. For example, in Buenos Aires another way to say **Está de moda** is to say **Está fashion** or **Es fashion.**

7-19 ¡Es una ganga! A Silvia le fue muy bien en las tiendas de la Recoleta. Termina los siguientes párrafos con las palabras de cada lista.

cara	hace juego	por ciento
de última moda	ofertas	queda
descuentos	probarse	talla

Cuando Silvia vio unas 1. __________ en su tienda favorita, no pudo resistir y entró. ¡Había (There were) *2. __________ de hasta el 20 3. __________! Silvia decidió 4. __________ una blusa 5. __________.*
La dependienta le dijo «Es su 6. __________, señora. La blusa le 7. __________ divinamente. Además, la blusa 8. __________ con los pantalones que lleva.»
«Me gusta mucho,» dijo Silvia. «¿Es muy 9. __________?»

cuánto le debo	gastar	tarjeta de crédito
cuesta	rebajamos	estilos
efectivo		

La dependienta le respondió, «No. Hoy nosotros 10. __________ todas las prendas que ve en esta sección. La blusa le 11. __________ 30 pesos. Tenemos otros 12. __________, pero son más caros.»
Entonces Silvia le dijo: «No puedo 13. __________ más de 30 pesos. Voy a llevarme esta blusa.»
«¿Algo más?», le preguntó la dependienta.
«No», dijo Silvia. «¿14. __________ por la blusa?»
La dependienta pensó un segundo y luego añadió, «Si usted paga en 15. __________, le puedo bajar el precio un poquito más.»
«Lo siento», dijo Silvia. «Creo que tengo que pagar con 16. __________. No tengo suficiente en efectivo.»

7-20 En la tienda Estás en Zara, tu tienda favorita, cuando oyes este anuncio sobre la gran liquidación que tiene la tienda. Mira la lista de artículos que buscas y marca con X las cosas mencionadas en el anuncio que puedes comprar en liquidación.

AUDIO CD
CD 2, TRACK 16

______ camisa a rayas
______ pantalones cortos
______ cartera
______ traje de baño
______ guantes
______ paraguas
______ chaleco
______ suéter
______ collar
______ reloj

¿Conoces las tiendas de ropa Zara?

Workbook *7-10 – 7-12*
Lab Manual *7-10 – 7-12*

¡A conversar!

7-21 En una tienda de ropa Habla con otro(a) compañero(a): una persona es el (la) dependiente(a) y la otra persona es el (la) cliente(a).

El/la dependiente(a)

1. Greet your customer.
3. Ask how you can help.
5. Inquire about size(s) using the chart below.
7. Find the correct size(s).
9. Ask about form of payment.
11. End the conversation.

El/la cliente(a)

2. Answer appropriately.
4. Say what you want to try on.
6. Respond to the question(s).
8. Decide whether or not to buy.
10. State method of payment.
12. Respond appropriately.

7-22 Comprando ropa Estás de vacaciones en Argentina y quieres comprar ropa para unos amigos y miembros de tu familia. Las tallas son diferentes de las tallas en los Estados Unidos, pero puedes usar la información de las tallas para damas *(women)* y caballeros *(men)* para determinar las tallas que necesitas. Prepara una lista de 4 personas para quienes quieres comprar un artículo de ropa. Para cada persona incluye la siguiente información:

- Su nombre
- Un artículo que quieres comprar para él (ella) y su talla en el sistema norteamericano
- La talla que necesitas buscar *(to look for)* en la tienda argentina
- Otro artículo que puedes comprar si no encuentras el primero
- La talla de ese artículo que necesitas buscar

LAS TALLAS DE ROPA

DAMAS									
Vestidos / Trajes									
Sistema norteamericano	6	8	10	12	14	16	18	20	
Sistema europeo	34	36	38	40	42	44	46	48	
Calcetines / Pantimedias									
Sistema norteamericano	8	8½	9	9½	10	10½			
Sistema europeo	0	1	2	3	4	5			
Zapatos									
Sistema norteamericano	6	6½	7	8	8½	9			
Sistema europeo	36	37	38	38½	39	40			
CABALLEROS									
Trajes / Abrigos									
Sistema norteamericano	36	38	40	42	44	46			
Sistema europeo	46	48	50	52	54	56			
Camisas									
Sistema norteamericano	14	14½	15	15½	16	16½	17	17½	18
Sistema europeo	36	37	38	39	41	42	43	44	45
Zapatos									
Sistema norteamericano	5	6	7	8	8½	9	9½	10½	11
Sistema europeo	37½	38	39½	40	41	42	43	44	46

Cultura

Sizes in European and in some Latin American countries run on an entirely different scale. In this case, a 36 would be equivalent to a woman's size 8.

Después de preparar la lista, conversa con un(a) compañero(a) sobre los artículos que Uds. van a buscar y las tallas que necesitan. Debes comentar sobre las ideas de tu compañero y él (ella) debe reaccionar a tus ideas.

Modelo **E1:** Para mi hermano Brian quiero comprar una camisa, talla 41 o un abrigo, talla 52.
E2: Ahora tienen rebajas en las tiendas de Recoleta. Debes comprar un abrigo. ¡Puede ser una ganga!

ESTRUCTURA 2

Direct object pronouns

In this section, you will learn how to simplify expressions by substituting direct objects with direct object pronouns.

The concept of direct objects

All sentences have a subject and a verb. Many sentences also have an object that receives the action of the verb. For example, in the sentence below, the direct object **(la blusa)** receives the action of the verb **(compró)** performed by the subject **(Silvia)**.

Subject	Verb	Direct Object
↓ Silvia	↓ compró	↓ la blusa

The direct object of a sentence is usually a person or a thing and it answers the questions *whom?* or *what?* in relation to the sentence's subject and verb.

Julio llamó a **su mamá.** *Whom did he call?* (his mom)
Silvia compró **la blusa.** *What did she buy?* (the blouse)

In Spanish, as in English, a direct object pronoun may be used in place of a direct object noun. The direct object pronoun will reflect the number and the gender of the direct object noun that it replaces.

Singular	Plural
me *me*	**nos** *us*
te *you* (informal)	**os** *you* (informal: Spain)
lo *you* (formal); *him; it* (masculine)	**los** *you; them* (masculine)
la *you* (formal); *her; it* (feminine)	**las** *you; them* (feminine)

Julio llamó a **su mamá.** Él **la** llamó.
Silvia compró **las blusas.** Ella **las** compró.

In the preceding sentences, the direct object pronouns **la** and **las** replace the direct object nouns **mamá** and **las blusas,** respectively.

Placement of the direct object pronouns

- Place the pronoun in front of the conjugated verb.

—¿Cambiaste los pantalones, Julio? *Did you exchange the pants, Julio?*
—Sí, **los cambié** anoche. *Yes, I exchanged them last night.*

- In negative sentences, place the **no** in front of the pronoun.

—¿Me llamaste, Silvia? *Did you call me, Silvia?*
—No, Julio. No **te** llamé. *No, Julio. I did not call you.*

- When the direct object pronoun is used with an infinitive or a present participle, place it either before the conjugated verb or attach it to the infinitive or the present participle. (A written accent is needed to retain the stressed vowel of a present participle when a direct object pronoun is attached to it.)

Lo voy a llamar mañana. **Voy a llamarlo** mañana.	*I'm going to call him tomorrow.*
Lo estoy llamando ahora. **Estoy llamándolo** ahora.	*I'm calling him now.*

Affirmative commands also require that the direct object pronoun be attached to the verb. You will learn more about commands and placement of pronouns in **Capítulo 9.**

- With reflexive verbs in the infinitive form, the direct object pronoun is placed after the reflexive pronoun at the end of the verb.

Voy a probarme el suéter.	*I'm going to try on the sweater.*
Voy a probármelo.	*I'm going to try it on.*

In the example above, a written accent must be added because the object pronoun was attached to the end of **probar,** resulting in a change of the natural stress. As a rule, words that end in a vowel, **-n** or **-s** have a natural stress (without written accent) on the next-to-last syllable. Words ending in consonants other than **n** or **s** have natural stress on the last syllable. The syllable that is stressed before a pronoun is attached retains the stress and it is necessary to add a written accent on that syllable, since the stress no longer falls there naturally.

Note that the direct object pronoun **lo** can be used to stand for actions or ideas in general.

—Julio, compré tres blusas nuevas.	*Julio, I bought three new blouses.*
—¡No puedo creer**lo!**	*I can't believe it! (it = the fact that the speaker bought three new blouses)*

¿Recuerdas?

Heinle/Cengage Learning

Julio: ¿Te acordás de la fiesta tan estupenda que dieron Jorge y Hortensia el año pasado cuando hacía tanto frío y llovía?

Silvia: Nunca **voy a olvidarla.** ¡Cómo nos divertimos! ¿No? Comimos tantas cosas ricas y conocimos a tanta gente, y vos, bailando con todo el mundo.

¡A practicar!

7-23 El asistente de Julio Julio está trabajando en la tienda con su nuevo asistente Rogelio. Están discutiendo dónde poner la nueva ropa que acaba de llegar. Completa las conversaciones con los pronombres **lo, la, los** o **las.**

1. —Julio, ¿usted vendió la última blusa de seda?
   —Sí, ______ vendí ayer.
2. —Rogelio, ¿terminó con las cuentas de ayer?
   —Yo ______ estoy haciendo ahora.
3. —Julio, ¿encontró los nuevos suéteres de algodón?
   —No, todavía ______ estoy buscando.
4. —Julio, mañana tengo que llevar a mi hermano al hospital. No puedo venir a trabajar hasta mediodía.
   —¡Yo no ______ creo! ¡Ud. no tiene hermanos!

7-24 Los Sepúlveda Completa los siguientes diálogos con el pronombre correcto.

En casa

Silvia: ¿Conoces a Ramón Sarmiento, Julio?

Julio: Pues... sí, ______ conozco un poco. ¿Por qué?

Silvia: Porque Ramón y su esposa ______ (a nosotros) invitaron a una fiesta.

Julio: Mmm... ______ conocimos el año pasado, ¿no?

Silvia: Sí, en una fiesta, pero nunca ______ visitamos. ¿Vamos a la fiesta?

Julio: Sí, cómo no. Vamos.

En la fiesta

Silvia: Gracias por tu invitación, Ramón. ______ recibimos la semana pasada.

Ramón: De nada, Silvia. ¿Conocen ustedes a mi hija Berta?

Berta: Mucho gusto.

Silvia: Berta, ¿no ______ recuerdas *(remember)*? Soy la señora Sepúlveda.

Berta: Ah, sí, señora Sepúlveda. Ahora ______ recuerdo. ¿Cómo está?

7-25 En la tienda La dependienta le hace muchas preguntas a una clienta en la tienda de ropa. Contesta las preguntas apropiadamente usando pronombres de objeto directo *(direct object pronouns).*

Modelo *—¿Busca Ud. los aretes?*
—Sí, ___los busco.___

1 —¿Ve las camisas?
  —Sí, ______________________.
2. —¿Va a comprar el traje de baño?
  —No, ______________________.
3. —¿Busca los vestidos?
  —Sí, ______________________.
4. —¿Tiene la tarjeta de crédito?
  —Sí, ______________________.

Workbook *7-13 – 7-16*
Lab Manual *7-13 – 7-15*

¡A conversar!

7-26 ¿Qué quieres? Tu compañero(a) va a ofrecerte *(offer you)* las siguientes cosas. Responde indicando si quieres comprar el objeto o no, sustituyendo el sustantivo *(noun)* por el pronombre *(pronoun)* correcto.

Modelo las camisetas
E1 *¿Quieres comprar las camisetas?*
E2: *Sí, las quiero comprar.* (o: *Sí, quiero comprarlas.*)
E2: *No, no las quiero comprar.* (o: *No, no quiero comprarlas.*)

1. el abrigo
2. las corbatas de seda
3. la chaqueta de cuero
4. el suéter de algodón
5. las medias de seda
6. las gafas de sol negras
7. los zapatos de tenis Adidas
8. la blusa Versace

Nota lingüística

In some Spanish-speaking countries, **las gafas (de sol)** are called **los lentes (de sol)** or **los anteojos (de sol).**

7-27 ¿Qué vas a comprar? Julio y Silvia están en su tienda favorita, pero no pueden decidir qué quieren comprar. En parejas, hagan y contesten las preguntas que ellos hacen, usando los elementos de la lista. Empieza con un verbo y selecciona un artículo de ropa para formar la pregunta. La otra persona contesta, empleando el pronombre apropiado.

Modelo **E1:** *¿Compras la blusa?*
E2: *No, no la compro.*
E1: *¿Compras los pantalones?*
E2: *Sí, los compro.*

Verbos: comprar, desear, necesitar, querer

Artículos

abrigo(s)	camiseta(s)	guantes	traje(s)
blusa(s)	chaleco(s)	impermeable(s)	suéter(es)
bota(s)	chaqueta(s)	pantalones	traje(s) de baño
calcetines	corbata(s)	sandalias	vestido(s)
camisa(s)	falda(s)	sombrero(s)	zapatos (de tenis)

7-28 Nuestras preferencias Habla con un(a) compañero(a) sobre los artículos que Uds. quieren comprar en la tienda Marisol. Emplea pronombres en las respuestas y comenta las características de los artículos.

Modelo **E1:** *¿Quieres comprar los pantalones? Son muy bonitos.*
E2: *No, no quiero comprarlos. Y tú, ¿quieres comprarlos?*
(o: *No, no los quiero comprar. Y tú, ¿los quieres comprar?*)
E2: *Sí, los quiero comprar.* (o: *Sí, quiero comprarlos.*) *Me gustan mucho.*

The imperfect tense

Spanish speakers use the imperfect tense to describe past actions, conditions, and events that were in progress or that occurred habitually or repeatedly.

To form the imperfect, add the following endings to the verb stem. Note the identical endings for **-er** and **-ir** verbs.

	jugar	hacer	divertirse
yo	jug**aba**	hac**ía**	me divert**ía**
tú	jug**abas**	hac**ías**	te divert**ías**
Ud., él/ella	jug**aba**	hac**ía**	se divert**ía**
nosotros(as)	jug**ábamos**	hac**íamos**	nos divert**íamos**
vosotros(as)	jug**abais**	hac**íais**	os divert**íais**
Uds., ellos(as)	jug**aban**	hac**ían**	se divert**ían**

Note that only three Spanish verbs are irregular in the imperfect:

	ir	ser	ver
yo	iba	era	veía
tú	ibas	eras	veías
Ud., él/ella	iba	era	veía
nosotros(as)	íbamos	éramos	veíamos
vosotros(as)	ibais	erais	veíais
Uds., ellos(as)	iban	eran	veían

—**¿Ibas** de compras a menudo cuando **eras** niña?
Did you use to go shopping often when you were a little girl?

—Sí, y mi familia y yo **comprábamos** mucha ropa.
Yes, and my family and I used to buy lots of clothes.

The imperfect tense of **hay** is **había.**

—**¿Había** muchas personas enfrente del Palacio del Congreso?
Were there a lot of people in front of the Palacio del Congreso?

—Sí, Silvia. **Había** mucha gente
Yes, Silvia. There were many people.

Cultura

The **Palacio del Congreso** is a majestic structure located in the **Plaza del Congreso.** The palace was completed in 1906 and is a major tourist attraction for those visiting Buenos Aires.

¿Recuerdas?

Heinle/Cengage Learning

Julio: ¡Claro que sí! ¿Te acordás de la fiesta tan estupenda que dieron Jorge y Hortensia el año pasado cuando **hacía** tanto frío y **llovía?**

Silvia: Nunca voy a olvidarla. ¡Cómo nos divertimos!

Talking about the past: the preterite and the imperfect

The preterite

You have learned that Spanish speakers use the preterite tense to describe the beginning or completion of past actions, conditions, and events. For example, notice how Silvia uses the preterite to tell what happened at her home this morning.

Esta mañana mi despertador **sonó** a las 7:00, como siempre. Me **levanté**, **fui** al baño, me **duché** y me **vestí**. Luego **desperté** a Juan Carlos y **preparé** el desayuno. Después de desayunar, nos **cepillamos** los dientes y **salimos** de casa. **Fuimos** en colectivo al centro.	*This morning my alarm went off at 7:00 as always. I got up, went to the bathroom, showered, and got dressed. Then, I awoke Juan Carlos and prepared breakfast. After we ate breakfast, we brushed our teeth and left the house. We went downtown by bus.*

Cultura

The easiest and most common way of getting around Buenos Aires is by buses called **colectivos**, or by subway, called **el subte.**

The imperfect

- Spanish speakers use the imperfect tense to express actions, conditions, and events that were in progress at some focused point in the past. For example, notice how Silvia uses the imperfect tense to tell what was going on when she got off the bus with her son.

Cuando nos bajamos del colectivo, **hacía** un poco de frío y **llovía.** Juan Carlos no **quería** ir de compras conmigo porque todavía **estaba** cansado.	*When we got off the bus, it was a little cold and it was raining. Juan Carlos didn't want to go shopping with me because he was still tired.*

- Spanish speakers also use the imperfect to describe actions, conditions, and events that occurred habitually or repeatedly in the past. Notice how Silvia uses the imperfect to describe how her life was when she was a girl.

Cuando **era** niña, todo **era** diferente de lo que es ahora. Yo **tenía** menos responsabilidades. Todos los sábados me **levantaba** tarde porque no **había** mucho que hacer en casa. Luego **iba** a la cocina, me **servía** un vaso de leche y **miraba** la tele. Por la tarde mis amigas y yo **jugábamos** juntas.	*When I was a child, everything was different from what it is now. I had fewer responsibilities. Every Saturday I would get up late because there wasn't much to do at home. Then, I would go to the kitchen, I would serve myself a glass of milk, and I would watch TV. In the afternoon my friends and I would play together.*

- Note that the imperfect tense can be translated in different ways, depending on the context. For example, read the following paragraph and notice the English meaning of the forms in parentheses.

  De niña yo **vivía** *(I lived)* en un pueblo cerca de Buenos Aires. Los sábados mi mamá y yo **íbamos** *(used to go)* de compras a la calle Florida donde **mirábamos** *(we would look at)* muchas cosas en las tiendas. Todos los domingos, cuando **caminábamos** *(we were walking)* por el barrio de San Telmo, **veíamos** *(we used to see)* la feria de antigüedades de la Plaza Dorrego.

¡A practicar!

7-29 Querido abuelo Cambia los verbos de la siguiente lista al imperfecto para completar el primer párrafo de una carta que Silvia le escribió a su abuelo.

escribir	ir	querer	trabajar
estar	llamar	tener	

¿Cómo estás, abuelito? Yo 1. ________ escribirte antes pero no lo pude hacer porque 2. ________ tantos quehaceres aquí en casa para prepararnos para la fiesta. Julio, Juan Carlos y mi trabajo me ocupan casi todo el tiempo. Ayer Julio 3. ________ preguntándome sobre ti y le dije que 4. ________ a escribirte muy pronto. Recuerdo que te 5. ________ cartas (letters) *y que te 6. ________ por teléfono más frecuentemente cuando no 7. ________ tanto como ahora.*

7-30 Silvia de niña Silvia está contándole a Juan Carlos algunas cosas que ella hacía de niña. ¿Qué le dice a su hijo?

Modelo yo / jugar con mis amigos
Yo jugaba con mis amigos.

1. mi familia y yo / vivir en una estancia veinte kilómetros al norte de Buenos Aires
2. (nosotros) no / tener auto, pero / tener muchos caballos
3. tu abuelo / ser agricultor *(farmer)*; también / comprar y / vender caballos
4. mis dos hermanos y yo / divertirse mucho / andar en bicicleta / montar a caballo
5. antes de acostarnos, mi mamá nos leer o / nos hablar de cuando ella / ser niña
6. a veces, mi papá / tocar el acordeón y / cantar viejas canciones *(songs)* italianas
7. yo / querer mucho a mis padres

Cultura

In Argentina and Uruguay, an **estancia** is a farm or ranch. Cattle ranching is very common in the center of Argentina, sheep ranching is more common in the south. Horses are very important animals on many ranches in Argentina and Uruguay.

7-31 ¿Pretérito o imperfecto? Julio está en la sala conversando con Juan Carlos sobre cómo llegaron a vivir en Buenos Aires. Completa su conversación, indicando los verbos correctos entre paréntesis.

Juan Carlos: Papá, ¿dónde (vivieron / vivían) tú y mamá después de casarse?

Julio: (Vivimos / Vivíamos) por un año y medio con mis padres cerca de Buenos Aires porque no (tuvimos / teníamos) mucho dinero.

Juan Carlos: ¿Qué tipo de trabajo (hiciste / hacías), papi?

Julio: (Trabajé / Trabajaba) como dependiente en una tienda. (Vendí / Vendía) zapatos allí. Nosotros (ganamos / ganábamos) poco dinero, pero (fue / era) suficiente para vivir.

Juan Carlos: ¿Cuándo (vinieron / venían) ustedes a vivir aquí en Buenos Aires?

Julio: Dos meses después de que (naciste / nacías), hijo.

Juan Carlos: ¿En diciembre?

Julio: Sí. Luego, tú, mamá y yo (pasamos / pasábamos) la Navidad *(Christmas)* juntos en esta casa. ¿Recuerdas eso?

Juan Carlos: ¿Cómo voy a recordar si solamente (tuve / tenía) dos meses?

Cultura

Around the turn of the twentieth century, many Italians immigrated to Argentina. People of Italian descent still make up a large portion of the Argentine population.

Workbook *7-17 – 7-20*
Lab Manual *7-16 – 7-18*

¡A conversar!

7-32 ¿Qué hacías? Dile a un(a) compañero(a) las actividades que tú hacías cuando eras más joven. ¿Hacían Uds. las mismas cosas?

Modelo Cuando vivía en... yo...
Cuando vivía en Vermont, yo compraba ropa para esquiar.

1. Cuando estudiaba en..., yo...
2. Vivía en... cuando mis hermanos(as)...
3. Compraba ropa... cuando nosotros(as)...
4. Me gustaba... cuando tenía...

7-33 Cuando era niño... Lee la carta que Emilio escribió sobre su niñez *(childhood)* en Argentina. Después, trabaja con un(a) compañero(a) de clase para comparar sus experiencias con las de Emilio.

Modelo **E1:** Emilio vivía en una estancia pero yo vivía en la ciudad cuando tenía seis años.
E2: Yo vivía en el campo como Emilio y yo también tenía una familia grande.

Cuando tenía seis años, mi familia y yo vivíamos en una estancia en Argentina. Éramos seis, mis padres, mis dos hermanas mayores, mi hermano menor y yo. Nuestra casa era vieja, pero era grande y cómoda. Mi papá trabajaba en el campo y mi mamá cuidaba la casa. En general la vida era muy buena. Me divertía mucho con mis hermanos y mis amigos y me gustaba ir a la escuela porque allí veía a mis amigos. Mi mejor amigo se llamaba Julio, pero tenía muchos otros amigos también. Jugábamos al fútbol muchísimo y me gustaba mucho montar a caballo. Ahora me gusta recordar esos días felices.

7-34 Entrevista Hazle estas preguntas a un(a) compañero(a) de clase.

1. **La familia:** ¿Dónde y con quién vivías cuando tenías seis años? ¿Cuántos hermanos tenías? ¿Quién era el menor? ¿y el mayor? ¿Qué tipo de trabajo hacía tu papá? ¿y tu mamá? ¿Dónde? ¿Cuándo visitabas a tus tíos y a tus abuelos? ¿Qué otras cosas hacías con tu familia?
2. **Las posesiones:** De niño(a), ¿tenías una bicicleta? (¿Sí? ¿De qué color era?) ¿Tenías un perro o un gato? (¿Sí? ¿Cómo se llamaba?) ¿Qué otras cosas tenías? ¿Cuál era la cosa más importante que tenías?
3. **Los amigos:** ¿Tenías muchos o pocos amigos en la escuela primaria? ¿Cómo te divertías con ellos? ¿Cómo se llamaba tu mejor amigo(a) de la escuela secundaria? ¿Dónde vivía? ¿Qué hacían ustedes juntos(as)? ¿Tenías novio(a)? (¿Sí? ¿Cómo se llamaba? ¿Cómo era él/ella?)
4. **Los pasatiempos:** De adolescente, ¿cómo pasabas el tiempo cuando no estudiabas o trabajabas? ¿Practicabas algún deporte? ¿Cuál? ¿Con qué frecuencia ibas al cine? ¿Qué tipo de películas veías? ¿Qué programas de televisión mirabas? ¿Qué otras cosas hacías para divertirte?

Heinle/Cengage Learning

¿Está de moda eso? En este segmento del video, Sofía y Alejandra hablan de la moda mientras se preparan para un día en la playa, y Antonio y Javier se visten con ropa especial. También, vas a ver escenas de todos los compañeros de casa vestidos de varias maneras.

Antes de ver

Expresiones útiles The following are some new expressions you will hear in the video.

Desde que salí del colegio...	*Since I graduated from high school . . .*
Ya pasó de moda.	*It's out of style.*
Playeras de algodón	*Cotton T-shirts*
Como digas.	*Whatever you say.*

Enfoque estructural The following are expressions in the video with direct object pronouns.

Alejandra: Parece que tenemos una crisis aquí ... ¡Te voy a llevar de compras!

Alejandra: Así se usa. Ese vestido lo compré hace poco. Es nuevo y siempre está de moda.

Sofía: Bueno, si tú lo dices ... me lo voy a probar.

Antonio: Oye, Sofía, ¡te ves muy bonita con esa ropa! Casi no te reconozo.

1. **Recordemos** ¿Qué compraste la última vez que fuiste de compras? ¿Te probaste mucha ropa? ¿Encontraste algo que te quedó bien? Con un compañero(a) de clase, hagan una lista de todas las prendas de ropa que compraron la última vez que fueron de compras. ¿Tienen algunas prendas en común?
2. **Practiquemos** Con un compañero de clase, identifica el objeto directo *(the direct object)* que cada pronombre subrayado identifica en las expresiones de **Enfoque estructural.** Luego, usa la lista que tu compañero hizo en **Recordemos** y hazle preguntas usando pronombres de objeto directo sobre dónde, cuándo y por qué él/ella compró esos artículos.
3. **Charlemos** Haz una encuesta a varios miembros de la clase sobre la ropa que está de moda para hombres y mujeres, a base de lo que ellos compraron la última vez que fueron de compras. ¿Qué prendas son las más populares para hombres y mujeres?

Después de ver

1. ¿Qué llevan puesto? Mira las fotos y describe con mucho detalle la ropa que lleva cada uno de los compañeros de casa.

Valeria lleva

____

____

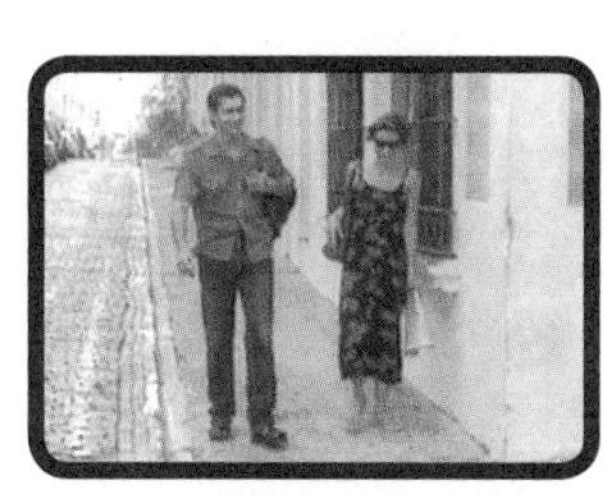

Sofía y Javier llevan

____

____

Alejandra lleva

____

____

Antonio lleva

____

____

2. Un estilo personal Ahora, según lo que viste en el video, describe el estilo personal de las tres compañeras de la Hacienda Vista Alegre: Alejandra, Sofía y Valeria. Luego compara tus descripciones con las de un(a) compañero(a). ¿Están de acuerdo?

Sofía: ____

Alejandra: ____

Valeria: ____

Entre nosotros En el video, Alejandra dijo que Sofía tenía que ir de compras. Escribe un párrafo en que identificas varios artículos de ropa o accesorios que Sofía debe comprar para lucir *(show off)* un estilo nuevo. Luego compara tus ideas con un(a) compañero(a). Según ustedes, ¿necesita Sofía las mismas cosas?

Presentaciones Con dos compañeros(as) de clase, selecciona a un miembro de la Hacienda de Vista Alegre que, en su opinión, necesita mejorar su estilo personal de moda. Hagan un dibujo de las prendas que recomiendan para el personaje. Luego, presenten el dibujo a la clase, justificando sus recomendaciones.

See the *Lab Manual,* **Capítulo 7, 7-22– 7-23** for additional activities.

Antes de leer

Strategy: Using background knowledge to anticipate content

The better you can anticipate what the topic of a reading selection will be, the more easily you will understand the main ideas of the passage. In addition to looking at the visuals, the title, and the subtitles of a selection, you should also think about what you already know about the topic.

Before reading the selection, consider the following:

1. the visuals
   a. Who is in the photos?
   b. What is the individual wearing?
   c. For which season is this collection appropriate?
2. the title
   a. What do you associate with the title?
   b. What type of clothing and which colors are typical for this season?
3. previous knowledge
   a. What do you know about today's fashion in terms of the popular styles and fabrics?
   b. What are the trendy colors?
   c. In your opinion, what clothing stores are the most popular?

Colección de otoño-invierno

Cognados Identifica cuatro cognados y su significado.

A completar Mientras lees las descripciones de la ropa, completa el siguiente cuadro con la moda para cada estación.

OTOÑO		
él/ella (día de semana)	él (fin de semana)	ella (fin de semana)

INVIERNO	
él/ella (día)	ella (noche)

Después de leer

A escoger Después de leer el texto, contesta las siguientes preguntas.

1. ¿Qué materiales se usan para las prendas de vestir en el invierno?
   a. algodón y seda
   b. lana y cuero
   c. cuero y algodón
2. ¿Qué colores son los preferidos para el otoño?
   a. colores vibrantes
   b. verde, azul y morado
   c. colores neutros

¡Descubre la nueva colección de otoño-invierno!

D

El Buenos Aires Fashion Week (BAFWEEK) nos trae las últimas tendencias de la moda para la próxima temporada *(season)*, otoño-invierno. El otoño está marcado por prendas simples y cómodas en colores neutros como el negro, blanco y beige. En contraste, el invierno nos trae una diversidad de colores para alegrar los fríos meses de julio y agosto.

Durante el otoño, para tener un *look* casual durante el día, puedes ponerte unos vaqueros clásicos, de color no muy oscuro, con una camiseta blanca y un cinturón de cuero.

Para esa cita tan especial durante el fin de semana, puedes usar una camisa de un solo color y vaqueros de moda (de preferencia de color oscuro). Evita *(Avoid)* combinar muchos colores y opta por llevar colores neutros y poco intensos.

Un *look* muy práctico para usar de día durante el fin de semana consiste en una camiseta de algodón con diseños monocromáticos, una chaqueta de seda y vaqueros. ¡No olvides añadir accesorios: las pulseras de plata, las gafas de sol extra grandes y los cinturones metálicos complementan este *look* súper bien!

El invierno nos trae colores vibrantes como el verde, el azul y el morado. ¡Los suéteres a rayas están *in!* ¡No olvides llevar bufandas de lana que hagan juego con los suéteres!

Para la noche, el color negro nunca pasa de moda, pues va muy bien con cualquier color. Un abrigo de lana negro y unas botas de cuero negras de tacón alto son básicos en tu guardarropa *(wardrobe)* para este invierno, ¡y cualquier invierno!

3. ¿Con qué prenda deben hacer juego las bufandas?
   a. con los suéteres
   b. con los vaqueros
   c. con las faldas
4. ¿Cuáles son los accesorios para la colección de otoño-invierno?
   a. aretes, pulseras, cinturones, bufandas
   b. pulseras, gafas de sol, anillos y collares
   c. gafas de sol, bufandas, pulseras y cinturones

¡A conversar! Comenta con tus compañeros de clase los siguientes temas.

1. Las semejanzas y diferencias entre la moda argentina y la moda estadounidense en relación con los colores, los materiales, las prendas de vestir y los accesorios.
2. ¿Es importante o no para ustedes estar a la moda?
3. Después de conversar sobre la moda, preparen un plan para un desfile de modas *(fashion show)*. ¿Qué prendas de vestir son importantes en la región donde ustedes viven? ¿Qué prendas no son tan importantes? ¿Qué accesorios están de moda?

Strategy: Editing your writing

Editing your written work is an important skill to master when learning a foreign language. You should plan on editing what you write several times. When checking your compositions, consider the following areas.

1. Content

a. Is the title of your composition captivating?
b. Is the information you wrote pertinent to the established topic?
c. Is your composition interesting?

2. Organization

a. Does each paragraph in the composition have a clearly identifiable main idea?
b. Do the details in each paragraph relate to a single idea?
c. Are the sentences in the paragraph ordered in a logical sequence?
d. Is the order of the paragraphs correct in your composition?

3. Cohesion and style

a. Does your composition as a whole communicate what you are trying to convey?
b. Does your composition "flow" easily and smoothly from beginning to end?
c. Are there transitions between the paragraphs?

4. Style and accuracy

a. Have you chosen the precise vocabulary words you need to express your ideas?
b. Are there grammatical errors in your composition?
c. Are there spelling errors in your composition?

If you consider these factors as you edit your written work, the overall quality of your compositions can increase dramatically!

Task: Simple reporting in the past

Simple reporting in the past occurs in a variety of contexts and focuses on the narration of a series of events. You will now prepare a short report about a recent shopping trip following the steps below and focusing on completed actions, such as where you went and what you did during your outing.

Paso 1 Antes de escribir, piensa en la última vez que fuiste de compras para buscar ropa. Contesta las siguientes preguntas.

¿Adónde fuiste de compras? (¿Cómo se llama el centro comercial o cómo se llaman las tiendas?)

¿Fuiste solo(a) o con otra persona?

¿A qué hora llegaste a la primera tienda?

¿Fuiste a otras tiendas?

¿Qué artículo(s) de ropa compraste? ¿Dónde compraste el artículo o los artículos?

¿Cuánto dinero gastaste en las compras que hiciste?

¿Cuánto tiempo pasaste en las compras?

¿Qué hiciste después?

Paso 2 Ahora escribe una composición de dos o tres párrafos sobre esta excursión. En tu composición, incluye la información que usaste para contestar las preguntas en **Paso 1.**

Paso 3 Ahora tienes que corregir tu composición. Usa las preguntas de la sección anterior (partes 1, 2, 3 y 4 de *Editing your writing*) como guía de corrección.

Paso 4 Intercambia tu composición con un(a) compañero(a) de clase. Cada persona debe usar la sección anterior para evaluar la composición de su compañero(a). Si hay partes de las composiciones que necesiten corrección, cada persona debe hacer los cambios necesarios.

Communicative Goals:

- Identify articles of clothing and accessories
- Communicate about shopping experiences
- Describe ongoing and habitual actions and feelings in the past

Paso 1

Review the Communicative Goals for **Capítulo 7** and determine if you are able to accomplish the goals. If you are not certain that you have achieved all of the goals, review the pertinent portions of the chapter.

Paso 2

Look at the components of a conversation which addresses the communicative goals for this chapter. The percentages will help you evaluate your ability to successfully participate in the conversation that is featured below. Your instructor may use the same rubric to assess your oral performance.

Components of the conversation	%
☐ Greetings, questions and answers about how the individuals are doing	10
☐ Statement of liking an article of clothing or accessory and questions about buying or receiving it	10
☐ Response with information about buying or receiving the item	10
☐ At least three questions about a recent shopping experience	20
☐ Answers to at least three questions about a recent shopping experience	20
☐ Question about feelings at the conclusion of the shopping experience and appropriate answer, followed by return of the question and offering of appropriate answer	20
☐ Appropriate conclusion of the conversation	10

En acción Think about a conversation in which two friends talk about clothing and a recent shopping experience. Consider the sort of information that might be exchanged and how the speakers might communicate the information. Work with a partner to carry out the conversation, being sure to include the following steps.

1. The friends greet one another and ask and answer questions about how they are doing.
2. One person states that he (she) likes an article of clothing or an accessory that the other person is wearing or has with him (her).
3. The second person responds appropriately and explains how and when he (she) bought it or received it.
4. One friend asks the other about a recent shopping experience, including questions about where the person went, what he (she) bought, and at least one additional detail.
5. The friend provides the information and, in return, asks similar questions.
6. One person asks the other how he (she) felt at the end of the shopping trip, the friend responds, and asks how the other felt.
7. The friend responds appropriately.
8. One friend states that he (she) must do something and both individuals conclude the conversation appropriately.

¡A REPASAR!

Stressed possessive adjectives

In Spanish, emphasis is placed on the possessive by using the following stressed forms:

Singular	Plural
mío(a)(s)	nuestro(a)(s)
tuyo(a)(s)	vuestro(a)(s)
suyo(a)(s)	suyo(a)(s)

The stressed possessive adjective must come after the noun and, like most other adjectives, agree in number and gender. The stressed possessives often function as pronouns, substituting the omitted noun.

¡A recordar! 1 When stressed possessive adjectives are used as pronouns, how are they modified?

Verbs irregular in the preterite

As you know, some Spanish verbs have irregular verb stems in the preterite. Furthermore, their endings have no accent marks.

dar	hacer	poner	ser	venir
decir	ir	querer	tener	
estar	poder	saber	traer	

¡A recordar! 2 When conjugating **andar** in the preterite, which verb listed above has the same pattern of endings? How are the preterite stems of **decir** and **traer** similar? Are there any verbs that have identical forms in the preterite? What is the preterite of **hay**?

Direct object pronouns

A direct object pronoun may be used in place of a direct object noun.

Singular	Plural
me	nos
te	os
lo/la	los/las

The direct object pronoun **lo** can be used to stand for actions or ideas in general.

¡A recordar! 3 How is the stressed vowel of a present participle marked when a direct object pronoun is attached to it?

The imperfect tense

Spanish speakers use the imperfect tense to describe past actions, conditions, and events that were in progress or that occurred habitually or repeatedly. To form the imperfect, add the following endings to the verb stem.

	jugar	hacer	divertirse
yo	jug**aba**	hac**ía**	me divert**ía**
tú	jug**abas**	hac**ías**	te divert**ías**
Ud., él, ella	jug**aba**	hac**ía**	se divert**ía**
nosotros(as)	jug**ábamos**	hac**íamos**	nos divert**íamos**
vosotros(as)	jug**abais**	hac**íais**	os divert**íais**
Uds., ellos(as)	jug**aban**	hac**ían**	se divert**ían**

¡A recordar! 4 Which three verbs are irregular in the imperfect? How are they conjugated?

Actividad 1 ¡A emparejar! Escoge la oración más apropiada de la segunda columna para cada oración de la primera columna. En la primera columna, el sujeto de cada oración es el (la) dueño(a) *(owner)* de cada artículo.

1. ____ Tengo las botas.
2. ____ Juan José tiene las camisas.
3. ____ Mis padres tienen la tarjeta de crédito.
4. ____ Isabel tiene el anillo.
5. ____ Los abuelos tienen los calcetines.
6. ____ Tienes el suéter.
7. ____ Alicia y yo tenemos los cinturones.
8. ____ Tienes la bolsa.
9. ____ Raúl y yo tenemos el paraguas.
10. ____ Tengo los vaqueros.

a. Son suyos.
b. Es tuya.
c. Son mías.
d. Son míos.
e. Son nuestros.
f. Es suya.
g. Es nuestro.
h. Son suyas.
i. Es suyo.
j. Es tuyo.

Actividad 2 Una fiesta Escoge la respuesta correcta para cada frase.

____ 1. Manolo y yo ____ una fiesta.
a. dijimos c. dimos
b. dijeron d. dieron

____ 2. Remi no ____ asistir.
a. puso c. pude
b. puse d. pudo

____ 3. Julieta ____ a dos fiestas esa noche.
a. fui c. hice
b. fue d. hizo

____ 4. Todos ____ comida riquísima.
a. trajo c. estuvo
b. trajeron d. estuvieron

____ 5. ____ una noche memorable para todos.
a. Fue c. Tuvo
b. Fuimos d. Tuvimos

Actividad 3 Un día de compras Escribe la forma correcta de cada verbo en el pretérito para narrar la historia de unas compras en Buenos Aires.

El sábado pasado mi amiga Eva _______ (1. venir) a mi casa a las diez de la mañana y nosotras _______ (2. ir) de compras. Yo _______ (3. querer) ir a la calle Florida para comprar unos regalos. Eva _______ (4. tener) que pasar por el banco primero porque no _______ (5. llevar) su tarjeta de crédito. Al llegar a la calle Florida nosotras _______ (6. ver) a muchas personas e inmediatamente _______ (7. saber) que ese día había una venta especial de sólo dos horas. Yo _______ (8. poder) comprar tres regalos a precios excelentes y me _______ (9. poner) contenta. Después de varias horas de compras, yo le _______ (10. decir) adiós a Eva y _______ (11. volver) a casa.

Actividad 4 Preguntas Contesta cada pregunta, cambiando los objetos directos a pronombres. Incluye el verbo y el pronombre en la respuesta.

1. —¿Tienes el reloj?
   —Sí, yo _______________.
2. —¿Tiene Sara las sandalias?
   —Sí, ella _______________.
3. —¿Estás comprando las gafas de sol?
   —Sí, yo _______________.
4. —¿Quiere los guantes tu papá?
   —No, él _______________.
5. —¿Lleva las sandalias la abuela?
   —No, ella _______________.
6. —¿Paquito va a usar el impermeable?
   —No, él _______________.

Actividad 5 Cuando era dependiente Combina cada frase de la primera columna con el verbo apropiado de la segunda columna.

1. Yo _____ en una tienda.	a. prefería
2. Nosotros _____ ropa para niños.	b. ibas
3. La ropa de la tienda _____ mucho.	c. trabajaba
4. Todos los dependientes _____ muy simpáticos.	d. hablábamos
	e. vendíamos
5. Nosotros _____ con muchos clientes todos los días.	f. costaba
	g. eran
6. Unos clientes _____ con tarjeta de crédito, otros en efectivo.	h. pagaban
7. Un cliente _____ pagar en efectivo.	
8. Tú _____ a esa tienda mucho, ¿no?	

Actividad 6 La vida en Mendoza, Argentina Completa el párrafo en el imperfecto para saber de la vida de un joven en Mendoza. Escoge el verbo apropiado y escribe la forma correcta.

divertirse	tener
esquiar	trabajar
estar	venir
ir	ver
ser	vivir

Cuando yo 1. _________ joven, mi familia y yo 2. _________ en Mendoza, en el oeste de Argentina. Nosotros 3. _________ una estancia pequeña, pero mi padre 4. _________ en un banco también. Yo 5. _________ a mis abuelos mucho porque ellos 6. _________ a Mendoza a visitarnos con frecuencia y yo siempre 7. _________ a su casa durante las vacaciones de la escuela. Mis amigos y yo 8. _________ en las montañas y siempre 9. _________. Todos nosotros 10. _________ contentos.

Refrán

_______ *(Shoemaker)* remendón,
ya en el oficio lleva el don.

VOCABULARIO ESENCIAL

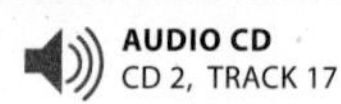
AUDIO CD
CD 2, TRACK 17

PERSONAL TUTOR

La ropa	Clothing
el abrigo	overcoat
la blusa	blouse
los calcetines	socks
la camisa	shirt
la camiseta	T-shirt
el chaleco	vest
la chaqueta	jacket
la corbata	necktie
la falda	skirt
el impermeable	raincoat
las medias	stockings
los pantalones	pants
los pantalones cortos	shorts
el suéter	sweater
el traje	suit
los vaqueros	jeans
el vestido	dress

Los zapatos	Shoes
las botas	boots
las sandalias	sandals
los zapatos	shoes
los zapatos de tenis	tennis shoes
los zapatos de taco/ tacón (alto)	(high) heels

Los accesorios	Accessories
el anillo	ring
los aretes	earrings
la bolsa	purse, bag
la bufanda	scarf
la cartera	wallet, purse
el cinturón	belt
el collar	necklace
las gafas de sol	sunglasses
la gorra (de béisbol)	(baseball) cap
los guantes	gloves
el paraguas	umbrella
la pulsera	bracelet
el reloj	watch
el sombrero	hat
el traje de baño	swimsuit

Estilos y telas	Styles and fabrics
a/de cuadros	plaid
a/de lunares	polka-dotted
a/de rayas	stripped
el algodón	cotton
el cuero	leather
la lana	wool
la seda	silk

Las compras	Shopping, purchases
Sustantivos	
el cheque	check
el (la) dependiente(a)	salesclerk
el descuento	discount
el efectivo	cash
la liquidación	sale (Lat. Am.), reduction (in price)
el número	shoe size
la oferta	sale (Lat. Am.)
el precio	price
el ... por ciento	. . . percent
la rebaja	sale (Spain), reduction (in price)
la talla	size (clothing)
la tarjeta de crédito	credit card
Adjetivos	
barato(a)	inexpensive, cheap
caro(a)	expensive
Verbos	
cambiar	to change, exchange
costar (ue)	to cost
gastar	to spend (money)
hacer juego con	to match
ir (bien) con	to go (well) with
llevar	to wear; to carry
mostrar (ue)	to show
ponerse	to put on
probarse (ue)	to try on
quedarle (a uno)	to fit (someone)
rebajar	to reduce (in price)
usar	to wear; use
Expresiones idiomáticas	
¿Cómo me queda?	How does it look/fit me?
¿Cuánto le debo?	How much do I owe you?
¿En qué puedo servirle?	How can I help you?
¡Es una ganga!	It's a bargain!
¡Está de (última) moda!	It's in style! (It's the latest style!)
¡Me quedan muy pequeños!	They're too small!

Adjetivos y pronombres posesivos enfáticos	
mío(a)(s)	my, (of) mine
tuyo(a)(s)	your [sing. informal], (of) yours
suyo(a)(s)	your [sing. formal], (of) yours; his, (of) his; her, (of) hers; its, (of) its
nuestro(a)(s)	our, (of) ours
vuestro(a)(s)	your [plural informal], (of) yours
suyo(a)(s)	your [plural], (of) yours; their, (of) theirs

Pronombres de complemento directo	
me	me
te	you [sing. informal]
lo	you [sing. formal, masc.]; him: it [masc.]
la	you [sing. formal, fem.]; her: it [fem.]
nos	us
os	you [plural informal: Spain]
los	you [plural, masc.]; them [masc.]
las	you [plural, fem.]; them [fem.]

CAPÍTULO 8

Fiestas y vacaciones

Guatemala y El Salvador

Plaza Mayor de la Constitución, Ciudad de Guatemala, Guatemala

Chapter Objectives

Communicative Goals

In this chapter, you will learn how to . . .

- Communicate about holidays, special events, and vacations
- Inquire and provide information about people and events
- Express affirmative and negative ideas
- Communicate about past events and activities

Structures

- Interrogative words
- The preterite vs. the imperfect
- Affirmative and negative expressions
- **Hace** + *period of time* + **que**

▲ ¿Cuál es el lugar más interesante que conoces? Descríbelo.

▲ ¿Qué lugares visitas y por qué te gusta visitarlos? ¿Visitas lugares históricos, parques nacionales, playas, montañas, etc.?

▲ ¿Te gusta estudiar o visitar las civilizaciones antiguas o modernas? ¿Por qué?

Visit it live on **Google Earth!**

Celebración del Día de Santo Tomás en Chichicastenango, Guatemala

In this section, you will learn how to talk about parties and celebrations while learning about the festivities surrounding a Mayan holiday in a small, mountain town. How do you celebrate special occasions?

Sustantivos

la celebración *celebration*
el cumpleaños *birthday*
el día feriado *official holiday*
la fiesta (sorpresa) *(surprise) party*

Verbos

celebrar *to celebrate*
cumplir años *to have a birthday*
dar (hacer) una fiesta *to give a party*
disfrazarse *to wear a costume*
olvidar *to forget*
pasarlo bien (mal) *to have a good (bad) time*
ponerse + *adjective* *to become, (to get) + adjective*
portarse bien (mal) *to behave well (poorly)*
reaccionar *to react*
recordar (ue) *to remember*
reunirse con *to get together with*

Expresiones idiomáticas

¡Felicitaciones! *Congratulations!*
Me pongo contento(a)/triste *I become happy/sad*

Nota lingüística

Generally, when people toast in Spanish they say **¡Salud!** In Spain, however, it is common to say **¡Salud, dinero y amor, y tiempo para gozarlos!** *(Health, love, and money, and time to enjoy them!)*

Cultura

The people of Santo Tomás de Chichicastenango combine ancient Mayan beliefs with a Christian ideology in their celebration of the December solstice. In this small Guatemalan village, the inhabitants celebrate the day of their patron saint and the Sun god who is honored so that that he continues to bless the town with light and warmth.

Algunas fiestas

el Año Nuevo *New Year*
el Día del Padre *Father's Day*
el Día de la Independencia *Independence Day*
el Día de las Madres *Mother's Day*
el Jánuca *Hanukkah*
la Navidad *Christmas*
el Ramadán *Ramadan*
la Semana Santa *Holy Week*

Palabras útiles

el Día de la Raza *Columbus Day*
el Día de los Muertos *Day of the Dead*
el Día de los Reyes Magos *Epiphany, Three Kings Day*
el Día de Todos los Santos *All Saints' Day (November 2)*
el Día del Santo *Saint's Day (the saint after whom one is named)*
la Nochebuena *Christmas Eve*
la Nochevieja *New Year's Eve*
la Pascua *Easter, Passover*

Palabras útiles are presented to help you enrich your personal vocabulary. The words here will help you talk about holidays.

¡A practicar!

8-1 Definiciones Escoge la definición apropiada para cada palabra.

1. ______ La persona que da una fiesta.
2. ______ Algo que cubre *(covers)* la cara.
3. ______ Cuando muchas personas no trabajan.
4. ______ Día celebrado con regalos y un pastel con velas.
5. ______ Comidas populares para fiestas.

a. el día feriado
b. el (la) anfitrión(a)
c. los entremeses
d. el cumpleaños
e. la máscara

8-2 Un cumpleaños Escoge la palabra adecuada/lógica para completar las siguientes oraciones.

1. Ayer fue el (disfraz / cumpleaños) de Tomás.
2. Hubo una (fiesta sorpresa / anfitriona) con todos sus amigos y parientes.
3. Vinieron muchos (brindis / invitados) a la fiesta.
4. Sus parientes le dieron (regalos / velas).
5. Su esposa le preparó un (día feriado / pastel de cumpleaños) muy grande con muchas (velas / celebraciones).
6. Su esposa Marta fue (la anfitriona / la procesión) de la fiesta.
7. La hermana de Tomás, Claudia, les ofreció (cohetes / entremeses) a los invitados que tenían hambre.
8. Los niños pequeños (se portaron / recordaron) bien durante la fiesta.
9. Todos los invitados (lo pasaron bien / lo pasaron mal) en esa (máscara / celebración).

Nota lingüística

Note that the word **desfile** is most used for a political or social parade, while the word **procesión** is used for a religious parade or celebration.

8-3 ¡Una fiesta sorpresa para Tomás! Este año Tomás cumplió treinta años. Describe los preparativos *(preparations)* que hizo su esposa para la fiesta sorpresa. No olvides usar los verbos en el pretérito donde sea necesario *(where it may be necessary)*.

asustarse	dar una fiesta	gritar	reaccionar
celebrar	disfrazarse	hacer un brindis	recordar
cumplir años	divertirse	llorar	reunirse

Este año mi esposa 1. ______________ para mi cumpleaños. Todos mis amigos 2. ______________ afuera de mi casa y me 3. ______________, «¡Feliz cumpleaños!». Después, encendieron unos cohetes, una tradición de Guatemala. Una niña 4. ______________ por el ruido y 5. ______________. Más tarde, mi mejor amigo, Rodrigo, 6. ______________ y luego nos contó la «Leyenda de la niña flor». Mi esposa 7. ______________ de una manera muy sentimental: ella 8. ______________ su fiesta de quince años. A las 12:00 de la noche, mi amigo Rodrigo y su esposa Claudia 9. ______________ de un matrimonio muy viejo para hacernos imaginar nuestra vida del futuro. Después, mi esposa sirvió un pastel con velas. Mis amigos me obligaron a comer un poquito antes de servirlo. Normalmente, no me gusta mucho 10. ______________, pero este año nosotros lo 11. ______________ con mucho entusiasmo y todos 12. ______________ muchísimo.

Cultura

The **fiesta de quince años**—a girl's 15th birthday—marks a girl's passage into womanhood. Though this tradition is more commonly associated with Mexico, it is also an important ritual in Guatemala and other Latin American countries.

Workbook *8-1 – 8-4*
Lab Manual *8-1 – 8-3*

¡A conversar!

8-4 **Mi día feriado favorito** Habla con un(a) compañero(a) de clase sobre su día feriado favorito. Luego, compartan esta información con la clase. ¿Cuál es el día feriado favorito de la clase?

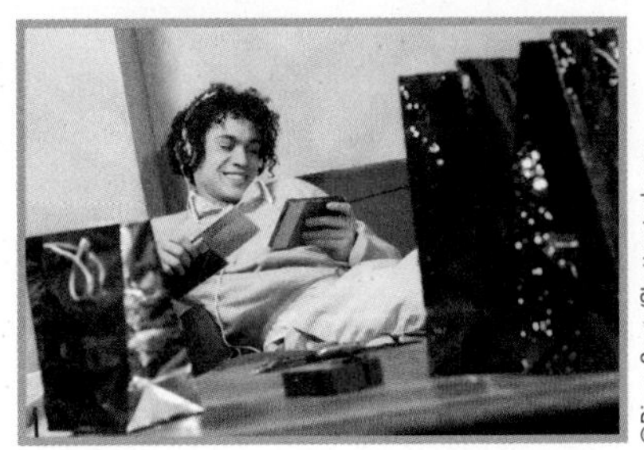
©Diego Cervo/Shutterstock.com

1. ¿Cuál es tu día feriado favorito? ¿Por qué?
2. ¿Cómo celebras esta ocasión especial? ¿Das una fiesta en tu casa? ¿Vas a un restaurante por la noche?
3. ¿Preparas una comida o bebida especial?
4. ¿Te pones muy contento(a) porque es un día especial?
5. ¿Qué hiciste el año pasado para celebrar ese día? ¿Recibiste regalos ese día? ¿Diste regalos?

8-5 **¿Cómo te pones?** Dile a un(a) compañero(a) de clase cómo reaccionas en las siguientes situaciones. Usa estos adjetivos u otros en la forma apropiada: asustado, contento, feliz, nervioso, preocupado, triste.

Modelo Estás en una fiesta y tu novio(a) está bailando con otra persona.
Me pongo furioso(a) con él (ella).

1. Das una fiesta y los invitados se comen toda la comida en media hora.
2. Es tu cumpleaños y tus amigos te hacen una fiesta sorpresa.
3. Estás en una fiesta y los invitados no se ríen, no sonríen y hablan muy poco.
4. Estás en una fiesta y pierdes un anillo muy caro.
5. No recuerdas que hoy es el cumpleaños de tu mejor amigo(a).
6. Estás en una fiesta hablando y conversando y alguien apaga *(turns off)* las luces.

8-6 **¡Vamos a hacer una fiesta!** Trabajen en grupos de tres o cuatro personas para planear una fiesta. Consideren los siguientes aspectos:

- El motivo *(reason)* de la fiesta
- Cuándo y dónde va a ser
- A quiénes van a invitar
- Quién(es) tiene(n) la responsabilidad de cada cosa y qué tiene(n) que hacer:
  - las invitaciones
  - las decoraciones
  - la comida
  - las bebidas
  - la música

Después de hacer los planes, compartan la información con la clase.

EN CONTEXTO

Tomás y Marta viven en Chichicastenango. Pilar, la madre de Tomás, decidió visitar a su hijo y a su esposa sin avisar. Ella vino para verlos a ellos y para asistir al festival de la Cofradía de Santo Tomás, que tiene lugar en diciembre en Chichicastenango.

CD 3, TRACK 2

Escucha el diálogo e indica si las siguientes oraciones son **ciertas** o **falsas**. Si la oración es falsa, ¡corrígela!

1. Hacía mal tiempo el día en que llegó Pilar.
2. Pilar causó el accidente entre el taxi y el autobús.
3. Pilar llegó rápidamente a la casa de su hijo.
4. Ella llegó en verano.
5. La madre de Tomás no tenía miedo de nada.
6. Tomás se puso triste cuando su mamá lo llamó.

Ayer fue domingo, 20 de diciembre. **Eran** las 11:40 de la mañana; la temperatura en Chichicastenango **estaba** a 14 grados centígrados y **llovía**. Marta **estaba duchándose** y Tomás **se estaba vistiendo** porque muy pronto **iban a ir** a la iglesia. De repente, **sonó el teléfono** y Tomás **fue a contestarlo.**

Comentario cultural Chichicastenango is a small town with a long history as a major center of commerce. With red tile roofs and cobblestone streets, it offers a colorful spectacle for tourists, especially on market days, which occur twice weekly. The **K'iche' Maya** of the surrounding region, as well as other indigenous groups from all over Guatemala, such as **Mam, Ixil,** and **Kaqchikel,** bring the marketplace to life by selling their wares and shopping.

Tomás: ¿Bueno?

Pilar: ¡Hola, hijo! Habla tu mamá.

Tomás: Mamá, ¿cómo estás?

Pilar: Bien, bien. Acabo de llegar de Quezaltenango. Estoy aquí en la parada de autobuses.

Tomás: ¡Mamá! ¿Estás aquí en Chichicastenango?

Pilar: Sí, hijo. **Decidí** venir a última hora. **Hace seis meses que no los veo** y, además, me encanta la Cofradía de Santo Tomás.

Comentario cultural Quezaltenango is the second-largest city of Guatemala and is located west of Guatemala City in the mountainous region of the country. It serves as an excellent base for tourists wishing to travel to nearby villages, which are noted for their handicrafts and hot springs.

Expresiones en contexto

a última hora *at the last minute*
casi *almost*
chocó con *crashed into*
Cofradía *Brotherhood*
de repente *suddenly*
hace tres meses que... *it has been three months since...*
insisto en que vengas en taxi *I insist that you come in a cab*
pararon *stopped*
¡Qué susto me dio el taxista! *What a scare the cab driver gave me!*
se subió *she got in (a vehicle)*
sin avisar *without prior notice*
te lo pago *I'll pay for it (the cab) for you*
tengo mucho equipaje *I have a lot of luggage*
voy a recogerte *I am going to pick you up*

Tomás: ¡Qué bueno, mamá! Voy a recogerte...

Pilar: No, mi hijo. Puedo ir a tu casa en taxi o en autobús porque vives muy lejos y tengo mucho equipaje.

Tomás: Bueno, pero insisto en que vengas en taxi. Yo te lo pago. Entonces te esperamos aquí en casa, ¿eh?

Pilar: Sí, sí. Nos vemos pronto. Hasta luego, hijo.

Tomás: Hasta luego, mamá.

Comentario cultural A popular means of travel in Guatemala are the so-called "chicken buses." These retired U.S. school buses are privately owned and offer inexpensive transportation to many of the smaller towns and villages. The colorfully decorated buses are modified for use in Guatemala with powerful engines, special transmissions, air brakes, longer seats, and a roof rack.

Pilar **encontró** un taxi en la plaza central y **se subió.** Luego ella le **dio** al taxista la dirección de la casa de Marta y Tomás. **Mientras** Pilar y el taxista **iban** a la casa, **conversaban** sobre el mal tiempo, pero el taxista **estaba** tan cansado que casi **se durmió** dos veces.

De repente, ¡pum! El taxi **chocó** con un autobús de turistas que **venían** de ver una procesión de la Cofradía de Santo Tomás en otra calle y los dos vehículos **pararon** inmediatamente. El taxista **estaba** tan cansado que **no vio** el autobús. Afortunadamente, **nadie se lastimó,** pero Pilar **se puso** nerviosa.

Comentario cultural The most important festival of Chichicastenango is the **Fiesta de Santo Tomás,** which honors the patron saint of the town. On December 21, the saint's image is carried in procession through the streets by the **Cofradía de Santo Tomás** *(Brotherhood of Saint Thomas).*

Dos horas más tarde, el taxi **llegó** finalmente a la casa de Marta y Tomás, quienes **esperaban** a Pilar en la puerta. Ella **salió** del taxi y todos **se saludaron** con abrazos y besos. Pilar **estaba** muy asustada y nerviosa, pero cuando **vio** a Marta y a Tomás **se puso** muy contenta.

Pilar: ¡Qué susto me **dio** el taxista!

Comentario cultural The specialty of Chichicastenango's market are the Chichicastenango **huipiles**—traditional, square-shaped shirts made from brightly colored fabric. Also of note are the sashes and the masks that often depict animals and are typically used in the festivals.

 **Recuerdos de una visita inesperada** Trabaja con un(a) compañero(a) de clase. Túrnense para narrar una visita sorpresa, usando verbos en el pretérito y en el imperfecto. Usen expresiones de **En contexto** como modelo para su diálogo.

Interrogative words

Throughout *Plazas* you have been using interrogative words to ask for information about people and events. Below is a summary of interrogative words and examples of their uses.

1. To ask *where* someone is going, use **¿Adónde?** If you are asking about the location of something, a person, or a place, use **¿Dónde?** If you are asking where someone is from, use **¿De dónde?**

¿Adónde? **¿Adónde** vas?	*Where (to)?* *Where are you going?*
¿Dónde? **¿Dónde** está el centro del pueblo?	*Where?* *Where is the center of town?*
¿De dónde? **¿De dónde** eres tú?	*From where?* *Where are you from?*

2. To ask *what* a person or thing is like, or *how* something is done, use **¿Cómo?**

¿Cómo es Miguel? **¿Cómo** lo hiciste?	*What is Miguel like?* *How did you do it?*

3. To ask *when* something is taking place, use **¿Cuándo?** To ask specifically *at what time* an event takes place, use **¿A qué hora?**

¿Cuándo es la fiesta? **¿A qué hora** es la fiesta?	*When is the party?* *What time is the party?*

4. To ask *How much?* or *How many?*, use a form of **¿Cuánto?** When a form of **¿Cuánto?** precedes a noun, it must agree in number and in gender.

¿Cuántos entremeses sirvieron?	*How many hors d'oeuvres did they serve?*
¿Cuántas personas vienen a la fiesta?	*How many people are coming to the party?*

5. To ask *who* does something, use **¿Quién?** if you are asking about one person, or **¿Quiénes?** if you are asking about more than one person. To ask *Whose?* use **¿De quién?**, or **¿De quiénes?** if you are asking about more than one person.

¿Quién es ella? **¿De quién** es la fiesta?	*Who is she?* *Whose party is it?*

6. To ask *Why?*, use **¿Por qué?** To ask *What for?*, use **¿Para qué?**

¿Por qué quieres ir a las montañas?	*Why do you want to go to the mountains?*
¿Para qué tienes los cohetes?	*What do you have the rockets/fireworks for?*

7. To ask *What?* or *Which?*, use **¿Qué?** or **¿Cuál?**

¿Qué quieres comer? **¿Cuál** es tu plato favorito?	*What do you want to eat?* *What is your favorite dish?*

As you can see, the choice of whether to use **¿Qué?** or **¿Cuál?** depends on the syntax of the question. Use **¿Qué?** before a verb to ask for a definition or explanation.

¿Qué quieres? — *What do you want?*

¿Qué es el *Popol Vuh*? — *What is the Popol Vuh?*

Note that **¿Cuál(es)?** is used much more frequently than the English *Which?* and can mean both *What?* and *Which?* **¿Cuál(es)?** cannot be used when the next word in the question is a noun. In such cases, **¿Qué?** must be used.

¿Qué libro quieres? — *Which book do you want?*

¿Cuál de los dos libros quieres? — *Which of the two books would you like?*

¿Cuál es la fecha? — *What is the date?*

Cultura

The *Popol Vuh* is the holy book of the **K'iche'**, a kingdom in the post-classic Maya civilization of Guatemala. The scripture tells of the creation of humans from corn.

¡A practicar!

8-7 **Un anuncio** Estás en Guatemala con un amigo que tiene ganas de participar en las actividades de Semana Santa. Escuchas este anuncio sobre la procesión y la gran fiesta. Después de escuchar el anuncio, escribe la información que tu amigo quiere saber.

AUDIO CD
CD 3, TRACK 3

¿Dónde? ____________________

¿Qué día? ____________________

¿A qué hora? ____________________

¿Cuánto cuesta? ____________________
____

¿Qué comidas/bebidas? ____________________
____

¿Quiénes participan? ____________________
____

8-8 **Preguntas de un turista** Dos turistas están hablando sobre lugares en o cerca del centro histórico de la Ciudad de Guatemala. Un turista le hace muchas preguntas al otro. Indica la palabra interrogativa correcta para completar cada pregunta.

1. —¿De dónde / ¿Dónde está el mejor hotel de la Ciudad de Guatemala?
   —Está en el centro histórico y es el Hotel Pan American.
2. —¿Cómo / ¿Cuándo son los cuartos en ese hotel?
   —Son grandes. También hay unas suites.
3. —¿Cuánto / ¿Cuántas cuesta el alojamiento *(lodging)* en el hotel?
   —Un cuarto cuesta alrededor *(around)* de 100 dólares por noche.
4. —¿Qué / ¿Quiénes van con nosotros a la discoteca esta noche?
   —Mis nuevos amigos que conocí en el Parque Central van con nosotros.
5. —¿Dónde / ¿Quién es tu amiga que sabe tanto sobre marimba?
   —Mi amiga Luisa es experta en marimba.
6. —¿Cuál / ¿Qué es tu monumento favorito en la Ciudad de Guatemala?
   —El monumento que más me gusta es la Catedral Metropolitana.

Workbook *8-5*
Lab Manual *8-4 – 8-6*

¡A conversar!

8-9 ***¿Qué o cuál(es)?*** Escoge la palabra correcta y luego hazle la pregunta a un(a) compañero(a) de clase.

1. ¿ ______ es el amor?
2. ¿ ______ es tu grupo de música favorito?
3. ¿ ______ clase tienes después de esta clase?
4. ¿ ______ son los videos más recientes que viste en las últimas tres semanas?
5. ¿ ______ es Internet?
6. ¿ ______ es tu número de teléfono?
7. ¿ ______ es la capital de El Salvador?
8. ¿ ______ ciudad es la capital de Guatemala?

8-10 **Quieres información** Con un(a) compañero(a), túrnense para hacerse preguntas sobre los siguientes temas. El (La) compañero(a) debe contestar apropiadamente.

- cantidad de regalos
- precio de un CD
- hora de un programa de TV
- lugares para ir a comer
- preferencias y gustos
- cumpleaños

Modelo: **E1:** *¿Cuándo es el cumpleaños de Sandra?*
E2: *Es el sábado.*

8-11 **¿Cuándo es la fiesta?** Habla con un(a) compañero(a) de clase. Una persona va a inventar detalles sobre una fiesta y la otra persona va a hacerle todas las preguntas posibles sobre esa fiesta.

Cultura

The **marimba** is the national instrument of Guatemala and has African and indigenous origins. It resembles a large xylophone with pipes of varying lengths under the keys.

The preterite vs. the imperfect

The choice of using the preterite tense or imperfect tense is not arbitrary. The choice depends on how a speaker or writer views the past actions, conditions, and events that he/she describes.

The following parameters may be used to distinguish between the use of the preterite and imperfect tenses:

Preterite	Imperfect
• **single, completed action (what someone did or didn't do)** Marta **dio** una fiesta sorpresa para su marido. *Marta gave a surprise party for her husband.*	• **habitual action or event (expresses the idea in English of something you *used to do* or *would always do* in the past)** Tomás y Marta siempre **celebraban** los cumpleaños. *Tomás and Marta always celebrated (used to celebrate) birthdays.*
• **highlighted, main action** Tomás **llegó** a casa y **entró.** *Tomás arrived home and went in.*	• **background action or description that sets the stage for main action (including time, location, age, weather, and physical and emotional states)** La noche de la fiesta **hacía** buen tiempo y Marta **estaba** muy contenta. *The night of the party the weather was nice and Marta was very happy.*
• **beginning or conclusion of an event** A las 11:00 de la noche **empezó** a llover. *At 11:00 at night, it began to rain.*	• **middle of an event or emphasis on indefinite continuation of event** En la fiesta, algunos de los invitados **hablaban** mientras otros **comían.** *At the party, some of the guests were talking while others were eating.*
• **action that interrupts another action** Cuando Tomás **entró** en la sala... *When Tomás entered the room . . .*	• **ongoing event or action in the past or event that is interrupted** ...los invitados **cantaban.** *. . . the guests were singing.* • **past actions, conditions, and events that were anticipated or planned** **Quería tomar un café, pero no tenía dinero.** I wanted to have a coffee, but I didn't have money.
• **with verbs associated with time expressions, such as *ayer, anteayer, anoche, una vez, dos veces, el mes pasado, and de repente* (suddenly).** El mes pasado, **fuimos** a Guatemala. *Last month we went to Guatemala.*	• **with verbs associated with time expressions such as *todos los días, cada semana, siempre, frecuentemente, de niño(a),* and *de joven.*** Todos los veranos mi esposa y yo **íbamos** de vacaciones a un país extranjero. *Every summer my wife and I would go on vacation to a foreign country.*

To describe two simultaneous actions that were occurring in the past, Spanish speakers often use **mientras** *(while)* to join the two clauses in the imperfect tense.

> Antonio y Mariana **hablaban mientras miraban** los fuegos artificiales.
> *Antonio and Mariana **talked while they watched** the fireworks.*

To describe an ongoing action in the imperfect that is interrupted by an event in the preterite, Spanish speakers often use the word **cuando** to introduce the preterite action.

> Claribel **servía** los entremeses **cuando** su mejor amigo **llegó** a la fiesta.
> *Claribel **was serving** the hors d'oeuvres **when** her best friend **arrived** at the party.*

When the verb **ir a** + infinitive is used in the imperfect, it translates as *was/were going to do something*. The implication is usually that something happened that prevented the intended action from taking place.

> Yo **iba** a mirar la procesión, pero un amigo me **llamó** pidiéndome ayuda.
> *I **was going** to watch the parade, but a friend **called** asking me for help.*

Verbs that refer to states or conditions

Verbs that normally refer to states or conditions **(saber, querer, tener, poder)** take on a special meaning in the preterite. When used in the preterite, they focus on completion of an action. In the imperfect, they emphasize the ongoing nature of an action or cognitive process.

Preterite		Imperfect	
supe	*I found out*	**sabía**	*I knew*
quise	*I wanted to* (and did)	**quería**	*I wanted to* (outcome undetermined)
pude	*I was able to* (and did)	**podía**	*I was able to* (outcome undetermined)
tuve que	*I had to* (and did)	**tenía que**	*I had to* (outcome undetermined)
tuve	*I got, received*	**tenía**	*I had* (in my possession)

The preterite and imperfect together

Spanish speakers often use the preterite and imperfect together to describe past experiences within the framework of the time they occurred. The following paragraph exemplifies many of the uses of the two tenses in the context of a single paragraph.

El segundo día de las vacaciones en El Salvador, **eran** las 2:15 de la tarde y Antonio e Isabela **tenían** mucha hambre. Por eso, **fueron** al restaurante Torremolinos. Isabela le **preguntó** a su marido si ellos **podían** sentarse en la terraza como lo **hacían** siempre que **almorzaban** allí. Antonio le **dijo** al camarero que su esposa **quería** sentarse en la terraza porque a ella le **gustaba** el papagayo que **tenían** allí. Antonio e Isabela **hablaban** sobre los acontecimientos de aquel día cuando **vino** el camarero con los entremeses.	*On the second day of the trip to El Salvador, **it was** 2:15 in the afternoon, and Antonio and Isabela **were** very hungry. So, they **went** to the restaurant Torremolinos. Isabela **asked** her husband if they **could sit** on the terrace as they always **used to** when they ate lunch there. Antonio **told** the waiter that his wife **wanted** to sit on the terrace because she **liked** the parrot they **had** out there. Antonio and Isabela **were talking** about the events of that day when the waiter **came** with the appetizers.*

¿Recuerdas?

Heinle/Cengage Learning

Pilar **encontró** un taxi en la plaza central y **se subió.** Luego ella le **dio** al taxista la dirección de la casa de Marta y Tomás.

Mientras Pilar y el taxista **iban** a la casa, **conversaban** sobre el mal tiempo, pero el taxista **estaba** tan cansado que casi **se durmió** dos veces.

¡A practicar!

8-12 La fiesta de mamá Decide si las partes subrayadas de las oraciones en inglés requieren *(require)* el pretérito o el imperfecto para describir las fiestas de cumpleaños en casa. Explica por qué es necesario usar cada forma que selecciones. Usa la frases subrayadas *(underlined)* para ayudarte.

1. Our family used to celebrate our birthdays together, and my mother would always make a cake.
2. When I was ten, my Aunt Jeanie hosted a big party for my mother.
3. It was a nice day, and we were all very excited.
4. We were all having a good time when my aunt brought in a large birthday cake.
5. My mom began to cry.
6. It was a wonderful party.

8-13 La primera cita de Antonio e Isabela Lee el siguiente párrafo una vez y luego selecciona el pretérito o el imperfecto, según el contexto.

Cultura

The **Plaza San Salvador** was built in honor of Dr. José Matías Delgado, the father of Independence in Central America.

Isabela 1. estaba / estuvo leyendo un libro en su apartamento cuando Antonio la 2. llamaba / llamó por teléfono. Antonio le 3. preguntaba / preguntó si 4. quería / quiso ir al parque cerca de la Plaza San Salvador con él. Isabela le 5. decía / dijo que sí, aunque 6. tenía / tuvo mucho que leer para la semana próxima.

Ahora contesta las siguientes preguntas sobre la primera cita de Antonio e Isabela.

1. ¿Qué hacía Isabela cuando Antonio la llamó?
2. ¿Qué le preguntó Antonio?
3. ¿Qué tenía que hacer Isabela para la semana próxima?

8-14 Preparativos para una fiesta de cumpleaños Decide qué tiempo verbal, pretérito o imperfecto, es necesario para completar las siguientes oraciones. Después, pon el verbo en la forma correcta. Recuerda que los verbos **tener, saber, querer** y **poder** tienen significados diferentes en el pretérito y el imperfecto.

Modelo Ayer, cuando Tomás llegó a casa, él *supo* (saber) que había una fiesta sorpresa para su cumpleaños.

1. Ayer, antes de la fiesta, yo ______ (tener) que limpiar la casa. Lo hice. Yo ______ (saber) que ______ (ir) a tener muchos invitados.
2. Ayer por la tarde nosotros ______ (saber) que los primos de Tomás ______ (querer) venir a la fiesta.
3. El año pasado, nosotros ______ (tener) que hacer planes con más tiempo porque ______ (querer) tener mucha gente para la celebración.
4. Cuando era niño, siempre ______ (tener) que limpiar mi habitación. Ahora vivo solo, por eso ayer ______ (tener) que limpiar la cocina antes de la fiesta.
5. Mi hermana no ______ (saber) que Andrea tiene un hermano. En la fiesta, mi hermana ______ (saber) que se llama Valentín.

Workbook *8-6 – 8-8*
Lab Manual *8-7 – 8-9*

¡A conversar!

8-15 Ocasiones memorables Hazle las siguientes preguntas a un(a) compañero(a) de clase y luego comparen sus respuestas. ¿Tienen mucho en común?

1. ¿Cuándo fue la primera vez que le enviaste una tarjeta *(sent a card)* a una persona para el Día de San Valentín? ¿Cómo reaccionó la persona? ¿Cómo te sentiste en aquel momento? ¿Recibiste alguna vez flores *(flowers)* de otra persona?
2. Cuando eras joven, ¿qué hacías para celebrar el Día de Acción de Gracias *(Thanksgiving)*? ¿Comías mucho pavo?
3. ¿Cuál fue el cumpleaños más memorable para ti? ¿Con quién lo celebraste? ¿Recibiste algunos regalos especiales? ¿Lo pasaste muy bien?
4. El año pasado, ¿qué hiciste para celebrar el Año Nuevo? ¿Qué hacías cuando el reloj dio las 12:00?

8-16 Entrevista: La niñez y la juventud Hazle a otro(a) compañero(a) las siguientes preguntas sobre experiencias y relaciones de la juventud.

1. **Su niñez:** ¿De dónde eres originalmente? ¿Por cuánto tiempo viviste allí? ¿Te gustaba vivir allí? ¿Qué cosas no te gustaban allí? ¿Vivías en una casa o en un apartamento? ¿Cómo era? ¿Tenías pocos o muchos amigos? ¿Cómo eran? ¿Cuántos años tenías cuando asististe a la escuela por primera vez? ¿Tenías miedo? ¿Cómo se llamaba la escuela? Durante tu niñez, ¿qué actividades hacías?
2. **Su adolescencia:** ¿Cuántos años tenías cuando comenzaste la escuela secundaria? ¿Cómo se llamaba la escuela y dónde estaba? ¿Dónde vivías? ¿Tenías novio(a) cuando eras adolescente? (¿Sí? Háblame de él/ella, por favor.) ¿Te llevabas bien con tus hermanos en esta época? Cuando eras adolescente, ¿qué hacías los fines de semana? ¿Adónde iban de vacaciones tú y tu familia? ¿Veías mucho a tus abuelos?

8-17 Las Fiestas Agostinas en El Salvador Trabaja con un(a) compañero(a) para contar *(tell)* qué pasó en las Fiestas Agostinas el año pasado. Incluye información sobre qué tiempo hacía, cómo se sentía la gente, qué tipo de ropa llevaban algunas personas y las actividades que varias personas hicieron.

Cultura

Las Fiestas Agostinas take place in San Salvador, El Salvador, August 1–6 each year in celebration of the patron saint, **el Divino Salvador del Mundo** *(the Divine Savior of the World)*. Activities include parades, sporting events, amusement park rides, and enjoyment of holiday foods.

Guatemala y El Salvador

Veamos los videos de Guatemala y El Salvador para luego comentarlos.

1. ¿Cómo son las ciudades de Antigua y Chichicastenango?
2. ¿Qué podemos comprar en los mercados guatemaltecos?
3. ¿Cómo es la ciudad de San Salvador, la capital de El Salvador?
4. ¿Por qué es importante visitar la Catedral Metropolitana?

See also the *Workbook,* **Capítulo 8, 8-16–8-19** for additional activities.

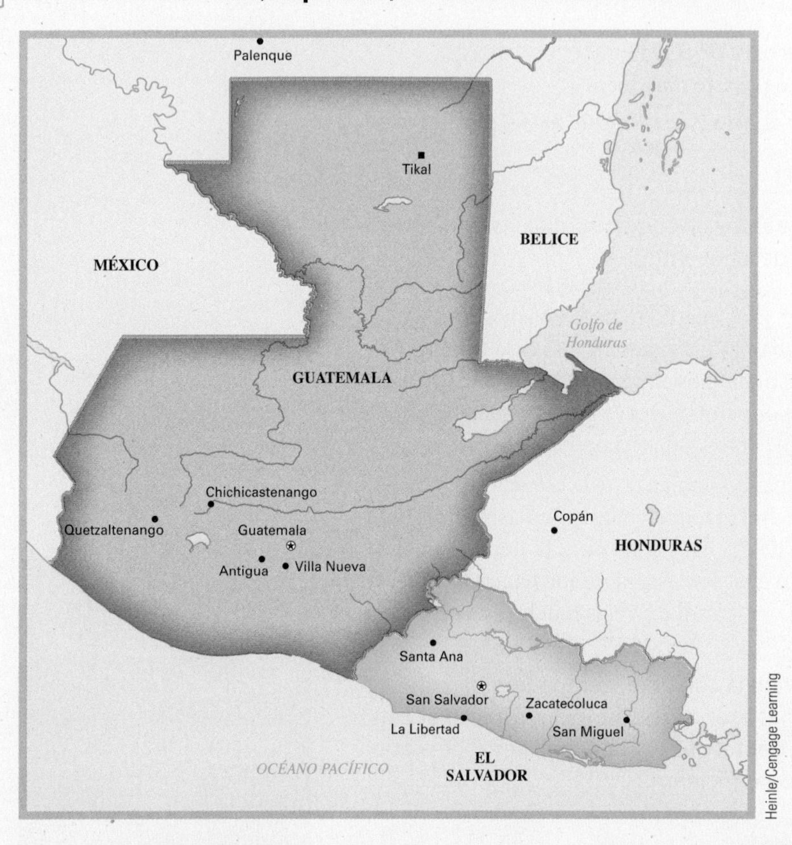

Guatemala

Población: 13.550.440 de habitantes

Área: 108.890 km^2, un poco más pequeña que Tennessee

Capital: Ciudad de Guatemala (3.700.000 habs.)

Moneda: el quetzal

Lenguas: el español y más de veinte lenguas indígenas

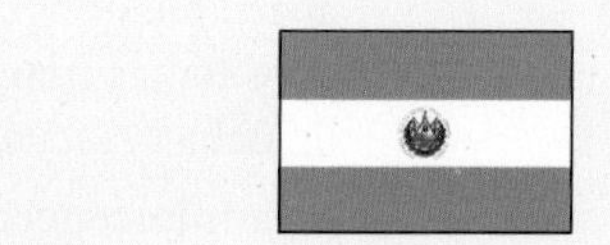

El Salvador

Población: 6.052.064 de habitantes

Área: 21.040 km^2, casi el tamaño de Massachusetts

Capital: San Salvador (2.200.000 habs.)

Moneda: el colón y el dólar estadounidense

Lenguas: el español y el náhuatl

Arzobispo Óscar Arnulfo Romero (1917 – 1980)

Personas notables El Arzobispo *(Archbishop)* Óscar Arnulfo Romero luchó *(fought)* por los derechos humanos *(human rights)* de los campesinos *(farmers)* y de los pobres en El Salvador. El Arzobispo Romero fue asesinado el 24 de marzo de 1980 en San Salvador, en una capilla *(chapel)* mientras daba la misa. La muerte del Arzobispo Romero dio comienzo al conflicto social en El Salvador que duró *(lasted)* del año 1980 al 1992 y que se transformó en una guerra civil *(civil war)* entre los ciudadanos oprimidos *(oppressed)* por el gobierno y las fuerzas militares del gobierno.

Nombra una persona ilustre que luchó por los derechos humanos en el pasado. ¿Puedes nombrar a otras personas que luchan por estos derechos hoy en día?

© Arte Maya Tz'utuhil. www.artemaya.com

Día de ceremonias en Chichicastenango de Pedro Rafael González Chavajay

Artes plásticas Pedro Rafael González Chavajay (1956) es considerado uno de los artistas mayas más importantes de la actualidad. Pertenece al grupo étnico Tz'utuhil, que es uno de los veintiún grupos indígenas mayas que habitan Guatemala. Comenzó a pintar desde muy niño por influencia de su abuelo, que era pintor. González Chavajay representa en su obra *(work)* la vida diaria, las costumbres y las tradiciones de los pueblos mayas de Santiago Atitlán y San Pedro la Laguna.

¿Qué hacen las personas de la pintura? ¿Dónde están?

Lugares mágicos Tikal es la ciudad antigua más grande de la cultura maya. Está situada en el departamento de El Petén, en Guatemala. La civilización maya se desarrolló entre los años 200 y 850 d.C. y tenía una población de 100.000 a 200.000 habitantes. Después de Tikal no se construyeron monumentos tan importantes. Todavía los visitantes pueden observar seis grandes templos en forma de pirámides, el palacio real, pirámides y palacios más pequeños, residencias y piedras talladas *(carved)*. Tikal significa «lugar de las voces» o «lugar de las lenguas» en maya.

¿Te gusta estudiar las civilizaciones antiguas?

© iStockphoto.com/v0v

Ruinas de Tikal

Visit it live on **Google Earth!**

© iStockphoto.com/lubilub

La marimba

Ritmos y música En Guatemala, en El Salvador y en otros países centroamericanos, la marimba *(xylophone)* es el instrumento principal de la música folclórica. La música centroamericana es una mezcla *(mix)* de la música maya, española y africana.

En Guatemala, el cantante y autor (cantautor) más famoso hoy en día es Ricardo Arjona, quien combina temas románticos con temas sociales y políticos. En esta oportunidad, vamos a escuchar la canción «Mojado», en la que el cantautor describe los sentimientos y los problemas que los inmigrantes sufren al cruzar la frontera de los Estados Unidos. *Access the iTunes playlist on the* ***Plazas*** *website.*

¿Te gustan las canciones con temas políticos o románticos? ¿Qué piensas de esta canción?

¡Busquen en Internet!

1. Personas notables: Arzobispo Óscar Arnulfo Romero
2. Artes plásticas: Pedro Rafael González Chavajay
3. Lugares mágicos: Tikal, Guatemala
4. Ritmos y música: la marimba, Ricardo Arjona

De vacaciones...

In this section, you will learn vocabulary and expressions to talk about outdoor activities at the beach and in the countryside. What do you like to do on vacation?

Palabras útiles

las aletas
fins
la arena
sand
el campo
countryside
la caña de pescar
fishing rod
las palmas
palm trees
el (la) salvavidas
life guard
la sombra
shade
la sombrilla (de playa / playera)
sun umbrella
la tabla de surf
surf board
el tanque
scuba tank
la toalla (de playa)
(beach) towel
ahogarse
to drown
armar una tienda de campaña
to pitch a tent

Palabras útiles are presented to help you enrich your personal vocabulary. The words here will help you talk about activities at the beach and in the countryside.

Nota lingüística

Hacer esnórquel is also known as **el buceo de superficie** in some Spanish-speaking countries or **caretear (Colombia)**. In some countries, **hacer surf** is used instead of **correr (las) olas**.

¡A practicar!

8-18 ¿Qué hace esta gente? Mira los siguientes dibujos y describe lo que estas personas hacen en la playa o en el campo. Usa el vocabulario que acabas de aprender.

1. Tomás

2. nosotros

3. José Carlos y Eva

4. tú

8-19 Unas vacaciones Completa el párrafo con la palabra apropiada.

bloqueador	lago	parrillada
camping	montañas	pescar

A la familia Gómez le gusta estar cerca del agua, pero no pueden ir a la playa. Deciden visitar un ________ en las ________. No necesitan hacer reservaciones en un hotel porque van a hacer ________. No quieren comer en un restaurante, van a hacer una ________. Van a ________ y, si tienen suerte, pueden cocinar y comer el pescado. Hace calor y sol y por eso necesitan el ________ solar.

Cultura

Both **el Río Dulce** and **el Lago de Izabal** in Guatemala are popular tourist destinations. **El Lago de Izabal** is the country's largest lake.

8-20 Asociaciones y preferencias Para saber un poco más de la variada geografía de Guatemala y para apreciar los lugares más famosos, haz la siguiente actividad. Puedes consultar un mapa del país si quieres.

Paso 1 Escoge la palabra que no va con el resto del grupo y explica por qué.

1. el océano Pacífico, las montañas, el Río Dulce, el Lago de Izabal
2. hacer camping en Tikal, hacer una parrillada, caminar por las montañas, bucear en la costa del Caribe
3. el balneario, la playa del Puerto de San José, caminar por las montañas, la costa
4. pasear en canoa, broncearse, tomar el sol en la playa, la crema bronceadora

Paso 2 Selecciona, de entre cada grupo de palabras de arriba, la palabra o expresión que te interesa más y explica por qué.

Workbook *8-9 – 8-10*
Lab Manual *8-10 – 8-12*

¡A conversar!

8-21 Problemas y soluciones Conversa con un(a) compañero(a). El estudiante 1 es un(a) cliente(a) en el balneario Hotel Playa del Tesoro en El Salvador y el estudiante 2 es el (la) director(a) de actividades del balneario. El (La) director(a) debe ofrecer una solución lógica a los problemas del (de la) cliente(a). Luego, cambien de papel y hagan otra conversación.

Modelo **E1:** No me gusta nadar en el mar.
E2: *Usted puede nadar en nuestra piscina.*

1. Quiero ir a la playa, pero no tengo traje de baño.
2. Tengo hambre y quiero comer comida salvadoreña, como pupusas.
3. No sé bucear, pero quiero ver los peces y otras cosas en el mar.
4. Quiero aprender a bucear, pero no sé adónde ir.
5. Siempre tengo miedo de broncearme mucho cuando voy a la playa.
6. Me gusta pasear en canoa, pero no quiero ir solo(a).
7. Quiero jugar al voleibol en la playa, pero no tengo una pelota *(ball)* y no tengo amigos aquí.

Cultura

Pupusa is a typical food from El Salvador. **Pupusas** are thick corn tortillas stuffed with cheese, beans, and any type of meat, fish or vegetable. **Chicharrón** *(fried pork rind)* is particularly popular as a filling.

8-22 ¡A pasarlo bien! Trabaja con otro(a) compañero(a). Ustedes van a pasar un fin de semana en un balneario o en el campo. Primero, hagan una lista de las actividades que ustedes van a hacer en ese lugar el sábado y el domingo. Luego hagan una lista de todo lo que ustedes van a llevar. Usen el vocabulario de este capítulo y del **Capítulo 3**. Al terminar, explíquenle el itinerario a la clase.

Modelo

Actividades	Cosas para llevar
sacar fotos	*una cámara*
tomar el sol	*un traje de baño*
comer mariscos	*200 dólares*

8-23 Definiciones Trabaja con un(a) compañero(a) de clase para describir las siguientes palabras e indicar qué te gusta y qué no te gusta. Un(a) estudiante mira el libro y escoge una palabra para definir o describir mientras el (la) otro(a), con su libro cerrado *(closed)*, escucha la información e identifica la palabra. Luego, los dos presentan sus opiniones y preferencias.

Modelo **E1:** Es un hotel en la playa con muchas cosas y actividades para turistas.
E2: Es un balneario. Me gusta pasar mis vacaciones en un balneario.
E1: No me gusta mucho. Prefiero hacer camping en las montañas.

1. el océano
2. la parrillada
3. bucear
4. broncearse
5. pescar
6. correr las olas

Affirmative and negative expressions

Below are some useful affirmative and negative expressions.

algo *something, anything*	**nada** *nothing, not anything at all*
alguien *somebody, anybody*	**nadie** *nobody, no one*
algún, alguno(a) *some, any*	**ningún, ninguno(a)** *none, not any*
o... o *either . . . or*	**ni... ni** *neither . . . nor*
siempre *always*	**nunca** *never*
también *also, too*	**tampoco** *neither, not either*

In Spanish, a negative sentence always has at least one negative word before the conjugated verb. Sometimes there are several negative words in one sentence.

Cultura

Las ruinas de Tazumal in El Salvador are Mayan ruins said to be the best preserved in Central America. According to archaeologists, they date back to 5000 b.c. and span a 1000-year period.

—¿Quieres beber **algo** antes de ir a las ruinas de Tazumal? *Do you want to drink something before going to the ruins of Tazumal?*

—**No, no** quiero **nada,** gracias. *No, thanks. I don't want anything.*

—¿Hay **alguien** en la oficina de turismo ahora? *Is there someone in the tourist office now?*

—**No,** ahora **no** hay **nadie, ni** en la oficina **ni** en el autobús. *No, there's no one in the office nor on the bus now.*

- If a negative word precedes the conjugated verb, the negative word **no** is omitted.

no + *verb* + *negative word*	*negative word* + *verb*
No viene nadie conmigo a nadar.	**Nadie viene** conmigo a nadar.
Nobody is coming to swim with me.	*Nobody is coming to swim with me.*

no + *verb* + *negative word*	*negative word* + *verb*
No voy nunca al gimnasio.	**Nunca voy** al gimnasio.
I never go to the gym.	*I never go to the gym.*

- Express *neither / not either* with a subject pronoun (**yo, tú, usted, él, ella,** etc.) + **tampoco.**

—Nunca voy al gimnasio. *I never go to the gym.*

—Yo **tampoco.** *Me neither. / Neither do I.*

- Place **ni** before a noun or a verb to express the idea of *neither . . . nor.*

—¿Quieres ir a correr o a levantar pesas? *Do you want to go running or lift weights?*

—No quiero **ni** ir a correr **ni** a levantar pesas. *I want neither to go running nor to lift weights.*

The words **algún, alguno, alguna, algunos,** and **algunas** are adjectives; use **algún** before a masculine singular noun.

—¿Hay **alguna** excursión al volcán de Izalco hoy?	*Is there any excursion to Izalco Volcano today?*
—No, pero hay **algunas** excursiones al lago del Ilopango.	*No, but there are some excursions to Ilopango Lake.*
—¿Hay **algún** restaurante cerca del lago?	*Is there any restaurant near the lake?*
—Hay **algunos** restaurantes en el área, pero no muy cerca del lago.	*There are some restaurants in the area but not very near the lake.*
—¿Hay **algún** café pequeño?	*Is there a small café?*

Note that the plural forms **ningunos** and **ningunas** are not used often; instead, use the singular form, and use **ningún** before a masculine singular noun.

—¿Cuántos campos de fútbol hay aquí?	*How many soccer fields are there here?*
—No hay **ningún** campo de fútbol aquí.	*There aren't any soccer fields here.*
—¿A qué hora viene mi entrenador?	*What time is my trainer coming?*
—No tengo **ninguna** idea sobre esto, Tomás.	*I have no idea about this matter, Tomás.*
—¿Cuántas piscinas tiene el balneario?	*How many swimming pools does the resort have?*
—No tiene **ninguna**.	*It doesn't have any.*

Ningunos and **ningunas** are used only with nouns that always come in pairs or plural. For example:

—¿Hay **algunos** zapatos de tenis para mí?	*Are there any tennis shoes for me?*
—No, no hay **ningunos.**	*No, there aren't any.*

Other nouns that always come in pairs or are always plural are **los guantes, los calcetines, las medias, los pantalones,** and **las vacaciones.**

Cultura

El volcán de Izalco has erupted at least 51 times, was active from 1945 to 1965, and still smolders today. **El lago de Ilopango** is a large scenic volcanic lake in central El Salvador. It is the largest lake in the country.

Nota lingüística

Spanish speakers will often say **No tengo la menor idea. / Ni idea.** *(I don't have the slightest idea.)* to emphatically express that they don't know the answer.

¿Recuerdas?

Heinle/Cengage Learning

De repente, ¡pum! El taxi chocó con un autobús de turistas que venían de ver una procesión de la Cofradía de Santo Tomás en otra calle y los dos vehículos pararon inmediatamente. El taxista estaba tan cansado que no vio el autobús. Afortunadamente, **nadie** se lastimó, pero Pilar se puso nerviosa.

¡A practicar!

8-24 Ideas opuestas Forma una oración con el significado opuesto sustituyendo las palabras afirmativas por palabras negativas.

Modelo Yo siempre voy con mi familia de vacaciones.
Yo nunca voy con mi familia de vacaciones.

1. Hay algunos libros sobre el turismo en El Salvador en la tienda del hotel.
2. Marta quiere comer algo en la playa.
3. Alguien en el balneario sabe correr las olas.
4. Rita quiere bucear o hacer esnórquel.
5. Tomás quiere bucear también.
6. Siempre es divertido pasear en velero.

8-25 Unas vacaciones memorables Recibes un mensaje telefónico de una amiga que está en la playa Sunzal, El Salvador, la playa que tú y tu familia van a visitar en dos semanas. Ustedes quieren saber cómo es la playa y qué pueden hacer allá. Escribe cinco datos *(pieces of information)* sobre la playa y las actividades que pueden hacer para luego decírselos a tu familia.

AUDIO CD
CD 3, TRACK 4

1. ______________________________
2. ______________________________
3. ______________________________
4. ______________________________
5. ______________________________

8-26 En el balneario Completa las dos conversaciones siguientes, usando **algo, nada, alguien, nadie, o... o, ni... ni, también, tampoco, siempre** y **nunca.**

—Tomás, voy al supermercado porque no hay casi 1. ______ en el refrigerador en nuestra habitación. ¿Quieres comer 2. ______ especial esta noche?

—No, gracias, Marta. No quiero comer 3. ______ porque comí mucho en el almuerzo.

—Pero, ¿qué te pasa, Tomás?

—4. ______. Es que no tengo hambre, Marta. 5. Tú sabes que ______ como tanta comida en el almuerzo.

(Más tarde...)

—¡Hola, Tomás! Conocí a 6. ______ en el supermercado cerca del balneario. Y 7. ______ es una persona que te conoce a ti.

—Ah, ¿sí? Debe ser 8. ______ un amigo 9. ______ un compañero de trabajo. ¿Quién es?

—Bueno, no es 10. ______ un amigo 11. ______ un compañero tuyo. Se llama Lucía.

—¿Cómo? ¿Lucía? No conozco a 12. ______ con ese nombre, ni tengo muchas amigas 13. ______.

—¿No? Pues, ella me dijo que fue tu novia.

—¿Mi novia? ¡Marta, 14. ______ estás inventando cosas!

—Yo 15. ______ invento historias sobre tu vida. ¿No recuerdas a Lucía? Era tu novia cuando ella tenía catorce años.

—Ah sí, ahora recuerdo, era muy amable conmigo y con mi mamá.

Workbook *8-11 – 8-13*
Lab Manual *8-13 – 8-15*

¡A conversar!

8-27 **De mal humor *(In a bad mood)*** Tú estás de mal humor hoy y, por eso, le contestas negativamente a tu compañero(a), que te hace preguntas con los siguientes elementos. **¡Ojo!** Tu compañero(a) necesita añadir *(add)* palabras para formar una pregunta completa.

Modelo ¿ir con alguien al cine esta noche?
E1: *¿Quieres ir con alguien al cine esta noche?*
E2: *No, no quiero ir con nadie al cine esta noche.*

1. ¿hacer la tarea?
2. ¿estudiar con otra persona de la clase?
3. ¿correr las olas o esquiar en el agua?
4. ¿hacer ejercicio?
5. ¿hacer algo hoy?
6. ¿nadar en alguna piscina?

8-28 **De vacaciones** Con un(a) compañero(a), comenta las siguientes fotografías del lago Atitlán, en Guatemala, y la playa Sunzal, en El Salvador. Contesta las preguntas sobre las fotos y conversa sobre tus propias *(own)* experiencias y preferencias.

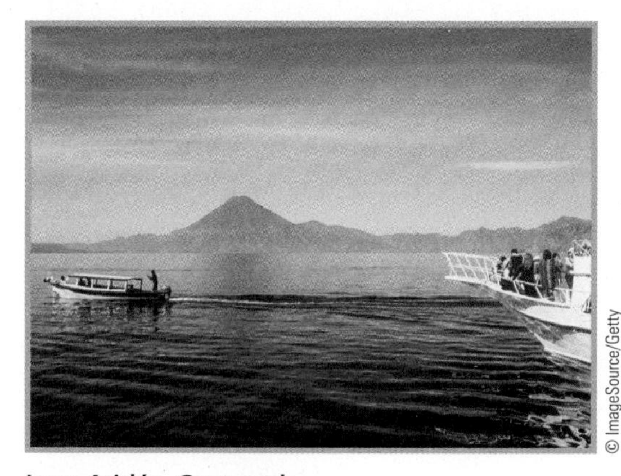

Lago Atitlán, Guatemala

Playa Sunzal, El Salvador

1. ¿Hay alguna persona en la foto del lago Atitlán? ¿Y en la foto de la playa Sunzal?
2. ¿Hay alguna montaña en la primera foto? ¿Y en la segunda? ¿Te gusta ir a las montañas en tus vacaciones? ¿Prefieres ir a la playa o a las montañas? ¿Qué actividades haces en esos lugares?
3. ¿Puedes ver algún animal en la foto? ¿Prefieres ver animales en un parque zoológico o en su hábitat natural?
4. ¿Crees que hay algunas familias en la foto del Lago Atitlán? ¿Vas de vacaciones con tu familia o con tus amigos? ¿Siempre te diviertes en las vacaciones? ¿Qué no haces nunca en las vacaciones?
5. ¿Piensas ir a Guatemala o El Salvador algún día? Si puedes ir, ¿quieres ver el lago Atitlán o la playa Sunzal? ¿Conoces lugares semejantes *(similar)* en los Estados Unidos?

Hace* + period of time + *que

The verb construction **hace** + period of time + **que** is used to talk about how long an event or condition has been taking place or how long it has been since an event or condition took place.

- **Hace** + period of time + **que** + present tense

  To indicate how long something has been happening, Spanish speakers use the construction **hace** + period of time + **que** + present tense.

  Hace seis años que vivo en San Salvador. (Vivo en San Salvador **hace seis años**). — *I've been living in San Salvador for six years.*

- **Hace** + period of time + **que** + preterite tense

  To express how long ago something occurred, Spanish speakers use the verb form **hace** + period of time + **que** + preterite tense.

  Hace un año que se mudaron. (Se mudaron hace un año). — *They moved a year ago.*

¿Cuánto tiempo hace que...?

Note that in order to ask about either (1) a period of time that continues into the present or (2) the amount of time since an event took place, you need to use the following model: **¿Cuánto tiempo hace que...?** The only feature that distinguishes the first scenario from the second is the choice of the present tense versus the past tense. Note the different implications for the following questions:

—**¿Cuánto tiempo hace que estudias** medicina? — *How long have you been studying medicine?* (You continue to study or be a student.)

—**Hace tres años que estudio** medicina. — *I have been studying medicine for three years.*

—**¿Cuánto tiempo hace que estudiaste** medicina? — *How long has it been since you studied medicine?* (You are no longer studying medicine.)

—**Hace dos años que estudié** medicina. — *It has been two years since I studied medicine.*

—**¿Cuánto tiempo hace que no visitas** a tu familia en San Salvador? — *How long has it been since you visited your family in San Salvador?*

—**Hace dos años que no visito** a mi familia en San Salvador. — *I haven't visited my family in San Salvador for two years.*

¿Recuerdas?

Heinle/Cengage Learning

Tomás: ¡Mamá! ¿Estás aquí en Chichicastenango?
Pilar: Sí, hijo. **Decidí** venir a última hora. **Hace seis meses que no los veo** y, además, me encanta la Cofradía de Santo Tomás.

¡A practicar!

8-29 ¿Cuánto tiempo hace que...? Completa las siguientes oraciones con el período de tiempo adecuado y la conjugación correcta del verbo en el presente.

Modelo Hace _un año_ que yo _estudio_ (estudiar) español.

1. Hace __________ que mi compañero(a) de cuarto y yo __________ (vivir) juntos.
2. Hace __________ que yo no __________ (vivir) con mis padres.
3. Hace __________ que el (la) profesor(a) __________ (enseñar) en esta universidad.
4. Hace __________ que nosotros __________ (practicar) español en esta sala.
5. Hace __________ que esta universidad __________ (ofrecer) clases.
6. Hace __________ que yo __________ (leer) novelas.
7. Hace __________ que mi mejor amigo(a) __________ (pasear) en velero.
8. Hace __________ que yo no __________ (ir) a la playa.

8-30 Hechos memorables ¿Cuánto tiempo hace que los siguientes acontecimientos *(events)* ocurrieron en el pasado?

Modelo yo / ir a la universidad por primera vez
Hace tres años que yo fui a la universidad por primera vez.

1. yo / conocer a mi mejor amigo(a)
2. mis amigos(as) / invitarme a una fiesta
3. el nuevo milenio / empezar
4. mis amigos(as) y yo / disfrazarse para una celebración
5. mi novio(a) / comprarme un regalo de cumpleaños
6. yo / venir a la universidad para estudiar
7. mis amigos(as) y yo / ponernos ropa elegante para una fiesta
8. mis padres / ir de vacaciones

Workbook *8-14 – 8-15*
Lab Manual *8-16 – 8-18*

¡A conversar!

8-31 ¿Hace cuánto tiempo que...? Pregúntale a un(a) compañero(a) de clase desde hace cuánto tiempo que hace o que hizo las siguientes cosas. Luego comparen sus respuestas. ¿Tienen mucho en común?

Modelo Conoces a tu novio(a)
E1: *¿Hace cuánto tiempo que conoces a tu novio(a)?*
E2: *Hace seis meses que conozco a mi novio(a).*
o **E1:** *¿Hace cuánto tiempo que conociste a tu novio(a)?*
E2: *Hace un año que conocí a mi novio(a).*

1. vivir en esta ciudad
2. conocer a tu mejor amigo(a)
3. visitar otro país
4. ir a un balneario
5. estudiar español
6. ir a la biblioteca

8-32 Entrevista Hazle preguntas a otro(a) compañero(a), usando **¿Cuánto tiempo hace que...?** para pedir información sobre las siguientes actividades. Debes hacer dos preguntas adicionales sobre cada actividad. Luego comparen sus respuestas. ¿Tienen mucho en común?

Modelo hacer esnórquel
—¿Cuánto tiempo hace que hiciste esnórquel? ¿Dónde lo hiciste? ¿Te divertiste?
—Hace tres años que yo hice esnórquel. Lo hice en Florida y me gustó mucho.

1. dar una fiesta
2. asustarse
3. llorar
4. caminar por las montañas
5. pasarlo bien
6. hacer una parrillada

¡A VER!

Heinle/Cengage Learning

El cumpleaños de Valeria En este segmento del video, vas a ver un flashback y aprender más del día de la lección de baile. ¿Recuerdas aquel día? Fue un día muy especial para Valeria, que estaba muy triste al principio porque todos sus amigos se olvidaron de su cumpleaños.

Antes de ver

Expresiones útiles The following are some new expressions you will hear in the video.

No lo tomes tan a pecho.	*Don't take it so hard.*
Un bizcocho	*A cake*
Ni tan siquiera	*Not even*

Enfoque estructural The following are expressions in the video with affirmative and negative expressions, the preterit tense, and the imperfect tense.

Valeria: **No, no** es eso. Es que **ninguno** de mis amigos en Venezuela **se acordó** de escribirme. **¡Nadie** me **felicitó!**

Alejandra: Cuando **era** pequeña, mi mamá me **celebraba** una fiesta de cumpleaños con mis compañeros de escuela. Ella **llegaba** como dos horas antes de que terminaran las clases, con un bizcocho de cumpleaños, refrescos y helados... y lo **celebrábamos** con mis compañeritos y con mi maestra.

1. **Recordemos** Algunas veces, hay ciertas circunstancias y los cumpleaños no resultan en días felices. ¿Conoces a alguien que se puso triste el día de su cumpleaños? ¿Qué pasó? ¿Cambió su estado de ánimo *(state of mind)* a lo largo del día? ¿Por qué? Cuéntale este acontecimiento a un(a) compañero(a).

2. **Practiquemos** Trabajando con un compañero de clase, identifica los usos del pretérito y del imperfecto en las expresiones del video. ¿Cómo se justifica la selección del pretérito o del imperfecto en cada caso?

3. **Charlemos** Describe la fiesta de cumpleaños más feliz que tuviste en tu vida a un compañero(a) de clase. ¿Qué pasó aquel día? ¿Hacía buen tiempo? ¿Estabas muy emocionado(a)? ¿A que hora empezó la fiesta? ¿Quiénes fueron tus invitados? ¿Recibiste algún regalo especial?

Después de ver

1. ¿Un cambio en el estado de ánimo de Valeria? Lee las siguientes oraciones sobre el cumpleaños de Valeria e indica si son **ciertas** o **falsas.** Corrige las oraciones falsas.

a. Muchos amigos la llamaron.
b. No recibió ningún correo electrónico.
c. No tenía pastel de cumpleaños.
d. Cumplió 26 años.
e. Habló con Sofía sobre las fiestas de cumpleaños que tenía cuando era niña.
f. Se puso feliz mientras bailaba con Antonio, Javier y Sofía.
g. Los compañeros de casa la sorprendieron con un regalo de cumpleaños después del baile.
h. Alejandra le entregó un disco compacto de música cubana.
i. Javier le regaló un ramo de flores.
j. Sofía le invitó a cenar.
k. Al final Valeria se divirtió mucho el día de su cumpleaños.

Heinle/Cengage Learning

2. Las experiencias de Valeria y Alejandra En el video, Valeria y Alejandra hablaron de cómo celebraban el cumpleaños cuando eran niñas, y parece que tenían experiencias diferentes. Lee los siguientes recuerdos y conjuga el verbo en el imperfecto. Luego indica si el comentario corresponde a Valeria o a Alejandra.

Valeria	Alejandra	
________	________	Mis padres siempre me ______ (**hacer**) una fiesta muy grande.
________	________	Mi mamá me _______ (**celebrar**) una fiesta de cumpleaños con mis compañeros de escuela.
________	________	Mi mamá me ______ (**traer**) un bizcocho de cumpleaños, refrescos y helados a la escuela.
________	________	Mi papá siempre me ______ (**llevar**) un ramo de flores a mi cuarto.
________	________	Mi mamá me ________ (**preparar**) mi comida favorita.

Entre nosotros En el video, Alejandra y Valeria describieron cumpleaños muy especiales. Con un compañero, piensen en una fiesta ideal, imaginaria o real, y luego hagan preguntas para adivinar los detalles de la fiesta. Por ejemplo: ¿Cuánto tiempo hace que ocurrió la fiesta? ¿Dónde la celebraron? ¿Vinieron algunas personas famosas? ¿Había algunos globos u otro decorado especial? ¿Había algún tipo de postre especial? Hicieron algunas actividades divertidas?

Presentaciones Con dos compañeros(as) de clase, seleccionen a un miembro de la Hacienda Vista Alegre que va a recibir una fiesta de sorpresa. Expliquen todos los preparativos que hicieron los otros miembros de la casa para este evento. Luego, escriban un párrafo corto explicando lo que pasó. ¿Salió bien la fiesta u ocurrió algo que interrupió la celebración?

See the *Lab Manual,* **Capítulo 8, 8-21– 8-22**

Antes de leer

Strategy: Guessing meaning from word roots *(raíces)*

Thus far, you have learned a large number of new Spanish words and are able to recognize a large number of cognates, even if they are new to you. You can guess the meaning of even more new Spanish words if you know the meaning of their roots. For example, in this chapter you learned the word **sorpresa;** based on your knowledge of this word, what would you guess that the verb **sorprender** means?

If you answered *to surprise,* then you are correct!

Words like **sorpresa, sorprender,** and **sorprendido(a)** that have the same root (e.g., **sorpr-**) are called "word families;" such words are closely related to one another.

Before reading the selection, respond to the following questions using your background information and prior knowledge:

1. What do you see in the photos?
2. What is the title of the piece?
3. What type of literary composition is the piece?
4. What do you know about El Salvador up to this point? (Think back to the chapter activities and the **Encuentro cultural.**)

Now, skim the selection and underline two words that have roots that you recognize.

If you underline words like: **memoria (memorizar), invento (inventar, inventor(a),** you are on the right track!

Flores del volcán

Cognados Escribe cinco cognados y sus significados.

1. ______________________________
2. ______________________________
3. ______________________________
4. ______________________________
5. ______________________________

Word roots Completa el siguiente cuadro para aumentar tu vocabulario. Puedes buscar palabras en este texto y también en los capítulos anteriores. ¿Qué significan estas palabras?

Verbo	Sustantivo *(Noun)*	Persona que hace la acción de...
memorizar		X
inventar		el/la inventor(a)
	el rugido	X
	la baba	X
morir		
traicionar		
	el cuento	

Después de leer

¿Cierto o falso? Indica si las siguientes oraciones son **ciertas** o **falsas**. Corrige las oraciones falsas.

1. ______ En el país de la escritora hay 15 volcanes.
2. ______ La escritora describe El Salvador como un lugar muy verde y pacífico.
3. ______ La escritora describe el volcán como una montaña violenta, que pide vidas humanas como el chacmol.
4. ______ La escritora describe a los niños como huérfanos y tristes.
5. ______ En este país mueren muchas personas.

Catorce volcanes se levantan
en mi país memoria
en mi país mito
que día a día invento.
Catorce volcanes de follaje *(foliage)* y piedra *(stone)*
donde nubes *(clouds)* extrañas se detienen
y a veces el chillido *(screech)*
de un pájaro extraviado *(lost bird)*.
¿Quién dijo que era verde mi país?
es más rojo
es más gris *(gray)*
es más violento:
el Izalco que ruge *(roars)*
exigiendo *(demanding)* más vidas.
Los eternos chacmol
que recogen la sangre *(blood)*
y los que beben sangre
del chacmol
y los huérfanos *(orphans)* grises
y el volcán babeando *(slobbering)*
toda esa lava incandescente
y el guerrillero muerto
y los mil rostros *(faces)* traicionados
y los niños que miran para contar la historia.

Claribel Alegría

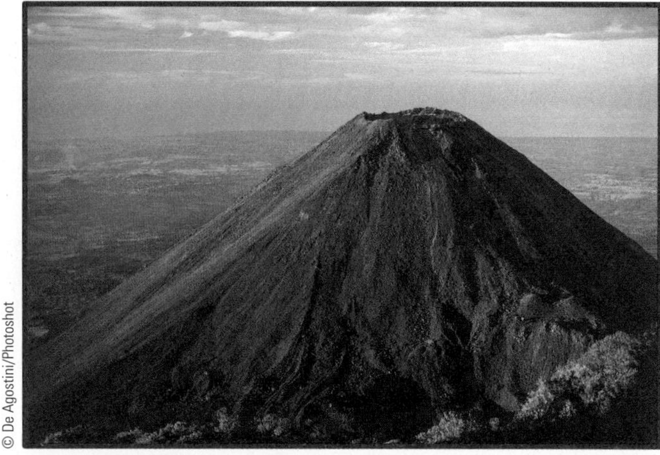

Volcán de Izalco

Cultura

Chacmol (or Chacmool, or Chac Mool) is a pre-Colombian statue of a seated figure that holds a plate in its hands. Some interpretations state that the plate was used to hold the heart and blood of individuals sacrificed to honor the gods of rain and agriculture.

¡A conversar! Con cuatro de sus compañeros de clase respondan las siguientes preguntas:

1. ¿Por qué compara Alegría el volcán con la guerra?
2. ¿Cómo utiliza los colores Alegría? ¿Qué significan los colores?
3. ¿Cómo describe Alegría a los niños, a los guerrilleros y a las demás personas?
4. ¿Por qué creen ustedes que el volcán tiene flores todavía?

¡A escribir! En grupos, escriban un *cinquain,* que es un poema de cinco líneas. En este poema ustedes hagan una descripción de algún aspecto de la geografía de su estado o región importante para ustedes. Sigan el siguiente ejemplo y reemplacen las palabras y frases con las suyas.

Montañas
[Sustantivo *(noun)*]
rojas, *hermosas*
[2 adjetivos *(adjectives)*, palabras descriptivas]
celebran, *gritan*, *recuerdan*
[3 verbos *(verbs)*, acciones]
y dan energía positiva a las personas que las visitan
(Frase para describir el sustantivo)
Sedona
[Sustantivo propio *(proper name)*]

Después de terminar, compartan su poema con la clase. ¿Qué opinan de los poemas de los otros grupos?

Strategy: Writing a summary

A good summary tells the reader the most important information about an event. The following is a list of important data that one should include in a summary.

- An interesting title or topic sentence
- Description of the setting: when and where the action took place, who was involved, any special conditions that were in existence
- What made the situation interesting or unique
- What actions took place, expected or unexpected
- How the event or situation ended or was resolved

Task: Writing a summary of an important event

Summaries of past events occur in a variety of contexts such as in newspapers or magazines or in letters to friends and family. The writer must present sufficient detail to capture and keep the interest of the reader but must not overwhelm the reader with unnecessary information. Follow the steps outlined below to prepare a summary of an important event in which you took part.

Paso 1 Piensa en una celebración que quieres describir en forma escrita. Trata de recordar detalles importantes, como el día o la fecha de la celebración, los preparativos *(preparations)*, las personas, las actividades, los problemas.

el día y la fecha	las actividades
los preparativos	los problemas (si hubo algunos)
las personas	la conclusión

Paso 2 Escribe un resumen de la celebración, contestando las siguientes preguntas.

1. ¿Qué día era o cuál era la fecha? ¿Qué hora era?
2. ¿Qué tiempo hacía?
3. ¿Dónde estabas tú? ¿Dónde estaban las otras personas? ¿Qué hacían todos?
4. ¿Cómo estaban las personas? ¿Por qué?
5. ¿Qué pasó en la celebración? ¿Qué hizo una persona o qué hicieron varias personas? ¿Qué hiciste tú? Menciona varias actividades y, si puedes, incluye información sobre cuándo ocurrieron.
6. ¿Ocurrió algo especialmente interesante?
7. ¿Cómo y cuándo terminó la celebración?
8. ¿Lo pasaste bien? Explica.

Paso 3 Lee la información que acabas de escribir y prepara un título o una oración de introducción para el resumen. Después, lee el resumen otra vez y haz las correcciones necesarias en el contenido, la organización, la gramática y la ortografía *(spelling)*.

Paso 4 Intercambia papeles con un(a) compañero(a) de clase. Lee el resumen de él/ella y después hazle preguntas sobre su resumen y contesta las preguntas que tenga *(may have)* sobre el tuyo.

¡A COMUNICARNOS!

Communicative Goals

- Communicate about holidays, special events and vacations
- Inquire and provide information about people and events
- Express affirmative and negative ideas
- Communicate about past events and activities

Paso 1

Review the Communicative Goals for **Capítulo 8** and determine if you are able to accomplish the goals. If you are not certain that you have achieved all of the goals, review the pertinent portions of the chapter.

Paso 2

Look at the components of a conversation which addresses the communicative goals for this chapter. The percentages will help you evaluate your ability to successfully participate in the conversation that is featured below. Your instructor may use the same rubric to assess your oral performance.

Components of the conversation	%
☐ Questions and answers about where you were when the memorable event took place	10
☐ Inclusion of information about at least one aspect of the setting (time of day, weather, other people present, reason for the celebration, etc.)	10
☐ Questions and answers about how you felt and why	20
☐ Statement of something that you or another person did and why	20
☐ Questions and answers about at least three additional things that some people did, about something that no one did, and about how the event came to an end	20
☐ Information about how you felt at the end of the event and why	20

En acción Think about a conversation in which two friends ask and answer questions about a memorable celebration from the past. Work with a partner to carry out the conversation, being sure to include the steps below. When you have concluded your conversation, change roles.

1. The first person asks the second person where he/she was when the memorable event took place and the second one responds.
2. The second person provides at least one piece of additional information, such as the time of day, the weather conditions, the reason for the event, who else was present, and the like.
3. The first person asks how the second person was feeling and the second person replies telling how he/she was feeling and explaining why.
4. The first person asks what happened next and the second person tells what he/she or another person did and explains why and also provides information about something that no one did and why.
5. The second person provides additional information by telling at least three additional things that he/she or other people did and explains how the event ended.
6. The first person asks how the second person felt at the end of the event and the second person replies with information about how he/she felt and why.

Interrogative words

To ask...
about the location of person or place → ***¿dónde?***
where someone is going → ***¿adónde?***
where someone is from → ***¿de dónde?***
what a person or thing is like or *how* something is done → ***¿cómo?***
when something is taking place → ***¿cuándo?***
at what time an event is taking place → ***¿a qué hora?***
how much or *how many* → a form of ***¿cuánto?***
who does something → ***¿quién?*** or ***¿quiénes?***
whose → ***¿de quién?*** or ***¿de quiénes?***
what or *which* → ***¿qué?*** or ***¿cuál?***

¡A recordar! 1 When should **¿qué?** be used instead of **¿cuál?**

Preterite vs. Imperfect

Preterite	Imperfect
single, completed action	habitual action or event
highlighted, main action	background action
beginning or end of an event	middle of an event
action that interrupts another	ongoing event or action

¡A recordar! 2 Which time expressions indicate the use of the preterite tense? Which indicate the use of the imperfect tense?

Affirmative and negative expressions

algo	**nada**
alguien	**nadie**
algún, alguno(a)(s)	**ningún, ninguno(a)(s)**
o... o	**ni... ni**
siempre	**nunca**
también	**tampoco**

¡A recordar! 3 When a negative word precedes the conjugated verb, is **no** omitted? When are the plural forms **ningunos** and **ningunas** used?

Hace + period of time + que

- **Hace** + period of time + **que** + present tense
- **Hace** + period of time + **que** + preterite tense

¡A recordar! 4 When do you use the present tense and when do you use the preterite tense in these types of constructions?

Actividad 1 Información sobre un festival Indica la palabra o la expresión interrogativa apropiada para cada pregunta.

1. —¿ ________ es el festival? —Es mañana.
2. —¿ ________ es? —Es en el centro de la ciudad.
3. —¿ ________ hora empieza? —Empieza a las dos de la tarde.
4. —¿ ________ es el nombre del festival? —Es La fiesta del pueblo.
5. —¿ ________ se llama la directora del festival? —Se llama Adela Gómez León.
6. —¿ ________ es ella? —Es de Antigua, pero ahora vive en Ciudad de Guatemala.
7. —¿ ________ es el supervisor de la música? —Es Alejandro Samoza.
8. —¿ ________ son los músicos? —Son Rafael Moreno y sus tres primos.

Actividad 2 ¿Qué pasó? Escoge la respuesta correcta para cada oración para saber qué pasó con unos amigos anoche. Presta atención al contexto para escoger las formas correctas de los verbos.

______ 1. Yo ________ un libro cuando Roberto me ______ anoche.
a. leí / llamó c. leía / llamaba
b. leía / llamó d. leí / llamaba

______ 2. Él me ______ que muchas personas ______ en la casa de Victoria, bailando y divirtiéndose.
a. dije / estuvieron c. decía / estaban
b. decía / estuvieron d. dijo / estaban

______ 3. Roberto me ______ a la casa de Victoria, pero yo ______ cansada.
a. invité / estuve c. invitaba / estaba
b. invitaba / estuve d. invitó / estaba

______ 4. Mi compañera de cuarto ______ ir porque ella no ______ ocupada.
a. decidió / estaba c. decidía / estuvo
b. decidía / estaba d. decidió / estuvo

______ 5. Muchas personas ______ cuando ella ______.
a. bailaron / llegó c. bailaban / llegaba
b. bailaban / llegó d. bailaron / llegaba

Actividad 3 Un correo electrónico de Guatemala Completa el correo electrónico que David le manda a su madre el segundo día de sus vacaciones en Ciudad de Guatemala. Escoge el pretérito o el imperfecto según el contexto.

Enviar | Guardar | Archivos

¡Hola, Mamá!

Yo ________ (1. llegar) a la capital ayer. ________ (2. Hacer) buen tiempo pero yo ________ (3. ir) directamente al hotel y ________ (4. descansar) por dos horas porque ________ (5. estar) cansado.

A las tres, mi amigo Manny me ________ (6. llamar) por teléfono y me ________ (7. decir) que él ________ (8. estar) en el centro, en un festival. Yo ________ (9. caminar) al centro e inmediatamente ________ (10. ver) a Manny, ¡bailando en la calle! Muchas personas ________ (11. estar) bailando, comiendo y divirtiéndose. Las mujeres ________ (12. llevar) vestidos tradicionales y los músicos ________ (13. tocar) música folclórica. Manny y su amiga Daniela me ________ (14. enseñar) unos bailes y nosotros ________ (15. bailar) dos horas. Después, nosotros ________ (16. comer) y ________ (17. beber) mucho porque ________ (18. tener) hambre y sed, y la comida ________ (19. estar) deliciosa. Yo ________ (20. volver) al hotel muy tarde, cansado pero alegre después de una experiencia memorable.

¡Escríbeme pronto!

Actividad 4 Un día en el balneario Dos amigos están hablando durante sus vacaciones. Completa las frases con la expresión afirmativa o negativa correcta y lógica.

1. —¿Quieres comer ________
   —No, no quiero comer ________ , gracias.
2. —¿Conoces ________ playa muy buena para correr las olas?
   —No, no conozco ________ playa buena cerca de aquí.
3. —¿________ tomas el sol en la playa?
   —No, ¡________ tomo el sol! ¡El sol es malo para la piel!
4. —¿Quieres esquiar ________ hacer esnórquel?
   —No, no quiero ________ esquiar ________ hacer esnórquel. Prefiero pescar o pasear en velero.
5. —Me gusta mucho la playa. Me gustan las montañas ________ pero no quiero ir a las montañas ahora porque estoy contento aquí.
   —No quiero ir a las montañas ________. Estoy bien aquí.

Actividad 5 ¿Cuánto hace? Completa las oraciones con la expresión **hace** + el tiempo correspondiente (minutos, horas, días, semanas, meses, años).

1. Hoy es 5 de julio. Viajé a El Salvador el 5 de julio del año pasado. Exactamente ____________.
2. Marisa estudió el lunes y el martes. Hoy es viernes por la noche. ____________ que Marisa no estudia.
3. Son las diez de la noche y la fiesta empezó a las seis de la tarde, ____________.
4. Hoy es 10 de septiembre y empiezan las clases. Volví de vacaciones el 10 de agosto. ____________ que volví de vacaciones.
5. ¡José! ¡Llegaste diez minutos tarde! ____________ que empezó la película.
6. ____________ que no como hamburguesas. ¡Exactamente catorce días!

Refrán

Heinle/Cengage Learning

"________ *(Not any)* persona ganó fama quedándose hasta *(remaining until)* las doce en la cama".

VOCABULARIO ESENCIAL

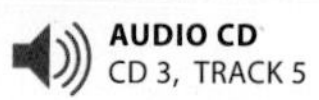
AUDIO CD
CD 3, TRACK 5

PERSONAL TUTOR

Fiestas y celebraciones — *Holidays and celebrations*

Sustantivos

el anfitrión	host
la anfitriona	hostess
el brindis	toast
la celebración	celebration
los cohetes	rockets, fireworks
el cumpleaños	birthday
el día feriado	holiday
el disfraz	costume
los entremeses	hors d'oeuvres
la fiesta (sorpresa)	(surprise) party
el (la) invitado(a)	guest
la máscara	mask
el pastel	cake
la procesión	religious parade
el regalo	gift
el traje típico	traditional /regional outfit
las velas	candles

Verbos

asustarse	to get frightened
celebrar	to celebrate
cumplir años	to have a birthday
dar (hacer) una fiesta	to give a party
disfrazarse	to wear a costume
gritar	to shout
hacer un brindis	to make a toast
llorar	to cry
olvidar	to forget
pasarlo bien (mal)	to have a good (bad) time
ponerse [adj.]	to become (get) [adj.]
portarse bien (mal)	to behave well (poorly)
reaccionar	to react
recordar (ue)	to remember
reunirse con	to get together with

Expresiones idiomáticas

¡Felicitaciones!	Congratulations!
Me pongo contento/ triste	I get happy/sad

Algunas fiestas

el Año Nuevo	New Year
el Día del Padre	Father's Day
el Día de la Independencia	Independence Day
el Día de las Madres	Mother's Day
el Jánuca	Hanukkah
la Navidad	Christmas
el Ramadán	Ramadan
la Semana Santa	Holy Week

De vacaciones — *On vacation*

Sustantivos

el balneario	beach resort
el bloqueador solar	sunblock
la costa	coast
la crema bronceadora	suntan lotion
el lago	lake
el mar	sea
el océano	ocean
la playa	beach
el río	river
la tienda de campaña	tent

Verbos

broncearse	to get a suntan
bucear	to scuba dive
correr las olas	to surf
escalar	to climb
hacer camping	to go camping
hacer esnórquel	to snorkel
hacer una parrillada	to have a cookout
pasear en canoa	to go canoeing
pasear en velero	to go sailing
remar	to row

Expresiones afirmativas

algo	something, anything
alguien	somebody, anybody
algún, alguno(a)(s)	some, any
o... o	either . . . or
siempre	always
también	also, too

Expresiones negativas

nada	nothing, not anything at all
nadie	nobody, no one
ningún, ninguno(a)(s)	none, not any
ni... ni	neither . . . nor
nunca	never
tampoco	neither, not either

Palabras interrogativas

¿A qué hora?	What time?
¿Adónde?	Where (to)?
¿Cómo?	What?
¿Cuál?	Which?, What?
¿Cuándo?	When?
¿Cuánto(a)?	How much?
¿Cuántos(as)?	How many?
¿De dónde?	From where?
¿De quién?	Whose?
¿Dónde?	Where?
¿Quién?	Who?
¿Por qué?	Why?
¿Para qué?	What for?
¿Qué?	What?

CAPÍTULO

De viaje por el Caribe

Cuba, Puerto Rico y la República Dominicana

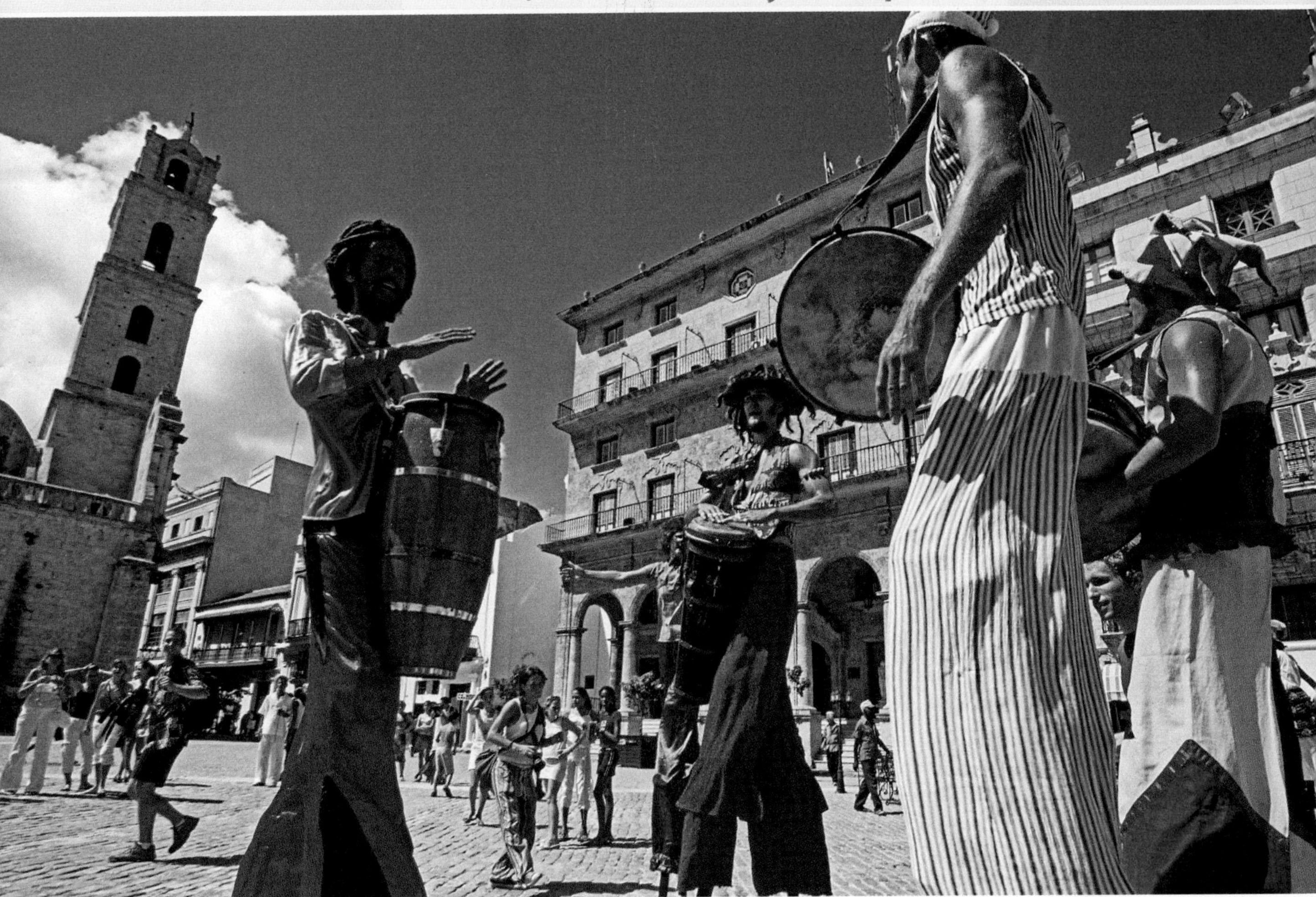

Plaza de San Francisco, La Habana, Cuba

Chapter Objectives

Communicative Goals

In this chapter, you will learn how to . . .

- Communicate about transportation, lodging, and other aspects of travel
- Request and provide information about getting around a city or town
- Give instructions

Structures

- Indirect object pronouns
- Double object pronouns
- Prepositions and adverbs of location
- Formal commands and negative **tú** commands

- Cuando vas de vacaciones, ¿qué te gusta hacer?
- ¿Te gusta viajar a otros países durante tus vacaciones?
- ¿Qué actividad o deporte nuevo quieres aprender en tus próximas vacaciones?

Visit it live on **Google Earth!**

En el aeropuerto Las Américas

In this section, you will learn vocabulary and expressions used for traveling by airplane. The drawing below represents a typical scene in main airports like the one in the Dominican Republic. Do you think flying is a convenient way to travel?

Cultura

Santo Domingo is the capital city of the Dominican Republic. The international airport is called **Las Américas,** and it is located about 20 minutes east of Santo Domingo.

Otros sustantivos

la aerolínea *airline*
el asiento *seat*
el boleto (billete) de ida *one-way ticket*
el boleto (billete) de ida y vuelta *round-trip ticket*
la llegada *arrival*
el pasillo *aisle*
la salida *departure*
el viaje *trip*
el vuelo (sin escala) *(nonstop) flight*

Otros verbos

bajar(se) (de) *to get off*
hacer escala (en) *to make a stop (on a flight) (in)*
ir en avión *to go by plane*
pasar por *to go through*
viajar *to travel*

Expresiones idiomáticas

¡Bienvenido(a)! *Welcome!*
¡Buen viaje! *Have a nice trip!*
Perdón. *Excuse me.*

Palabras útiles

abrocharse el cinturón de seguridad *to buckle the seatbelt*
aterrizar *to land*
con destino a *departing for*
la demora *delay*
despegar *to take off*
procedente de *arriving from*
la salida de emergencia *emergency exit*

Palabras útiles are presented to help you enrich your personal vocabulary. The words here will help you talk about air travel.

¡A practicar!

Nota lingüística

In Latin America, the words **boleto** and **billete** are used to talk about an airplane ticket. In Spain, it is more common to use **el pasaje.**

9-1 Un viaje en avión a Santo Domingo Teresita, una mujer puertorriqueña, hizo un viaje a Santo Domingo para visitar a unos familiares el verano pasado. Pon sus acciones en un orden lógico.

_____ Facturó el equipaje.
_____ Abordó el avión con destino a Santo Domingo.
_____ Fue a la agencia de viajes.
_____ Compró un boleto de ida y vuelta.
_____ Hizo las maletas.
_____ Recibió una invitación de sus parientes de Santo Domingo.
_____ Pasó por el control de seguridad.

9-2 Nuestra luna de miel *(honeymoon)* Teresita y su esposo Manny fueron a La Habana, la capital de Cuba, para pasar su luna de miel. Completa el párrafo usando las siguientes palabras.

agente de la aerolínea	boleto	llegada
agente de viajes	equipaje de mano	salida
asiento de pasillo	hacer escala	viaje
Bienvenidos	inmigración	vuelo sin escalas

El mes pasado, Manny y yo fuimos a La Habana, Cuba, para nuestra luna de miel. Nuestro 1. _____ nos reservó un 2. _____ en la aerolínea Cubana de Aviación. Yo estaba contenta porque a mí no me gusta 3. _____. Tampoco me gusta mirar afuera del avión cuando vuelo, así que yo pedí un 4. _____. Antes de la 5. _____ del vuelo, le enseñamos el pasaporte y el 6. _____ a un 7. _____. No teníamos muchas maletas, pero Manny llevó 8. _____ con las cosas más necesarias. Durante el vuelo, esperamos con mucha emoción la 9. _____ a Cuba. Al llegar a La Habana, el piloto nos dijo: "¡10. _____ a Cuba!" Tuvimos que pasar por la oficina de 11. _____, pero fue fácil. Total, nuestra luna de miel en La Habana fue el mejor 12. _____ de mi vida.

Cultura

Travel from the U.S. to Cuba has been restricted since 1961. Official government travel and travel by professional journalists, researchers, and educators is allowed with required visas. In 2009, President Obama lifted a broad set of sanctions against Cuba, which included eliminating restrictions on gifts and money sent by U.S. relatives to the island.

9-3 En el aeropuerto Estás en el aeropuerto cuando escuchas información sobre el vuelo que tú y tu amigo van a tomar a Puerto Rico. Tu amigo no está en el aeropuerto y por eso necesitas mandarle un mensaje de texto *(text message)* con la información necesaria. Escucha la información y escribe cinco datos (*pieces of information*) importantes.

AUDIO CD
CD 3, TRACK 6

1. _____
2. _____
3. _____
4. _____
5. _____

Workbook *9-1 – 9-3*
Lab Manual *9-1 – 9-3*

¡A conversar!

9-4 **En el aeropuerto** Haz esta actividad con dos compañeros(as). Dos personas son pasajeros en el aeropuerto y la otra persona es el (la) agente de la aerolínea.

Agente	Pasajeros
1. Greet your passengers.	2. Respond appropriately.
3. Find out where they are going.	4. Answer the question.
5. Ask for their tickets and passport.	6. Do what the agent asks and say something appropriate.
7. Ask their seating preference (window/aisle).	8. Answer, then ask if your plane will leave on time.
9. Answer the question, then check in their luggage.	10. Ask how the weather is at your destination.
11. Respond, then say where they should board the airplane.	12. Ask for directions to your departure gate.
13. Explain, then return their travel documents.	14. Ask what time it is. Express appreciation.
15. Respond, then wish them a good trip.	16. Express your appreciation.
17. Say good-bye.	18. Answer appropriately.

9-5 **¡Vamos a Santo Domingo!** Tienes la oportunidad de viajar de Nueva York a Santo Domingo, República Dominicana. El (La) agente de viajes recomienda un itinerario, pero no estás contento(a) con los detalles. Trabaja con un(a) compañero(a) para comentar el itinerario y pedir cambios. Decidan ustedes las fechas, las horas, el precio, el número de pasajeros y cualquier otra *(any other)* información. El (La) viajero(a) debe pedir todos los cambios que quiere y el (la) agente puede aceptarlos o no.

Modelo **E1:** Agente de viajes: *El vuelo es el miércoles, 15 de noviembre.*
E2: Viajero(a): *Prefiero el jueves, 16 de noviembre. ¿Es posible cambiarlo?*
E1: Agente de viajes: *Sí, es posible, pero el precio es mejor el miércoles.*

Por favor, revisa y confirma tu selección

Itinerario

IDA

Salida	07:40 LUN, 15-Nov	Nueva York - JFK (John F Kennedy Intl Airport)	Estados Unidos	e	Sin escala
Llegada	12:20 LUN, 15-Nov	Santo Domingo - SDQ (Las Américas)	República Dominicana		Clase: Turista

VUELTA

Salida	13:30 MAR, 30-Nov	Santo Domingo - SDQ (Las Américas)	República Dominicana	e	Sin escala
Llegada	16:15 MAR, 30-Nov	Nueva York - JFK (John F Kennedy Intl Airport)	Estados Unidos		Clase: Turista

Presupuesto

Precio total*: $374,44
Tasas y gastos incluidos

Número de pasajeros: 1
* El precio total incluye los gastos de servicio de $12,00 por pasajero y trayecto.

EN CONTEXTO

Sharon y su amiga Kate son estudiantes de la Universidad Internacional de la Florida en Miami, donde hace tres años que estudian español. Ahora ellas están de vacaciones en Santo Domingo, visitando la Ciudad Colonial. Lo que sigue es una parte del diario que grabó Sharon en su iPod.

AUDIO CD
CD 3, TRACK 7

Escucha el diálogo y contesta las siguientes preguntas.

1. ¿Cuáles son algunos sitios de interés turístico que ofrece Santo Domingo?
2. ¿Cuáles son los lugares que Sharon y Kate visitaron durante su viaje a Santo Domingo y las actividades que ellas hicieron allí? Haz una lista.
3. ¿Por qué Sharon se enojó un poco con Kate?
4. Imagínate que tú estás en Santo Domingo ahora. De las cosas que Sharon y Kate vieron e hicieron, ¿cuáles quieres ver y hacer?

27 de junio. Kate y yo estamos en el Hotel Montesinos. Cuando llegamos aquí anoche, estábamos tan cansadas que nos acostamos inmediatamente. Esta mañana caminamos por la Ciudad Colonial y vimos algunas plazas e iglesias coloniales.

Comentario cultural The old section of Santo Domingo, in the seaport district, served as the first capital of the new territories discovered by Christopher Columbus. Santo Domingo was also the first city in the New World to establish a university, a cathedral, a fort, a monastery, a hospital, and a palace.

En una librería **cerca de** La Plaza de la Cultura compramos tarjetas postales para **mandarles a nuestros padres y amigos.** Luego tomamos un autobús a la Fortaleza de Ozama, desde donde vimos el Río Ozama.

Comentario cultural Fort Ozama is the oldest military fortress in the New World. It was built on the banks of the Ozama River in 1502 to protect the city of Santo Domingo from pirate attacks. "Ozama" means "navegable waters" to the Taíno people, the first inhabitants of the island.

Yo saqué una foto de Kate **enfrente de** la fortaleza y **se la mandé** por correo electrónico a un amigo que tenemos, llamado Rodrigo Enrique. Después, Kate me dijo otra vez: «**No te olvides** de **enviarles la foto a los miembros de mi familia** también». Yo le respondí: «**¡No me pidas** más este favor si no puedes recordar las direcciones de correo electrónico!»

Comentario cultural Fort Ozama has the distinction of having never been taken by force of arms, despite all the military intervention it has suffered over the centuries.

Expresiones en contexto

antes de irse *before leaving*
charlamos *we chatted*
desde donde *from where*
hacer algunas compras *to purchase a few things*
mercado de artesanías *arts and crafts market*
no deberíamos haber llevado *we shouldn't have worn*

En la Plaza de la Hispanidad conocí a Eduardo Pérez, a su esposa Gabriela y a sus dos hijas. Ellos son amigos íntimos de nuestro profesor en la Universidad Internacional de la Florida. **Se los presenté a Kate** cuando ella volvió de la Plaza España de hacer algunas compras. Ellos nos invitaron a su casa para cenar.

Comentario cultural The Plaza de la Hispanidad in Santo Domingo features a statue commemorating Columbus's arrival on the island of Hispaniola on his first voyage to the Americas in December of 1492. Hispaniola, which includes the Dominican Republic and Haiti, is the second-largest island in the Antilles.

28 de junio. Esta mañana visitamos muchas iglesias, como la Capilla de Nuestra Señora de los Remedios. ¡No deberíamos haber llevado ropa tan informal a las iglesias!

Por la tarde, fuimos al mercado de artesanías, en el Parque Colón, para comprar algunos recuerdos. Yo compré un anillo y unos aretes, y **se los di a Kate.** Luego, ella **me compró** un sombrero y una camiseta muy bonita.

Comentario cultural Most churches and other holy monuments in Latin America and Spain have strict dress codes. Their policies often prohibit shorts, sandals, bare shoulders, and hats.

Heinle/Cengage Learning

Allí en el parque conocimos a Juan Ochoa Valderrama y a José Hernández Lillo, que son empleados del Museo Casas Reales. Juan tiene veintitrés años y José tiene veinte. Ellos nos invitaron a tomar café en un pequeño restaurante, donde charlamos por dos horas. Antes de irse, Juan nos invitó a una fiesta en su casa.

Hemos estado en Santo Domingo solamente dos días y ya tenemos seis amigos. ¡Qué simpáticos son los dominicanos!

Comentario cultural The Museo Casas Reales provides a unique understanding of Santo Domingo's colonial heritage through exhibitions of artifacts dating from 1492 through 1821.

 **Narración de un viaje inolvidable** Con un(a) compañero(a) de clase, túrnense para hablar de experiencias sobre un viaje imaginario, parecidas a las descripciones que acaban de escuchar en **En contexto.** Deben cambiar las nacionalidades y los destinos. Usen expresiones de **En contexto** como modelo.

ESTRUCTURA 1

Indirect object pronouns

The concept of indirect objects

Most sentences have a subject and a verb. As you learned in **Capítulo 7,** many sentences also have a direct object or a pronoun that replaces the direct object (the direct object pronoun).

Subject	Verb	Direct Object	Subject	D.O.P.	Verb
↓ Manny	↓ compró	↓ un boleto.	↓ Manny	↓ lo	↓ compró.
Manny	*bought*	*a ticket.*	*Manny*		*bought it.*

Note below that some sentences also have an indirect object.

Subject	Indirect Object Pronoun	Verb	Direct Object	Indirect Object
↓ Manny	↓ le	↓ compró	↓ un boleto	↓ a su esposa.
Manny		*bought*	*a ticket*	*for his wife.*

Indirect object pronouns refer to people already mentioned as indirect objects; that is, the pronoun tells *to whom* or *for whom* the action of the verb is performed.

To whom did he give the tickets?

Manny **le** dio los boletos **a su esposa.** — *Manny gave the tickets* ***to his wife.***

Él **le** dio los boletos. — *He gave the tickets* ***to her.***

For whom did he buy the souvenirs?

Manny **les** compró recuerdos **a sus hermanos.** — *Manny bought souvenirs* ***for his brothers.***

Él **les** compró los recuerdos. — *He bought the souvenirs* ***for them.***

Indirect object pronouns

In the preceding examples, the indirect object pronouns **le** and **les** replace the indirect object nouns **esposa** and **hermanos,** respectively.

Singular	Plural
me *to/for me*	**nos** *to/for us*
te *to/for you* (informal)	**os** *to/for you* (informal: Spain)
le *to/for you* (formal), *him, her*	**les** *to/for you, them*

Note that indirect object pronouns are placed in the same positions as direct object pronouns.

1. Place the pronoun in front of the conjugated verb.

   —¿Marta **te dio** esa maleta? — *Did Marta* ***give you*** *that suitcase?*

   —Sí. También **me compró** estos sombreros. — *Yes. She also* ***bought me*** *these hats.*

2. In negative sentences, place the **no** in front of the pronoun.

   —Le di el boleto a mi esposo. — *I gave my husband the ticket.*

   —¿Por qué **no nos** diste uno? — *Why didn't you give us one?*

3. When the pronoun is used with an infinitive, a present participle, or an affirmative command, either place it before the conjugated verb or attach it to the infinitive, the present participle, or the command.

   Le voy a escribir. / Voy a escribir**le.** — *I'm going to write* ***to him.***

   Le estoy escribiendo ahora. / Estoy escribiéndo**le** ahora. — *I'm writing* ***to him*** *now.*

   ¡Escríbe**le** ahora! — *Write* ***to him*** *now!*

Also note that since **le** and **les** can have different meanings, you may add the expressions **a él, a ella, a usted, a ellos, a ellas,** or **a ustedes** to the sentence for clarification or emphasis.

For clarification

—¿**Le** prometiste el viaje **a él o a ella?** — *Did you promise the trip* ***to him or her?***

—**Le** prometí el viaje **a ella.** — *I promised the trip* ***to her.***

For emphasis

—¿A quién **le** está comprando este recuerdo? — *For whom are you buying this souvenir?*

—Estoy comprándo**le** este recuerdo **a usted.** — *I'm buying this souvenir* ***for you.***

A written accent is needed to mark the stressed vowel of a present participle or an affirmative command when an indirect object pronoun is attached to it.

Indirect object pronouns are often used with the verbs **dar** *(to give)* and **decir** *(to say; to tell)*. Other verbs that frequently employ indirect object pronouns are:

escribir *to write*
explicar *to explain*
mandar *to send*
ofrecer (zc) *to offer*
pedir (i, i) *to request; to ask for*
preguntar *to ask a question*
prestar *to lend*
prometer *to promise*
recomendar (ie) *to recommend*
regalar *to give (as a gift)*
servir (i, i) *to serve*

Ofrecer, like **conocer**, undergoes the change of **c** to **zc** in the **yo** form: **yo ofrezco. Pertenecer** *(to belong)* follows this pattern as well.

¿Recuerdas?

Heinle/Cengage Learning

En una librería cerca de La Plaza de la Cultura compramos tarjetas postales para **mandarles a nuestros padres y amigos.** Luego tomamos un autobús a la Fortaleza de Ozama, desde donde vimos el Río Ozama.

¡A practicar!

9-6 De viaje por el Caribe Imagínate que vas de viaje por las islas del Caribe y quieres describir lo que haces allá. Completa las frases, usando el pronombre de objeto indirecto correcto.

Cultura

A **guayabera** is a typical dress shirt worn by men, and lately by women in form of a dress, in the Caribbean. They are usually made of light-weight material and have four pockets embroidered on the front. Today, they come in different colors as well.

Modelo Yo *les* escribo postales del Caribe. (a mis padres)

1. Yo ______ hago muchas preguntas al agente de viajes sobre Santo Domingo. (a él)
2. Él ______ recomienda visitar la Fortaleza Ozama, que fue la primera construcción militar de América. (a mí)
3. Yo ______ prometo comprar cosas típicas, como guayaberas dominicanas, cubanas y puertorriqueñas. (a ti)
4. Los padres de mis compañeros de viaje ______ piden fotos de La Habana. (a sus hijos)
5. En Cuba, el botones *(bellhop)* del hotel ______ recomienda tomar un helado en el Café Coppelia de La Habana. (a nosotros)

9-7 En una tienda del aeropuerto Teresita y Manny deciden a última hora comprarle un recuerdo de Cuba al hermano de Teresita. Llena los espacios en blanco, conjugando los verbos entre paréntesis (si es necesario) y colocando *(placing)* el pronombre de objeto indirecto en el lugar correcto.

Modelo **Dependiente:** ¿Puedo *recomendarles* (recomendar/les) algo?

Dependiente: Hola, ¿en qué puedo ______ (1. servir/les)?

Teresita: Queremos ______ (2. comprar/le) un regalo a mi hermano.

Dependiente: Bien. ¿Qué tipo de regalo ______ (3. dar/le) Uds.?

Teresita: Pues, a mi hermano y a mí ______ (4. gustar/nos) mucho la ropa.

Dependiente: ¿Qué tipo de ropa ______ (5. gustar/les) a Uds., por ejemplo?

Teresita: Bueno, el año pasado él ______ (6. regalar/me) un sombrero de Perú y ahora quiero ______ (7. dar/le) a él un sombrero cubano.

Dependiente: Bueno, ¿a Ud. ______ (8. gustar/le) éste?

Teresita: ¡Sí! Y pienso que a él también ______ (9. ir a gustar/le). ¿Puedo ______ (10. probar/me) el sombrero? Mi esposo quiere ______ (11. regalar/me) uno a mí también.

Manny: Y tú ______ (12. poder/me) regalar una guayabera, ¿no?

9-8 ¡Ayúdanos! Teresita y Manny están muy cansados después de su luna de miel y te piden ayuda. Explica lo que tú haces por ellos, y lo que ellos hacen por ti, usando el pronombre de objeto indirecto correcto.

Modelo (a ellos) hacer las reservas para el vuelo *Les hago las reservaciones para el vuelo.*

1. (a Teresita) bajar las maletas
2. (a ellos) llamar un taxi
3. (al agente) preguntar el horario
4. (a Teresita y Manny) prometer escribir una carta
5. (a nosotros) Teresita dar un beso
6. (a mí) Manny y Teresita regalar una guayabera cubana por ayudarlos

Workbook *9-4 – 9-6*
Lab Manual *9-4 – 9-6*

¡A conversar!

9-9 **Un esposo preocupado** Es el día del regreso, y Manny está preocupado. Responde a sus preocupaciones desde la perspectiva de Teresita, diciéndole a Manny que todo está bien. Sigue el modelo.

Modelo —¿Les compramos los regalos a nuestros amigos?
—Sí, les compramos los regalos ayer. Les compramos las carteras. ¿No te acuerdas?

1. ¡Ay! Me olvidé de decirles el número del vuelo a nuestros amigos.
2. ¡Caramba! Yo quería comprarme una camiseta de Cuba.
3. También quería comprarme una caja de puros *(cigars)* de aquí.
4. No le di una propina al camarero en el restaurante esta mañana.
5. Tenemos que mandarle una tarjeta postal a mi abuelo.
6. Tenemos que explicarle al agente de vuelos que llevamos mucho equipaje.

9-10 **¿Me puede ayudar?** Un turista en San Juan, Puerto Rico, habla con un policía y le pide ayuda. Trabajando en parejas, narren lo que dicen este turista (y otros) y cómo responde el policía. También deben ofrecer comentarios personales sobre la información.

Modelo El turista / preguntarle al policía: dónde está el Capitolio Viejo // El policía / decirle: en la Avenida Muñoz Rivera
El turista le pregunta al policía dónde está el Capitolio Viejo y el policía le dice que está en la Avenida Muñoz Rivera. Si voy a Puerto Rico, quiero ver el Capitolio Viejo.

1. el turista / preguntarle al policía: cuál es la moneda nacional de Puerto Rico // El policía / decirle: el dólar estadounidense
2. otro turista / preguntarle al policía: qué es El Morro // El policía / informarle: la fortaleza más famosa de Puerto Rico
3. varios turistas / preguntarle al policía: dónde está la Iglesia de San Francisco // El policía / decirles: en la Calle San Francisco
4. yo / preguntarle al policía: cuántas personas viven en San Juan // El policía / informarme: unas 500.000 personas
5. el policía / explicarnos: es fácil caminar por el Viejo San Juan // Nosotros / decirle: gracias
6. el policía / ofrecerles a muchos turistas: recomendaciones de restaurantes y cafés // Los turistas / pedirle: recomendaciones de hoteles también

Cultura

Because Puerto Rico is a commonwealth (**estado libre asociado** in Spanish) of the United States, no passport is needed when U.S. citizens travel to Puerto Rico. For the same reason, residents of Puerto Rico do not need a passport to enter any part of the United States.

9-11 **Preguntas personales** Hazle las siguientes preguntas sobre su vida personal a uno(a) de tus compañeros. Túrnense para contestarse las preguntas.

Tus amigos ¿Les hablas a tus amigos sobre tu vida personal? ¿Te ayudan tus amigos con algunos problemas? ¿Les ayudas a ellos con sus problemas? ¿Cuándo fue la última vez que un amigo te hizo un favor? ¿Les prestas dinero a tus amigos? ¿Por qué sí o por qué no?

Tus padres ¿Les haces muchos favores a tus padres? ¿Ellos te hacen favores a ti? ¿Qué tipo de favores? ¿Te escriben cartas o correos electrónicos de vez en cuando? ¿Les escribes a ellos? ¿Te hicieron una visita sorpresa alguna vez? ¿Qué pasó?

Double object pronouns

Sometimes you may want to use both direct and indirect object pronouns together in the same sentence. In this case, note that indirect object pronouns always precede direct object pronouns.

Indirect		Direct
me		
te		lo
le (se)	+	la
nos		los
os		las
les (se)		

In the examples below, notice that the indirect object pronouns **le** and **les** always change to **se** when they are used together with the direct object pronouns **lo, la, los,** and **las.**

Teresita **le** compró **un regalo a su hermano.** — *Teresita bought a gift for her brother.*

Se lo compró ayer en el aeropuerto. — *She bought it for him yesterday in the airport.*

También **le** compró **una camiseta a su madre.** — *She also bought a shirt for her mother.*

Teresita **se la** compró en una tienda en el centro. — *Teresita bought it for her in a store downtown.*

Also note that in a sentence with an infinitive or a present participle, pronouns may be placed before conjugated verbs or attached to the infinitive or present participle.

Teresita quiere compra**rle** un sombrero a Humberto. — *Teresita wants to buy Humberto a hat.*

Se lo va a comprar hoy.
Va a comprár**selo** hoy. — *She's going to buy it for him today.*

Se lo está comprando ahora.
Está comprándo**selo** ahora. — *She is buying it for him now.*

In the case of affirmative commands, the pronouns must be attached to the command form. Note that when two pronouns are attached, an accent mark is written over the stressed vowel.

Teresita, cómpra**selo** en esa tienda. — *Teresita, buy it for him in that store.*

¿Recuerdas?

Heinle/Cengage Learning

28 de junio. Esta mañana visitamos muchas iglesias, como la Capilla de Nuestra Señora de los Remedios. ¡No deberíamos haber llevado ropa tan informal a las iglesias! Por la tarde, fuimos al mercado de artesanías, en el Parque Colón, para comprar algunos recuerdos. Yo compré un anillo y unos aretes, y **se los di a Kate.** Luego, ella me compró un sombrero y una camiseta muy bonita.

¡A practicar!

9-12 ¿Qué hicieron Manny y Teresita en Cuba? Lee las siguientes preguntas. Subraya *(underline)* el objeto directo y haz un círculo alrededor del objeto indirecto. En tu respuesta, sustitúyelos por los pronombres de objeto directo e indirecto necesarios para hacer la oración más corta.

Modelo ¿Les venden los agentes de viaje los boletos (a los turistas)?
Sí, *se* *los* venden.

1. ¿Le explicó Manny a Teresita los detalles del viaje?
   Sí, _____ _____ explicó.
2. ¿Le compró Teresita una guayabera cubana a Manny?
   Sí, _____ _____ compró.
3. ¿Teresita y Manny nos trajeron un recuerdo a nosotros?
   Sí, _____ _____ trajeron.
4. ¿Les trajo Manny dos botellas de ron a sus amigos?
   Sí, _____ _____ trajo.
5. ¿Manny va a prestarte a ti su nueva guayabera?
   No, no _____ _____ va a prestar.
6. ¿Le envió Manny las fotos a su familia?
   Sí, _____ _____ envió.

9-13 La mandona *(bossy one)* Teresita se pone muy mandona con Manny. Para cada situación, cambia el verbo a un mandato *(command)* de **tú.** Sustituye los objetos directos e indirectos por los pronombres necesarios.

Modelo mandar la carta a mi mamá *¡Mándasela!*

1. plancharme la blusa
2. servirnos el desayuno
3. mandar el dinero a Visa
4. prepararte las maletas
5. darles la comida a los perros
6. comprar una maleta nueva para mí
7. prometerme un regalo
8. prestarle el sombrero al tío Daniel

Workbook *9-7 – 9-10*
Lab Manual *9-7 – 9-9*

¡A conversar!

9-14 Preguntas y preguntas... Lee las preguntas que la madre de Manny le hace sobre el viaje y contéstalas usando pronombres de objeto directo e indirecto. ¡Sé *(Be)* creativo(a) con las explicaciones!

Modelo ¿Compraste un regalo para tu padre?
Sí, mamá, se lo compré porque...
o *No, mamá, no se lo compré porque...*

1. ¿Trajiste las fotos de La Habana para mí?
2. ¿Le diste las gracias al recepcionista del hotel?
3. ¿Le regalaste las guayaberas a la familia de Teresita?
4. ¿Me trajiste el sombrero que te pedí?
5. ¿Te trajo Teresita tu pasaporte?
6. ¿Le explicaste el problema al señor de la aduana?
7. ¿Nos compraste recuerdos a tu padre y a mí?

9-15 Entrevista Hazle las siguientes preguntas a un(a) compañero(a). Intenta usar pronombres de objeto directo e indirecto cuando sea posible.

1. Cuando necesitas dinero para un viaje, ¿a quiénes se lo pides? ¿Te lo dan? ¿Se lo pides con mucha o con poca frecuencia?
2. Cuando vas de viaje, ¿a quiénes les compras regalos? ¿Qué cosas les compras? ¿A quiénes les compraste regalos la última vez que viajaste?
3. ¿Se te olvidó algo importante en un viaje? ¿Se te perdieron unas cosas?
4. Cuando estás en el aeropuerto, ¿haces muchas preguntas? ¿A quién se las haces? ¿Te dan respuestas importantes? ¿Te las explican claramente?
5. Cuando un amigo o familiar viene a visitarte a tu ciudad, ¿le ofreces cosas de tu casa? ¿Le preguntas si quiere ir a lugares especiales? ¿Le recomiendas actividades? ¿Le escribes instrucciones para ir a lugares? ¿Le sirves comida en tu casa?

ENCUENTRO CULTURAL

Cuba, Puerto Rico y la República Dominicana

Veamos los videos de Cuba, Puerto Rico y la República Dominicana para luego comentarlos.

1. ¿Qué pueden visitar en La Habana Vieja, Cuba? Describan La Habana Vieja.
2. ¿Qué es y qué representa el Fuerte de San Felipe del Morro en San Juan de Puerto Rico?
3. ¿Qué son «bacalaítos» y «piraguas» en Puerto Rico?
4. ¿Cuáles fueron los primeros edificios que hicieron los españoles en Santo Domingo, República Dominicana?

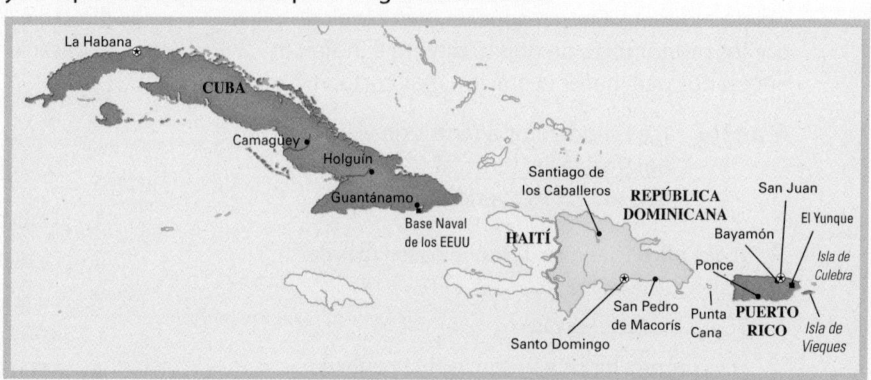

Heinle/Cengage Learning

See the *Workbook*, **Capítulo 9, 9-19–9-21** for additional activities.

Cuba 

Población: 11.477.459 habs.

Área: 110.992 km², casi el tamaño de Pennsylvania

Capital: La Habana (2.400.300 habs.)

Moneda: el peso cubano

Lengua: el español

Puerto Rico 

Población: 3.977.663 habs.

Área: 8.897 km², casi tres veces el tamaño de Rhode Island

Capital: San Juan (2.221.616 habs.)

Moneda: el dólar estadounidense

Lenguas: el español y el inglés

República Dominicana 

Población: 9.794.487 habs.

Área: 48.582.477 km², el tamaño de New Hampshire y Vermont juntos

Capital: Santo Domingo (2.252.400 habs.)

Moneda: el peso dominicano

Lengua: el español

© iStockphoto.com/TexPhoto

Capitolio Viejo en San Juan, Puerto Rico

Historia Desde 1952, Puerto Rico mantiene el estatus de estado libre asociado *(territory with commonwealth status)* con respecto a los Estados Unidos. Esto significa que los puertorriqueños son ciudadanos *(citizens)* de los Estados Unidos, con los mismos derechos y deberes que los ciudadanos estadounidenses, excepto que tienen que residir en los Estados Unidos para poder votar en las elecciones presidenciales. Los puertorriqueños que residen en la isla de Puerto Rico votan para elegir a su gobernador(a) cada cuatro años.

¿Qué piensas del estatus de la isla de Puerto Rico con respecto a los EE.UU.?

La jungla de Wifredo Lam

Artes plásticas Wifredo Lam (1902–1982), de padre chino y madre de origen africano, europeo e indígena, es el artista cubano más reconocido mundialmente. Visitó y vivió en España, Francia, Martinica, Haití y nuevamente Cuba, donde comenzó a incluir elementos africanos en sus pinturas y a mezclarlos de manera abstracta con figuras humanas, animales y vegetales. Lam ganó muchos premios y sus obras están expuestas en museos como el Instituto de Arte de Chicago, el Museo de Arte de San Francisco, el Museo Guggenheim de New York, entre otros. En esta obra, «La jungla», aparecen figuras cubistas con máscaras africanas que se mezclan con la caña de azúcar *(sugar cane)* y el bambú.

¿Qué elementos culturales identificas en esta pintura?

Lugares mágicos Santo Domingo fue fundada *(was founded)* entre 1494 y 1498 por Bartolomé Colón, hermano de Cristóbal Colón. En el sector colonial, los edificios *(buildings)* importantes son la fortaleza Ozama, que fue la primera *(first)* construcción militar del Nuevo Mundo; el hospital de San Nicolás de Bari, que fue el primer hospital; y el Monasterio de San Francisco. En 1521 se construyó la primera catedral, y en 1538 se fundó la primera universidad de las Américas, con el nombre de Santo Tomás de Aquino.

Fortaleza Ozama

¿Cuando se fundó tu universidad?

Visit it live on **Google Earth!**

Ritmos y música Los ritmos caribeños de las islas de Cuba, Puerto Rico y la República Dominicana tienen influencias de los instrumentos de percusión de los indígenas, de los instumentos de los españoles, como la guitarra y el violín, y de los ritmos e instrumentos africanos. De ellos salen los ritmos caribeños y latinoamericanos como el merengue, la bachata, la rumba, el son y la samba.

Juan Luis Guerra es uno de los más famosos cantantes dominicanos de los últimos treinta años. Por medio de su música, los ritmos de la bachata y del merengue se hicieron famosos en todo el mundo. Ahora el Grupo Aventura de Nueva York, cuyos *(whose)* padres son de origen dominicano y puertorriqueño, los interpreta con mucho éxito. Escuchen su canción «Dile al amor», que es un ritmo de bachata romántico. *Access the iTunes playlist on the* **Plazas** *website.*

¿Cuál es el tema de esta canción? ¿Te gusta el ritmo del merengue?

¡Busquen en Internet!

1. Historia: Puerto Rico, «estado libre asociado»
2. Artes plásticas: Wifredo Lam, arte cubano
3. Lugares mágicos: Santo Domingo, República Dominicana
4. Ritmos y música: ritmos caribeños, Juan Luis Guerra, Grupo Aventura

En el Hotel Nacional de Cuba, La Habana

In this section, you will learn vocabulary and expressions associated with lodging by observing scenes from Teresita and Manny's honeymoon in La Habana. When you make hotel reservations, what questions do you ask?

Cultura

Two forms of currency exist in Cuba, the Cuban peso or **moneda nacional** used by Cubans, and the convertible **peso** or CUC used by citizens of other countries.

Heinle/Cengage Learning

Sustantivos

el aire acondicionado *air-conditioning*
el ascensor *elevator*
la cama sencilla (doble) *single (double) bed*
el hotel de cuatro estrellas *four-star hotel*
la llave *key*
la recepción *front desk*
el (la) recepcionista *receptionist*
la reserva *reservation*

Adjetivos

arreglado(a) *neat, tidy*
cómodo(a) *comfortable*
limpio(a) *clean*
lujoso *luxurious*
privado(a) *private*
sucio(a) *dirty*

Verbos

quedarse *to stay*
quejarse (de) *to complain (about)*
registrarse *to register*
reservar *to reserve*
subir(se) (a) *to go up, to climb, to get on*

Palabras útiles

la caja fuerte *security box*
el centro de negocios *business center*
las comodidades *amenities, features*
el servicio de cuarto/ habitación *room service*

Palabras útiles are presented to help you enrich your personal vocabulary. The words here will help you talk about visits to hotels.

> **Nota lingüística**
> In addition to **el cuarto**, another term commonly used for a hotel room is **la habitación.**

¡A practicar!

9-16 **¿Cierto o falso?** Según lo que aprendiste del viaje de Teresita y Manny, indica si las siguientes oraciones son **ciertas** o **falsas.** Si la oración es falsa, corrígela.

Modelo Teresita y Manny piden dos cuartos para dos personas.
Es falso. Piden un cuarto para dos personas.

1. Teresita y Manny no necesitan un baño privado.
2. El cuarto tiene aire acondicionado porque es un hotel de cuatro estrellas.
3. El cuarto cuesta 100 dólares al día.
4. Hay otro cuarto con cama doble más barato en el hotel.
5. Para llegar a su cuarto, Teresita y Manny tienen que subir la escalera.
6. El cuarto no estaba arreglado cuando Teresita y Manny entraron.

9-17 **Definiciones** Busca las palabras del vocabulario que corresponden a las definiciones que están a continuación. Luego compara tu lista con la de un(a) compañero(a) de clase. ¿Están de acuerdo?

Modelo Nosotros dormimos en esta cosa.
la cama

1. Es una cama para una persona.
2. Entramos en esto para subir o bajar.
3. En este lugar uno se registra.
4. Es un baño que no hay que compartir con otros.
5. Es un hotel muy lujoso.
6. Es un objeto de metal que abre la puerta.
7. Cuando nadie limpia el cuarto, el cuarto está...

9-18 **Una visita al Hotel Nacional de Cuba** Completa el párrafo con las palabras apropiadas.

arreglados	doble	recepcionista
ascensor	privados	reserva
cuartos	quedarse	sencilla

La familia Sanz llega al Hotel Nacional de Cuba. El padre habla con el __________ y le dice que tiene una __________. Van a __________ tres días. Pide dos __________, uno con cama __________ para los padres y uno con dos camas __________ para la abuela y el niño. Toman el __________ y llegan a sus cuartos. Los dos cuartos tienen baño __________. Cuando llegan a los cuartos, están __________ y toda la familia está contenta.

Hotel Nacional de Cuba

Workbook *9-11 – 9-12*
Lab Manual *9-10 – 9-12*

¡A conversar!

9-19 ¡Bienvenido a La Habana! Habla con un(a) compañero(a) de clase. Imagínense que una persona es el (la) cliente(a) que busca una habitación en un hotel y la otra es el (la) recepcionista.

Cliente(a)	**Recepcionista**
1. Greet the receptionist.	2. Return the greeting.
3. Ask for a single room with a private bath.	4. Ask how many days he/she is going to stay.
5. Find out how much the room costs.	6. Inform your guest about your various room rates.
7. Ask about the hotel amenities.	8. Answer your guest's questions.
9. Describe the kind of room you want.	10. Respond, then say the number and floor of the room.
11. Express your appreciation.	12. Respond, then say something to make your guest feel welcome.

9-20 Una visita al Apartahotel Morasol Lee la información sobre el Apartahotel Morasol, y luego trabaja con un(a) compañero(a) para presentar una escena en el hotel. Una persona es el (la) recepcionista y la otra es el (la) cliente(a). La conversación debe tener de 8 a 10 preguntas con respuestas. Si prefieren trabajar en un grupo de tres, dos personas pueden ser los (las) clientes(as).

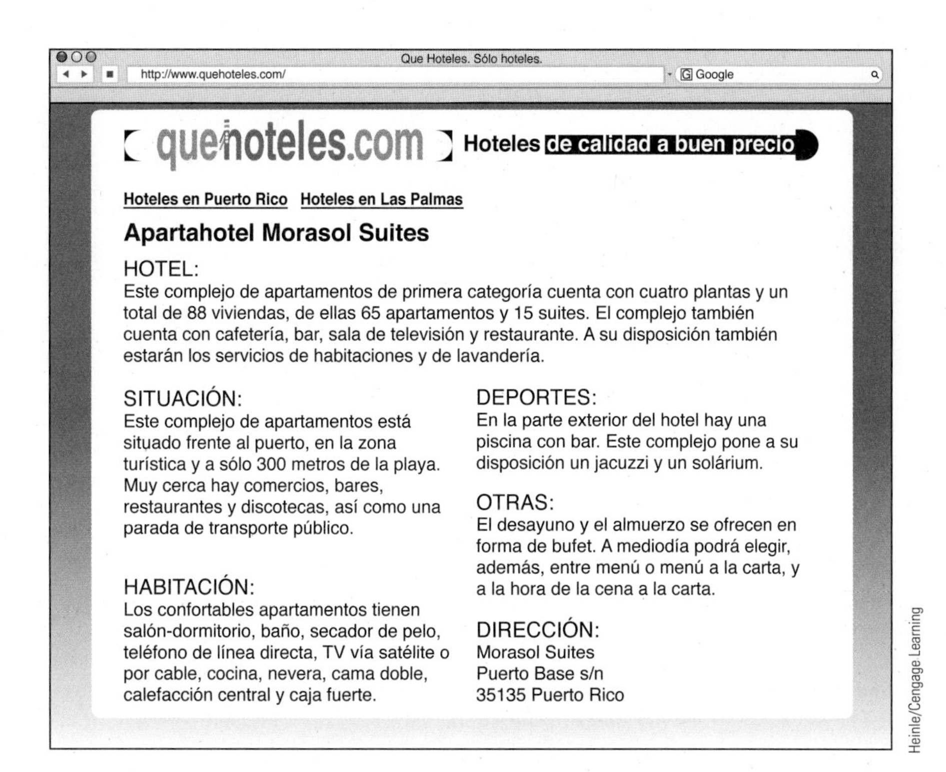

Heinle/Cengage Learning

Cultura

Un apartahotel is an accommodation that includes apartments rather than simple hotel rooms but rents by the night or week as a hotel room would. Many condominium rentals in the United States would be comparable to an **aparthotel**.

9-21 Planes para un viaje Basándote en la información sobre el Apartahotel Morasol, decide si quieres planear unas vacaciones allí. Explícale a un(a) compañero(a) por qué quieres quedarte allí o por qué no, y pregúntale a él/ella si quiere ir o no.

Prepositions of location, adverbs, and relevant expressions

In this section, you will learn how to ask for and give street directions. Look at the map below and read the accompanying description of El Viejo San Juan in Puerto Rico with the prepositions of place highlighted.

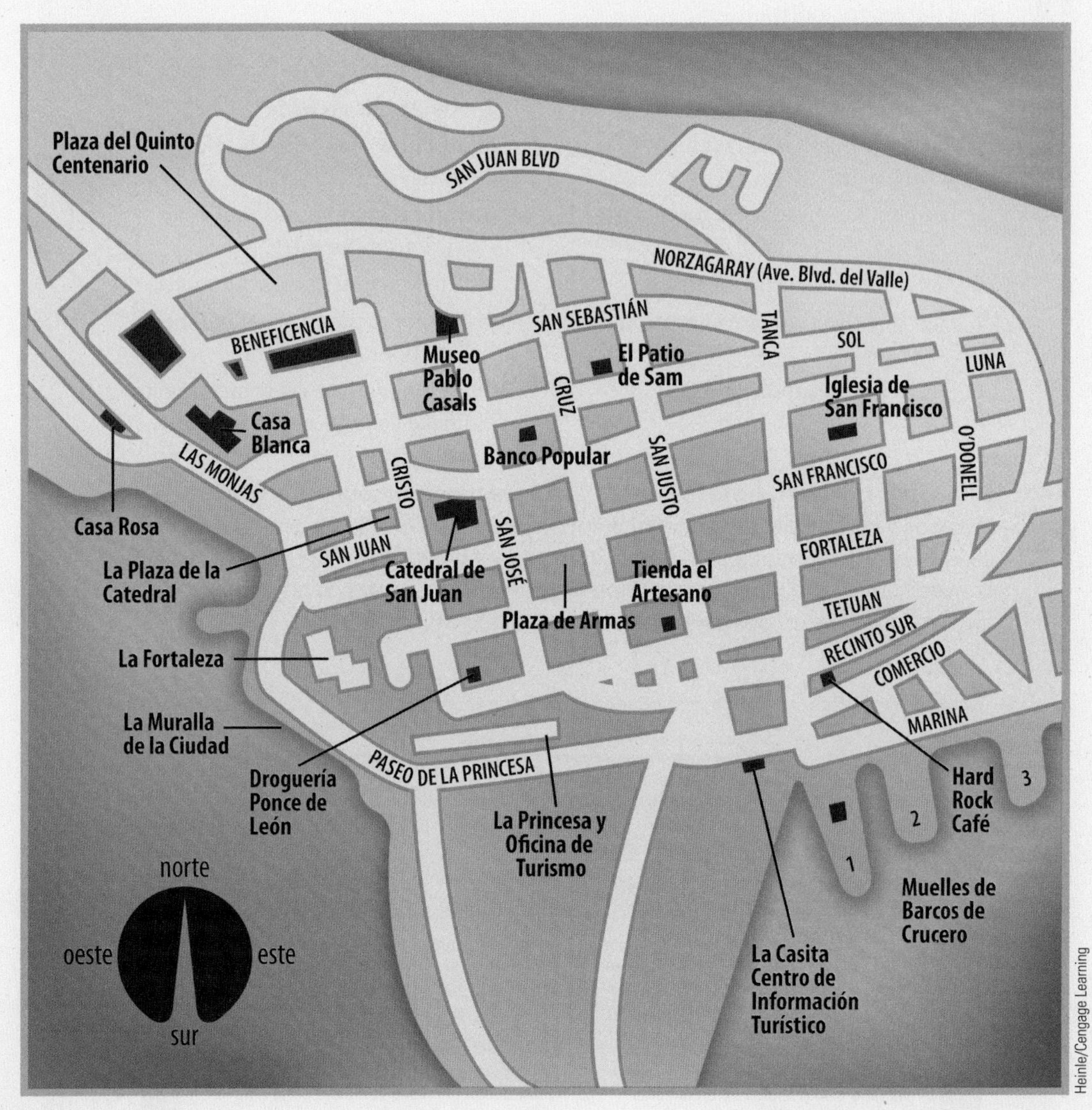

El mapa

La Plaza de Armas está en el centro de la ciudad. **Hacia** *(Toward)* el **sur** *(south)* de la ciudad, el Paseo de la Princesa está **detrás de** *(behind)* la Muralla de la Ciudad *(City Wall)*. En el **norte** *(north)* de la ciudad, el restaurante el Patio de Sam está **entre** *(between)* las calles San Justo y Cruz. Los muelles de barcos de crucero están **enfrente de** *(across from)* la calle Marina. La Plaza de la Catedral está **a la izquierda de** *(to the left of)* la Catedral de San Juan. La Catedral de San Juan está **a la derecha de** *(to the right of)* la Plaza de la Catedral. El mar está **al lado de** *(next to)* los muelles de barcos de crucero. El Museo Pablo Casals está **cerca del** *(near the)* Patio de Sam. San Juan Bulevar está **delante de** *(in front of)* la calle Norzagaray. El aeropuerto está **lejos de** *(far from)* la ciudad.

Asking for directions

In the following dialogue, Manny asks for directions from the Plaza de Armas to the Casa Blanca.

Manny: Perdón, ¿dónde está la Casa Blanca?
Excuse me, where is the Casa Blanca?

Señor: Está en la calle Monjas. **Suba tres cuadras** por la calle San José. **Doble** en la calle Sol, **cruce** la calle y **siga derecho.**
It's on Monjas Street. Go up three blocks on San José Street. Turn on Sol Street, cross the street, and continue straight ahead.

Manny: Eso es **hacia** el **este,** ¿verdad?
That is going toward the east, right?

Señor: No, es **hacia** el **oeste.**
No, it's toward the west.

Manny: Muchísimas gracias.
Thank you very much.

Nota lingüística

In Spain, it is more common to say **recto** *(straight ahead)*, whereas in Latin America, **derecho** is more commonly used. Likewise in Spain, it is more common to say **la manzana,** instead of **la cuadra,** for *block*.

Suba, doble, cruce, and **siga** are formal commands that you will be learning later in this chapter.

The following are additional words and phrases related to talking about location and giving directions:

Otros lugares

la estación de trenes	*train station*
el puerto	*port*
la terminal de autobuses	*bus station*

Verbos

cruzar	*to cross*
doblar	*to turn*
parar(se)	*to stop*
seguir (i, i)	*to continue*
subir(se) (a)	*to go up*

Medios de transporte

a pie	*on foot*
en autobús	*by bus*
en barco	*by boat*
en bicicleta	*by bike*
en coche	*by car*
en metro	*by subway*
en taxi	*by taxi*
en tren	*by train*

Nota lingüística

In Puerto Rico, buses are called **las guaguas;** in Argentina and El Salvador, **los colectivos;** in Mexico, **los camiones;** and in other countries like Cuba, the terms **el ómnibus** and **el microbús** are common.

¡A practicar!

9-22 ¿Cierto o falso? Mira el mapa de la página 302 y lee las oraciones para ver si son **ciertas** o **falsas.** Si una oración es falsa, corrígela.

1. La Plaza de la Catedral está a la derecha de la Catedral de San Juan.
2. Los muelles de barcos de crucero están lejos de la Casa Rosa.
3. El Banco Popular está al norte de la ciudad.
4. La casita centro de información turística está cerca de la Plaza del Quinto Centenario.
5. La calle San Justo está entre la calle Cruz y la calle Tanca.
6. La Plaza de la Catedral está al oeste de la Iglesia de San Francisco.

9-23 Lugares y transporte Usa una palabra del vocabulario para completar las siguientes oraciones. Luego compara tus respuestas con las de un(a) compañero(a). ¿Están de acuerdo?

1. Tengo mucha prisa; no quiero tomar el autobús y no tengo tiempo para ir a pie. Voy a pedir un ______________.
2. Compré ayer un boleto para el tren que sale a las 5:00. ¿Dónde está la ______________?
3. No sé dónde está la estación, pero tengo aquí un ______________ de la ciudad. Podemos mirarlo, si quieres.
4. Voy de San Juan a Ponce en autobús. Pero no sé dónde está la ______________.
5. Uy, hay mucho tráfico. Yo quiero cruzar la ciudad por debajo de la tierra. Voy ______________.

Cultura

Ponce is the second-largest city in Puerto Rico and is a popular tourist destination.

9-24 Opuestos *(Opposites)* Dos amigos están hablando de dónde están varios lugares, pero uno está muy confundido. Busca la respuesta con la palabra opuesta para contestar cada pregunta.

______ 1. ¿El hotel está cerca de la estación de trenes?	a. No, hacia el oeste.
______ 2. ¿El restaurante está a la izquierda del museo?	b. No, está lejos.
______ 3. ¿Ponce está al norte de San Juan?	c. No, está detrás.
______ 4. ¿Caminamos hacia el este?	d. No, está al sur.
______ 5. ¿El banco está enfrente de la terminal de autobuses?	e. No, doblamos aquí.
______ 6. ¿Seguimos derecho para ir a la catedral?	f. No, a la derecha.

© Lori Froeb/Shutterstock

Calle del Viejo San Juan

Workbook *9-13 – 9-15*
Lab Manual *9-13 – 9-14*

¡A conversar!

9-25 **¿Dónde está?** Trabajas en una oficina de turismo en el Viejo San Juan y tienes que indicarle a un(a) compañero(a) de clase dónde están los siguientes lugares en el mapa de la página 302. Usa **al lado de, cerca de, delante de, detrás de, enfrente de, entre** y **lejos de.**

Modelo el aeropuerto
El aeropuerto está lejos del centro de la ciudad.

1. la Plaza del Quinto Centenario
2. el Patio de Sam
3. el Banco Popular
4. la droguería Ponce
5. la Catedral de San Juan
6. la Calle San Francisco
7. el Museo Pablo Casals
8. la Fortaleza

9-26 **¿Te gusta el hotel?** Vas a hacer un viaje con un(a) amigo(a) y quieres recomendarle un hotel. Tienes una foto de un cuarto, pero hablas con tu amigo(a) por teléfono y él/ella no puede verla. Trabaja con un(a) compañero(a) para decidir si les gusta el cuarto o no. Una persona mira la foto del cuarto, pero la otra no la ve. La primera persona tiene que decirle a la otra dónde están las cosas y la segunda persona tiene que dibujar el cuarto. Al terminar la descripción, compara el dibujo con la foto. Indica dónde están las siguientes cosas e incluye tanta información como sea posible.

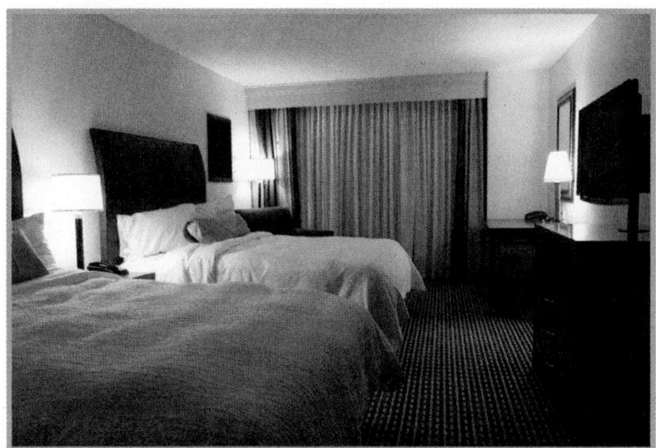

Modelo las lámparas
Una lámpara está entre las camas, la otra lámpara está cerca de la ventana y la otra está encima del escritorio.

las camas
la mesa
el televisor
la mesa de noche
el cuadro
la cómoda

9-27 **Una comparación** Piensa en el cuarto de hotel ideal para ti y compáralo con el cuarto de la foto. Habla con un(a) compañero(a) e indica dónde están las cosas importantes en cada cuarto. Explícale dónde está tu hotel favorito diciendo, por ejemplo, si está cerca de la playa, lejos de la universidad, al norte o al sur de donde vives ahora, etcétera.

Formal commands and negative *tú* commands

In **Capítulo 4**, you learned how to form informal affirmative commands. In this section, you will learn how to form affirmative and negative formal commands and negative **tú** commands.

I. Formal commands

When we give advice to others or ask them to do something, we often use commands, such as *Take bus No. 25* and *Give me your address.* Spanish speakers use formal commands when they address people as **usted** or **ustedes.**

To form formal commands for most Spanish verbs, drop the **-o** ending from the present tense **yo** form and add the following endings to the verb stem:

-e/**-en** for **-ar** verbs

-a/**-an** for **-er** and **-ir** verbs

To form the negative, simply place **no** before the verb.

	Infinitive	Present-tense *yo* form	*usted*	*ustedes*
-ar verbs	hablar	hablo	(no) habl**e**	(no) habl**en**
-er verbs	volver	vuelvo	(no) vuelv**a**	(no) vuelv**an**
-ir verbs	venir	vengo	(no) veng**a**	(no) veng**an**

Vengan a San Juan a visitarme pronto. — ***Come*** *to San Juan to visit me soon.*

No olvide mi dirección. — ***Don't forget*** *my address.*

Note that verbs ending in **-car, -gar,** and **-zar** have a spelling change: the **c** changes to **qu, g** changes to **gu,** and **z** changes to **c,** respectively.

Infinitive	Present-tense *yo* form	*usted*	*ustedes*
sacar	saco	sa**que**	sa**quen**
llegar	llego	lle**gue**	lle**guen**
comenzar	comienzo	comien**ce**	comien**cen**

Saque una foto del parque. — ***Take*** *a picture of the park.*

Lleguen a tiempo, por favor. — ***Arrive*** *on time, please.*

No comience a caminar todavía. — ***Don't start*** *walking yet.*

There are several irregular verbs:

Infinitive	*usted*	*ustedes*
dar	**dé**	**den**
estar	**esté**	**estén**
ir	**vaya**	**vayan**
saber	**sepa**	**sepan**
ser	**sea**	**sean**

Sean buenos estudiantes. — ***Be*** *good students.*

Vaya al banco. — ***Go*** *to the bank.*

In affirmative commands, attach reflexive and object pronouns to the end of the command, thus forming one word. If the command has three or more syllables, write an accent mark over the stressed vowel. In negative commands, place the pronouns separately in front of the verb.

Póngase el abrigo. — ***Put on** your overcoat.*

No se ponga el abrigo. — ***Don't put on** your overcoat.*

Cómprelo ahora. — ***Buy it** now.*

No lo compre mañana. — ***Don't buy it** tomorrow.*

II. Negative *tú* commands

To form negative informal commands, you'll be using the same strategy as you would to form either affirmative or negative formal commands.

As you recall from the previous section, to form both affirmative and negative formal commands for most Spanish verbs, you drop the **-o** ending from the present-tense **yo** form and add the following endings to the verb stem: **-e/-en** for **-ar** verbs and **-a/-an** for **-er** and **-ir** verbs. Negative informal commands drop the **-o** ending from the present-tense **yo** form and add the following endings to the stem: **-es/-éis** for **-ar** verbs and **-as/-áis** for **-er** and **-ir** verbs. Remember that there are also spelling changes for verbs ending in **-car, -gar,** and **-zar** and that there are irregular verbs such as **dar, estar, ir, saber,** and **ser.**

The chart below, graphically illustrates the similarities among the negative informal command forms and all the formal command forms.

Infinitive	Informal command *(tú/vosotros)* (+)	(–)	Formal command *(usted/ ustedes)* (+)	(–)
hablar	**habla**	**no hables**	**hable**	**no hable**
	hablad	**no habléis**	**hablen**	**no hablen**
comer	**come**	**no comas**	**coma**	**no coma**
	comed	**no comáis**	**coman**	**no coman**
vivir	**vive**	**no vivas**	**viva**	**no viva**
	vivid	**no viváis**	**vivan**	**no vivan**
dormir	**duerme**	**no duermas**	**duerma**	**no duerma**
	dormid	**no durmáis**	**duerman**	**no duerman**
ir	**ve**	**no vayas**	**vaya**	**no vaya**
	id	**no vayáis**	**vayan**	**no vayan**

Nota lingüística

Remember that the **vosotros** form is generally used in Spain when addressing a group of friends. **Ustedes** is considered the more formal manner of address in Spain but is generally used when addressing groups in Latin America both formally and informally.

As you can see from the chart above, only the affirmative informal commands **(habla/hablad, come/comed, vive/vivid, duerme/dormid,** and **ve/id)** deviate from the endings used in the remaining command forms.

Note that, as with negative formal commands, we place reflexive or object pronouns before the negated verb.

—No **te** olvides de escribirme. — *Don't forget to write me.*

—No **le** hables. — *Don't talk to him.*

—¿Debo llamar**te**? — *Should I call you?*

—No, no **me** llames. — *No, don't call me.*

¡A practicar!

9-28 Consejos para el hermano de Manny El hermano de Manny va a San Juan para visitar a la pareja. Con el infinitivo, forma mandatos negativos informales que Manny le ofrece a su hermano.

1. No ______ **(decir)** tonterías *(silly things)* en la aduana.
2. No ______ **(hablar)** tanto con los asistentes de vuelo en el avión.
3. No ______ **(comer)** en el aeropuerto.
4. No ________ **(dormirte)** en el autobús.
5. No ______ **(contestar)** el teléfono en inglés.
6. No ______ **(hacer)** muchas preguntas sobre la habitación en el hotel.

9-29 Para llegar al laboratorio Acabas de llegar al aeropuerto de Mayagüez, Puerto Rico, con otro estudiante de tu universidad. Uds. van a reunirse con un profesor de la Universidad de Puerto Rico, para hablar sobre las investigaciones de su laboratorio. Encuentras un mensaje telefónico con direcciones al laboratorio. Escucha la información y dibuja un mapa de la ruta.

AUDIO CD
CD 3, TRACK 8

© Robert Fried/Alamy

Universidad de Puerto Rico–Mayagüez

9-30 Consejos para turistas en Santo Domingo Completa los mandatos de un guía de turistas en la ciudad de Santo Domingo, usando mandatos formales o informales, según lo indicado.

Modelo (ustedes) caminar para ver todo lo que ofrece la ciudad
Caminen para ver todo lo que ofrece la ciudad.
(tú) caminar para ver todo lo que ofrece la ciudad
Camina para ver todo lo que ofrece la ciudad.

1. (tú) salir temprano del hotel
2. (usted) ir a un mercado
3. (tú) no sacar fotos sin pedir permiso
4. (tú) descansar un poco por la tarde
5. (ustedes) no subirse a un autobús sin saber la ruta
6. (usted) no andar en bicicleta; es muy peligroso
7. (tú) pararse si pasa una procesión
8. (usted) no cruzar las calles sin mirar en las dos direcciones
9. (ustedes) ser amables con la gente de la ciudad, y ellos los van a tratar bien a Uds.

Workbook *9-16 – 9-18*
Lab Manual *9-15 – 9-17*

¡A conversar!

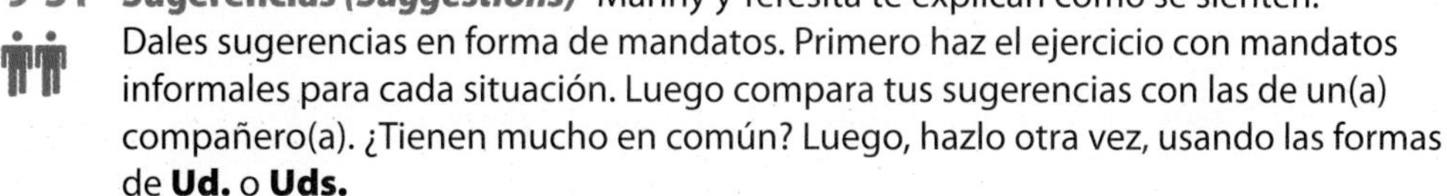

9-31 **Sugerencias *(Suggestions)*** Manny y Teresita te explican cómo se sienten. Dales sugerencias en forma de mandatos. Primero haz el ejercicio con mandatos informales para cada situación. Luego compara tus sugerencias con las de un(a) compañero(a). ¿Tienen mucho en común? Luego, hazlo otra vez, usando las formas de **Ud.** o **Uds.**

Modelo Estoy cansado de caminar y tomar el autobús.
a. *¡Toma un taxi entonces!*
b. *¡Tome Ud. un taxi entonces!*

1. Tengo muchas ganas de comer comida china.
2. Queremos quedarnos en un hotel lujoso.
3. Necesito cambiar dinero. ¿Dónde está el banco?
4. Tengo ganas de beber algo.
5. Necesito comprar regalos para mi familia.
6. Necesitamos confirmar nuestro vuelo.

Nota lingüística

You can soften commands to make them sound more like requests than demands, by using **usted** or **ustedes** after the command form or by adding **por favor: Pasen ustedes por aquí,** or **Pasen por aquí, por favor.** *(Come this way, please.)* **No hable usted tan rápido.** or **No hable tan rápido, por favor.** *(Don't speak so fast, please.)*

9-32 **Un agente de turismo** Trabajen en grupos de tres personas. Una persona es un(a) agente de turismo. Los otros estudiantes van a presentarle una situación que contiene una necesidad o un problema que tienen. El (La) agente entonces va a ofrecerles consejos en forma de mandatos. Hagan el ejercicio usando primero mandatos formales y luego mandatos informales.

Modelo **E1:** *No puedo descansar en mi habitación.*
E2: *Busque/Busca otro hotel.*
E3: *Mi compañero de cuarto y yo nunca podemos desayunar antes de salir por la mañana.*
E2: *Levántense más temprano.*

9-33 **En el balneario** Trabajen en grupos de 3 ó 4 personas. Una persona trabaja en un balneario en Puerto Rico, las otras son clientes(as) que necesitan ayuda. Un(a) cliente(a) es adulto(a) y la(s) otra(s) persona(s) es (son) jóvenes. Los (Las) clientes(as) le hacen preguntas al (a la) empleado(a) (*employee*) y él (ella) contesta con mandatos formales e informales apropiadamente. Después de hacer varias preguntas y respuestas, cambien papeles. Pueden usar la lista a continuación para formular sus preguntas.

bailar
beber algo
comer
comprar regalos
conseguir información turística
correr
escuchar música
hacer ejercicio
ir al museo
llegar al restaurante
nadar
tomar un taxi al centro

Modelo **E1:** *Señor, me llamo Paco. Quiero nadar.*
E2: *Paco, nada en la piscina. Está al lado del gimnasio. No nades en el mar.*
E3: *Señor, ¿cómo se llega a la estación de trenes?*
E2: *Señora, siga derecho y doble a la izquierda en la calle Colón.*

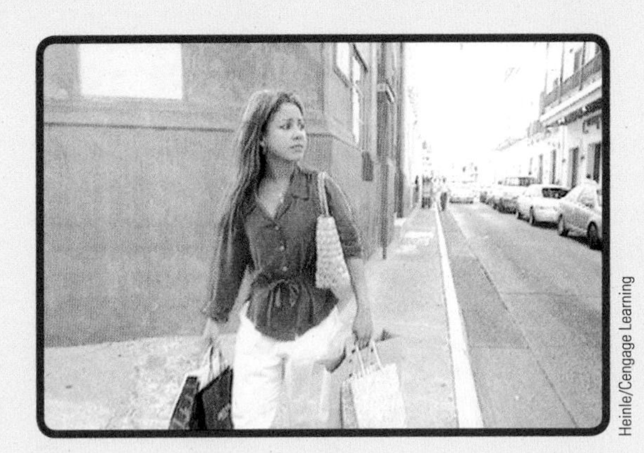

Heinle/Cengage Learning

El Viejo San Juan En este segmento del video, Valeria, Antonio y Javier están en la ciudad de San Juan. Valeria va de compras mientras Javier y Antonio visitan una agencia de viajes.

Antes de ver

Expresiones útiles Las siguientes son expresiones nuevas que vas a escuchar en el video.

Me doy cuenta de	*I realize*
¿Te perdiste?	*Did you get lost?*
Será que le duele la mano	*Her hand probably hurts*
Algo no salió bien	*Something didn't go well*

Enfoque estructural The following are expressions in the video with indirect object pronouns:

Antonio: Javier está planeando ir a vivir a otro país. Todavía no sabe dónde. Estamos leyendo sobre diferentes lugares que **le** interesan para establecer su agencia de ecoturismo.

Javier: **Me** gustaría tomar un avión a Centroamérica.

Valeria: ***Me*** *duelen los brazos de tanto cargar bolsas.*

Antonio: ¡Será que **le** duele la mano de tanto usar la tarjeta de crédito!

1. **Recordemos** ¿Quieres visitar muchos lugares exóticos? Haz una lista de los lugares que quieres visitar en los próximos cinco años. Incluye el modo de transporte que vas a usar para esos viajes. Luego compara tu lista con la lista de un(a) compañero(a). ¿Tienen mucho en común?

2. **Practiquemos** Trabajando con un compañero de clase, explica los usos de los pronombres de objeto indirecto en las oraciones de **Enfoque estructural.** Por ejemplo, ¿por qué se necesita un pronombre de objeto indirecto con los verbos gustar y doler?, y en la última frase, ¿a quién se refiere **le**?

3. **Charlemos** Describe a un compañero(a) los preparativos que haces para viajar a algún destino exótico. ¿Les pides permiso, dinero o el uso del coche a tus padres? ¿Les dices a tus amigos tus planes, o no le dices nada a nadie? ¿Buscas la ayuda de una agencia de viajes o haces todo por Internet?

Después de ver

1. **Planes para un viaje** En el video, Javier habla de sus planes para un viaje. Lee las siguientes oraciones y pon el número apropiado en el espacio para indicar el orden cronológico de los planes de Javier.

   _______ Pienso recorrer la costa pacífica de Costa Rica en bicicleta.
   _______ Voy a visitar Belice, Honduras y Costa Rica.
   _______ Voy a tomar un tren a Machu Picchu.
   _______ Voy a tomar un avión a Centroamérica.
   _______ Voy a tomar un avión a Cusco.

2. **¡Valeria está perdida!** En el video Valeria se perdió en San Juan mientras iba de compras y tuvo que pedirle ayuda a una señora. Ahora imagínate que tú eres la persona que la está ayudando. Completa tu conversación con Valeria poniendo los verbos en la forma correcta del mandato formal.

Valeria: Señora, ¿cómo hago para llegar a la Plaza de la Rogativa?

Señora: No 1. ______________ (preocuparse), es muy fácil. De esta esquina, 2. ______________ (caminar) tres cuadras. De allí, 3. ______________ (doblar) a la izquierda y 4. ______________ (seguir) tres cuadras más.

Valeria: Gracias.

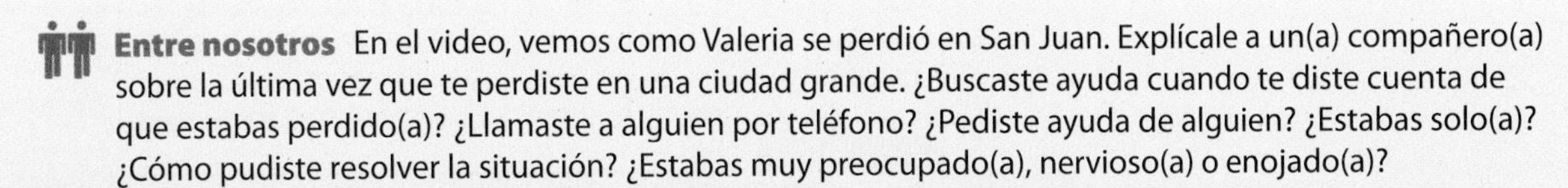

Entre nosotros En el video, vemos como Valeria se perdió en San Juan. Explícale a un(a) compañero(a) sobre la última vez que te perdiste en una ciudad grande. ¿Buscaste ayuda cuando te diste cuenta de que estabas perdido(a)? ¿Llamaste a alguien por teléfono? ¿Pediste ayuda de alguien? ¿Estabas solo(a)? ¿Cómo pudiste resolver la situación? ¿Estabas muy preocupado(a), nervioso(a) o enojado(a)?

Presentaciones Como ya sabes, no es nada agradable perderse en un lugar que no conoces. ¿Cómo puedes ayudar a los nuevos estudiantes para que ellos no se pierdan cuando llegan a tu universidad? Trabaja con dos compañeros(as) de clase y preparen una guía para que los nuevos estudiantes de tu universidad no se pierdan. Su guía debe incluir cinco mandatos sobre lo que uno debe hacer para no perderse.

See the *Lab Manual,* **Capítulo 9, 9-21– 9-22** for additional activities.

Antes de leer

Strategy: Using format clues

Printed material often contains different kinds of cues that can help you skim, scan, and guess meaning. For example, some words and phrases appear in large, boldface, or italic print to attract the reader's attention; some words are repeated several times to persuade the reader; and other words appear together with a graphic design to help the reader remember a particular concept. Before reading the selection, consider and discuss the following:

1. What is the title of the selection? Which headings stand out the most?
2. What words are repeated?
3. What do the photographs show?
4. The selection presents information in various sections; what are these sections?

Ofertas de viaje

Cognados Escribe cinco cognados y sus significados.

Detalles A medida que lees las secciones, contesta las siguientes preguntas.

1. ¿Cuál es el país que se menciona en la lectura?
2. ¿Cuál es el tema principal de la lectura?
3. ¿A qué tipo de lectores *(readers)* está dirigida la lectura?

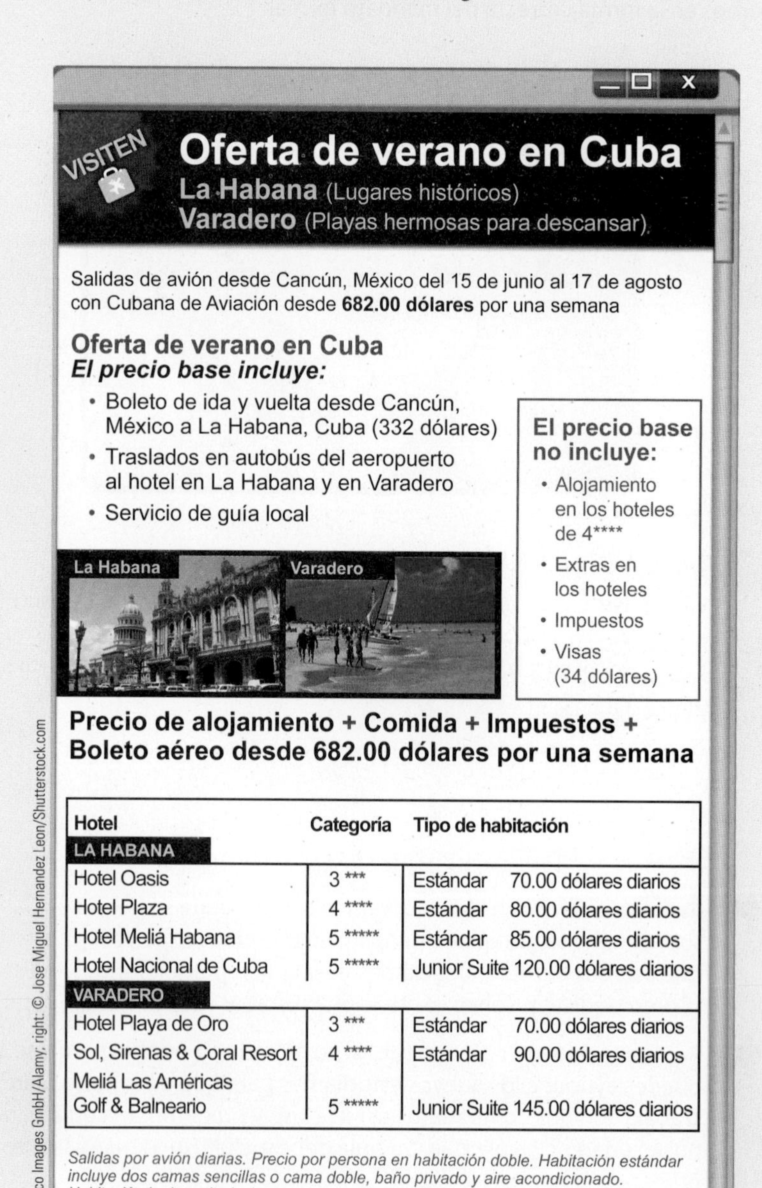

VISITEN

Oferta de verano en Cuba

La Habana (Lugares históricos)
Varadero (Playas hermosas para descansar)

Salidas de avión desde Cancún, México del 15 de junio al 17 de agosto con Cubana de Aviación desde **682.00 dólares** por una semana

Oferta de verano en Cuba
El precio base incluye:

- Boleto de ida y vuelta desde Cancún, México a La Habana, Cuba (332 dólares)
- Traslados en autobús del aeropuerto al hotel en La Habana y en Varadero
- Servicio de guía local

El precio base no incluye:

- Alojamiento en los hoteles de 4****
- Extras en los hoteles
- Impuestos
- Visas (34 dólares)

Precio de alojamiento + Comida + Impuestos + Boleto aéreo desde 682.00 dólares por una semana

Hotel	Categoría	Tipo de habitación	
LA HABANA			
Hotel Oasis	3 ***	Estándar	70.00 dólares diarios
Hotel Plaza	4 ****	Estándar	80.00 dólares diarios
Hotel Meliá Habana	5 *****	Estándar	85.00 dólares diarios
Hotel Nacional de Cuba	5 *****	Junior Suite	120.00 dólares diarios
VARADERO			
Hotel Playa de Oro	3 ***	Estándar	70.00 dólares diarios
Sol, Sirenas & Coral Resort	4 ****	Estándar	90.00 dólares diarios
Meliá Las Américas Golf & Balneario	5 *****	Junior Suite	145.00 dólares diarios

Salidas por avión diarias. Precio por persona en habitación doble. Habitación estándar incluye dos camas sencillas o cama doble, baño privado y aire acondicionado. Habitación junior suite incluye cuatro camas sencillas o dos camas dobles, baño privado, refrigerador pequeño y aire acondicionado. (Para 4 personas)

Después de leer

A escoger. Después de leer el texto, contesta las siguientes preguntas.

1. En Cuba, ¿dónde están las playas hermosas?
   a. en Varadero
   b. en La Habana
   c. en La Habana Vieja
2. ¿Qué incluye el pago de 332.00 dólares?
   a. un hotel de tres estrellas en La Habana
   b. un hotel de tres estrellas en Varadero
   c. un boleto de ida y vuelta de México a La Habana
3. El precio base incluye:
   a. boleto, traslado al aeropuerto y visas
   b. boleto, traslado al aeropuerto y servicio de guía local
   c. boleto, traslado al aeropuerto y extras en el hotel
4. El precio base no incluye:
   a. las visas, los impuestos y los extras en los hoteles
   b. las visas, el servicio de guía local y los impuestos
   c. las visas, el traslado al aeropuerto y los impuestos

¿Cierto o falso? Indica si las siguientes oraciones son **ciertas** o **falsas**. Corrige las oraciones falsas.

1. ______ Usted puede visitar Cuba desde 682 dólares por una semana.
2. ______ El hotel Meliá Habana tiene 4 estrellas y cuesta 80.00 dólares.
3. ______ En Varadero, el hotel Playa de Oro tiene cinco estrellas y cuesta 90.00 dólares.
4. ______ La habitación estándar incluye dos camas sencillas o una cama doble, baño privado y aire acondicionado.
5. ______ La habitación Junior Suite incluye cinco camas sencillas o dos camas dobles, baño privado, refrigerador grande y aire acondicionado. (Para 6 personas).

¡A conversar! Con cuatro de sus compañeros de clase comenten y diseñen un anuncio para dar a conocer el próximo viaje que ofrece su universidad a los estudiantes de español. Comenten los siguientes puntos:

- Línea aérea
- Tipo y precio del boleto
- Tipo y cantidad de equipaje
- Tipo y precio del hotel
- Tipo de cuarto
- Atracciones turísticas y restaurantes

El anuncio debe atraer la atención de los estudiantes. ¡Usen su creatividad y sean orginales! Ustedes pueden mencionar que los precios del viaje son muy económicos, que los lugares que van a visitar son totalmente increíbles o que las clases de lenguas son las más dinámicas del país. Presenten el anuncio a toda la clase. Los estudiantes van a decidir el lugar que quieren visitar.

Strategy: Using commands to give directions

If you're traveling in a Spanish-speaking country or city, chances are you might need to ask for directions. In addition, you might even have to give directions! The most important element of explaining to someone how to get from one place to another is accuracy. If you explain your directions clearly and concisely, people will be able to follow them easily.

Here are six basic requirements for giving directions to a place:

1. Choose the easiest route.
2. Be very clear in your directions.
3. Give the directions in chronological order.
4. Use linking expressions such as: **Primero…, Luego…, Después de eso…, Entonces…, Usted debe…, Después…, Finalmente…**
5. Identify clearly visible landmarks such as: **la avenida** *(avenue)*, **el bulevar** *(boulevard)*, **la calle** *(street)*, **el camino** *(road)*, **la colina** *(hill)*, **el cruce de caminos** *(intersection)*, **el edificio** *(building)*, **el letrero** *(sign)*, **el puente** *(bridge)*, **el semáforo** *(traffic light)*.
6. When possible, include a sketch of the route.

Task: Giving directions from the airport to your house or a hotel

Paso 1 Vas a escribir una composición en que le explicas a un viajero hispanohablante cómo ir del aeropuerto de tu ciudad hasta tu residencia o hasta un hotel de tu ciudad. Antes de empezar, vuelve a leer los seis puntos y el párrafo anterior.

Paso 2 Dibuja un mapa de la ruta a seguir, mientras escribes las direcciones.

Paso 3 Escribe un párrafo siguiendo el modelo anterior e incluyendo los seis puntos. Emplea mandatos formales.

____
____
____
____
____
____
____
____
____

Paso 4 Repasa y corrige tu composición. Puedes consultar la siguiente lista:

______ easiest route	______ chronological order
______ correct punctuation	______ correct spelling
______ linking expressions	______ clear directions
______ visible landmarks	______ correct grammar

Paso 5 Trabaja con un(a) compañero(a) de clase. Intercambien sus composiciones, pero no compartan los mapas que dibujaron. Cada persona debe leer la composición de la otra persona y dibujar un mapa de la ruta explicada. Si ustedes encuentran errores o problemas en las composiciones, hagan las correcciones y después hablen sobre los cambios.

Communicative Goals

- Communicate about transportation, lodging, and other aspects of travel
- Request and provide information about getting around a city or town
- Give instructions

Paso 1

Review the Communicative Goals for **Capítulo 9** and determine if you are able to accomplish the goals. If you are not certain that you have achieved all of the goals, review the pertinent portions of the chapter.

Paso 2

Look at the components of a conversation which addresses the communicative goals for this chapter. The percentages will help you evaluate your ability to successfully participate in the conversation that is featured below. Your instructor may use the same rubric to assess your oral performance.

Components of the conversation	%
☐ Questions and answers about a desired destination and the people traveling	20
☐ Information on flight schedule	10
☐ At least two questions and answers about preferences regarding airline travel	15
☐ At least two questions and answers about desires for hotel features	15
☐ Request for directions from airport to hotel and response which includes three or four pieces of information	15
☐ Instructions about at least three things the traveler must do to prepare for the trip	15
☐ Polite conclusion of the conversation	10

En acción Think about a conversation in which a travel agent and a client discuss plans for a trip to a specific destination in the Spanish-speaking world. Note that the conversation takes place in a professional setting and therefore includes formal forms of address. Work with a partner. Be sure to include the steps below. When you finish, change roles.

1. The travel agent asks the client who plans to travel and what destination is desired.
2. The client specifies the destination, tells the travel agent that he/she and a friend plan to travel there, and indicates that he/she is going to make the plans, purchase both tickets, and give one to the friend.
3. The travel agent provides information on flight schedule then indicates the price of the tickets and the client agrees to purchase them.
4. The travel agent asks at least two questions about the client's preferences regarding travel by air and the client responds.
5. The travel agent asks at least two questions about the client's preferences regarding features in a hotel for the trip and the client responds.
6. The client asks for directions from the airport to the hotel and the travel agent gives directions, providing three or four pieces of information about how to get to the hotel.
7. The travel agent tells the client to do at least three things in order to prepare for the trip.
8. The travel agent and the client thank one another and conclude the conversation politely.

¡A REPASAR!

Indirect object pronouns

Indirect object pronouns replace indirect objects; they indicate *to whom* or *for whom* the action of the verb is performed.

me	nos
te	os
le	les

¡A recordar! 1 Where in relation to the verb are indirect object pronouns placed? Which verbs often require the use of indirect object pronouns?

Double object pronouns

Indirect object pronouns always precede direct object pronouns. The indirect object pronouns **le** and **les** change to **se** when they are used together with the direct object pronouns **lo, la, los,** and **las.**

me te le (se) nos os les (se)	+	lo la los las

¡A recordar! 2 Where are pronouns placed in relation to the verb of a sentence?

Expressions of location

a la derecha de	a la izquierda de	al lado de
cerca de	delante de	detrás de
enfrente de	entre	hacia
lejos de	el este	el norte
el oeste	el sur	

¡A recordar! 3 How many modes of transportation can you recall from the chapter?

Formal commands and negative *tú* commands

To form formal commands for most Spanish verbs, drop the **-o** ending from the present tense **yo** form and add the following endings to the verb stem: **-e/-en** for **-ar** verbs; **-a/-an** for **-er** and **-ir** verbs. The following have irregular formal command forms:

Infinitive	*usted*	*ustedes*
dar	**dé**	**den**
estar	**esté**	**estén**
ir	**vaya**	**vayan**
saber	**sepa**	**sepan**
ser	**sea**	**sean**

To form negative informal commands, use the same strategy as you would to form either affirmative or negative formal commands, but add **-es/-éis** for **-ar** verbs and **-as/-áis** for **-er** and **-ir** verbs. Remember that there are also spelling changes for verbs ending in **-car, -gar,** and **-zar** and that there are irregular verbs such as **dar, estar, ir, saber,** and **ser**.

¡A recordar! 4 Where are pronouns placed with affirmative commands? Where are pronouns placed with negative commands?

Actividad 1 Un viaje a San Juan Escribe el pronombre de objeto indirecto apropiado para completar cada oración.

1. El agente de viajes ________ recomendó un viaje a San Juan (a mí).
2. Yo ________ hice muchas preguntas (a él).
3. Yo ________ pedí a mis padres una maleta nueva como regalo de Navidad.
4. Salimos el 2 de enero. En el avión los asistentes de vuelo ________ sirvieron bebidas (a nosotros).
5. En San Juan fui de compras y ________ compré un regalito (a ti).
6. Luisa ________ escribió un mensaje de texto a su madre cada día.
7. Hacía mucho calor en San Juan. Una joven simpática ________ ofreció una botella de agua (a mí).
8. Ella ________ recomienda (a los visitantes) visitar El Morro dos o más veces.

Actividad 2 En un viaje Subraya la respuesta correcta para cada oración para indicar qué hacen varias personas en sus viajes.

1. Mi hermano me presta dinero a veces. → Mi hermano ______ presta.

   a. se lo b. se la c. me lo d. me la

2. En una excursión, le hacemos preguntas al guía. → ______ hacemos.

   a. Nos las b. Nos la c. Se las d. Se la

3. ¿Estás preparándonos el itinerario? → ¿Estás ______?

   a. preparándonoslos c. preparándoselos

   b. preparándonoslo d. preparándoselo

4. Te voy a dar la información pronto. → ______ voy a dar pronto.

   a. Te la b. Te las c. Se la d. Se las

5. El agente de viajes le recomendó unos hoteles a Raúl. → El agente de viajes ______ recomendó.

   a. me los b. me lo c. se lo d. se los

Actividad 3 ¿Dónde está? Completa cada oración con la palabra apropiada.

cerca	derecha	este	lejos	oeste
delante	entre	izquierda	norte	sur

1. Puerto Rico no está lejos de la República Dominicana, está ________.
2. La República Dominicana no está al oeste de Cuba, está al ________.
3. México no está al sur de Guatemala, está al ________.
4. Colombia no está al este de Venezuela, está al ________.
5. Argentina no está al norte de Bolivia, está al ________.
6. España no está cerca de Chile, está ________.
7. En el mapa, Portugal no está a la derecha de España, está a la ________.
8. El Océano Atlántico está ________ Europa y América.
9. En el mapa, Uruguay no está a la izquierda de Argentina, está a la ________.
10. Cuando nuestro(a) profesor(a) presenta la lección de geografía, no está detrás de la clase, está ________ de la clase.

Actividad 4 Instrucciones para los viajeros Llena los espacios en blanco con los mandatos formales plurales (la forma de **Uds.**). Escoge el verbo lógico de la lista y escribe el mandato apropiado.

comer	ir	ponerse	quitarse	subir
dormir	llegar	presentar	seguir	tener

1. Señores, ________ al aeropuerto dos horas antes del vuelo.
2. ________ el boleto y el pasaporte al agente.
3. ________ las instrucciones de los agentes.
4. ________ los zapatos antes de pasar por el control de seguridad.
5. ________ los zapatos otra vez al salir del control de seguridad.
6. ________ a la puerta de embarque de su vuelo.
7. ________ algo, porque no sirven comida en el avión.
8. ________ paciencia.
9. ________ al avión cuidadosamente *(carefully)*.
10. ________ la siesta en el avión si pueden.

Actividad 5 Consejos para todos Escribe los mandatos correctos para saber qué les dice la guía a los turistas. Escoge la forma correcta (singular o plural, formal o informal) para cada mandato.

1. Señorita Alonso, no ________ (acostarse) muy tarde.
2. Rique, no ________ (tocar) nada en el museo.
3. Señor Baez, no ________ (hacer) ejercicio en el calor tropical.
4. Mariana, no ________ (correr) en el centro comercial.
5. Señores Montoya, no ________ (ir) al restaurante sin hacer una reserva.
6. Susi, no ________ (cruzar) la calle sola.
7. Doctora Salgado, no ________ (conducir) muy rápido en la zona turística.
8. Señores Pino, no ________ (pedir) la llave en la recepción; yo la tengo.
9. Señorita Calderón, no ________ (salir) sola por la noche.
10. Pepe, no ________ (nadar) solo.
11. Señor Fernal, no ________ (quedarse) en el hotel todo el día. ¡Hay mucho que hacer!
12. Señores, no ________ (olvidar) los documentos importantes.

Refrán

«No ________ *(leave)* para mañana, lo que ________ *(you can)* hacer hoy».

VOCABULARIO ESENCIAL

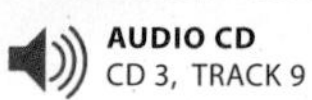
AUDIO CD
CD 3, TRACK 9

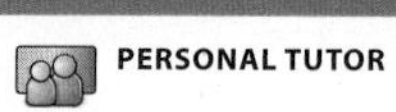
PERSONAL TUTOR

Viajar en avión	Airplane travel
Sustantivos	
la aduana	customs
la aerolínea	airline
la agencia de viajes	travel agency
el (la) agente de la aerolínea	airline agent
el (la) agente de viajes	travel agent
el asiento	seat
el (la) asistente de vuelo	flight attendant
el avión	plane
el boleto (billete) de ida	one-way ticket
el boleto (billete) de ida y vuelta	round-trip ticket
el control de seguridad	security
el equipaje	luggage
el equipaje de mano	carry-on baggage
el horario	schedule
la llegada	arrival
la maleta	suitcase
la oficina de inmigración	immigration; passport control
el (la) pasajero(a)	passenger
el pasaporte	passport
el pasillo	aisle
la puerta (de embarque)	gate
la salida	departure
la tarjeta de embarque	boarding pass
la ventanilla	airplane window
el viaje	trip
el vuelo (sin escala)	(nonstop) flight
Verbos	
abordar	to board
bajar(se) (de)	to get off
facturar el equipaje	to check the luggage
hacer escala (en)	to make a stop (in) (on a flight)
hacer la(s) maleta(s)	to pack one's suitcase(s)
ir en avión	to go by plane
pasar por	to go through
recoger el equipaje	to pick up, to claim the luggage
viajar	to travel
Expresiones idiomáticas	
¡Bienvenido(a)!	Welcome!
¡Buen viaje!	Have a nice trip!
Perdón.	Excuse me.

El hotel	The hotel
Sustantivos	
el aire acondicionado	air-conditioning
el ascensor	elevator
la cama sencilla (doble)	single (double) bed
el hotel de cuatro estrellas	four-star hotel
la llave	key
la recepción	front desk
el (la) recepcionista	receptionist
la reserva	reservation
Adjetivos	
arreglado(a)	neat, tidy
cómodo(a)	comfortable
limpio(a)	clean
lujoso	luxurious
privado(a)	private
sucio(a)	dirty
Verbos	
quedarse	to stay
quejarse (de)	to complain (about)
registrarse	to register
reservar	to reserve
subir(se) (a)	to go up, to climb, to get on

Medios de transporte	Transportation
ir...	to go . . .
a pie	on foot
en autobús	by bus
en barco	by boat
en bicicleta	by bike
en coche	by car
en metro	by subway
en taxi	by taxi
en tren	by train

Cómo llegar a un lugar	Directions
Verbos	
bajar	to go down
cruzar	to cross
doblar	to turn
parar(se)	to stop
seguir (i, i)	to continue
subir	to go up
Expresiones de lugar	
a la derecha de	to the right of
a la izquierda de	to the left of
al lado de	next to
cerca de	near
delante de	in front of
detrás de	behind
enfrente de	across from
entre	between
hacia	toward
lejos de	far from
el este	east
el norte	north
el oeste	west
el sur	south

Otros verbos	
ofrecer	to offer
prestar	to lend
prometer	to promise
regalar	to give (as a gift)

Las relaciones sentimentales

Honduras y Nicaragua

Plaza Central, León, Nicaragua

Chapter Objectives

Communicative Goals

In this chapter, you will learn how to . . .

- Communicate about personal relationships and marriage
- Indicate things that people do for one another
- Share information about events that have taken place
- Express frequency of actions and state how they are done

Structures

- The present perfect tense
- Reciprocal constructions with **se, nos,** and **os**
- Adverbs and adverbial expressions of time and sequencing of events
- Relative pronouns

- ▲ ¿Qué planes haces cuando sales con una persona por primera vez?
- ▲ ¿Te gusta salir solo(a) o con tus amigos en la primera cita *(date)*?
- ▲ ¿Crees en el amor a primera vista *(love at first sight)?*
- ▲ ¿Qué país quieres visitar en tu luna de miel *(honeymoon)*?

 Visit it live on **Google Earth!**

El noviazgo de Francisco Morazán y Celia Herrera

In this section, you will learn vocabulary associated with courtship and marriage. You will then learn how to talk about romantic relationships by following an imagined version of the courtship of Francisco Morazán and his wife, Celia Herrera de Morazán. How would you describe the perfect relationship?

Cultura

Francisco Morazán (1792–1842), a Honduran soldier and statesman, is considered a national hero of Honduras. Morazán was the guiding force behind the Central American Federation (1823–1839), which united Costa Rica, El Salvador, Guatemala, Honduras, and Nicaragua. Disputes between liberals and conservatives and among the five national groups finally broke up the federation in 1839. Morazán was also president of Costa Rica for a few months before he was assassinated in 1842.

Sustantivos

la amistad *friendship*
el amor *love*
la boda *wedding*
el cariño *affection*
el compromiso *engagement*
el divorcio *divorce*
la flor *flower*
la luna de miel *honeymoon*
el matrimonio *marriage*
la novia *bride*
el noviazgo *courtship*
el novio *groom*
los novios *engaged couple, newlyweds*
la pareja *couple*
la primera cita *first date*
los recién casados *newlyweds*
la separación *separation*
la vida *life*

Verbos

abrazar(se) *to hug (each other)*
amar(se) *to love (each other)*
besar(se) *to kiss (each other)*
casarse (con) *to get married, to marry*
darse la mano *to shake hands*
divorciarse (de) *to get divorced (from)*
enamorarse (de) *to fall in love (with)*
llevarse bien (mal) (con) *to get along well (poorly) (with)*
querer (ie) *to love*
romper (con) *to break up (with)*
salir (con) *to go out (with)*
separarse (de) *to separate (from)*
tirar *to throw*

Expresión idiomática

a primera vista *at first sight*

¡A practicar!

10-1 Definiciones Busca las palabras de la lista de la derecha que vayan con la definición de la izquierda. Luego compara tus definiciones con las de un(a) compañero(a) de clase. ¿Están de acuerdo?

Nota lingüística

Some other ways of talking about romantic breakups are **dejar a alguien** and **cortar con alguien.** You can also say that a relationship ended by stating **se acabó/se terminó la relación** (the relationship has ended).

1. ______ cuando dos personas empiezan a quererse
2. ______ tener una boda
3. ______ hacer planes con otra persona para salir o hacer algo
4. ______ cuando dos personas se enamoran la primera vez que se ven
5. ______ tener mucho amor por alguien es como tenerle mucho...
6. ______ una muestra de amor con los labios
7. ______ una muestra de amor con los brazos
8. ______ cuando dos personas siempre se pelean y no les gusta estar juntas
9. ______ cuando una persona decide terminar una relación sentimental
10. ______ un verbo que indica amor
11. ______ una manera de saludar a una persona con la mano

a. casarse
b. darse la mano
c. amar
d. romper con alguien
e. querer
f. abrazarse
g. besarse
h. llevarse mal
i. enamorarse
j. el amor a primera vista
k. la cita
l. cariño

10-2 Preparativos de una boda Completa el párrafo con las palabras o las frases adecuadas de la lista. Luego compara tu párrafo con el de un(a) compañero(a). ¿Están de acuerdo?

Nota lingüística

The term **novio(a)** is used for *boyfriend* or *girlfriend*, and is also used when two people are very close to getting married. **Prometido(a)** is *fiancé/fiancée*. The verb **comprometerse** means to become engaged or to be engaged to be married. In Chile, the word **el (la) pololo(a)** can be used to say *boyfriend/girlfriend*, as can the word **el (la) enamorado(a)** in Ecuador.

boda flores luna de miel novia novio recién casados

Normalmente, los preparativos de una 1. ________ consumen mucho tiempo y mucha energía. Primero, la 2. ________ tiene que comprar su vestido y también tiene que pedir las 3. ________ para la recepción. El 4. ________ compra un traje nuevo o puede alquilar un smoking (tuxedo). *Finalmente, los novios planean la 5. ________, según el dinero que tengan* (may have). *A veces, los 6. ________ van a otro país, pero frecuentemente lo pasan muy cerca de su ciudad o pueblo.*

10-3 La pareja más romántica Radio Honduras va a regalarle una boda y una luna de miel a la pareja considerada la más romántica de Honduras. Escucha las presentaciones de tres parejas, escribe dos datos importantes sobre cada pareja y decide qué pareja debe ganar. Después, habla con un(a) compañero(a) para ver si tiene la misma opinión sobre qué pareja debe ganar.

AUDIO CD
CD 3, TRACK 10

1. ____________________ ____________________
2. ____________________ ____________________
3. ____________________ ____________________

En mi opinión, ____________________ porque ____________________.

Workbook *10-1 – 10-3*
Lab Manual *10-1 – 10-3*

¡A conversar!

10-4 **Entrevista** Hazle a un(a) compañero(a) las siguientes preguntas sobre el matrimonio y comparen sus respuestas para ver si tienen mucho en común.

1. ¿Eres soltero(a) o casado(a)?
2. Si eres soltero(a), ¿tienes novio(a) ahora? Si estás casado(a), ¿cuándo y dónde te casaste?
3. Para ti, ¿es importante casarse? ¿Por qué?
4. Para ti, ¿qué es una familia? En tu opinión, ¿qué futuro tiene la familia en nuestra sociedad?
5. ¿Por qué hay tantos divorcios?
6. ¿Qué se puede hacer para tener éxito en el matrimonio?
7. Para ti, ¿cuál es el lugar ideal para casarse?
8. ¿Cuál es el lugar ideal para pasar una luna de miel?

10-5 **¿Parejas?** En grupos de dos o tres, lean los anuncios de dos personas que deciden salir juntas. Preparen una narración breve (de cuatro a seis oraciones) sobre lo que hacen en la cita, cómo se sienten y por qué. Luego, indiquen qué pasa después de la cita: ¿Se enamoran? ¿Se llevan bien? ¿Se casan?

© Jenkedco/Shutterstock.com

Heinle/Cengage Learning

10-6 **Y tú, ¿qué buscas?** Prepara un anuncio personal para expresar lo que tú buscas en una pareja o, si prefieres, prepara un anuncio para un personaje famoso. Sigue el modelo de los anuncios personales de la actividad anterior. Trabaja con un(a) compañero(a) para leer los anuncios y comentarlos. Después, compartan el anuncio con el resto de la clase.

EN CONTEXTO

El 14 de marzo, Claudia Ortega, la novia de Jorge Ramírez, recibió una invitación de su amigo Felipe. La invitación llegó a su casa, en Managua, Nicaragua. Claudia estaba muy emocionada y llamó por teléfono a Jorge para comunicarle las buenas noticias.

AUDIO CD
CD 3, TRACK 11

Escucha el diálogo y contesta las siguientes preguntas en oraciones completas.

1. ¿Cuál es el tema principal de este diálogo?
2. ¿Por qué llamó Claudia a su novio?
3. ¿Por qué conoce Jorge a Marisol?
4. ¿Por qué quieren casarse Felipe y Marisol?
5. ¿Piensas que Jorge quiere casarse ahora con Claudia?
6. ¿Cuál es un título adecuado para el diálogo?

Jorge: Aló.

Claudia: Hola, Jorge, ¿cómo estás?

Jorge: Bien, mi amor. ¿Qué tal?

Comentario cultural Aló Nicaragua is the country's largest wireless provider. Like for young people in the United States, communication via cell phone (including text messaging) is the preferred form of communication for young people in Nicaragua who can afford it. **Aló** is also used as an expression to answer the phone, favored slightly over other expressions, such as **sí, bueno,** and **diga,** used in other Spanish-speaking countries.

Claudia: Muy bien. Oye, Jorge, ¿sabes qué? **He recibido** muy buenas noticias de mi amigo Felipe Vega. Se casará el próximo mes con Marisol Flores.

Comentario cultural During the Sandinista regime, from 1979 until 1990, the communist doctrine of the party was at odds with the Catholic Church. During that time, civil ceremonies were common. Since the end of the regime in 1990, couples have returned to the Church in growing numbers for weddings.

Jorge: ¡No me digas! ¿Es la chica **con quien** estaba Felipe en la discoteca O.M. la semana pasada?

Comentario cultural Fancy nightclubs, such as O.M. in Managua, are becoming increasingly popular among Nicaraguans in big cities. These clubs, featuring European or American accents, such as red-carpet entrances, are relatively new to Nicaragua and are only affordable to the upper class or foreigners.

Expresiones en contexto

con quien *with whom*
felicitarlo *congratulate him*
la misma *the same one*
llevan un año de novios *they have been engaged (in a serious relationship) for one year*
locamente *wildly*
mi amor *my love*
pasarlo bien *have a good time*
Yo te lo explico todo *I'll explain everything to you*

Claudia: Sí, la misma. Él me **ha hablado** mucho de ella. Parece muy simpática. Llevan un año de novios y, según él, están locamente enamorados.

Jorge: ¿Un año de novios? No es mucho tiempo. Para mí, dos años, como mínimo...

Claudia: Sí, mi amor, ya sabemos lo que piensas tú.

Comentario cultural Nicaraguans, like other people from Latin America, view marriage as a very serious commitment. When two Nicaraguans are identified as **novios—novio y novia** *(fiancé and fiancée)*—, they intend to marry. Typically, couples will declare themselves **novios** for at least a year, often longer, before they are married. Despite the longer engagement period, the divorce rate in Nicaragua continues to rise. By the end of the 1980s, when unilateral divorce was legalized, 20 percent of marriages ended in divorce; that said, this percentage still remains lower than that in the United States.

Jorge: ¿Cuándo es la boda?

Claudia: **Han decidido** casarse el 16 de abril en la Catedral de Managua. La recepción será en el Hotel Crowne Plaza. Los padres de ella deben de ser muy ricos. ¿Quieres ir a la boda conmigo?

Comentario cultural After the end of the Sandinista period in Nicaragua in 1990, the Catholic Church reaffirmed its position in Nicaragua by building a massive modern cathedral with money donated by the United States. To be married in this cathedral is a sign of wealth and status in Managua.

Jorge: Pues, claro que sí, Claudia. ¡Muchas gracias! Pero, ¿sabes qué? Nunca **he asistido** a una boda.

Claudia: No importa. Yo te lo explico todo. Vamos a pasarlo bien. Bueno, ahora voy a llamar a Felipe para felicitarlo. Chao, Jorge.

Jorge: Chao, Claudia.

Nota lingüística

In addition to **mi amor,** Spanish speakers use many terms of endearment, for example, **mi amorcito, mi vida, cariño, mi negrito(a), viejo(a), querido(a), cielo, corazón, corazoncito.**

Diálogo entre dos novios de distintos países

Trabaja con un(a) compañero(a) de clase y túrnense para practicar el diálogo que acaban de estudiar en **En contexto.** Una persona debe ser norteamericana y la otra nicaragüense. Usen expresiones de **En contexto** como modelo para su diálogo, pero traten de representar de una manera realista las actitudes de cada uno.

The present perfect tense

Spanish speakers use the present perfect indicative tense to describe what has and has not happened recently. Unlike the preterite tense, which is used to make time-specific references to either the beginning or end of an action or event in the past, the present perfect merely establishes the fact that an action has taken place sometime in the past before the present. The emphasis is placed on the fact that the action took place, not *when* it took place. Consider the following examples:

Present perfect	Yo **he comido.**	***I have eaten.*** (past action with no specific reference to time)
Preterite	Yo **comí** a las 7:00.	***I ate at 7:00.*** (past action with specific reference to time)

How to form the present perfect

Use the present-tense forms of the auxiliary verb **haber** *(to have)* with the past participle of a verb.

	Present of **haber**	+	Past participle
yo	**he** *I have*		
tú	**has** *you* (informal) *have*		**hablado** *spoken*
Ud., él/ella	**ha** *you* (formal) *have, he/she has*		**comido** *eaten*
nosotros(as)	**hemos** *we have*		**vivido** *lived*
vosotros(as)	**habéis** *you* (informal: Spain) *have*		
Uds., ellos(as)	**han** *you have, they have*		

Regular past participles

Add **-ado** to the stem of **-ar** verbs, and **-ido** to the stem of **-er** and **-ir** verbs.

-ar verb	stem + **-ado**	**-er/-ir** verb	stem + **-ido**
habl-	habl**ado**	com-	com**ido**

—¿**Has hablado** con el novio de Ana? *Have you* ***spoken*** *to Ana's boyfriend?*

—No, pero ellos **han ido** a la casa de mi hermano antes. *No, but they* ***have come to*** *my brother's house before.*

Note that **-er** and **-ir** verbs have an accent mark on the **í** of their past participles when the ending is preceded by **a, e,** or **o.**

leer	→	leído *read*	traer	→	traído *brought*
creer	→	creído *believed*	reír	→	reído *laughed*

—Te **he traído** un regalo, Celia. ***I've brought*** *a gift for you, Celia.*

—¿Qué me **has traído,** mi amor? *What* ***have you brought me,*** *my love?*

Irregular past participles

Some verbs have irregular past participles. Here are some of the most common ones.

abrir	→	**abierto** *opened*
decir	→	**dicho** *said; told*
escribir	→	**escrito** *written*
hacer	→	**hecho** *done; made*
morir	→	**muerto** *died*
poner	→	**puesto** *put*
ver	→	**visto** *seen*
volver	→	**vuelto** *returned*

—¿Qué **han hecho** ustedes hoy? *What **have you done** today?*

—**Hemos visto** una película. *We **have seen** a movie.*

Past participles used as adjectives

The past participle can be used as an adjective to modify a noun. When used as an adjective, the past participle must agree in number and in gender with the noun that it modifies.

Voy a escuchar **canciones escritas** en español.
*I'm going to listen to **songs written** in Spanish.*

Ramón tiene dos **cuadros pintados** en Nicaragua.
*Ramón has two **paintings painted** in Nicaragua.*

The past participle is also frequently used with the verbs **estar** and **ser.** When used with the verb **estar,** the emphasis is placed on the result of an action of the verb, as opposed to the action itself. When a past participle is used with the verb **ser,** the emphasis is placed on the action rather than the result of the action; Spanish speakers often use the preposition **por** with this agent of the action.

Compare the following examples:

Result of an action

La puerta **está cerrada.** *The door **is closed.***

Emphasis on the action itself

La puerta **fue cerrada por el dueño** de la casa. *The door **was closed by the owner** of the house.*

¿Recuerdas?

Heinle/Cengage Learning

Claudia: Muy bien. Oye, Jorge, ¿sabes qué? **He recibido** muy buenas noticias de mi amigo Felipe Vega. Se casará el próximo mes con Marisol Flores.

¡A practicar!

Cultura

Las Islas de la Bahía off the Caribbean coast of Honduras are a popular tourist destination. The beautiful coral reefs make the area very appealing to scuba divers and the lovely beaches attract tourists from all over the world.

10-7 **En una terraza en las Islas de la Bahía, Honduras** Completa la siguiente conversación durante la luna de miel de Francisco y Celia con la forma correcta de **haber: he, has, ha, hemos** o **han.**

Camarero: ¿1. ______ estado Uds. en estas islas antes?

Celia: Sí, señor. Nosotros 2. ______ venido aquí antes.

Camarero: Oiga, señora, ¿3. ______ visto nuestras flores en la terraza?

Celia: Sí, sí. Yo las 4. ______ visto. Y nosotros 5. ______ decidido pasar la tarde entre las flores.

Francisco: Mejor dicho, tú 6. ______ decidido venir aquí, Celia.

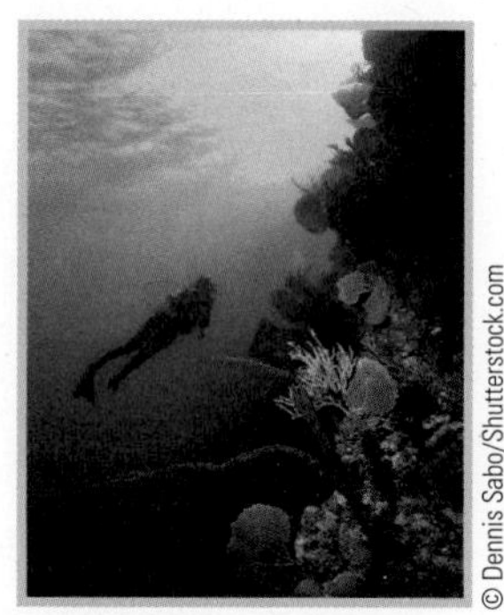

Arrecife de coral cerca de las Islas de la Bahía

10-8 **Mis queridos amigos...** Celia está escribiéndoles a sus amigos sobre algunas actividades que Francisco y ella han hecho en las Islas de la Bahía. ¿Qué les dice en su carta?

Modelo Yo ___*he hecho*___ (hacer) mucho ejercicio aquí.

Yo ______ (1. nadar) en la piscina del hotel y ______ (2. jugar) al tenis con Francisco. Él ______ (3. montar) en bicicleta dos veces esta semana. Francisco y yo ______ (4. divertirse) mucho. Esta tarde ______ (5. almorzar) en un buen restaurante y ______ (6. pasar) toda la tarde en una terraza magnífica. El camarero nos ______ (7. traer) mucha comida. Pienso que él ______ (8. creer) que teníamos mucha hambre. Nosotros ______ (9. reírse) mucho. En total, lo ______ (10. pasar) muy bien aquí en esta isla maravillosa. Nosotros ______ (11. hacer) muchas actividades diferentes y ______ (12. ver) unos paisajes (landscapes) muy bonitos.

10-9 **¿Cómo está todo?** Completa la siguiente descripción que Celia preparó sobre su luna de miel en las Islas de la Bahía escribiendo los participios pasados apropiados.

Ahora Francisco y yo estamos un poco ______ (1. cansar) pero muy contentos. La puerta al balcón está ______ (2. abrir) y podemos ver el mar. Las luces están ______ (3. apagar) porque una vela está ______ (4. encender). ¡Qué romántico! Estoy leyendo un libro ______ (5. escribir) por un hombre que conoce esta región muy bien. Es fascinante y he aprendido mucho. Estamos ______ (6. sentar) en unas sillas ______ (7. hacer) aquí en Honduras. Mañana voy a comprar un cuadro *(painting)* ______ (8. pintar) por un artista local. Siempre voy a recordar este lugar.

Workbook *10-4 – 10-9*
Lab Manual *10-4 – 10-6*

¡A conversar!

10-10 ¿Cómo está la clase? Indica si las siguientes oraciones son **ciertas** o **falsas** para tu clase en este momento.

1. Las ventanas están abiertas.
2. Todos los libros de los estudiantes están cerrados.
3. Las luces están apagadas.
4. El (La) profesor(a) está sentado(a).
5. Hay algunas palabras escritas en la pizarra.
6. Todos los estudiantes tienen los zapatos puestos.
7. Algo en la clase está roto.
8. Las persianas *(blinds)* están cerradas.
9. Los estudiantes están muertos de hambre.
10. Mi tarea para hoy ya está hecha.

10-11 La luna de miel José Luis y Raquel están en Roatán, las Islas de la Bahía, Honduras, para su luna de miel. Es el cuarto día de su viaje y han hecho muchas actividades, pero hay varias cosas que todavía no han hecho. Con un(a) compañero(a), formen oraciones para expresar lo que han hecho y lo que no han hecho hasta ahora.

Lo que han hecho:	**Lo que no han hecho:**
nadar mucho	correr las olas
practicar el buceo	hacer una parrillada
tomar el sol	pescar
comer mucho pescado	escribir muchas cartas
bailar todas las noches	hacer camping
caminar en la playa	correr en la playa
hablar con su familia por teléfono	comprar regalos para todos sus parientes
ir de compras	pasear en canoa
¿ ... ?	¿ ... ?

10-12 ¿Qué has hecho? Trabajen en parejas para hacer y contestar las siguientes preguntas. Comparen sus respuestas y compartan *(share)* la información que ya saben sobre los temas.

1. ¿Has visto fotos de Managua, la capital de Nicaragua? ¿Has visto fotos de Tegucigalpa, la capital hondureña? ¿Has visto fotos de las capitales de otros países hispanos? ¿Has visitado la capital de un país hispano?
2. ¿Has leído la poesía de Rubén Darío, Ernesto Cardenal, Gioconda Belli o de otro poeta nicaragüense? ¿Has escrito poesía?
3. ¿Has comido muchas bananas de Honduras y Nicaragua? ¿Has bebido mucho café?
4. ¿Qué has aprendido sobre la civilización maya? ¿Qué has aprendido sobre las Islas de la Bahía?

Cultura

Nicaragua is known as "**la tierra de los poetas**" because it has produced an impressive number of outstanding poets, such as Rubén Darío, from the late nineteenth and early twentieth centuries, and the contemporary poets Ernesto Cardenal and Gioconda Belli.

Reciprocal constructions with *se, nos,* and *os*

Spanish speakers express the idea of *each other* or *one another* with the plural reflexive pronouns **se, nos,** and **os.** Verbs that are not normally reflexive are frequently used to express reciprocal actions. Consider the following examples:

Osvaldo y Lola **se miran** el uno al otro.

Osvaldo and Lola look at each other.

Mi novio y yo **nos besamos.**

My boyfriend and I kiss each other.

¿**Os habláis** mucho por teléfono?

Do you all talk to each other on the phone a lot?

The phrase **el uno al otro** *(each other)* is sometimes added to reciprocal actions for clarification.

Verbs that are often reflexive can also be used in this way, but only in the plural form and with the meaning of *each other* or *one another* rather than *oneself, yourselves, themselves, ourselves,* and the like. Note the following example:

> Los esposos **se cuidan el uno al otro** cuando están enfermos.
>
> *The husband and wife take care of each other when they are sick.*

Context will usually allow you to determine if a sentence that includes **se, nos,** or **os** and a plural verb is reflexive or reciprocal. You can see the differences in these examples:

> Los niños **se miran** en el espejo cuando se peinan.
>
> *The children look at themselves in the mirror when they comb their hair.*

> Los novios **se miran** cariñosamente cuando hablan de su amor.
>
> *The sweethearts look at one another affectionately when they talk about their love.*

¡A practicar!

10-13 Amor a primera vista Forma oraciones para saber la historia de amor entre Alicia y Emilio. Ojo con el uso del pretérito.

Modelo Alicia y Emilio / conocerse / en un café
Alicia y Emilio se conocieron en un café.

1. Alicia y Emilio / verse / una tarde de julio en un café
2. no hablarse / pero / ellos mirarse profundamente
3. inmediatamente / la muchacha y el muchacho / enamorarse
4. ellos / abrazarse / y / besarse / aquella tarde
5. Pronto Alicia explicó a sus padres: «Emilio y yo / enamorarse / Fue un amor a primera vista.»
6. Los padres / mirarse / sorprendidos
7. No se preocupen; Emilio y yo ya / sentarse / a hablar: ¡Todavía no nos vamos casar!

10-14 ¿La pareja ideal? Indica si estás de acuerdo con las siguientes cualidades de la pareja ideal. Si no estás de acuerdo, explica por qué. Luego compara tu razonamiento *(reasoning)* con el de un(a) compañero(a) de clase. ¿Piensan igual?

Modelo Ellos nunca se miran a los ojos cuando se hablan.
No es una cualidad de la pareja ideal, porque dos personas de una pareja ideal siempre se miran cuando se hablan.

1. Ellos se comunican todas sus ideas y opiniones.
2. Ellos se ayudan con problemas difíciles.
3. Ellos siempre se dicen la verdad.
4. Ellos no se contradicen *(contradict one another)* con frecuencia.
5. A veces se besan en público.
6. Se enamoraron a primera vista.
7. Nunca se separan cuando van juntos a una fiesta.
8. Se casan después de un noviazgo largo.
9. Ellos se sientan a charlar cuando tienen opiniones diferentes.
10. Ellos siempre se van de vacaciones juntos.

Workbook *10-10 – 10-11*
Lab Manual *10-7 – 10-9*

¡A conversar!

10-15 Mis relaciones sentimentales Forma preguntas con los siguientes elementos para hacérselas a un(a) compañero(a) de clase sobre sus relaciones sentimentales.

Modelo tú y tus amigos / verse frecuentemente
E1: *¿Se ven tú y tus amigos frecuentemente?*
E2: *Sí, nos vemos frecuentemente los fines de semana.*

1. tú y tus padres / hablarse por teléfono una vez a la semana
2. tú y tu mejor amigo(a) / escribirse durante las vacaciones
3. tú y tus abuelos / conocerse muy bien; respetarse
4. tú y tus hermanos / ayudarse con problemas económicos
5. tú y tu compañero(a) de cuarto / hablarse sinceramente
6. tú y tu novio(a) / mirarse cariñosamente; quererse
7. tú y tus compañeros de clase / darse la mano en clase
8. ¿...?

10-16 ¿Qué hacen? Trabaja con un(a) compañero(a) para describir las siguientes relaciones familiares y sociales. Hablen de las actividades que las personas hacen y de las que no hacen.

Modelo *Los buenos amigos se hablan mucho por teléfono.*

Relaciones: los buenos amigos, los parientes, los esposos, los padres y los niños, los profesores y los estudiantes, los estudiantes de una clase, los jefes *(bosses)* y los empleados, los(las) compañeros(as) de cuarto o de casa, los(las) atletas en un equipo de deportes

Actividades: (no) escribirse, (no) hablarse (por teléfono), (no) verse, (no) darse regalos, (no)ayudarse, (no) abrazarse, (no) besarse, (no) decirse la verdad, (no) gritarse

Honduras y Nicaragua

Veamos los videos de Honduras y Nicaragua para luego comentarlos.

1. Describan algunos ejemplos de arquitectura colonial en Tegucigalpa, la capital de Honduras.
2. ¿Qué pueden comprar en el Mercado la Isla en Tegucigalpa?
3. ¿Por qué se conoce Nicaragua?
4. ¿Cómo es el ambiente de Managua? ¿Qué pueden ver y visitar en Managua, la capital de Nicaragua?

See the *Workbook*, **Capítulo 10, 10-20–10-22** for additional activities.

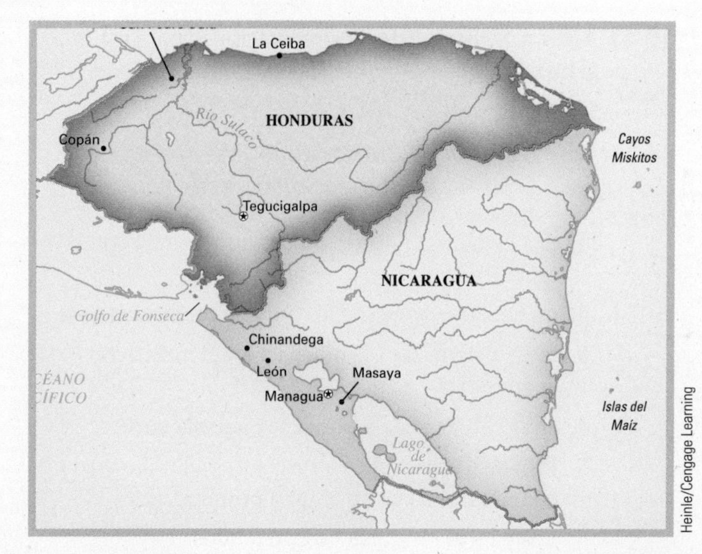

Heinle/Cengage Learning

Honduras

Población: 7.989.414 de habitantes

Área: 112.090 km^2, un poco más grande que el estado de Tennessee

Capital: Tegucigalpa (1.300.000 habs.)

Ciudades principales: San Pedro de Sula (638.259 habs.); Choloma (228.828 habs.); La Ceiba (174.006 habs.)

Moneda: la lempira

Lenguas: el español y varias lenguas indígenas

Nicaragua

Población: 5.995.928 de habitantes

Área: 129.494 km^2, un poco más pequeño que el estado de Nueva York

Capital: Managua (1.098.000 habs.)

Ciudades principales: León (139.433 habs.); Chinandega (95.614 habs.); Masaya (92.598 habs.)

Moneda: el córdoba

Lenguas: el español y varias lenguas indígenas

© Hulton Archive/Getty Images

Poeta nicaragüense Rubén Darío

Personas notables El poeta Rubén Darío (1867–1916) nació en Metapa, Nicaragua y es conocido como el «Príncipe de las letras hispanas» de Latinoamérica. Darío es considerado como el máximo representante del modernismo literario en español y uno de los poetas más influyentes de su generación. El tema principal en sus poemas es el amor, el cual describe por medio de símbolos y metáforas. La siguiente es una estrofa *(stanza)* de uno de los poemas de Darío titulado «Amo, amas».

> Amar, amar, amar, amar siempre, con todo
> el ser y con la tierra y con el cielo,
> con lo claro del sol y lo oscuro del lodo *(mud)*:
> amar por toda ciencia y amar por todo anhelo *(wish, desire)*.

¿Qué piensas de esta estrofa? ¿Qué significa el símbolo del lodo? ¿Qué es el amor para ti?

© Da Vinci Gallery of Art

Pintura sin título de Benigno Gómez López

Artes plásticas El pintor hondureño Benigno Gómez López nació en la ciudad de Naranjito en 1934. Estudió arte en la Escuela Nacional de Bellas Artes en Tegucigalpa y diez años más tarde continuó sus estudios en la Academia de Bellas Artes de Roma, Italia, por medio de una beca *(scholarship)*. En 1977, la Organización de las Naciones Unidas *(United Nations)* escogió una de sus obras, "Las Palomas", como imagen para una estampilla *(stamp)* conmemorativa de esa organización. En su obra *(work)*, normalmente usa tonos azules, grises y amarillos, y representa la realidad por medio de símbolos.

¿Puedes distinguir qué hacen las personas en la pintura? ¿Dónde están? Crea un título apropiado para esta pintura.

© J Marshall/Tribaleye Images/Alamy

Escultura en Copán, Honduras

Historia Las ruinas mayas de Copán, en Honduras, son de gran importancia histórica para toda la región. La ciudad de Copán era el centro de la civilización maya. Ellos usaban la escritura jeroglífica, un calendario avanzado y una astronomía compleja. La división social era muy definida; la mujer tenía un puesto inferior al hombre. La mujer hacía los trabajos de la casa, como la limpieza, el cuidado de los hijos y de los animales; además, estaba encargada de *(in charge of)* cultivar y hacer la comida. La civilización desapareció debido a la sobrepoblación, a la contaminación del agua, a las luchas políticas y a la guerra *(war)*. Hoy en día, se puede visitar el Museo de Escultura de Copán, construido por el gobierno de Honduras en 1996. El museo está dentro del Parque Nacional de Copán. En el parque hay también vegetación original de la zona, y así los visitantes pueden experimentar cómo vivían los mayas.

¿Has visitado ruinas o sitios arqueológicos en los Estados Unidos o en otros países? ¿Qué te parece la idea de construir un museo dentro de la zona arqueológica?

Visit it live on **Google Earth!**

Ritmos y música La música y la danza nicaragüenses son una mezcla de elementos españoles, africanos e indígenas de la región. La música es una parte muy importante de las celebraciones nicaragüenses. Los instrumentos que se usan son la marimba, la guitarra, la flauta y las maracas.

Uno de los grupos folclóricos de Nicaragua es el grupo Nicaragua Libre, que en esta oportunidad presenta una selección instrumental, usando la marimba como instrumento principal. La canción se llama «La danza del cielo». *Access the iTunes playlist on the **Plazas** website.*

¿Crees que el sonido de la marimba es similar a algún otro instrumento? ¿A cuál?

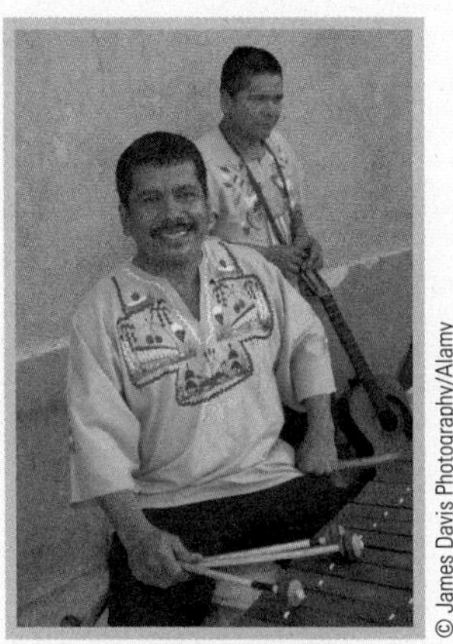
© James Davis Photography/Alamy

Músicos nicaragüenses con marimba y guitarra

¡Busquen en Internet!

1. Personas notables: Rubén Darío
2. Artes plásticas: Benigno Gómez López
3. Historia: Copán, Honduras
4. Ritmos y música: marimba, Nicaragua Libre

VOCABULARIO 2

La recepción de Rubén y Rafaela

In this section, you will practice vocabulary used to describe receptions and banquets by observing Carolina's memories of her best friend's wedding reception. Have you ever attended a banquet or a wedding reception? What was it like?

Todas las personas importantes de Managua **asistieron a la recepción** de Rubén y Rafaela.

Los invitados **felicitaron** a los recién casados cuando llegaron a la recepción.

El banquete fue **elegante** y los invitados estaban **vestidos de gala. La orquesta** de la ciudad tocó para la celebración.

Rafaela tiró **el ramo** de flores y una chica lo **agarró**. ¡Todos **aplaudieron**!

La recepción de la pareja **tuvo lugar** en el hotel InterContinental Metrocentro de Managua.

El padre de Rafaela la **acompañó** al coche que esperaba afuera del hotel. Así **terminó** una celebración perfecta.

Heinle/Cengage Learning

Sustantivos

el banquete *banquet*
el champán *champagne*
los detalles *details*
la orquesta *band*
el pastel de boda(s) *wedding cake*
el primer baile *first dance*
el ramo *bouquet*
la recepción *reception*
los recuerdos *(wedding) favors*

Adjetivos

clásico(a) *classic*
elegante *elegant*
moderno(a) *modern*
sencillo(a) *simple*

Verbos

acompañar *to accompany*
agarrar *to catch*
aplaudir *to applaud*
asistir (a) *to attend (a function)*
felicitar *to congratulate*
partir *to cut*
tener lugar *to take place*
terminar *to end*

Expresión idiomática

vestido(a) de gala *dressed elegantly*

¡A practicar!

10-17 ¿Qué palabra no pertenece aquí? Identifica la palabra o expresión de cada grupo que no pertenezca y explica por qué.

1. agarrar, el ramo, tirar, tener lugar
2. felicitar, vestirse de gala, hacer un brindis, aplaudir
3. la pareja, terminar, los invitados, la orquesta
4. asistir, ir, acompañar, recepción
5. detalles, banquete, champán, pastel de bodas
6. terminar, partir, acompañar, el primer baile
7. clásico, elegante, champán, sencillo

10-18 ¿En qué palabra estoy pensando? Busca la palabra adecuada del nuevo vocabulario que defina cada oración.

1. dos palabras que se refieren a la fiesta que se da después de una boda ______________
2. un grupo de dos personas ______________
3. el grupo musical que toca en fiestas o en conciertos ______________
4. con ropa elegante ______________
5. Los ______________ son la gente que va a una boda o a otro evento.
6. levantar las copas en honor a una persona ______________
7. objetos que se guardan para acordarse de un evento ______________
8. que tiene elementos comunes, que no es ni moderno, ni antiguo, ni extraordinario ______________
9. postre principal que se come en una boda y se corta en porciones ______________

Cultura

Managua is the capital and largest city of Nicaragua. It is located along the southern shore of Lake Managua. It was chosen to be the capital of Nicaragua in 1857 in order to resolve a dispute over the location of the capital in one of the two then larger cities of Granada and León.

10-19 La perspectiva de un músico Félix, un miembro de la orquesta que tocó para los recién casados, narra la historia de la recepción. Usa los siguientes verbos para completar su historia, escogiendo entre el pretérito o el imperfecto.

acompañar	aplaudir	felicitar	terminar
agarrar	asistir a	tener lugar	

Más de 300 personas 1. ____________ la recepción de Rubén y Rafaela. La celebración 2. ____________ en el elegante Hotel InterContinental Metrocentro de Managua. Nosotros, los músicos, 3. ____________ a un cantante en una canción de amor cuando los novios entraron. Todos los invitados 4. ____________ con alegría. El padre de la novia los 5. ____________ con un brindis. Una chica joven 6. ____________ el ramo de flores que Rafaela tiró. La fiesta 7. ____________ cuando Rubén y Rafaela se fueron de la recepción.

Workbook *10-12 – 10-13*
Lab Manual *10-10 – 10-12*

¡A conversar!

10-20 Planes, planes y planes Felipe y Gabriela están organizando la recepción de su boda y siempre hay un poquitín de desacuerdo. Con un(a) compañero(a), hagan los papeles de Felipe y Gabriela y hablen de los planes para la fiesta. Hagan preguntas con la información dada. ¡Sean creativos!

Modelo Fecha

Felipe: *¿Cuándo quieres tener la recepción?*
Gabriela: *Yo quiero tener la recepción el día de la boda por la noche.*
Felipe: *¡Ay que no, mi amor! Yo prefiero tenerla por la tarde.*

Preguntas de Felipe	Respuestas de Gabriela	Desacuerdo de Felipe
el lugar	sala de baile, Palacio Nacional	....
el número de invitados	50 personas	....
la cena	cena de cinco platos	....
el tipo de ropa	ropa muy formal	....
el tipo de música	merengue	....
tirar arroz	no tirar arroz	....

10-21 Entrevista Con un(a) compañero(a) de clase, contesta las siguientes preguntas sobre bodas para ver si tienen mucho en común.

1. ¿Estás casado(a)? Si no, ¿piensas casarte algún día? ¿Cómo vas a celebrar? Si estás casado(a), ¿cómo celebraste la boda? ¿Hubo una fiesta grande? ¿Quiénes asistieron a tu boda? ¿Cómo te vestiste tú? ¿Cómo se vistieron los invitados?
2. ¿Fuiste a una boda alguna vez? ¿De quién? ¿Lo pasaste bien? ¿Hubo mucha gente? ¿Qué tipo de ropa llevaban los invitados? ¿Dónde se celebró la boda?
3. ¿Fuiste alguna vez a una recepción o un banquete para celebrar una boda? ¿Había una orquesta? ¿Bailaron juntos los novios? ¿Cómo trataron los invitados a los novios? ¿Les tiraron mucho arroz?

10-22 ¿Qué deben hacer? Trabajen en grupos para leer y considerar las siguientes situaciones. Discutan lo que Uds. creen que las personas deben hacer.

Pareja 1:
Están muy enamorados, pero son estudiantes y no tienen dinero. Quieren una boda memorable, pero simplemente no pueden pagarla. ¿Deben casarse ahora sin tener la boda y la recepción que quieren, o deben esperar varios años para tener la boda de sus sueños?

Pareja 2:
También están muy enamorados y quieren casarse. Viven lejos de sus familias y no pueden decidir dónde celebrar la boda. Si la celebran donde viven sus familias, muchos de sus amigos no van a poder asistir porque no tienen dinero para viajar muy lejos. Si la celebran donde viven sus padres van a poder venir, pero otros parientes y amigos de su pueblo no van a poder asistir. ¿Qué lugar deben escoger para la boda y recepción, o deben celebrar dos bodas y dos recepciones?

Pareja 3:
Esta pareja también está enamorada y quiere casarse, pero tiene ideas muy diferentes a las de sus padres sobre la boda ideal. Los padres desean una boda tradicional para sus hijos, pero la pareja prefiere una ceremonia muy moderna. Los padres van a pagar la boda y la recepción y por eso piensan que los novios deben respetar sus preferencias. ¿Qué deben hacer los novios?

ESTRUCTURA 2

Adverbs and adverbial expressions of time and sequencing of events

Adverbs

An adverb is a word that modifies a verb, an adjective, or another adverb. It may describe *how, when, where, why,* or *how much.* You already know many adverbs such as **muy, poco, siempre, después, mucho, bien, mal, tarde, temprano, mejor,** and **peor.**

- To form most other Spanish adverbs, add **-mente** *(-ly)* to an adjective.

natural	**naturalmente**	*naturally*
frecuente	**frecuentemente**	*frequently*

Mi amiga habla de su novio **constantemente.**
My friend talks about her boyfriend constantly.

Los estudiantes llegan a clase **puntualmente.**
*The students arrive to class **on time (in a timely manner).***

- If an adjective ends in **-o,** change the **-o** to **-a,** then add **-mente.**

perfecto	**perfectamente**	*perfectly*

Todos deben hacer la tarea **cuidadosamente.**
*Everyone must do the homework **carefully.***

Cuando estoy cansado, camino **lentamente.**
*When I am tired, I walk **slowly.***

- If an adjective has an accent mark, the adverb retains it.

fácil	**fácilmente**	*easily*
rápido	**rápidamente**	*rapidly*

Mis compañeros de cuarto corren **rápidamente.**
*My classmates run **rapidly (quickly).***

La profesora contesta las preguntas **honestamente.**
*The teacher responds to the questions **honestly.***

Note that adverbs modifying a verb are generally placed immediately after the verb, whereas adverbs modifying adjectives or other adverbs are placed directly before them.

Ellos salieron **rápidamente** de la sala.
*They left the room **quickly.***

Rubén estaba **muy** enojado.
*Rubén was **very** mad.*

¿Recuerdas?

Heinle/Cengage Learning

Claudia: Sí, la misma. Él me ha hablado mucho de ella. Parece muy simpática. Llevan un año de novios y, según él, ellos están **locamente** enamorados.

Adverbial expressions of time and sequencing of events

In previous chapters, you learned many of the following adverbs and adverbial expressions with their English equivalents.

- Use the following adverbs to express how often something is done.

cada día (semana, mes, etc.)	*each day (week, month, etc.)*
todos los años (días, meses, etc.)	*every year (day, month, etc.)*
dos (tres, etc.) veces	*twice (three times, etc.)*
nunca	*never*
otra vez	*again*
(casi) siempre	*(almost) always*
solamente	*only, just*
a veces	*sometimes*
una vez	*once*
muchas veces	*many times, very often*

—Hablo con mi novio **todos los días.**
*I talk to my boyfriend **every day.***

—**Siempre** voy con él al cine los fines de semana.
*I **always** go to the movies with him on the weekend.*

—También hablo con mis padres **cada día.**
*I also speak to my parents **every day.***

—**Casi siempre** voy al gimnasio después de clase.
*I **almost always** go to the gym after class.*

—He esquiado en el agua **tres veces,** pero mis amigos lo han hecho **muchas veces.**
*I've water skied **three times,** but my friends have done it **many times.***

—He esquiado en la nieve **solamente una vez** y **nunca** he practicado *snowboarding.*
*I've skied on snow **only once** and I've **never** practiced snowboarding.*

- Use the following adverbs to express the order of events.

primero	*first*
entonces	*then; so*
luego	*then*
después	*afterward*
finalmente	*finally*
por fin	*at last, finally*

—¿Adónde vamos **primero,** mi amor?
*Where are we going **first,** my love?*

—Al cine. **Luego** a la discoteca.
*To the movies. **Then** to the disco.*

—¿Y **después**?
*And **afterward**?*

—Volvemos a casa.
We're going back home.

¡A practicar!

10-23 Impresiones de una boda Vas a describir lo que pasó en la boda de Francisco Morazán y Celia Herrera. Para darle más énfasis, convierte el adjetivo en adverbio y luego incorpóralo en la oración.

Modelo fabuloso / Celia se vestía
fabulosamente / Celia se vestía fabulosamente.

1. puntual / Francisco llegó a la iglesia
2. elegante / Celia caminó
3. constante / Las dos madres lloraban *(cried)*
4. sincero / Francisco y Celia hablaron
5. perfecto / Ellos dijeron sus votos *(vows)*
6. alegre / Todos salieron de la iglesia

10-24 Los preparativos de Paulina Tu amiga Paulina va a casarse y tú vas a ayudarla con los preparativos. Ella te deja un mensaje telefónico para decirte varias cosas que ya ha hecho. En la lista de preparativos, marca con una X las cosas que Paulina dice que ha hecho.

AUDIO CD
CD 3, TRACK 12

_______ hablar con la organizadora de la boda
_______ pedir el pastel
_______ pedir las invitaciones
_______ pedir las flores
_______ hablar con el director de la orquesta
_______ asistir a un concierto de la orquesta
_______ escuchar unas canciones de la orquesta
_______ ver fotos de la boda de su prima
_______ hablar con su tío
_______ planear todo el menú para el banquete

10-25 Un fracaso amoroso Luis Eduardo nos cuenta de una relación amorosa que terminó mal para él. Pon el relato en orden. Después, vuelve a contar la historia y añade palabras como **primero, un día, entonces, luego, después, finalmente** y **por fin** para hacerla más completa.

_______ Me fui corriendo de su casa. Me puse muy triste. ¡Yo quería casarme con esta chica!
_______ ¡La encontré en los brazos de mi hermano, Raúl!
_______ La invité a cenar conmigo.
_______ Después de salir con ella por algunas semanas, yo me enamoré perdidamente de ella.
_______ Un día, salí temprano del trabajo y pasé por su casa para sorprenderla *(surprise her)*.
_______ Conocí a Raquel, la mujer más guapa del mundo, el año pasado.
_______ Después de comer, fuimos a tomar un café y hablamos toda la noche.
_______ Decidí romper con ella para siempre.
_______ Empezamos a salir todas las noches.

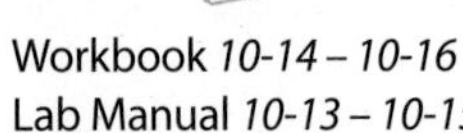
Workbook *10-14 – 10-16*
Lab Manual *10-13 – 10-15*

¡A conversar!

10-26 ¿Cómo haces esas cosas? Con un(a) compañero(a), busca el adverbio que corresponda con las siguientes palabras para describir cómo hacen Uds. las siguientes cosas. **¡Ojo!** Algunas de las palabras no requieren cambios: ya son adverbios.

Modelo jugar con los niños pequeños
E1: *¿Cómo juegas con los niños pequeños?*
E2: *Juego pacientemente con los niños pequeños. ¿Y tú?*
E1: *Yo juego mal con los niños pequeños; no me gustan los niños.*

bien	fácil	frecuente	mal	mejor	natural
paciente	peor	perfecto	rápido	tarde	

1. hablar español
2. conducir
3. hablar con gente del sexo opuesto
4. estudiar para mis clases
5. tocar el piano
6. bailar

10-27 Un día perfecto ¿Cómo es un día perfecto para ti? Prepara una lista con las actividades necesarias para tener un día absolutamente perfecto. Empieza con la primera actividad del día y prepara una lista cronológica con un mínimo de seis actividades. Utiliza las expresiones **primero, después, por fin, entonces, luego** y **finalmente**, y explícale a tu compañero(a) tu día perfecto. Puedes usar esas expresiones más de una vez si lo necesitas. Después de presentar sus listas, comparen Uds. sus opiniones sobre lo que constituye un día perfecto.

10-28 La boda de Ana Eres reportero(a) y tu reportaje para el programa *¡Hoy!* en la tele es sobre la boda de Ana Mendoza, hija de una familia prominente de su pueblo. Refiérete a la foto de la boda, y empezando desde ese momento cuando la novia y su familia caminan a la iglesia, prepara un reportaje de siete a diez oraciones sobre la boda y la recepción. Explica cronológicamente qué hacen la novia y el novio, sus parientes y los invitados e incluye tantos elementos de las listas como sea posible.

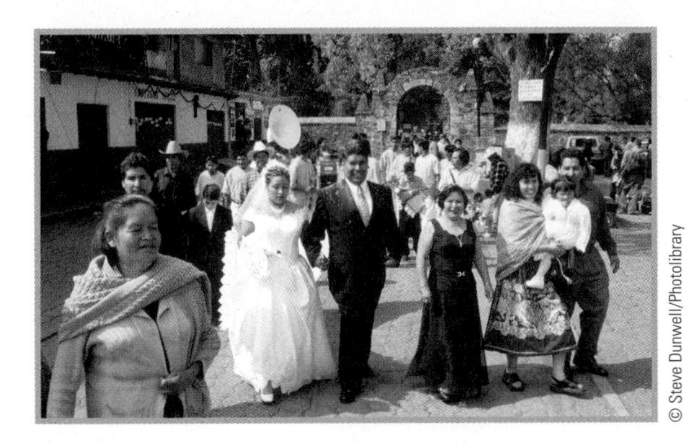

Nota lingüística
Married couples are referred to as **el matrimonio**. Some Spanish-speaking countries also use the word **el matrimonio,** rather than the more common words **la boda** or **el casamiento,** for *wedding.*

¿Qué hacen?

abrazar(se)
bailar
caminar
casarse
comer
entrar
felicitar
hablar
llegar
mirar(se)
salir
tirar

¿Cómo lo hacen?

cariñosamente
constantemente
elegantemente
inmediatamente
pacientemente
perfectamente
puntualmente
rápidamente
sinceramente
totalmente

Relative pronouns

Relative pronouns are used in joining two clauses together. There are four primary relative pronouns in English: *who, whom, that,* and *which.* Their Spanish equivalents are words you already know.

que	refers to people and things
quien(es)	refers only to people
lo que	refers to an entire idea, concept, or situation

¿Quién es el hombre **que** hablaba contigo? ↑ (first clause) ↑ (second clause)	*Who is the man who was talking with you?*
Ella es la mujer **con quien** yo bailaba. ↑ (first clause) ↑ (second clause)	*She is the woman with whom I was dancing.*
No sabemos **lo que** él hizo en la fiesta. ↑ (first clause) ↑ (second clause)	*We don't know what he did at the party.*

- Note that in distinguishing between the use of the relative pronouns **que** or **quien,** both of which can be used to refer to people, Spanish speakers use **quien** *(who/whom)* only when it is preceded by a preposition. Compare the following examples:

Es una mujer **que** tiene muchos amigos.	*She is a woman who has many friends.*
Es la mujer **con quien** yo bailaba. (**quien** preceded by the preposition **con**)	*She is the woman with whom I was dancing.*

- **Lo que** at the beginning of a sentence translates into English as *what* or *the thing that.*

Lo que me gusta de la clase es la cultura.	*What (The thing that) I like about the class is the culture.*

¿Recuerdas?

Heinle/Cengage Learning

Jorge: ¡No me digas! ¿Es la chica **con quien** estaba Felipe en la discoteca O.M. la semana pasada?

¡A practicar!

10-29 Una mujer misteriosa Usa el pronombre relativo adecuado para completar las siguientes oraciones.

1. ¿Quién es la mujer ________ lleva el vestido azul?
2. Creo que es la mujer con ________ Ramón hablaba el otro día.
3. Dicen que es la mujer ________ se divorció de Juan Medellín porque él no era muy fiel. *(faithful)*
4. No debes creer ________ dice la gente. Otras personas dicen que Juan salía con una chica ________ era la amiga de esa mujer.
5. La persona con ________ bailaba Cecilia era su ex novio. Él me dijo que siempre le fue fiel a la mujer con ________ se casó.
6. No creas todo ________ Juan dice.
7. Juan es una persona ________ nunca miente.
8. Cristina y Mabel son ________ almuerzan con Juan todos los días.
9. ¡No importa! Juan solamente se sienta a comer. ¡________ hace no está mal!
10. No te enojes. La gente es ________ dice que Juan es infiel; no yo.

10-30 La civilización maya Usa el pronombre relativo adecuado para completar el siguiente párrafo que describe la civilización de los mayas.

La civilización maya, ________ se desarrolló en México, Guatemala, Belice y Honduras, era una civilización muy avanzada. Esta civilización tuvo su mayor desarrollo en los años 300 a 900 después de Cristo. ________ distinguió a esta civilización fue su arquitectura. Construyeron pirámides de piedra ________ servían para celebraciones religiosas, templos y esculturas. Además, los mayas fueron grandes matemáticos y astrólogos ________ explicaron sus descubrimientos con su escritura de símbolos o jeroglíficos. En el siglo XVI, los españoles conquistaron esta civilización y, hoy en día, los descendientes (descendants) *de los mayas ________ viven en estos países todavía conservan algunas de sus tradiciones culturales.*

Workbook *10-17 – 10-19*
Lab Manual *10-16 – 10-18*

¡A conversar!

10-31 Lo que necesitamos es amor Completa las siguientes preguntas con **que, lo que** o **quien.** Después, contéstalas con un(a) compañero(a) de clase para expresar sus opiniones personales. ¿Tienen mucho en común?

Modelo **E1:** ¿Tu mejor amiga es la persona ___*que*___ sabe más de ti?
E2: *Sí, mi mejor amiga sabe todos mis secretos.*
o **E2:** *No, yo le cuento más a mi mamá que a mi mejor amiga.*

1. ¿Es el amor ________ da felicidad en la vida?
2. ¿Es el divorcio ________ está destruyendo nuestra sociedad?
3. ¿Piensas casarte con una persona ________ tenga los mismos gustos que tú?
4. ¿Es tu novio(a) ________ te conoce mejor?
5. ¿Son tus padres las personas en ________ más confías *(trust)*?
6. ¿Te parece que el dinero es ________ debe tener una pareja para ser feliz?
7. Si tienes un problema de pareja, son tus padres con ________ debes hablar primero?
8. ¿Quiénes son las personas ________ pueden vivir con una pareja?

10-32 La pareja ideal ¿Cómo es la pareja ideal? Con un(a) compañero(a) de clase, completen las siguientes oraciones para describir la pareja ideal.

Modelo Dos personas que...
Dos personas que se comunican mucho son la pareja ideal.

1. El amor que...
2. El matrimonio es lo que...
3. La persona con quien...
4. El amor a primera vista es lo que...
5. La amistad que...
6. La pareja ideal que...
7. La comunicación es lo que...
8. Los amigos son quienes...

Heinle/Cengage Learning

¿Algo más que amigos? En este segmento del video, Valeria y Antonio hablan sobre las relaciones sentimentales. Los dos han tenido malas experiencias amorosas y parece *(it seems)* que se sienten mejor al compartir esta información. A ver si los buenos amigos pueden llegar a ser algo más...

Antes de ver

Expresiones útiles Las siguientes son expresiones nuevas que vas a escuchar en el video.

Es el colmo	*It's an outrage*
Puedo hacerte compañía	*I can keep you company*

Enfoque estructural The following are expressions in the video with adverbial expressions of time:

Valeria: Ya mira, a veces quisiera largarme de esta casa. Y **ahora**, ni siquiera puedo hablar por teléfono.

Antonio: Los tres éramos bien unidos, **siempre** estábamos juntos.

Antonio: ¿Quieres hacer algo **esta noche?**

1. **Recordemos** Las relaciones sentimentales no son fáciles y a veces no terminan bien. Haz una lista de posibles causas del fracaso *(failure)* de una relación sentimental y comparte tu lista con un(a) compañero(a). ¿Hay causas comunes en sus listas?
2. **Practiquemos** Con un compañero de clase, inventen una historia de amor entre Valeria y Antonio con expresiones adverbiales de tiempo. Por ejemplo: *Primero Valeria y Antonio decidieron ir juntos a una película. Luego,... Entonces,...*
3. **Charlemos** Describe a un compañero(a) tu cita ideal. Explica la secuencia de todos los sucesos de la cita. Luego tu compañero(a) debe aclarar detalles de los sucesos usando el tiempo verbal perfecto.

Modelo **E1:** Primero, paso por la casa de Natasha.
E2: ¿Vas en coche o a pie?
E1: Voy en coche. Luego,...

Después de ver

1. Valeria y Antonio En el video, viste los comienzos de una relación sentimental entre Valeria y Antonio. Pon las siguientes oraciones en orden cronológico para contar exactamente lo que pasó. Luego, no te olvides de añadir *(add)* en los espacios en blanco las expresiones adverbiales apropiadas: **después, entonces, finalmente, luego, primero.**

_______________, los dos decidieron cenar juntos y pasear por la playa.

_______________, Antonio le preguntó si se sentía bien y Valeria explicó por qué la relación con César había terminado.

_______________, Valeria dijo que se sentía muy sola y Antonio respondió que no debía sentirse así y ofreció acompañarla esa noche.

_______________, Valeria estaba hablando con su ex-novio César por teléfono cuando descubrió que Antonio estaba escuchando la conversación. Colgó con César y empezó a gritarle a Antonio.

_______________, Antonio contó lo que pasó con su ex-novia Raquel y cómo ella se enamoró de su mejor amigo Rubén. A pesar de eso *(in spite of that)*, Antonio perdonó a los dos.

2. Acciones y reacciones Piensa en el comportamiento *(behavior)* de Antonio y Valeria durante este segmento del video e indica si las siguientes oraciones son **ciertas** o **falsas.** No te olvides de corregir las oraciones falsas.

- Antonio y Valeria se miran mientras hablan sobre sus ex novios.

  ____

- Antonio besa a Valeria.

  ____

- Ellos caminan en la playa.

  ____

- Valeria abraza a Antonio.

  ____

Entre nosotros Escoge uno de los temas presentados a continuación y explícale a un(a) compañero(a) lo que pasó primero, segundo, luego, etc., a lo largo de *(throughout)* esa relación personal. ¿Han tenido experiencias similares? ¿Sus experiencias siguieron el mismo orden? ¿Por qué crees que hay diferencias?

- Cuando conocí a mi mejor amigo(a)
- Cuando conocí a mi novio(a) / esposo(a)

Presentaciones Con un grupo de tres personas, hagan una historia de amor ficticia, o básenla en algunos detalles cómicos/interesantes de **Entre nosotros** o invéntenla totalmente. Los miembros de cada grupo deben turnarse para describir cada suceso de la situación. Al terminar, compartan su historia con la clase para ver qué grupo tiene la historia más interesante. No se olviden de dar nombres a las personas en la historia e incluir muchos detalles.

See the *Lab Manual,* **Capítulo 10, 10-21– 10-22** for additional activities.

Antes de leer

Strategy: Summarizing a reading passage

Summarizing in English a reading passage that you have read in Spanish can help you synthesize its most important ideas. Here are some guidelines you can follow:

- Underline the main ideas.
- Circle the key words and expressions.
- Write the summary of the passage in your own words.
- Do not include your personal reactions to the selection.

In addition, the summary should not be longer than the original passage so you should not include too many details. Finally, verify that the key terms and expressions are included in your summary.

Use this strategy to summarize the reading passage about Ernesto Cardenal's life.

Ernesto Cardenal (1925–) Nació en Granada, Nicaragua, y es uno de los poetas más reconocidos y más importantes del siglo XX. Al terminar sus estudios de secundaria viajó a México, donde estudió en la Facultad de Filosofía y Letras de la Universidad Nacional Autónoma de México. De 1947 a 1949 estudió en la Universidad de Columbia en Nueva York. Entre 1949 y 1950 viajó por España, París e Italia, y en 1950, cuando regresó a Nicaragua, comenzó a escribir poemas históricos, poemas amorosos y poemas políticos en contra de la dictadura de la familia Somoza que gobernó al país por cuarenta y tres años. En 1956 decidió hacerse sacerdote *(to become a priest)* y así comenzó a escribir poemas religiosos. En 1966 fundó una comunidad política, social y religiosa para los campesinos nicaragüenses en una de las islas de Solentiname en el Lago de Nicaragua. En 1979, cuando triunfó la Revolución Sandinista en contra de Somoza, Cardenal fue nombrado ministro de Cultura. Ernesto Cardenal continua siendo una figura muy importante y polémica de Nicaragua, y ha recibido premios y reconocimientos de distintas partes del mundo.

Epigrama V

Poeta nicaragüense Ernesto Cardenal

La selección de Ernesto Cardenal es un poema en forma de epigrama. Un epigrama es una composición poética corta que expresa con precisión un solo pensamiento principal, que puede ser un pensamiento alegre o satírico. Ahora lee el poema y emplea las estrategias que están a continuación.

1. Lee el poema y subraya la idea principal.
2. Lee el poema una vez más y haz un círculo alrededor de las palabras claves.
3. Escribe en tus propias palabras la idea principal.

Al perderte yo a ti tú y yo hemos perdido:
yo porque tú eras lo que yo más amaba
y tú porque yo era el que te amaba más.
Pero de nosotros dos tú pierdes más que yo:
porque yo podré amar a otras como te amaba a ti
pero a ti no te amarán como te amaba yo.

Después de leer

A escoger Después de leer el epigrama, contesta las siguientes preguntas.

1. ¿Qué tipo de epigrama es?
   a. alegre y satírico
   b. triste y satírico
   c. pesimista y satírico
2. ¿Quién(es) perdió/perdieron en esta relación que se termina?
   a. el poeta
   b. la mujer
   c. el poeta y la mujer
3. ¿Quién(es) tiene(n) la esperanza *(hope)* de volver a amar?
   a. el poeta
   b. la mujer
   c. el poeta y la mujer
4. ¿Quién(es) en esta relación pierde más, según el autor?
   a. el poeta
   b. la mujer
   c. el poeta y la mujer

¿Cierto o falso? Indica si las siguientes oraciones son **ciertas** o **falsas.** Corrige las oraciones falsas.

1. ______ Al terminar esta relación, el hombre y la mujer no van a perder nada en el amor.
2. ______ El hombre y la mujer se amaban mucho.
3. ______ El hombre va a amar a otras mujeres como amaba a esta mujer.
4. ______ La mujer va a encontrar a otra persona que la ame como este hombre la amó.

¡A conversar! Con sus compañeros(as) de clase, conversen sobre los siguientes temas.

Las diferencias entre lo que piensa el poeta sobre la mujer (que no va a encontrar a nadie que la ame tanto como él) y lo que ustedes piensan que ella cree. ¿Qué nos indica la actitud del poeta sobre su personalidad? ¿Cómo es el poeta? ¿Es una persona sencilla, arrogante, confiada, etcétera?

¡A escribir! Después de conversar con sus compañeros(as) de clase, escriban:

1. **La respuesta de la mujer** Escriban otro epigrama contestándole al poeta lo que ustedes piensan que la mujer le va a contestar al poeta.
2. **El amor ideal** Escriban un anuncio romántico para buscar el amor ideal. Preséntenle el anuncio a toda la clase. ¿Están de acuerdo todos con la descripción del amor ideal? ¿Cuál es el mejor anuncio y por qué?

Strategy: Using expressions of frequency in descriptions of activities

Descriptive paragraphs occur in many contexts. They are often found in works of fiction such as novels and short stories, but they also appear in newspaper articles, advertising materials, educational publications, and personal letters. A descriptive paragraph contains sentences that describe people, places, things, and/or events. In this chapter, we will focus on describing events. To express how often events take place or how often you or others do something, you can use adverbs of frequency such as the following:

a veces	*sometimes*	raras veces	*rarely, infrequently*
cada año	*each year*	siempre	*always*
dos veces a la semana	*twice a week*	todos los días	*every day*
muchas veces	*often*	una vez al mes	*once a month*
nunca	*never*		

Remember that you can also modify these expressions to describe a wide variety of time frames: **dos veces al mes, tres veces a la semana, cada mes,** and so on.

Task: Writing a descriptive paragraph

Paso 1 Ahora, vas a escribir un párrafo para describir unas actividades que tú haces con tu familia o con otras personas importantes de tu vida. Para empezar, identifica a las personas que vas a incluir en la composición. Después, escribe una lista de actividades que tú haces con esas personas. Incluye un mínimo de ocho actividades.

Paso 2 Indica con qué frecuencia haces cada actividad de la lista. Puedes referirte a la lista de palabras y expresiones de arriba.

Paso 3 Escribe un párrafo bien planeado en el cual describas las actividades que haces, las personas con quienes las haces y la frecuencia de cada actividad. Puedes organizar el párrafo basándote en las actividades o en las personas que hacen las actividades contigo.

Paso 4 Intercambia papeles con un(a) compañero(a) de clase. Lee el párrafo de la otra persona para ver si ha incluido la información necesaria en su composición. Si es necesario hacer algunos cambios, hazlos.

Paso 5 Habla con tu compañero(a) sobre las actividades que cada persona ha incluido en su composición y la frecuencia identificada para cada actividad. Comparen y contrasten las actividades que hacen y la frecuencia con que las hacen.

Communicative Goals

- Communicate about personal relationships and marriage
- Indicate things that people do for one another
- Share information about events that have taken place
- Express frequency of actions and state how they are done

Paso 1
Review the Communicative Goals for **Capítulo 10** and determine if you are able to accomplish the goals. If you are not certain that you have achieved all of the goals, review the pertinent portions of the chapter.

Paso 2
Look at the components of a conversation which addresses the communicative goals for this chapter. The percentages will help you evaluate your ability to successfully participate in the conversation that is featured below. Your instructor may use the same rubric to assess your oral performance.

Components of the conversation	%
☐ Questions and answers about when, where and how you met someone who is very important to you	20
☐ Information about at least three things you do for one another and the frequency with which you do them	20
☐ Questions and answers about at least three things the two of you have done recently and information about how you have done them	20
☐ Questions and answers about a special event you have attended or in which you have participated, including at least three details	20
☐ Information about at least two other people who are important to you, who they are, what they are like, and why they are important	20

En acción Think about a conversation in which two friends (A and B) tell one another about people who are very important to them. Consider the sort of information that might be presented and how the speakers ask and answer questions to share information. Work with a partner to carry out the conversation, being sure to include the steps below. When you have concluded your conversation, change roles and carry out the conversation again.

1. A asks B about one individual who is very important to him/her and B responds with information about the person and tells how, where and when they met.
2. B shares information about at least three things that he/she and the important person do for one another and indicates how often they do them.
3. A asks what B and his/her important person have done recently and B responds with information about at least three activities they have done and about how they have done them.
4. A asks about a special event that B and his/her special person have attended or in which they have participated and B responds with at least three details about the event and their involvement.
5. A asks B about other people who are important to him/her and B provides information about at least two other people, explaining who each is and telling why he/she is important.
6. The friends conclude the conversation in an appropriate manner.

¡A REPASAR!

Present perfect tense

Use the present-tense forms of the auxiliary verb **haber** *(to have)* with the past participle of a verb.

yo	**he**		
tú	**has**		**hablado**
Ud., él, ella	**ha**	+	**comido**
nosotros(as)	**hemos**		**vivido**
vosotros(as)	**habéis**		
Uds., ellos(as)	**han**		

¡A recordar! 1 Which **-er** and **-ir** verbs have an accent mark on the **í** of their past participles? What are eight common irregular past participles?

Reciprocal constructions with *se, nos* and *os*

Spanish speakers express the idea of *each other* or *one another* with the plural reflexive pronouns **se, nos,** and **os.** Verbs that are not normally reflexive are frequently used to express reciprocal actions.

¡A recordar! 2 Why is the phrase **el uno al otro** sometimes added to reciprocal expressions?

Adverbial expressions of time and sequencing of events

To form most Spanish adverbs, add **-mente** to an adjective.

frecuente **frecuentemente**

If an adjective ends in **-o,** change the **-o** to **-a,** then add **-mente.**

perfecto **perfectamente**

If an adjective has an accent mark, the adverb retains it.

fácil **fácilmente**

Use the following adverbs to express how often something is done.

a veces
dos (tres, etc.) veces
solamente
(casi) siempre
cada día (semana, mes, etc.)
todos los años (días, meses, etc.)
una vez
muchas veces
otra vez
nunca

Use the following adverbs to express the order of events.

primero **entonces** **finalmente**
luego **después** **por fin**

¡A recordar! 3 What determines where an adverb is placed in a sentence?

Relative pronouns

Relative pronouns are used to join two clauses together. There are four primary relative pronouns in English: ***who, whom, that,*** and ***which.*** Their Spanish equivalents are words you already know: **que** refers to people and things; **quien** refers only to people; and **lo que** refers to an entire idea, concept or situation.

¡A recordar! 4 How do you distinguish between the use of **que** or **quien**? How do you express the idea of *What* or *The thing that* at the beginning of a sentence in Spanish?

Actividad 1 La luna de miel Completa la tarjeta postal que Ceci les escribe a sus padres durante su luna de miel en Roatán, Honduras. Emplea el presente perfecto.

¡Hola, papis!

Nuestra luna de miel 1. ______________ (ser) estupenda. Fernando y yo 2. ______________ (divertirse) mucho. Nosotros 3. ______________ (jugar) al tenis y también 4. ______________ (nadar) cada día. Yo 5. ______________ (caminar) en la playa mucho y Fernando 6. ______________ (correr) varias veces. Nuestros amigos nuevos Gerardo y Carolina nos 7. ______________ (enseñar) a hacer esnórquel. Nosotros 8. ______________ (ver) peces bonitos y otras cosas increíbles. Estoy cansada porque 9. ______________ (acostarse) tarde, pero estoy contenta porque Fernando y yo 10. ______________ (bailar) cada noche. ¿Qué 11. ______________ (hacer) Uds. esta semana? Papi, ¿12. ______________ (trabajar) en tu jardín? Mami, ¿13. ______________ (terminar) el libro que leías? Estamos en un café y el mesero nos 14. ______________ (traer) la comida. ¡Hasta pronto!

Actividad 2 ¿Qué hacen estas personas? Forma oraciones con los elementos dados, incluyendo la forma recíproca de los verbos.

1. Ana y Sole / decirse / secretos
2. Mi primo y yo / escribirse / correos electrónicos
3. Mis padres / besarse / cada día
4. Muchos amigos / ayudarse / con los problemas
5. Mi esposa y yo / llamarse / mucho por teléfono
6. Mis amigos y yo / verse / en la biblioteca

Actividad 3 El día de la boda Completa cada frase con la forma apropiada de **estar** en el primer espacio y la forma correcta del participio pasado en el segundo blanco.

1. La novia ________ un poco ________ (preocupar) por su vestido.
2. Las puertas de la iglesia ________ ________ (abrir).
3. Las luces ________ ________ (apagar) porque hay muchas velas.
4. El pobre novio ________ ________ (morir) de hambre porque no ha comido nada en todo el día.
5. Yo ________ ________ (cansar) después de tantas horas de preparativos.

Actividad 4 ¿Cómo lo hacen? Cambia los adjetivos a adverbios y escribe el adverbio apropiado para completar cada oración.

alegre	inmediato	perfecto	rápido
fácil	paciente	puntual	regular

1. Estela corre una milla en menos de seis minutos. Corre ______________.
2. Nosotros siempre llegamos a clase a tiempo. Llegamos______________.
3. David estudia español todos los días a la misma hora. Estudia ______________.
4. La clase no es difícil para Horacio. Hace la tarea ______________.
5. Ana María vuelve a casa a las tres y empieza la tarea a las tres y un minuto. Empieza la tarea ______________.
6. Luis siempre recibe 100% en su examen. Completa los exámenes ______________.
7. Estoy contento en la clase y me gusta participar. Participo ______________.
8. La profesora tiene mucha paciencia. Contesta nuestras preguntas ______________.

Actividad 5 Hagamos planes Escoge la(s) palabra(s) correcta(s) para completar cada oración.

_____ 1. Conozco un lugar _____ es perfecto para la luna de miel.
a. que
b. quien
c. quienes
d. lo que

_____ 2. Mi amigo Carlos, _____ viaja conmigo, lo recomienda también.
a. quienes
b. quién
c. quien
d. quiénes

_____ 3. La boda de Felipe y Andrea es un evento _____ no quiero perder.
a. quien
b. que
c. lo que
d. con quien

_____ 4. _____ más me gusta del lugar es la tranquilidad.
a. Que
b. quien
c. Lo que
d. Quienes

_____ 5. Ramón es la persona _____ le recomendé el lugar el año pasado. Le gustó mucho.
a. quién
b. quien
c. de quien
d. a quien

_____ 6. La persona _____ hablaba la novia de Raúl era su tío.
a. quién
b. quien
c. con quién
d. con quien

Refrán

Los ______________ *(newlyweds)* casa quieren.

VOCABULARIO ESENCIAL

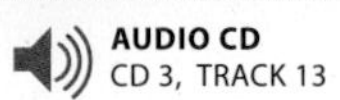
AUDIO CD
CD 3, TRACK 13

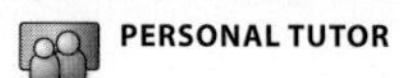
PERSONAL TUTOR

Las relaciones sentimentales — *Relationships*

Sustantivos	
la amistad	friendship
el amor	love
la boda	wedding
el cariño	affection
la cita	date (social)
el compromiso	engagement
el divorcio	divorce
la flor	flower
la luna de miel	honeymoon
el matrimonio	marriage
la novia	bride
el noviazgo	courtship
el novio	groom
los novios	engaged couple, newlyweds
la pareja	couple
los recién casados	newlyweds
la separación	separation
la vida	life
Verbos	
abrazar(se)	to hug (each other)
amar(se)	to love (each other)
besar(se)	to kiss (each other)
casarse (con)	to get married, marry
darse la mano	to shake hands
divorciarse (de)	to get divorced (from)
enamorarse (de)	to fall in love (with)
llevarse bien (con)	to get along well (with)
llevarse mal (con)	to get along poorly (with)
querer (ie)	to love
romper (con)	to break up (with)
salir (con)	to go out (with)
separarse (de)	to separate (from)
tirar	to throw
Expresión idiomática	
a primera vista	at first sight

En la recepción — *At the reception*

Sustantivos	
el banquete	banquet
el champán	champagne
los detalles	details
la orquesta	band
el pastel de boda(s)	wedding cake
el primer baile	first dance
el ramo	bouquet
la recepción	reception
los recuerdos	(wedding) favors
Adjetivos	
clásico(a)	classic
elegante	elegant
moderno(a)	modern
sencillo(a)	simple
Verbos	
acompañar	to accompany
agarrar	to catch
aplaudir	to applaud
asistir (a)	to attend (a function)
felicitar	to congratulate
interrumpir	to interrupt
partir	to take place
tener lugar	to end
terminar	
Expresión idiomática	
vestido(a) de gala	dressed elegantly

Expresiones adverbiales de tiempo

a veces	sometimes
cada día	each day
después	afterward
dos veces	twice
entonces	then; so
luego	then
muchas veces	very often
nunca	never
otra vez	again
por fin	at last, finally
primero	first
(casi) siempre	(almost) always
solamente	only, just
todos los años	every year
una vez	once

For more detailed explanations of these grammar points, consult the Index to find the pages where they are explained fully in the body of the textbook.

ACTIVE VOICE (La voz activa) A sentence written in the active voice identifies a subject that performs the action of the verb.

Juan	cantó	la canción.
Juan	***sang***	***the song.***
subject	**verb**	**direct object**

In the sentence above Juan is the performer of the verb **cantar.**
(*See also* **Passive voice.**)

ADJECTIVES (Los adjetivos) are words that modify or describe **nouns** or **pronouns** and agree in **number** and generally in **gender** with the nouns they modify.

Las casas **azules** son **bonitas.**
*The **blue** houses are **pretty.***

Esas mujeres **mexicanas** son mis amigas **nuevas.**
*Those **Mexican** women are my **new** friends.*

Plazas es un libro **interesante** y **divertido.**
***Plazas** is an **interesting** and **fun** book.*

- **Demonstrative adjectives (Los adjetivos demostrativos)** point out persons, places, or things relative to the position of the speaker. They always agree in **number** and **gender** with the **noun** they modify. The forms are: **este, esta, estos, estas / ese, esa, esos, esas / aquel, aquella, aquellos, aquellas.** There are also neuter forms that refer to generic ideas or things, and hence have no gender: **esto, eso, aquello.**

Este libro es fácil.	***This** book is easy.*
Esos libros son difíciles.	***Those** books are hard.*
Aquellos libros son pesados.	***Those** books **(over there)** are boring.*

  Demonstratives may also function as **pronouns,** replacing the **noun** but still agreeing with it in **number** and **gender. Demonstrative pronouns** once carried accents to distinguish them from the demonstrative adjectives, but in 2005, the **Real Academia Española** ruled that accents are not necessary unless there is room for confusion.

Me gustan esas blusas verdes.	*I like those green blouses.*
¿Cuáles, **estas?**	*Which ones, **these?***
No. Me gustan **esas.**	*No. I like **those.***

- **Stressed possessive adjectives (Los adjetivos posesivos acentuados)** are used for emphasis and follow the noun that they modifiy. These adjectives may also function as pronouns and always agree in **number** and in **gender.** The forms are: **mío, tuyo, suyo, nuestro, vuestro, suyo.** Unless they are directly preceded by the verb **ser,** stressed possessives must be preceded by the **definite article.**

Ese perro pequeño es **mío.**	*That little dog is **mine.***
Dame el **tuyo;** el **nuestro** no funciona.	*Give me **yours; ours** doesn't work.*

- **Unstressed possessive adjectives (Los adjetivos posesivos no acentuados)** demonstrate ownership and always precede the **noun** that they modify.

La señora Elman es **mi** profesora.	*Mrs. Elman is **my** professor.*
Debemos llevar **nuestros** libros a clase.	*We should take **our** books to class.*

ADVERBS **(Los adverbios)** are words that modify **verbs, adjectives,** or other adverbs and, unlike **adjectives,** do not have **gender** or **number.** Here are examples of different classes of adverbs:

Practicamos **diariamente.**	*We practice **daily.*** (adverb of manner)
Ellos van a salir **pronto.**	*They will leave **soon.*** (adverb of time)
Jennifer está **afuera.**	*Jennifer is **outside.*** (adverb of place)
No quiero ir **tampoco.**	*I don't want to go **either.*** (adverb of negation)
Paco habla **demasiado.**	*Paco talks **too much.*** (adverb of quantity)

AGREEMENT **(La concordancia)** refers to the correspondence between parts of speech in terms of **number, gender,** and **person.** Subjects agree with their verbs; articles and adjectives agree with the nouns they modify, etc.

Toda**s** la**s** lengua**s** so**n** interesante**s.**	*All languages are interesting.* (number)
Ella es bonit**a.**	*She is pretty.* (gender)
Nosotros somos de España.	*We are from Spain.* (person)

ARTICLES **(Los artículos)** precede nouns and indicate whether they are definite or indefinite persons, places, or things.

- **Definite articles** **(Los artículos definidos)** refer to particular members of a group and are the equivalent of *the* in English. The definite articles are: **el, la, los, las.**

El hombre guapo es mi padre.	***The** handsome man is my father.*
Las mujeres de esta clase son inteligentes.	***The** women in this class are intelligent.*

- **Indefinite articles** **(Los artículos indefinidos)** refer to any unspecified member(s) of a group and are the equivalent of *a(n)* and *some.* The indefinite articles are: **un, una, unos, unas.**

Un hombre vino a nuestra casa anoche.	***A** man came to our house last night.*
Unas niñas jugaban en el parque.	***Some** girls were playing in the park.*

CLAUSES **(Las cláusulas)** are subject and verb combinations; for a sentence to be complete it must have at least one main clause.

- **Main clauses** (Independent clauses) **(Las cláusulas principales)** communicate a complete idea or thought.

Mi hermana va al hospital.	*My sister goes to the hospital.*

- **Subordinate clauses** (Dependent clauses) **(Las cláusulas subordinadas)** depend upon a main clause for their meaning to be complete.

Mi hermana va al hospital	con tal que no llueva.
My sister goes to the hospital	*provided that it's not raining.*
main clause	**subordinate clause**

In the sentence above, *provided that it's not raining* is not a complete idea without the information supplied by the main clause.

COMMANDS **(Los mandatos)** (*See* **Imperatives.**)

COMPARISONS **(Las formas comparativas)** are statements that describe one person, place, or thing relative to another in terms of quantity, quality, or manner.

- **Comparisons of equality** **(Las formas comparativas de igualdad)** demonstrate an equal share of a quantity or degree of a particular characteristic. These statements use a form of **tan(to)(ta)(s)** and **como.**

Ella tiene **tanto** dinero **como** Elena.	*She has **as much** money **as** Elena.*
Fernando trabaja **tanto como** Felipe.	*Fernando works **as much as** Felipe.*
Jim baila **tan** bien **como** Anne.	*Jim dances **as** well **as** Anne.*

- **Comparisons of inequality** **(Las formas comparativas de desigualdad)** indicate a difference in quantity, quality, or manner between the compared subjects. These statements use **más/menos... que** or comparative **adjectives** such as **mejor/peor, mayor/menor.**

España tiene **más** playas que México.	*Spain has **more** beaches **than** Mexico.*
Tú hablas español **mejor que** yo.	*You speak Spanish **better than** I.*

(*See also* **Superlatives.**)

CONJUGATIONS **(Las conjugaciones)** represent the inflected form of the verb as it is used with a particular subject or **person.**

Yo bailo los sábados.	***I dance** on Saturdays.* (1st-person singular)
Tú bailas los sábados.	***You dance** on Saturdays.* (2nd-person singular)
Ella baila los sábados.	***She dances** on Saturdays.* (3rd-person singular)
Nosotros bailamos los sábados.	***We dance** on Saturdays.* (1st-person plural)
Vosotros bailáis los sábados.	***You dance** on Saturdays.* (2nd-person plural)
Ellos bailan los sábados.	***They dance** on Saturdays.* (3rd-person plural)

CONJUNCTIONS **(Las conjunciones)** are linking words that join two independent **clauses** together.

Fuimos al centro **y** mis amigos compraron muchas cosas.
*We went downtown **and** my friends bought a lot of things.*

Yo quiero ir a la fiesta, **pero** tengo que estudiar.
*I want to go to the party, **but** I have to study.*

CONTRACTIONS **(Las contracciones)** in Spanish are limited to preposition/article combinations, such as **de + el = del** and **a + el = al,** or preposition/pronoun combinations such as **con + mí = conmigo** and **con + ti = contigo.**

DIRECT OBJECTS **(Los objetos directos)** in sentences are the direct recipients of the action of the verb. Direct objects answer the questions *What?* or *Whom?*

¿Qué hizo?	*What did she do?*
Ella hizo **la tarea.**	*She did her **homework.***
Y luego llamó a **su amiga.**	*And then called **her friend.***

(*See also* **Pronouns, Indirect object, Personal a.**)

EXCLAMATION WORDS **(Las palabras exclamativas)** communicate surprise or strong emotion. Like interrogative words, exclamatives also carry accents.

¡**Qué** sorpresa!	***What** a surprise!*
¡**Cómo** canta Miguel!	***How well** Miguel sings!*

(*See also* Interrogatives.)

GENDER **(El género)** is a grammatical feature of Romance languages that classifies words as either masculine or feminine. The gender of the word is sometimes used to distinguish meaning (**la papa** = *the potato,* but **el Papa** = *the Pope;* **la policía** = *the police force,* but **el policía** = *the policeman*). It is important to memorize the gender of nouns when you learn the nouns.

GERUNDS **(Los gerundios)** are the Spanish equivalent of the *-ing* verb form in English. Regular gerunds are created by replacing the **infinitive** endings **(-ar, -er/-ir)** with **-ando** or **-iendo.** Gerunds are often used with the verb **estar** to form the present progressive tense. The present progressive tense places emphasis on the continuing or progressive nature of an action.

Miguel está **cantando** en la ducha.	*Miguel is **singing** in the shower.*

(*See also* **Present participle.**)

IDIOMATIC EXPRESSIONS (Las frases idiomáticas) are phrases in Spanish that do not have a literal English equivalent.

Hace mucho frío. — *It is very cold.* (Literally, *It makes a lot of cold.)*

IMPERATIVES (Los imperativos) represent the mood used to express requests or commands. It is more direct than the **subjunctive** mood. Imperatives are commonly called commands and fall into two categories: affirmative and negative. Spanish speakers must also choose between using formal commands and informal commands based upon whether one is addressed as **usted** (formal) or **tú** (informal).

Habla conmigo.	**Talk** to me. (informal, affirmative)
No me hables.	**Don't talk to me.** (informal, negative)
Hable con la policía.	**Talk** to the police. (formal, singular, affirmative)
No hable con la policía.	**Don't talk** to the police. (formal, singular, negative)
Hablen con la policía.	**Talk** to the police. (formal, plural, affirmative)
No hablen con la policía.	**Don't talk** to the police. (formal, plural, negative)

(*See also* **Mood.**)

IMPERFECT (El imperfecto) The imperfect tense is used to make statements about the past when the speaker wants to convey the idea of 1) habitual or repeated action, 2) two actions in progress simultaneously, or 3) an event that was in progress when another action interrupted. The imperfect tense is also used to emphasize the ongoing nature of the middle of the event, as opposed to its beginning or end. Age and clock time are always expressed using the imperfect.

Cuando María **era** joven, ella **cantaba** en el coro.
*When María **was** young, she **used to sing** in the choir.*

Aquel día **llovía** mucho y el cielo **estaba** oscuro.
*That day **it was raining** a lot and the sky **was** dark.*

Juan **dormía** cuando sonó el teléfono.
*Juan **was sleeping** when the phone rang.*

(*See also* **Preterite.**)

IMPERSONAL EXPRESSIONS (Las expresiones impersonales) are statements that contain the impersonal subjects of *it* or *one.*

Es necesario estudiar.	***It is necessary*** *to study.*
Se necesita estudiar.	***One needs to*** *study.*

(*See also* **Passive voice.**)

INDEFINITE WORDS (Las palabras indefinidas) are **articles, adjectives, nouns** or **pronouns** that refer to unspecified members of a group.

Un hombre vino.	***A*** *man came.* (indefinite article)
Alguien vino.	***Someone*** *came.* (indefinite noun)
Algunas personas vinieron.	***Some*** *people came.* (indefinite adjective)
Algunas vinieron.	***Some*** *came.* (indefinite pronoun)

(*See also* **Articles.**)

INDICATIVE (El indicativo) The indicative is a mood, rather than a tense. The indicative is used to express ideas that are considered factual or certain and, therefore, not subject to speculation, doubt, or negation.

Josefina **es** española. (present indicative) — *Josefina **is** Spanish.*

(*See also* **Mood.**)

INDIRECT OBJECTS **(Los objetos indirectos)** are the indirect recipients of an action in a sentence and answer the questions *To whom?* or *For whom?* In Spanish it is common to include an indirect object **pronoun** along with the indirect object.

Yo **le** di el libro a **Sofía.**	*I gave the book* ***to Sofía.***
Sofía **les** guardó el libro **a sus padres.**	*Sofía kept the book* ***for her parents.***

(*See also* **Direct objects** and **Pronouns.**)

INFINITIVES **(Los infinitivos)** are verb forms that are uninflected or not **conjugated** according to a specific **person.** In English, infinitives are preceded by *to: to talk, to eat, to live.* Infinitives in Spanish end in **-ar (hablar), -er (comer),** and **-ir (vivir).**

INTERROGATIVES **(Las formas interrogativas)** are used to pose questions and carry accent marks to distinguish them from other uses. Basic interrogative words include: **quién(es), qué, cómo, cuánto(a)(s), cuándo, por qué, dónde.**

¿**Qué** quieres?	***What*** *do you want?*
¿**Cuándo** llegó ella?	***When*** *did she arrive?*
¿De **dónde** eres?	***Where*** *are you from?*

(*See also* **Exclamatives.**)

MOOD **(El modo)** is like the word *mode,* meaning *manner* or *way.* It indicates the way in which the speaker views an action, or his/her attitude toward the action. Besides the **imperative** mood, which is simply giving commands, you learn two basic moods in Spanish: the **subjunctive** and the **indicative.** Basically, the subjunctive mood communicates an attitude of uncertainty or negation toward the action, while the indicative indicates that the action is certain or factual. Within each of these moods there are many **tenses.** Hence you have the present indicative and the present subjunctive, the present perfect indicative and the present perfect subjunctive, etc.

- **Indicative mood** **(El indicativo)** implies that what is stated or questioned is regarded as true.

Yo **quiero** ir a la fiesta.	***I want*** *to go to the party.*
¿**Quieres** ir conmigo?	***Do you want*** *to go with me?*

- **Subjunctive mood** **(El subjuntivo)** indicates a recommendation, a statement of doubt or negation, or a hypothetical situation.

Yo recomiendo que tú **vayas** a la fiesta.	*I recommend* ***that you go*** *to the party.*
Dudo que **vayas** a la fiesta.	*I doubt that* ***you'll go*** *to the party.*
No creo que **vayas** a la fiesta.	*I don't believe that* ***you'll go*** *to the party.*
Si **fueras** a la fiesta, te divertirías.	*If* ***you were to go*** *to the party, you would have a good time.*

- **Imperative mood** **(El imperativo)** is used to make a command or request.

¡**Ven** conmigo a la fiesta!	***Come*** *with me to the party!*

(*See also* **Indicative, Imperative,** and **Subjunctive.**)

NEGATION **(La negación)** takes place when a negative word, such as **no,** is placed before an affirmative sentence. In Spanish, double negatives are common.

Yolanda va a cantar esta noche.	*Yolanda will sing tonight.* (affirmative)
Yolanda **no** va a cantar esta noche.	*Yolanda will* ***not*** *sing tonight.* (negative)
Ramón quiere algo.	*Ramón wants something.* (affirmative)
Ramón **no** quiere **nada.**	*Ramón* ***doesn't*** *want* ***anything.*** (negative)

NOUNS **(Los sustantivos)** are persons, places, things, or ideas. Names of people, countries, and cities are proper nouns and are capitalized.

Alberto	*Albert* (person)
el pueblo	*town* (place)
el diccionario	*dictionary* (thing)

ORTHOGRAPHY **(La ortografía)** refers to the spelling of a word or anything related to spelling such as accentuation.

PASSIVE VOICE **(La voz pasiva),** as compared to **active voice (la voz activa),** places emphasis on the action itself rather than the agent of the action (the person or thing that is indirectly responsible for committing the action). The passive **se** is used when there is no apparent agent of the action.

Luis vende los coches.	*Luis sells the cars.* (active voice)
Los coches **son vendidos por** Luis.	*The cars **are sold by** Luis.* (passive voice)
Se **venden** los coches.	*The cars **are sold.*** (passive voice)

(*See also* **Active voice.**)

PAST PARTICIPLES **(Los participios pasados)** are verb forms used in compound tenses such as the **present perfect.** Regular past participles are formed by dropping the **-ar** or **-er/-ir** from the **infinitive** and adding **-ado** or **-ido.** Past participles are the equivalent of verbs ending in *-ed* in English. They may also be used as **adjectives,** in which case they agree in **number** and **gender** with their nouns. Irregular past participles include: **escrito, roto, dicho, hecho, puesto, vuelto, muerto, cubierto.**

Marta ha **subido** la montaña.	*Marta has **climbed** the mountain.*
Hemos **hablado** mucho por teléfono.	*We have **talked** a lot on the phone.*
La novela **publicada** en 1995 es su mejor novela.	*The novel **published** in 1995 is her best novel.*

PERFECT TENSES **(Los tiempos perfectos)** communicate the idea that an action has taken place before now (present perfect) or before a moment in the past (past perfect). The perfect tenses are compound tenses consisting of the verb **haber** plus the **past participle** of a second verb.

Yo **he comido.**	***I have eaten.*** (present perfect indicative)
Antes de la fiesta, yo **había comido.**	*Before the party **I had eaten.*** (past perfect indicative)
Yo espero que **hayas comido.**	*I hope that **you have eaten.*** (present perfect subjunctive)
Yo esperaba que **hubieras comido.**	*I hoped that **you had eaten.*** (past perfect subjunctive)

PERSON **(La persona)** refers to changes in the subject pronouns that indicate if one is speaking (first person), if one is spoken to (second person), or if one is spoken about (third person).

Yo hablo.	*I speak.* (1st-person singular)
Tú hablas.	*You speak.* (2nd-person singular)
Ud./Él/Ella habla.	*You/He/She speak(s).* (3rd-person singular)
Nosotros(as) hablamos.	*We speak.* (1st-person plural)
Vosotros(as) habláis.	*You speak.* (2nd-person plural)
Uds./Ellos/Ellas hablan.	*They speak.* (3rd-person plural)

PREPOSITIONS **(Las preposiciones)** are linking words indicating spatial or temporal relations between two words.

Ella nadaba **en** la piscina.	*She was swimming **in** the pool.*
Yo llamé **antes de** las nueve.	*I called **before** nine o'clock.*
El libro es **para** ti.	*The book is **for** you.*
Voy **a** la oficina.	*I'm going **to** the office.*
Jorge es **de** Paraguay.	*Jorge is **from** Paraguay.*

PRESENT PARTICIPLE (*See* **Gerunds.**)

PRETERITE **(El pretérito)** The preterite tense, as compared to the **imperfect tense,** is used to talk about past events with specific emphasis on the beginning or the end of the action, or emphasis on the completed nature of the action as a whole.

Anoche yo **empecé** a estudiar a las once y **terminé** a la una.
Last night I ***began*** *to study at eleven o'clock and* ***finished*** *at one o'clock.*

Esta mañana **me desperté** a las siete, **desayuné, me duché** y **vine** al campus para las ocho.
This morning ***I woke up*** *at seven,* ***I ate*** *breakfast,* ***I showered,*** *and* ***I came*** *to campus by eight.*

PERSONAL A **(La *a* personal)** The personal **a** refers to the placement of the preposition **a** before the name of a person when that person is the **direct object** of the sentence.

Voy a llamar **a** María. — *I'm going to call María.*

PRONOUNS **(Los pronombres)** are words that substitute for **nouns** in a sentence.

Yo quiero **este.** — *I want* ***this one.*** (demonstrative—points out a specific person, place or thing)

¿Quién es tu amigo? — ***Who*** *is your friend?* (interrogative—used to ask questions)

Yo voy a llamar**la.** — *I'm going to call* ***her.*** (direct object—replaces the direct object of the sentence)

Ella va a dar**le** el reloj. — *She is going to give* ***him*** *the watch.* (indirect object—replaces the indirect object of the sentence)

Juan **se** baña por la mañana. — *Juan bathes* ***himself*** *in the morning.* (reflexive—used with reflexive verbs to show that the agent of the action is also the recipient)

Es la mujer **que** conozco. — *She is the woman* ***that*** *I know.* (relative—used to introduce a clause that describes a noun)

Nosotros somos listos. — **We** are clever. (subject—replaces the noun that performs the action or state of a verb)

SUBJECTS **(Los sujetos)** are the persons, places, or things that perform the action or state of being of a verb. The **conjugated** verb always agrees with its subject.

Carlos siempre baila solo. — ***Carlos*** *always dances alone.*
Colorado y **California** son mis estados preferidos. — ***Colorado*** *and* ***California*** *are my favorite states.*
La cafetera produce el café. — *The* ***coffee pot*** *makes the coffee.*

(*See also* **Active voice.**)

SUBJUNCTIVE **(El subjuntivo)** The subjunctive mood is used to express speculative, doubtful, or hypothetical situations. It also communicates a degree of subjectivity or influence of the main clause over the subordinate clause.

No creo que **tengas** razón. — *I don't think that* ***you're*** *right.*
Si yo **fuera** el jefe, pagaría más a mis empleados. — *If I* ***were*** *the boss, I would pay my employees more.*
Quiero que **estudies** más. — *I want* ***you to study*** *more.*

(*See also* **Mood, Indicative.**)

SUPERLATIVE STATEMENTS **(Las frases superlativas)** are formed by adjectives or adverbs to make comparisons among three or more members of a group. To form superlatives, add a definite article **(el, la, los, las)** before the comparative form.

Juan es **el más alto** de los tres.	*Juan is* ***the tallest*** *of the three.*
Este coche es **el más rápido** de todos.	*This car is* ***the fastest*** *of them all.*

(*See also* **Comparisons.**)

TENSES **(Los tiempos)** refer to the manner in which time is expressed through the **verb** of a sentence.

Yo estudio.	*I study.* (present tense)
Yo estoy estudiando.	*I am studying.* (present progressive)
Yo he estudiado.	*I have studied.* (present perfect)
Yo había estudiado.	*I had studied.* (past perfect)
Yo estudié.	*I studied.* (preterite tense)
Yo estudiaba.	*I was studying.* (imperfect tense)
Yo estudiaré.	*I will study.* (future tense)
Yo estudiaría.	*I would study.* (conditional tense)

VERBS **(Los verbos)** are the words in a sentence that communicate an action or state of being.

Helen **es** mi amiga y ella **lee** muchas novelas.
Helen ***is*** *my friend and she* ***reads*** *a lot of novels.*

AUXILIARY VERBS **(Los verbos auxiliares)** or helping verbs are verbs such as **estar** and **haber** used to form the present progressive and the present perfect, respectively.

Estamos estudiando mucho para el examen mañana.
We are *studying a lot for the exam tomorrow.*

Helen **ha** trabajado mucho en este proyecto.
Helen ***has*** *worked a lot on this project.*

REFLEXIVE VERBS **(Los verbos reflexivos)** use reflexive **pronouns** to indicate that the person initiating the action is also the recipient of the action.

Yo **me afeito** por la mañana.	***I shave (myself)*** *in the morning.*

STEM-CHANGING VERBS **(Los verbos con cambios de raíz)** undergo a change in the main part of the verb when conjugated. To find the stem, drop the **-ar**, **-er**, or **-ir** from the **infinitive: dorm-**, **empez-**, **ped-**. There are three types of stem-changing verbs: **o** to **ue**, **e** to **ie** and **e** to **i.**

dormir: Yo d**ue**rmo en el parque.	*I sleep in the park.* (**o** to **ue**)
empezar: Ella siempre emp**ie**za su trabajo temprano.	*She always starts her work early.* (**e** to **ie**)
pedir: ¿Por qué no p**i**des ayuda?	*Why don't you ask for help?* (**e** to **i**)

Apéndice B: Los verbos regulares

Infinitive	Present indicative	Imperfect	Preterite	Future	Conditional	Present subjunctive	Past subjunctive	Commands
hablar	hablo	hablaba	hablé	hablaré	hablaría	hable	hablara	habla
to speak	hablas	hablabas	hablaste	hablarás	hablarías	hables	hablaras	(no hables)
	habla	hablaba	habló	hablará	hablaría	hable	hablara	hable
	hablamos	hablábamos	hablamos	hablaremos	hablaríamos	hablemos	habláramos	hablad
	habláis	hablabais	hablasteis	hablaréis	hablaríais	habléis	hablarais	(no habléis)
	hablan	hablaban	hablaron	hablarán	hablarían	hablen	hablaran	hablen
aprender	aprendo	aprendía	aprendí	aprenderé	aprendería	aprenda	aprendiera	aprende
to learn	aprendes	aprendías	aprendiste	aprenderás	aprenderías	aprendas	aprendieras	(no aprendas)
	aprende	aprendía	aprendió	aprenderá	aprendería	aprenda	aprendiera	aprenda
	aprendemos	aprendíamos	aprendimos	aprenderemos	aprenderíamos	aprendamos	aprendiéramos	aprended
	aprendéis	aprendíais	aprendisteis	aprenderéis	aprenderíais	aprendáis	aprendierais	(no aprendáis)
	aprenden	aprendían	aprendieron	aprenderán	aprenderían	aprendan	aprendieran	aprendan
vivir	vivo	vivía	viví	viviré	viviría	viva	viviera	vive
to live	vives	vivías	viviste	vivirás	vivirías	vivas	vivieras	(no vivas)
	vive	vivía	vivió	vivirá	viviría	viva	viviera	viva
	vivimos	vivíamos	vivimos	viviremos	viviríamos	vivamos	viviéramos	vivid
	vivís	vivíais	vivisteis	viviréis	viviríais	viváis	vivierais	(no viváis)
	viven	vivían	vivieron	vivirán	vivirían	vivan	vivieran	vivan

Compound Tenses

Present progressive	estoy	estamos	hablando	aprendiendo	viviendo
	estás	estáis			
	está	están			
Present perfect indicative	he	hemos	hablado	aprendido	vivido
	has	habéis			
	ha	han			
Present perfect subjunctive	haya	hayamos	hablado	aprendido	vivido
	hayas	hayáis			
	haya	hayan			
Past perfect indicative	había	habíamos	hablado	aprendido	vivido
	habías	habíais			
	había	habían			

Apéndice C: Los verbos con cambios en la raíz

Infinitive Present participle Past participle	*Present indicative*	*Imperfect*	*Preterite*	*Future*	*Conditional*	*Present subjunctive*	*Past subjunctive*	*Commands*
pensar	**pienso**	pensaba	pensé	pensaré	pensaría	**piense**	pensara	**piensa**
to think	**piensas**	pensabas	pensaste	pensarás	pensarías	**pienses**	pensaras	**(no pienses)**
e → ie	**piensa**	pensaba	pensó	pensará	pensaría	**piense**	pensara	**piense**
pensando	pensamos	pensábamos	pensamos	pensaremos	pensaríamos	pensemos	pensáramos	pensad
pensado	pensáis	pensabais	pensasteis	pensaréis	pensaríais	penséis	pensarais	**(no penséis)**
	piensan	pensaban	pensaron	pensarán	pensarían	**piensen**	pensaran	**piensen**
acostarse	me **acuesto**	me acostaba	me acosté	me acostaré	me acostaría	me **acueste**	me acostara	**acuéstate (no**
to go to bed	te **acuestas**	te acostabas	te acostaste	te acostarás	te acostarías	te **acuestes**	te acostaras	**te acuestes)**
o → ue	se **acuesta**	se acostaba	se acostó	se acostará	se acostaría	se **acueste**	se acostara	**acuéstese**
acostándose	nos acostamos	nos acostábamos	nos acostamos	nos acostaremos	nos acostaríamos	nos acostemos	nos acostáramos	**acostaos (no os**
acostado	os acostáis	os acostabais	os acostasteis	os acostaréis	os acostaríais	os acostéis	os acostarais	**acostéis)**
	se **acuestan**	se acostaban	se acostaron	se acostarán	se acostarían	se **acuesten**	se acostaran	**acuéstense**
sentir	**siento**	sentía	sentí	sentiré	sentiría	**sienta**	**sintiera**	**siente (no**
to feel	**sientes**	sentías	sentiste	sentirás	sentirías	**sientas**	**sintieras**	**sientas)**
e → ie, i	**siente**	sentía	**sintió**	sentirá	sentiría	**sienta**	**sintiera**	**sienta**
sintiendo	sentimos	sentíamos	sentimos	sentiremos	sentiríamos	**sintamos**	**sintiéramos**	**sentaos (no**
sentido	sentís	sentíais	sentisteis	sentiréis	sentiríais	**sintáis**	**sintierais**	**sintáis)**
	sienten	sentían	**sintieron**	sentirán	sentirían	**sientan**	**sintieran**	**sientan**
pedir	**pido**	pedía	pedí	pediré	pediría	**pida**	**pidiera**	**pide** (no
to ask for	**pides**	pedías	pediste	pedirás	pedirías	**pidas**	**pidieras**	**pidas)**
e → i, i	**pide**	pedía	**pidió**	pedirá	pediría	**pida**	**pidiera**	**pida**
pidiendo	pedimos	pedíamos	pedimos	pediremos	pediríamos	**pidamos**	**pidiéramos**	**pedid** (no
pedido	pedís	pedíais	pedisteis	pediréis	pediríais	**pidáis**	**pidierais**	**pidáis)**
	piden	pedían	**pidieron**	pedirán	pedirían	**pidan**	**pidieran**	**pidan**
dormir	**duermo**	dormía	dormí	dormiré	dormiría	**duerma**	**durmiera**	**duerme (no**
to sleep	**duermes**	dormíais	dormiste	dormirás	dormirías	**duermas**	**durmieras**	**duermas)**
o → ue, u	**duerme**	dormía	**durmió**	dormirá	dormiría	**duerma**	**durmiera**	**duerma**
durmiendo	dormimos	dormíamos	dormimos	dormiremos	dormiríamos	**durmamos**	**durmiéramos**	dormid **(no**
dormido	dormís	dormíais	dormisteis	dormiréis	dormiríais	**durmáis**	**durmierais**	**durmáis)**
	duermen	dormían	**durmieron**	dormirán	dormirían	**duerman**	**durmieran**	**duerman**

Apéndice D: Los verbos con cambios de ortografía

Infinitive *Present participle* *Past participle*	*Present indicative*	*Imperfect*	*Preterite*	*Future*	*Conditional*	*Present subjunctive*	*Past subjunctive*	*Commands*
comenzar (e → ie) *to begin* **z → c** **before e** comenzando comenzado	comienzo comienzas comienza comenzamos comenzáis comienzan	comenzaba comenzabas comenzaba comenzábamos comenzabais comenzaban	**comencé** comenzaste comenzó comenzamos comenzasteis comenzaron	comenzaré comenzarás comenzará comenzaremos comenzaréis comenzarán	comenzaría comenzaríais comenzaría comenzaríamos comenzaríais comenzarían	**comience** **comiences** **comience** **comencemos** **comencéis** **comiencen**	comenzara comenzaras comenzara comenzáramos comenzarais comenzaran	comienza **(no** **comiences)** **comience** comenzad **(no** **comencéis)** **comiencen**
conocer *to know* **c → zc** **before a, o** conociendo conocido	**conozco** conoces conoce conocemos conocéis conocen	conocía conocías conocía conocíamos conocíais conocían	conocí conociste conoció conocimos conocisteis conocieron	conoceré conocerás conocerá conoceremos conoceréis conocerán	conocería conocerías conocería conoceríamos conoceríais conocerían	**conozca** **conozcas** **conozca** **conozcamos** **conozcáis** **conozcan**	conociera conocieras conociera conociéramos conocierais conocieran	conoce **(no** **conozcas)** **conozca** conoced **(no** **conozcáis)** **conozcan**
construir *to build* **i → y,** **y inserted** **before a, e, o** **construyendo** construido	**construyo** **construyes** **construye** construimos construís **construyen**	construía construías construía construíamos construíais construían	construí construiste **construyó** construimos construisteis **construyeron**	construiré construirás construirá construiremos construiréis construirán	construiría construirías construiría construiríamos construiríais construirían	**construya** **construyas** **construya** **construyamos** **construyáis** **construyan**	**construyera** **construyeras** **construyera** **construyéramos** **construyerais** **construyeran**	**construye (no** **construyas)** **construya** construíd **(no** **construyáis)** **construyan**
leer *to read* **i → y;** **stressed** **i → í** **leyendo** **leído**	leo lees lee leemos leéis leen	leía leías leía leíamos leíais leían	leí leíste **leyó** leímos leísteis **leyeron**	leeré leerás leerá leeremos leeréis leerán	leería leerías leería leeríamos leeríais leerían	lea leas lea leamos leáis lean	**leyera** **leyeras** **leyera** **leyéramos** **leyerais** **leyeran**	lee (no leas) lea leed (no leáis) lean

Infinitive *Present participle* *Past participle*	*Present indicative*	*Imperfect*	*Preterite*	*Future*	*Conditional*	*Present subjunctive*	*Past subjunctive*	*Commands*
pagar *to pay* **g → gu** **before e** pagando pagado	pago pagas paga pagamos pagáis pagan	pagaba pagabas pagaba pagábamos pagabais pagaban	**pagué** pagaste pagó pagamos pagasteis pagaron	pagaré pagarás pagará pagaremos pagaréis pagarán	pagaría pagarías pagaría pagaríamos pagaríais pagarían	**pague** **pagues** **pague** **paguemos** **paguéis** **paguen**	pagara pagaras pagara pagáramos pagarais pagaran	paga **(no pagues)** **pague** pagad **(no paguéis)** **paguen**
seguir *to follow* (e → i, i) **gu → g** **before a, o** siguiendo seguido	**sigo** **sigues** **sigue** seguimos seguís **siguen**	seguía seguías seguía seguíamos seguíais seguían	seguí seguiste **siguió** seguimos seguisteis **siguieron**	seguiré seguirás seguirá seguiremos seguiréis seguirán	seguiría seguirías seguiría seguiríamos seguiríais seguirían	**siga** **sigas** **siga** **sigamos** **sigáis** **sigan**	**siguiera** **siguieras** **siguiera** **siguiéramos** **siguierais** **siguieran**	sigue **(no sigas)** **siga** seguid **(no sigáis)** **sigan**
tocar *to play; to touch* **c → qu** **before e** tocando tocado	toco tocas toca tocamos tocáis tocan	tocaba tocabas tocaba tocábamos tocabais tocaban	**toqué** tocaste tocó tocamos tocasteis tocaron	tocaré tocará tocarás tocaremos tocaréis tocarán	tocaría tocarías tocaría tocaríamos tocaríais tocarían	**toque** **toques** **toque** **toquemos** **toquéis** **toquen**	tocara tocaras tocara tocáramos tocarais tocaran	toca **(no toques)** **toque** tocad **(no toquéis)** **toquen**

Apéndice E: Los verbos irregulares

Infinitive Present participle Past participle	*Present indicative*	*Imperfect*	*Preterite*	*Future*	*Conditional*	*Present subjunctive*	*Past subjunctive*	*Commands*
andar	ando	andaba	**anduve**	andaré	andaría	ande	**anduviera**	anda (no andes)
to walk	andas	andabas	**anduviste**	andarás	andarías	andes	**anduvieras**	ande
andando	anda	andaba	**anduvo**	andará	andaría	ande	**anduviera**	andad (no andéis)
andado	andamos	andábamos	**anduvimos**	andaremos	andaríamos	andemos	**anduviéramos**	anden
	andáis	andabais	**anduvisteis**	andaréis	andaríais	andéis	**anduvierais**	
	andan	andaban	**anduvieron**	andarán	andarían	anden	**anduvieran**	
*caer	**caigo**	caía	caí	caeré	caería	**caiga**	**cayera**	cae **(no caigas)**
to fall	caes	caías	**caíste**	caerás	caerías	**caigas**	**cayeras**	**caiga**
cayendo	cae	caía	**cayó**	caerá	caería	**caiga**	**cayera**	caed **(no caigáis)**
caído	caemos	caíamos	**caímos**	caeremos	caeríamos	**caigamos**	**cayéramos**	**caigan**
	caéis	caíais	**caísteis**	caeréis	caeríais	**caigáis**	**cayerais**	
	caen	caían	**cayeron**	caerán	caerían	**caigan**	**cayeran**	
*dar	**doy**	daba	**di**	daré	daría	**dé**	**diera**	da (no des)
to give	das	dabas	**diste**	darás	darías	**des**	**dieras**	**dé**
dando	da	daba	**dio**	dará	daría	**dé**	**diera**	dad **(no deis)**
dado	damos	dábamos	**dimos**	daremos	daríamos	**demos**	**diéramos**	den
	dais	dabais	**disteis**	daréis	daríais	**deis**	**dierais**	
	dan	daban	**dieron**	darán	darían	**den**	**dieran**	
*decir	**digo**	decía	**dije**	**diré**	**diría**	**diga**	**dijera**	**di (no digas)**
to say, tell	**dices**	decías	**dijiste**	**dirás**	**dirías**	**digas**	**dijeras**	**diga**
diciendo	**dice**	decía	**dijo**	**dirá**	**diría**	**diga**	**dijera**	decid **(no digáis)**
dicho	decimos	decíamos	**dijimos**	**diremos**	**diríamos**	**digamos**	**dijéramos**	**digan**
	decís	decíais	**dijisteis**	**diréis**	**diríais**	**digáis**	**dijerais**	
	dicen	decían	**dijeron**	**dirán**	**dirían**	**digan**	**dijeran**	
*estar	**estoy**	estaba	**estuve**	estaré	estaría	**esté**	**estuviera**	**está (no estés)**
to be	**estás**	estabas	**estuviste**	estarás	estarías	**estés**	**estuvieras**	**esté**
estando	**está**	estaba	**estuvo**	estará	estaría	**esté**	**estuviera**	estad **(no estéis)**
estado	estamos	estábamos	**estuvimos**	estaremos	estaríamos	**estemos**	**estuviéramos**	**estén**
	estáis	estabais	**estuvisteis**	estaréis	estaríais	**estéis**	**estuvierais**	
	están	estaban	**estuvieron**	estarán	estarían	**estén**	**estuvieran**	

*Verbs with irregular **yo** forms in the present indicative

Infinitive Present participle Past participle	*Present indicative*	*Imperfect*	*Preterite*	*Future*	*Conditional*	*Present subjunctive*	*Past subjunctive*	*Commands*
haber *to have* habiendo habido	**he** **has** **ha [hay]** **hemos** **habéis** **han**	había habías había habíamos habíais habían	**hube** **hubiste** **hubo** **hubimos** **hubisteis** **hubieron**	**habré** **habrás** **habrá** **habremos** **habréis** **habrán**	**habría** **habrías** **habría** **habríamos** **habríais** **habrían**	**haya** **hayas** **haya** **hayamos** **hayáis** **hayan**	**hubiera** **hubieras** **hubieran** **hubiéramos** **hubierais** **hubieran**	
*hacer *to make; to do* haciendo **hecho**	**hago** haces hace hacemos hacéis hacen	hacía hacías hacía hacíamos hacíais hacían	**hice** **hiciste** **hizo** **hicimos** **hicisteis** **hicieron**	**haré** **harás** **hará** **haremos** **haréis** **harán**	**haría** **harías** **haría** **haríamos** **haríais** **harían**	**haga** **hagas** **haga** **hagamos** **hagáis** **hagan**	**hiciera** **hicieras** **hiciera** **hiciéramos** **hicierais** **hicieran**	**haz (no hagas)** **haga** haced **(no hagáis)** **hagan**
ir *to go* **yendo** ido	**voy** **vas** **va** **vamos** **vais** **van**	**iba** **ibas** **iba** **íbamos** **ibais** **iban**	**fui** **fuiste** **fue** **fuimos** **fuisteis** **fueron**	iré irás irá iremos iréis irán	iría irías iría iríamos iríais irían	**vaya** **vayas** **vaya** **vayamos** **vayáis** **vayan**	**fuera** **fueras** **fuera** **fuéramos** **fuerais** **fueran**	**ve (no vayas)** **vaya** id **(no vayáis)** **vayan**
*oír *to hear* **oyendo** **oído**	**oigo** **oyes** **oye** **oímos** **oías** **oyen**	oía oías oía oíamos oíais oían	oí **oíste** **oyó** **oímos** **oísteis** **oyeron**	oíré oirás oirá oiremos oiréis oirán	oiría oirías oiría oiríamos oiríais oirían	**oiga** **oigas** **oiga** **oigamos** **oigáis** **oigan**	**oyera** **oyeras** **oyera** **oyéramos** **oyerais** **oyeran**	**oye (no oigas)** **oiga** oíd **(no oigáis)** **oigan**

*Verbs with irregular **yo** forms in the present indicative

Infinitive *Present participle* *Past participle*	*Present indicative*	*Imperfect*	*Preterite*	*Future*	*Conditional*	*Present subjunctive*	*Past subjunctive*	*Commands*
poder **(o → ue)** *can, to be able* **pudiendo** podido	**puedo** **puedes** **puede** podemos podéis **pueden**	podía podías podía podíamos podíais podían	**pude** **pudiste** **pudo** **pudimos** **pudisteis** **pudieron**	**podré** **podrás** **podrá** **podremos** **podréis** **podrán**	**podría** **podrías** **podría** **podríamos** **podríais** **podrían**	**pueda** **puedas** **pueda** podamos podáis **puedan**	**pudiera** **pudieras** **pudiera** **pudiéramos** **pudierais** **pudieran**	
*poner *to put, place* poniendo **puesto**	**pongo** pones pone ponemos ponéis ponen	ponía ponías ponía poníamos poníais ponían	**puse** **pusiste** **puso** **pusimos** **pusisteis** **pusieron**	**pondré** **pondrás** **pondrá** **pondremos** **pondréis** **pondrán**	**pondría** **pondrías** **pondría** **pondríamos** **pondríais** **pondrían**	**ponga** **pongas** **ponga** **pongamos** **pongáis** **pongan**	**pusiera** **pusieras** **pusiera** **pusiéramos** **pusierais** **pusieran**	**pon (no pongas)** **ponga** poned **(no pongáis)** **pongan**
querer **(e → ie)** *to want, to wish* queriendo querido	**quiero** **quieres** **quiere** queremos queréis **quieren**	quería querías quería queríamos queríais querían	**quise** **quisiste** **quiso** **quisimos** **quisisteis** **quisieron**	**querré** **querrás** **querrá** **querremos** **querréis** **querrán**	**querría** **querrías** **querría** **querríamos** **querríais** **querrían**	**quiera** **quieras** **quiera** querramos querráis **quieran**	**quisiera** **quisieras** **quisiera** **quisiéramos** **quisierais** **quisieran**	**quiere (no quieras)** **quiera** quered (no queráis) **quieran**
reír **(e → i)** *to laugh* **riendo** **reído**	**río** **ríes** **ríe** **reímos** reís **ríen**	reía reías reía reíamos reíais reían	reí **reíste** **rió** **reímos** **reísteis** **rieron**	reiré reirás reirá reiremos reiréis reirán	reiría reirías reiría reiríamos reiríais reirían	**ría** **rías** **ría** **riamos** **riáis** **rían**	**riera** **rieras** **riera** **riéramos** **rierais** **rieran**	**ríe (no rías)** **ría** reíd **(no riais)** **rían**

*Verbs with irregular **yo** forms in the present indicative

Infinitive *Present participle* *Past participle*	*Present indicative*	*Imperfect*	*Preterite*	*Future*	*Conditional*	*Present subjunctive*	*Past subjunctive*	*Commands*
*saber *to know* sabiendo sabido	**sé** sabes sabe sabemos sabéis saben	sabía sabías sabía sabíamos sabíais sabían	**supe** **supiste** **supo** **supimos** **supisteis** **supieron**	**sabré** **sabrás** **sabrá** **sabremos** **sabréis** **sabrán**	**sabría** **sabrías** **sabría** **sabríamos** **sabríais** **sabrían**	**sepa** **sepas** **sepa** **sepamos** **sepáis** **sepan**	**supiera** **supieras** **supiera** **supiéramos** **supierais** **supieran**	sabe **(no sepas)** **sepa** sabed **(no sepáis)** **sepan**
*salir *to go out* saliendo salido	**salgo** sales sale salimos salís salen	salía salías salía salíamos salíais salían	salí saliste salió salimos salisteis salieron	**saldré** **saldrás** **saldrá** **saldremos** **saldréis** **saldrán**	**saldría** **saldrías** **saldría** **saldríamos** **saldríais** **saldrían**	**salga** **salgas** **salga** **salgamos** **salgáis** **salgan**	saliera salieras saliera saliéramos salierais salieran	**sal (no salgas)** **salga** salid **(no salgáis)** **salgan**
ser *to be* siendo sido	**soy** **eres** **es** **somos** **sois** **son**	**era** **eras** **era** **éramos** **erais** **eran**	**fui** **fuiste** **fue** **fuimos** **fuisteis** **fueron**	seré serás será seremos seréis serán	sería serías sería seríamos seríais serían	**sea** **seas** **sea** **seamos** **seáis** **sean**	**fuera** **fueras** **fuera** **fuéramos** **fuerais** **fueran**	**sé (no seas)** **sea** sed **(no seáis)** **sean**
*tener *to have* teniendo tenido	**tengo** **tienes** **tiene** tenemos tenéis **tienen**	tenía tenías tenía teníamos teníais tenían	**tuve** **tuviste** **tuvo** **tuvimos** **tuvisteis** **tuvieron**	**tendré** **tendrás** **tendrá** **tendremos** **tendréis** **tendrán**	**tendría** **tendrías** **tendría** **tendríamos** **tendríais** **tendrían**	**tenga** **tengas** **tenga** **tengamos** **tengáis** **tengan**	**tuviera** **tuvieras** **tuviera** **tuviéramos** **tuvierais** **tuvieran**	**ten** (no tengas) **tenga** tened **(no tengáis)** **tengan**

*Verbs with irregular **yo** forms in the present indicative

Infinitive Present participle Past participle	*Present indicative*	*Imperfect*	*Preterite*	*Future*	*Conditional*	*Present subjunctive*	*Past subjunctive*	*Commands*
*traer *to bring* **trayendo** **traído**	**traigo** traes trae traemos traéis traen	traía traías traía traíamos traíais traían	**traje** **trajiste** **trajo** **trajimos** **trajisteis** **trajeron**	traeré traerás traerá traeremos traeréis traerán	traería traerías traería traeríamos traeríais traerían	**traiga** **traigas** **traiga** **traigamos** **traigáis** **traigan**	**trajera** **trajeras** **trajera** **trajéramos** **trajerais** **trajeran**	trae (**no traigas**) **traiga** traed (**no traigáis)** **traigan**
*venir *to come* **viniendo** venido	**vengo** **vienes** **viene** venimos venís **vienen**	venía venías venía veníamos veníais venían	**vine** **viniste** **vino** **vinimos** **vinisteis** **vinieron**	**vendré** **vendrás** **vendrá** **vendremos** **vendréis** **vendrán**	**vendría** **vendrías** **vendría** **vendríamos** **vendríais** **vendrían**	**venga** **vengas** **venga** **vengamos** **vengáis** **vengan**	**viniera** **vinieras** **viniera** **viniéramos** **vinierais** **vinieran**	**ven (no vengas)** venga venid (**no vengáis)** **vengan**
ver *to see* viendo **visto**	**veo** ves ve vemos veis ven	**veía** **veías** **veía** **veíamos** **veíais** **veían**	**vi** **viste** **vio** **vimos** **visteis** **vieron**	veré verás verá veremos veréis verán	vería verías vería veríamos veríais verían	**vea** **veas** **vea** **veamos** **veáis** **vean**	viera vieras viera viéramos vierais vieran	ve (**no veas)** **vea** ved (**no veáis)** **vean**

*Verbs with irregular **yo** forms in the present indicative

Glosario español-inglés

This Spanish-English Glossary includes all the words and expressions that appear in the text except verb forms, regular superlatives and diminutives, and most adverbs ending in **-mente.** Only meanings used in the text are given. Gender of nouns is indicated except for masculine nouns ending in **-o** and feminine nouns ending in **-a.** Feminine forms of adjectives are shown except for regular adjectives with masculine forms ending in **-o.** Verbs appear in the infinitive form. Stem changes and spelling changes are indicated in parentheses: e.g., **divertirse (ie, i); buscar (qu).** The number following each entry indicates the chapter in which the word with that particular meaning first appears. The following abbreviations are used:

adj.	*adjective*	*m.*	*masculine*	*prep.*	*preposition*
adv.	adverb	*f.*	feminine	*pron.*	pronoun
conj.	conjunction	*pl.*	plural	*s.*	singular
def. art.	definite article	*p.p.*	past participle		
indef. art.	indefinite article				

A

a *prep.* at, to
a cambio de in exchange for
a cuadros plaid, 7
a fin de que *conj.* so that, 13
a la derecha de *prep.* to the right of, 9
a la izquierda de *prep.* to the left of, 9
a lunares polka-dotted, 7
a menos que *conj.* unless, 13
a menudo frequently
a primera vista at first sight, 10
¿A qué hora? At what time?, 1
a rayas striped, 7
a tiempo on time, 1
a última hora at the last minute, 8
a veces *adv.* sometimes, 3
abajo *adv.* below
abierto *p.p.* opened
abogado(a) lawyer, 11
abordar to board, 9
aborto abortion, 14
abrazar(se) to hug (each other), 10
abrigo overcoat, 7
abril April, 3
abrir to open
abrir un documento (un programa) to open a document (program), 15
abrochar el cinturón de seguridad to buckle the seat belt, 9
abuela grandmother, 2
abuelo grandfather, 2
aburrido *adj.* bored, 2
aburrir to bore, 13
acabar to run out, 12
acabar de + *infinitive* to have just (done something)
accesorio accessory, 7
acción *f.* action
accionista *m./f.* stockbroker, 11
aceite *m.* oil, 6
acelerado *adj.* accelerated, 12
acercar (qu) to approach, move closer
acompañar to accompany, 10
acostarse (ue) to go to bed, 5
acostumbrarse to get used to
actividad *f.* activity, 3
actor *m.* actor, 13
actriz *f.* actress, 13
actual *adj.* current, 14
actuar to act
además de in addition to
Adiós. Good-bye., P
adivinanza riddle, 2
administración *(f.)* **de empresas** business administration, 1
¿Adónde? Where (to)?, 8
aduana customs, 9
aerolínea airline, 9
aeropuerto airport, 9
afán *m.* desire, 12
afeitarse to shave, 5
aficionado(a) fan (sports), 3
agarrar to catch, 10
agencia de viajes travel agency, 9
agente *(m./f.)* **de la aerolínea** airline agent, 9
agente de viajes travel agent, 9
agosto August, 3
agricultor(a) farmer, 12
agua *f.* **mineral con/sin gas** carbonated/noncarbonated mineral water, 6
aguacate *m.* avocado, 6
ahijado(a) godchild, 2
ahora *adv.* now, 1
ahorrar to save, 11
aire *m.* air, 12
aire acondicionado air conditioning, 9
ajo garlic, 6
al aire libre outdoors, 4
al día up to date, 14
al lado de *prep.* next to, beside, 4
alarma alarm, 15
alcalde(sa) mayor, 14
alegrarse (de) to be glad, 12
alemán *m.* German (language), 1
alemán(ana) *adj.* German, 2
alergia allergy, 5
alfabetismo literacy, 14
alfombra carpet, 4; rug, floor covering, 8
algo something, anything, 8
algodón *m.* cotton, 7
alguien somebody, someone, anybody, anyone, 8
algún, alguno(a/os/as) some, any, 8
alianza alliance
allí *adv.* there, 1
alma soul
almacén store, 7
almorzar (ue) to have (eat) lunch, 6
almuerzo lunch, 6
alrededor de around
altavoces *m.* speakers, 15
alto(a) *adj.* tall, 2
amable *adj.* friendly, 2
amar(se) to love (each other), 10
amarillo *adj.* yellow, 1
ambulancia ambulance, 5
amigo(a) friend, 1
amistad *f.* friendship, 10
amor *m.* love, 10
analfabetismo illiteracy, 14
analista de sistemas *m./f.* systems analyst, 11
anaranjado *adj.* orange, 1
andar en bicicleta to ride a bike, 3
anfitrión *m.* host, 8
anfitriona hostess, 8
anillo ring, 7
animal *m.* animal, 12
anoche *adv.* last night, 6
anteayer *adv.* the day before yesterday, 6
antena parabólica satellite dish, 15
antes (de) que *conj.* before
antiácido antacid, 5
antibiótico antibiotic, 5
antigüedad *f.* antique, 7
antipático *adj.* unpleasant, 2
anuncio commercial, 13
año year, 3
Año Nuevo New Year, 8
apagado *adj.* off, 15
apagar (ue) to turn off, 15
apartamento apartment, 1
apellido last name, 2
aplaudir to applaud, 10
apoyar to support, 14
apoyo support, 13
apreciar to appreciate, 13
aprender to learn, 2
apretón *(m.)* **de manos** handshake
aprobar (ue) to approve; to pass, 14
aprovechar to take advantage, 14
apuntes *m.* notes
aquél (aquélla) *adj.* that (over there), 5
aquel (aquella) *pron.* that (over there), 5
aquí *adv.* here, P
árabe *adj.* Arab, 2
árbol *m.* tree, 12
archivar to file, 11; to save, 15
archivo file, 11
arena sand, 6
arepas cornmeal pockets, 6
arete *m.* earring, 7
argentino *adj.* Argentine, 2
armario wardrobe, armoire, closet, 4
arquitecto(a) architect, 11
arquitectura architecture, 13
arreglado *adj.* neat, tidy, 9
arrogante *adj.* arrogant, 2
arroyo stream, 12
arroz *m.* rice, 6
arte *m./f.* art, 1
artista *m./f.* artist, 13
artístico *adj.* artistic, 2
ascensor *m.* elevator, 9
Así así. So-so., P
así como just like
Así que... So . . . , 2
asiento seat, 9
asistente de vuelo *m./f.* flight attendant, 9

asistir a to attend, 2
aspiradora vacuum cleaner, 4
aspirina aspirin, 5
asustarse to be frightened, 8
aterrizar to land, 9
atlético *adj.* athletic, 2
aumentar to increase, 14
aún *adv.* still
aunque *conj.* although, even though, 13
auriculares *m.* headphones, 15
autobús *m.* bus *(Spain)*,
automóvil *m.* car
autor(a) author, 13
avance *m.* advance, 15
avergonzado: Me pongo avergonzado. I get embarrassed., 8
avión *m.* plane, 9
avisar to warn
ayer *adv.* yesterday, 6
ayudante *m./f.* assistant
ayudar(se) to help (each other), 1
azúcar *m.* sugar, 6
azul *adj.* blue, 1

B

babear to spew
bailar to dance, 3
bailarín *m.* dancer, 13
bailarina dancer, 13
baile *m.* dance, 3
bajar(se) (de) to get off, 9
bajo *adj.* short (height), 2
balcón *m.* balcony, 4
ballet *m.* ballet, 13
balneario beach resort, 8
baloncesto basketball, 3
banana/banano banana, 6
banco bank, 3
banquero(a) banker, 11
banquete *m.* banquet, 10
bañarse (en la tina) to take a bath, 5
bañera bathtub, 4
barato *adj.* inexpensive, cheap, 7
barrer el piso to sweep the floor, 4
barrio neighborhood, P
Bastante bien. Rather well., P
basura trash, 12
beber to drink, 2
bebida beverage, 6
béisbol *m.* baseball, 3
bello *adj.* beautiful, 12
beneficios benefits, 11
besar(se) to kiss (each other), 10
biblioteca library, 1
bibliotecario(a) librarian, 11
bicicleta bicycle, 3
bien *adv.* well, fine
  Bastante bien. Rather well., P
  bien cocido well done, 6
  Bien, gracias. Fine, thanks., P
  Muy bien. Very well., P
¡Bienvenido! Welcome!, 9
bilingüe *adj.* bilingual, 2
billete *m.* ticket, 9
  billete de ida one-way ticket, 9
  billete de ida y vuelta round-trip ticket, 9
biología biology, 1
bistec *m.* steak, 6
blanco *adj.* white, 1
bloqueador solar *m.* sunblock, 8
blusa blouse, 7
boca mouth, 5
boda wedding, 10
boleto ticket, 3
  boleto de ida one-way ticket, 9
  boleto de ida y vuelta round-trip ticket, 9
bolígrafo ballpoint pen, 1
boliviano *adj.* Bolivian, 2
bolsa purse, bag, 7
bolsillo pocket, 7
bombero(a) firefighter, 11
bonito *adj.* pretty, 2
borrador *m.* eraser, 1
bosque *m.* forest, 12
bota boot, 7
botella bottle, 6
botón *m.* button, 7
brasileño *adj.* Brazilian, 2
brazo arm, 5
brindis *m.* toast, 8
broma *joke*, 1
broncearse to get a suntan, 8
bucear to scuba dive, 8
¡Buen provecho! Enjoy your meal!, 6
¡Buen viaje! Have a nice trip!, 9
Buenas noches. Good evening/ night., P
Buenas tardes. Good afternoon., P
bueno *adj.* good, 2
Buenos días. Good morning., P
bufanda scarf, 7
bufete *m.* law office, 11
buscar (qu) to look for, 1
búsqueda de trabajo job hunt, 11

C

cabello hair, 5
cabeza head, 5
cabina cabin, 9
cada *adv.* each
  cada día (semana, etc.) every day (week, etc.), 10
cadera hip, 5
café *m.* café, 3; coffee, 6
cafetería cafeteria, 1
caja box, 6
  caja fuerte security box, 9
cajero automático ATM, 11
cajero(a) cashier, 11
calamares (fritos) *m.* (fried) squid, 6
calcetines *m. pl.* socks, 7
calculadora calculator, 1
calendario calendar, 1
caliente *adj.* hot (temperature), 6
callarse to quiet
calle *f.* street, 3
cama bed, 4
  cama sencilla (doble) single (double) bed, 9
cámara camera, 3
  cámara digital digital camera, 15
cámara web web camera, 15
camarero(a) waiter (waitress), 6
camarones (fritos) *m.* (fried) shrimp, 6
cambiar to change, 7
camello camel, R3
cámara de representantes (diputados) house of representatives, 14
caminar to walk, 1
  caminar por las montañas to hike/walk in the mountains, 3
caminata walk
camión *m.* bus (Mexico)
camisa shirt, 7
camiseta T-shirt, 7
campaña campaign, 14
campesino(a) farm worker, peasant, 12
campo country, 8
  campo de fútbol (de golf) football field (golf course), 3
campus *m.* campus
canadiense *adj.* Canadian, 2
canal *m.* channel (TV), 13
cancha (de tenis) (tennis) court, 3
canción *f.* song
candidato(a) candidate, applicant, 11
cansado *adj.* tired, 4
cantante *m./f.* singer, 13
cantar to sing, 1
capa de ozono ozone layer, 12
capítulo episode, 13
cara face, 5
cargar (un archivo) to upload a file, 15
cargo charge, 11
cariño affection, 10
carne (de res) *f.* meat (beef), 6
carnicería butcher shop, 3
caro *adj.* expensive, 7
carpintero(a) carpenter, 11
carrera major, field of study
carretera highway, 12
carro car, P
carta letter (correspondence), 2
cartera wallet, 7
cartón *m.* cardboard
casa house, 4
  casa de ancianos nursing home
casado *adj.* married, 2
casarse (con) to get married, to marry, 10
casi (siempre) *adv.* almost (always), 10
catarata waterfall, 12
catarro cold, 5
catorce fourteen, P
cebolla onion, 6
cebra zebra
cejas eyebrows, 5
celebración *f.* celebration, 8
celebrar to celebrate, 8
cena dinner, supper, 6
cenar to have (eat) supper (dinner), 6
centro downtown, 3
  centro comercial mall, 3
  centro de negocios business center, 9
  centro estudiantil student center, 1
cepillarse los dientes to brush one's teeth, 5
cerca de *prep.* near, 4
cerebro brain
cero zero, P
cerrar (ie) to close
cerveza beer, 6
chaleco vest, 7
champán *m.* champagne, 10
champiñón *m.* mushroom, 6
chaqueta jacket, 7
Chao. (informal) Bye., P
cheque *m.* check, 7
  cheque de viajero traveler's check, 11
¡Chévere! Cool!, 3
chico(a) boy (girl), 1
chileno *adj.* Chilean, 2
chimenea fireplace, chimney, 4
chino Chinese (language), 1; *adj.* Chinese, 2
chuleta (de cerdo) (pork) chop, 6
ciberespacio cyberspace, 15
ciclismo cycling, 3
ciencia (la) science, 1
cien/ciento one hundred, 2
cierre *m.* zipper, 7
ciervo deer
cinco five, P
Cinco de Mayo Cinco de Mayo, 8
cincuenta fifty, 2
cine *m.* movie theater, 3; movies, 13
cinturón *m.* belt, 7
cita date (social), 10
  cita de negocios job appointment, 1
ciudadano(a) citizen, 14
clásico *adj.*, classical, 10
cobarde *adj.* cowardly
coche *m.* car, 4
cocina kitchen, 4
cocinar to cook, 6
cocinero(a) cook, chef, 11
cocodrilo crocodile, 12
codo elbow, 5
cognado falso false cognate, 1
cohete *m.* rocket, 8
colina hill, 12
collar *m.* necklace, 7
colombiano *adj.* Colombian, 2
color *m.* color, 1
comedia comedy, 13
comedor *m.* dining room, 4
comenzar (ie) to start, begin, 4
comer to eat, 2
  No puedo (comer) más. I can't (eat) any more, 6
comerciante *m./f.* merchant, 11
cómico *adj.* humorous, 2
comida food, meal, 6

¿Cómo? How? P
¿Cómo está usted? How are you? (formal), P
¿Cómo estás? How are you? (informal), P
¿Cómo me queda? How does it look/ fit me?, 7
¡Cómo no! Of course!, 6
¿Cómo se llama usted? What's your name? (formal), P
¿Cómo te llamas? What's your name? (informal), P
¿Cómo te va? How's it going? (informal), P
cómoda dresser, 4
comodidad *f.* comfort *pl.* ammenities, features, 9
cómodo *adj.* comfortable, 9
compañero(a) de clase classmate, 1
compañero(a) de cuarto roommate, 1
compositor(a) composer, 13
comprar to buy, 1
compras: de compras shopping, 7
comprender to understand, 2
comprometido *adj.* engaged, 10
compromiso engagement, 10
computación *f.* computer science, 1
computadora computer, 1
computadora portátil laptop computer, 15
con *prep.* with, 4
con destino a departing for, 9
con permiso pardon me, excuse me, P
con respecto a with regard to, 11
con tal (de) que *conj.* provided (that), 13
concierto concert, 13
condimento condiment, 6
condominio condominium, 4
conectar to connect, 15
conexión *f.* connection, 15
conexión de alta velocidad high-speed connection, 15
conexión inalámbrica wireless connection, 15
congestión (de tráfico) *f.* (traffic) congestion
congestionado *adj.* congested, 5
Congreso congress, 14
conocer(se) to know (each other); to meet, 3
conseguir (i) to get, to obtain, 6
consejero(a) advisor, 1
conservación *f.* conservation, 12
conservador(a) *adj.* conservative, 14
conservar to conserve, 12
constitución *f.* constitution, 14
construir to construct, 12
contabilidad *f.* accounting, 1
contador(a) accountant, 11
contaminación *f.* pollution, 12
contaminado *adj.* polluted, 12
contaminar to pollute, 12
contar (ue) to count; to tell
contar con to count on
contento *adj.* happy, 4
Me pongo contento. I get happy., 8
contestador automático *m.* answering machine, 15
contestar to answer, 1
contra *prep.* against, 1
contratar to hire, 11
control *(m.)* **remoto** remote control, 15
control *(m.)* **de seguridad** security, 9
copa goblet, wine glass, 6
corazón *m.* heart, 5
corbata necktie, 7
coreano *adj.* Korean, 2
correo electrónico email, 11
correr to run, 3
correr las olas to surf, 8
corrupción *f.* corruption, 14
cortar el césped to mow the lawn, 4
corto *adj.* short (length), 2
costa coast, 8
costar (ue) to cost, 4
costarricense *adj.* Costa Rican, 2
costo expense
cotidiano *adj.* daily, 13
crecer to grow up
crecimiento growth
creer to believe, 2
crema bronceadora suntan lotion, 8
cremallera zipper, 7
criado(a) servant; maid, 11
crimen *m.* crime, 14
cruzar to cross, 9
cuaderno notebook, 1
cuadra city block, 9
cuadro painting, 4
¿Cuál(es)? Which?, P
¿Cuál es tu dirección? (informal) What's your address? (informal), P
¿Cuál es tu nombre? What's your name? (informal), P
¿Cuál es tu número de teléfono? What's your telephone number? (informal), P
cuando *conj.* when, 13
¿Cuándo? When?, P
¿Cuánto(a)? How much?, P
¿Cuántos(as)? How many?, P
¿Cuánto le debo? How much do I owe you?, 7
¿Cuántos años tienes tú? How old are you?, P
cuarenta forty, 2
cuarto room, 1
cuarto de baño bathroom, 4
cuatro four, P
cuatrocientos four hundred, 4
cubano *adj.* Cuban, 2
cuchara spoon, 6
cucharada tablespoon, 6
cucharadita teaspoon, 6
cuchillo knife, 6
cuello neck, 5
cuenta check, bill, 6; account, 11
cuenta corriente checking account, 11
cuenta de ahorros savings account, 11
La cuenta, por favor. The check, please., 6
cuento story
cuero leather, 7
cuerpo humano body, 5
cuidar(se) to take care (of oneself), 5
culebra snake, 12
cultivar to plant, 5; to cultivate; to grow (plants), 12
cumpleaños *m.* birthday, 8
cumplir años to have a birthday, 8
cumplir con to honor
cuñada sister-in-law, 2
cuñado brother-in-law, 2
currículum *m.* résumé, 11
curso course, 1

D

danza dance, 13
dar to give, 3
dar una fiesta to give a party, 8
dar un paseo to go for a walk, 3
darse cuenta to realize
darse la mano to shake hands, 10
de from, of
de cuadros plaid, 7
¿De dónde? From where?, P
¿De dónde eres tú? Where are you from? (informal), P
¿De dónde es usted? Where are you from? (formal), P
de la (mañana, tarde, noche) in the (morning, afternoon/evening), 1
de lunares polka-dotted, 7
¿De quién(es)? Whose?, 8
de rayas striped, 7
de repente suddenly, 8
de tiempo completo full-time, 11
de tiempo parcial part-time, 11
de vez en cuando occasionally, 6
debajo de *prep.* under, below, 4
debate *m.* debate, 14
deber ought to, must, 2
deber *m.* noun duty, 14
debilidad *f.* weakness
decano(a) dean, 1
decir (i) to say; to tell, 4
¡No me digas más! Say no more!
dedo finger, 5
dedo del pie toe, 5
defender (ie) to defend, 14
defensa defense, 14
dejar to quit, 11; to leave; to let, to allow, 13
dejar una (buena) propina to leave a (good) tip, 6
delante de *prep.* in front of, 4
delgado *adj.* thin, 2
demandar to sue
demasiado *adv.* too much, 9
democracia democracy, 14
demócrata *adj.* democratic, 14
demora delay, 9
denso *adj.* dense, 12
dentista *m./f.* dentist, 11
departamento apartment, 4
dependiente *m./f.* salesclerk, 7
deporte *m.* sport, 3
deportiva *adj.* sports, 3
depositar to deposit (money), 11
derecha: a la derecha de *prep.* to the right of, 9
derecho law, 1; straight, 9
derechos humanos (civiles) human (civil) rights, 14
desafío challenge, 14
desarrollar to develop, 12
desarrollo development, 12
desayunar to have (eat) breakfast, 6
desayuno breakfast, 6
descansar to rest, 1
descargar (un archivo) to download (a file), 15
desconectar to disconnect, 15
desconocido *adj.* unknown
descuento discount, 7
desde *prep.* from, 1
desear to want, to wish, 1
desempleo unemployment, 14
desenchufar to unplug, 15
desigualdad *f.* inequality, 14
desmedro impairment
desordenado *adj.* messy, 4
despedir (i) to fire, 11
despegar to take off, 9
desperdicio waste, 12
despertador *m.* alarm clock, 4
despertarse (ie) to wake up, 5
después *adv.* afterward, 10
después (de) (que) *conj.* after, 13
destrucción *f.* destruction, 12
destruido *adj.* destroyed, 12
destruir to destroy, 12
desventaja disadvantage, 15
detalle *m.* detail, 10
detrás de *prep.* behind, 4
día *m.* day, 1
al día up to date, 14
Día de la Independencia Independence Day, 8
Día de la Raza Columbus Day, 8
Día de las Madres Mother's Day, 8
Día de los Muertos Day of the Dead, 8
Día de los Reyes Magos Day of the Magi (Three Kings), 8
Día de Todos los Santos All Saints' Day, 8
Día del Padre Father's Day, 8
Día del santo saint's day, 8
día feriado *m.* holiday, 8

diagnóstico diagnosis, 5
diariamente daily, 3
dibujar to draw, 1
dibujo animado cartoon, 13
diccionario dictionary, 1
dicho *p.p.* said; told, 10
díciembre December, 3
dictador(a) dictator, 14
dictadura dictatorship, 14
diecinueve nineteen, P
dieciocho eighteen, P
dieciséis sixteen, P
diecisiete seventeen, P
diente *m.* tooth, 5
dieta diet, 5
diez ten P
dinero money, 1
¡Dios mio! My god! My goodness!, P
diputado(a) representative, 14
director(a) director, 13
dirigir to direct, 13
disco compacto compact disc (CD), 15
disco duro hard drive, 15
disculpe pardon me, P
discurso speech, 14
discutir to argue, to discuss, 14
disfraz *m.* costume, 8
disfrazarse to wear a costume, 8
disfrutar to enjoy, 9
divertido *adj.* fun, 2
divertirse to have fun, 6
divorciado *adj.* divorced, 2
divorciarse (de) to get divorced (from), 10
divorcio divorce, 10
doblar to turn, 9
doce twelve, P
documental *m.* documentary, 13
dolerle (ue) (a alguien) to be painful (to someone), 5
dolor (de oídos, de cabeza) *m.* ache, pain (earache, headache), 5
domingo Sunday, 1
dominicano *adj.* Dominican (from the Dominican Republic), 2
¿Dónde? Where?, P
dormir (ue) to sleep, 6
dormirse (ue) to fall asleep, 5
dormitorio bedroom, 4
dos two, P
doscientos(as) two hundred, 4
drama *m.* drama, play, 13
dramático(a) *adj.* dramatic, 2
dramaturgo *m./f.* playwright, 13
drogadicción *f.* drug addiction, 14
ducha shower, 4
ducharse to take a shower, 5
dulce *adj.* sweet
durante *prep.* throughout

E

ecología ecology, 12
economía economics, 1
económico *adj.* economic, 5
ecuatoriano Ecuadorian, 2
edad *f.* age, 2
edificio building, 1
educación *f.* education, 1
efectivo cash, 7
egipcio *adj.* Egyptian, 2
ejército army, 14
el, la, los, las *def. art.* the
él *pron.* he, P
elecciones *f.* elections, 14
electricista *m./f.* electrician, 11
electrodomésticos electric appliance, 4
elefante *m.* elephant, 12
elegante *adj.* elegant, 10
elegir (i, i) to elect, 14
El gusto es mío. The pleasure is mine., P
eliminar to eliminate, 14
ella *pron.* she, P
ellos(as) *pron.* they, P
emocionado *adj.* excited, 4
empezar (ie) to begin, 4
empleado(a) employee, 11
empleo employment, 14
empresa corporation; business, 11
en in; on, 4
en caso (de) que *conj.* in case (of), 13
en contra against
en cuanto a in regard to, 13
en frente de in front of, 9
en punto on time, 1
¿En qué puedo servirle? How can I help you?, 7
enamorarse (de) to fall in love (with), 10
Encantado(a). Nice to meet you. P
encarcelamiento imprisonment, 14
encender to turn on, 15
encendido *adj.* on, 15
enchufado *adj.* plugged in, 15
enchufar to plug in, 15
encima de *prep.* on top of, 4
encontrar to find, 5
energía solar solar energy, 12
enero January, 3
enfermarse to get sick, 5
enfermedad *f.* illness, 5
enfermería infirmary, 9
enfermero(a) nurse, 5
enfermo *adj.* sick, 4
enfrentar to face
enfrente de *prep.* across from, 9
enmendar (ie) to amend, 14
enmienda amendment, 14
enojado *adj.* angry, 4
ensalada salad, 6
enseguida right away, 6
enseñar to teach, 1
entender (ie) to understand, 4
entonces *adv.* then; so, 10
entrar to enter, 1
entre *prep.* between, among, 4
entremés *m.* hors d'oeuvre, 8
entrevista interview, 11
equilibrio balance, 12
equipaje (de mano) *m.* (carry-on) baggage, luggage, 9
equipo equipment, 15
escalar to climb, 8
escalera stairs, 4
escáner *m.* scanner, 15
escasez *f.* lack, shortage, 12
escenario stage, 13
escoger to choose, 9
escribir to write, 2
escrito *p.p.* written, 10
escritor(a) writer, 13
escritorio desk, 4
escuchar (música) to listen (to music), 1
escuela school, 1
escuela politécnica technical school
esculpir to sculpt, 13
escultor(a) sculptor, 13
escultura sculpture, 13
hacer escultura to sculpt, 13
ese(a) *adj.* that, 5
ése(a) *pron.* that, 5
espacio space, 4
espacio cibernético cyberspace, 15
espalda back, 5
español *m.* Spanish (language), 1
español *adj.* Spanish, 2
especialidad *(f.)* **de la casa** house specialty, 6
especialización *f.* major, 1
especies *f.* species, 12
espectáculo show
espectador(a) viewer, 13
espejo mirror, 4
esperar to hope; to wait
espiritualmente spiritually, 2
esposa wife, 2
esposo husband, 2
esquiar (en el agua) to (water) ski, 3
está despejado/nublado it's clear/cloudy, 3
estación *f.* season, 3
estación de trenes *f.* train station, 9
estadio stadium, 3
estadounidense *adj.* from the United States, 2
estante *m.* bookshelf, 4
estar to be, 3
estar conectado(a) (en línea) to be online, 15
estar de acuerdo to agree, 10
estar congestionado to be congested, 5
estar enfermo(a) to be sick, 5
estar resfriado(a) to have a cold, 5
estar sano(a) to be healthy, 5
este *m.* east, 9
éste *pron.* this one, 5
este(a) *adj.* this, 5
estéreo stereo, 15
estilo style, 7
estómago stomach, 5
estornudar to sneeze, 5
Estoy a dieta. I'm on a diet., 6
Estoy satisfecho(a). I'm satisfied. I'm full., 6
estudiante *m./f.* student, 1
estudiar to study, 1
estudio study, 1
estufa stove, 4
examen *m.* test, 1
examinar to examine, 5
explicar (qu) to explain, 9
explotar to exploit, 12
extinción: en peligro de extinción in danger of extinction, 12
extrovertido(a) *adj.* outgoing, 2

F

fábrica factory, 12
factura bill, 11
facturar el equipaje to check the luggage, 9
facultad *f.* department, school, 2
falda skirt, 7
falta lack
familia family
farmacia pharmacy, 5
fáx *m.* fax machine, 11
febrero February, 3
¡Felicitaciones! Congratulations!, 8
felicitar to congratulate, 10
feo *adj.* ugly, 2
ferretería hardware store, 3
fiebre fever, 5
fiesta (de sorpresa) (surprise) party; holiday, 8
filosofía philosophy, 1
fin *(m.)* **de semana** weekend, 1
finalmente *adv.* at last, finally, 10
finanzas personales personal finances, 11
finca farm, 12
firmar to sign, 11
física physics, 1
flan (casero) *m.* (homemade) caramel custard, 6
flor *f.* flower, 10
folclórico *adj.* folkloric, 13
fotocopiadora photocopier, 11
fotografía photography, 13
fotógrafo(a) photographer, 11
francés *m.* French (language), 1
francés(esa) *adj.* French, 2
frasco jar, pot, jug, 6
fresco *adj.* fresh, 6
frontera border, 12
fruta fruit, 6
frutería fruit store, 3
fuente *f.* source, 12; fountain, 4
funcionar to function (to work), 15
furioso *adj.* furious, 4
fútbol (americano) *m.* soccer (football), 3

G

gafas de sol sunglasses, 7
galón *m.* gallon, 6
ganador(a) winner, 13
ganar to win, 3
ganga: ¡Es una ganga! It's a bargain!, 7
garaje *m.* garage, 4
garganta throat, 5
gasolinera gas station, 3
gastar to spend (money), 7
gasto expense, 11
gato cat, 2
gemelo cufflink, 7
generoso(a) *adj.* generous, 2
gente *f.* people, P
geografía geography, 1
gerente *m./f.* manager, 11
gimnasio gymnasium, 1
gobernador(a) governor, 14
gobernar (ie) to govern, 14
gobierno government, 14
golf *m.* golf, 3
gordo *adj.* fat, 2
gorila *m.* gorilla, 12
gorra de béisbol baseball cap, 7
grabar to word record, 15
gramo gram, 6
grande *adj.* big, large, 2
gratis *adj.* free, 1
gritar to shout, 8
grupo paramilitar paramilitary group, 14
guagua bus *(Puerto Rico)*, P
guante *m.* glove, 7
guapo *adj.* good-looking, 2
guardaparques *m./f.* park ranger, 12
guardar to save, 15
guardar cama to stay in bed, 5
guatemalteco *adj.* Guatemalan, 2
guerra war, 14
guerrillero *m./f.* guerrilla, 14
guineano(a) guinean, 2
guión *m.* script, 13
guitarra guitar, 3
  tocar la guitarra to play the guitar, 3
gustar to be pleasing (to someone), 3
  (no) me gusta + *infinitive* I (don't) like + infinitive, 3
gusto: El gusto es mío. The pleasure is mine, P

H

haber to have (auxillary verb), 10
habitación (bed) room, 4
hablar(se) to speak, to talk (with each other), 9
habla tan bien speak so well, P
hace buen tiempo it's nice, 3
  hace calor it's hot, 3
  hace fresco it's cool, 3
  hace frío it's cold, 3
  hace sol it's sunny, 3
  hace viento it's windy, 3
hacer to do; to make, 3
  hacer (un picnic, planes, ejercicio) to go on a picnic, to make plans, to exercise, 3
  hacer camping to go camping, 8
  hacer clic (sobre) to click (on), 15
  hacer escala (en) to make a stop (on a flight) (in), 9
  hacer esnórquel to snorkel, 8
  hacer juego con to match, 7
  hacer la cama to make one's bed, 4
  hacer la(s) maleta(s) to pack one's suitcase(s), 9
  hacer un brindis to make a toast, 8
  hacer una fiesta to give a party, 8
  hacer una parrillada to have a cookout, 8
hacia *adv.* toward, 9
haitiano *adj.* Haitian, 2
hamburguesa hamburger, 6
hambre *f.* hunger, 5
harina de maíz corn flour
hasta *adv.* up to, until
  Hasta luego. See you later, P
  Hasta mañana. See you tomorrow, P
  Hasta pronto. See you soon, P
  hasta que *conj.* until, 13
hay there is, there are, P
hecho *p.p.* done; made, 10
helado ice cream, 6
hermana sister, 2
hermanastra stepsister, 2
hermanastro stepbrother, 2
hermano brother, 2
hierba herb, 5;
hija daughter, 2
hijo son, 2
hipopótamo hippopotamus, 12
hipoteca mortgage, 11
hispanohablante *m./f.* native Spanish speaker
historia history, 1; story, 4
historial clínica *f.* medical history, 5
hogar *m.* home, 4
hoja leaf, 5
¡Hola! Hi! (informal), P
hombre *m.* man, 1
hombre de negocios businessman, 11
hondureño *adj.* Honduran, 2
honesto(a) *adj.* honest, 2
hora hour, time
  ¿A qué hora? At what time?, 1
  ¿Qué hora es? What time is it?, 1
horario schedule, 9
horno (microondas) (microwave) oven, 4
hotel de cuatro estrellas *m.* four-star hotel, 9
hoy *adv.* today, 1
huelga strike, 14
hueso bone, 5
huevo duro hard-boiled egg, 6
humanidades *f. pl.* humanities, 1
humilde *adj.* humble, 2

I

ideología ideology, 14
iglesia church, 3
igualdad *f.* equality, 14
impermeable *m.* raincoat, 7
importante *adj.* important, 12
imposible *adj.* impossible, 12
impresora printer, 15
imprimir to print, 11
impuestos taxes, 14
imunidad *f.* immunity
incluir to include, 2
indeciso(a) *adj.* indecisive, 2
indio *adj.* Indian, 2
inflación *f.* inflation, 14
informar to inform, 14
informe *m.* report, 11
ingeniería engineering, 1
ingeniero(a) engineer, 11
inglés *m.* English (language), 1
inglés(esa) *adj.* English, 2
ingreso income, 12
injusticia injustice, 14
inmigración *f.* passport control, immigration, 14
inodoro toilet, 4
inseguridad *f.* insecurity, lack of safety, 14
intelectual *adj.* intellectual, 2
inteligente *adj.* intelligent, 2
interesante *adj.* interesting, 2
Internet *m.* Internet
interpelar to question
interpretar to play a role, 13
intérprete *m./f.* interpreter, 11
introvertido(a) introverted, 2
intuitivo *adj.* intuitive, 2
inventar to invent, 3
investigar to investigate, 14
invierno winter, 3
invitado *m./f.* guest, 8
invitar: Te invito. It's on me (my treat)., 6
inyección *f.* shot (injection), 5
ir to go, 3
  ir al cine to go to the movies, 3
  ir a pie to go on foot, 9
  ir a tomar un café to drink coffee, 3
  ir a un bar to go to a bar, 3
  ir a un club to go to a club, 3
  ir a un concierto to go to a concert, 3
  ir a una discoteca to go to a disco, 3
  ir a una fiesta to go to a party, 3
  ir (bien) con to go well with, 7
  ir de compras to go shopping, 3
  ir en autobús to go by bus, 9
  ir en avión to go by plane, 9
  ir en barco to go by boat, 9
  ir en bicicleta to go by bike, 9
  ir en coche to go by car, 9
  ir en metro to go by subway, 9
  ir en taxi to go by taxi, 9
  ir en tren to go by train, 9
irresponsable *adj.* irresponsible, 2
isla island, 9
italiano Italian (language), 1; *adj.* Italian, 2
izquierda: a la izquierda de *prep.* to the left of, 9

J

jaguar *m.* jaguar, 12
jamón *m.* ham, 6
Jánuca *m.* Hanukkah, 8
japonés *m.* Japanese (language), 1
japonés(esa) *adj.* Japanese, 2
jarabe *m.* cough syrup, 5
jardín *m.* garden, 4
jeans *m. pl.* blue jeans, 7
jefe *m./f.* boss, 11
jerarquía hierarchy, 11
joven *adj.* young, 2
joya gem
joyas jewelry, 7
joyería jewelry store, 3
jubilarse to retire, 11
juego game, 3
jueves *m.* Thursday, 1
juez *m./f.* judge, 10
jugador(a) player, 3
jugar (ue) to play, 4
  jugar al baloncesto to play basketball, 3
  jugar al béisbol to play baseball, 3
  jugar al fútbol to play soccer, 3
  jugar al fútbol americano to play football, 3
  jugar al golf to play golf, 3
  jugar al tenis to play tennis, 3
  jugar al voleibol to play volleyball, 3
jugo de fruta fruit juice, 6
julio July, 3
junio June, 3
justicia justice, 14

K

kilo(gramo) kilogram, 6

L

labios lips, 5
lado: al lado de *prep.* next to, 9
lago lake, 8
lámpara lamp, 4
lana wool, 7
langosta lobster, 6
lápiz *m.* pencil, 1
largo *adj.* long, 2
lástima: es una lástima it's a shame
lata can, 6
lavabo bathroom sink, 4
lavadora washing machine, 4
lavaplatos *m.* dishwasher, 4
lavar (los platos, la ropa, las ventanas) to wash (dishes, clothes, windows), 4
lavarse to wash up, 5
lección *f.* lesson, 1
leche *f.* milk, 6
lechuga lettuce, 6
leer to read, 2

lejos (de) *prep.* far (away) (from), 4
lengua language, 1; tongue, 5
lenguas extranjeras foreign languages, 1
lentillas/lentes *(m.)* **de contacto** contact lenses, 5
león *m.* lion
levantar pesas to lift weights, 3
levantarse to get up, 5
levemente lightly, 11
ley *f.* law, 14
liberal *adj.* liberal, 15
libertad *f.* **de la prensa** freedom of the press, 14
libra pound, 6
librería bookstore, 1
libro (de texto) (text)book, 1
ligero *adj.* light (meal, food), 6
limosna charity
limpiar la casa to clean the house, 4
limpio *adj.* clean, 4
liquidación *f.* sale *(Lat. Am.)*, reduction (in price), 7
listo *adj.* smart; ready, 2
literatura literature, 1
litro liter, 6
llamar to call, to phone, 1
Me llamo... My name is . . . , P
llamar por teléfono to make a phone call, 11
llano plain, 12
llave *f.* key, 9
llegada arrival, 9
llegar to arrive, 1
llenar to fulfill, 7; to fill out (a form), 11
llevar to wear, to carry, 7
llevar a cabo to take place, 8
llevar una vida tranquila to lead a peaceful life, 12
llevarse bien (mal) (con) to get along well (poorly) (with) each other, 10
llorar to cry, 8
llover (ue) to rain, 4
lluvia rain, 3
lo que *pron.* what, 10
lobo wolf
Localizador Uniforme de Recursos *m.* URL, 15
lógico *adj.* logical, 12
lograr to succeed
luchar (contra/por) to fight (against/for), 14
luego *adv.* then, 10
lugar *m.* place, 3
lujoso *adj.* luxurious, 7
luna de miel honeymoon, 10
lunes *m.* Monday, 1
luz *f.* light, 1

M

madrastra stepmother, 2
madre *f.* mother, 2
madrina godmother, 2
maestro(a) teacher, 1
maleta suitcase, 9
malo *adj.* bad, 2
mamá mother, 2
mamífero mammal
mandar to command, 11
mandar (cartas) to send (letters), 1
manifestación *f.* demonstration, 14
mano *f.* hand, 5
manta blanket, 8
mantel *m.* tablecloth, 6
mantequilla butter, 6
manzana apple, 6
mañana *adv.* tomorrow, 1
mapa *m.* map, 1
maquillarse to put on makeup, 5
mar *m.* sea, 8
marcador *m.* marker, 1
mareado *adj.* dizzy, 5
mareo dizziness, 5
mariposa butterfly, 12
mariscos shellfish, seafood, 6
marrón *adj.* brown, 1
martes *m.* Tuesday, 1
marzo March, 3
Más o menos. So-so., P
más... que more . . . than, 6
máscara mask, 8
mascota pet
masticar (qu) to chew, 5
matemáticas math, 1
materias subject, courses, 1
matrícula tuition, 1
matrimonio marriage, 10
mayo May, 3
mayor older, 6
el mayor oldest, 6
mayoría majority, 1
mecánico(a) mechanic, 11
medianoche *f.* midnight, 1
medias stockings, 7
medicina medicine, 1
médico *m./f.* physician, doctor, 5; *adj.* medical, 5
seguro médico medical insurance, 11
medio ambiente environment, 12
mediodía *m.* noon, 1
medio(a) hermano(a) half brother (sister), 2
medios de comunicación means of communication, 14
mejillas cheeks, 5
mejor better, 6
el mejor best, 6
menor younger, 6
el menor youngest, 6
menos... que less . . . than, 6
mensaje *m.* message, 15
mensaje de texto text message, 15
menú *m.* menu, 6
mercado (al aire libre) (outdoor) market, 3
merienda snack time, 3
mes *m.* month, 3
el mes pasado last month, 6
mesa table, 4
mesero(a) waiter (waitress), 6
mesita coffee (side) table, 4
metrópolis *f.* metropolis, 12
mexicano *adj.* Mexican, 2
mi *adj.* my, 2
micrófono microphone, 15
miércoles *m.* Wednesday, 1
mil one thousand, 4
millón million, 4
ministro(a) minister, 14
mío *adj.* my, mine, 7
mirar to watch, 1
mirarse to look at each other, 10
mismo *adj.* same, 10
mitad *f.* half, 15
mochila backpack, 1
moda: ¡Está de última moda! It's the latest style!, 7
módem *m.* modem, 15
moderno(a) *adj.* modern, 10
molestar to bother, 12
molesto: Me pongo molesto. I get annoyed., 8
monarquía monarchy, 14
monitor *m.* monitor, 15
mono monkey, 12
montañas mountains, 8
montar a caballo to go horseback riding, 3
morado *adj.* purple, 1
moreno(a) *adj.* dark-haired, 2
morir (ue) to die, 6
mostrar (ue) to show, 7
mover (ue) to move, 3
muchacho(a) boy (girl), 1
Mucho gusto. Nice to meet you, P
muebles *m.* furniture, 4
muerte *f.* death
muerto *adj.* dead, 4; *p.p.* died, 10
mujer *f.* woman, 1
mujer de negocios businesswoman, 11
mundo world, 9
murciélago bat
músculo muscle, 5
museo museum, 3
música music, 1
musical *m.* musical (play), 13
músico *m./f.* musician, 13
muslo thigh, 5
muy *adv.* very, P

N

nacer to be born, 2
nacionalidad *f.* nationality, 2
nada nothing, not anything, at all, 8
nadar to swim, 3
nadie nobody, no one, 8
naranja orange, 6
nariz *f.* nose, 5
natación *f.* swimming, 3
naturaleza nature, 12
naturalista *m./f.* naturalist, 12
navegar la Red to surf the Net, 15
Navidad *f.* Christmas, 8
necesario *adj.* necessary, 12
necesitar to need, 1
negocios business, 1
negro *adj.* black, 1
nevera refrigerator, 4
ni... ni neither . . . nor, 8
ni siquiera not even, 4
nicaragüense *adj.* Nicaraguan, 2
nieta granddaughter, 2
nieto grandson, 2
nieva it's snowing, 3
nieve *f.* snow, 3
niñero nanny, 11
ningún, ninguno(a) none, not any, 8
niño(a) boy (girl), child, 2
Noche Vieja *f.* New Year's Eve, 8
Nochebuena Christmas Eve, 8
nombre *m.* first name, 2
norte *m.* north, 9
norteamericano *adj.* North American, American, 2
nosotros(as) *pron.* we, P
noticias news, 13
noticiero newscast, 14
novecientos nine hundred, 4
noventa ninety, 2
novia girlfriend, 1; bride, 10
noviazgo courtship, 10
noviembre November, 3
novio boyfriend, 1; groom, 10
nublado cloudy, 3
nuera daughter-in-law, 2
nuestro *adj.* our, 2
nueve nine, P
nuevo *adj.* new, 2
número number, P; shoe size, 7
nunca *adv.* never, 8
nunca más *adv.* never again, 3

O

o *conj.* or, 3
o... o either . . . or, 8
objeto object, 1
obra (de arte) work (of art), 13
obra maestra masterpiece, 13
obrero(a) worker; laborer, 11
océano ocean, 8
ochenta eighty, 2
ocho eight, P
ochocientos eight hundred, 4
octubre October, 3
ocupado *adj.* busy, 4
oeste *m.* west, 9
oferta sale *(Lat. Am.)*, 7
oferta de trabajo job offer, 11
oficina office, 1
oficina de correos post office, 3
ofrecer (zc) to offer, 9

oído inner ear, 5
ojalá que I wish that, 12
ojo eye, 5
oler to smell, 4
olvidar to forget, 8
once eleven, P
onza ounce, 6
ópera opera, 13
oponer to oppose, 14
oposición *f.* opposition, 14
orar to pray, 8
ordenado *adj.* neat, 4
oreja (outer) ear, 5
órgano organ, 5
orgulloso *adj.* proud
orquesta band, 10
orquídea orchid, 12
oso bear
otoño fall, 3
otra vez *adv.* again, 10

P

paciente *adj.* patient, 2; noun *m./f.* patient, 5
padrastro stepfather, 2
padre *m.* father, 2
padres parents, 2
padrino(a) godfather (godmother), 2
pagar to pay, 1
  pagar a plazos to pay in installments, 11
página de bienvenida (de entrada, de presentación, inicial, principal, de la Red) home page, 15
  página web web page, 15
paisaje *m.* landscape, 12
pájaro bird, 12
palabra word, 1
pan (tostado) *m.* bread (toast), 6
panameño *adj.* Panamanian, 2
panelista *m./f.* guest on a talk show, 13
pantalla screen, 15
pantalones (cortos) *m.* pants (shorts), 7
pantera panther
pantorrilla calf (of leg), 5
papá *m.* father, 2
papas (fritas) (french fried) potatoes, 6
papel *m.* paper, 1; role, 13
papelería stationery store, 3
par *m.* pair, 7
para *prep.* for
  para colmo on top of that, 4
  para disculparse to excuse yourself, P
  para que *conj.* so that, 13
  ¿Para qué? For what purpose?, 8
paraguas *m.* umbrella, 7
paraguayo *adj.* Paraguayan, 2
parar(se) to stop, 9
parecer to appear, 1
parecido *adj.* similar
pared *f.* wall, 4
pareja couple, 10
pariente *m./f.* relative, 2
parque *m.* park, 3
participar to take part, to participate, 14
partido game, 3
  partido político political party, 14
partir to cut, 10
pasado: (la semana, el mes, el año) pasado(a) last (week, month, year), 6
pasajero(a) passenger, 9
pasaporte *m.* passport, 9
pasar to spend (time); to pass, 1
  pasar la aspiradora to vacuum, 4
  pasar por to go through, 9
  pasarlo bien (mal) to have a good (bad) time, 8
pasatiempo pastime, 3
Pascua Easter, Passover, Christmas, 8
pasear en canoa/velero to go canoeing/sailing, 8
paseo stroll, 7
pasillo aisle, 9
paso step, 7
pastel *m.* cake, 8
  pastel de boda(s) *m.* wedding cake, 10
pastilla pill, 5
patinar (en línea) to (in-line) skate, 3
patrón *m.* pattern, 7
pavo turkey, 6
paz *f.* peace, 14
pecho chest, 5
pedir (i, i) to ask for, 4; to order (food), 6; to request, 9
  pedir prestado to borrow, 11
  pedir un aumento to ask for a raise, 11
peinarse to comb one's hair, 5
película movie, film, 13
  película clásica classic film, 13
  película de acción action film, 13
  película de ciencia ficción science fiction film, 13
  película de terror horror film, 13
  película de intriga (misterio) mystery film, 13
  película fantástica fantasy film, 13
  película extranjera foreign film, 13
  película romántica romantic film, 13
peligro: en peligro de extinción in danger of extinction, 12
peligroso *adj.* dangerous
pelo hair, 5
peluquería hair salon, 3
peluquero(a) hairstylist, 11
pensar (ie) to think, 4
peor worse, 6
  el peor worst, 6
pequeño *adj.* small, 2
  ¡Me quedan muy pequeños! They're too small!
perder (ie) to lose; to miss (a function), 4
perdón pardon me, excuse me, P
perezoso(a) *adj.* lazy, 2
periódico newspaper, 14
periodismo journalism, 1
periodista *m./f.* journalist, 11
período de sequía dry season, 5
pero *conj.* but, 3
perro dog, 2
peruano *adj.* Peruvian, 2
pesado *adj.* heavy (meal, food), 6
pescado fish (when caught), 6
pescar (qu) to fish, 3
pestañas eyelashes, 5
petróleo petroleum, 12
pez *m.* fish (alive), 2
picar (qu) to eat appetizers; to nibble, 6; to bite, 12
pie *m.* foot, 5
piedra stone, 4
piel *f.* skin, 5
pierna leg, 5
piloto *m./f.* pilot, 9
pimentero pepper shaker, 6
pimienta pepper, 6
pintarse to put on makeup, 5
pintor(a) painter, 13
pintura painting, 1
piscina pool, 3
piso floor, 4
pizarra chalkboard, 1
plancha iron, 4
planchar (la ropa) to iron (clothes), 4
plan de retiro retirement plan, 11
plataforma de operación operating platform (system), 15
plato plate, 6
  plato principal main dish, 6
playa beach, 8
plaza plaza, 3
plomero(a) plumber, 11
pluma fountain pen, 1
pobre *adj.* poor, 2
poder (ue) to be able, 4
  No puedo (comer) más. I can't (eat) any more., 6
poder *m.* power, 14
poesía poetry, 13
poeta *m./f.* poet, 13
policía *m.* **(mujer** *f.* **policía)** police officer, 11
política politics, 14
  política internacional international policy, 14
político *m./f.* politician, 14
pollo (asado) (roast) chicken, 6
poner to put (on), 3; to turn on (TV); to show (a movie), 13
  poner la mesa to set the table, 4
ponerse + *adjective* to become, to get + adjective, 8
  ponerse (la ropa) to put on (one's clothes), 5
popular *adj.* popular, 13
por prep. for
  por ciento percent, 7
  por ejemplo for example, 11
  por eso that's why, 11
  por favor please, P
  por fin *adv.* finally, 10
  por la (mañana, tarde, noche) in the (morning, afternoon/evening), 1
  por otro lado on the other hand
  ¿Por qué? Why?, P
  porque because, 3
  por supuesto of course, 2
portarse bien (mal) to behave well (poorly), 8
portugués *m.* Portuguese (language), 1
postal *m.* postcard, 2
postre *m.* dessert, 6
practicar (qu) to practice, 1
practicar deportes to play sports, 3
precio price, 7
preferir (ie) to prefer, 6
pregunta question, P
preguntar to ask (a question), 1
prenda article of clothing, 7
prender to turn on, 15
prendido *adj.* on, 15
prensa press, 14
preocuparse to worry, 11
preocupado *adj.* worried, 4
preparar to prepare, 6
presidente *m./f.* president, **14**
  de la universidad of the university, 1
préstamo loan, 11
prestar to loan, 11
presupuesto budget, 11
primavera spring, 3
primero first, 10
  a primera vista at first sight, 10
  primer baile first dance, 10
  primera vez first time, 5
primo(a) cousin, 2
privado *adj.* private, 9
probarse (ue) to try on, 7
problema *m.* problem, 5
procedente de arriving from, 9
procesión *f.* parade, 8
profesión *f.* profession, 11
profesor(a) professor, 1
programa (de CD-ROM) *m.* (CD-ROM) program, 15
  programa de concursos game show, 13
  programa de entrevistas talk show, 13
  programa deportivo sports program, 13
  programa de realidad reality (TV) show, 13
programador(a) programmer, 11
programar to program, 15
progresista *adj.* progressive
prometer to promise, 10
pronóstico del tiempo weather report (forecast), 13

propina: dejar una (buena) propina to leave a (good) tip, 6
propósito purpose, 2
proteger to protect, 12
protestar to protest, 14
proveedor *m.* **de servicios Internet** Internet service provider, 15
proyecto project, 11
pueblo town, 3
puerta door, 4; gate, 9
puerto port, 9
  puerto USB USB port, 15
puertorriqueño *adj.* Puerto Rican, 2
puesto stand, 7; job, position, 11; *p.p.* put, 10
pulmones *m.* lungs, 5
pulsera bracelet, 7
pupitre *m.* student desk, 1
puro *adj.* pure, 12

Q

que *pron.* that, which, who, 3
¿Qué? What? Which?, P
  ¡Qué bueno! Wonderful!, 2
  ¡Qué casualidad! What a coincidence!, P
  ¿Qué hay? What's new? (informal), P
  ¿Qué hora es? What time is it?, 1
  ¡Qué padre! Cool!, 2
  ¿Qué tal? What's up? (informal), P
quedarle (a uno) to fit (someone), 7
  ¿Cómo me queda? How does it look?, 7
quedarse to stay, 9
quehacer doméstico *m.* chore, 4
quejarse de to complain about, 9
quemar to burn, 8
querer (ie) to want; to love, 4
  Yo quisiera... I would like . . ., 6
queso cheese, 6
quien *pron.* who, 10
  ¿Quién(es)? Who?, P
química chemistry, 1
quince fifteen, P
quinientos five hundred, 4
quitar el programa to quit the program, 15
quitar la mesa to clear the table, 4
quitarse (la ropa) to take off (one's clothes), 5

R

radiografía X-ray, 5
raíz *f.* root
Ramadán *m.* Ramadan, 8
ramo bouquet, 10
rana frog, 12
ranchero(a) rancher, 11
rascacielos *m.* skyscraper, 12
rato: un buen rato a good time, 3
ratón *m.* mouse (of computer), 15
razón *f.* reason, 12
reaccionar to react, 8
rebaja sale *(Spain)*, reduction (in price), 7
rebajar to reduce (in price), 7
rebelde *adj.* rebellious
rebotar to bounce (a check), 11
recepción *f.* front desk, 9; reception, 10
recepcionista *m./f.* receptionist, 9
receta prescription, 5
recibir to receive, 2
recibo receipt, 11
reciclar to recycle, 12
recién casados *m.* newlyweds, 10
recoger (j) to pick up; to claim, 12
recomendar (ie) to recommend, 6
recordar (ue) to remember, 8
rector(a) de la universidad president of the university, 1
recuerdo souvenir, wedding favor, 10
recursos naturales natural resources, 12
red social *f.* social network, 15
reducir to reduce, 14
reforestar to reforest, 12
reforma reform, 14
refresco soft drink, 6
refrigerador *m.* refrigerator, 4
refugio natural wildlife preserve, 12
regalar to give (as a gift), 9
regalo gift, 8
regar (ie) las plantas to water the plants, 4; to irrigate, 12
registrarse to register, 9
regresar (a casa) to return (home), 1
reinar to rule
reírse to laugh, 6
relaciones sentimentales *f.* relationships, 10
rellenar to stuff, 6
reloj *m.* clock, 1; watch, 7
remar to row, 8
renunciar to resign, 11
reportaje *m.* report, 14
reportero(a) reporter, 11
reproductor de DVD DVD player, 15
reproductor de MP3 MP3 player, 15
republicano *adj.* republican, 14
reserva reservation, 9
reservado(a) *adj.* reserved, 2
resfriarse to catch a cold, 5
resfrío cold, 5
residencia dormitory, 1
resolver (ue) to solve, resolve, 12
respeto respect, 11
responsable *adj.* responsible, 2
restaurante *m.* restaurant, 3
restaurar to refresh, 5
retrato portrait, 13
  retrato al óleo oil painting, 13
reunión *f.* meeting, 11
reunirse con to get together with, 8; to meet, 11
revista magazine, 14
rico *adj.* rich, 2; delicious, 6
ridículo *adj.* ridiculous, 12
rinoceronte *m.* rhinoceros, 12
río river, 8
rodeado *adj.* surrounded, 11
rodear to surround, 11
rodilla knee, 5
rojo *adj.* red, 1
romper (con) to break up (with), 10
ropa clothes, 5
rubio(a) *adj.* blond(e), 2
ruido noise, 12
ruso Russian (language), 1; *adj.* Russian, 2

S

sábado Saturday, 1
saber to know (how), 3
sabor *m.* flavor, 5
sabroso *adj.* tasty, 6
sacar (qu) to withdraw (money), 11
  sacar fotos to take pictures, 3
  sacar la basura to take out the garbage, 4
sagrado *adj.* sacred, 8
sal *f.* salt, 6
sala living room, 4
  sala de clase classroom, 1
  sala de conferencias / para banquetes conference / banquet room, 9
  sala de espera waiting room, 5
  sala de emergencia emergency room, 5
salario salary, 11
salero salt shaker, 6
salida departure, 9
  salida de emergencia emergency exit, 9
salir (con) to leave, to go out (with), 3
  salir del programa to quit the program, 15
salón (la sala) de charla *m.* chat room, 15
salsa sauce, 6
salud *f.* health, 5
  ¡Salud! Cheers!, 6
saludar(se) to greet (each other), P
salvadoreño *adj.* Salvadorean, 2
sandalia sandal, 7
sándwich *m.* sandwich, 6
sano *adj.* healthy, 5
santo(a) saint, 2
sapo toad, 12
satélite *m.* satellite, 15
sciencias science, 1
secadora clothes dryer, 4
secarse (qu) to dry off, 5
sección *f.* **de (no) fumar** *f.* (non)smoking section, 9
secretario(a) secretary, 11
seda silk, 7
segundo *adj.* second, 2
seguir (i) to follow, to continue, 4
seguridad *f.* security, safety, 14
seguro surely, 4
seis six, P
seiscientos six hundred, 4
selva jungle, 12
  selva nubosa tropical rain forest, 12
semana week, 1
  Semana Santa Holy Week, 8
sembrar (ie) to plant, 12
senado senate, 14
senador(a) senator, 14
sencillez *f.* simplicity
sencillo *adj.* simple, 10
sensible sensitive, 3
sentir (ie) to be sorry, 6
  sentirse (bien/mal) to feel (good/bad), 5
señor (Sr.) Mr., sir, P
señora (Sra.) Mrs., ma'am, P
señorita (Srta.) Miss, P
separación *f.* separation, 10
separado *adj.* separated, 2
separarse (de) to separate (from), 10
septiembre September, 3
ser to be, P
servicio de habitación (cuarto) room service, 9
servidor *m.* server, 15
servilleta napkin, 6
servir (i) to serve, 6
sesenta sixty, 2
setecientos seven hundred, 4
setenta seventy, 2
si if, 15
sí yes, P
sicología psychology, 1
sicólogo psychologist, 11
siempre always, 8
siete seven, P
silla chair, 4
sillón *m.* easy chair, arm chair, 4
simpático *adj.* nice, 2
sin *prep.* without, 8
  sin esfuerzo alguno effortless
  sin que *conj.* without, 13
sincero(a) *adj.* sincere, 2
sino *conj.* rather, 5
síntoma *m.* symptom, 5
sinvergüenza *m./f.* shameless person, 4
siquiatra *m./f.* psychiatrist, 11
sistema *(m.)* **nervioso** nervous system, 5
sobre *prep.* about, on; over
sobrepoblación *f.* overpopulation, 12
sobrina niece, 2
sobrino nephew, 2
sociología sociology, 1
sofá *m.* sofa, couch, 4
soldado (la mujer soldado) soldier, 11
solicitar un puesto to apply for a job, 11

solicitud *f.* application (form), 11
solo *adj.* alone, 5
sólo only, P
soltero *adj.* single, 2
sombrero hat, 7
sonreír to smile, 6
sopa soup, 6
sorprender to surprise, 12
sorteo raffle, 7
sótano basement, 4
(Yo) Soy de... I'm from..., P
su *adj.* his, her, its, their, your (formal), 2
suavidad *f.* smoothness, 3
subida climb, 5
subir to climb, to go up, 9
sugerir to suggest, 6
sucio *adj.* dirty, 4
suegra mother-in-law, 2
suegro father-in-law, 2
sueldo salary, 11
suelo floor, 4
suéter *m.* sweater, 7
sufrir to suffer, 9
supermercado supermarket, 3
suplir to supply
sur *m.* south, 9
suyo *adj.* your, yours, his, her, hers, its, 7

T

tabla de planchar ironing board, 4
tacaño *adj.* stingy, 2
tajada slice, 6
talar to cut down (trees), 12
talla size (clothing), 7
también *adv.* also, too, 8
tampoco *adv.* neither, not either, 8
tan pronto como *conj.* as soon as, 13
tan... como as . . . as, 6
tanto(a)... como as much . . . as, 6
tantos(as)... como as many . . . as, 6
tarde *adv.* late, 1
tarea homework, 1
tarjeta card
  tarjeta de cajero automático ATM card, 11
  tarjeta de crédito credit card, 7
  tarjeta de cheque check card, 11
  tarjeta de presentación business card, 2
taza cup, 6
té (helado) *m.* (iced) tea, 6
teatro theater, 13
techo roof, 4
teclado keyboard, 15
técnico *m./f.* technician, 11
tecnológico technological, 15
tela fabric, 7
teléfono phone
  teléfono celular cellular phone, 15
  teléfono inteligente smartphone, 15
telenovela soap opera, 13
teleserie *f.* TV series, 13
teletrabajar to telecommute, 15
televidente *m./f.* television viewer, 13
televisor (de pantalla plana) *m.* (flat-screen) TV, 15
temprano *adv.* early, 1
tenedor *m.* fork, 6
tener (ie) to have, 2
  tener calor to be hot, 4
  tener celos to be jealous, 4
  tener dolor de cabeza to have a headache, 5
  tener escalofríos to have chills, 5
  tener éxito to be successful, 2
  tener fiebre to have a fever, 5
  tener frío to be cold, 2
  tener ganas de to feel like (doing something), 4
  tener gripe to have a cold, 5
  tener hambre to be hungry, 2
  tener lugar to take place, 10
  tener miedo (de) to be afraid (of something), 4
  tener náuseas to be nauseous, 5
  tener paciencia to be patient, 4
  tener prisa to be in a hurry, 2
  tener que to have to (do something), 3
  tener razón to be right, 2
  tener sed to be thirsty, 2
  tener sueño to be tired, sleepy, 2
  tener tos to have a cough, 5
tercero *adj.* third, 2
terminal de autobuses *f.* bus station, 9
terminar to finish, end, 1
terraza terrace, 4
terrorismo terrorism, 14
testigo *m./f.* witness, 10
tía aunt, 2
tiempo weather, 3
tienda store, 3
tienda de antigüedades (de música [de discos], de ropa) antique (music, clothing) store, 3
tienda de campaña tent, 8
tierra land, earth, 12
tigre *m.* tiger, 12
tímido(a) *adj.* shy, timid, 2
tío uncle, 2
tirar to throw, 10
tiza chalk, 1
tobillo ankle, 5
tocador *m.* dresser, 4
tocar (qu) to touch; to play an instrument, 1
tocar la guilarra to *play the guitar,* 3
todos all
  todos los años (días, meses, etc.) every year (day, month, etc.), 10
tolerante *adj.* tolerant, 2
tomar (clases/exámenes) to take (classes/tests); to drink, 1
  tomar el sol to sunbathe, 3
  tomarle la temperatura (a alguien) to take (someone's) temperature, 5
tomate *m.* tomato, 6
tonto(a) *adj.* silly, foolish, 2
tortuga turtle, 12
tos *f.* cough, 5
toser to cough, 5
tostadora toaster, 4
trabajador *adj.* hardworking, 2
trabajar to work, 1
trabajo work, 11
traductor(a) translator, 11
traer to bring, 3
tráfico traffic, 12
traje *m.* suit, 7
  traje de baño bathing suit, 7
  traje típico traditional outfit, 7
tranquilo *adj.* tranquil, peaceful, 12
transferir (ie, i) (fondos) to transfer (funds), 11
transporte *m.* **público** public transportation, 12
tratamiento treatment, 5
trece thirteen, P
treinta thirty, P
tres three, P
trescientos three hundred, 4
triste *adj.* sad, 4
tu *adj.* your (informal), 2
tú *pron.* you, P
tumba tomb, 7
turismo tourism, 1
tuyo *adj.* your, yours, 7

U

un(a) *indef. art.* a, an
universidad *f.* university, 1
uno one, P
unos(as) *indef. art.* some
uña fingernail, 5
uruguayo *adj.* Uruguayan, 2
usar to use, 1; to wear, 7
usted(es) *pron.* you, P

V

vago *lazy*
valiente *adj.* brave
valle *m.* valley, 12
vamos a ver let's see, 7
various several, 1
vaqueros jeans, 7
vaso glass, 6
vegetal *m.* vegetable, 6
veinte twenty, P
veinticuatro twenty-four, P
veinticinco twenty-five, P
veintidós twenty-two, P
veintinueve twenty-nine, P
veintiocho twenty-eight, P
veintiséis twenty-six, P
veintisiete twenty-seven, P
veintitrés twenty-three, P
veintiuno twenty-one, P
vela candle, 8
vendedor(a) salesperson, 11
vender to sell, 2
venezolano(a) *adj.* Venezuelan, 2
venir (ie) to come, 4
  ¡Venga! Come on!, 3
ventaja advantage, 7
ventana window, 4
ventanilla window, 9
ver to see, 3
  Nos vemos. See you later., P
  ver la tele to watch television, 3
verano summer, 3
verdad *f.* truth, 1
verde *adj.* green, 1
verdura vegetable, 6
vestido dress, 7
vestido de gala dressed elegantly, 10
vestirse (i) to get dressed, 5
veterinario *m./f.* veterinarian, 11
vez time
  a la vez at the same time
  a veces sometimes, 10
  de vez en cuando occasionally, 6
  dos (tres, etc.) veces twice (three times, etc.), 10
  muchas veces often, 10
  otra vez *adv.* again
  raras veces rarely, infrequently, 10
  una vez *adv.* once, 10
viajar to travel, 1
viaje *m.* trip, 9
vida life, 10
videocámara digital digital video camera, 15
videocasete *m.* videotape, 15
videocasetera VCR, 15
videojuego video game, 15
videollamada video call, 15
viejo(a) *adj.* old, 2
viernes *m.* Friday, 1
vigente *adj.* existing, 14
vinagre *m.* vinegar, 6
vino (blanco, tinto) (white, red) wine, 6
visitar to visit, 1
  visitar un museo to visit a museum, 3
visto *p.p.* seen, 10
  a primera vista at first sight, 10
viuda widow
viudo *adj.* widowed, 2; *noun* widower
vivienda housing, 4
vivir to live, 2
volcán *m.* volcano, 12
vólibol *m.* volleyball, 3
volver (ue) to return, 4
vosotros(as) *pron.* you, P
votar to vote, 14

voto vote, 14
vuelo (sin escala) (nonstop) flight, 9
vuelto *p.p.* returned, 10
vuestro *adj.* your, yours, 2

Y

y and, 3
ya *adv.* already, 9
y usted and you (formal) P
yerno son-in-law, 2
yo *pron.* I, P
yunta cufflink, 7

Z

zapatería shoe store, 7
zapato shoe, 7
 zapato de tacón (alto) high heels, 7
 zapato de tenis (deportivo) tennis shoe (sneaker), 7
zoología zoology, 1
zorro fox

Glosario inglés-español

A

a, an un(a) *indef. art.*
abortion aborto, 14
about sobre *prep.*
accelerated acelerado *adj.*, 12
accessory accesorio, 7
accompany acompañar, 10
account cuenta, 11
accountant contador(a), 11
accounting contabilidad *f.*, 1
ache dolor *m.*, 5
across from enfrente de *prep.*, 9
act actuar; interpretar, 13
action acción *f.*
activity actividad *f.*, 3
actor actor *m.*, 13
actress actriz *f.*, 13
advance avance *m.*, 15
advantage ventaja, 7
advisor consejero(a), 1
affection cariño, 10
after después (de) (que) *conj.*, 13
afterward después *adv.*, 10
again otra vez *adv.*, 10
against contra *prep.*, 1
age edad *f.*, 2
agree estar de acuerdo, 10
air aire *m.*, 12
air conditioning aire acondicionado, 9
airline aerolínea, 9
airline agent agente *m.f.* de la acrolínea, 9
airport aeropuerto, 9
aisle pasillo, 9
alarm alarma, 15
alarm clock despertador *m.*, 4
all todos
  All Saints' Day Día de Todos los Santos, 8
allergy alergia, 5
alliance alianza
alligator caimán *m.*, 12
allow dejar, 13
almost (always) casi (siempre) *adv.*, 10
alone solo *adj.*, 5
already ya *adv.*, 9
also también *adv.*, 8
although aunque *conj.*, 13
always siempre, 8
ambulance ambulancia, 5
amend enmendar (ie), 14
amendment enmienda, 14
ammenities comodidades *f.*, 9
among entre *prep.*, 4
and y, 3
angry enojado *adj.*, 4
animal animal *m.*, 12
ankle tobillo, 5
annoyed: I get annoyed. Me pongo molesto., 8
answer contestar, 1
answering machine contestador automático *m.*, 15
antacid antiácido, 5
antibiotic antibiótico, 5
antique antigüedad *f.*, 7
antique store tienda de antigüedades, 3
any algún, alguno(a/os/as), 8
anybody, anyone alguien, 8
anything algo, 8
apartment apartamento, departamento 1
appear parecer, 1
applaud aplaudir, 10
apple manzana, 6
applicant candidato(a), 11
application (form) solicitud *f.*, 11
apply for a job solicitar un puesto, 11
appreciate apreciar, 13
approach acercar (qu)
approve aprobar (ue), 14
April abril, 3
Arab árabe *adj.*, 2
architect arquitecto(a), 11
architecture arquitectura, 13
Argentine argentino *adj.*, 2
argue discutir, 14
arm brazo, 5
arm chair sillón *m.*, 4
armoire armario, 4
army ejército, 14
around alrededor de
arrival llegada, 9
arrive llegar, 1
arriving from procedente de, 9
arrogant arrogante *adj.*, 2
art arte *m./f.*, 1
article of clothing prenda, 7
artist artista *m./f.*, 13
artistic artístico(a) *adj.*, 2
as . . . as tan... como, 6
as many . . . as tantos(as)... como, 6
as much . . . as tanto(a)... como, 6
as soon as tan pronto como *conj.*, 13
ask (a question) preguntar, 1
ask for pedir (i, i), 4
  ask for a raise pedir un aumento, 11
aspirin aspirina, 5
assistant ayudante *m./f.*
at a *prep.*
  at first sight a primera vista, 10
  at last finalmente *adv.*, 10
  at the last minute a última hora, 8
  at the same time a la vez
  At what time? ¿A qué hora?, 1
athletic atlético *adj.*, 2
ATM cajero automático, 11
  ATM card tarjeta de cajero automático, 11
attend asistir a, 2
August agosto, 3
aunt tía, 2
author autor(a), 13
avocado aguacate *m.*, 6

B

back espalda, 5
backpack mochila, 1
bad malo *adj.*, 2
bag bolsa, 7
baggage (carry-on) equipaje (de mano) *m.*, 9
balance equilibrio, 12
balcony balcón *m.*, 4
ballet ballet *m.*, 13
ballpoint pen bolígrafo, 1
banana banana/banano, 6
band orquesta, 10
bank banco, 3
banker banquero(a), 11
banquet banquete *m.*, 10
  banquet room sala para banquetes, 9
bargain: It's a bargain! ¡Es una ganga!, 7
baseball béisbol *m.*, 3
baseball cap gorra de béisbol, 7
basement sótano, 4
basketball baloncesto, 3
bat murciélago
bathing suit traje de baño, 7
bathroom cuarto de baño, 4
bathroom sink lavabo, 4
bathtub bañera, 4
be ser, P; estar, 3
  be able poder (ue), 4
  be afraid (of something) tener miedo (de), 4
  be born nacer, 2
  be cold tener frío, 2
  be delayed demorarse, 13
  be frightened asustarse, 8
  be glad alegrarse (de), 12
  be healthy estar sano(a), 5
  be hot tener calor, 4
  be hungry tener hambre, 2
  be in a hurry tener prisa, 2
  be jealous tener celos, 4
  be nauseous tener náuseas, 5
  be online estar conectado(a) (en línea), 15
  be painful (to someone) dolerle (ue) (a alguien), 5
  be patient tener paciencia, 4
  be pleasing (to someone) gustar, 3
  be right tener razón, 2
  be sick estar enfermo(a), 5
  be sleepy tener sueño, 2
  be sorry sentir (ie), 6
  be successful tener éxito, 2
  be thirsty tener sed, 2
  be tired tener sueño, 2
beach playa, 8
beach resort balneario, 8
bear oso
beautiful bello *adj.*, 12
because porque, 3
become + *adjective* ponerse + *adjective*, 8
bed cama, 4
bedroom dormitorio, 4 habitación , 4
beer cerveza, 6
before antes (de) que *conj.*
begin comenzar (ie), empezar (ie), 4
behave well (poorly) portarse bien (mal), 8
behind detrás de *prep.*, 4
believe creer, 2
below abajo *adv.*; debajo de *prep.*, 4
belt cinturón *m.*, 7
benefits beneficios, 11
beside al lado de *prep.*, 4
best el mejor, 6
better mejor, 6
between entre *prep.*, 4
beverage bebida, 6
bicycle bicicleta, 3
big grande *adj.*, 2
bilingual bilingüe *adj.*, 2
bill cuenta, 6; factura, 11
biology biología, 1
bird pájaro, *m.*, 12
birthday cumpleaños *m.*, 8
bite picar (qu), 12
black negro *adj.*, 1
blanket manta, 8
blond(e) rubio *adj.*, 2
blouse blusa, 7
blue azul *adj.*, 1
blue jeans jeans *m. pl.*, 7
board abordar, 9
boardinghouse pensión *f.*, 1
body cuerpo humano, 5
Bolivian boliviano *adj.*, 2
bone hueso, 5
book (text) libro (de texto), 1
bookshelf estante *m.*, 4
bookstore librería, 1
boot bota, 7
border frontera, 12
bore aburrir, 13
bored aburrido *adj.*, 2
borrow pedir prestado, 11
boss jefe *m./f.*, 11
bottle botella, 6
bother molestar, 12
bounce (a check) rebotar, 11
bouquet ramo, 10
box caja, 6
boy chico, muchacho, 1; niño, 2
boyfriend novio, 1
bracelet pulsera, 7
brain cerebro
brave valiente *adj.*
Brazilian brasileño *adj.*, 2
bread (toast) pan (tostado) *m.*, 6
break up (with) romper (con), 10
breakfast desayuno, 6
bride novia, 10
bring traer, 3
brother hermano, 2
brother-in-law cuñado, 2
brown marrón *adj.*, 1

brush one's teeth cepillarse los dientes, 5
buckle the seat belt abrochar el cinturón de seguridad, 9
budget presupuesto, 11
building edificio, 1
burn quemar, 8
bus autobús *m. (Spain)*, P; camión *m. (Mexico)*, P; guagua *(Puerto Rico)*, P
bus station terminal de autobuses *f.*, 9
business negocios, 1; empresa, 11
  business administration administración *f.* de empresas, 1
  business card tarjeta de presentación, 2
  business center centro de negocios, 9
  businessman hombre de negocios, 11
  businesswoman mujer de negocios, 11
busy ocupado *adj.*, 4
but pero *conj.*, 3
butcher shop carnicería, 3
butter mantequilla, 6
butterfly mariposa, 12
button botón *m.*, 7
buy comprar, 1
Bye. Chao. (informal), P

C

cabin cabina, 9
café café *m.*, 3
cafeteria cafetería, 1
cake pastel *m.*, 8
calculator calculadora, 1
calendar calendario, 1
calf (of leg) pantorrilla, 5
call llamar, 1
camera cámara, 3
campaign campaña, 14
campus campus *m.*
can lata, 6
Canadian canadiense *adj.*, 2
candidate candidato(a), 11
candle vela, 8
car automóvil *m.*; carro; coche *m.*
caramel custard (homemade) flan (casero) *m.*, 6
card tarjeta
cardboard cartón *m.*
carpet alfombra, 4
carpenter carpintero(a), 11
carry llevar, 7
cartoon dibujo animado, 13
cash efectivo, 7
cashier cajero(a), 11
cat gato, 2
catch a cold resfriarse, 5
catch agarrar, 10
celebrate celebrar, 8
celebration celebración *f.*, 8
cellular phone teléfono celular, 15
chair silla, 4
chalk tiza, 1
chalkboard pizarra, 1
challenge desafío, 14
champagne champán *m.*, 10
change cambiar, 7
channel (TV) canal *m.*, 13
charge cargo, 11
charity limosna
chat room salón (la sala) de charla *m.*, 15
cheap barato *adj.*, 7
check cuenta, 6; cheque *m.*, 7
  check card tarjeta de cheque, 11
  The check, please. La cuenta, por favor., 6
check the luggage facturar el equipaje, 9
checking account cuenta corriente, 11
cheeks mejillas, 5
Cheers! ¡Salud!, 6
cheese queso, 6
chemistry química, 1
chest pecho, 5
chew masticar (qu), 5
chicken (roast) pollo (asado), 6
Chilean chileno *adj.*, 2
chimney chimenea, 4
Chinese chino *adj.*, 2; **(language)** chino, 1
choose escoger, 9
chore quehacer doméstico *m.*, 4
Christmas Eve Nochebuena, 8
Christmas Pascua, Navidad *f.*, 8
church iglesia, 3
citizen ciudadano(a), 14
city block cuadra, 9
claim recoger (j), 12
classical clásico *adj.*, 10
classmate compañero(a) de clase, 1
classroom sala de clase, 1
clean limpio *adj.*, 4
clean the house limpiar la casa, 4
clear the table quitar la mesa, 4
clear: it's clear está despejado, 3
click (on) hacer clic (sobre), 15
climb subida, 5
  climb escalar, 8; subir, 9
clock reloj *m.*, 1
close cerrar (ie)
closet armario, 4
clothes dryer secadora, 4
clothes ropa, 5
clothing store tienda de ropa, 3
cloudy: it's cloudy está nublado, 3
coast costa, 8
coffee café *m.*, 6
coincidence: What a coincidence! ¡Qué casualidad!, P
cold resfrío, catarro, 5
  it's cold hace frío, 3
Colombian colombiano *adj.*, 2
color color *m.*, 1
Columbus Day Día de la Raza, 8
comb one's hair peinarse, 5
come venir (ie), 4
  Come on! ¡Venga!, 3
comedy comedia, 13
comfort comodidad *f.*
comfortable cómodo *adj.*, 9
command mandar, 11
commercial anuncio, 13
compact disc (CD) disco compacto, 15
complain about quejarse de, 9
composer compositor(a), 13
computer computadora, 11
computer science computación *f.*, 1
concert concierto, 13
condiment condimento, 6
condominium condominio, 4
conference room sala de conferencias, 9
congested congestionado *adj.*, 5
congestion (traffic) congestión (de tráfico) *f.*, 12
congratulate felicitar, 10
  Congratulations! ¡Felicitaciones!, 8
Congress congreso, 14
connect conectar, 15
connection conexión *f.*, 15
conservation conservación *f.*, 12
conservative conservador(a) *adj.*, 14
conserve conservar, 12
constitution constitución *f.*, 14
construct construir, 12
contact lenses lentillas/lentes *m.* de contacto, 5
continue seguir (i), 4
cook cocinar, 6
cook, chef cocinero(a), 11
Cool! ¡Chévere!, 3
¡Que padrel!, 2
cool: it's cool hace fresco, 3
corn flour harina de maíz
cornmeal pockets arepas, 6
corporation empresa, 11
corruption corrupción *f.*, 14
cost costar (ue), 4
Costa Rican costarricense *adj.*, 2
costume disfraz *m.*, 8
cotton algodón *m.*, 7
couch sofá *m.*, 4
cough syrup jarabe *m.*, 5
cough tos *f.*, 5
  cough toser, 5
count contar (ue)
  count on contar con
country campo, 8
couple pareja, 10
course curso, 1
court (tennis) cancha (de tenis), 3
courtship noviazgo, 10
cousin primo(a), 2
cowardly cobarde *adj.*
credit card tarjeta de crédito, 7
crime crimen *m.*, 14
crocodile cocodrilo, 12
cross cruzar, 9
cry llorar, 8
Cuban cubano *adj.*, 2
cufflink gemelo, yunta, 7
cultivate cultivar, 12
cup taza, 6
current actual *adj.*, 14
customs aduana, 9
cut cortar, partir 10
cut down (trees) talar, 12
cyberspace espacio cibernético, ciberespacio, 15
cycling ciclismo, 3

D

daily cotidiano *adj.*, 13; *adv.* diariamente, 3
dance bailar, 3
  dance baile *m.*, 3; danza, 13
dancer bailarín *m.*, bailarina, 13
dangerous peligroso *adj.*
dark-haired moreno *adj.*, 2
date (social) cita, 10
daughter hija, 2
daughter-in-law nuera, 2
day before yesterday anteayer *adv.*, 6
day día *m.*, 1
  Day of the Dead Día de los Muertos, 8
  Day of the Magi (Three Kings) Día de los Reyes Magos, 8
dead muerto *adj.*, 4
dean decano(a), 1
death muerte *f.*
debate debate *m.*, 14
December diciembre, 3
deer ciervo
defend defender (ie), 14
defense defensa, 14
delicious rico *adj.*, 6
democracy democracia, 14
democratic demócrata *adj.*, 14
demonstration manifestación *f.*, 14
dense denso *adj.*, 12
dentist dentista *m./f.*, 11
departing for con destino a, 9
department facultad *f.*
departure salida, 9
deposit (money) depositar, 11
desire afán *m.*, 12
desk escritorio, 1
  student desk pupitre *m.*, 1
dessert postre *m.*, 6
destroy destruir, 12
destroyed destruido *adj.*, 12
destruction destrucción *f.*, 12
detail detalle *m.*, 10
develop desarrollar, 12
development desarrollo, 12
diagnosis diagnóstico, 5
dictator dictador(a), 14
dictatorship dictadura, 14
dictionary diccionario, 1
die morir (ue), 6
died *p.p.* muerto, 10

diet dieta, 5
digital camera cámara digital, 15
dining room comedor *m.*, 4
dinner cena, 6
direct dirigir, 13
director director(a), 13
dirty sucio *adj.*, 4
disadvantage desventaja, 15
disconnect desconectar, 15
discount descuento, 7
discuss discutir, 14
dishwasher lavaplatos *m.*, 4
divorce divorcio, 10
divorced divorciado *adj.*, 2
dizziness mareo, 5
dizzy mareado *adj.*, 5
do hacer, 3
doctor médico *m./f.*, 5
documentary documental *m.*, 13
dog perro, 2
Dominican (from the Dominican Republic) dominicano *adj.*, 2
done hecho *p.p.*, 10
door puerta, 4
dormitory residencia, 1
double bed cama doble, 9
download (a file) descargar (un archivo), 15
downtown centro, 3
drama drama *m.*, 13
dramatic dramático(a) *adj.*, 2
draw dibujar, 1
dress vestido, 7
  dressed elegantly vestido de gala, 10
dresser cómoda, tocador *m.*, 4
drink tomar, 1; beber, 2
  drink coffee ir a tomar un café, 3
drug addiction drogadicción *f.*, 14
dry off secarse (qu), 5
dry season período de sequía, 5
duty deber *m.* noun, 14
DVD player reproductor de DVD, 15

E

each cada *adv.*
ear (outer) oreja, 5; **(inner)** oído, 5
earache dolor de oídos *m.*, 5
early temprano *adv.*, 1
earring arete *m.*, 7
earth tierra, 12
east este *m.*, 9
Easter Pascua, 8
easy chair sillón *m.*, 4
eat comer, 2
  eat appetizers picar (qu), 6
  eat breakfast desayunar, 6
  eat lunch almorzar (ue), 6
  eat supper (dinner) cenar, 6
  I can't (eat) any more. No puedo (comer) más., 6
ecology ecología, 12
economic económico *adj.*, 5
economics economía, 1
Ecuadorian ecuatoriano, 2
education educación *f.*, 1
effortless sin esfuerzo alguno
egg: hard-boiled egg huevo duro, 6
Egyptian egipcio *adj.*, 2
eight hundred ochocientos, 4
eight ocho, P
eighteen dieciocho, P
eighty ochenta, 2
either . . . or o... o, 8
elbow codo, 5
elect elegir (i, i), 14
elections elecciones *f.*, 14
electric appliance electrodomésticos, 4
electrician electricista *m./f.*, 11
elegant elegante *adj.*, 10
elephant elefante *m.*, 12
elevator ascensor *m.*, 9
eleven once, P
eliminate eliminar, 14
email correo electrónico, 11
embarrassed: I get embarrassed. Me pongo avergonzado., 8
emergency exit salida de emergencia, 9
emergency room sala de emergencia, 5
employee empleado(a), 11
employment empleo, 14
end terminar, 1
engaged comprometido *adj.*, 10
engagement compromiso, 10
engineer ingeniero(a), 11
engineering ingeniería, 1
English (language) inglés *m.*, 1; inglés(esa) *adj.*, 2
enjoy disfrutar, 9
  Enjoy your meal! ¡Buen provecho!, 6
enter entrar, 1
environment medio ambiente, 12
episode capítulo, 13
equality igualdad *f.*, 14
equipment equipo, 15
eraser borrador *m.*, 1
even though aunque *conj.*, 13
every day (week, etc.) cada día (semana, etc.), 10
  every year (day, month, etc.) todos los años (días, meses, etc.), 10
examine examinar, 5
excited emocionado *adj.*, 4
excuse me perdón, con permiso, P
exercise hacer ejercicio, 3
existing vigente *adj.*, 14
expense gasto; costo, 11
expensive caro *adj.*, 7
explain explicar (qu), 9
exploit explotar, 12
extinction: in danger of extinction en peligro de extinción, 12
eye ojo, 5
eyebrows cejas, 5
eyelashes pestañas, 5

F

fabric tela, 7
face enfrentar
  cara, 5
factory fábrica, 12
fall otoño, 3
fall asleep dormirse (ue), 5
fall in love (with) enamorarse (de), 10
false cognate cognado falso, 1
family familia
fan (sports) aficionado(a), 3
far (away) (from) lejos (de) *prep.*, 4
farm finca, 12
farm worker campesino(a), 12
farmer agricultor(a), 12
fat gordo *adj.*, 2
father papá, padre, *m.*, 2
  Father's Day Día del Padre, 8
father-in-law suegro, 2
fax machine fax *m.*, 11
features comodidades *f.*, 9
February febrero, 3
feel (good/bad) sentirse (bien/mal), 5
feel like (doing something) tener ganas de, 4
fever fiebre, 5
fifteen quince, P
fifty cincuenta, 2
fight luchar, 14
file archivar, 11
  archivo, 11
fill out (a form) llenar, 11
film película, 13
  action film película de acción, 13
  classic film película clásica, 13
  fantasy film película fantástica, 13
  foreign film película extranjera, 13
  horror film película de terror, 13
  mystery film película de intriga (misterio), 13
  romantic film película romántica, 13
  science fiction film película de ciencia ficción, 13
finally por fin, finalmente *adv.*, 10
find encontrar, 5
fine bien *adv.*
  Fine, thanks. Bien, gracias., P
finger dedo, 5
fingernail uña, 5
finish terminar, 1
fire despedir(i), 11
firefighter bombero(a), 11
fireplace chimenea, 4
first primero, 10
  first dance primer baile, 10
  first time primera vez, 5
first name nombre *m.*, 2
fish pescar (qu), 3
  (alive) pez *m.*, 2
  (when caught) pescado, 6
fit (someone) quedarle (a uno), 7
five cinco, P
five hundred quinientos, 4
flavor sabor *m.*, 5
flight (nonstop) vuelo (sin escala), 9
flight attendant asistente de vuelo *m./f.*, 9
floor piso, 4/suelo, 4
floor covering alfombra, 8
flower flor *f.*, 10
folkloric folclórico *adj.*, 13
follow seguir (i), 4
food comida, 6
foolish tonto *adj.*, 2
foot pie *m.*, 5
football field campo de fútbol, 3
for para, por, *prep.*
  for example por ejemplo, 11
  For what purpose? ¿Para qué?, 8
foreign languages lenguas extranjeras, 1
forest bosque *m.*, 12
forget olvidar, 8
fork tenedor *m.*, 6
forty cuarenta, 2
fountain fuente *f.*, 4
fountain pen pluma, 1
four cuatro, P
four hundred cuatrocientos, 4
fourteen catorce, P
fox zorro
free gratis *adj.*, 1
freedom of the press libertad *f.* de la prensa, 14
French (language) francés *m.*, 1; francés(esa) *adj.*, 2
frequently a menudo
fresh fresco *adj.*, 6
Friday viernes *m.*, 1
friend amigo(a), 1
friendly amable *adj.*, 2
friendship amistad *f.*, 10
frog rana, 12
from de, desde *prep.*, 1
  I'm from... Soy de..., P,
  From where? ¿De dónde?, P
front desk recepción *f.*, 9
fruit fruta, 6
fruit juice jugo de fruta, 6
fruit store frutería, 3
fulfill llenar, 7
full-time de tiempo completo, 11
fun divertido *adj.*, 2
function (to work) funcionar, 15
furious furioso *adj.*, 4
furniture muebles *m.*, 4

G

gallon galón *m.*, 6
game juego, partido, 3
game show programa de concursos, 13
garage garaje *m.*, 4
garden jardín *m.*, 4

garlic ajo, 6
gas station gasolinera, 3
gate puerta, 9
gem joya
generous generoso(a) *adj.*, 2
geography geografía, 1
German (language) alemán *m.*, 1; alemán(ana) *adj.*, 2
get conseguir (i), 4; + *adjective* ponerse + *adjective*, 8
get a suntan broncearse, 8
get along well (poorly) (with) each other llevarse bien (mal) (con), 10
get divorced (from) divorciarse (de), 10
get dressed vestirse (i), 5
get married casarse (con), 10
get off bajar(se) (de), 9
get sick enfermarse, 5
get together with reunirse con, 8
get up levantarse, 5
get used to acostumbrarse
gift regalo, 8
girl chica, muchacha, 1; niña, 2
girlfriend novia, 1
give dar, 3
give (as a gift) regalar, 9
give a party dar/hacer una fiesta, 8
glass vaso, 6
glove guante *m.*, 7
go ir, 3
go by bike (boat, bus, car, plane, subway, taxi, train) ir en bicicleta (barco, autobús, coche/carro, avión, metro, taxi, tren), 9
go camping hacer camping, 8
go canoeing/sailing pasear en canoa/velero, 8
go for a walk dar un paseo, 3
go horseback riding montar a caballo, 3
go on a picnic hacer un picnic, 3
go on foot ir a pie, 9
go out (with) salir (con), 3
go shopping ir de compras, 3
go through pasar por, 9
go to a bar (club, concert, disco, party) ir a un bar (club, concierto, discoteca, party), 3
go to bed acostarse (ue), 5
go to the movies ir al cine, 3
go up subir, 9
go well with ir (bien) con, 7
goblet copa, 6
godchild ahijado(a), 2
godfather padrino, 2
godmother madrina, padrina, 2
golf golf *m.*, 3
golf club palo de golf, 3
golf course campo de golf, 3
good bueno *adj.*, 2
Good afternoon. Buenas tardes., P
Good evening (night). Buenas noches., P
Good morning. Buenos días., P
Good-bye. Adiós., P
good-looking guapo *adj.*, 2
gorilla gorila *m.*, 12
govern gobernar (ie), 14
government gobierno, 14
governor gobernador(a), 14
gram gramo, 6
granddaughter nieta, 2
grandfather abuelo, 2
grandmother abuela, 2
grandson nieto, 2
green verde *adj.*, 1
greet (each other) saludar(se), P
groom novio, 10
grow (plants) cultivar, 12
grow up crecer
growth crecimiento
Guatemalan guatemalteco *adj.*, 2
guerrilla guerrillero *m./f.*, 14
guest invitado *m./f.*, 8
guest on a talk show panelista *m./f.*, 13
Guinean Guineano(a), 2
guitar guitarra, 3
gymnasium gimnasio, 1

H

hair cabello, pelo, 5
hair salon peluquería, 3
hairstylist peluquero(a), 11
Haitian haitiano *adj.*, 2
half brother (sister) medio(a) hermano(a), 2
half mitad *f.*, 15
ham jamón *m.*, 6
hamburger hamburguesa, 6
hand mano *f.*, 5
handshake apretón m. de manos
Hanukkah Jánuca *m.*, 8
happy contento *adj.*, 4
I get happy. Me pongo contento., 8
hard drive disco duro, 15
hardware store ferretería, 3
hardworking trabajador(a) *adj.*, 2
hat sombrero, 7
have tener (ie), 3; *(auxillary verb)* haber, 10
have a birthday cumplir años, 8
have a cold estar resfriado, tener gripe, 5
have a cookout hacer una parrillada, 8
have a cough tener tos, 5
have a fever tener fiebre, 5
to have fun divertirse, 6
have a good (bad) time pasarlo bien (mal), 8
have a headache tener dolor de cabeza, 5
Have a nice trip! ¡Buen viaje!, 9
have chills tener escalofríos, 5
have just (done something) acabar de + *infinitive*
have to (do something) tener que, 3
he él *pron.*, P
head cabeza, 5
headache dolor de cabeza *m.*, 5
headphones auriculares *m.*, 15
health salud *f.*, 5
healthy sano *adj.*, 5
heart corazón *m.*, 5
heavy (meal, food) pesado *adj.*, 6
help (each other) ayudar(se), 1
her su *adj.*, 2
herb hierba, 5
here aquí *adv.*, P
hers suyo *adj.*, 7
Hi! ¡Hola!, P
hierarchy jerarquía, 11
high heels zapato de tacón (alto), 7
high-speed connection conexión de alta velocidad *f.*, 15
highway carretera, 12
hike in the mountains caminar por las montañas, 3
hill colina, 12
hip cadera, 5
hippopotamus hipopótamo, 12
hire contratar, 11
his su *adj.*, 2; suyo *adj.*, 7
history historia, 1
holiday fiesta, día feriado *m.*, 8
Holy Week Semana Santa, 8
home hogar *m.*, 4
home page página de bienvenida (de entrada, de presentación, inicial, principal, de la Red), 15
homework tarea, 1
Honduran hondureño *adj.*, 2
honest honesto(a) *adj.*, 2
honeymoon luna de miel, 10
honor cumplir con, 10
hope esperar
hors d'oeuvre entremés *m.*, 8
host anfitrión *m.*, 8
hostess anfitriona, 8
hot (temperature) caliente *adj.*, 6
it's hot hace calor, 3
hotel: four-star hotel hotel de cuatro estrellas *m.*, 9
hour hora, 1
house casa, 4
house of representatives cámara de representantes (diputados), 14
house specialty especialidad *f.* de la casa, 6
housing vivienda, 4
How ¿Cómo?, P
How are you? ¿Cómo está usted?, ¿Cómo estás?, P
How can I help you? ¿En qué puedo servirle?, 7
How does it look? ¿Cómo me queda?, 7
How many? ¿Cuántos(as)?, P
How much do I owe you? ¿Cuánto le debo?, 7
How much? ¿Cuánto(a)?, 8
How old are you? ¿Cuántos años tienes tú?, P
How's it going? ¿Cómo te va?, P
hug (each other) abrazar(se), 10
human (civil) rights derechos humanos (civiles), 14
humanities humanidades *f. pl.*, 1
humble humilde *adj.*, 2
humorous cómico *adj.*, 2
hunger hambre *f.*, 5
husband esposo, 2

I

I yo *pron.*, P
ice cream helado, 6
ideology ideología, 14
if si, 15
illiteracy analfabetismo, 14
illness enfermedad *f.*, 5
immigration inmigración *f.*, 14
immunity inmunidad *f.*
impairment desmedro
important importante *adj.*, 12
impossible imposible *adj.*, 12
imprisonment encarcelamiento, 14
in en, 4
in addition to además de
in case (of) en caso (de) que *conj.*, 13
in exchange for a cambio de
in front of delante de / enfrente de *prep.*, 4
in regard to en cuanto a, 13
in the (morning, afternoon/evening) de/por la (mañana, tarde, noche), 1
include incluir, 2
income ingreso, 12
increase aumentar, 14
indecisive indeciso *adj.*, 2
Independence Day from Spain Día de la Independencia de España, 8
Indian indio *adj.*, 2
inequality desigualdad *f.*, 14
inexpensive barato *adj.*, 7
infirmary enfermería, 9
inflation inflación *f.*, 14
inform informar, 14
injustice injusticia, 14
insecurity inseguridad *f.*, 14
intellectual intelectual *adj.*, 2
intelligent inteligente *adj.*, 2
interesting interesante *adj.*, 2
international policy política internacional, 14
Internet Internet *m.*
Internet service provider proveedor *m.* de servicios Internet, 15
interpreter intérprete *m./f.*, 11
interview entrevista, 11
introverted introvertido, 2
intuitive intuitivo *adj.*, 2
invent inventar, 3
investigate investigar, 14
iron plancha, 4
iron (clothes) planchar (la ropa), 4

Glosario inglés-español

ironing board tabla de planchar, 4
irresponsible irresponsable *adj.*, 2
irrigate regar (ie) las plantas, 12
island isla, 9
Italian (language), italiano, 1; italiano, *adj.*, 2
its su *adj.*, 2; suyo *adj.*, 7

J

jacket chaqueta, 7
jaguar jaguar *m.*, 12
January enero, 3
Japanese (language) japonés *m.*, 1; japonés(esa) *adj.*, 2
jar frasco, 6
jeans vaqueros, 7
jewelry joyas, 7
jewelry store joyería, 3
job puesto, 11
job appointment cita de negocios, 1
job hunt búsqueda de trabajo, 11
job offer oferta de trabajo, 11
joke broma, 1
journalism periodismo, 1
journalist periodista *m./f.*, 11
judge juez *m./f.*, 10
July julio, 3
June junio, 3
jungle selva, 12
just like así como
justice justicia, 14

K

key llave *f.*, 9
keyboard teclado, 15
kilogram kilo(gramo), 6
kiss (each other) besar(se), 10
kitchen cocina, 4
knee rodilla, 5
knife cuchillo, 6
know (each other) conocer(se), 3
know (how) saber, 3
Korean coreano *adj.*, 2

L

laborer obrero(a), 11
lack falta
lake lago, 8
lamp lámpara, 4
land aterrizar, 9
tierra, 12
landscape paisaje *m.*, 12
language lengua, 1
laptop computer computadora portátil, 15
large grande *adj.*, 2
last (week, month, year) (la semana, el mes, el año) pasado(a), 6
last name apellido, 2
last night anoche *adv.*, 6
late tarde *adv.*, 1
laugh reírse, 6
law derecho, 1; ley *f.*, 14
law office bufete *m.*, 11
lawyer abogado(a), 11
lazy perezoso *adj.*, 2
vago
lead a peaceful life llevar una vida tranquila, 12
leaf hoja, 5
learn aprender, 2
leather cuero, 7
leave salir, 3; dejar, 13
leave a (good) tip dejar una (buena) propina, 6
left: to the left of a la izquierda de *prep.*, 9
leg pierna, 5
less . . . than menos... que, 6
lesson lección *f.*, 1
let dejar, 13
let's see vamos a ver, 7
letter (correspondence) carta, 2
lettuce lechuga, 6
liberal liberal *adj.*, 15
librarian bibliotecario(a), 11
library biblioteca, 1
life vida, 10
lift weights levantar pesas, 3
light (meal, food) ligero *adj.*, 6
light luz *f.*, 1
lightly levemente, 11
like: I (don't) like + infinitive (no) me gusta + *infinitive*, 1
I would like...yo quisiera..., 6
lion león *m.*
lips labios, 5
listen (to music) escuchar (música), 1
liter litro, 6
literacy alfabetismo, 14
literature literatura, 1
live vivir, 2
living room sala, 4
loan préstamo, 11
prestar, 11
lobster langosta, 6
logical lógico *adj.*, 12
long largo *adj.*, 2
look for buscar (qu), 1
look at each other mirarse, 10
lose perder (ie), 4
love querer (ie), 4; amar, 10
amor *m.*, 10
lunch almuerzo, 6
lungs pulmones *m.*, 5
luxurious lujoso *adj.*, 7

M

made hecho *p.p.*, 10
magazine revista, 14
main dish plato principal, 6
major especialización *f.*, 1
major, field of study carrera
majority mayoría, 1
make hacer, 3
make a phone call llamar por teléfono, 11
make a stop (on a flight) (in) hacer escala (en), 9
make a toast hacer un brindis, 8
make one's bed hacer la cama, 4
make plans hacer planes, 3
mall centro comercial, 3
mammal mamífero
man hombre *m.*, 1
manager gerente *m./f.*, 11
map mapa *m.*, 1
March marzo, 3
marker marcador *m.*, 1
market (outdoor) mercado (al aire libre), 3
marriage matrimonio, 10
married casado *adj.*, 2
marry casarse (con), 10
mask máscara, 8
masterpiece obra maestra, 13
match hacer juego con, 7
math matemáticas, 1
May mayo, 3
mayor alcalde(sa), 14
meal comida, 6
means of communication medios de comunicación, 14
meat (beef) carne (de res) *f.*, 6
mechanic mecánico(a), 11
medical médico *adj.*, 5
medical history historial clínica *f.*, 5
medical insurance seguro médico, 11
medicine medicina, 1
meet conocer(se), 3; reunirse con, 11
meeting reunión *f.*, 11
menu menú *m.*, 6
merchant comerciante *m./f.*, 11
message mensaje *m.*, 15
messy desordenado *adj.*, 4
metropolis metrópolis *f.*, 12
Mexican mexicano *adj.*, 2
microphone micrófono, 15
midnight medianoche *f.*, 1
milk leche *f.*, 6
million millón, 4
mine mío *adj.*, 7
minister ministro *m./f.*, 14
mirror espejo, 4
miss (a function) perder (ie), 4
Miss señorita (Srta.), P
modem módem *m.*, 15
modern moderno(a) *adj.*, 10
monarchy monarquía, 14
Monday lunes *m.*, 1
money dinero, 1
monkey mono, 12
monitor monitor *m.*, 15
month mes *m.*, 3
more . . . than más... que, 6
mortgage hipoteca, 11
mother mamá, madre, *f.*, 2
Mother's Day Día de las Madres, 8
mother-in-law suegra, 2
mountains montañas, 8
mouse (of computer) ratón *m.*, 15
mouth boca, 5
move mover (ue), 3
movie película, 13
movie theater cine *m.*, 3
movies cine *m.*, 13
mow the lawn cortar el césped, 4
MP3 player reproductor de MP3, 15
Mr., sir señor (Sr.), P
Mrs, ma'am señora (Sra.), P
muscle músculo, 5
museum museo, 3
mushroom champiñón *m.*, 6
music música, 1
music store tienda de música (de discos), 3
musical (play) musical *m.*,13
musician músico *m./f.*, 13
must deber, 2
my mi *adj.*, 2; mío, 7
My God! My goodness! ¡Dios Mío!, P

N

name: My name is . . . Me llamo..., P
nanny niñero, 11
napkin servilleta, 6
nationality nacionalidad *f.*, 2
native Spanish speaker hispanohablante *m./f.*
natural resources recursos naturales, 12
naturalist naturalista *m./f.*, 12
nature naturaleza, 12
near cerca de *prep.*, 4
neat ordenado *adj.*, 4; arreglado *adj.*, 9
necessary necesario *adj.*, 12
neck cuello, 5
necklace collar *m.*, 7
necktie corbata, 7
need necesitar, 1
neighborhood barrio, P
neither . . . nor ni... ni, 8
neither, not either, 8 tampoco *adv.*, 8
nephew sobrino, 2
nervous system sistema *m.* nervioso, 5
never nunca *adv.*, 8
never again nunca más *adv.*, 3
new nuevo *adj.*, 2
New Year Año Nuevo, 8
New Year's Eve Noche Vieja *f.*, 8
newlyweds recién casados *m.*, 10
news noticias, 13
newscast noticiero, 14
newspaper periódico, 14
next to al lado de *prep.*, 9
nibble picar (qu), 6
Nicaraguan nicaragüense *adj.*, 2
nice simpático *adj.*, 2
it's nice hace buen tiempo, 3
Nice to meet you. Encantado(a)., Mucho gusto., P
niece sobrina, 2
nine hundred novecientos, 4

nine nueve, P
nineteen diecinueve, P
ninety noventa, 2
nobody, no one nadie, 8
noise ruido, 12
none, not any ningún, ninguno(a), 8
nonsmoking section sección *f.* de no fumar *f.*, 9
noon mediodía *m.*, 1
North American norteamericano *adj.*, 2
north norte *m.*, 9
nose nariz *f.*, 5
not even ni siquiera, 4
notebook cuaderno, 1
notes apuntes *m.*
nothing, not anything, at all nada, 8
November noviembre, 3
now ahora *adv.*, 1
number número, P
nurse enfermero(a), 5
nursing home casa de ancianos, 2

O

object objeto, 1
obtain conseguir (i), 6
occasionally de vez en cuando, 6
ocean océano, 8
October octubre, 3
of de
  of course por supuesto, 2; ¡Cómo no!, 6
off apagado *adj.*, 15
offer ofrecer (zc), 9
office oficina, 1
often muchas veces, 10
oil aceite *m.*, 6
oil painting retrato al óleo, 13
old viejo(a) *adj.*, 2
older mayor, 6
oldest el mayor, 6
on en, 4; encendido *adj.*, prendido *adj.*, 15; sobre *prep.*
  on the other hand por otro lado
  on time a tiempo, 1; en punto, 1
  on top of encima de *prep.*, 4
  on top of that para colmo, 4
once una vez *adv.*, 10
one hundred cien/ciento, 2
one thousand mil, 4
one uno, P
one-way ticket billete/boleto de ida, 9
onion cebolla, 6
only sólo, P
open abrir
  open a document (program) abrir un documento (un programa), 15
opened abierto *p.p.*
opera ópera, 13
operating platform (system) plataforma de operación, 15
oppose oponer, 14
opposition oposición *f.*, 14
or o *conj.*, 3
orange anaranjado *adj.*, 1
orange naranja, 6
orchid orquídea, 12
order (food) pedir (i, i), 6
organ órgano, 5
ought to deber, 2
ounce onza, 6
our nuestro *adj.*, 2
outdoors al aire libre, 4
outgoing extrovertido *adj.*, 2
oven (microwave) horno (microondas), 4
over sobre *prep.*
overcoat abrigo, 7
overpopulation sobrepoblación *f.*, 12
owl búho, 12
ozone layer capa de ozono, 12

P

pack one's suitcase(s) hacer la(s) maleta(s), 9
pain dolor *m.*, 5
painter pintor(a), 13
painting pintura, 1; cuadro, 4
pair par *m.*, 7
Panamanian panameño *adj.*, 2
panther pantera
pants (shorts) pantalones (cortos) *m.*, 7
paper papel *m.*, 1
Paraguayan paraguayo *adj.*, 2
paramilitary group grupo paramilitar, 14
pardon me disculpe, con permiso, perdón, P
parents padres, 2
park parque *m.*, 3
park ranger guardaparques *m./f.*,12
part-time de tiempo parcial, 11
participate participar, 14
party (surprise) fiesta (de sorpresa), 8
pass pasar, 1; aprobar (ue), 14
passenger pasajero(a), 9
Passover Pascua, 8
passport pasaporte *m.*, 9
  passport control inmigración *f.*, 9
pastime pasatiempo, 3
patient paciente *adj.*, 2; paciente *m./f.*, 5
pattern patrón *m.*, 7
pay pagar, 1
  pay in installments pagar a plazos, 11
peace paz *f.*, 14
peaceful tranquilo *adj.*, 12
peasant campesino(a), 12
pencil lápiz *m.*, 1
people gente *f.*, P
pepper pimienta, 6
pepper shaker pimentero, 6
percent por ciento, 7
personal finances finanzas personales, 11
Peruvian peruano *adj.*, 2
pet mascota
petroleum petróleo, 12
pharmacy farmacia, 5
philosophy filosofía, 1
phone llamar, 1
photocopier fotocopiadora, 11
photographer fotógrafo(a), 11
photography fotografía, 13
physician médico *m./f.*, 5
physics física, 1
pick up recoger (j), 12
pill pastilla, 5
pilot piloto *m./f.*, 9
place lugar *m.*, 3
plaid a/de cuadros, 7
plain llano, 12
plane avión *m.*, 9
plant cultivar, 5; sembrar (ie), 12
plate plato, 6
play drama *m.*, 13
play jugar (ue), 4
  play a role interpretar, 13
  play an instrument tocar (qu), 1
  play basketball jugar al baloncesto, 3
  play baseball jugar al béisbol, 3
  play football (soccer) jugar al fútbol (americano), 3
  play golf jugar al golf, 3
  play tennis jugar al tenis, 3
  play volleyball jugar al voleibol, 3
  play the guitar tocar la guitarra, 3
  play sports practical deportes, 3
player jugador(a), 3
playwright dramaturgo *m./f.*, 13
plaza plaza, 3
please por favor, P
pleasure: The pleasure is mine. El gusto es mío., P
plug in enchufar, 15
  plugged in enchufado *adj.*, 15
plumber plomero(a), 11
pocket bolsillo, 7
poet poeta *m./f.*, 13
poetry poesía, 13
police officer policía *m.* (mujer *f.* policía), 11
political party partido político, 14
politician político *m./f.*, 14
politics política, 14
polka-dotted a/de lunares, 7
pollute contaminar, 12
polluted contaminado *adj.*, 12
pollution contaminación *f.*, 12
pool piscina, 3
poor pobre *adj.*, 2
popular popular *adj.*, 13
pork chop chuleta de cerdo, 6
port puerto, 9
portrait retrato, 13
Portuguese (language) portugués *m.*, 1
position puesto, 11
post office oficina de correos, 3
postcard postal *m.*, 2
potatoes (french fried) papas (fritas), 6
pound libra, 6
power poder *m.*, 14
practice practicar (qu), 1
pray orar, 8
prefer preferir (ie), 6
prepare preparar, 6
prescription receta, 5
President president, 14
president of the university presidente *m./f.* de la universidad, 1
press prensa, 14
pretty bonito(a) *adj.*, 2
price precio, 7
print imprimir, 11
printer impresora, 15
private privado *adj.*, 9
problem problema *m.*, 5
profession profesión *f.*, 11
professor profesor(a), 1
program programar, 15
  (CD-ROM) programa (de CD-ROM) *m.*, 15
programmer programador(a),11
progressive progresista *adj.*
project proyecto, 11
promise prometer, 10
protect proteger, 12
protest protestar, 14
proud orgulloso *adj.*
provided (that) con tal (de) que *conj.*, 13
psychiatrist siquiatra *m./f.*, 11
psychologist sícologo, 11
psychology sicología, 1
public transportation transporte público *m.*, 12
Puerto Rican puertorriqueño *adj.*, 2
pure puro *adj.*, 12
purple morado *adj.*, 1
purpose propósito, 2
purse bolsa, 7
put puesto *p.p.*, 10
put (on) poner, 3
  put on (one's clothes) ponerse (la ropa), 5
  put on makeup pintarse, maquillarse, 5

Q

question interpelar; pregunta, P
quiet callarse
quit dejar, 11
  quit the program quitar el programa, 15

R

raffle sorteo, 7
rain llover (ue), 4
rain lluvia, 3
  rain forest selva nubosa tropical, 12
raincoat impermeable *m.*, 7
Ramadan Ramadán *m.*, 8
rancher ranchero(a), 11
rarely raras veces, 10

rather sino *conj.*, 5
Rather well. Bastante bien., P
react reaccionar, 8
read leer, 2
ready listo(a) *adj.*, 2
reality (TV) show programa de realidad, 13
realize darse cuenta
reason razón *f.*, 12
rebellious rebelde *adj.*
receipt recibo, 11
receive recibir, 2
reception recepción *f.*, 10
receptionist recepcionista *m./f.*, 9
recommend recomendar (ie), 6
record grabar, 15
recycle reciclar, 12
red rojo *adj.*, 1
reduce reducir, 14
reduce (in price) rebajar, 7
reforest reforestar, 12
reform reforma, 14
refresh restaurar, 5
refrigerator refrigerador *m.*, 4 nevera, 4
register registrarse, 9
relationships relaciones sentimentales *f.*, 10
relative pariente *m./f.*, 2
remember recordar (ue), 8
remote control control *m.* remoto, 15
report informe *m.*, 11; reportaje *m.*, 14
reporter reportero(a), 11
representative diputado(a), 14
republican republicano *adj.*, 14
request pedir (i, i), 9
reservation reserva, 9
reserved reservado(a) *adj.*, 2
resign renunciar, 11
respect respeto, 11
responsible responsable *adj.*, 2
rest descansar, 1
restaurant restaurante *m.*, 3
résumé currículum *m.*, 11
retire jubilarse, 11
retirement plan plan de retiro, 11
return volver (ue), 4
return (home) regresar (a casa), 1
returned vuelto *p.p.*, 10
rhinoceros rinoceronte *m.*, 12
rice arroz *m.*, 6
rich rico(a) *adj.*, 2
riddle adivinanza, 2
ride a bike andar en bicicleta, 3
ridiculous ridículo *adj.*, 12
right: to the right of a la derecha de *prep.*, 9
right away enseguida, 6
ring anillo, 7
river río, 8
rocket cohete *m.*, 8
role papel *m.*, 13
roof techo, 4
room cuarto, 1
room service servicio de habitación (cuarto), 9
roommate compañero(a) de cuarto, 1
root raíz *f.*
round-trip ticket billete/boleto de ida y vuelta, 9
row remar, 8
rug alfombra, 8
rule reinar
run correr, 3
run out acabar, 12
Russian (language), ruso, 1; ruso *adj.*, 2

S

sacred sagrado *adj.*, 8
sad triste *adj.*, 4
said dicho *p.p.*, 10
saint santo(a), 2
saint's day Día del santo, 8
salad ensalada, 6
salary salario, sueldo, 11
sale oferta, liquidación *f. (Lat. Am.)*; rebaja *(Spain)*, 7
salesclerk/person dependiente *m./f.*, 7; vendedor(a), 11
salt sal *f.*, 6
salt shaker salero, 6
Salvadorean salvadoreño *adj.*, 2
same mismo *adj.*, 10
sand arena, 6
sandal sandalia, 7
sandwich sándwich *m.*, 6
satellite satélite *m.*, 15
satellite dish antena parabólica, 15
satisfied: I'm satisfied. I'm full. Estoy satisfecho(a)., 6
Saturday sábado, 1
sauce salsa, 6
save ahorrar, 11; archivar, 15; guardar, 15
savings account cuenta de ahorros, 11
say decir (i), 4
Say no more! ¡No me digas más!
scanner escáner *m.*, 15
scarf bufanda, 7
schedule horario, 9
school escuela, 1
science ciencias, 1
screen pantalla, 15
flat screen pantalla plana, 15
script guión *m.*, 13
scuba dive bucear, 8
sculpt esculpir, hacer escultura, 13
sculptor escultor(a), 13
sculpture escultura, 13
sea mar *m.*, 8
seafood mariscos, 6
season estación *f.*, 3
seat asiento, 9
second segundo *adj.*, 2
secretary secretario(a), 11
security control *m.* de seguridad, 9
security box caja fuerte, 9
see ver, 3
See you later. Hasta luego., Nos vemos., P
See you soon. Hasta pronto., P
See you tomorrow. Hasta mañana., P
seen visto *p.p.*, 10
sell vender, 2
senate senado, 14
senator senador(a), 14
send (letters) mandar (cartas), 1
sensitive sensible, 3
separate (from) separarse (de), 10
separated separado *adj.*, 2
separation separación *f.*, 10
September septiembre, 3
servant criado(a), 11
series (TV) (tele)serie *f.*, 13
serve servir (i), 6
server servidor *m.*, 15
set the table poner la mesa, 4
seven hundred setecientos, 4
seven siete, P
seventeen diecisiete, P
seventy setenta, 2
several varios, 1
shake hands darse la mano, 10
shame: it's a shame es una lástima
shameless person sinvergüenza *m./f.*, 4
shave afeitarse, 5
she ella *pron.*, P
shellfish mariscos, 6
shirt camisa, 7
shoe zapato, 7
shoe size número, 7
shoe store zapatería, 7
shopping de compras, 7
short (height) bajo(a) *adj.*, 2; **(length)** corto(a) *adj.*, 2
shortage escasez *f.*, 12
shot (injection) inyección *f.*, 5
shout gritar, 8
show espectáculo, 14
show mostrar (ue), 7
show (a movie) poner, 13
shower ducha, 4
shrimp (fried) camarones (fritos) *m.*, 6
shy tímido(a) *adj.*, 2
sick enfermo *adj.*, 4
sign firmar, 11
silk seda, 7
silly tonto(a) *adj.*, 2
similar parecido *adj.*
simple sencillo *adj.*, 10
simplicity sencillez *f.*
sincere sincero *adj.*, 2
sing cantar, 1
singer cantante *m./f.*, 13
single soltero *adj.*, 2
single bed cama sencilla, 9
sister hermana, 2
sister-in-law cuñada, 2
six hundred seiscientos, 4
six seis, P
sixteen dieciséis, P
sixty sesenta, 2
size (clothing) talla, 7
skate (in-line) patinar (en línea), 3
ski (water) esquiar (en el agua), 3
skin piel *f.*, 5
skirt falda, 7
skyscraper rascacielos *m.*, 12
sleep dormir (ue), 4
slice tajada, 6
small pequeño *adj.*, 2
smart listo(a) *adj.*, 2
smell oler, 4
smile sonreír, 6
smoking section sección *f.* de fumar *f.*, 9
smoothness suavidad *f.*, 3
snack time merienda, 3
snake culebra, 12
sneeze estornudar, 5
snorkel hacer esnórquel, 8
snow nieve *f.*, 3
it's snowing nieva, 3
so entonces *adv.*, 10
So . . . Así que..., 2
So-so. Así así., Más o menos., P
so that a fin de que, para que *conj.*, 13
soap opera telenovela, 13
soccer (football) fútbol (americano) *m.*, 3
social network red social *f.*, 15
sociology sociología, 1
socks calcetines *m. pl.*, 7
sofa sofá *m.*, 4
soft drink refresco, 6
solar energy energía solar, 12
soldier soldado (la mujer soldado), 11
solve, resolve resolver (ue), 12
some unos(as) *indef. art.*; algún, alguno(a/os/as), 8
somebody, someone alguien, 8
something algo, 8
sometimes a veces *adv.*, 10
son hijo, 2
song canción *f.*, 13
son-in-law yerno, 2
soul alma
soup sopa, 6
source fuente *f.*, 12
south sur *m.*, 9
space espacio, 4
Spanish (language) español *m.*, 1; español(a) *adj.*, 2
speak (with each other) hablar(se), 9
speak so well habla tan bien, P
speakers altavoces *m.*, 15

species especies *f.*, 12
speech discurso, 14
spend (money) gastar, 7
spend (time) pasar, 1
spiritually espiritualmente, 2
spoon cuchara, 6
sport deporte *m.*, 3
sports deportiva *adj.*, 3
 sports program programa deportivo, 13
spring primavera, 3
squid (fried) calamares (fritos) *m.*, 6
stadium estadio, 3
stage escenario
stairs escalera, 4
stand puesto, 7
start comenzar (ie), 4
stationery store papelería, 3
stay quedarse, 9
 stay in bed guardar cama, 5
steak bistec *m.*, 6
step paso, 7
stepbrother hermanastro, 2
stepfather padrastro, 2
stepmother madrastra, 2
stepsister hermanastra, 2
stereo estéreo, 15
still aún *adv.*
stingy tacaño(a) *adj.*, 2
stockbroker accionista *m./f.*, 11
stockings medias, 7
stomach estómago, 5
stone piedra, 4
stop parar(se), 9
store tienda, 3; almacén, 7
story cuento; historia
stove estufa, 4
straight derecho, 9
stream arroyo, 12
street calle *f.*, 3
strike huelga, 14
striped a/de rayas, 7
stroll paseo, 7
student estudiante *m./f.*, 1
 student center centro estudiantil, 1
study estudiar, 1
 study estudio, 1
stuff rellenar, 6
style estilo, 7
 It's the latest style! ¡Está de última moda!, 7
subjects (courses) materias, 1
succeed lograr
suddenly de repente, 8
sue demandar
suffer sufrir, 9
sugar azúcar *m.*, 6
suggest sugerir, 6
suit traje *m.*, 7
suitcase maleta, 9
summer verano, 3
sunbathe tomar el sol, 3
sunblock bloqueador solar *m.*, 8
Sunday domingo, 1
sunglasses gafas de sol, 7
sunny: it's sunny hace sol, 3
suntan lotion crema bronceadora, 8
supermarket supermercado, 3
supper cena, 6
supply suplir
support apoyar, 14
 support apoyo, 13
surf correr las olas, 8
 surf the Net navegar la Red, 15
surprise sorprender, 12
surround rodear
surrounded rodeado *adj.*, 9
sweater suéter *m.*, 7
sweep the floor barrer el piso, 4
sweet dulce *adj.*
swim nadar, 3
swimming natación *f.*, 3
symptom síntoma *m.*, 5
systems analyst analista de sistemas *m./f.*, 11

T

table mesa, 4
 table (side, cofee) mesita, 4
tablecloth mantel *m.*, 6
tablespoon cucharada, 6
take (classes/tests) tomar (clases/ exámenes), 1
 take (someone's) temperature tomarle la temperatura (a alguien), 5
 take a bath bañarse (en la tina), 5
 take a shower ducharse, 5
 take advantage aprovechar, 14
 take care (of oneself) cuidar(se), 5
 take off (one's clothes) quitarse (la ropa), 5; despegar, 9
 take out the garbage sacar la basura, 4
 take part participar, 14
 take pictures sacar fotos, 3
 take place tener lugar, 10; llevar a cabo, 8
talk (with each other) hablar(se), 9
talk show programa de entrevistas, 13
tall alto *adj.*, 2
tasty sabroso *adj.*, 6
taxes impuestos, 14
tea (iced) té (helado) *m.*, 6
teach enseñar, 1
teacher maestro(a), 1
teaspoon cucharadita, 6
technical school escuela politécnica
technician técnico *m./f.*, 11
technological tecnológico, 15
telecommute teletrabajar, 15
television viewer televidente *m./f.*, 13
tell contar (ue), 4; decir (i), 4
ten diez, P
tennis shoe (sneaker) zapato de tenis (deportivo), 7
tent tienda de campaña, 8
terrace terraza, 4
terrorism terrorismo, 14
test examen *m.*, 1
text message mensaje de texto, 15
that ese(a) *adj.*, 5; **(over there)** aquel (aquella) *adj.*, 5
that que *pron.*, 3; ése(a) *pron.*, 5; **(over there)** aquél (aquélla) *pron.*, 5
 that's why por eso, 11
the el, la, los, las *def. art.*
The pleasure is mine. El gusto es mío., P
theater teatro, 13
their su *adj.*
then luego, entonces *adv.*, 10
there allí *adv.*, P
there is, there are hay, P
they ellos(as) *pron.*, P
thigh muslo, 5
thin delgado *adj.*, 2
think pensar (ie), 4
third tercero *adj.*, 2
thirteen trece, P
thirty treinta, P
this este(a) *adj.*, 5
 this one éste *pron.*, 5
three tres, P
three hundred trescientos, 4
throat garganta, 5
throughout durante *prep.*
throw tirar, 10
Thursday jueves *m.*, 1
ticket boleto, 3; billete *m.*, 9
tidy arreglado *adj.*, 9
tiger tigre *m.*, 12
time hora; vez
 a good time un buen rato, 3
timid tímido *adj.*, 2
to a *prep.*
toad sapo, 12
toast brindis *m.*, 8
toaster tostadora, 4
today hoy *adv.*, 1
toe dedo del pie, 5
toilet inodoro, 4
told dicho *p.p.*, 10
tolerant tolerante *adj.*, 2
tomato tomate *m.*, 6
tomb tumba, 7
tomorrow mañana *adv.*, 1
tongue lengua, 5
too también *adv.*, 8
 too much demasiado *adv.*, 9
tooth diente *m.*, 5
touch tocar (qu), 1
tourism turismo, 1
toward hacia *adv.*, 9
town pueblo, 3
traditional outfit traje típico, 7
traffic tráfico, 12
train station estación de trenes *f.*, 9
tranquil tranquilo *adj.*, 12
transfer (funds) transferir (ie, i) (fondos), 11
translator traductor(a), 11
trash basura, 12
travel viajar, 1
 travel agency agencia de viajes, 9
 travel agent agente de viajes, 9
traveler's check cheque de viajero, 11
treatment tratamiento, 5
tree árbol *m.*, 12
trip viaje *m.*, 9
truth verdad *f.*, 1
try on probarse (ue), 7
T-shirt camiseta, 7
Tuesday martes *m.*, 1
tuition matrícula, 1
turkey pavo, 6
turn doblar, 9
 turn off apagar (ue), 15
 turn on encender, prender, 15; **(TV)** poner, 13
turtle tortuga, 12
tuxedo esmoquin *m.*
twelve doce, P
twenty veinte, P
twenty-eight veintiocho, P
twenty-five veinticinco, P
twenty-four veinticuatro, P
twenty-nine veintinueve, P
twenty-seven veintisiete
twenty-one veintiuno, P
twenty-six veintiséis, P
twenty-three veintitrés, P
twenty-two veintidós, P
twice (three times, etc.) dos (tres, etc.) veces, 10
two dos, P
two hundred doscientos(as), 4

U

ugly feo *adj.*, 2
umbrella paraguas *m.*, 7
uncle tío, 2
under debajo de *prep.*, 4
understand comprender, 2; entender (ie), 4
unemployment desempleo, 14
United States: from the United States estadounidense *adj.*, 2
university universidad *f.*, 1
unknown desconocido *adj.*
unless a menos que *conj.*, 13
unpleasant antipático *adj.*, 2
unplug desenchufar, 15
until hasta *adv.*; hasta que *conj.*
up to hasta *adv.*, 9
 up to date al día, 14
upload (a file) cargar un archivo, 15
URL Localizador Uniforme de Recursos *m.*, 15
Uruguayan uruguayo *adj.*, 2
USB port puerto USB, 15
use usar, 1

V

vacuum pasar la aspiradora, 4
vacuum cleaner aspiradora, 4
valley valle *m.*, 12
VCR videocasetera, 15
vegetable verdura, vegetal *m.*, 6
Venezuelan venezolano *adj.*, 2
very muy *adv.*, P
Very well. Muy bien., P
vest chaleco, 7
veterinarian veterinario *m./f.*, 11
video call videollamada, 15
video camera (digital) videocámara (digital), 15
video game videojuego, 15
videotape videocasete *m.*, 15
viewer espectador(a), 13
vinegar vinagre *m.*, 6
visit visitar, 1
visit a museum visitar un museo, 3
volcano volcán *m.*, 12
volleyball vólibol *m.*, 3
vote votar, 14
vote voto, 14

W

wait esperar
waiter (waitress) camarero(a), 6
waiting room sala de espera, 5
wake up despertarse (ie), 5
walk caminar, 1
walk caminata, 7
walk in the mountains caminar por las montañas, 3
wall pared *f.*, 4
wallet cartera, 7
want desear, 1; querer (ie), 4
war guerra, 14
wardrobe armario, 4
warn avisar
wash (dishes, clothes, windows) lavar (los platos, la ropa, las ventanas), 4
wash up lavarse, 5
washing machine lavadora, 4
waste desperdicio, 12
watch mirar, 1
watch reloj *m.*, 7
watch television ver la tele, 3
water the plants regar (ie) las plantas, 4
water: carbonated/noncarbonated mineral water agua *f.* mineral con/sin gas, 6
waterfall catarata, 12
we nosotros(as) *pron.*, P
weakness debilidad *f.*
wear llevar, usar, 7
wear a costume disfrazarse, 8
weather tiempo, 3
weather report (forecast) pronóstico del tiempo, 13
web camera cámara web, 15
web page página web, 15
wedding boda, 10 **wedding cake** pastel de boda(s) *m.*, 10 **wedding favor** recuerdo, 10
Wednesday miércoles *m.*, 1
week semana, 1
weekend fin *m.* de semana, 1
Welcome! ¡Bienvenido!, 9
well bien *adv.*
well done bien cocido, 6
west oeste *m.*, 9
what lo que *pron.*, 10
What time is it? ¿Qué hora es?, 1
What? Which? ¿Qué?, P
What's new? (informal) ¿Qué hay?, P
What's up? (informal) ¿Qué tal?, P
What's your address? (informal) ¿Cuál es tu dirección? (informal), P
What's your name? ¿Cómo se llama usted?, ¿Cuál es tu nombre?, ¿Cómo te llamas?, P
What's your telephone number? (informal) ¿Cuál es tu número de teléfono?, P
when cuando *conj.*, 13
When? ¿Cuándo?, P
Where? ¿Dónde?, P
Where (to)? ¿Adónde?, 8
Where are you from? ¿De dónde es usted?, ¿De dónde eres tú?, P
which que *pron.*, 3
Which? ¿Cuál(es)?, P
white blanco *adj.*, 1
who que *pron.*, 3; quien *pron.*, 10
Who? ¿Quién(es)?, P
Whose? ¿De quién(es)?, 8
Why? ¿Por qué?, P
widow viuda
widowed viudo *adj.*, 2
widower viudo
wife esposa, 2
wildlife preserve refugio natural, 12
win ganar, 3
window ventana, 4; ventanilla, 9
windy: it's windy hace viento, 3
wine (white, red) vino (blanco, tinto), 6
wine glass copa, 6
winner ganador(a), 13
winter invierno, 3
wireless connection conexión inalámbrica *f.*, 15
wish desear, 1
I wish that ojalá que, 12
with con *prep.*, 4
with regard to con respecto a, 11
withdraw (money) sacar (qu), 11
without sin *prep.*, 8; sin que *conj.*, 13
witness testigo *m./f.*, 10
wolf lobo
woman mujer *f.*, 1
Wonderful! ¡Qué bueno!, 2
wool lana, 7
word palabra, 1
work trabajar, 1
work trabajo, 11
work (of art) obra (de arte), 13
worker obrero(a), 11
world mundo, 9
worried preocupado *adj.*, 4
worry preocuparse, 11
worse peor, 6
worst el peor, 6
write escribir, 2
writer escritor(a), 13
written escrito *p.p.*, 10

X

X-ray radiografía, 5

Y

year año, 3; **year before** el año pasado, 15
yellow amarillo *adj.*, 1
yes sí, P
yesterday ayer *adv.*, 6
you tú, usted(es), vosotros(as) *pron.*, P
and you? ¿y usted? (formal), P
young joven *adj.*, 2
younger menor, 6
youngest el menor, 6
your (formal) su *adj.*, 2; vuestro *adj.*, 2; tuyo, suyo *adj.*, 7
yours vuestro *adj.*, 2; tuyo, suyo *adj.*, 7

Z

zebra cebra
zero cero, P
zipper cremallera, cierre *m.*, 7
zoology zoología, 1

El alfabeto en español

The Spanish alphabet contains twenty nine letters:

a	a	América Central
b	be	Buenos Aires
c	ce	Costa Rica
ch	che	Chile
d	de	Durango
e	e	Ecuador
f	efe	fútbol
g	ge	Guatemala, Gibraltar
h	hache	Honduras
i	i (i latina)	isla
j	jota	Juárez
k	ka	kilo
l	ele	León
ll	elle	Manzanillo
m	eme	México
n	ene	Nicaragua
ñ	eñe	España
o	o	océano
p	pe	Paraguay
q	cu	Quito
r	ere	río Grande
s	ese	San José
t	te	Tegucigalpa
u	u	Uruguay
v	ve (ve chica, ve corta, uve)	Venezuela
w	doble ve (doble uve)	Washington
x	equis	Extremadura
y	i griega	Yucatán
z	zeta	Zaragoza

- All letters in the alphabet are feminine: **la a, la be, la ce,** etc.
- As opposed to the English alphabet, there are three more letters in the Spanish alphabet: **ch, ll,** and **ñ.** In all dictionaries published prior to 1995, you will find separate sections for words beginning with **ch** and **ll** (**ñ** has always had its own section). Most dictionaries published after 1995 do not treat **ch** and **ll** separately.
- The letters **k** and **w** are not common and appear only in words of foreign origin, such as **karate** and **whiski.**